SOUTH ASIAN HISTORY, 1750-1950

SOUTH ASIAN HISTORY

1750-1950

A Guide to Periodicals

Dissertations and

Newspapers

MARGARET H. CASE

PRINCETON UNIVERSITY PRESS

PRINCETON, NEW JERSEY

1968

Second Printing, with corrections, 1969

Printed in the United States of America
by Princeton University Press

FOREWORD

BY STEPHEN N. HAY

This volume greatly extends our bibliographical control over several types of source material important for the study of the history of the India-Pakistan subcontinent during the past two centuries. Because modern South Asian history is a relatively new field of historical study, and because the sources for it are widely scattered, reference works such as this *Guide* are of unusual value.

The principal portions of the work, systematically arranged under twelve major headings and one hundred forty-four sub-headings, refer us to over six thousand articles and dissertations, most of them little known. Many scholars using this book may experience the same mixture of delight and dismay with which I discovered, even in those sections closest to my own research interests, important articles of which I previously had no knowledge. By guiding us to these sources of information and interpretation Mrs. Case is in effect opening up a series of Pandora's boxes, whose contents will force research scholars to consider many questions and problems hitherto overlooked.

The listing of nineteenth and twentieth century South Asian newspapers which concludes the volume draws our attention to a still larger, and even less-explored, body of source material. Tragically, many if not most of these newspapers no longer exist in complete files, and even now the climate and vermin of South Asia are steadily reducing to powder innumerable unique pages of newsprint. To halt this irreparable loss, these newspapers must be microfilmed—an immense task now being undertaken by various institutions, but most actively by the Inter Documentation Company of Zug, Switzerland. Such efforts at preservation will be greatly aided by the future, complete census of South Asian newspapers for which Mrs. Case's preliminary listing provides a solid foundation.

We have here a *Guide* in the best sense of the word: not a complete inventory, but a careful selection, evaluation, and arrangement of those items of a particular kind which the researcher should be aware of from the outset of his inquiry. What Mrs. Case has done for periodicals, dissertations, and newspapers other scholars have done and are doing for monographs, reference works, government documents, archival holdings, and pamphlets. To name only a few of the bibliographic projects now underway: J. D. Pearson of the School of Oriental and African Studies, London, has in view a complete index to the periodical literature relating to all periods of South Asian history; Henry Scholberg of the University of Minnesota has in press a bibliography of the gazetteers of India; V. C. Joshi of the National Archives of India is preparing a guide to archival collections in India; and Katharine S. Diehl at the University of Chicago is compiling a guide to reference works on modern South Asian history. More such aids to research are needed, both to bring order into the immense body of unreferenced sources already extant and to cope with the increasing flow of new publications being issued in all parts of the world. Students of the history of India and Pakistan can only say of the small but devoted band of bibliographers now at work on South Asian source materials: "May their tribe increase!"

University of California,
Santa Barbara

CONTENTS

CONTENTS

PART II · DISSERTATIONS

CONTENTS

PART III · NEWSPAPERS

CONTENTS

CONTENTS

SOUTH ASIAN HISTORY, 1750-1950

INTRODUCTION

The main purpose of this guide is to aid scholars of modern South Asian history to find material relevant to their research from the vast periodical literature in Western languages. The guide also lists doctoral dissertations on South Asian history and files of newspapers published in South Asia since the beginning of the nineteenth century.

PERIODICALS

In the field of modern South Asian history, there is a great deal of periodical literature which has been difficult to use because it has not been indexed. Articles have been included here from 351 periodicals published between 1800 and 1965, and from 26 books of collected essays and encyclopedias. In the case of about a third of the periodicals, as many volumes as were available in the United States and London were thoroughly searched; the volumes seen are indicated in the list of abbreviations of articles and books. Access to the remaining journals was through existing general bibliographies and readers' guides, but virtually every article obtained from these sources was examined. About 3100 of the more than 5400 article entries have been annotated.

By far the greatest number of articles listed here are in English; a few in other Western languages are included, but there are fewer than a dozen Indian-language articles. The indexing of scholarly Indian-language periodical material can best be done in the libraries of India and Pakistan, and such a project would be a great service to historians of South Asia.

The articles indexed in this guide deal with events and people in the period 1750-1950. Although 1750 is a conventional date rather than a milestone in Indian history, the mid-eighteenth century was a time of transition. It saw the beginnings of a new order built on the wreckage of the Mughal Empire and the first important European involvement in the politics of India, which was to influence profoundly the future of South Asia. The middle of the century seems a convenient point from which to begin, and the abundance of source material in Western languages dealing with the period since about 1750 substantiates the usefulness of this periodization for purposes of this guide. The year 1950 was chosen as a cut-off date so that Partition and its immediate aftermath could be included; the material on independent India and Pakistan, which would fill a book in itself, has been excluded.

This guide was designed primarily to aid scholars doing research on modern South Asian history; it is, therefore, deliberately selective. The general principle for selecting articles has been to include those written on the basis of archival research, responsible contemporary reporting, or direct personal observation. In the fringe areas of historical writing, such as surveys for the general reader, editorial observations on the current scene, and eulogies of political or literary figures, only exceptionally good articles were taken. Probably 95 percent of all articles purporting to be on history proper are included. A much smaller percentage, perhaps 30 to 40 percent, of the articles written in the past on contemporary affairs are included here. The general criterion for selection was the article's contribution of fact or original interpretation. Some more specific guidelines to the range of articles included within certain subjects are as follows:

A. *Areas not primarily under British control.* This covers the administrative, political, and military history of the Mughals (after 1750), the continental European powers in India, the South Asian powers, and the frontier areas. All articles on politics and administration were taken; articles dealing with military history were taken selectively, and detailed descriptions of individual battles were generally omitted.

B. *Areas primarily under British control.* This section covers the political and administrative history of the British in India. It includes substantial articles of contemporary comment on British policy; brief (1-2 page) comments and critiques, unless especially cogent, were generally omitted. Likewise, brief articles on minor points of British administration were usually left out.

C. *Nationalism and politics.* This section deals with South Asian politics, as distinct from the politics of the British in India. Muslim activities after 1875 that were politically important are included here; Muslim movements before 1875 are listed under Cultural History.

D. *Economic history.* All articles dealing with economic history in noneconomic journals were included. The literature in specialized economic journals is vast and technical, and the entries from them are selective. A comprehensive bibliography is readily available in the *Index of Economic Journals* (Homewood, Ill., 1961-62).

E. *Social History.* As can be seen from the length of this section, this is the most neglected area of South Asian historical studies. Articles on population, histories of families and groups (but not ethnology), and studies of British-Indian social relations and social reforms are the core of the section. The periphery includes miscellaneous observations on the life of the Indians and the British in India.

F. *Cultural history.* A distinction has been made between cultural history and literary or artistic criticism. The former is included, the latter is not. The history of religious movements is included; philosophic and theological discourses are not. Intellectual history is not fairly represented, for an intellectual historian will want to study all the writings of a person or an era, whether that person or the people of that era wrote about modern South Asia or other subjects. Articles by such writers on subjects outside modern South Asian history have not been included here.

INTRODUCTION

I am indebted to Mary Carmen Lynn for undertaking the task of combing through the volumes of the *Modern Review*, as well as some journals on art history. Manisha Das Gupta searched for titles in the volumes of the *Readers' Guide to Periodical Literature* and the *International Index to Periodicals*, and annotated entries on Bengali articles. Mary Alice Kopf assisted in searching a number of journals. Katherine Bason and John Harrison helped to tote books and copy titles at the New York Public Library. Ann Irschick examined some articles at Berkeley and Stephen N. Hay did the same at Harvard. I am very grateful to all of them for their assistance.

In a few cases, when I was unable to examine the volumes themselves, I worked from Xerox copies of the tables of contents. These were supplied by Louis Jacob, University of California at Berkeley; Karen Leonard, University of Chicago; Henry Scholberg, University of Minnesota; and Stanley Sutton, India Office Library. Maureen Patterson and the staff of the South Asian Collection at the University of Chicago Library were helpful at several stages of the work, as were Cecil Hobbs and a number of staff members of the Library of Congress. Hugh McLean and Caroline Mason, University of Chicago, translated some Slavic titles. Richard C. Howard, Cornell University Library, sent proofs of the 1965 *Bibliography of Asian Studies*, which helped to bring the guide up to date. Alicia Coppola typed a section of the manuscript. I wish to thank them, and all the others who answered questions and helped with various problems.

Each article is listed only once. A subject index has been included to help locate materials that could have been entered under alternative subject headings.

DISSERTATIONS

Although a number of lists of dissertations in this area exist, they are limited to the dissertations accepted by one institution or within one country in any one year. This guide brings together information on about 650 dissertations in the field of modern South Asian history.

Dissertations accepted through 1965 for the Ph.D. and D.Litt. degrees are included. I am grateful to the many scholars at Indian, American, and Australian universities who supplied lists of dissertations recently accepted by their departments. Dr. S. P. Sen, Institute of Historical Studies, Calcutta, was particularly helpful in obtaining information from India. S. M. Master, Columbia University Libraries, kindly supplied some printed indexes of dissertations.

Over half the titles were collected from published lists, which are not entirely reliable. The original intention was to list only the titles of unpublished dissertations, but when this list had nearly been completed, it was urged by some scholars in the field that it would be useful to include published dissertations as well. The major sources were retraced, but a few published works may, regrettably, have been missed.

A number of the dissertations listed here have been published; a prospective user should check the Library of Congress or British Museum catalogue before trying to obtain a copy of the original dissertation.

The dissertations are listed by subject. An index of dissertations by university has been provided.

NEWSPAPERS

This guide lists 341 English and bilingual English- and Indian-language newspapers, and 251 Indian-language papers published in South Asia since the beginning of the nineteenth century. Those English papers were listed for which there were known holdings within or outside South Asia. Indian-language papers held outside South Asia or in the National Library, Calcutta, were also listed. Information on about 500 additional newspapers held in three or four smaller Indian libraries was gathered, but this represents only a small fraction of the newspapers that have been published in the last century, and so was omitted. A comprehensive census of newspapers in South Asian libraries would greatly extend the range of information available to scholars. The more complete files of these papers should then be filmed, for the urgency of preserving these rapidly deteriorating sources grows more acute each year.

The holdings of the following libraries were checked from newspaper accession records: the University of Chicago Library, the Midwest Inter-Library Center (now the Center for Research Libraries), the New York Public Library, and the Library of Congress. A number of people provided lists of holdings for other institutions: Ann Irschick for the University of California Library, Berkeley; Henry Scholberg for the Ames Library of South Asia, University of Minnesota, Minneapolis; Lan-Hiang Tan for the East-West Center Library, Honolulu; W. J. Watson for the Institute of Islamic Studies, McGill University, Montreal; and V. C. Joshi for (1) the Secretariat Record Office, Maharashtra, Elphinstone College Building, Bombay; and (2) the Asiatic Society of Bombay, Town Hall, Bombay. I thank all of them for their assistance. Holdings of other libraries were obtained from printed reference works. I am very grateful to Mary Alice Kopf for collating the information from all these sources.

Monographic works have not been included in this guide. The following bibliographies are helpful in finding books on South Asian subjects:

Mahar, J. Michael. *India, a Critical Bibliography*. Tucson, University of Arizona Press, 1964. 119 pp.

Patterson, Maureen L. P., and Inden, Ronald B. *South Asia: an Introductory Bibliography*. Chicago: University of Chicago Press, Syllabus

Division, November 1962 ("Introduction to the Civilization of India").
412 pp. An enlarged second edition is in progress.

Wilson, Patrick. *Government and Politics in India and Pakistan 1885-1955; a Bibliography in Western Languages.* Berkeley: South Asia Studies, Institute of East Asia Studies, University of California, 1956. 356 pp.

————. "A Survey of Bibliographies on Southern Asia," *Journal of Asian Studies*: 18 (1959), 365-76.

The annual *Bibliography of Asian Studies,* published by the *Journal of Asian Studies,* is useful in bringing the material in these bibliographies, as well as the present guide, up to date.

Funds for the preparation of this guide were provided by the Committee on Southern Asian Studies at the University of Chicago from a grant made by the Ford Foundation for the support of South and Southeast Asian studies.

The original planning of the guide was done together with Stephen N. Hay at the University of Chicago, and the work has greatly benefited from his advice and encouragement at every stage. I am most grateful to him.

Margaret H. Case

Washington, D.C.
November 1966

PART I • ARTICLES

INDEXES OF PERIODICALS

ASIATIC SOCIETY OF BENGAL. *Centenary Review of the Asiatic Society of Bengal from 1784 to 1883.* Calcutta: Thacker, Spink & Co., 1885. 762 pp. Part I, Appendix D, "Index to the Papers and Contributions to the Asiatick Researches and the Journal and Proceedings of the . . . Society," pp. 106-95. Author index. Part II is followed by a "Classified Index to the Scientific Papers in the Society's Publications from 1788-1883." Subject index.

CALCUTTA REVIEW. "Articles Published in the Calcutta Review from 1844 to 1912 on Subjects of Indian History, Administration, Education and Culture," *Calcutta Review*, May 1944, pp. 122-43.

CALCUTTA REVIEW. *Index to Calcutta Review, v. 1-50.* Calcutta: City Press, 1873. Part I: list of all articles with analysis of their contents, arranged alphabetically by title; author not given. Also lists reviews of books by author of book. 196 pp. Part II: subject index, i.e., subjects other than those that fall naturally under the title. 47 pp.

CHAUDHURI, SIBDAS. *Index to the Publications of the Asiatic Society, 1788-1953.* Calcutta: Asiatic Society, 1956- .
Vol. I, part 1: 1956, 336 pp., 5139 entries. Author index to *Asiatick Researches*, vol. 1-20; *Journal*, series 1-3 (through 1953); *Memoirs*; *Miscellaneous Publications.*
Vol. I, part 2: 1959, 472 pp., entries 5140-7161. Index to *Bibliotheca Indica, Monograph Series, Proceedings, Yearbooks, Miscellaneous Notes* in the *Journal* and *Miscellaneous Publications.*
Vol. I, part 3 (projected). Index to plates, addenda and corrigenda; analytical classified index.
Vol. II (projected). Subject index.

CHOUDHURY, G. R., comp. *Index to Articles Published in the Journal of the Bihar Research Society,* vol. *I-XLVII (1915-1961).* Ed. S. V. Sohono.

HARI RAO, R. "Bibliography of Articles Published in *The Quarterly Journal of the Mythic Society* on the History, Art, and Culture of Karnātaka and on Kannaḍa Language and Literature," *Quarterly Journal of the Mythic Society:* 44 (1957-58), 150-75.

INDEX OF ECONOMIC JOURNALS. Homewood, Illinois: Richard D. Irwin, Inc., 1961-62. Vol. I, 1886-1924; vol. II, 1925-1939; vol. III, 1940-1949; vol. IV, 1950-1954; vol. V, 1954-1959. By subject and author; English language periodicals only.

INTERNATIONAL INDEX TO PERIODICALS. New York, H. W. Wilson Co.

JOURNAL OF ASIAN STUDIES. *Bibliography of Asian Studies.* Annual bibliography of books and articles.

PARGITER, FREDERICK EDEN, ed. *Centenary Volume of the Royal Asiatic Society of Great Britain and Ireland, 1823-1923.* London: the Society, 1923. xxviii, 186 pp. Section III, index to articles and contributions, India.

PEARSON, JAMES, comp., with the assistance of Julia F. Ashton. *Index Islamica, 1906-1955; a Catalogue of Articles on Islamic Subjects in Periodicals and other Collective Publications.* Cambridge, Eng.: W. Heffer, c. 1958. 897 pp. India, pp. 619-65. *Supplement, 1956-1960,* 1962. 316 pp. Indexes periodicals in Western languages.

PUNJAB UNIVERSITY HISTORICAL SOCIETY. *Journal,* vol. I, no. 1 (April 1932), 81-85. Index to *Journal* of the Punjab Historical Society, vol. 1-11 (1911-1931).

READERS' GUIDE TO PERIODICAL LITERATURE. New York: H. W. Wilson Co.

REVUE LINGUISTIQUE. Tome 32 (1899), 1-38. Index for *Madras Journal of Literature and Science,* 1833-1866.

ROSE, H. A. "Index to Panjab Notes and Queries, Indian and North Indian Notes and Queries," Asiatic Society of Bengal, *Journal,* NS 4 (1908), extra pp. 1-124. Detailed subject index.

ROYAL ASIATIC SOCIETY OF GREAT BRITAIN AND IRELAND, BOMBAY BRANCH. "Index to the Transactions of the Literary Society of Bombay, v. 1-3 and of the Journals of the Bombay Branch, Royal Asiatic Society, v. i-xvii. With a Historical Sketch of the Society." Bombay, 1886. 50, 82, xlvii, 17 pp. Subject index, index of proper names, index of authors and papers.

SCHOLBERG, HENRY. Card index of *Journal of Indian History* by author and subject. Located at Ames Library, University of Minnesota, Minneapolis, Minnesota.

ABBREVIATIONS OF PERIODICALS AND BOOKS

A   *Asia.* New York, 1898-1946. *, ‡ vol. 1-46.

AfQ   *Africa Quarterly.* New Delhi, April/June 1961-.

AnSB   Anthropological Society of Bombay, *Journal.* Bombay, vol. 1-15, 1886-1936; NS vol. 1-, 1946-.

Ar   *Arena.* Boston, vol. 1-41, Dec. 1889-Aug. 1909. *

ArQ   *Army Quarterly.* London, Oct. 1920-. ‡ 1920-1965.

AsR   *Asiatick Researches.* London, vol. 1-20, 1801-1836; vol. 7-11 called *Asiatic Researches.* ‡ vol. 1-12; vol. 1-20 indexed in Asiatic Society of Bengal, *Centenary Review,* which was searched.

AuQ   *Australian Quarterly.* Sydney, 1929-.

AA   *American Anthropologist.* Menasha, Wisconsin, vol. 1-11, Jan. 1888–Dec. 1898; NS vol. 1-, Jan. 1899-. **

AAG   Association of American Geographers, *Annals.* Washington, D.C., 1911-.

AAAPSS   American Academy of Political and Social Science, *Annals.* Philadelphia, July 1890-. *

AAR   *Asiatic Annual Register.* London, 1800-1812. ‡ vol. 1-12, 1800-1812.

AAS   *Azia i afrika segodnia.* Moscow, July 1957-; until 1961 called *Sovremennyi vostok.* Indexed in SPA, below.

AAWA   *Afro-Asian and World Affairs.* New Delhi, March 1964-.

AES   American Ethnological Society, *Bulletin of the Proceedings.* New York, Sept. 1860–Jan./March 1863.

AH   *Agricultural History.* Chicago, vol. 1, 1927; Baltimore, vol. 2, 5, 6, 1928, 1931, 1932.

AHR   *American Historical Review.* New York, Oct. 1895-. *, ‡ vol. 1-70 (1965).

AHRS   Andhra Historical Research Society, *Journal.* Rajahmundry, Madras, July 1926-. ‡ vol. 1-29 (1963/64).

AIIS   Aligarh, Institute of Islamic Studies, *Bulletin.* Aligarh, 1957-. ‡ vol. 1-5 (1961).

AIOC   All India Oriental Conference, *Proceedings and Transactions.* Poona, etc., 1920-1937.

AJIL   *American Journal of International Law.* Washington, D.C., Jan. 1907-. **

AJLH   *American Journal of Legal History.* Philadelphia, Jan. 1957-.

* Indexed in *Readers' Guide to Periodical Literature.*
** Indexed in *International Index to Periodicals.*
† Indexed in *Index of Economic Journals.*
‡ Volumes indicated were searched for articles.
Journals not otherwise marked were indexed in the *Bibliography of Asian Studies* and other indexes of periodicals listed in the previous section.

AJPH   *Australian Journal of Politics and History.* Brisbane, Nov. 1955-.

AJS   *American Journal of Sociology.* Chicago, July 1895-. *

AKR   *Aoyama Keizai Ronshu* [Aoyama Economic Journal]. Tokyo, Nov. 1949-.

AL   *American Literature.* Durham, N.C., March 1929-.

AM   *Atlantic Monthly.* Boston, Nov. 1857-. *

AO   *Archiv Orientálni.* Prague, March 1929-.

AOS   American Oriental Society, *Journal.* New Haven, 1843/49-. **

AP   *Aryan Path.* Bombay, Bangalore, Jan. 1930-.

APS   American Philosophical Society, *Proceedings.* Philadelphia, 1838/40-.

APSR   *American Political Science Review.* Menasha, Wisconsin, Nov. 1906-. *, **

AQ   *American Quarterly.* Minneapolis, Spring 1949-.

AQR   *Asiatic Quarterly Review.* London, vol. 1-10, Jan. 1886–Oct. 1890. Continued as AR, below. ‡ vol. 1-10.

AR   *Asian Review.* London. Successor to AQR; 2nd ser., vol. 1-10, Jan. 1891–Oct. 1895, and 3rd ser., vol. 1-34, Jan. 1896–Oct. 1912 called *The Imperial and Asiatic Quarterly Review* or *Oriental and Colonial Record*; new ser., vol. 1-, Jan. 1913- called *Asiatic Review* through 1952, thereafter *Asian Review.* ‡ 1891-1964. **

ASB   Asiatic Society of Bengal, *Journal.* Calcutta, vol. 1-74, 1832-1904; NS vol. 1-30, 1905-1934; 3rd ser., vol. 1-24, 1935-1958; 4th ser., vol. 1-, 1959-. 1936 to July 1951 called Royal Asiatic Society of Bengal; 1951- called Asiatic Society, Calcutta. ‡ vol. 1-74, NS vol. 1-30, 3rd ser., vol. 1-24, 4th ser., vol. 1-4 (Sept. 1964).

ASBP   Asiatic Society of Bengal, *Proceedings.* Calcutta, 1865-1904 (previously and subsequently pub. tog. with ASB). Index, 1865-1883. ‡ Index and 1884-1886.

ASP   Asiatic Society of Pakistan, *Journal.* Dacca, 1956-. ‡ vol. 1-10, no. 1 (June 1965).

AT   *Anthropology Tomorrow.* Chicago, 1952-.

AUJR   *Agra University Journal of Research (Letters).* Agra, Nov. 1952-. ‡ vol. 1-7, no. 1; 8-12, no. 1.

AV   *Artha Vijñāna.* Poona, 1959-. Chiefly in English. †, ‡ vol. 1-7 (1965).

B   *Bookman.* London, vol. 1-87, Oct. 1891–Dec. 1934.

BABO   Association of British Orientalists, *Bulletin.* London, 1951-1961; NS vol. 1-, March 1963-. Title varies: 1951, *Bulletin of Near Eastern and Indian Studies*; 1954/55-1961, *Bulletin of Oriental Studies*; not issued 1952/53, 1958. ‡ NS vol. 1 (1963).

BGM   *Bombay Geographical Magazine.* Bombay, Oct. 1953-. ‡ vol. 1-11 (1964).

BHS   Bombay Historical Society, *Journal.* Bombay, 1928-.

BIN   *Bulletin of International News.* London, Feb. 1925–June 1945; name changed to *World Today* July 1945.

BJES   *British Journal of Educational Studies.* London, Nov. 1952-.

BJS   *British Journal of Sociology.* London, March 1950-.

BM   *Blackwood's Magazine.* Edinburgh, 1817-. ‡ 1817-1963, *, **.

BORS   Bihar and Orissa Research Society, *Journal.* Bankipore, 1915-1917; Patna, 1917-; in 1943, became BRS. ‡ vol. 1-28, Sept. 1915–June 1943.

BP   *Biśbabhārati Patrikā.* Calcutta, 1942-.

BPP   *Bengal: Past and Present.* Calcutta, June 1907-. ‡ vol. 1-85 (1965).

BQ   *Baptist Quarterly.* London, NS 1-, Jan. 1922- (supersedes Baptist Historical Society, *Transactions*).

BRS   Bihar Research Society, *Journal.* Patna, vol. 29-, 1943-; see BORS. ‡ vol. 29-49 (1963).

BSOAS London, University, School of Oriental and African Studies, *Bulletin.* London, 1939-. ‡ 1939-1964.

BSOS   London, University, School of Oriental Studies, *Bulletin.* London, 1917-1938; became BSOAS.

BTLV   *Bijdragen tot de Taal-, Land-, en Volkenkunde van Nederlandsch-Indië.* The Hague, 1853-. **

BUJ   Bombay University, *Journal.* Bombay, 1932-. ‡ vol. 1-32 (1963).

BV   *Bhāratīya Vidyā.* Bombay, 1939-. ‡ vol. 1-16, 19 (1959).

C   *Commonweal.* London, 1885-. *

Co   *Comprendre.* Venice, 1950-.

Con   *Confluence. An International Forum.* Cambridge, Mass., 1952-.

CoR   *Contemporary Review.* New York, July 1879-. ‡ 1879-1964.

CAR   *Central Asian Review.* London, Jan./March 1953-. ‡ vol. 1-13 (1965).

C&AR   *Colonial and Asiatic Review.* London, July 1852–June 1853. ‡ vol. 1, 2.

CC   *Christian Century.* Chicago, 1884-. *, **

CE   *Ceylon Economist.* Dehiwela, Ceylon, Aug. 1950-.

CH   *Current History.* New York, 1941-. *

CHJ   *Cambridge Historical Journal.* London, vol. 1-13 (1923-1957); became HJ. ‡ vol. 1-13.

CHM   *Cahiers d'histoire mondiale; Journal of World History; Cuadernos de historia mundial.* Paris, July 1953-. ‡ vol. 1-6.

CIEH   *Contributions to Indian Economic History.* Calcutta, 1961, 1963-. ‡ 1961, 1963.

CJA   Marius B. Jansen, ed. *Changing Japanese Attitudes Toward Modernization*. Princeton, N.J., 1965.

CJEPS   *Canadian Journal of Economics and Political Science*. Toronto, 1935-.

CJHSS   *Ceylon Journal of Historical and Social Studies*. Peradeniya, Ceylon, Jan. 1958-. ‡ vol. 1-7 (1964).

CL   *Comparative Literature*. Eugene, Oregon, Winter 1949-.

CM   *Cornhill Magazine*. London, Jan. 1860-.

CR   *Calcutta Review*. Calcutta, vol. 1-135 (May 1844–Oct. 1912); NS vol. 1-32 (Jan. 1913–Oct. 1920); 3rd ser., vol. 1- (Oct. 1921-); Index vol. 1-50. ‡ vol. 1-45, vol. 46-50 searched in index; ‡ vol. 51-80; xerox copies of tables of contents of vol. 81-108 searched; ‡ vol. 109-129, NS vol. 1-29, 3rd ser.: 1-176 (Aug. 1965).

CSA   Calcutta Statistical Association, *Bulletin*. Calcutta, Aug. 1947-.

CSSH   *Comparative Studies in Society and History*. The Hague, Oct. 1958-. ‡ vol. 1-6 (1964).

D   *Dial*. Chicago and New York, vol. 1-86, no. 7 (May 1880–July 1929). *

DA   *Dissertation Abstracts*. Ann Arbor, Michigan, 1938-; vol. 1-11 known as *Microfilm Abstracts*. ‡ vol. 1-26.

DCI   *Deuxième conférence internationale d'histoire économique* (*Aix-en-Provence*). Paris, Mouton, 1952.

DCRI   Deccan College Postgraduate and Research Institute, *Bulletin*. Poona, Dec. 1939-. ‡ vol. 1-8, 11, 21-23.

DR   *Dalhousie Review*. Halifax, April 1921-.

DS   *Difesa sociale*. Rome, 1922-.

E   *Encounter*. London, Oct. 1957-.

EaW   *Eastern World*. London, 1947-.

EcHR   *Economic History Review*. London, Jan. 1927-. ‡ 1945-1965.

En   *Enquiry*. Delhi, vol. 1-6, 1959-1963; NS vol. 1-, Feb. 1964-.

EnR   *English Review*. London, vol. 1-64, no. 7 (Dec. 1908–July 1937).

Es   *Esprit. Revue internationale*. Paris, Oct. 1932-.

Eu   *Europe*. Paris, Feb. 15, 1923-.

EA   *Eastern Anthropologist*. Lucknow, Sept. 1947-. ‡ vol. 1-4, 7, 8, 13, 14.

EB   *Encyclopedia Britannica*. 11th ed., New York, 1910-11.

EDCC   *Economic Development and Cultural Change*. Chicago, March 1952-. ‡ vol. 1-11 (July 1963).

EE   *Eastern Economist*. New Delhi, May 21, 1943-.

EG   *Economic Geography*. Concord, N.H. and Worcester, Mass., March 1925-. **

EHR   *English Historical Review*. London, 1886-. ‡ vol. 1-80 (1965). **

EI   *Encyclopedia of Islam*. New ed., Leiden and London, 1960-. ‡ vol. 1, 2 (through "G").

EJ   *Economic Journal.* London, New York, 1891-. **

ER   *Edinburgh Review.* Edinburgh, 1802-. ‡ vol. 1–date. *

EW   *Economic Weekly.* Bombay, Jan. 1949-.

E&W   *East and West.* Bombay, 1905-1921. ‡ vol. 4-8.

F   *Folk-lore.* Calcutta, 1960-. In 1958, 1959, known as *Indian Folk-lore.* ‡ vol. 1-4 (1963).

Fo   *Forum.* New York, vol. 1-103, no. 6 (March 1886–June 1940); merged into CH. *

Fr   *Frontsoldat erzählt.* Kiel, 1932-.

FrA   *France-Asie.* Saigon, April 15, 1946-. ‡ 1946-1963.

FA   *Foreign Affairs.* New York, Sept. 15, 1922-. *, **

FAR   *Foreign Affairs Reports.* New Delhi, July/Aug. 1952-.

FEQ   *Far Eastern Quarterly.* Ann Arbor, Michigan, Nov. 1941–May 1956; thereafter called JAS. ‡ 1941-1956.

FES   *Far Eastern Survey.* New York, March 3, 1932-. until Dec. 21, 1934, called Institute of Pacific Relations, *Memoranda.*

FI   *Foro internacional.* Mexico City, July/Sept. 1960-.

FPR   *Foreign Policy Reports.* New York, Oct. 5, 1925-. *, **

FR   *Fortnightly Review.* London, vol. 1-182, May 15, 1865–Dec. 1954; absorbed by CoR. After July 1934 called *Fortnightly.*

GeM   *Geographical Magazine.* London, May 1935-.

GJ   *Geographical Journal.* London, Jan. 1893-. **

GKSV   *O genezise kapitalizma v stranakh vostoka (xv-xix vv.).* (On the Genesis of Capitalism in the Countries of the East, 15-19 centuries). Moscow, 1962.

GM   *Gandhi Marg. A Quarterly Journal of Gandhian Thought.* New Delhi, Jan. 1957-. ‡ vol. 1-7 (1963).

GO   *Geographical Outlook.* Ranchi, 1956-.

GR   *Geographical Review.* New York, Jan. 1916-. **

GRI   *Geographical Review of India.* Calcutta, Sept. 1936-.

GRS   Gujarat Research Society, *Journal.* Bombay, 1939?-.

GUJ   Gauhati University, *Journal.* Gauhati, 1950-. ‡ vol. 1-3, 5-8.

GUOS   Glasgow University Oriental Society, *Transactions.* Glasgow, 1907-. ‡ vol. 1-14 (1950/52).

H   *History.* London, vol. 1-4, Jan. 1912–Dec. 1915; NS vol. 1-, April 1916-.

HiR   *Hitotsubashi Ronsō* Hititsubashi Review). Tokyo, Jan. 1938-.

HmJ   *Himalayan Journal.* Calcutta, April 1929-. ‡ vol. 3-22.

Hn   *Historian.* Albuquerque, N.M., Winter 1938-. ‡ vol. 17-26 (1954-1964).

HuR   *Human Relations; Studies towards the Integration of the Social Sciences.* London, June 1947-.

HA   *Historical Abstracts, 1775-1945.* Santa Barbara, California, March 1955-. ‡ vol. 1-12.1 (March 1966).

HFM   *History of the Freedom Movement.* Karachi, Pakistan Historical Society.

HIPC   C. H. Philips, ed. *Historians of India, Pakistan and Ceylon.* London, Oxford University Press, 1961.

HJ   *The Historical Journal.* Cambridge, England, 1958-. Supersedes CHJ.

HJE   *Hitotsubashi Journal of Economics.* Tokyo, Oct. 1960-.

HL   *Harvard Library Bulletin.* Cambridge, Mass., Winter 1947-.

HM   *Harpers Magazine.* New York, June 1850-. *

HR   *Hindustan Review.* Patna, 1900-1954. ‡ vol. 23, 25-39, 81, 82.

HS   *Historical Studies, Australia and New Zealand.* Melbourne, 1940-.

HT   *History Today.* London, Jan. 1951-. ‡ vol. 1-15 (1965).

HYUC   Gupta, Pratulchandra and Niharranjan Ray, eds. *Hundred Years of the University of Calcutta.* Calcutta University, 1957.

I   *Iqbal.* Lahore, July 1952-; Urdu and English, alternate issues.

In   *Indonesië: Tweemaandelijks tijdschrift gewijd aan het Indonesisch cultuurgebied.* The Hague, 1947-.

InAf   *Indian Affairs.* London, vol. 1-2, no. 3 (March 1930–Jan. 1932). ‡ vol. 1, 2.

InC   *International Conciliation.* New York, 1907-. *

IAn   *Indian Antiquary.* Bombay, vol. 1-62, 1872-1933. Index vol. 1-50 (1872-1921). ‡ vol. 1-62.

IAC   *Indo-Asian Culture.* New Delhi, 1953?-. ‡ vol. 1-12 (1963).

IAEH   [India: Articles in Economic History], Moscow, 1958 (in Russian).

IAL   *Indian Arts and Letters* and *Arts and Letters, India and Pakistan.* London, 1925-1947, 1948-. ‡ vol. 1-35 (1959).

IAP   *Islamic Academy Patrika.* Dacca, April/June 1961-.

IAQR   *Imperial and Asiatic Quarterly Review.* See AR.

IC   *Islamic Culture.* Hyderabad, A.P., Jan. 1927-. ‡ vol. 1-38 (1964).

IEJ   *Indian Economic Journal.* Bombay, July 1953-. †

IER   *Indian Economic Review.* Delhi, Feb. 1952-. †

IEvR   *Indian Evangelical Review.* Calcutta, 1873-. ‡ vol. 23-29 (1896/97-1902/03).

IESHR   *Indian Economic and Social History Review.* Delhi, July/Sept. 1963-. ‡ vol. 1, 2.

IG   *Indian Geographer.* New Delhi, Aug. 1956-. ‡ vol. 1-6, no. 1 (1961).

IHCP   Indian History Congress, *Proceedings.* Allahabad, etc., 1935-. ‡ 1935-.

IHQ   *Indian Historical Quarterly.* Calcutta, March 1925-. ‡ vol. 1-38 (1962).

IHRB   Institute of Historical Research, *Bulletin.* London, 1938-. ‡
        vol. 1-38 (1965).

IHRC   Indian Historical Records Commission, *Proceedings.* New
        Delhi, 1919-. ‡ vol. 1-16 (1963); all pp. given below are in
        part 2 of the *Proceedings.*

II   *Indo-Iranica.* Calcutta, 1946-. ‡ vol. 1-17 (1964).

IIJ   *Indo-Iranian Journal.* The Hague, 1957-. ‡ vol. 1-6.

IJAE   *Indian Journal of Agricultural Economics.* Bombay, July 1946-.

IJE   *Indian Journal of Economics.* Allahabad, 1916-. †

IJHM   *Indian Journal of the History of Medicine.* Madras, 1956-. ‡
        vol. 1-6 (1961).

IJPA   *Indian Journal of Public Administration.* New Delhi, Jan./
        March 1955-. ‡ vol. 1-10 (1964), 11.2.

IJPS   *Indian Journal of Political Science.* Lucknow, 1939-. ‡ vol. 1-12,
        15, 19-26 (1965).

IL   *Indian Literature.* Delhi, 1957-. ‡ vol. 1-6 (1963).

ILn   *Indian Librarian.* Jullundur City and Simla, 1946-.

ILA   Indian Library Association, *Journal.* Calcutta, 1956-.

ILI   Indian Law Institute, *Journal.* Delhi, 1958.

ILR   *International Labour Review.* Geneva, Jan. 1921.

IQ   *India Quarterly.* New Delhi, Jan. 1945-. ‡ vol. 2-21 (1965).

IR   *The Indian Review.* Madras, 1905-. ‡ vol. 9-31.

IRM   *The International Review of Missions.* Edinburgh, 1912-. ‡
        Indexes, 1912-1931 (in vol. 10, 20), **

IRSH   *International Review of Social History.* Assen, 1956-.

IS   *International Studies.* Bombay, 1959-. ‡ vol. 1-5 (1964).

ISPP   *Indian Studies: Past and Present.* Calcutta, 1959/60-. ‡ vol.
        1-7, no. 1 (Dec. 1964).

ISSB   *International Social Science Bulletin.* Paris, 1949-. After 1959
        called *International Social Science Journal.*

ITC   Institute of Traditional Cultures, *Bulletin.* Madras, 1957-.

IUF   Turner, Roy, ed. *India's Urban Future.* Berkeley and Los
        Angeles, University of California Press, 1962.

IYBIA   *Indian Year Book of International Affairs.* Madras, 1952-. ‡
        vol. 1-13 (1964).

JAS   *Journal of Asian Studies.* Ann Arbor, Michigan, Nov. 1941-.
        Through May 1956, called FEQ. ‡ 1956-1965.

JBR   *Journal of Bible and Religion.* Garden City, N.Y., 1933-.

JCPS   *Journal of Commonwealth Political Studies.* Leister, England,
        1961-. ‡ vol. 1-3.

JDS   *Journal of Development Studies.* London, Oct. 1964-.

JEH   *Journal of Economic History.* New York, May 1941-.

JEcH   *Journal of Ecclesiastical History.* London, April 1950-.

JESHO   *Journal of the Economic and Social History of the Orient.*
        Leiden, 1958-. ‡ vol. 1-7 (1964).

JIH	*Journal of Indian History.* Trivandrum, Nov. 1921-. ‡ vol. 1-43 (1965).
JITH	*Journal of Indian Textile History.* Ahmedabad, 1955-. ‡ vol. 1-6. (1961).
JJS	*Jewish Journal of Sociology.* London, 1959-.
JMH	*Journal of Modern History.* Chicago, 1929-. ‡ vol. 7-19, 21-34.
JNB	*J.N. Banerjea Memorial Volume.* Calcutta, Alumni Association, Department of Ancient History and Culture, Calcutta University, 1960.
JPE	*Journal of Political Economy.* Chicago, Dec. 1892-. *
JPHS	Punjab Historical Society, *Journal.* Lahore, vol. 1-11, no. 1 (1911-1931). ‡ vol. 1-11.
JPUHS	Punjab University Historical Society, *Journal.* Lahore, 1931- (none pub. 1936/37, 1939). ‡ vol. 1-11.
JQ	*Journalism Quarterly.* Iowa City, 1924-.
JRL	John Rylands Library, *Bulletin.* Manchester, Eng., April/June 1903-. **
JSH	*Journal of Southern History.* Baton Rouge, La., Feb. 1935-.
JSS	*Jewish Social Studies.* New York, 1939-.
JUP	University of Poona, *Journal (Humanities).* Poona, 1953-. ‡ vol. 1, 3, 5, 7, 9, 11, 13, 19.
KS	*Kratkie soobshcheniia* (Communications of the Institute of Oriental Studies). Moscow, 1951-.
KU	Karnatak University, *Journal (Humanities).* Dharwar, Nov. 1956-. ‡ vol. 1-7 (1963).
L	*The Listener.* London, 1929-.
Li	*Libri.* Copenhagen, 1950-.
LA	*Living Age.* Boston, New York, vol. 1-360 (May 11, 1844– Aug. 1941).*
LBP	Saggi, P.D., ed. *A Nation's Homage; Life and Work of Lal, Bal, and Pal.* New Delhi, Overseas Publishing House, 1962.
LD	*Literary Digest.* New York, vol. 1-125, no. 8 (March 1, 1890– Feb. 19, 1938), merged into *Time.*
LM	*Labour Monthly.* London, July 1921-. **
LQ	*Library Quarterly.* Chicago, Jan. 1931-. **
LSBT	Literary Society of Bombay, *Transactions.* London, vol. 1-3, 1819-1823; reprinted at Bombay Education Society's Press, 1877. ‡ vol. 1-3.
LSGI	Local Self-Government Institute, *Quarterly Journal.* Bombay, July 1930-; indexes in vol. 11, 22. ‡ vol. 1-34.
LY	*Li-shih Yen-chiu.* Peking, Jan. 1954-. Additional tables of contents in Russian and English.
M	*Mankind.* Hyderabad, Aug. 1956-.
Mi	Akademie der Wissenschaften, Berlin, Institut für Orientforschung. *Mitteilungen.* Berlin.

MsR   *Muslim Review.* Calcutta, vol. 1-4, 1926-1930. ‡ vol. 1-4.

MA   *Modern Age.* New York, vol. 1-3, Jan. 1883–June 1884.

MAKA   Humayun Kabir, ed. *Maulana Abul Kalam Azad. A Memorial Volume.* New York, Asia Publishing House, 1959.

MEJ   *Middle East Journal.* Washington, D.C., Jan. 1947-.

MIF   *Munshi Indological Felicitation Volume. Bharātīya Vidya,* vol. 20-21, 1960-61 (issued 1963).

MII   *Man in India.* Ranchi, 1921-.

MIQ   *Medieval India Quarterly.* Aligarh, July 1950-.

MIW   O'Malley, L.S.S., ed. *Modern India and the West; a Study of the Interaction of their Civilizations.* London, etc., Oxford University Press, 1941.

MJLS   *Madras Journal of Literature and Science.* Madras, 1834-1894; suspended pub. 1866-77, 1881-85. Index for 1833-66 in *Revue linguistique* (Paris) tome 32 (1899), 1-38. ‡ Index, 1878-81, 1886-94.

MLR   U.S. Bureau of Labor Statistics, *Monthly Labor Review.* Washington, D.C., July 1915-. *

MM   *Macmillan's Magazine.* London, vol. 1-92 (Nov. 1859–Oct. 1905); NS vol. 1-2 (Nov. 1905–Oct. 1907).

MP   *Modern Philology.* Chicago, June 1903-.

MQ   *Midwest Quarterly.* Lincoln, Nebraska, vol. 1-5, Oct. 1913–July 1918.

MR   *Modern Review.* Allahabad, 1907; Calcutta, 1908-. ‡ vol. 1-19, 21, 23-66, 69-72, 74, no. 3-118 (1965).

MRW   *Missionary Review of the World.* Princeton, N.J. and London, vol. 1-62 (1878–Dec. 1939). *

MS   Mythic Society, *Quarterly Journal.* Bangalore, Oct. 1909-. ‡ vol. 1-53 (1963).

MSESS   *Manchester School of Economic and Social Studies.* Manchester, 1930-.

MSUB   Maharaja Sayajirao University of Baroda, Oriental Institute, *Journal.* Baroda, Sept. 1951-.

MUJ   Madras University, *Journal.* Madras, 1928-1942; 1943- in 2 sections: A, Humanities; B, Science. ‡ vol. 1-16, 17, no. 2, 18, no. 2, 23-28, 29, no. 1, 30-32, 34, no. 2.

MW   *Moslem World.* London, 1911-. From vol. 38, called *Muslim World.* ‡ vol. 1-32, 34-55 (1965). **

N   *Nation.* New York, 1865-. *

NA   *North American Review.* Boston and New York, vol. 1-248 (May 1815–Winter 1939/40). *

NAA   *Narody Azii i Afriki* (Peoples of Asia and Africa). Moscow, 1959-; supersedes SV. Indexed in SPA. Title also in Chinese, Hindi, Urdu; tables of contents also in English, Chinese; summaries in English.

NC   *Nineteenth Century*. London, March 1877–Dec. 1900; Jan. 1901-1950 called *The Nineteenth Century and After*; thereafter called *Twentieth Century*. Index, vol. 1-50. ‡ 1877-1963. *

NE   Howe, Suzanne. *Novels of Empire*. New York, Columbia University Press, 1949.

NEI   *Near East and India*. London, NS vol. 28-45, July 2, 1925–Sept. 19, 1935 (previous issues called *Great Britain and the East* and *Near East*.) **

NEM   *New England Magazine*. Boston, vol. 1-6, Jan. 1884–Oct. 1888; NS vol. 1-56, no. 6 (Sept. 1889–March 1917). *

NEQ   *New England Quarterly*. Portland, Maine, Jan. 1928-. **

NGJI   *National Geographic Journal of India*. Banaras, 1955-.

NLM   [National-Liberation Movement in India and Bal Gangadhar Tilak]. Moscow, 1958 (in Russian).

NO   *Nový orient*. Prague, Jan. 1945-.

NR   *National Review*. London, March 1883-.

NRp   *New Republic*. New York, Nov. 7, 1914-.

NSI   Numismatic Society of India, *Journal*. Banaras, 1931-.

NT   *New Times*. Moscow, 1943?-.

Or   *Orient*. Paris, Jan. 1957-. ‡ vol. 1-9 (1965).

Ou   *Outlook*. London, vol. 1-61 (Feb. 5, 1898–June 30, 1928). **

Ov   *Overland Monthly*. San Francisco, vol. 1-15, July 1868–Dec. 1875; 2nd ser., vol. 1-33, no. 4 (1883–July 1935); suspended 1876-1882. *

OC   *Open Court*. Chicago, vol. 1-50, Feb. 17, 1887–Oct. 1936. **

OG   *Oriental Geographer*. Dacca, Jan. 1957-. Index vol. 1-4 in vol. 4.

OH   *Oriental Herald and Journal of General Literature*. London, vol. 1-23 (Jan. 1824–Dec. 1829). ‡ vol. 1-7.

OHRJ   *Orissa Historical Research Journal*. Bhubaneswar, 1952-. ‡ vol. 1-8, 10 (1961/62).

OM   *Oriente moderno*. Rome, June 1921-.

OMRR   *Oriental Magazine, Review and Register*. Calcutta, vol. 1-8, 1823-1827.

ONU   *Obshchestvennye nauki v Usbekistane*. Tashkent.

ORLD   *Orient Review and Literary Digest*. Calcutta, 1955-. ‡ vol. 1-5 (1959).

OSEI   *Die Ökonomische und Soziale Entwicklung Indiens: Sowietische Beiträge zur Indischen Geschichte*. Band I. Herausgegeben von Walter Ruben. Akademie-Verlag, Berlin, 1959.

P   *The Pamphleteer*. London, vol. 1-29, March 1813-Dec. 1828. Index in vol. 29.

Po   *Il politico*. Pavia, April, 1928-.

PoQ   *Political Quarterly*. London, Jan. 1930-. **

PoR   *Population Review*. Madras, Jan. 1957-.

PoS   *Political Studies.* Oxford, Feb. 1953-.

PrlA   *Parliamentary Affairs.* London, Winter 1947-.

PubA   *Public Administration.* Kanpur, Jan. 1963-.

PA   *Pacific Affairs.* Honolulu; Camden, N.J., NS Jan. 1928-. ‡ NS vol. 20-38 (1965); vol. NS 1-19 exclusively on the Far East.

PB   *Prabuddha Bhārata.* Calcutta, 1937-.

PEJ   *Pakistan Economic Journal.* Lahore, July 1949-. †

PGR   *Pakistan Geographical Review.* Lahore, 1942-. 1942, 1947-48, called *Panjab Geographical Review*; suspended 1943-46.

PH   *Pakistan Horizon.* Karachi, March 1948-.

PHR   *Pacific Historical Review.* Glendale, Calif., March 1932-. **, ‡ vol. 1-23, 25-32 (1963).

PHS   Pakistan Historical Society, *Journal.* Karachi, Jan. 1953-. ‡ vol. 1-13 (1965).

PHSM   Pakistan Historical Society, *Memoir.* Karachi, 1956-.

PI   Cumming, John Ghest., ed. *Political India, 1832-1932.* London, etc., Oxford University Press, 1932.

PIS   *Prepodavanie istorii v shkole.* Moscow, 1946-.

PO   *Przeglad orientalistczny.* Warsaw, 1948-.

POr   *Poona Orientalist.* Poona, April 1936-.

PPHC   Pakistan History Conference, *Proceedings.* Karachi, 1951-. ‡ vol. 1-6 (1956).

PQ   *Pakistan Quarterly.* Karachi, April 1949-. Index for vol. 1-11 in vol. 11 (Summer 1963), 61-73. ‡ Index and vol. 12-13.

PR   *Pakistan Review.* Lahore, 1953-. ‡ April, May, Oct.–Dec. 1954; March–May 1955; Jan.–Aug., Oct. 1956; 1957-1958; May 1959; Oct.–Dec. 1960; Feb. 1961; Feb.–Dec. 1962; Jan.–Oct., Dec. 1963; 1964; 1965.

PS   *Population Studies.* London, 1947-.

PSI   Philips, C.H., ed. *Politics and Society in India.* London, George Allen and Unwin, 1963.

PSQ   *Political Science Quarterly.* New York, March 1886-. *

PSR   *Political Science Review.* Jaipur, 1962-. ‡ vol. 1-4 (1965).

PSS   Poona Sarvajanik Sabha, *Quarterly Journal.* Poona, vol. 1-13, 1878-1890. ‡ vol. 1-8.

PU   Patna University, *Journal.* Patna, July 1944-. English and Sanskrit.

Q   *Quest.* Bombay, Aug. 1955-. ‡ vol. 15-47 (1965).

QJE   *Quarterly Journal of Economics.* Cambridge, Mass., 1886-. *, †

QJPSS   *Quarterly Journal of Political and Social Science.*

QQ   *Queen's Quarterly.* Kingston, Ontario, 1893-. *

QR   *Quarterly Review.* London, Feb. 1809-. *, **

QRHS   *Quarterly Review of Historical Studies.* Calcutta, April/June 1961-. ‡ vol. 1-5 (1965/66).

R   *Race.* London, Nov. 1959-.

RdE *Revue des études islamiques.* Paris, 1927-. Supersedes RMM.

Reb. Joshi, P. H., ed. *Rebellion 1857: A Symposium.* Bombay, People's Publishing House, 1957.

RAS Royal Asiatic Society of Great Britain and Ireland, *Journal.* London, 1834-. Index in the society's centenary volume, 1923. ‡ 1834-1965.

RASB Royal Asiatic Society, Bombay Branch, *Journal.* Bombay, vol. 1-26, 1841-1923; NS vol. 1-, 1924-. ‡ vol. 1-26, NS vol. 1-37 (1961/62, issued 1964).

RCAS Royal Central Asian Society, *Journal.* London, 1914-. ‡ vol. 1-52 (1965).

RE *Revue encyclopédique.* Paris, vol. 1-61, 1819-1835.

REJ *Revue des études juives.* Paris, 1880-.

REL *Review of English Literature.* London, 1960-.

RHS Royal Historical Society, *Transactions.* London, 1869-1882; NS 1884-1907; 3rd ser., 1908-.

RIGB Royal Institution of Great Britain, *Proceedings.* London, 1851-.

RK *Rekishigaku kenkyu; the Journal of the Historical Science Society.* Tokyo, Nov. 1933-.

RMM *Revue du monde musulman.* Paris, vol. 1-66, 1906-1926. Became RdE. Index, vol. 1-66 in vol. 65/66.

RP *Review of Politics.* Notre Dame, Indiana, Jan. 1939-.

RPI *Revue politique internationale.* Lausanne, vol. 1-13, 1914-1920.

RS *Reference Shelf,* no. 16.3 (1943); comp. J. E. Johnson.

RSA Royal Society of Arts, *Journal.* London, Nov. 26, 1852-.

RSS Royal Statistical Society, *Journal.* London, 1838-. **

RT *Round Table.* London, 1910-. ‡ 1910-1965. **

RU Rajasthan University, *Studies: Arts.* Jaipur, 1951-. 1951-1955 called University of Rajputana *Studies.* ‡ 1951-1962.

S *Survey.* New York, vol. 1-68, Dec. 1897–1932. *

Sa *Sankhya.* Calcutta, 1933-.

Se *Seminar.* Bombay, 1959-.

Sh *Shakti.* New Delhi, Dec. 1964-.

Sm *Saeculum.* Freiburg, 1950-.

StOA *Studies on Asia.* Lincoln, Nebraska, 1960-, ed. Robert K. Sakai. ‡ 1960-1965.

SA *Scientific American.* New York, vol. 1-14, Aug. 28, 1845–June 25, 1859; NS vol. 1-, July 2, 1859-. *

SAA Iyer, Raghavan, ed. *South Asian Affairs, No. 1* (St. Antony's Papers, No. 8), London, Chatto and Windus, 1960.

SAHR Society for Army Historical Research, *Journal.* London, 1921-. Index vol. 1-12. ‡ Index and vol. 13-40 (1962).

SANJ *South Australian Numismatic Journal.* Adelaide, Jan. 1950-. After Jan. 1958 called *Australian Numismatic Journal.*

SAQ *South Atlantic Quarterly.* Durham, N.C., Jan. 1902-. **

SBR   Gupta, Atulchandra, ed. *Studies in the Bengal Renaissance; in Commemoration of the Birth Centenary of Bipinchandra Pal.* Jadavpur, National Council of Education, 1958.

S&C   *Science and Culture.* Calcutta, 1935-.

SE   *Social Education.* Crawfordsville, Indiana, Jan. 1937-.

SEJ   *Southern Economic Journal.* Chapel Hill, N.C., Oct. 1933-. †

SGM   *Scottish Geographical Magazine.* Edinburgh, Jan. 1885-. **

SI   *Studia Islamica.* Paris, 1953-. ‡ vol. 1-19 (1963).

SIS   Butt, Abdullah, ed. *Aspects of Shah Ismail Shaheed.* Lahore: Qaumi Kutub Khana, 1943.

SOA   Society of Arts, *Journal.* London, Nov. 26, 1852-. After 1908, called RSA.

SP   *Sovetskaia pedagogika.* Moscow, July 1937-.

SPA   *Soviet Periodical Abstracts: Asia, Africa, Latin America.* New York, vol. 2-, May 1962-. See SSAB. ‡ vol. 2-4, no. 2; 5, no. 1, 2.

SR   *Sewanee Review.* Sewanee, Tenn., Nov. 1892-.

SS   *Science and Society.* New York, 1936-.

SSAB   *Selective Soviet Annotated Bibliographies.* New York, vol. 1 (May 1961–March 1962). Became SPA.

SV   *Sovetskoe vostokovedenie* (Soviet Orientology). Moscow, Leningrad, 1940-1958? Superseded by NAA.

SWJ   *Sir William Jones: Bicentenary of His Birth Commemoration Volume 1746-1946.* Calcutta: Royal Asiatic Society of Bengal, 1948.

SZ   *Shigaku-zasshi.* Tokyo, Dec. 1889-.

TwC   *Twentieth Century.* See NC

TBKK   *Toyo bunka kenkyusho kiyo* (Memoirs of the Institute for Oriental Culture). Tokyo, Dec. 1943-. Tables of contents also in English; summaries in English.

TC   *Tamil Culture.* Tuticorin, 1952-. ‡ vol. 1-11 (1964/65).

TG   *Toyo gakuho.* Tokyo, Jan. 1911-.

UB   *Uttara Bharati.* Lucknow, 1954-. ‡ vol. 1, 2, scattered later issues.

UDA   *University Debaters Annual.* New York, vol. 1-37 (1914/15–1950/51). *

UPHS   Uttar Pradesh Historical Society, *Journal.* Lucknow, vol. 1-24/25, Sept. 1917–1951/52; NS vol. 1-, 1953-. Early volumes issued by United Provinces Historical Society. ‡ vol. 1-23, NS vol. 1-5, 8.

US   *University Studies.* Karachi, April 1964-.

USI   Royal United Service Institution of India, *Journal.* Simla, 1871/72-. Also called *U.S.I. Journal.*

USOE   United States Office of Education, *Bulletin.* Washington, D.C., 1906-. *

UTQ   *University of Toronto Quarterly*. Toronto, July 1900-.

UZIV   *Uchenye zapiski instituta vostokovedeniia* (Memoirs of the Institute of Oriental Studies). Moscow.

VBA   *Visva Bharati Annals*. Santiniketan, 1948-. ‡ vol. 2-10 (1961).

VBB   *Visva Bharati Bulletin*. Calcutta, 1924-.

VBN   *Visva Bharati News*. Calcutta, July 1932-.

VBQ   *Visva Bharati Quarterly*. Calcutta, vol. 1-84, April 1923–Jan. 1932; NS vol. 1-, May/June 1935-.

VIs   *Voprosy istorii* (Problems of History). Moscow, 1945-.

VIMK   *Vestnik istorii mirovoi kul'tury*. Moscow.

VF   *Voprosy filosofii* (Problems of Philosophy). Moscow.

VLU   *Vestnik Leningradskogo universiteta (Istorii, iazik, literatura)*. Leningrad.

VMU   *Vestnik Moskovskogo universiteta, seriia 9, Istoriia*. Moscow.

VMUE   *Vestnik Moskovskogo universiteta, Ekonomika, Filosofiia*.

VS   *Victorian Studies*. Bloomington, Indiana, 1957-.

VSU   *Vierteljahresschrift für Sozial- u Wirtschaftsgeschichte*. Leipzig, 1903-. Suspended 1945-1948.

VZ   *Vierteljahrshefte für Zeitgeschichte*. Stuttgart, Jan. 1953-.

W   *Westminster Review*. London, vol. 1-180, 181, no. 1 (Jan. 1824–Jan. 1914). *

WA   *World Affairs Quarterly*. London, 1935-.

WAG   *Die Welt als Geschichte*. Stuttgart, Jan. 1935-.

WI   *Die Welt des Islams*. Berlin, 1913-.

WP   *World Politics*. New Haven, Conn., Oct. 1948-.

WPQ   *Western Political Quarterly*. Salt Lake City, Utah, March 1948-.

WSC   *Wên shih chê* (Shantung Ta-hsüeh hsüeh-pao). Tsingtao, May 1951-.

WSM   *Walpole Society Magazine* (Annual volume), Oxford, 1911/12-.

WZHUB   *Wissenschaftliche Zeitschrift der Humboldt-Universität zu Berlin*. Berlin.

YR   *Yale Review*. New Haven, Conn., vol. 1-19, May 1892–Feb. 1911; NS vol. 1-, Oct. 1911-. *

A. AREAS NOT PRIMARILY UNDER BRITISH CONTROL

1. *MUGHALS*

A1 ABDUL ALI, A. F. M. "Mirza Najaf Khan," BPP:55 (Jan.-June 1938), 118-24. Late 18th cent. contemporary of Shah 'Alam.

A2 ———. "Prince Jawan Bakht Jahandar Shah," BPP:54 (July-Dec. 1937), 9-17.

A3 ANSARI, A. S. BAZMEE. "Ghulām Kādir Rohilla," EI:2, 1092. Founder of Nadjībābād; remembered for his cruel treatment of Shah 'Alam and his family.

A4 ———. "Sayyid Ghulām Husayn Khān," EI:2, 1091-92. Bakhshi to Shah 'Alam.

A5 ASKARI, SYED HASAN. "A Copy of Dastur-ul-Amal," IHRC:18 (Jan. 1942), 178-87. Manuscript on last days of Mughals.

A6 ———. "Nawab Munir-ud-dowla. A Minister of Shah Alam," BORS: 27 (1941), 187-220.

A7 ———. "A Newly Discovered Letter of Shah Alam to George III," IHRC:20 (1943), 47-49.

A8 BANNERJI, R. D. "Mir Shihabuddin," MsR:2 (April-June 1928), 21-31. Wazir at Mughal court, mid-18th cent.

A9 ·BHARGAVA, K. D. "British Attitude to Mughal Firmans," IHRC:33 (1958), 36-38. Extracts.

A10 BUCKLER, F. W. "The Historical Antecedents of the *Khilāfat* Movement," CR:121 (May 1922), 603-11. A sketch of 18th and 19th century Mughal politics in the light of Sunni-Shiah conflicts and Otto-man-Safavi-Mughal diplomatic history. Not reliable, but interesting.

A11 BULLOCK, H. "Captain Manuel Deremao," JPUHS:1 (Dec. 1932), 155-71. Succeeded to a jagir near Delhi.

A12 CHATTERJI, NANDALAL. "Shah Alam at Allahabad (1767-69)," UPHS:12 (Dec. 1939), 60-86. Persian manuscripts.

A13 COTTON, JULIAN JAMES (ed.). "General de Boigne and the Taj," BPP:33 (Jan.-June 1927), 12-24. Correspondence on the condition of the Mughal royal family.

A14 DATTA, KALIKINKAR. "Delhi Restoration, 1772," JIH:43 (April 1965), 71-86.

A15 ———. "Factors in the Eighteenth Century History of India," CR:62 (March 1937), 309-20. Thoughts on the general trends of history in this period.

A16 ———. "Provision for Shah Alam II and His Family at Delhi in 1804," BPP:67 (1948), 22-31. National Archive records.

A17 FRANKLIN, WILLIAM. "An Account of the Present State of Delhi," AsR:4 (1795), 417-31. Description of city, palace, and an audience with 72-year-old Shah 'Alam in travels of Capt. Reynolds.

A18 "The Great Anarchy," CR:108 (Jan., April 1899), 1-16, 216-35; 109 (July-Oct. 1899), 1-18, 193-216; 110 (Jan., April 1900), 1-22, 193-217; 111 (July 1900), 1-11. On the last half of the 18th cent.

A19 GUPTA, HARI RAM. "Adina Beg Khan; The Last Mughal Viceroy of the Punjab," IC:13 (July 1939), 323-38. Biography of 18th cent. officer.

A20 GUPTA, P. C. "An English Manuscript on Shah Alam II," IHRC:21 (1944), 20-21. A description of manuscript dated 1790.

A21 HABIBULLAH, A. B. M. "Shah Alam's Letter to George III," IHRC:16 (1939), 97-98. Tr. part of letter.

A22 HAQ, S. MOINUL. "The Last Days of the Mughal Dynasty," HFM:2 (1831-1905), Part 1, 1-26.

A23 HODIVALA, S. H. "A Portrait of Shāh 'Ālam II," ASB: NS 29 (1933), Numism. Supp. 44, 39N-42N.

A24 IRVINE, WILLIAM. "The Later Mughals (1707-1803)," ASB:65 (1896), 136-212; 67 (1898), 141-66; 72 (1903), 33-64; 73 (1904), 282-361; I Ext. 28-61; NS 4 (1908), 511-88; ASBP (1903), pp. 134-36; (1904), pp. 67-68.

A25 ———. "Note on the Official Reckoning of the Reigns of the Later Moghul Emperors and Some of Their Mint Towns," ASB:62 (1893), 256-65. Note on paper by A. F. R. Hoernle, ASB:62 (1893), 265-67.

A26 KEMAL, R. "The Evolution of British Sovereignty in India," IYBIA:6 (1957), 143-71. British relations with Mughals.

A27 KHAN, IMTIAZ MOHAMAD. "Ali Ibrahim Khan; A Forgotten Administrator and Writer," CR:39 (April 1931), 67-82. A disorganized, laudatory biographical sketch based on contemporary (late 18th cent.) records.

A28 MODAVE, L.-L. DOLISY DE. "The Delhi Empire a Century after Bernier; Translated from the French Manuscript by Sir Jadunath Sarkar," IC:11 (July 1937), 382-92.

PART I: ARTICLES

A29 [MORRISON]. "Major John Morrison, 'Ambassador from the Great Moghul,'" BPP:41 (Jan.-June 1931), 71-73. Worked for alliance with Mughals.

A30 NAWAZ, M. K. "Some Legal Aspects of Anglo-Mogul Relations," IYBIA:5 (1956), 70-83.

A31 "ORME'S Historical Fragments," ER:9 (Jan. 1807), 391-419.

A32 PAWAR, A. G. "Some Documents Bearing on Imperial Mughal Grants to Raja Shahu (1717-24)," IHRC:17 (1940), 204-15.

A33 QEYAMUDDIN, AHMAD. "Public Opinion as a Factor in the Government Appointments in the Mughal State," IHRC:31 (1955), 142-47. On Bihar in 18th cent., from materials in Patna.

A34 QURESHI, ISHTIAQ HUSAIN. "A Year in Pre-Mutiny Delhi (1837 A.C.)," IC:17 (July 1943), 282-97. Based on a volume of the Delhi Akhbār.

A35 RAHMAN, A. F. M. KHALILUR. "Najib-ud Daula, 1739-70," BPP:62 (1942), 1-24. The career of the Regent of the Empire in Delhi. Persian manuscript in British Museum.

A36 RIZAWI, M. H. "A Brief Note on Two Manuscripts in the National Archives of India," IHRC:31 (1955), 156-58. Late Mughal records.

A37 ROSS, E. DENISON. "Faqīr Khayr-ud-Din Muhammad, The Historian of Shāh 'Ālam," ASB:71 (1902), 136-41. Persian text of Khātima giving the Faqīr's life with English summary thereof.

A38 SAMADI, S. B. (tr.) "A Firman of Shah Alam Dated 1759 A.D.," UPHS:18 (1945), 202-03.

A39 SARKAR, JADUNATH. "A Correct Chronology of Delhi History, 1739-1754," BORS:18 (1932), 80-96. A political chronology with sources of information on each date indicated.

A40 ———. "Delhi during the Anarchy, 1749-1788, As Told in Contemporary Records," IHRC:3 (1921), 4-9; MR:29 (Feb. 1921), 204-07. Discussion of a contemporary chronicle at Patna.

A41 ———. "India's Military Decline in the 18th Century," MR:74 (Aug., Dec. 1943), 97-100, 417-20.

A42 ———. "Life of Najib-ud-daulah; the Last Phase," IC:8 (April 1934), 237-57.

A43 ———. "Mission of James Browne to the Delhi Court, 1783-1785," IHRC:14 (1937), 12-19; BPP:54 (July-Dec. 1937), 1-8. From Persian, Maratha, English records.

[29]

A44 ———(ed. and tr.). "Najib-ud-daulah as the Dictator of Delhi, 1761-1770," IC:7 (Oct. 1933), 613-39.

A45 ———(tr.). "Najib-ud-daulah, Ruhela Chief," IC:10 (Oct. 1936), 648-58.

A46 ———. "The Rise of Najib-ud-daula," IHQ:9 (Dec. 1933), 866-71.

A47 ———. "Zābita Khān, the Ruhela Chieftain," IHQ:2 (Dec. 1935), 640-51. Translation of a Persian MS in British Museum—continuation of translation in IHQ 1933 (on Najib-ud-daula).

A48 SPEAR, T. G. P. "Bahādur Shāh II," EI:1, 914. The last Mughal Emperor, reigned 1837-1857.

A49 ———. "The Grounds of Political Obedience in the Indian State," JPUHS:4 (April 1935), 4-23. Penetrating and challenging thoughts on political history and the requirements of Indian political life, especially as appreciated and used by the Mughals and their successors, the British.

A50 ———. "The Mogul Family and the Court in 19th Century Delhi," JIH:20 (April 1941), 38-60. The social and cultural history of the royal family, pointing not only to its decadence but to its continued role as "a school for manners" and a source of cultural patronage.

A51 ———. "Some Aspects of Late Mughal Delhi," JPUHS:5 (April 1938), 1-18. Covers 1772-1857; based on Home Misc. Series and other English records. Discussion of Rammohun Roy's role in negotiations on royal stipend, as a prelude to Mutiny.

A52 ———. "The Twilight of the Moghuls," BPP:39 (Jan.-June 1930), 124-143; MR:4 (Jan.-March 1930), 1-23. A brief history of the court in the 19th cent.

A53 SRIVASTAVA, A. L. "The Failure of Shah Alam II's First Expedition to Delhi (1765-66)," IHRC:17 (1940), 195-98.

A54 TAYLOR, G. P. "List Complementary to Mr. Whitehead's 'Mint Towns of the Mughal Emperors of India,'" ASB: NS:10 (May 1914), 178-95. "List exhibiting for each reign its active mints and their metals."

A55 ———. "Some Dates Relating to the Mughal Emperors of India," ASB: NS 3 (1907), 57-64. Exact dates of accession and death in A.H. and A.D.

2. THE DUTCH

A56 CHATTERJEE, NANDALAL. "Anglo-Dutch Disputes during Verelst's Administration in Bengal (1767-69)," IHCP:3 (1939), 1433-50. Bengal records.

A57   COTTON, EVAN. "A Forgotten Sea-fight in the 'Bengal River,'" BPP:53 (Jan.-June 1937), 1-6. British-Dutch, 1759.

A58   DAS GUPTA, ASHIN. "Dutch Materials and Modern Indian History," QRHS:3 (1963-64), 47-50. Brief survey of works based on Dutch sources.

A59   DATTA, KALIKINKAR. "Capture of the Dutch Settlements in Bengal and Bihar 1781," BORS:27 (1941), 398-415; 27 (1941), 521-42. Based on unpublished records of the Imperial Records Department, Delhi.

A60   ———. "The Dutch in Bengal after Bedara," IHQ:14 (Sept. 1938), 536-44. A summary of relations, 1759-1825.

A61   ———. "A Memorial of the Dutch to Warren Hastings and the Council in Calcutta," IHRC:18 (Jan. 1942), 166-77.

A62   ———. "The Ostend Company in Bengal," IHQ:16 (Sept. 1940), 629-30. A note on Flemish Netherland's activities in 1730's.

A63   ———. "Situation of the Dutch in Bengal, 1740-1756 A.D. (Part I, Early Relationships; Part II, Critical Months 1756-57; Part III, Alarums and Excursions after Plassy)," BPP:43 (Jan.-June, 1932), 76-82; 44 (July-Dec. 1932), 29-41, 165-68. Based on British records.

A64   HOBBS, H. "Clive's Quarrel with the Dutch in 1759," BPP:50 (July-Dec. 1935), 101-10; 51 (Jan.-June 1936), 36-42. From the *London Magazine* 1762.

A65   HODENPIJL, A. K. A. GIJSBERITI. "De handhaving der neutraliteit van de Nederlandsche loge te Houghly, bij de overrompeling van de Engelsche kolonie Calcutta, in Juni 1756" [The Maintenance of Neutrality of the Dutch Lodge at Houghly at the Sacking of the English Colony, Calcutta, in June 1756], BTLV:76 (1920), 258-83.

A66   HOSTEN, H. "Dutch Records from the Dutch and the British East India Company Commissions of 1762-63 on Their Affairs in Bengal," IHRC:5 (1923), 104-06. Describes a collection of manuscripts in Goethals Indian Library, St. Xavier's College, Calcutta.

A67   [MILLES]. "Colonel Milles, Soldier of Fortune and the Ostend East India Company," BPP:34 (July-Dec. 1927), 40-43. Mid-18th cent.

A68   SRINIVASACHARI, C. S. "Dutch Intervention in the Southern Poligar Wars," IHCP:7 (1944), 427-37. Military and diplomatic history in Carnatic.

A69   VAN DER KEMP, P. H. "De jaren 1817-1825 der nederlandsche factorijen van Hindostans oostkust naar onuitgegeven stukken" [The Years 1817-1825 of the Dutch Factories of the Hindostan East Coast according to Unpublished Documents], BTLV:74 (1918), 1-137.

3. *THE FRENCH*

A70 [ANTONOVA, K. A.]. "Tipu Sultan and the French; Hitherto Unpublished Documents in the Leningrad Institute of History," CAR 11:1 (1963), 72-88. On documents mentioning missions to the French in 1793 and 1795-96, hitherto unknown.

A71 BALASUBRAMANIAM PILLAI, A. "The Adventurous Life of Dom Antonio José de Noronha, Bishop of Halicarnassus and Pseudo Nephew of Madam Dupleix (1720-1776)," BPP:56 (Jan.-June 1939), 37-41; IHRC:15 (Dec. 1938), 130-34. Brief life, based on a Portuguese biography.

A72 BOWRING, LEWIN B. "The French in India," FR:61 (Jan.-June 1894), 83-92. Summary of activity.

A73 "Bussy and the Fall of Dupleix," CR:44 (Feb. 1867), 443-504.

A74 CHANDY, KORA. "A Collection of Original Letters of the Abbé Dubois in the Mysore Residency," IHRC:20 (1943), 62-65. Includes extracts.

A75 CHATTERJI, NANDALAL. "Some Anglo-French Disputes in Bengal during Post-Diwany Period," IHQ:17 (Sept. 1941), 324-39. Political and diplomatic history. Based on Bengal records.

A76 CHOWDHURI, NANI GOPAL. "The Anglo-French Disputes in Bengal during the Administration of Cartier (December, 1769-April, 1772)," IHCP:7 (1944), 448-55. From Bengal records.

A77 ———. "The French Menace to Bengal during the Rule of Cartier (December, 1769-April, 1772)," IHRC:21 (1944), 25-27. From Bengal records.

A78 COTTON, EVAN. "A Begum of Sussex (The Strange Tale of de Boigne's Indian Wife)," BPP:46 (July-Dec. 1933), 91-94.

A79 ———. "Benoi de Boigne. 'Guereggio in Asia, e non vi cambio o merco'" [Benoi de Boigne. "I Fight in Asia and I Won't Turn Around or Negotiate"], IHRC:9 (1926), 8-22; BPP:33 (Jan.-June 1927), 92-105. Biography.

A80 ———. "The Memoires of Gentil," IHRC:10 (1927), 7-30; BPP:34 (July-Dec. 1927), 77-87. Summary of memoirs of a French colonel in Deccan, 18th cent.

A81 DAS GUPTA, S. N. "Charles Desvoeux at Achin 1772-73," IHRC:27 (1950), 1-12. From Madras records.

A82 DATTA, K. K. "The French Menace and Warren Hastings, 1778-79," IHRC:22 (1945), 40-42.

A83 ———. "A Letter of the Council in Calcutta to Marquis de Bussy," IHQ:19 (Dec. 1943), 368-72. Diplomatic history.

A84 DE CUNHA, J. GERSON. "The Diary of a French Missionary in Bombay, from November 8th, 1827, to May 12th, 1828," RASB:18 (1890-94), 350-69. Summary of diary of Abbé Denis Louis Cottineau de Kloguen.

A85 ———. "Madame Dupleix and the Marquise de Falaiseau," RASB: 18 (1890-94), 370-401. A comparative biography.

A86 [DU BOIS]. "Inconsistencies of the Abbé Du Bois in His Letters on India," OH:2 (June 1824), 218-28.

A87 [DUPLEIX]. "The Struggles of Dupleix with Adversity," CR 44:87 (1866), 56-104.

A88 "F. M. S." "Notes on the Position of the French in Bengal during the Early British Period," BPP:45 (Jan.-June 1933), 31-36. Midnapur records.

A89 "The First Struggle in the Carnatic," CR 43:85 (1866), 227-58.

A90 FRENCH, J. C. "Napoleon's Indian Plan Seen in the Light of Contemporary Foreign Politics," NR:112 (May 1934), 614-21. On possible invasion routes from northwest.

A91 "French India at Its Zenith," CR 43:86 (1886), 318-56.

A92 "French Notions of India," CR 21:41 (1853), 77-97.

A93 "French Pictures of the English in India," CR 5:10 (1846), 317-47. On "L'Inde anglaise en 1843-44" by Comte Edouarde Warren.

A94 "From Godeheu to Lally," CR:45 (May 1867), 1-55. English-French conflict.

A95 GHOSAL, HARI RANJAN. "Some Unpublished Documents Relating to the French in Bengal, Bihar and Orissa (1784-87)," IHQ:28 (Dec. 1952), 319-26. Documents in record room of Muzaffarpur Collectorate; summarized, not printed.

A96 HALIM, A. "General de Boigne's Endowment of Two Villages to a Muslim Shrine," IHRC:25 (Dec. 1948), 81-86.

A97 ———. "General Perron's Memories in Aligarh," IHRC:20 (1943), 34-37. French Commander-in-Chief of Sindhia's troops, 1796-1803.

A98 HATALKAR, V. G. "French Documents Throwing Fresh Light on the Embassy of M. de St. Lubin to the Maratha Court 1777-78," IHRC:31 (1955), 45-49. Diplomatic history.

A99 ———. "Tipu Sultan's Embassy to France, 1787-89," IHRC:33 (1958), 94-99. From National Archives in Paris.

A100 KARPELES, SUZANNE. "A Note on Some French Correspondence Preserved in the Royal Asiatic Society of Bengal (1794-1850)," IHRC:23 (1946), 26-28.

A101 KEENE, H. G. "General de Boigne," CR 66:133 (1878), 458-78.

A102 KHAN, MOHIBBUL HASAN. "The French in the Second Anglo-Mysore War," BPP:65 (1945), 55-65. Pondicherry records.

A103 "La Bourdonnais and Dupleix," CR 42:84 (1865), 425-74.

A104 "The Last Struggle for Empire," CR:45 (Aug. 1867), 237-95. On the French in India.

A105 "Late French Writers on India," CR:27 (Dec. 1856), 336-55.

A106 MALLESON, G. B. "French Mariners on the Indian Seas," CR 64:127 (1877), 24-64. On naval battles.

A107 "Malleson's French in India," ER:127 (April 1868), 537-59.

A108 MITRA, R. C. "Some Light on the Third Anglo-Mysore War from French Sources," IHCP:14 (1951), 232-38. From Pondicherry archives.

A109 NILAKANTA SASTRI, K. A. "French Policy in India in 1777," IHRC:13 (1930), 115-20. From Pondicherry records.

A110 ———. "New Pages from Ananda Ranga Pillai's Diary," MUJ:14 (July 1942) Supplement, 49 pp. With English translation of Tamil text.

A111 OWEN, SIDNEY JAMES. "Count Lally," EHR:6 (July 1891), 495-534. Frenchman who opposed Dupleix's policies in India, for which he was beheaded.

A112 PARKER, R. H. "The French and Portuguese Settlements in India," PoQ:26 (Oct.-Dec. 1955), 389-98. Brief historical résumé discusses the condition of the settlements in 1947. Summary of Jaipur Resolution of Congress (18th December 1948).

A113 RAMSBOTHAM, R. B. "Chittagong in 1784; 'The War' against Jan Baksh Khan," BPP:39 (Jan.-June 1930), 83-90. French letters.

A114 RANGASWAMI, A. "The Political System of French India," CR: 111 (Oct. 1900), 281-306.

A115 "The Rise of the French Power in India," CR 42:83 (1865), 126-77.

A116 SACHSE, F. M. "The Passing of the French Factory in Dacca in 1774," BPP:42 (July-Dec. 1931), 49-54.

A117 SARKAR, JADUNATH. "De Boigne," IHRC:17 (1940), 1-3. After 1788.

A118 ———. "French Mercenaries in the Jat Campaign of 1775-76," BPP:51 (Jan.-June 1936), 114-26. Translation from manuscript journal of the Comte de Modave.

A119 ———. "General de Boigne in India," IHRC:15 (Dec. 1938), 9-12. Chronology and some details.

A120 ———. "General de Boigne's First Wife," BPP:50 (July-Dec. 1935), 111-13.

A121 ———. "The Lakheri Campaign of de Boigne: A New Study," MR:77 (Feb. 1945), 59-63.

A122 ———(tr.). "Memoir of Monsieur Rene Madec II (After the Battle of Buxar)," BPP:52 (July-Dec. 1936), 61-66; 53 (Jan.-June 1937), 69-80; 55 (Jan.-June 1938), 1-10. Records in Bibliothèque Nationale in Paris.

A123 ———. "Some Frenchmen in India," BPP:51 (Jan.-June 1936), 1-6.

A124 ———. "A Prisoner of Tipu Sultan," BPP:50 (July-Dec. 1935), 75-85. Account by a Frenchman, Burette.

A125 SEN, S. P. "The Correspondence of Modave," IHRC:27 (1950), 13-21. A Frenchman in India, second half of 18th cent.

A126 ———. "The Diplomatic Intrigues of Chevalier, Governor of Chandernagore (1767-1778)," IHRC:29 (1953), 120-29. Manuscript in Bibliothèque Nationale.

A127 ———. "Franco-Mysore Relations from 1785-93," IHRC:31 (1955), 32-39. From Pondicherry archives.

A128 ———. "A French Project for the Conquest of Sind," IHRC:25 (Dec. 1948), 73-78. From Pondicherry records.

A129 ———. "A 'Memoire' on Franco-Maratha Negotiations from 1770 to 1783," IHRC:28 (1951), 78-83.

A130 ———. "A Picture of Chandernagore and Subordinate French Factories in Bengal—1765 to 1778," BPP:72 (1953), 63-71.

A131 ———. "Pondicherry: 1765 to 1778," BPP:71 (1952), 15-33. Description, government, and history.

A132 ———. "Private Correspondence of Montreau, A French Officer in Maratha Service," IHCP:10 (1947), 431-36. Letters of 1780's and 90's on military and political affairs.

A133 ———. "A Proposed Treaty of Alliance between the French and the Marathas (1782)," CR:99 (May 1946), 67-74. Translation of text.

A134 ———. "The Relations between the French and Hyderabad, 1785-1793," IHRC:30 (1954), 141-49.

A135 SHARADAMMA, M. "Historical Importance of the Abbé Duboies–Alexander Read (Correspondence published in the Baramahal Records)," IHRC:18 (Jan. 1942), 297-300.

A136 SINHA, H. N. "A Little Known Factor That Contributed to the Defeat of the French in the Carnatic Wars," IHRC:24 (Feb. 1948), 79-81. On the supply of saltpeter.

A137 SRINIVASACHARI, C. S. "The Abbé Dubois in the Baramahal Records," IHRC:9 (1926), 68-72. Description of the Abbé's book on his stay in India.

A138 ———. "The Later Representatives of a Great Family of Courtiers of Pondicherry. Diwan Savari Muthu Mudaliar and Appaswami," IHRC:18 (Jan. 1942), 53-61.

A139 THOMPSON, J. P. (tr.). "An Autobiographical Memoir of Louis Bourquien," JPHS:9 (1923), 36-70. French soldier in North India in late 18th cent.

A140 [TOCQUEVILLE]. "Remains of Alexis de Tocqueville," ER:113 (April 1861), 427-68. Includes letter by de Tocqueville on British rule in India, pp. 446-47.

A141 TRILOKEKAR, M. K. "Mons de St. Luvin, A French Adventurer at the Maratha Court," BHS:3 (Mar. 1930), 51-76: In 1770's—based on selections of various records and printed materials.

A142 WADIA, C. N. "Career of Bishop Noronha (1752-1762)," JIH:30 (Dec. 1952), 273-86.

4. THE MARATHAS

A143 ABDUL ALI, A. F. M. "Commercial and Social Intercourse between the Honorable East India Company and the Poona Court in the Eighteenth Century," IHRC:11 (1928), 175-90. BPP:37 (Jan.-June 1929), 19-34; MsR:3 (Jan.-Mar. 1929), 63-81.

A144 ATHAVALE, S. N. "A Scrutiny of the Policy of Nana Fadnis in the North Indian Enterprise of the Marathas," IHCP:14 (1951), 238-54. 1775-95; from Maratha records.

A145 BANERJEE, ANIL CHANDRA. "A Contemporary Account of the Origin of the First Anglo-Maratha War," IHRC:20 (1943), 31-33. From a Maratha document.

A146 ———. "Peshwa Madhav Rao I and Raghunath Rao," IHCP:4 (1940), 306-15. 1760's; based on Peshwa Daftar and Maratha sources.

A147 ———. "Peshwa Madhav Rao I's Relations with the English," IHCP:3 (1939), 1469-1507.

A148 ———. "Revival of Maratha Power in the North (1761-1769)," IHQ:17 (Sept. 1941), 311-23. Selections from Peshwa Daftar, Sarkar's works, Malcolm's Memoir of Central India.

A149 BANERJI, BRAJENDRANATH. "A Chapter of the East India Company and Diplomacy: The Begam of Sardhana," MR:37 (May 1925), 521-30. 1782-1805, following Treaty of Salbai.

A150 BENNELL, A. S. "The Anglo-Maratha Confrontation of June and July 1803," RAS (Oct. 1962), pp. 107-31. Based on Wellesley papers and IOL records.

A151 ———. "Factors in the Marquis Wellesley's Failure against Holkar, 1804," BSOAS:28 (1965), 553-81.

A152 BHANU, DHARMA. "The Mughal-Maratha Treaty of April, 1752," PPHC:2 (1952), 349-60. From printed English-language sources.

A153 CASI, RAJA. "An Account of the Battle of Paniput, and of the Events Leading to It. Written in Persian by Casi Raja Pundit, who was present at the battle," AsR:3 (1792), 91-139. Tr., Col. James Browne.

A154 CHATTERJEE, NONDITA. "Anglo-Maratha Relations during Maratha-Mysore War (1785-1787)," JIH:39 (April 1961), 129-36. Diplomatic history.

A155 CHATTERJI, NANDALAL. "The Failure of Anglo-Maratha Negotiations Regarding the Cession of Cuttack," BPP:61 (Jan.-June 1939), 58-64; IHRS:15 (Dec. 1938), 79-84. Based on Bengal records.

A156 CHITALE, V. S. "Relations between Madhav Rao and Janoji Bhonsle," IHRC:28 (1951), 13-18. In 1760's.

A157 COATS, THOMAS. "Notes Respecting the Trial by Panchayat and the Administration of Justice at Poona, under the Late Peshwa," LSBT:2 (old ed., 273-80; new ed., 189-96).

A158 DATTA, KALIKINKAR. "The Marathas in Bengal (1740-1765)," BHS:3 (Sept. 1930), 201-22; 4 (1931), 1-18, 192-208.

A159 ———. "The Marathas in Bengal after 1751," JIH:15 (1936), 387-409. Persian records in Calcutta; diplomatic history.

A160 ———. "Social, Economic and Political Effects of the Maratha Invasions between 1740 and 1764 on Bengal, Bihar and Orissa," AIOC:6 (Dec. 1930), 189-98. Bengali and English sources.

A161 DIGHE, V. G. "Jamav Daftar—An Important Source for the Social History of the Marathas," BV:9 (1948), 143-47. Brief description.

A162 DIKSHIT, M. G. "Early Life of Peshwa Savai Madhav-rao (II)," DCRI:7 (Dec. 1946), 225-48.

A163 DISKALKAR, D. B. (ed.). "James Grant Duff's Private Correspondence with Maharaja Pratapsimha of Satara," JIH:15 (1936), 221-36. Grant Duff's friendly advice to the Maharaja on his duties, after Duff's return to England.

A164 EDWARDES, S. M. "The Marathas at the Close of the Eighteenth Century as Described by a Soldier of Fortune," IAn:53 (March 1924), 69-77. From an account by William Henry Tone.

A165 FUKAZAWA, HIROSHI. "18 Seiki Marātā ōkoku no nuhi ni kansuru ichi oboegaki" [Gulāms and Batkas, or Kanbinas, of the Maratha Kingdom in the 18th Century], HiR:45 (1961), 73-86. HA:8 (No. 1406): "An analysis of the slave (Gulām and Batika) in the Maratha Kingdom in the 18th century."

A166 ———. [State and Caste System in the 18th Century Maratha Kingdom], HiR 49:5 (1963). Review in QRHS 4:1&2 (1964/65), 92: "The author proves that the caste life . . . was not always autonomous."

A167 GOKHALE, D. V. "A Letter from the Maratha Agent with the Mughal Vazir Safdarjang (1751 A.D.)," IHRC:23 (1946), 10-11.

A168 GUPTA, PRATUL CHANDRA. "The Administration of Poona under Baji Rao II," IHRC:16 (1939), 99-101. Brief summary.

A169 ———. "The Commissioners at Bithur (1811-51)," IHCP:6 (1943), 275-81. Carefully documented political history of British commissioners at the court of pensioner Peshwa Baji Rao II. Records in Imperial Record Department.

A170 ———. "Peshwa Bajee Rao II, The Gaikwad and the English," CR:54 (March 1935), 283-304.

A171 ———. "Sir John Low's Services at Bithur 1818-25," IHCP:5 (1941), 495-503. The Commissioner at the court of the ex-Peshwa; supplements material in the personal biography of Low by his granddaughter. Archives at Bombay and New Delhi.

A172 HATALKAR, V. G. "Souillac's Fresh Approach to Maratha-Franco Relations," IHRC:32 (1956), 28-32.

A173 JOSHI, R. M. "Two Unpublished Akhbars from Poona," IA:10 (1956), 17-19. Related to the death of Peshwa Madhavarao II.

A174 JOSHI, SHANKAR NARAYAN. "Maratha Ambassadors during the Reign of Peshwa Madhavrao I (1761 to 1772 A.D.)," IHCP:14 (1951), 285-94. Analysis of terms and titles, analysis of vakils' duties, income, and table of all ambassadors and agents to or from the Peshwa.

A175 KALE, D. V. "Development of Constitutional Ideas in the History of the Marathas," BUJ:2 (Jan. 1934), 239-51. From M.A. thesis on social life and manners (1928).

A176 KARKARIA, R. P. "Lieut.-Col. Thomas Best Jervis (1796-1857) and His Manuscript Studies on the State of the Maratha People and Their History," CR:123 (April 1906), 240-77; RASB:22 (1905), 43-66.

A177 KHARE, G. H. "Some New Records on the Mahratta-Jaipur Relations," IHRC:24 (Feb. 1948), 5-8. 18th cent. records from a private collection.

A178 KHONDEKAR, GANPAT RAO GOPAL. "Gopal Sambhaji," IHCP:3 (1939), 1283-90. A biography of an 18th cent. Maratha government servant from family records and Peshwa Daftar.

A179 MACMUNN, GEORGE. "Battle of Kirkee, November 5, 1817," CM:65 (Nov. 1928), 583-94.

A180 MADHAV RAO, P. SETHU. "Maratha-Nizam Relations; Two Persian Sources: The Tarikhe Rahatafza and the Tarikh-e-Zafrah," BUJ: 28 (Jan. 1960), 1-35. Summary of information therein.

A181 "The Mahratta History and Empire—Recent Operations in the Kolapoor and Sawunt-waree Countries," CR 4:7 (1845), 178-240.

A182 "The Mahratta War: The Origin, Progress, and Termination of the Late War between the British Government in India and the Mahratta Princes, Dowlut Rao, Scindeah, and Ragojee Bounsla," AAR:5 (1903), 1-77. Followed by 87-page appendix of official documents.

A183 "MARATHA." "How the Marquess Wellesley Ensnared the Peishwa," MR:28 (Oct.-Dec. 1920), 364-70, 474-80, 587-94.

A184 ———. "The Last of the Peishawas," MR:31 (March-May 1922), 285-91, 438-46, 575-83.

A185 MAWJEE, P. V. "Sir Charles Malet, the First English Resident at the Court of the Peshwa," MR:6 (July 1909), 68-75.

A186 NARAYANA RAO, GONDKER. "The Second Invasion of Pēṣwa Mādhava Rao against Mysore, 1767," MS:37 (Jan.-April 1947), 171-89. From Marathi sources.

A187 ———. "The Third Invasion of Pēṣwa Mādhava Rao against Mysore, 1769-1770," MS:39 (1948-1949), 101-16, 172-86, 254-63.

A188 OTURKAR, R. V. "Scope of State Activity under the 18th Century Maratha Rule," IHCP:13 (1950), 202-04. Based on Marathi manuscripts; survey of miscellaneous state activities.

A189 PARASNIS, D. B. "Maratha Historical Literature," RASB:22 (1905), 168-78. Surveys Western and Indian works published 1804-1904.

A190 ——. "Maratha Historical Literature," MR:1 (Jan. 1907), 104-11.

A191 ——. "Original Correspondence between the English and the Marathas," IHRC:5 (1923), 91-99. Prints some documents of the 18th cent.

A192 PERTSMAKKER, V. V. "Iz istorii bor'by Maratkhov s evropeïskimi zakhvatchikami (1698-1756)" [From the History of the Struggle of the Mahratta with the European Plunderers (1698-1756)], NAA:3 (1962), 73-82.

A193 QANUNGO, S. N. "Some Sidelights on the Battle of Indore (14th October, 1801)," UB:10 (Aug. 1963), 89-93. Details of the battle between Holkar and Sindhia.

A194 RAMALINGAM, J. A. "The Battle of Sitabaldi 26th and 27th November, 1817," IHQ:36 (Dec. 1960), 227-37. A detailed report on a battle against the Marathas in Nagpur.

A195 RAMANUJAM, CHIDAMBARAM S. "Was Nana the Cause of Maratha Downfall?" JIH:39 (Dec. 1961), 407-12. From British records.

A196 RANADE, M. G. "Introduction to the Peshwa's Diaries," RASB:20 (1902), 448-79. Summarizes information in 22,000 pp. of selections covering 1708-1817, prepared by Rao Bahadur Wad from the Marathi original.

A197 RAO, P. SETU MADHAVA. "Maratha-Nizam Relations—A Persian Source, the Tuzuke Asafia of Tajalli Shah," BUJ: NS 27 (Jan. 1959), 1-25. On military relations, 1750's-1780's.

A198 ——. "Maratha-Nizam Relations. The Masire Asafi of Laxmi Narayan Shafiq Aurangabadi," JIH:39 (April 1961), 53-78.

A199 ——. "Maratha-Nizam Relations. Nizam-ul Mulk's Letters," JIH: 40 (1963), 131-50. "Translation of 9 letters on the Marathas, from the Musawi Khan collection, Hyderabad."

A200 RAO, VASANT D. "A Maker of Modern Maharashtra; Hon'ble Shri Jugannath Sunkersett (February 10, 1803 to July 31, 1865)," JIH:43 (April 1965), 201-17.

A201 SAMADDAR, J. N. "The Maratha Invasion of Bengal in 1748; As Told in the Maharastra Purana," BPP:27 (Jan.-March 1924), 34-55. Translation of a Bengali manuscript by poet Gangaram.

A202 SARDESAI, GOVIND S. "The Battle of Panipat—Its Causes and Consequences," MR:54 (Sept. 1933), 269-74.

A203 ———. "The Historical Records in Kotah," MR:94 (Dec. 1953), 451. Historical papers in Marathi, important for the student of Maratha history and north Indian history in general during the 18th cent.

A204 ———. "A Life-Sketch of Nana Fadnis," MR:48 (Nov. 1930), 523-26.

A205 SARKAR, BENOY KUMAR. "The Maratha Political Ideas of the Eighteenth Century," IHQ:12 (March 1936), 88-103. An analysis of the political ideas in *Sambhāji's Ādnāpatra* (known as the *Rājanīti*) issued in 1716, believed to have been written by Rāmachandrapant Amātya; also some discussion of the Peshwa's diaries (1708-1817).

A206 SARKAR, JADUNATH. "Battle of Panipat: The Victor's Despatches," MR:79 (May 1946), 337-39.

A207 ———. "Events Leading up to the Battle of Panipat, 1761," IHQ:2 (Sept. 1935), 547-58. Translation of Kashiraj's Persian account of events Oct. 17, 1760 to Jan. 14, 1761; earlier portion of manuscript published in IHQ, June 1934.

A208 ———. "The Historian Rajwade," MR:41 (Feb. 1927), 184-87. Collected sources for Maratha history.

A209 ———. "Maratha History Newly Presented," MR:80 (Dec. 1946), 461-62. On historiography.

A210 ———. "A New Source of Maratha History," MR:77 (Jan. 1945), 13-15. Letters and papers of the Maratha national leaders (Bara-bhai) from the rise of Mahadaji Sindhia in 1771.

A211 ———. "Pānipat, 1761," IHQ:10 (June 1934), 258-73. Translation of Persian manuscript by Kāshirāj Shivdev, sec'y of Shujā-ud-Daulah, Nawab of Oudh, written in 1780.

A212 ———. "Salabat Jang's First War with the Peshwa," IC:11 (April 1937), 180-87. Translated from a French manuscript dated 1751.

A213 ———. "A Sketch of the Battle of Dig, 13 November 1804," IA:9 (July-Dec. 1955), 113-20. Based on sketches, maps, and charts in the Historical Map Records of the Survey of India at the National Archives, and additional dispatches, etc., pertaining to the Anglo-Maratha War.

A214 ———. "Sources of Maratha History [Sources in the Persian Language]," BUJ:10 (July 1941), 1-22. Discusses Persian and Marathi sources, problems of Marathi historiography.

A215 ———. "True Sources of Maratha History," MR:47 (March 1930), 305-09. On the 19th cent. revolution in the writing of Maratha history.

A216 ———. "Warren Hastings as Seen by the Maratha Envoy," BPP: 72 (1953), 30-38. Five dispatches to Nana Fadnis, 1779-84, describing Hastings' activities.

A217 "Satara—and British Connexion Therewith," CR 10:20 (1848), 437-95.

A218 SEN, SURENDRANATH. "The Theory of the Maratha Constitution," MR:27 (June 1920), 640-46. On succession and legitimacy.

A219 SETH, D. R. "Wellington's Indian Campaign," USI:86 (1956), 190-98. Summary in HA:4 (No. 2463); on second Maratha war, 1803.

A220 SHEJWALKAR, T. S. "The Bengal Episode in Maratha History," DCRI:2 (June 1941), 361-82. Books and selections from Peshwa's Daftar.

A221 ———. "The Surat Episode of 1759," DCRI:8 (Aug. 1947), 173-203. From printed documents.

A222 SRIVASTAVA, A. L. "The Marathas and Najīb-ud-daulah (1757-1760)," IC:20 (Jan. 1946), 49-57.

A223 "The Struggle for Empire with the Mahrattas," W:91 (Jan. 1869), 1-48.

A224 TAMBE, G. K. "The Regime of Vinayak Ganesh Chandorkar as the Deputy Governor of the Saugor Territory 1795-1819," IHCP:14 (1951), 259-63. Materials on British protectionist policy vis-à-vis Maratha dependencies.

A225 TEMPLE, RICHARD. "Personal Traits of Mahratta Brahman Princes," RHS: NS 1 (1884), 289-308. Sketch of Peshwas, 1714-1818.

5. OUDH, 1750–1800

A226 ABDUL ALI, A. F. M. "The Last Will and Testament of Bahu Begum," IHRC:6 (1924), 149-56. 18th cent., wife of Shuja-ud-Daulah.

A227 ———. "Shuja-ud-Daulah, Nawab Vazir of Oudh (1754-75)," MsR:1 (April-June 1927), 63-72; 2 (Oct.-Dec. 1927), 67-72. Also: IHRC: 9 (1926), 116-29; BPP:33 (Jan.-June 1927), 39-51. From English records.

A228 ANSARI, A. S. BAZMEE. "Faydābād (Fyzabad)," EI:2, 870. On Shuja-ud-Daulah's capital.

A229 ———. "Ghāzī'l-dīn Ḥaydar," EI:2, 1045-46. Nawab Wazir of Oudh.

A230 ASKARI, HASAN. "Chait Singh and Hastings (from Persian Sources)," IHRC:30 (1954), 15-24. Persian MSS.

A231 ———. "The Political Significance of Hazin's Career in Eastern India," BPP:62 (1943), 1-10. The advice given to Shuja-ud-Daulah by a Persian poet who lived in India, 1733-60. Persian MSS.

A232 BANERJI, BRAJENDRA NATH. "The Last Days of Rajah Chait Singh (Based on Unpublished State Records)," IHRC:11 (1928), 167-75; BPP:37 (Jan.-June 1929), 35-42.

A233 BASU, P. "Some Aspects of the Administration of Oudh under Asafuddaula, 1775-1797," UPHS:11 (Dec. 1938), 27-44. From author's thesis.

A234 "The Begum of Sardhana," CR:98 (April 1894), 310-26.

A235 BHATNAGAR, G. D. "The Annexation of Oudh," UB:3 (Aug. 1956), 55-66. From British and Persian records.

A236 CHATTERJI, NANDALAL. "A Forgotten Treaty between Shu-jauddaulah and the English," IHQ:16 (Sept. 1940), 610-28. Diplomatic history, 1767-68.

A237 ———. "Lord Hastings and the Oudh Loans," IHCP:12 (1949), 214-15.

A238 ———. "Lord Hastings, Colonel Baillie and the Oudh Loans," UPHS: NS 1 (1953), 52-62. The role of the Resident at Lucknow in Lord Hastings' dealings with the Nawab.

A239 ———. "Nawab Shujauddaulah of Oudh and His Alliance with Mir Qasim against the British," UPHS:8 (July 1935), 24-29. From Persian records.

A240 ———. "Shuja-ud-daulah of Oudh in the Eyes of a Contemporary English Governor," UPHS:10 (July 1937), 33-37. Extracts from Verelst's letters, 1768 and 1769.

A241 ———. "Vazir Ali's Plans against the Company's Power," JIH:43 (April 1965), 285-97. In Oudh, 1797-99.

A242 ———. "Verelst's Observations on Shuja-ud-Daulah's Character," IHRC:14 (1937), 68-71. Extracts from letters.

A243 ———. "Wazir Ali's Conspiracy against the English," UPHS:9 (July 1936), 50-63. Benares, 1799.

A244 CHAUDHURI, S. B. "The Outbreak at Benares in 1799," MR:94 (Sept. 1953), 205-09. Information from the monograph *Vizier Ali Khan on the Massacre at Benares: A Chapter in British Indian History*, by Sir J. F. Davis.

A245 COHN, BERNARD S. "Political Systems in Eighteenth Century India; The Banaras Region," AOS:82 (July-Sept. 1962), 312-20. A study of the political structure behind the political events.

A246 DATTA, KALIKINKAR. "Some Unpublished Documents Relating to the Conspiracy of Wazir Ali," IHRC:14 (1937), 75-87; BPP:55 (Jan.-June 1938), 137-50. Papers at Patna.

A247 ————. "Two Brothers of Sa'ādat Alī, Nawab of Oudh," IHCP:3 (1939), 1546-53. The role of the British Magistrate at Patna in the political intrigues among Shuja-ud-Daulah's sons. "Based on unpublished English Records."

A248 ————. "Wazir Ali's Family," IHCP:13 (1950), 272-77. Oudh politics and British intervention in the first quarter of the 19th cent.; appendix contains excerpts from British correspondence.

A249 DAVIES, C. COLLIN. "Awadh (Oudh)," EI:1, 756-58. Useful brief history.

A250 DISKALKAR, D. B. (ed.). "Mahadji Sindia's Supersession of the Nabob of Lucknow," UPHS:10 (Dec. 1937), 17-29. A paper in the Satara Museum dated March 16, 1785.

A251 D'SOUZA, A. W. P. "Raja Chait Singh of Benares under the Nawab of Oudh (1770-1775)," BUJ:1 (July 1932), 19-47. Archival sources.

A252 GURBAX, Gope Ramkrishna. "Sadat Ali Khan, Nawab Vazir of Oudh and Wellesley," IHRC:18 (Jan. 1942), 246-49. From Persian records.

A253 [HASTINGS]. "Controversy between Lord Hastings and Colonel Baillie, the Late Resident at the Court of Lucknow," OH:7 (Dec. 1825), 401-27. Detailed account.

A254 "History of Oude," AAR:8 (1806), 1-36. 1758-1800.

A255 IRVINE, WILLIAM. "The Bangash Nawābs of Farrukhābād—A Chronicle (1713-1857)," ASB:47 (1878), 259-383; 48 (1879), 49-170. With tables; a very full chronicle from Persian sources.

A256 "The Massacre at Benares," CR:1 (May 1844), 246-50. Of 1799.

A257 MUKHERJEE, ANSHUMAN. "Life and Career of Wazir Ali Khan, the Rebel Nawab of Oudh," BRS:43 (Sept.-Dec. 1957), 323-28. Late 18th cent.; Persian and English sources.

A258 NIGAM, KRISHNA CHARAN. "An Unpublished Persian Work on the Nawabs of Oudh," UPHS:14 (July 1941), 39-47. "Tarikh Mohtasham," a history of Oudh, 1732-1837, by Mohtasham Khan.

A259 QANUNGO, K. R. "Some Side-Lights on the History of Benares, Political and Social, Thrown by the Selections from the Peshwa's Daftar, Poona," IHRC:14 (1937), 65-68. 18th cent.

A260   RAHMAN, A. F. M. KHALILUR. "Shuja-ud-daula as a Diplomat (1754-65)," IHQ:19 (March 1943), 39-49. Based on Persian MSS in the British Museum.

A261   RAJ, JAGDISH. "The Revenue System of the Nawabs of Oudh," JESHO:2 (1959), 92-104. A study of relationships between Nawabs and subjects, methods of assessment, mode of collection as observed by the British; the general state of corruption and abuse before the British took over. Based on English accounts.

A262   RASHID, SH. ABDUR. "Mirat-ul-Auza," IHRC:30 (1954), 98-108. Administration of Oudh under the Nawabs.

A263   SKRINE, FRANCIS H. "The Benares Massacre of 1799: A Study in Eighteenth Century Politics," AR, Ser. 3:18 (July 1904), 87-105.

A264   SRIVASTAVA, A. L. "A Critical Examination of the Various Versions of Shujā-ud-daulah's Death," IC:19 (April 1945), 242-44.

A265   ———. "Rise and Fall of Maharajah Beni Bahadur, 1759-1767," IHCP:3 (1939), 1034-42. A biography of Shuja-ud-daulah's deputy in Oudh and Allahabad, from Persian, Marathi, English, and French sources.

A266   ———. "Shuja-ud-Daulah's Policy during the Maratha Invasion of 1770-71," IHRC:8 (1942), 332.

A267   ———. "The Treaty of Faizabad between Asaf-ud-Daulah and the English East India Company, May 21, 1775," AUJR:1 (Nov. 1952), 15-23.

6. CENTRAL PROVINCES AND BERAR

A268   ABDUL ALI, A. F. M. "Mahadji Sindhia of Gwalior," MsR:4 (Oct.-Dec. 1929), 31-40; IHRC:12 (1929), 108-16; BPP:39 (Jan.-June 1930), 3-11.

A269   ———. "The Pindaris," IC:11 (July 1937), 370-72. A summary of their activities.

A270   ANSARI, A. S. BAZMEE. "Barōda," EI:1, 1053.

A271   ———. "Bhōpāl," EI:1, 1195-97.

A272   ———. "Burhānpūr," EI:1, 1330-31.

A273   "The Baroda Blunder," W:104 (Oct. 1875), 391-414. In 1874-75.

A274   BASU, BASANTA KUMAR. "The Side-Light on the Life of Daulat Rao Sindhia, Maharajah of Gwalior (1794-1824)," BPP:39 (Jan.-June 1930), 144-49. Letter from Wellesley, 1803.

A275 BOULGER, DEMETRIUS C. "The Murat of the Marathas," ArQ: 5 (Oct. 1922), 83-98. Diplomatic and military activities of Holkar, 1800-1805; based on political records of the government of India.

A276 "Central India under British Supremacy," CR 14:27 (1850), 91-115.

A277 "The Central Provinces," CR 38:76 (1863), 213-37.

A278 CHATTERJI, HIRA LAL. "Ten Years in Gwalior," MR:60 (Nov. 1936), 529-31.

A279 DAVIES, C. COLLIN, "Berār," EI:1, 1170.

A280 FERNANDEZ, T. "Negotiations between the Hon'ble East India Company and the Bhosla Rajahs Regarding the Establishment of a Subsidiary Force in the Nagpur State," IHRC:11 (1928), 72-79. Copies of dispatches, 1803-16.

A281 GUPTA, HIRA LAL. "Bhopal Succession (1819-20)," IHRC:32 (1956), 13-19. Persian MSS.

A282 ———. "Holkar Succession, 1844," IHRC:33 (1958), 85-93. British records.

A283 GUPTA, S. C. "The Events Leading to the Conclusion of the Treaty between Bhopal and the English," IHRC:29 (1953), 45-55.

A284 "Gwalior," EB:12, 748-49. Fairly detailed history.

A285 HAIG, WOLSELEY. "The Berar Question Again," NC:95 (April 1924), 592-98. Relates historical background.

A286 "History of the Bhonsla Family of Nagpore," MJLA:22 (1854?), 213-25.

A287 HUNTER, WILLIAM. "Narrative of a Journey from Agra to Oujein," AsR:6 (1801), 7-76.

A288 "Indian Affairs—Gwalior," BM:55 (May 1844), 579-92. On Sindhia and the British.

A289 JOSHI, C. V. "Life and Fortunes of Sevaram Jagadeesh," IHRC: 18 (Jan. 1942), 316-20. Prominent in the military history of Baroda during the last twenty years of the 18th cent.

A290 KAUL, IQBAL. "Investigation Regarding the Death of Nawab Nazar Muhammad Khan of Bhopal State," AHRS:26 (1960-61), 145-48. An incident of 1819-20.

A291 ———. "Nawab Hayat Muhammad Khan and the Ministerial Era in Bhopal State (1778-1808)," AHRS:27 (1961-62), 131-43.

A292 ———. "Transitional Period in the History of Bhopal State (1808-1818)," AHRS:26 (1960-61), 139-44. From Persian and English sources.

A293 ———. "Two Rulers of Bhopal and the Stabilisation of the Illegitimate Line in the State (1726-1777)," AHRS:27 (1961-62), 56-69. Largely from Bhopal State Gazetteer and a Persian source.

A294 KIBE, MADHAV RAO VENAYEK. "The Consolidation of the British Supremacy in Central India," CR:119 (July 1904), 336-73.

A295 KIBE, SARDAR RAO BAHADUR M. V. "Fragments from the Records of Devi Shri Ahilya Bai Holkar," IHRC:13 (1930), 132-39. Dispatches in English and Hindi.

A296 LANDGE, D. G. "Did Khandoji Bhonsle of Nagpur Ruling Family Go to Bengal in 1764," IHRC:33 (1958), 112-14.

A297 LUARD, C. ECKFORD. "Some Views of an Indian Ruler on the Administration of an Indian State," AR: NS 22 (1926), 278-87; discussion, pp. 288-96. The views of Maharaja Sindhia.

A298 [MADHAVA RAO]. "V. P. Madhava Rao," MR:15 (June 1914), 659-62. Biography of the Dewan of Baroda; also administered Travancore and Mysore.

A299 MAHAJAN, D. B. "A Copper Plate Record (Magajarnmā) of 1756 A.D. in Berar," IHPC:17 (1954), 292-95. Annotated translation of a lease on a village.

A300 MEHTA, MAKRAND J. "Gangadhar Shastri Patwardhan," JIH: 41 (April 1963), 223-26. A politician in Baroda, early 19th cent.

A301 NARAIN, B. "New Constitutional Reforms in Gwalior," IJPS:1 (Oct. 1939), 231-37.

A302 "ONE WHO KNOWS." "In the Public Eye: Mr. Madhava Rao, C.I.E.: The New Dewan of Baroda," HR:19 (March 1914), 324-49.

A303 RAMALINGAM, JOHN A. "British Policy in the Context of Bhonsla-Bhopal Relations, 1810-1914," IC:36 (April 1962), 129-42; IHQ: 38 (March 1962), 8-28.

A304 RAY, N. B. "Marquess Wellesley's Policy towards Sindia in the War with Holkar (1804-05)," IHRC:16 (1939), 80-90.

A305 SAHAY, CHANDRA BANSI. "The Progress of the Baroda State," HR:32 (Aug. 1915), 322-25.

A306 SARDESAI, G. S. "The Rise of Mahadji Sindhia," MR:75 (March 1944), 209-11.

A307 SARKAR, JADUNATH. "The Battle of Lakhere, 1793, or Campoo *Versus* Campoo," MR:75 (Feb. 1944), 97-104. One of a series of articles on Sindhia's battles, complete with battle plans.

A308 ———. "English Residents with Mahadji Sindhia," IHRC:11 (1928), 10-14. Names and personalities of residents.

A309 ———. "Mahadji Sindhia's End," MR:75 (March 1944), 177-79. In February 1794.

A310 SHEJWALKAR, T. S. "Danger to Jhansi in 1774-75," IHRC:27 (1950), 49-53.

A311 [SINDIA]. "Madhajee Sindia," CR:49 (Oct. 1933), 49-82. His role in the 1760's.

A312 SINGH, NIHAL. "H. H. The Maharaja-Gaekwar's Administrative Record," MR:21 (March-April 1917), 308-13, 441-48.

A313 SINHA, H. N. "The Newly Discovered Autograph Letters of Wellington," BPP:39 (Jan.-June 1930), 91-99. Relations with Bhonsla.

A314 SRIVASTAVA, SATYA PRAKASH. "The Jhansi State and Its Annexation," IHCP:7 (1944), 457-65. British motives and justifications.

A315 TROMBRE, R. K. "The Sovereignty over Berar and the Question of the Retrocession of Berar to the Nizam," MR:82 (July 1947), 31-35. Historical background.

A316 WARD, H. C. E. "An Indian Sensation," BM:164 (Aug. 1898), 206-19. Royal doings in Central India.

7. MYSORE

A317 ACHUTA RAO, D. S. "Haidar Āli: Character, Personality, Public and Private Life," MS:31 (July 1940), 25-35. Uses both manuscripts and secondary sources; includes bibliography.

A318 ———. "Haidar Āli—His Relations with the Crown," IHRC:18 (Jan. 1942), 301-04.

A319 ———. "Haidar Āli: His Religious Disposition," MS:29 (1938-39), 452-65. From Persian MS, the *Haidar-Nāma*.

A320 ASKARI, S. H. "Some Letters of, and Relating to, Tipu Sultan," IHRC:32 (1956), 50-57. Persian MSS at Patna.

A321 AYYAR, K. R. VENKATARAMA. "Some Little Known but Vital Incidents in Haidar Ali's Carnatic Campaign (1780-82)," IHRC:21 (1944), 91-93. Based on Persian records.

A322 BAILEY, T. GRAHAME. "Two Indian Standards of the Eighteenth Century, with Facsimiles and Translations of Tracings from Arabic Inscriptions," BSOS 2:3 (1921-23), 549-54. The standards of Haidar Ali and Tipu Sultan.

A323 BAQA'I, IRSHAD HUSAIN. "A Conference between Brigadier-General MacLeod and Tīpū Sulṭān," IC:17 (Jan. 1943), 88-95. In 1873.

A324 ———. "The Death of Haidar 'Alī," IC:21 (April 1947), 167-71.

A325 ———. "Tīpū's Relations with the Niẓām and the Marathas during the Period 1785-87," IC:17 (Oct. 1943), 414-21.

A326 BENNELL, A. S. "Wellesley's Settlement of Mysore, 1799," RAS (1952), pp. 124-32. An examination of his aims and diplomacy.

A327 BOULGER, DEMETRIUS C. "Constitutional Government in Mysore," CoR:87 (March 1905), 402-12. An account of the government and the state.

A328 "Buchanan's *Travels in the Mysore*," ER:13 (Oct. 1808), 82-100. Reviews his travels to investigate for Wellesley, after Tipu Sultan was killed.

A329 CADELL, P. R. (ed.). "A Prisoner of War in India, 1782-4. By Lieut.-Colonel Robert Cameron," SAHR:10 (Jan. 1931), 17-34. A narrative of a Mysore POW.

A330 CAMPBELL, R. H. "Tipoo Sultan; The Fall of Seringapatam and the Restoration of the Hindu Raj," MS:10 (Oct. 1919), 12-33. M. Kantarāj Urs, "Remarks," MS:10 (Oct. 1919), 33-36.

A331 CHETTY, A. SUBBARAYA. "Tippu's Endowments to the Hindus and the Hindu Institutions," IHCP:7 (1944), 416-19. A list of Tipu Sultan's grants to temples and Brahmins.

A332 GATES, ROSALIE PRINCE. "Tipu Sultan of Mysore and the Revolutionary Governments of France, 1793-1799," BPP:83 (Jan. 1964), 7-19.

A333 GOODALL, F. "Mysore," CR 68:135 (1879), 137-51. General description.

A334 ———. "British Prisoners in Mysore Fortresses," MS:6 (1915-16), 203-21. POW's of Hydar Ali and Tipu Sultan.

A335 HICKSON, SAMUEL. "Diary of Samuel Hickson, 1777-1785," BPP:49 (Jan.-June 1935), 5-54. On campaigns in Mysore; printed in full.

A336 HULTZSCH, E. "The Names of Coins of Tipu Sultan," IAn:18 (Oct. 1889), 313-15.

A337　HUSAIN, MAHMUD. "Regulations of Tipu Sultan's Navy," PHS:3 (Oct. 1955), 211-18. Ordinances for a projected building program.

A338　HUSAIN, YOUSUF. "Copy of a Letter of Tipu Sultan Addressed to Nawab Nizam Ali Khan," IHCP:14 (1951), 301-04. Tr. of 1791(?) letter on relations with British.

A339　KHAN, MOHIBUL HASAN. "Tipu Sultan and His English Prisoners of War," BPP:62 (1942), 124-28. Argues that Tipu treated POW's well.

A340　KIRKPATRICK, JAMES ACHILLES (tr.). "Biographical Anecdotes to the Late Tippoo Sultaun, Together with an Account of His Revenues, Establishment of His Troops, etc.," AAR:1 (1799), "Characters," 1-6. Translated from the Persian.

A341　KRISHNA, M. H. "The *Hyder-Nāma* on the Administration of Hyder Ali," IHCP:3 (1939), 1554-64.

A342　———. "Tipoo's Army in 1793 A.D.," IHRC:19 (Dec. 1942), 134-38.

A343　KUNJU, A. P. IBRAHIM. "Relations between Travancore and Mysore in the 18th Century," IHCP 23:2 (1961), 56-61. A reinterpretation of records, justifying Tipu Sultan's invasion of Travancore in 1790. Based on Cochin state records and other local records.

A344　LETHBRIDGE, ROPER. "Progress in Mysore: The Success of the Rendition Policy," AR:2 (Jan. 1895), 21-28.

A345　MARTIN, ERNEST J. (ed.). "An Engineer in the Mysore War of 1791-1792," SAHR:22 (1943/44), 324-38. Letters.

A346　MORAES, GEORGE M. "Muslim Rulers of Mysore and Their Christian Subjects," IHCP:7 (1944), 442-48; BUJ:14 (Jan. 1946), 1-5. Political history based on Portuguese records.

A347　———. "Muslim Rulers of Mysore and Their Christian Subjects: Appendix," BUJ:15 (July 1946), 53-56. Translation of a letter from Father Miranda (Superior of Seminary at Monte Mariano) to Portuguese Viceroy.

A348　MORLEY, JOHN. "England and the Annexation of Mysore," FR:6 (Sept. 15, 1866), 257-71.

A349　"Mysore," CR 46:92, 328-48. General history.

A350　NAIDU, B. M. RANGIAH. "The Letters and Memoirs of Tipoo Sultān," MS:13 (Jan. 1923), 628-44.

A351　NATARAJAN, B. "Land Revenue Administration under Haider Ali (1760-82)," MUJ:10 (Jan. 1938), 43-53. From published British sources.

A352 "One Who Knows Him." "In the Public Eye: Sir M. Visvesvaraya: Dewan of Mysore," HR:35 (Jan. 1917), 68-76.

A353 RAMACHANDRA RAO, P. B. "History of the Organisation and Growth of Departments of the Government of Mysore and Its Archives," MS (Culture and Heritage No., 1956), 170-78.

A354 RAO, RAGHAVENDRA V. "Haidar Āli and the First Mahrātta War, 1779-1782 A.D.," MS:31 (April 1941), 415-20.

A355 SAJAN LAL, K. "Hyder Ali's Appeal to the Hon'ble East India Co. 1764," IHQ:19 (June 1943), 184-87. A note based on the Public Department Diary.

A356 SALETORE, B. A. "The Mysore Rising of 1830," IHRC:31 (1955), 184-88. Summary of report by Special Committee of Inquiry.

A357 ———. "Tipu Sultan as a Defender of the Hindu Dharma," MIQ:1 (Oct. 1950), 43-55.

A358 SALETORE, G. N. "The British Expedition against Dhondji Vagh," BUJ:15 (Jan. 1947), 5-17. Part of mopping-up after defeat of Tipu Sultan. Records in Imperial Record Department.

A359 SARKAR, JADUNATH. "Haidar 'Ali's Invasion of the Eastern Carnatic, 1780," IC:15 (April 1941), 217-28. From a French manuscript.

A360 SASTRI, K. N. V. "Dadabhai Naoroji's Papers on the Mysore Rendition of 1881," IHCP:10 (1947), 443-47. Naoroji on the rights of the Raja of Mysore.

A361 ———. "The Disappearance of Mysore Postal System," IHRC:24 (Feb. 1948), 106-09. Description of the *Anche* (local mail service) in 1863.

A362 ———. "History of Mysore in the 19th Century Illustrated from Contemporary Newspapers," IHRC:22 (1945), 74-75. A few tidbits of information.

A363 ———. "A Social Background to Haidar Āli and Tipu Sultan," MS (Culture & Heritage No., 1956), 144-55. A sketch of 18th cent. Mysore.

A364 ———. "Some Particulars Relating to Tippo Sultan, His Revenue, Establishment of Troops, etc., etc.," MS:30 (July 1939), 91-98. Extract of an account of one of Tipu's officers, dated Madras, Dec. 1, 1790. First pub. in Dalrymple's *Oriental Repertory*:1, 1793, 229ff.

A365 SEN, SURENDRA NATH. "Hyder Ali's Fleet," IHQ:6 (June 1930), 309-17. History of the fleet. Based on Portuguese records and English published sources.

A366 ———(tr. & ed.). "A Portuguese Account of Haidar Ali," CR:65 (Dec. 1937), 253-60. Tr. from an MS in the Archivo Ultramarino of Lisbon.

A367 ———. "Tipu Sultan's Letters at Sringeri," IAn:48 (June 1919), 102-03. About letters to Peshwa's guru.

A368 SEN GUPTA, SURATH CHARAN. "Siege of Bednore, 1783," IHQ:2 (Dec. 1926), 797-808; 3 (March 1927), 134-43. From Tipu Sultan's *Memoirs*; combination of translation and paraphrase, with notes; also two English accounts.

A369 SINGH, NIHAL. "The Evolution of Modern Institutions in Mysore," MR:60 (Nov., Dec. 1936), 537-41, 650-55.

A370 SINHA, NARENDRA KRISHNA. "Hyder Ali's Relations with the British (1760-67)," IHRC:17 (1940), 67-72. Records in Government Record Office, Madras.

A371 ———. "Hyder Ali's Relations with the British (1775-80)," IHRC: 15 (Dec. 1938), 126-30; BPP:56 (Jan.-June 1939), 18-22. Records in Imperial Record Department.

A372 ———. "Hyder 'Ali's Relations with the British Government (1769-75)," IHQ:15 (March 1939), 55-64. Records in Imperial Record Department.

A373 ———. "Hyder Ali's Relations with Marathas, 1763-65," IHRC:16 (1939), 76-79. From the Peshwa Daftar.

A374 ———. "Hyder Ali's Relations with the Marathas (1766-67)," IHQ:16 (March 1940), 1-8. From the Peshwa Daftar and other records.

A375 ———. "Hyder Ali's Relations with the Marathas (1766-67)," 16 (Dec. 1940), 719-26.

A376 TABARD, A. M. "Tippū Sultān's Embassy to the French Court in 1788," MS:7 (Jan. 1917), 77-101.

A377 THURSTON, EDGAR. "Note on a Tour in Mysore in 1891," MJLS (1889-94), 35-48. Descriptive.

A378 [TIPU]. "Further Anecdotes of Tippoo Sultaun Extracted from Colonel Beatson's Account of the Late War in Mysore," AAR:2 (1800), "Characters," 10-16.

A379 "Treatment of a Native Indian Prince," OH:1 (Feb. 1824), 308-14. On Tipu Sultan.

8. HYDERABAD

A380 ASKARI, SYED HASSAN. "The Nizam and Cornwallis," IHCP:14 (1951), 217-24. Military and diplomatic history of the Northern Circars.

A381 BRADLEY, W. H. "Statistics of the Circar of Dowlatabad," MJLS: 15 (1847), 481-551.

A382 BURTON, R. G. "The Romance of an Indian State," FR:116 (Feb. 1922), 204-18. Traces history of Hyderabad, its wars and occupations.

A383 DAS, TARAKNATH. "The Status of Hyderabad during and after British Rule in India," MR:85 (Jan. 1949), 21-30; AJIL:43 (Jan. 1949), 57-72.

A384 DAVIES, C. COLLIN (ed.). "Correspondence of William Palmer with Sir Henry Russell, Formerly Resident at Hyderabad, 1836-1847," IA:13 (1959), 29-64. Excerpts from 24 letters.

A385 ————. "Correspondence of Henry Russell with Major Robert Pitman Commanding the Berar Division of the Nizam's Army," IA:12 (1958), 28-44. Excerpts from 16 letters.

A386 EAGLETON, C. "Case of Hyderabad before the Security Council," AJIL:44 (April 1950), 277-302. A historical summary of the case from its submission to the Security Council on August 21, 1948.

A387 "Further Development of the Iniquitous Conduct of the Indian Government, as Connected with the Transactions at Hyderabad," OH:4 (March 1825), 471-502.

A388 GORST, J. E. "The Kingdom of the Nizam," FR:41 (Jan.-June 1884), 522-30. On its political and economic condition.

A389 GRAY, GEORGE. "British Embassy to the Court of Hyder," RASB 25:72 (1918-19), 346-57. "A copy of the journal of Mr. George Gray, sent as a vakeel to Hyder Ali by Sir Thomas Rumbold." Covers Jan. 14 to March 19, 1780; MS from Lord Macartney's collection.

A390 "HISTORICUS." "Lord Mornington's Treatment of the Nizam," MR:28 (Aug. 1920), 143-51.

A391 HUSAIN KHAN, YUSUF. "Some Unpublished Documents in the Imperial Record Department of the Government of India Having a Bearing on Anglo-Nizam Relations," IC:23 (Jan. & April 1949), 37-47.

A392 "Hyderabad:—the Nizam's Contingent," CR 11:21 (1849), 141-219.

A393 "In the Nizam's Country," CR 63:126 (1876), 217-39.

A394 "Lord Hastings—Sir Charles Metcalfe—Mr. Adam—and the Contractors for the Hyderabad Loan," OH:3 (Nov. 1824), 368-82.

A395 "The Nizam's Dominions," CR 53:105 (1871), 90-128.

A396 RAO, P. SETU MADHVA (tr.). "Anecdotes of Nizam-ul-Mulk," JIH:39 (Dec. 1961), 413-66. Translated from Persian manuscript, "Masire Nizami."

A397 ——— (tr.). "Maratha-Nizam Relations: Nizam-ul-Mulk's Letters," JIH:41 (April 1963), 131-50. Translated from the Persian.

A398 REGANI, SAROJINI. "The Appointment of Diwans in Hyderabad State (1803-1887)," AHRS:25 (1958-60), 11-18.

A399 ——— (tr.). "An Unpublished Letter of the Resident Henry Russell 1811-20," AHRS:25 (1958-60), 46-51. "The object of this paper is to throw light on the extent to which the British Resident often interfered in the internal affairs of Hyderabad State in order to promote the British interests." Letter dated Poona, 12th Oct., 1810, from Resident-designate Henry Russell to his assistant, Charles Russell.

A400 ROCK, JOSEPH. "The New Era in Hyderabad," FR:67 (Jan.-June 1897), 911-22. Administration after the death of Salar Jang.

A401 [SALAR JANG]. "Sir Salar Jang's Administration," PSS:3 (No. 3, 1880), 30-50.

A402 SARKAR, JADUNATH (ed. & tr.). "General Raymond of the Nizam's Army," IC:7 (Jan. 1933), 95-113. Letters dated 1792 and 1793.

A403 ———(ed.). "Haidarabad and Golkonda in 1750 as Seen through French Eyes (From the Unpublished Diary of a French Officer of Bussy's Army, Preserved in the Bibliothèque Nationale, Paris)," IC:10 (April 1936), 234-47.

A404 ——— (tr.). "Old Hyderabad," IC:11 (Oct. 1937), 521-28. 1776-77 manuscript.

A405 "Selections from the Mass of Papers Laid Before the Proprietors of East India Stock, Relating to the Transactions at Hyderabad," OH:4 (Mar. 1825), 517-49.

A406 SHAUKAT, SAMEENA. "Maharaja Chandu Lal Shadan (The Minister-Poet of Hyderabad): His Ancestry, Parentage and Family," AHRS:27 (1961-62), 90-100. Family history in 18th and 19th centuries.

A407 SHERWANI, H. K. "The Evolution of the Legislature in Hyderabad," IJPS:1 (April 1940), 424-38.

A408 SMITH, WILFRED CANTWELL. "Hyderabad: Muslim Tragedy," MEJ:4 (Jan. 1950), 27-51. Detailed account of political background and events of the 1948 take-over.

A409 STEUART, A. FRANCIS (ed.). "Letters from the Nizam's Camp, 1791-1794," AR, Ser. 3:34 (July 1912), 114-51. Written by William Steuart, a Company soldier.

PART I: ARTICLES

A410   STRACHEY, EDWARD. "The Romantic Marriage of Major James Achilles Kirkpatrick, Sometime British Resident at the Court of Hyderabad," BM:154 (July 1893), 18-29.

A411   WALKER, A. "Aurangabad (Statistics of the City of)," MJLS:16 (1850?), 1-33.

A412   ———. "Hyderabad (N. and E.), Statistical Report," MJLS:16 (1848?), 182-235.

A413   ———. "Statistical Report on the Sircar of Kummemmet," MJLS:16 (1848?), 179-81.

A414   ———. "Statistical Report on the Sircar of Nelgoondah," MJLS:16 (1848?), 173-78.

A415   ———, and FRANZER, MAJOR GENERAL. "Statistical Report on the Sircar of Warungal," MJLS:15 (1847?), 219-301.

9. SIKHS AND THE PUNJAB, 1750–1850

A416   ABDUL ALI, A. F. M. "Notes on the Life and Times of Ranjit Singh," BPP:31 (Jan.-June 1926), 42-65; IHRC:8 (Nov. 1925), 211-35; MR:1 (July-Sept. 1926), 75-90. Based on British records.

A417   AHLUWALIA, M. L. "Mai Chand Kaur's Rule in the Punjab—An Estimate," IHRC:31 (1955), 65-74. 19th cent. political history; based on British records.

A418   ———. "Sher Singh and the First War of Succession for the Lahore Throne, 1841," IHRC:32 (1956), 107-21. British records.

A419   ———. "Some Facts behind the Second Anglo-Sikh War," IHRC:35 (1960), 1-10. Summaries of letters on secret negotiations.

A420   ANDERSON, WILLIAM. "Sketch of the Recorded Revenues of the States beyond the Sutlej about 1750-1800," ASB:18 (Aug. 1849), 822-26.

A421   "Another Chapter in the History of the Conquest of the Punjab," CR:108 (April 1899), 316-37.

A422   BAKSHI, S. R. "Metcalfe's Mission to the Court of Maharaja Ranjit Singh," MR:118 (Dec. 1965), 32-36.

A423   BANERJEE, INDUBHUSHAN. "The Calcutta Review and the First Sikh War," CR (Centenary No., 1944), 69-91. Reporting of the war in CR.

A424   ———. "The Kashmir Rebellion and the Trial of Raja Lal Singh," IHCP:3 (1939), 1308-29. British relations with Sikhs in the 1840's.

A425 BHASIM, A. S. "Macauliffe and the Adi Granth," JPUHS:12 (June 1961), 39-43.

A426 BROWNE, JAMES. "History of the Origin and Progress of the Sikhs." Edited and annotated [with an introduction] by Ganda Singh. ISPP:2 (April, July 1961), 535-42, 549-83. "The first regular treatise on the Sikhs written by an Englishman. The greater part of it is the translation of the abridged Persian version of a Devinagri manuscript in the possession of two Hindus with whom he came into contact in 1783." Originally published in 1788.

A427 BRUCE, J. F. and SURI, VIDYASAGAR. [Catalogue of Original Sources of the History of the Punjab], JPUHS:8 (April 1944), 1-121 & 1-6.

A428 "The Campaign of the Sutlej," BM:59 (July 1846), 625-44. Extensive extracts from Maj. Bradfoot's letters, Nov.-Dec. 1845, and from the Governor-General to the Secret Committee.

A429 "A Chapter in the History of the Conquest of the Panjab," CR:107 (Oct. 1898), 257-93.

A430 "The Countries betwixt the Sutlej and the Jumna," CR 5:10 (1846), 348-72.

A431 "Court and Camp of Runjeet Sing," ER:71 (April 1840), 263-75.

A432 "The Court and Camp of Runjeet Sing," CR:31 (Dec. 1858), 247-302.

A433 "Cunningham's History of the Sikhs," CR 11:22 (1849), 523-58.

A434 DIVER, MAUD. "The British Subaltern in India," BM:257 (June 1945), 385-98. Largely on Herbert Edwardes and the Sikhs in the 1840's.

A435 GARRETT, H. L. O. "An Italian in India: Paolo di Avitabile," AR: NS 37 (1941), 361-65. In the service of the Sikhs in early 19th cent., Governor of Wazirabad and Peshawar.

A436 GOSWAMY, KARUNA. "The Bāthū Shrine and the Rajas of Guler: A Brief Study of a Vaishnava Establishment," JIH:43 (Aug. 1965), 577-85. With paintings of Duleep Singh.

A437 GREWAL, J. S. "J. D. Cunningham and His British Predecessors on the Sikhs," BPP:83 (July-Dec. 1964), 101-14.

A438 GUPTA, HARI RAM. "Lieutenant-Colonel Stuart in Sikh Captivity, from 3rd January to 24th October, 1791," CR:82 (Jan. 1942), 58-66. Narrative taken from Imperial Records.

A439 ———. "Origin of Sikh Territorial Chieftainships, 1748-1759," IHCP:3 (1939), 1172-88. Rise of the Sikh powers; English and Persian sources.

A440 ISLAM, ZAFARUL. "The End of Sikh Rule," HFM:2 (1831-1905), Part 1, 72-96.

A441 [JACQUEMONT]. "Victor Jacquemont's Interview with Maharaja Ranjit Singh at Lahore," MR:50 (Nov. 1931), 503-04. Entry in his diary, Lahore, 11th March 1831; tr. from the French by B. R. Chatterji.

A442 KHANNA, K. C. "The Multan Outbreak of April 1848," JPUHS:2 (Dec. 1933), 166-74.

A443 KHASH ALEE, SHEKH. "Account of the Esafzai-Affghans Inhabiting Sama (the Plains), Swat, Bunher and the Chamla Valley, Being a Detail of Their Clans, Villages, Chiefs and Force, and the Tribute They Pay to the Sikhs. By Shekh Khash Alee, a follower of the fanatic Syud Ahmed. Prepared in 1837." ASB:14 (July-Dec. 1845), 736-46.

A444 KHERA, P. N. "Mr. C. T. Metcalfe in the Panjab, 1801-9," IHCP:4 (1940), 359-67. Punjab Government Records.

A445 KOHLI, SITA RAM. "The Army of Maharaja Ranjit Singh," JIH:1 (Feb. 1922), 189-225—organization and pay of the army, with tables of figures; JIH:1 (Sept. 1922), 397-418—artillery; JIH:2 (May 1923), 178-205—cavalry; JIH:4 (Jan. 1926), 105-17—recruitment; JIH:5 (1926), 20-35—pay and discipline; JIH:13 (1934), 358-79—attack and defense of fortified places; JIH:14 (1935), 400-25—deductions, fines, rewards. Well-written and factual.

A446 ———. "A Book of Military Parwanas," IHCP:4 (1940), 367-71. Suggestions of what sorts of social and economic information can be gleaned from a manuscript collection of Ranjit Singh's military orders.

A447 ———. "Document Regulating Succession to the Throne of Lahore, Nov. 1840," IHRC:32 (1956), 1-6. Transcription, translation, and discussion of its background.

A448 ———. "Land Revenue Administration under Maharajah Ranjit Singh," JPHS 7:1 (1918), 74-90. Includes "Statement showing the Annual Receipts and Disbursements of the Khalsa Exchequer for the Sambat 1877 (1821 A.D.)."

A449 ———. "The Multan Outbreak and the Trial of Diwan Mul Raj," JPUHS:1 (April 1932), 32-48. 1848 outbreak by Sikhs.

A450 ———. "A Trained Infantry Battalion; Its Composition, Constitution and Cost of Maintenance," IHRC:31 (1955), 1-11. Based on Khalsa Darbar Records (of the Sikh army).

A451 LAHIRI, REBATI MOHAN. "Teerat Singh and the Khasi Rebellion (1829-1833)," MR:77 (April 1945), 174-76.

A452 "The Lahore Blue Book," CR 8:15 (1847), 231-82. On 1846 agreement.

A453 "Macgregor's Sikhs—Political Agency in the East," CR 7:14 (1847), 283-320.

A454 MACKESON, F. "Survey of the Satlaj River," ASB:6 (Jan.-June 1837), 169-217.

A455 MADHAVA RAO, P. SETU. "The Punjab (1758 to 1763): from the Tahmasnama Abridged and Translated," RASB: NS 38 (1963), 85-115.

A456 MAHAJAN, JAGMOHAN LAL. "The Anglo-Sikh War of 1845-46: A Re-Orientation," CR:95 (June 1945), 89-96.

A457 ———. "The Private Correspondence of Sir Frederick Currie, 1846-1848," JUPHS:10 (April 1947), 1-25. Political agent at Lahore, 1846-48, thereafter British Resident. Letters from Lord Hardinge showing connivance at taking control of the Sikh kingdom.

A458 "Malcolm's *Sketch of the Sikhs*," ER:21 (July 1913), 432-44.

A459 MATHUR, GIRISH PRASAD. "Maharaja Ranjit Singh," MR:66 (Aug. 1939), 161-65.

A460 MOJUMDAR, KANCHANMOY. "Maharanee Chanda Kaur in Nepal," BPP:83 (Jan. 1964), 20-24; BRS:47 (1961), 241-45. Queen of Maharaja Ranjit Singh; 1849.

A461 NAIR, LAJPAT RAI. "Ranjit Singh and Shah Shujah's Expedition to Kandhar (1831-34)," IHCP:4 (1940), 372-83. Correspondence and treaties printed.

A462 "The Punjab," ER:89 (Jan. 1849), 184-221. Review of "Papers Relating to the Treaties of Lahore"; history of Sikh state.

A463 QANUNGO, S. N. "Ranjit Singh and the Fall of Sikh Power," MR:116 (Oct. 1964), 287-89.

A464 ———. "Some Sidelights on the Fall of the Sikh Power," VBQ:28 (1962-63), 167-74. On Ranjit Singh's failures.

A465 RAI, GULSHAN. "The Mughal Province of Multan and Its Subsequent History (1707-1849)," JPUHS:2, Pt. 1:3 (April 1933), 51-71. With fold-out map.

A466 "Ranjit Singh: 'The Lion of the North,'" CR:93 (Oct. 1891), 377-402.

A467 RANKEN, G. P. "The Punjab under Native Rule," ER:238 (Oct. 1923), 334-47. On conditions under Sikh rule.

A468 "Recent History of the Punjab," CR:1 (Aug. 1844), 449-507.

A469 REHATSEK, EDWARD. "A Notice of the *Zafarnama-i-Ranjit-Singh* of Kanhayya Lal," IAn:16 (Oct., Nov. 1887), 303-12, 334-40; 17

(Jan.-April 1888), 18-23, 54-60, 81-88, 98-100. A translation of a poem in praise of Ranjit Singh.

A470 "The Reigning Family of Lahore," CR 9:18 (1848), 511-24.

A471 SACHCHIDANAND. "Balwant Singh and the English," PU:5 (Jan. 1950), 25-35.

A472 SALUJA, JAGAT. "The Unpublished Letters of Sardar Chatar Singh Atariwala," JPHS:11 (1931), 17-29. Written in 1840's.

A473 SARDESAI, G. S. "Career of Ranjit Singh and Its Effect on Indian Politics," BV:1 (May 1940), 156-61. Pictured as a successful politician vis-à-vis Great Britain.

A474 SARKAR, JADUNATH. "Guide to Indian Historical Literature," MR:2 (Oct. 1907), 392-95. Bibliography of historical works bearing on the Punjab from the rise of the Sikhs to British annexation.

A475 SAXENA, S. K. "Dr. Lord's Interview with Maharaja Ranjit Singh at Amritsar in 1838 on His Mission to Peshawar," IHRC:22 (1945), 66-67. His report of it in a letter.

A476 "The Second Punjab War," CR 12:23 (1849), 238-96.

A477 "The Second Sikh War," CR 15:30 (1851), 253-98.

A478 "The Seikhs and Their Country," CR:2 (Oct. 1844), 153-208.

A479 SEMENOVA, N. I. "Sel'skaia obshchina i feodal'noe semlevladenie v gosudarstve Randzhit Singa [Rural Communities and Feudal Land Ownership in the State of Ranjit Singh]," UZIV:12 (1955), 61-98. Summary in HA:4: "Examines the different types, the occurrence and the functional and social structure of village communities in Punjab during the first half of the 19th century. Based on C. L. Tupper's Punjab Customary Law, H. K. Trevaskis' The Land of the Five Rivers, and gazetteers."

A480 SEN, S. N. "A Note on General Ventura's Jagir," IHCP:5 (1941), 511-16. On the fortune acquired by a French adventurer in Ranjit Singh's service.

A481 SETHI, R. R. "The Treaty of Bhyrowal or Second Treaty of Lahore—Dec. 1846," JPUHS:2, part 1:3 (April 1933), 43-50.

A482 "The Sikh Invasion of British India in 1845-1846," CR 6:11 (1846), 241-304.

A483 [SINGH]. "Maharaja Duleep Singh's Letter, May 1887," BPP:84 (July-Dec. 1965), foll. p. 187. Facsimile of letter to Alexander III of Russia.

A484 SINGH, GANDA (ed.). "Colonel Polier's Account of the Sikhs," ASB, Ser. 4:1 (1959), 73-87. "First known connected account of Sikh people written by a European," written c. 1780.

A485 ———. "The Maratha-Sikh Treaty of 1785," IHCP:3 (1939), 1265-82. Prints the various versions of the treaty and correspondence about negotiations.

A486 ———. "Some New Lights on the Treaty of Bhyrowal (Dec. 16, 1846) Thrown by the Private Letters of Sir Henry Hardinge," IHRC:17 (1940), 91-98. On the British garrisons and "regency" in Lahore during the minority of Maharajah Duleep Singh.

A487 ———. "Three Letters of Maharani Jind Kaur," IHCP:13 (1950), 304-13; JIH:42 (1964), 265-80. Letters from mother of Dulip Singh to British in 1847.

A488 [SINGH, GULAB]. "Maharaja Gulab Singh and the Second Sikh War," JPUHS:4, part 1:7 (April 1935), 51-62.

A489 SINGH, NIHAL. "The Progressive Ruler of Nabha," MR:19 (April 1916), 367-72. Biography of Maharaja Ripudaman Singh, ruler of one of the Punjab states.

A490 SINHA, NARENDRA KRISHNA. "Ranjit Singh and the North-West Frontier Problem," IHQ:5 (Sept. 1929), 513-17. "Based solely on the records in the Imperial Record Department." Includes figures on revenue and expenditure of administration at Peshawar.

A491 SMITH, G. C. MOORE (ed.). "Correspondence of Sir Henry Hardinge, Sir Hugh Gough, and Sir Harry Smith during the Sutlej Campaign, 1846," EHR:17 (Oct. 1902), 737-52. Prints letters. Note on correspondence: "The Campaign on the Sutlej, 1845-6," by Robert S. Rait. EHR:18 (Jan. 1903), 130-31.

A492 TEMPLE, R. C. "The Coins of the Modern Native Chiefs of the Panjab," IAn:18 (Nov. 1889), 321-41. With plates and map showing Punjab states' mint towns.

A493 VERMA, BIRENDRA. "Afghan-Sikh Relations," PU:19 (July 1964), 63-75. 1756-1785.

A494 WILLIAMS, G. R. C. "Historical Sketches: The Sikhs in the Upper Doab," CR 60:119 (1875), 21-36; 61:121 (1875), 39-55; 61:122 (1875), 346-68.

10. RAJPUT STATES

A495 ALAEV, L. B. "Sobstvennost' na zemliu v kniazhostvakh radzhputany v pervoĭ polovine XIX v. (po knige Dzh. Toda 'Annaly i drevnosti Radzhastkhana')" [Property in the Land in the Rajput Kingdoms in the First Half of the 19th Century (according to J. Tod's 'Annals and Antiquities of Rajasthan')], KS:51 (1962), 133-50.

A496 ANSARI, A. S. BAZMEE. "Djaypur," EI:2, 503-04 Jaipur.

A497 ASKARI, SYED HASAN. "Unpublished Correspondence Relating to Maharaja Madho Singh of Jaipur and Some of His Contemporaries," IHRC:24 (Feb. 1948), 73-78. Durrani-Rajput relations, 1759-61.

A498 BANERJEE, ANIL CHANDRA. "British Alliance with Udaipur, 1818," IHRC:21 (1944), 22-24. Extracts from documents.

A499 ———. "The Subsidiary System in Marwar (1803-1843)," IHQ:22 (Sept. 1946), 180-90. The rule of Maharaja Man Singh; based on government records in Delhi, Tod's *Annals of Marwar*, treaties.

A500 ———. "The Subsidiary System in Mewar, 1818-1828," IHQ:21 (Sept. 1945), 184-92. Administrative history.

A501 ———. "The Subsidiary System in Rajputana," IHQ:23 (March, June 1947), 17-32; 93-112. Political and diplomatic history.

A502 "Character of the Rajpoots," ER:56 (Oct. 1832), 73-98. Review of Tod's *Annals*, vol. 2.

A503 CHOWDHURI, R. N. "A Glimpse of Jaipur—A Century Ago," IHCP:14 (1951), 355-62. Brief history, 1818-52. Based on British records.

A504 DAVIES, C. COLLIN. "Djōdhpur or Mārwār," EI:2, 567. Jodhpur.

A505 "Dixon's Mairwara," CR 15:30 (1851), 456-74. On Ajmer and Marwar.

A506 GUPTA, HIRA LAL. "Banswara Successions, 1838-1844," JIH:42 (Dec. 1964), 763-70. A Rajput state.

A507 ———. "The Plunder of Bharatpur," IHCP:13 (1950), 277-80. Documentation of British looting in 1826.

A508 HASAN, NURUL. "Adjmēr," EI:1, 208. History and description of Rajastani state, 1100-1818.

A509 KHADGAWAT, N. R. "An Introduction to Rajasthan State Archives," IA:13 (1959), 1-11.

A510 PANIKKAR, K. N. "Sir David Ochterlony and British Interference in Jaipur (1818-1821)," JIH:42 (Dec. 1964), 921-30.

A511 "The Rajpūt States of India," ER:144 (July 1876), 169-203. On their history and government.

A512 "The Romance of Mairwara," BM:73 (Feb. 1853), 207-15. Public works and revenue, 1835-1847.

A513 RUDOLPH, SUSANNE HOEBER. "The Princely States of Rajputana: Ethic, Authority and Structure," IJPS:24 (Jan. 1963), 14-32.

A514 SARKAR, JADUNATH. "A Proposal for a Subsidiary Alliance in Rajputana, in 1794," IHRC:16 (1939), 1-4.

A515 SHARMA, G. N. "Political and Social Condition of Rajasthan in the 19th Century, as Revealed from Havālā-Bahies," UB:7 (Dec. 1960), 93-103. Based on *bahies* in Marwari found in Pustak Prakash Library, Jodhpur. Deals with local government, revenue and the judicial systems, and living standards, 1843-73.

A516 [TOD]. "Colonel Tod's *Annals of Rajpootana*," ER:53 (Oct. 1830), 86-109.

11. NORTHWEST FRONTIER AND AFGHANISTAN

A517 "The Afghan Tribes on Our Trans-Indus Frontier," W:92 (Oct. 1869), 438-94.

A518 "The Afghan War and Its Authors," BM:125 (Jan. 1879), 112-40.

A519 "The Afghan War: Passages from the Note-Book of a Staff Officer," BM:127 (March, April, June 1880), 364-77, 464-78, 757-67.

A520 ALLAN, JAMES J. "The Strategic Principles of Lord Lytton's Afghan Policy," RCAS:24 (July 1937), 429-36.

A521 ANSARI, A. S. BAZMEE. "Ambāla," EI:1, 432-33.

A522 ———. "Chitral," EI:2, 29-31.

A523 ———. "Dīr," EI:2, 316-17. Princely state which acceded to West Pakistan; pro-British in 20th century.

A524 ANWAR KHAN, MOHAMMAD. "The Russophobia of Lord Ellenborough, 1828-1830," ASP:8 (June 1963), 73-81. Papers in Public Record Office.

A525 "B.G." "Afghanistan and Scinde," W:41 (June 1844), 521-52.

A526 BARTON, WILLIAM P. "India's North-west Frontier," GeM:15 (July 1942), 97-105. On the Durand Line, with photos.

A527 BASU, B. D. "The Causes of the Second Afghan War," MR:44 (July-Sept. 1928), 36-41, 129-33, 265-69.

A528 ———. "Evacuation of Afghanistan after the Second Afghan War," MR:44 (Nov. 1928), 522-29.

A529 ———. "The Second Afghan War," MR:43 (May 1928), 531-36; 44 (Oct. 1928), 387-95.

A530 BEAUCHAMP, HENRY K. "North-west Frontier of India," FR:63 (May 1895), 721-32. On its strategic strength.

A531 BYRT, A. H. "Indian North-west Frontier under Modern Political Conditions," RCAS:28 (July 1941), 270-94. Paper followed by discussion.

A532 "The Campaign of Pānipat," CR 68:135 (1879), 91-103. The battle of 1760.

A533 CHAKRABARTI, B. P. "An Unpublished Demi-Official Report on Peshawar Disturbance, 1860," IHRC:22 (1945), 63-65.

A534 CHAND, BOOL. "The North-Western Question of Indian History 1798-1830," CR:77 (Nov., Dec. 1940), 141-56, 289-302. A survey.

A535 CHATTERJI, NANDALAL. "The Second Afghan War and the Patriotic Fund," IHCP:14 (1951), 211-13; JIH:30 (Dec. 1952), 259-61. An attempt by officials to raise funds to aid war victims. Based on U.P. records.

A536 CHAUDHURI, NIRAD C. "The Military Background of the Third Afghan War, 1919," MR:52 (Oct. 1932), 407-14.

A537 CHOPRA, JANKI. "Dost Muhammad Khan in India," IHRC:19 (Dec. 1942), 82-86.

A538 GOLVIN, AUCKLAND. "The Problem beyond the Indian Frontier," NC:42 (Dec. 1897), 845-68.

A539 CURZON, GEORGE N. "The Scientific Frontier of India, An Accomplished Fact," NC:23 (June 1888), 901-17.

A540 DACOSTA, J. "Rectification of Frontier," W:137 (March 1892), 313-17. On British claims against Afghanistan.

A541 DAMES, M. LONGWORTH, and GIBB, H. A. R. "Afghānistān: History," EI:1, 225-33. Includes relations with India.

A542 DAVIES, C. COLLIN. "Aḥmad Shāh Durrāni," EI:1, 295-97.

A543 ———. "The Amir and the Frontier Tribesmen of India," ArQ: 12 (April 1926), 44-54. Argues Amir can control tribesmen.

A544 ———. "Amīr Khān, 1768-1839," EI:1, 444. Pathan chief, founder of state of Tonk.

A545 ———. "Coercive Measure on the Indian Borderland: Blockading the Mahsuds," ArQ:16 (April 1928), 81-95.

A546 ———. "An Imperial Problem: The North-West Frontier of India," ArQ:15 (Oct. 1927), 28-41.

A547 ———. "Lord Curzon's Frontier Policy and the Formation of the North-West Frontier Province, 1901," ArQ:13 (Jan. 1927), 261-73. With map.

A548 DISKALKAR, D. B. "Some Letters about the First Afghan War 1838-1842," JIH:12 (Dec. 1933), 251-68. Three letters from a deputy adjutant general in the field.

A549 DIVER, MAUD. "A Hundred Years of the Khyber Pass," BM:255 (March 1944), 157-71. Popular history and description.

A550 DIXON, F. "Sir Herbert Edwardes at Peshawar and Treaty with Afghanistan, 1857," MM:63 (Nov. 1890–April 1891), 291-98.

A551 DURAND, A. G. A. "North-west Frontier Policy," QR:191 (April 1900), 467-91.

A552 "The Evacuation of Afghanistan," BM:53 (Feb. 1843), 266-79. Cites in full Lord Ellenborough's proclamation of Oct. 1, 1842.

A553 "The Fear of Russia and the Defence of India," BM:177 (April 1905), 589-96. With map of Russian railroads to Afghan border.

A554 GORDON-POLONSKAYA, L. R. [Socio-Economic Order of Afghan Tribes in India in the Second Half of the 19th Century], VIs 3:3 (1950).

A555 GOSSE, EDMUND. "The Baluch and Afghan Frontiers of India," FR:51 (March 1889), 292-324. Maps.

A556 GRANTOVSKIĬ, E. A. "Iz istorii vostochno-iranskikh plemen na granitsakh Indii" [On the History of East-Iranian Tribes on the Borders of India], KS:61 (1963), 8-30.

A557 GRIFFIN, LEPEL H. "The Breakdown of the Forward Frontier Policy," NC:42 (Oct. 1897), 501-16. Against the background of British Muslim policy.

A558 GUPTA, H. R. "Some Observations on the Life and Letters of Mohan Lal Kashmerian," CR:77 (Dec. 1940), 317-28; 78 (Jan. 1941), 51-62. The career of a Delhi Hindu munshi who became involved in the diplomacy of the Northwest Frontier, visited England in 1844 and finally converted to Shi'i faith.

A559 "H.R.S." "Unrest in the Peshawar District, 1930-1932," RCAS:19 (1932), 624-42. On the Red Shirt movement.

A560 HAMILTON, ANGUS. "Habib Ullah and the Indo-Afghan Frontier," FR:89 (June 1908), 973-81.

A561 ———. "Indo-Afghan Relations under Lord Curzon," FR:86 (Dec. 1906), 984-1000.

A562 HAYE, KHWAJA A. "British Interest in Afghanistan," HFM:2 (1831-1905), Part 1, 27-46.

A563 HERAS, J. "Durrānī Influence in Northern India," IC:11 (Oct. 1937), 498-515; 12 (Jan. 1938), 17-32.

A564 HOBSON, WILLIAM A. "Warden of the Khyber; or, The Story of a Distinguished Anglo-Indian Soldier," CR:284 (April 1916), 209-14. Biography of Sir Robert Warburton.

A565 HOLDICH, THOMAS HUNGERFORD. "Baluchistan: History," EB:3, 295-96. Largely history of relations with British.

A566 "India and Afghanistan," BM:124 (Nov. 1878), 603-27.

A567 "India, Persia, and Afghanistan," ER:105 (Jan. 1857), 266-304.

A568 "AN INDIAN CORRESPONDENT." "Why We Went to Chitral," BM:158 (Sept. 1895), 402-19.

A569 "AN INDIAN OFFICER." "Our True Policy in India," FR:51 (Feb. 1889), 275-81. Afghans and Russian threat.

A570 INNES, J. M'LEOD. "Lord Roberts and Indian Frontier Policy," FR:68 (Nov. 1897), 750-65. With diagrams of battles.

A571 IRVINE, WILLIAM. "Aḥmad Shah, Abdālī, and the Indian Wazīr, 'Imād-ul-Mulk (1756-7)," IAn:34 (Jan.-March 1907), 10-18, 43-51, 55-70. Account of Abdali invasion, from Persian MS.

A572 "The Kabul Tragedy; From the Papers of a Survivor of the Massacre in Afghanistan, 1841-42," BM:179 (March 1906), 347-68.

A573 KHANNA, K. C. "The Sikh Darbar and the First Afghan War," JPUHS:2, part 1 (April 1933), 1-22. The part played by the Lahore Durbar in British policy toward Afghanistan, 1838-42.

A574 KHERA, P. N. "Origins of the First Afghan War," JPUHS:1 (Dec. 1932), 87-107.

A575 KHOSLA, JAGANATH. "Provincial Autonomy in the N.-W.F.P.," IJPS:1 (Jan. 1940), 324-32. On administrative developments in the late 1930's.

A576 "Lord Mayo and the Umballa Durbar," BM:107 (Jan. 1870), 61-74. On his Afghan policy.

A577 "Lumsden of the Guides," BM:165 (June 1899), 1003-15. Soldier on the Northwest Frontier.

A578 [MACNAGHTEN]. "Sir W. H. Macnaghten," CR:2 (Oct. 1844), 209-65. On policy on North-west Frontier.

A579 MAURICE, J. F. "Frontier Policy and Lord Lytton's Indian Administration, 1876-1880," ER:191 (Jan. 1900), 226-46.

A580 ———. "Our True Policy in India; a Reply," FR:51 (Feb. 1889), 282-92. On the Afghan border and Russian threat.

A581 MONCRIEFF, G. K. SCOTT. "Some Punjab Frontier Recollections," BM:176 (Nov. 1904), 597-613. About 1880.

A582 NAPIER, R. W. N. "Brief Note on the North-West Frontier Policy," NC:43 (March 1898), 371-75.

A583 "The North-West Frontier of India," CR 69:138 (1879), 280-93.

A584 OLIVIER, EDWARD E. "Punitive Expeditions on the North-West Frontier of India," FR:56 (July 1891), 89-100. On pros and cons of annexation.

A585 OSBORN, ROBERT D. "India and Afghanistan," CoR:36 (Oct. 1879), 193-211. Somewhat acid history of border wars in 1870's.

A586 ———. "The Last Phase of the Afghan War," CoR:38 (Sept. 1880), 434-45. Urges abandonment of Afghans' country so that they might establish new institutions in peace.

A587 "The Pathans of the North-West Frontier of India," BM:125 (May 1879), 595-610.

A588 RAWLINSON, H. G. "The Results of the Afghan War," NC:6 (Aug. 1879), 377-400.

A589 "Recent Campaigns in India," W:55 (April 1851), 49-69. In northwest.

A590 REHATSEK, EDWARD. "The Reign of Ahmad Shah Durrani; Translated from the Tārīkh Sultānī of Sultān Muḥammad Khāṅ Bārukzai," IAn:16 (Sept., Oct. 1887), 263-74, 298-303.

A591 REPINGTON, C. à C. "Northwest Frontier," NC:95 (Feb. 1924), 269-72. Need for a consistent policy and strategy there.

A592 ROBINSON, E. KAY. "The Afghan Alliance," FR:64 (Nov. 1895), 707-16.

A593 RODGERS, J. "The Coins of Ahmad Shāh Abdālī or Ahmad Shāh Durranī," ASB:54 (1885), 67-76. With plate.

A594 ROOMAN, M. ANWAR. "Ghulam Hussain (Masoori Bugti). The Baluch Hero," PPHC:1 (1950), 361-67. A frontier chieftain of 1860's and 70's as a freedom fighter.

A595 SARKAR, JADUNATH (tr.). "An Original Account of Ahmad Shah Durrani's Campaigns in India and the Battle of Panipat. (From the Persian Life of Najib-ud-daulah, British Museum Persian MS 24,410)," IC:7 (July 1933), 431-56.

A596 SETHI, R. R. "The Ambela Campaign, 1863," JPUHS:3, part 1: 5 (April 1934), 20-30; BPP:47 (Jan.-June 1934), 111-19.

A597 ———. "Events Leading to the Ambela Expedition—1863," JPUHS:2, part 2:4 (Dec. 1933), 131-41; BPP:46 (July-Dec. 1933), 14-22.

A598 ———. "Panic of Sir Robert Montgomery, 1863," JPUHS:3, part 2:6 (Dec. 1934), 119-23.

A599 SHAND, ALEXANDER INNES. "Field-Marshal Sir Neville Chamberlain," CM, Ser. 3:12 (May 1902), 598-617. His operations in the Northwest in the 1840's.

A600 SINHA, NARENDRA KRISHNA. "The Durrani Menace and the British North-West Frontier Problem in the Eighteenth Century," IHQ:10 (Dec. 1934), 624-41.

A601 "A SUBALTERN." "The Agra Durbar," BM:181 (March 1907), 391-99. Meeting between Viceroy and Amir, 1907.

A602 THORBURN, S. S. "Our Last War with the Mahsuds," BM:158 (July 1895), 76-91. In Afghanistan.

A603 THORNTON, A. P. "Afghanistan in Anglo-Russian Diplomacy, 1869-1873," CHJ:9 (1954), 204-18.

A604 "The Unrest on the Indian Frontier," RT:21 (1930-31), 351-70.

A605 YAPP, M. E. "Disturbances in Eastern Afghanistan, 1839-42," BSOAS:25 (1962), 499-523. Based on British correspondence in India Office Library.

A606 YOUNGHUSBAND, G. J. "Permanent Pacification of the Indian Frontier," NC:43 (Feb. 1898), 250-55.

A607 ZAIDI, Z. H. "Negotiations between Dost Mohammad Khan, Amir of Kabul and the British Government Leading up to the Treaty of 1855," PPHC:6 (1956), 197-212.

12. HIMALAYA AND NORTHEAST FRONTIER

A608 "The Abode of Snow," BM:116 (Aug., Oct.-Dec. 1874), 127-45, 410-31, 560-82, 703-22; 117 (Jan.-May 1875), 69-87, 219-37, 336-61, 508-25, 600-15; 118 (July 1875), 60-81. Travel in the Himalayas.

A609 APPADORAI, A. & others. "Bases of India's Title on the North-East Frontier," IS:1 (1959-60), 351-87. History and international law; with map.

A610 BANERJI, ALBION. "The Problem of Kashmir," NC:112 (Aug. 1932), 180-89.

A611 BANON, H. M. "Fifty Years in Kulu," HmJ:17 (1952), 126-30. Geographical and social account of the valley.

A612 BARPUJARI, H. K. "The Early Phase of the Resistance Movement in the North-East Frontier 1828-30," IHRC:31 (1955), 8-11. British records; letters printed.

A613 ———. "The Genesis of the NEFA," IHRC:35 (1960), 39-43. Negotiations of Lt. Neufville in 1826.

A614 BARTON, WILLIAM P. "Pakistan's Claim to Kashmir," FA:28 (Jan. 1950), 299-308. Summary of the early days of the Pakistan debacle.

A615 BHADURI, MANINDRA BHUSHAN. "Bagchi-levi in Nepal: A Glimpse of Rana Rule in the Early Twenties," CR:166 (July 1962), 31-36.

A616 BHATTACHARYA, S. S. "The McMahon Line," MR:117 (Feb. 1965), 140-45. Its history and description.

A617 BUCHAN, W. H. "A Journey in Sikhim," BM:191 (April 1912), 470-85.

A618 CHAKRAVERTI, BISHNUPADA. "Maulavi Qader's Nepal Embassy, 1795—A Forgotten Episode," CR:86 (Jan. 1934), 43-49. Based on political consultations.

A619 CHATTERJI, NANDALAL. "A Forgotten English Expedition against Prithvi Narayan," UPHS:11 (Dec. 1938), 45-65. A 1767 military expedition against the Gurkhas.

A620 ———. "The Military Operations of 1824-5 on the North-East Frontier of India," JIH:41 (Aug. 1963), 371-89. A chronicle.

A621 DIGBY, SIMON. "Pir Hasan Shah and the History of Kashmir," IESHR:1 (Jan. 1964), 95-100. With historiographical comment on other histories of Kashmir.

A622 GANKOVSKII, IU. V. "'Azad Kashmir' 1947-1958 gg (k istorii kashmiriskogo voprosa)" ["Azad Kashmir" 1947-1958 (On the History of the Kashmir Question)], KS:51 (1962), 167-82.

A623 GANNON, J. R. C. "A Frontier Tour," HmJ:3 (1931-32), 63-76. Travel account, with historical sketches.

A624 GUIMBRETIÈRE, ANDRÉ. "Le Problème du Cachemire" [The Problem of Kashmir], Or:9 (3° trimestre 1965), 7-32.

A625 GUPTA, SISIR. "The Kashmir Question; 1947-60 Survey of Source Material," IS:3 (Oct. 1961), 184-93. Lists documents and documentary volumes, books on historical background, pamphlets, articles in periodicals.

A626 HUTCHINSON, J. and VOGEL, J. PH. "History of Jammu State," PHS:8 (1921), 103-51. A large portion of it on modern history.

A627 HUTTENBACK, ROBERT A. "Gulab Singh and the Creation of the Dogra State of Jammu, Kashmir, and Ladakh," JAS:20 (Aug. 1961). The political history of British-Ladakh conflict in 1830's and '40's. Based on manuscripts in National Archives.

A628 ISLAM, M. ZIAUL. "The Sale of Kashmir," HFM:2 (1831-1905), Part 1, 97-126.

A629 KAK, RAM CHANDRA. "The Jammu and Kashmir State, I—1846-1890," AR:NS 33 (1937), 775-86.

A630 "Kashmir and the Countries around the Indus," CR:2 (Dec. 1844), 469-535.

A631 KENNION, R. L. "England and Nepal," NC:91 (Jan. 1922), 45-56. Historical survey of their relations.

A632 "Kirkpatrick's Account of Nepaul," ER:18 (Aug. 1811), 425-45. Observations made on a mission in 1793.

A633 KUMAR, SATISH. "The Nepalese Monarchy from 1769 to 1951," IS:4 (July 1962), 46-73. Based on Nepali printed sources, English records, and interviews.

A634 LEE-WARNER, WILLIAM. "Maharaja Sir Jung Bahadur (1816-1877)," EB:15, 556. Prime minister of Nepal, loyal in Mutiny.

A635 MOJUMDAR, KANCHANMOY. "Nepal and the Sikh-Tibetan War, 1841-42," BPP:82 (Jan.-June 1963), 12-25. Based on India Office Library records.

A636 MORRIS, C. J. "A Bibliography of Nepal," RCAS:18 (1931), 547-59.

A637 ———. "A Note on the Unknown Nepal," HmJ:6 (1934), 77-80. Geography and society of Nepal.

A638 "North-East Frontier," CR 48:96, 141-86.

A639 "Our North-East Frontier," CR 38:76 (1863), 264-85.

A640 PAL, DHARM. "The Bhootan War (1864-65)," CR:101 (Dec. 1946), 235-49. From Government of India archives.

A641 ———. "The North-East Frontier Policy of Sir John Lawrence (1864-1868)," IHQ:21 (June 1945), 105-17. Pacification of the Nagas; based on Bengal government records.

A642 PHILLIMORE, R. H. "Survey of Kashmir and Jammu, 1855 to 1865," HmJ:22 (1959-60), 95-102. Reprinted from *Journal of the Institution of Surveyors.*

A643 RAHUL, R. "The Himalaya Frontier in the Nineteenth Century," QRHS 4:3 (1964-65), 138-51.

A644 RODGERS, CHARLES J. "Some Coins of Ranjit Deo, King of Jummu a Hundred Years Ago," ASB:54 (1885), 60-66. With plate.

A645 ROY, N. B. "The Early Inroads of the Naga Sannyasis in Bengal 1760-73," IHRC:31 (1955), 148-55.

A646 SEN, SIVA NARAYANA. "Nepal, a Historical Sketch," MR:88 (Dec. 1950), 465-78.

A647 SETHI, R. R. "The Revolt in Kashmir—1847," SAHR:11 (1932), 158-67. The same (dated 1846), PUHS:1 (April 1932), 19-31. Based on Punjab government records.

A648 ———. "The Trial of Raja Lal Singh—1846," SAHR:11 (1932), 228-37; JPUHS:1 (Dec. 1932), 113-22.

A649 THORNER, ALICE. "The Kashmir Conflict," MEJ:3 (Jan., April 1949), 17-30, 164-80. Chronicle of events.

A650 "Works on the Himalaya," CR 4:7 (1845), 162-77.

13. *OTHER PRINCELY STATES*

A651 "AUTHORITY." "Our Relations with Manipur," AR, Ser. 2:2 (July 1891), 6-38.

A652 BLUNT, W. S. "Ideas about India: IV. The Native States," FR:43 (Feb. 1885), 234-48.

A653 BRETT-JAMES, ANTHONY. "Disaster in Manipur: An Imperial Episode," HT:12 (Jan. 1962), 48-55. 1891 rebellion.

A654 CHATTERJEE, RAMANANDA. "The Indian States," MR:50 (July 1931), 29-43.

A655 DE, S. C. (ed.). "Feudatory States of Orissa: Extract of a Report from the Late Commissioner at Cuttack Dated the 20th December, 1914," OHRJ:7 (July 1958), 91-104.

A656 ELLIOT, F. A. H. "Native States of India," ER:186 (July 1897), 188-212. Review of books by William Lee-Warner, Charles L. Tupper, B. H. Baden Powell.

A657 GARRATT, G. T. "Indian India," A:30 (Nov. 1930), 782-89, 804-06. Photographs of princes and of coronation durbar.

A658 GRIFFIN, LEPEL. "Indian Princes at Home," FR:40 (Oct. 1883), 482-96. Compares English and princely systems of government.

A659 ———. "Native India: Princes and People," AR:2 (July 1886), 1-46. On their condition.

A660 KIBE, M. V. "Principles of Taxation in Native States," HR:31 (April 1915), 377-81.

A661 KITTOE, MARKHAM. "Account of a Journey from Calcutta *via* Cuttack and Pooree to Sumbulpur, and from Thence to Mednipur through the Forests of Orissa," AsB:8 (May-July 1839), 367-83, 474-80, 606-20; OHRJ:1 (Jan. 1953), Appendix 1, extra pp. 1-24.

A662 KURIYAN, GEORGE. "Urban Centres in Kerala," MUJ:11 (1939), 90-111. Tables showing distribution of population: density, trade, religion.

A663 LAHIRI, P. C. "Orissa States and British Policy," MR:47 (May, June 1930), 616-20, 712-16; 48 (Sept. 1930), 286-90. Based on government minutes and law reports.

A664 LAWRENCE, W. R. "Indian States," ER:248 (July 1928), 23-37.

A665 MAJUMDAR, R. C. "The Manipur Rebellion of 1891," BPP:78 (Jan.-June 1959), 1-29.

A666 ———. "Rebellion in Manipur, 1891," IHRC:35 (Feb. 1960), 140-50.

A667 MOTTE, THOMAS. "A Narrative of a Journey to the Diamond Mines at Sumbhulpur," OHRJ:1 (Oct. 1952), Appendix 2, 49 pp. Reprinted from *Asiatick Miscellany*:2 (Calcutta 1786).

A668 MUKHERJI, TARIT KUMAR. "Boundary Disputes between the British and Mayurbhanj in the 18th Century," IHRC:27 (1950), 73-77. Based on Midnapur district records.

A669 "Native Government in Native States," CR:44 (Feb. 1867), 387-423.

A670 "A Native Statesman," CR 55:110 (1872), 225-63. On Sir Madhava Rao, Dewan in Travancore, mid-19 cent.

A671 RAHMAN, CHOUDHURY SHAMSUR. "Majnoo Shah Mastana: The Faqir Leader," PR:11 (Aug. 1963), 13-16. 18th cent. raider.

A672 RAJ KUMAR, N. V. "Evolution and Working of the Government in Travancore," IJPS:2 (Oct. 1940), 217-40.

A673 "The Rajasthanik Court and Progress in Kathiawar," CR:108 (April 1899), 380-83.

A674 "A Run Through Kathiawar," BM:120 (Aug., Oct., Nov. 1876), 141-210, 399-416, 577-600. On princely states in Gujarat.

A675 SAHANI, T. K. "Western India States—Kathiawar: Administration Review," IJPS:3 (July 1941), 83-89. Includes figures on finance.

A676 SHAH, A. M. "Political System in Eighteenth Century Gujarat," En: NS 1 (Spring 1964), 83-95. Situation at mid-century.

A677 SINGH, A. "Twilight of the Princes," A:37 (May 1937), 366-70. With photos.

A678 SINGH, NIHAL. "United States of India," A:35 (July 1935), 414-21. On princely states.

A679 STEWART, COSMO. "A Great Indian Prince and Reformer," BM:224 (Dec. 1928), 831-48. On Maharaja Sir Shahu Chhatrapati, Prince of Kolhapur.

A680 "The Travancore-Cochin Arbitration," CR 76:152 (1883), 285-99. On a boundary dispute.

14. INDIANS OVERSEAS

A681 AIYAR, P. S. "A Review of the Indian Problem in South Africa," MR:43 (Feb. 1928), 160-69. By the editor of African Chronicle.

A682 ANDREWS, C. F. "Indian Labour in Fiji," MR:24 (Sept., Dec. 1918), 267-75, 622-30; 25 (May 1919), 467-72.

A683 ———, and PEARSON, W. W. "Report on Indentured Labour in Fiji," MR:19 (March-June 1916), 333-39, 392-402, 514-25, 615-24.

A684 BALGOBIN, S. "Mauritius Politics Reach the Turning-Point," MR:86 (Nov. 1949), 384-86. With brief history of Indians in Mauritius.

A685 BALLHATCHET, K. A. "Raja Ram Roy's Visit to England," BSOAS:20 (1957), 69-71. Short account of Rammohun Roy's adopted son's service in the offices of the Board of Control 1835-37.

A686 BANERJEE, ANIL CHANDRA. "Position of Indians in Separated Burma," MR:57 (March 1935), 296-301.

A687 BANERJEE, INDUBHUSHAN. "An Indian in England in the Eighteenth Century," CR:24 (Sept. 1927), 351-53. Hanumant Row gave evidence at Supreme Court of Judicature in 1781.

A688 BANERJEE, KALYAN KUMAR. "East Indian Immigration into America; Beginnings of Indian Revolutionary Activity," MR:116 (Nov. 1964), 355-61. Extensively documented.

A689 BANNERJI, INDU PRAKAS. "Hindu Immigration," MR:17 (May 1915), 608-16. With special reference to the history of Hindu immigration into the United States.

A690 BISSOONDOYAL, B. "Indians in Mauritius," CoR:187 (June 1955), 402-05.

A691 BOSE, SUDHINDRA. "Exclusion of the Indians from America," MR:15 (June 1914), 624-28. On the Raker Bill.

A692 ——. "Professor Jagadis Chandra Bose in America," MR:17 (May 1915), 559-64.

A693 CHATTOPADHYAYA, HARAPRASAD. "Negro Slavery and Indian Immigrants in Mauritius," BPP:78 (July-Dec. 1959), 98-110. Coolie emigration in the 1830's and '40's: terms and conditions of labor.

A694 CUMPSTON, I. M. "A Survey of Indian Immigration to British Tropical Colonies to 1910," PS:10 (1956), 158-65. Summary in HA:3 (No. 126): "Discusses local origins, conditions of service, and development" of indentured Indian labor.

A695 DAS, HARIHAR. "The Early Indian Visitors to England," CR:13 (Oct. 1924), 83-114.

A696 ——. "Some More Early Indian Visitors to England, CR:27 (April 1928), 72-73.

A697 DAS, SARANGADHAR. "Why We Must Emigrate to the United States," MR:10 (July 1911), 69-80. With lists of graduates of American universities and résumés of positions held after graduation. Shiv Narayan, "Emigration to America—A Rejoinder," MR:10 (Aug. 1911), 210-11.

A698 DAYAL, R. "Status of Indians Abroad," MR:41 (Jan. 1927), 39-44. An historical survey.

A699 DE SILVA, K. M. "Indian Immigration to Ceylon—The First Phase c. 1840-1855," CJHSS:4 (July-Dec. 1961), 106-37. A well-documented account.

A700 DIGBY, WILLIAM. "Indian Emigration to Ceylon," CR 65:129 (1877), 51-74.

A701 DOCTOR, MANILAL M. "Indian Peasant Proprietors in Mauritius," MR:9 (Feb. 1911), 183-85. From the Report of the Mauritius Royal Commission of 1909.

A702 "Emigration from British India," SA:Supp. 53 (Mar. 22, 1902), 219-30. Figures on emigration 1885-1901, with destinations.

A703 GELL, C. W. M. "The Indians in South Africa," FR:176 (July, Sept. 1951), 429-38, 633. Brief history with many facts and figures.

A704 GILLION, K. L. "The Sources of Indian Emigration to Fiji," PS:10 (Nov. 1956), 139-57. On geographical sources, causes of emigration from different areas—with tables. Based on Emigration proceedings; archives in New Delhi, Calcutta, Madras; emigration statistics; and journals.

A705 "The History of Indian Immigration on the Pacific Coast of America," MR:5 (Jan. 1909), 55-57. Interview with Girindra Nath Mukerji, Indian Immigration Officer, San Francisco, 1907-1908.

A706 HOLLAND, ROBERT. "Indian Immigration into Canada: The Question of Franchise," AR:NS 39 (1943), 167-72.

A707 "Indians Abroad," MR:43 (June 1928), 731. Population statistics from the journal *Indians Abroad*.

A708 IYER, C. P. SESHA. "The Status and Condition of Indians Abroad," HR:32 (July 1915), 17-25. Review of a commission report.

A709 "Journal of a Residence in Great Britain, by Jehungeer Nowrajee and Hirjeebhoy Merwanjee, of Bombay, Naval Architects," CR:4 (1845), i-xii.

A710 LINDSAY, DARCY. "The Indian Question in South Africa and the Round Table Conference," AR:NS 23 (April 1927), 177-90.

A711 ———. "Indians Overseas," PI, pp. 247-57.

A712 MASÈ, EZIO. "L'emigrazione indiana oltremare, con particolare riferimento alle isole Figi" [Indian Overseas Emigration, with Special Reference to the Fiji Islands], DS:42 (July-Sept. 1963), 162-87.

A713 MENON, C. NARAYANA. "The Indians Abroad," IJPS:1 (Oct. 1939), 206-11. A survey of their sorry state.

A714 MUKERJEE, RADHAKAMAL. "Indian and Chinese Labour in the Agriculture of South-East Asia," MR:54 (Dec. 1933), 669-74.

A715 MUKHERJEE, SUDHANSU BIMAL. "Early Years of Indian Immigration to Mauritius (1837-1842)," CR:149 (Dec. 1958), 275-84.

A716 ———. "Indian Labourers in Mauritius (1870-1915)," CR:153 (Nov. 1959), 165-78.

A717 ———. "Indians in Mauritius, 1842-1870," IQ:15 (Oct.-Dec. 1959), 367-81.

A718 ———. "Indians in South Africa—Beginnings of Bitterness (1800-1900)," CR:145 (Dec. 1957), 243-57.

A719 ———. "Indians in South Africa. Lake Success and After (1946-1956)," CR:144 (Aug. 1957), 134-59.

A720 MUTHANNA, I. M. "The First Indian Princess in England: Victoria Gowramma," MR:116 (Aug. 1964), 134-36; IR:63 (Sept. 1964), 315-16. From Coorg.

A721 NAINAR, S. M. H. "Indians in Indonesia," IAC:6 (Oct. 1957), 157-79.

A722 NARAIN, IQBAL. "Beginning of Emigration to Natal," IQ:11 (Jan.-March 1955), 31-55.

A723 ———. "Beginning of Indian Emigration to Natal (South Africa)," AUJR:6 (July 1958), 149-83. A re-interpretation of the causes of emigration, based on British source material.

A724 ———. "Disfranchisement of the Natal Indians," IQ:17 (Oct.-Dec. 1961), 396-402.

A725 ———. "The Imposition of £ 3 Tax on Indians in Natal," AUJR:6 (Jan. 1958), 71-89. In 1894.

A726 ———. "Indians in the Orange Free State and the Cape (A Study of Their Status up to 1909)," UB:4 (Dec. 1957), 83-96. (Appendix pp. 94-96). Cites official dispatches and other types of government documents.

A727 ———. "Indians in the Transvaal," UB:4 (March 1958), 67-94, appendix pp. 91-94; 5 (July 1958), 73-116. Petitions sent by British to government and schemes for solving "coloured" question.

A728 ———. "Years without Discrimination in Natal," AUJR:5 (Jan. 1957), 66-83. Beginnings of Indian labor in South Africa; source: government archives.

A729 "An Old Bengalee in Switzerland," CR:45 (Aug. 1867), 327-81. Journal of an 1866 trip.

A730 PACHAI, BRIDGLAL. "South African Indians and Citizenship: a Historical Survey—1855-1934," AfQ:4 (Oct.-Dec. 1964), 167-78.

A731 PEARSON, W. W. "Report on My Visit to South Africa," MR:15 (June 1914), 629-42.

A732 POCOCK, DAVID. "Slavery and Indo-Arab Relations in 19th Century Zanzibar," EW:11 (1959), 165-72.

A733 PROCTOR, JESSE HARRIS. "East Indians and the Federation of the British West Indies," IQ:17 (Oct.-Dec. 1961), 370-95.

A734 RAO, P. KODANDA. "Indians Abroad," IYBIA:4 (1955), 42-54. Briefly reviews history and present status of subject with regard to political status, restrictions.

A735 ———. "Indians Overseas," AAAPSS:233 (May 1944), 200-67.

A736 ROY, JAY NARAIN. "Indians in Mauritius," IAC:9 (July 1960), 88-92. Sketch of Indian culture in Mauritius.

A737 RUDD, DOROTHEA. "The Indians in South Africa," QR:271 (Oct. 1938), 332-42.

A738 SEN, PRIYA RANJAN. "Indians in Mauritius," MR:75 (April 1944), 274-75. On societies formed there.

A739 SILVA, NIMALASIRI. "The Problem of Indian Immigration to Ceylon," SAA:1, 141-53. The historical background to the India-Ceylon problem.

A740 SINGH, NIHAL. "Anti-Indian Moves in Ceylon," MR:44 (Dec. 1928), 621-30.

A741 ———. "The Indian Immigration Crisis in South Africa; Its Effect on Indo-British Relations," FR:101 (Jan.-June 1914), 487-97. Treated as a problem of Empire relations.

A742 ———. "Moves to Make Indians in Ceylon Political Helots," MR:45 (June 1929), 657-67.

A743 "South Africa: The Indian Question," RT:16 (June 1926), 633-54. Historical.

A744 SPEIGHT, W. L. "Indians in South Africa," NC:107 (Feb. 1930), 197-204. On Areas Reservation and Immigration (Further Provision) Bill, problems arising from it and why it was passed in the first place.

A745 STANLEY, E. LYULPH. "The Treatment of Indian Immigrants in Mauritius," FR:23 (Jan.-June 1875), 794-819. Gives a number of figures on living conditions.

A746 STONE, F. G. "The Asiatic Invasion of South Africa," NC:90 (July 1921), 118-30. Legal position of Indians in South Africa and recommendations of the Asiatic Enquiry Commission, 1920.

A747 SUNDARAM, LANKA. "The International Aspects of Indian Emigration," AR:NS 26 (1930), 741-48; NS 27 (1931), 113-21, 287-96, 588-98.

A748 TAIFOOR, SYED A. S. M. "Sheikh I. Tesamuddin of Nadia; The First Indian to Visit London; Accounts of His Travels in England and Scotland," BPP:49 (Jan.-June 1935), 117-29. A 1766-67 visitor, from a Persian manuscript.

A749   VANDEN DRIESEN, I. H. " 'Indian Immigration to Ceylon, The First Phase c. 1840-1855'—A Comment," CJHSS:7 (July-Dec. 1964), 218-29. Comment on de Silva's article; critique of James Emerson Tennent's role.

A750   VANE, MICHAEL. "The Indians in Natal," CoR:174 (July 1948), 43-47. Review of their problems there and government acts related thereto.

B. Areas Primarily Under British Control

1. BRITISH EXPANSION AND RULE, GENERAL

B1 ALLEN, GRANT. "Why Keep India?" CoR:38 (Oct. 1880), 544-56. "India has been a false lure which tempted us from peaceful paths."

B2 ARNOLD, EDWIN. "Duty and Destiny of England in India," NA:154 (Feb. 1892), 168-88. Imperialist apologia.

B3 "The British Conquest of Hindustan," CR:81 (Oct. 1885), 227-40.

B4 CRANE, ROBERT I. "India: a Study of the Impact of Western Civilization," SE:15 (1951), 365-71, 374. A summary of the changes wrought by British rule and the general problems of contemporary India.

B5 CURZON, LORD. "The True Imperialism," NC:63 (Jan. 1908), 151-66. Full text of speech delivered 1907.

B6 DAY, WINIFRED M. "Relative Permanence of Former Boundaries in India," SGM:65 (Dec. 1949), 113-22. With maps.

B7 DESAI, MAHANDRA V. "La Rencontre de l'Inde et de la Grande-Bretagne" [The Encounter of India and Great Britain], Co:13/14 (1955), 52-62.

B8 GAMIAUNOV, L. S. [Review of *Novaia Istoriia Indii* (Modern History of India) (Moscow, 1961, 834 p.)], NAA:1 (1962), 176-84. Summary in SPA:2 (Oct. 1962), 15. Summary of another review of same book, SPA:2 (Oct. 1962), 27.

B9 GHOSE, DILIP KUMAR. "The Forward Policy," IHCP:17 (1954), 350-57. Origin and development of a school of British foreign policy in India, 1849-1877.

B10 GOKHALE, B. G. "John Bright and India (1848-1861)," JIH:41 (April 1963), 57-67. Views of a "radical," anti-imperialist.

B11 HALIFAX, EARL OF. "India: Two Hundred Years," FA:26 (Oct. 1947), 104-15. An *ave atque vale* to India.

B12 HARNETTY, PETER. "The British Period of Indian History: Some Recent Interpretations; a Review Article," PA:37 (Summer 1964), 179-94.

B13 KOMAROV, E. N. [British Rule and Its First Socio-Economic Consequences in India in the Late 18th and First Half of the 19th Centuries], PUI.

B14 ———. "V. I. Lenin ob angliiskoi gospodstve v Indii" [V. I. Lenin on British Rule in India], SV:2 (1955), 40-46. Summary in HA:4

(No. 2952): "Survey of Lenin's remarks . . . in the period 1900-1923. Based on V. I. Lenin's Complete Works, 4th ed."

B15 MAHMOOD, SYED. "British Rule in India: Does It Owe Its Origin to Conquest, and Its Maintenance to Physical Force?" CR 68:135 (1879), 1-11. Answer: no.

B16 MASUI, TSUNEO. "Morison to Rindorē—Indo to Chūgoku to ni okeru igirisu ginjin" ["Morrison and Lindley—The British Soldiers in India and China"], *Kanazawa Daigaku Hobungakubu Ronshu* (Tetsugak-shingaku-hen 5) 1957, 24-41. HA:4, 1134: "An Analysis of John Morrison's *The Advantages of an Alliance with the Great Mogul's Forces* (1774) and Augustus Lindley's *Ti-Ping Tien-kuoh: The History of the Ti-Ping Revolution* (1866). Whereas Morrison's view of India was characterized by conservatism, Lindley's was more objective and regarded China with affection."

B17 NIVEDITA, SISTER. "On the Influence of History in the Development of Modern India," MR:50 (Aug. 1931), 129-33.

B18 O'MALLEY, L. S. S. "The Impact of European Civilization," MIW, pp. 44-106.

B19 PHELPS, E. M. (ed.). "British Colonial Policy in India," UDA (1945-46), pp. 301-29. "Resolved that this house favors the British Colonial Policy in India," University of British Columbia vs. Linfield College.

B20 "PHI OMEGA." "An Eighteenth Century Indian View of British Rule in India," CR:284 (April 1916), 113-28. Précis of and excerpts from *Seir-ul-mutaquherin* by Saiyid Gholam Hossein Khan, published 1789.

B21 "Present State and Prospects of British India," ER:71 (July 1840), 327-70. On the policy of expansion.

B22 QURESHI, I. H. "The Impact of British Rule upon the Muslims," HFM:2, 1831-1905, part 2, 333-65.

B23 RAJASEKHARIAH, A. M. "The Political and Administrative Impact of British Rule on India," KU:8 (1964), 286-98.

B24 SAY, JEAN-BAPTISTE. "Essai historique sur l'origine, les progrès, et les résultats probables de la souveraineté des Anglais aux Indes" [Historical Essay on the Origin, Progress, and Probable Results of the Sovereignty of the English in India], RE:23 (July 1824), 281-91; English tr. in OH:3 (Nov. 1824), 348-60.

B25 [STEWART]. "Colonel Stewart on the Policy of the Government of India," OH:6 (Sept. 1825), 423-37. Comment on imperialist policies.

B26 "Two Anglo-Indian Empire Builders," CR:108 (Jan. 1899), 129-38.

2. *ADMINISTRATION AND CONSTITUTIONAL LAW, GENERAL*

B27 AHMAD, A. F. SALAHUDDIN. "The Origins of Communal Representation in India," PHS:12 (Oct. 1964), 311-41.

B28 AHMAD, M. B. "Constitutional Changes (1831-1905)," HFM:2, 1831-1905, part 2, 556-80.

B29 "The Character of British Rule in India," W:90 (July 1868), 1-36. Discussion of Hunter's *Annals of Rural Bengal.*

B30 CHAUDHURI, M. A. "The Growth of the Civil Service in British India and Pakistan," ASP:5 (1960), 72-127. A history of its organization.

B31 COTTON, HENRY. "The Indian Civil Service," CoR:104 (Oct. 1913), 477-86.

B32 [COTTON]. "The Late Sir Henry Cotton—the Man and His Work:—A Study," HR:32 (Dec. 1915), 465-71. A leader of ICS reform.

B33 DHAR, GOKULNATH. "The Post Office in India," CR:291 (Jan. 1918), 108-15. A brief history.

B34 "Early British Administration in India," CR:88 (April 1889), 412-38.

B35 GHOSAL, A. K. "Indianisation of the Civil Services," CR:96 (Sept. 1945), 63-78; 97 (Oct., Dec. 1945), 13-20, 89-99; 99 (April 1946), 25-34.

B36 [GHOSE]. "Ram Gopal Ghose," CR 46:92, 505-25. Merchant and public figure.

B37 ISLAM, ZAFARUL, and JENSEN, RAYMOND L. "Indian Muslims and the Public Service 1871-1915," ASP:9 (June 1964), 85-149. Includes employment statistics.

B38 KAMESVARA AIYAR, B. K. "Sir A. Sashiah Sastri, K.C.S.I.—a Few Reminiscences," CR:118 (April 1904), 180-89. South Indian public figure.

B39 LEE-WARNER, W. "Civil Service of India," NC:74 (Aug. 1913), 233-43. History of recruitment.

B40 LOVETT, H. VERNEY. "India from Curzon's Days to These," QR:251 (July 1928), 175-94.

B41 MALHAN, PRAN NATH. "The Position of the Government Members in the Legislative Council of the Governor-General (Established under the Act of 1861)," IHCP:4 (1940), 322-34. Questions of principle in the modification of cabinet government.

B42 MISRA, B. B. "Efforts for Administrative Reforms before Independence," IJPA:9 (July 1963), 311-35.

B43 ———. "The Evolution of the Office of Collector," IJPA:11 (July 1965), 345-67.

B44 PARSHAD, BAINI. "The Indian Civil Service and Some Extra-Departmental Activities of Its Members," BPP:64 (1944), 1-17. Recruitment to the ICS and scholarly activities of its most prominent members.

B45 PATRA, ATUL CHANDRA. "Landmarks in the Constitutional History of India," ILI:5 (Jan.-March 1963), 81-131. Important dates from 1600.

B46 "POLITICUS." "The Indian Civil Service," MR:21 (June 1917), 717-29.

B47 PRINSEP, H. T. "The Indian Civil Service, a Retrospect and a Prospect," NC:73 (March 1913), 694-704.

B48 "Public Works in Pre-British, Native, and British India," MR:5 (May 1909), 387-96.

B49 RAI, HARIDWAR. "The Changing Role of the District Officer (1860-1960)," IJPA:9 (April 1963), 238-57. Changes in the regulations.

B50 ROY, NARESH CHANDRA. "The Indian Civil Service," MR:42 (Nov. 1927), 521-26.

B51 ROY CHOUDHURY, P. C. "The District Gazetteers of India: The Relation of Information to Administration," Sh:2 (June 1965), 27-30. The history of the gazetteers.

B52 SALDANHA, J. A. "Survival of Portuguese Institutions in British Western India," RASB 25:71 (1917-18), 153-60. Sketches ecclesiastical and revenue institutions which survived into British times.

B53 SAPRU, TEJ BAHADUR. "The Indian Constitution," AAAPSS:145 (Supplement, Sept. 1929), 9-18. Historical survey of constitutional development.

B54 SARKAR, JADUNATH. "William Irvine, I.C.S.," MR:15 (Jan. 1914), 40-46. Biography and evaluation of his work by a personal friend.

B55 SEN, S. P. "Effects on India of British Law and Administration in the 19th Century," CHM:4 (1958), 849-80. An outline of the following factors: 1) structure of administration; 2) land tenure; 3) judicial organization; 4) codification of laws; 5) new system of education. Not a study in depth.

B56 "The Settlement of Europeans in India," MR:4 (July 1908), 35-44. Historical review.

B57 "Simla, Calcutta, and Darjeeling as Centres of Government," CR:83 (Oct. 1886), 398-419.

B58 SUBRAMANIAN, V. "The Evolution of Minister–Civil Servant Relations in India," JCPS:1 (1962), 223-32. Summary in HA:10 (No. 420): "Based on government reports and administrative histories."

B59 ———. "Graduates in the Public Services. A Comparative Study of Attitudes," PubA:35 (1957), 373-93. Summary in HA:8 (No. 1143).

B60 "The Surveys of India," CR:95 (July 1892), 1-9.

B61 TINKER, HUGH. "People and Government in Southern Asia," RHS:6 (1959), 141-67. Long summary in HA:8 (No. 1199). On British attitudes and Indian reactions.

B62 "AN UNCOVENANTED." "Position of Indians in British Indian Administration," CR:262 (Oct. 1910), 505-70. Includes accounts of the careers of several British civil servants in India.

3. ADMINISTRATION TO 1857

B63 "The Acts of the Governor General of India in Council," CR:8 (1847), 344-78; 9 (1848), 138-62, 390-414; 11 (1849), 55-72. Criticism of government policies.

B64 "The Administration of India," BM:88 (Nov. 1860), 542-64. A criticism.

B65 AHLUWALIA, M. L. "Changing Style of Correspondence between the India House and Fort William Authorities," IA:12 (1958), 54-62. Changes in forms of address, arrangement, referencing, and tone of letters.

B66 "Alison's Chapters of Indian History," CR:4 (1845), 128-61. On chapters 51-52 of Archibald Alison's History of Europe.

B67 ARBUTHNOT, A. J. "Lord Ellenborough's Indian Administration," CoR:24 (Aug. 1874), 374-96.

B68 BAGAL, JOGESH C. "The Charter Act of 1833 and Indian Public Opinion," MR:53 (March 1933), 281-83.

B69 BEARCE, GEORGE D., JR. "Lord William Bentinck: the Application of Liberalism to India," JMH:28 (Sept. 1956), 234-46. Stresses Bentinck's relations with the Company and government, and his own outlook.

B70 BENNELL, A. S. "Wellesley," HT:9 (1959), 94-102. Summary in HA:5 (No. 1495).

B71 [BENTINCK]. "Lord William Bentinck's Administration," CR:1 (Aug. 1844), 337-71.

B72 "The British in India," W:4 (Oct. 1825), 261-93. On Company policy.

B73 "British India," QR:104 (July 1858), 224-76. On administrative policies.

B74 "The Buchanan Records," CR:99 (July 1894), 1-17.

B75 [CAMPBELL]. "Mr. Campbell's Modern India," CR:17 (1852), 452-88. Review of a general book.

B76 "Centralization: an Indian Problem," CR:31 (Dec. 1858), 466-84. On government reform.

B77 CHAKRAVARTI, M. K. "Macaulay on India, 1833," MR:57 (May 1935), 532-34.

B78 CHAKRAVORTY, U. N. "Sir John's Work," CR:173 (Dec. 1964), 223-26. On Sir John Malcolm.

B79 CHAR, S. V. DESIKA. "The First Indian Law Commission," IA:7 (Jan.-June 1953), 48-51. Cites materials on or by the Commission, constituted 1835.

B80 "Charters and Patriots," CR 18:36 (1852), 403-26. On government reform.

B81 CHATTERJI, NANDALAL. "The Beginnings of a British Postal System in India," JIH:33 (Aug. 1955), 171-74. The regulations under Clive.

B82 "Cheap and Uniform Postage in India," CR 10:20 (1848), 521-66.

B83 "Civis on Indian Affairs," CR 13:26 (1850), 406-41. On the general state of British India.

B84 "The Clapham Sect," ER:80 (July 1844), 251-307. Includes material on John Shore.

B85 COLEBROOKE, EDWARD. "Memoir of the Honourable Mountstuart Elphinstone," RAS:18 (1861), 221-344. Biography and letters.

B86 "Colonial and Indian Blue Books," CR:30 (June 1858), 253-65. On British policy, 1840-56.

B87 "Colonization and Commerce of British India," W:11 (Oct. 1829), 326-53.

B88 "The Company's Government," CR 19:38 (1853), 298-44.

B89 "The Company's Raj," BM:82 (Nov. 1857), 615-42. Also "Note," BM:83 (Jan. 1858), 137-38. On administration.

B90 "Constitution and Government of India," W:17 (July 1832), 75-103. On Mughal and British practice.

B91 [DALHOUSIE]. "The Administration of Lord Dalhousie," CR 22:43 (1854), 1-74.

B92 ———. "A Great Proconsul," BM:175 (June 1904), 863-80. On Dalhousie.

B93 ———. "India under Lord Dalhousie," BM:80 (Aug. 1856), 233-56. On his public works.

B94 ———. "India under Lord Dalhousie," ER:117 (Jan. 1863), 1-42.

B95 ———. "Lord Dalhousie," CR:33 (Dec. 1859), 396-439.

B96 ———. "Mr. Mead on Lord Dalhousie," CR:30 (March 1858), 231-51. Henry Mead on the subject of 1857.

B97 ———. "Sir Charles Jackson and Lord Dalhousie," CR 42:83 (1865), 178-203. On Jackson's defense of Dalhousie's administration.

B98 DAS, DAYAL. "The Administration of Sir Charles Metcalfe," UB:5 (July 1958), 141-46.

B99 DAS, M. N. "Dalhousie and the Reform of the Postal System," IHCP:21 (1958), 488-95. The conditions necessitating and the reforms establishing regular postal service. Based on Dalhousie papers and *Friend of India*.

B100 DATTA, V. N. "Grounds for Differences between Malcolm and Bentinck," IHCP:21 (1958), 447-52. Examines their respective views with respect to general policy toward Indian culture. Source: Bentinck papers.

B101 DESIKACHAR, S. V. "Macaulay on the Executive vis-à-vis the Legislature under the Charter Act of 1833," IHRC:32 (1956), 91-95. Copy of a minute.

B102 "The Directors of the East India Company and Their Retired Civil Servants," C&AR:11 (May 1853), 363-77.

B103 "The East India Company and Its Charter," CR:15 (1851), 320-33; 16 (1851), 77-118; 17 (1852), 422-51.

B104 "East Indian Monopoly," ER:19 (Nov. 1811), 229-45. In the guise of a review of a book on the Indian Archipelago, a virulent attack on the East India Company's monopoly.

B105 "East Indian Monopoly," ER:20 (Nov. 1812), 471-93. On the renewal of the Charter Act.

B106 [ELLENBOROUGH]. "The Administration of Lord Ellenborough," CR:1 (Aug. 1844), 508-62.

B107 ———. "Lord Ellenborough's Indian Administration," ER:141 (Jan. 1875), 31-52. Review of Lord Colchester's *History* (London, 1874).

B108 [ELPHINSTONE]. "Life of Mountstuart Elphinstone," ER:160 (July 1884), 116-50. Review of T. E. Colebrooke's *Life*.

B109 "AN ENGLISH BENCHER." "Governor Elphinstone and Governor-General Adam," OH:3 (Dec. 1824), 521-36.

B110 "The English in India," CR:1 (May 1844), 1-41. Reviews 4 books.

B111 "The English in India," W:69 (Jan. 1858), 180-209. Reviews 14 assessments of the British in India published in 1857.

B112 FORREST, G. W. "The Marquess of Dalhousie," FR:94 (July-Dec. 1910), 1056-73. Based on a published volume of private papers.

B113 [FRANCIS]. "Memoirs of Sir Philip Francis," ER:127 (Jan. 1868), 166-212.

B114 ———. "Sir Philip Francis," CR:2 (Dec. 1844), 561-608. Review of his correspondence.

B115 FURBER, HOLDEN. "Edmund Burke and India," BPP:76 (Jubilee No., 1957), 11-21. Asks what his real role and attitude were. Based on Macartney Papers at U. of Pennsylvania and other MSS.

B116 ——— (ed.). "The East India Directors in 1784," JMH:5 (Dec. 1933), 479-95. Reprints 2 confidential letters from Richard Atkinson to Henry Dundas bearing on Pitt's India Act.

B117 "Future Government of India," W:19 (July 1883), 107-46. On the administration.

B118 GHOSAL, A. K. "The Civil Service of India at the Beginning of the Crown's Rule," CR:96 (July 1945), 9-16.

B119 ———. "Constitutional Relation between the Court of Directors and the Board of Control with Special Reference to the Dispute over Fort William College," IJPS:4 (Oct. 1942), 170-82.

B120 GOKHALE, BALKRISHNA GOVIND. "India, America and Cornwallis," JIH:39 (April 1961), 29-44. The influence of Cornwallis's American experience on his Indian policy.

B121 GOPAL, S. "Dalhousie," HT:9 (1959), 186-94. Summary in HA:5.

B122 GOPAL, S. "Lord Ellenborough and the Home Authorities," IHRC:29 (1953), 32-35. From Gladstone papers.

B123 "Government of British India," ER:53 (June 1831), 438-77. A discussion of what form of government is appropriate.

B124 "Government of British India," ER:84 (Oct. 1846), 452-79. Review of a French attack on British policy.

B125 "Government of India," QR:35 (Jan. 1827), 32-66.

B126 "The Government of India," W:57 (April 1852), 357-405.

B127 "The Government of India in England," QJPSS:7 (July 1884), 1-65.

B128 "Government of India—Its Constitution and Departments," ER: 76 (Oct. 1842), 171-202. A descriptive survey.

B129 "The Government of the East India Company—the Lords' Report," CR 18:36 (1852), 439-92.

B130 "Grant on Maintaining the Indian System," QR:9 (March 1813), 225-53. Review of book by Robert Grant on administration and trade.

B131 GROVER, B. L. "District Daks in India (1757-1858)," UB:6 (Dec. 1959), 119-29. On organization of mail service.

B132 GUHA, RANAJIT. "An Administration Blueprint of 1785," BPP: 74 (1955), 68-78. A description of a plan by a member of the Supreme Council in Calcutta, Charles Stuart, to solve administrative problems in the light of Pitt's India Act of 1784.

B133 GUPTA, PRATUL CHANDRA. "Lord Hastings' 'Summary of Administration' with Low's Comments," IHQ:23 (Dec. 1947), 327-32. Discussion of an MS with John Low's marginal notes, differing with Lord Hastings' appraisal of Indian administration. Plates reproduce some of the comments; others are quoted.

B134 HALL, D. G. E. "The Dalhousie-Phayre Correspondence, 1852-56," BPP:37 (Jan.-June 1929), 9-14.

B135 [HARDINGE]. "Lord Hardinge's Administration," CR 8:16 (1847), 451-547.

B136 HARRIS, ABRAM L. "John Stuart Mill: Servant of the East India Company," CJEPS:30 (May 1964), 185-202.

B137 [HASTINGS]. "Observations on the Defence Put Forth by the Marquess of Hastings," OH:2 (May 1824), 35-57. Text of a pamphlet.

B138 "HISTORICUS." "Cornwallis the Civil Ruler," MR:14 (Dec. 1913), 571-75.

B139 ———. "Cornwallis the Warrior," MR:14 (Nov. 1913), 466-75.

B140 ———. "The First Lord Minto's Indian Administration," MR:30 (Aug.-Dec. 1921), 204-10, 282-87, 410-13, 555-60, 647-52.

B141 ———. "The Marquess Wellesley's Appointment as Governor General of India," MR:15 (Feb. 1914), 153-58.

B142 "The House of Commons and the Legislative Council," CR 27:54 (Dec. 1856), 314-35.

B143 HUNTER, WILLIAM WILSON, and COTTON, J. S. "India: History (Under the British)," EB:14, 407-17. Military and political history.

B144 "The India Bill in the Commons," CR:21 (1853), 284-328.

B145 "Indian Administration," QR:92 (Dec. 1852), 46-76.

B146 "The Indian Civil Service," BM:79 (April 1856), 456-70.

B147 "The Indian Civil Service," CR:27 (Dec. 1856), 356-75.

B148 "The Indian Civil Service—Its Rise and Fall," BM:89 (Jan., March 1861), 115-30, 261-76.

B149 JERVIS, TH. B. "Origin, Progress and Present State of the Surveys in India," MJLS:7 (1839?), 424-41.

B150 JOSHI, V. V. "Marquess of Wellesley and the Conquest of India," BUJ:9 (Jan. 1941), 8-48.

B151 "Kaye's *Life of Malcolm*," ER:105 (April 1857), 391-419. An extensive review thereof.

B152 KEENE, H. G. "Company and Crown (An Object Lesson)," W: 152 (July 1899), 11-25. Largely on Lord Moira and the relative merits of British and princely rule.

B153 LAHIRI, R. M. "The Relation between the East India Company and Their Servants in India," MR:89 (Feb. 1951), 123-24. Based on MSS in the National Archives.

B154 LAL, MUKUT BEHARI. "The Fourth Ordinary Member of the Supreme Council (1834-1853)," IHRC:19 (Dec. 1942), 61-64.

B155 [LAUDERDALE]. "Lord Lauderdale on Indian Affairs," ER:16 (Jan. 1810), 235-51.

B156 "Law and Constitution of India," OH:6 (Sept. 1825), 443-55. Comments on a pamphlet from London.

B157 LEE-WARNER, WILLIAM. "Dalhousie, James Andrew Brown Ramsay, 1st Marquess and 10th Earl of (1812-1860)," EB:7, 764-67.

B158 LEVIN, SANDER M. "The Administration of Lord Wellesley and the Establishment of British Rule in India," CR:131 (May 1954), 156-73. Discusses the extent to which British expansion was inevitable.

B159 "M." "Lord William Bentinck's Indian Administration," MR:24 (Aug. 1918), 108-16.

B160 "Macfarlane's 'Indian Empire,' " CR:2 (Dec. 1844), 443-68. Largely on Bentinck's administration.

B161 "The Madras and Bengal Governments, and Their Relative Positions," CR 16:32 (1851), 446-82.

B162 MAJUMDAR, R. C. "Lord William Cavendish-Bentinck—A Revised Estimate of His Administration (1828-35)," JIH:40 (Dec. 1962), 803-18. A revision of his good reputation in the light of his "imperialist"—though bloodless—annexations.

B163 MALCOLM, JOHN. "Etiquette for Civil Servants," IJPA:10 (Jan. 1964), 92-100. Extract from Notes of Instructions to Assistants and Officers Acting under Orders of Major-General Sir John Malcolm, 1821.

B164 "Malcolm on India," ER:20 (July 1812), 38-54. Review of his History since 1784.

B165 [MALCOLM]. "Sir John Malcolm," CR:29 (Sept., Dec. 1857), 157-206, 305-53.

B166 ———. "Sir John Malcolm's Life of Lord Clive," ER:70 (Jan. 1840), 295-362.

B167 MALHAN, P. N. "The Two Councils Theory of Lords Macaulay and Dalhousie," CR:86 (Jan. 1943), 12-20.

B168 MALLET, CHARLES. "Macaulay," CoR:153 (March 1938), 299-307. Brief review of life and writings.

B169 MARSHALL, P. J. "Indian Officials under the East India Company in Eighteenth-Century Bengal," BPP:84 (July-Dec. 1965), 95-120.

B170 MARX, KARL. "India under British Rule; Prophecy of 1853," LA:328 (Jan. 23, 1926), 177-83. Marx's letters to the New York Tribune.

B171 "Marx and Engels on India," LM:15 (June-Aug. 1933), 392-99, 453-57, 512-17. A collection of excerpts from their writings; does not include the Tribune letters.

B172 "Maurice's Modern India," ER:5 (Jan. 1805), 288-301. Critical review.

B173 MEHTA, B. N. "Lord Wellesley's Policy and Its Reversal," JIH:32 (Aug. 1954), 171-90. An essay on subsidiary alliances showing that if anyone "reversed" the system, it was Wellesley in his own last months.

B174 [METCALFE]. "Lord Metcalfe," CR 24:47 (1855), 121-64.

B175 ———. "The Opinions of Lord Metcalfe," CR 24:48 (1855), 234-64.

B176 "Mill's *British India*," ER:31 (Dec. 1818), 1-44. A summary.

B177 "Ministerial Misrepresentations Regarding the East," ER:77 (Feb. 1843), 261-300. On military and financial policies of the British in India and China.

B178 [MINTO]. "Lord Minto in India," ER:151 (Jan. 1880), 228-56.

B179 MISRA, G. S. "Effect of the French Revolutionary War on Sir John Shore's Administration," UPHS: NS 2 (1944), 35-46.

B180 MOORE, R. J. "The Abolition of Patronage in the Indian Civil Service and the Closure of Haileybury College," HJ:7 (1964), 246-57.

B181 M[UDDIMAN], A. P. M. "The Governor-General of a Day," BPP:1 (1907), 47-53. June 20, 1777; General Clavering and Warren Hastings both claimed the Governor-Generalship.

B182 [MUNRO]. "Life and Correspondence of Sir Thomas Munro," ER:51 (April 1830), 247-86.

B183 [NAPIER]. "Sir Charles Napier's Posthumous Work," CR 22:43 (1854), 208-90. On defects in the Indian government.

B184 NARAIN, V. A. "Restrictions on the Settlement of Europeans in India till 1800," JIH:41 (Aug. 1963), 481-87. History of the regulations.

B185 "Native Petitions from India," C&AR:10 (April 1853), 300-08. Comment on petitioners to Parliament.

B186 O'MALLEY, L. S. S. "A Great Civilian: George Carnac Barnes, C.B., I.C.S.," BPP:43 (Jan.-June 1932), 1-9.

B187 "The Old Company and the New India Bill," CR:31 (Dec. 1858), 412-42.

B188 "Origin and Progress of English Connexion with India," CR:7 (1847), 220-82.

B189 "Our Indian Empire," BM:80 (Dec. 1856), 636-59. The administration thereof.

B190 "Our Indian Empire," BM:82 (Dec. 1857), 643-64. Its growth and effect on India.

B191 "Our Indian Empire," QR:103 (Jan. 1858), 253-78. On the administration.

B192 "Papers Respecting the E. I. Company's Charter," QR:8 (Dec. 1812), 239-86.

B193 "The Patronage of the East India Company," CR 18:35 (1852), 1-48.

B194 PHILIPS, C. H. "Clive in the English Political World, 1761-64," BSOAS:12 (1948), 695-702. The East India Company in London.

B195 ——. "The Correspondence of David Scott, Chairman and Director of the East India Company, 1787-1805," IA:4 (July-Dec. 1950), 202-18. A brief biography based on his letters.

B196 —— (ed.). "The New East India Board and the Court of Directors, 1784," EHR:55 (July 1940), 438-46.

B197 ——. "The Secret Committee of the East India Company," BSOS:10 (1940), 299-315, 699-716. On its powers and policies.

B198 PHILIPS, C. H., and PHILIPS, D. "Alphabetical List of Directors of the East India Company from 1758 to 1858," RAS (1941), pp. 325-36. Dates of service and year of death.

B199 "POLITICUS." "Hundred Years Ago," MR:18 (Dec. 1915), 615-25. The private journal of the Marquess of Hastings, 1814-1818: a discussion, with quotations.

B200 ——. "Sir Thomas Munro," MR:14 (July 1913), 41-47. Letters and minutes are the source.

B201 "Religious Aspect of the Charter Question," CR 19:37 (1853), 105-55. On Company charter renewal.

B202 ROY, P. C. "A Landmark in Indian Archive-Keeping," IA:8 (Jan.-June 1954), 8-13. How the Court of Directors prohibited Wellesley from taking with him letters and records in 1807.

B203 ROY CHOUDHURY, P. C. "William Taylor—a Colourful Personality," MR:95 (Feb. 1954), 151-52. Arrived in India in 1829 as a civil servant.

B204 SAJANLAL, K. "A Few Unpublished Letters of Sir Thomas Munro," IHRC:31 (1955), 106-12. A summary.

B205 SANIAL, S. C. (ed.). "The Governor-General of a Day," BPP:12 (Jan.-June 1916), 1-31. Verbatim minutes of Consultations of the Governor-General's Council, June 20, 1777.

B206 SARVADHIKARI, D. P. "Acts of Pains and Penalties in the Past," BPP:36 (July-Dec. 1928), 81-86; 37 (Jan.-June 1929), 15-18. Dalhousie correspondence on the Turton embezzlement case.

B207   SASTRI, K. N. V. "Petrie Papers," IHRC:18 (Jan. 1942), 288-96. A few letters from Wm. Petrie of the Madras Council to Henry Dundas and Lord Mornington, 1790-1802.

B208   "Secret Politics of the East India House," OH:5 (April 1825), 92-95.

B209   SEN, AMIYAKUMAR. "Violation of Common Justice and a Breach of Faith by the Supreme Government of India: Resumption of Rent-Free Lands, 1793-1833," CR:171 (June 1964), 215-28.

B210   SEN, S. N. "A Note on Major Polier's Resignation," IHRC:20 (1943), 75-78. Chief engineer of Calcutta.

B211   SINHA, N. K. "India in 1844," CR (Centenary No., 1944), 14-25.

B212   SINHA, SACHCHIDANANDA. "India under the First Lord Hardinge," HR:23 (Jan. 1911), 74-83.

B213   SMITH, THOMAS. "'Khond' Macpherson," CoR:2 (May-Aug. 1866), 212-39. Short sketch, based on memoirs and correspondence, of Major Samuel Charters Macpherson, political agent at Gwalior in 1857; worked to suppress human sacrifice in Orissa.

B214   SOVANI, N. V. "British Impact on India before 1850-57," CHM:1 (April 1954), 857-82. "The source material for the period is mainly in English by Englishmen. Indian source material is not available and in some cases non-existent." An attempt to isolate the impact of British bureaucracy from the impact of the industrial revolution and the social and cultural impact.

B215   SPEAR, T. G. P. "Lord Ellenborough and Lord William Bentinck," IHCP:3 (1939), 1360-74. On Ellenborough's attitudes toward India in his years as president of the India Board. Based on Bentinck papers.

B216   ———. "Lord William Bentinck," JIH:19 (April 1940), 100-11; UPHS:12 (Dec. 1939), 1-14. Examines his motives and the extent to which the work of his administration was his own.

B217   STOKES, ERIC. "Macaulay: the Indian Years, 1834-38," REL:1 (Oct. 1960), 41-50. The influence of his relationship with his sisters during his years in India as a major factor in the shaping of his character thereafter.

B218   SUTHERLAND, LUCY STUART. "Lord Shelburne and East India Company Politics, 1766-9," EHR:49 (July 1934), 450-86. Fully documented.

B219   [TEIGNMOUTH]. "Lord Teignmouth," CR:1 (May 1844), 42-93. On John Shore.

B220 "Three Letters of Historical Importance," BPP:83 (July-Dec. 1964), 153-54. 2 from Claude Russell to Vansittart, 1767; 1 from T. B. Macaulay to Sir Charles Wood, 1857, on the closing of Haileybury.

B221 [TUCKER]. "Henry St. George Tucker," CR 22:44 (1854), 379-414. On the Accountant-General of Bengal, a Director of the East India Company.

B222 [VERELST]. "Governor Verelst," CR:35 (Sept. 1860), 1-37.

B223 [WELLESLEY]. "Lord Wellesley's Administration," CR:9 (1848), 29-102.

B224 ———. "The Marquess Wellesley," BM:59 (April 1846), 385-407. Biographical sketch.

B225 ———. "Marquis Wellesley's Indian Administration," ER:63 (July 1836), 537-59.

B226 ———. "Marquess Wellesley's Indian Administration," ER:148 (July 1878), 1-57.

B227 WELLS, J. "Macaulay and Hastings," ER:242 (Oct. 1925), 339-49. A review of treatments of the quarrel by historians.

B228 WHEATLEY, JOHN. "Colonization of India," OH:1 (Feb. 1824), 275-84. In favor thereof.

4. WARREN HASTINGS

B229 BANERJEE, D. N. "The Court of Directors and Warren Hastings' *Supposed* Resignation of the Office of Governor-General of Bengal," IHRC:20 (1943), 23-25.

B230 BEVERIDGE, H. "Warren Hastings in Lower Bengal," CR 65:130 (1877), 205-29; 66:132 (1878), 273-311; 68 (1879), 282-305.

B231 BULLOCK, H. "Some New Hastings Letters," BPP:52 (July-Dec. 1936), 1-9.

B232 [BURKE]. "Edmund Burke: Part IV," BM:34 (Sept. 1833), 317-43. On Burke and Hastings.

B233 "Burke and the Impeachment of Hastings," BPP:29 (April-June 1925), 201-06. Burke correspondence.

B234 [COLEBROOKE]. "Warren Hastings in Benares, 1781," AR:4 (Oct. 1887), 279-312. With a long letter by Edward Colebrooke.

B235 COTTON, EVAN. "Warren Hastings and His Friends," BPP:36 (July-Dec. 1928), 1-7. Miscellaneous letters.

B236 ———. "Warren Hastings through German Eyes," BPP:37 (Jan.-June 1929), 86-89. Describes a play in which Hastings is the central figure.

B237 COTTON, JAMES SUTHERLAND. "Warren Hastings (1732-1818)," EB:13, 55-59.

B238 DAVIES, C. COLLIN. "Warren Hastings and the Rohilla War," AQ:36 (July 1938), 273-88. From MSS in the British Museum.

B239 ———. "Warren Hastings and the Younger Pitt," EHR:70 (Oct. 1955), 609-22. Prints a letter from Hastings to Pitt, Dec. 11, 1784, just before his resignation.

B240 DODWELL, H. "Warren Hastings and the Assignment of the Carnatic," EHR:40 (July 1925), 375-96. Based on Madras military consultations and British Museum MSS.

B241 "The Father of Warren Hastings," BPP:46 (July-Dec. 1933), 48-50.

B242 GHOSH, JAMINI MOHAN. "The Site Where Nanda Kumar Was Executed," BPP:83 (July-Dec. 1964), 141-43. With sketch map.

B243 GRIER, SYDNEY C. [pseud. of Hilda Gregg]. "A Friend of Warren Hastings," BM:175 (April 1904), 497-514. Dr. Tyson Saul Hancock.

B244 ———. "Some Fresh Light on the Second Mrs. Hastings and Her Family," BPP:5 (1910), 333-34.

B245 HODSON, V. C. P. "A Letter of Warren Hastings," BPP:47 (Jan.-June 1934), 124-25. On Hercules Durham.

B246 HUTTON, W. H. (ed.). "A Letter of Warren Hastings on the Civil Service of the East India Company," EHR:44 (Oct. 1929), 633-41. On the institution of a college in Bengal.

B247 HYDE, H. B. "First Marriage of Warren Hastings," ASBP (July 1899), pp. 79-81. On the identity of his wife.

B248 MARSHALL, P. J. "'Nobkissen versus Hastings,'" BSOAS:27 (1964), 382-96. On the loan to Hastings from Maharaja Nabakrishna.

B249 ———. "Personal Fortune of Warren Hastings," EcHR, Ser. 2:17 (Dec. 1964), 284-300.

B250 MERCER, WILLIAM. "The Letters of Captain William Mercer; Aide-de-Camp to Warren Hastings, and Lieutenant in the Governor-General's Body-Guard," BPP:44 (July-Dec. 1932), 1-28, 120-55. With a note by Major V. C. Hodson.

B251 MORLEY, VISCOUNT (of Blackburn). "Burke, Edmond (1729-1797)," EB:4, 824-35. Pp. 830-31 on his part in the impeachment of Hastings.

B252 NEILL, J. W. "Warren Hastings," H:NS 3 (April 1918), 36-47. A "revision" of Macaulay's judgment on Hastings.

B253 ROBERTS, P. E. "Warren Hastings and His Accusers," JIH:3 (March 1924), 91-134. An evaluation of his character and career in India on the basis of three crucial incidents.

B254 SUTHERLAND, LUCY. "The Resignation on Behalf of Warren Hastings, 1776; George Vansittart's Evidence," BPP:76 (Jubilee No., 1957), 22-29. Prints a letter from Vansittart to Hastings in 1780, not among Hastings's papers in the British Museum.

B255 "Warren Hastings," ER:74 (Oct. 1841), 160-255. Review of his memoirs.

B256 "Warren Hastings in Slippers," CR:26 (March 1856), 59-141.

B257 "Warren Hastings on British Indian Administration," BPP:79 (Jan.-June 1960), 18-25.

5. ADMINISTRATION AND REFORMS, 1858 TO 1898

B258 "Administrative Reform for India," CR:36 (March 1861), 1-18.

B259 BADEN-POWELL, B. H. "English Legislation in India," AR:2 (Oct. 1886), 365-80. On need for reform.

B260 BADEN-POWELL, GEORGE. "A New Title for the Crown," NC:21 (May 1887), 775-80. On Victoria's crowning as empress.

B261 BAINES, J. A. "India under Lord Elgin," QR:189 (April 1899), 313-36.

B262 BAKER, SAMUEL W. "Reflections in India, 1880-1888," FR:50 (July-Dec. 1888), 211-28. General observations on British rule.

B263 BALFOUR, ARTHUR JAMES. "The Indian Civil Service—A Reply," FR:28 (July-Dec. 1877), 244-58. In defense of ICS exam regulations.

B264 BELL, NANCY FITZJAMES. "Sir James Fitzjames Stephen, Bart., K.C.S.I. A Pioneer of Indian Legal Reform," E&W:8 (June 1909), 511-26. Biography and tribute.

B265 BLUNT, W. S. "Ideas about India: V. The Future of Self-Government," FR:43 (March 1885), 386-98.

B266 BRACKENBURY, H. "Lord Lytton's Indian Administration," BM:166 (Dec. 1899), 852-70.

B267 "British Settlers," CR:36 (March 1861), 19-52.

B268 "Can India Be Colonized by Europeans?" CR 39:77 (1864), 143-66.

B269 CHAKRAVARTI, TRIPURARI. "The Calcutta Review and the Problem of Indian Constitutional Reform in the Nineteenth Century," CR:91 (Centenary No., 1944), 99-110. Quotations from the CR.

B270 CHAUDHARY, V. C. "Lytton's Indian Problems in 1876," CR:174 (March 1965), 244-50.

B271 [CHESNEY]. "Major Chesney's Indian Polity," CR 48:95, 1-31.

B272 CHESNEY, GEORGE. "The Indian Services," NC:5 (June 1879), 1038-59. Critical of the civil service.

B273 COLLINS, J. CHURTON. "The New Scheme for the Indian Civil Service Examinations," CoR:59 (June 1891), 836-51.

B274 "Colonisation and Settlement in India," CR:34 (March 1860), 16-33.

B275 "Colonisation in India," CR:30 (March 1858), 163-88. Pro and con.

B276 "The Competition System and the Indian Civil Service," CR 40:79 (1864), 11-31.

B277 "The Connection of India with England," CR 41:81 (1865), 69-94.

B278 "The Constitution and Functions of Our Legislative Councils," QJPSS:7 (Nov. 1884), 18-65.

B279 "COVENANTED." "The Moral Progress of Indian Administration," CR 80:160 (1885), 349-68.

B280 DAVIES, C. C. "India and Queen Victoria," AsR:NS 33 (July 1937), 482-504. The Queen's attitudes toward India.

B281 DE, BARUN. "Brajendranath De and John Beams—a Study in the Reactions of Patriotism and Paternalism in the I.C.S. at the Time of the Ilbert Bill," BPP:81 (Jan.-June 1962), 1-31.

B282 DE, BRAJENDRA NATH. "Reminiscences of an Indian Member of the Indian Civil Service," CR:127 (April-June 1953), 43-56, 233-40; 128 (July-Sept. 1953), 141-50; 129 (Oct.-Dec. 1953), 155-69, 253-67; 130 (Jan.-March 1954), 16-26, 141-53, 265-80; 131 (April-June 1954), 25-38, 227-42; 132 (July-Sept. 1954), 85-98, 171-85; 133 (Oct.-Dec. 1954), 82-96, 220-34; 134 (Jan.-March 1955), 49-62, 162-78, 278-86; 135 (April-June 1955), 25-31, 147-54, 275-84; 136 (July-Sept. 1956), 27-36. The 8th Indian to enter the ICS, served 1875-1910.

B283 "The Dehra Doon as a Seat of European Colonization in India," CR:31 (Dec. 1858), 485-98. Its desirability.

B284 "The Delhi Durbar: a Retrospect," BM:173 (March 1903), 311-23. An evaluation of the extravaganza of 1876-77.

B285 DIXON, FREDERICK. "Sir Eyre Coote and the 'Dictionary of National Biography,'" EHR:10 (April 1895), 336-38. Corrects errors therein.

B286 DUFF, M. E. GRANT. "A Bird's Eye View of India," NC:25 (June 1889), 813-26. Review of book by Sir John Strachey.

B287 ———. "India: Political and Social," CoR:26 (Nov. 1875), 857-86. Perceptive observations on the English in India.

B288 [DUFFERIN]. "India under the Marquis of Dufferin," ER:169 (Jan. 1889), 1-43.

B289 ———. "An Outline Sketch of the Viceroyalty of the Marquess of Dufferin and Ava (December 1884 to December 1888)," CR:88 (Jan. 1889), 156-70.

B290 "English Rule in India," W:78 (July 1862), 112-39.

B291 "English Statesmanship and Indian Policy," CR:30 (March 1858), 66-120.

B292 "The Examination System," CR:32 (June 1859), 380-99. On Civil Service exams.

B293 "The Government of India," CR:35 (Dec. 1860), 427-44.

B294 "The Government of India in England," QJPSS:7 (Oct. 1884), 1-43.

B295 "Government of the Indian Empire," ER:159 (Jan. 1884), 1-41.

B296 "Governors and Governed," CR 47:94, 116-35. On ways and means to hold India.

B297 GRIFFIN, LEPEL H. "India in 1895," AR, Ser. 2: 9 (April 1895), 273-96. Survey of administration.

B298 ———. "The Indian Civil Service Examinations," FR:23 (Jan.-June 1875), 522-36. On their subject matter and grading.

B299 ———. "The Public Service of India," AR:3 (April 1887), 250-83. On the Indianization of the civil service.

B300 GUJRAL, LALIT. "Background to the Appointment of Sir John Strachey as Finance Member in 1876," JIH:40 (Aug. 1962), 357-63. Largely from Lytton-Salisbury correspondence.

B301 HAGGARD, A. H. "Europeans and Natives in India," CoR:44 (Aug. 1883), 264-78. Discusses the Indianization of the services; comments on the Ilbert Bill.

B302 HAMBLY, G. R. G. (ed.). "The Growth of Bureaucracy in Indian Administration after 1858; a Private Criticism by A. O. Hume," BPP:80 (July-Dec. 1961), 79-85. A letter dated Aug. 1, 1872, to Lord Northbrook, "which shows that in the period when he was an influential member of the Supreme Government, he already had profound misgivings as to the direction which British rule was taking in India."

B303 ———. "Lord Lytton and the Indian Civil Service; Some New Evidence from the Lytton-Stephen Correspondence," BPP:79 (Jan.-June 1960), 1-17.

B304 HUNTER, W. W. "The Present Problem in India," CoR:54 (Sept. 1888), 313-34. Says Indians are getting Westernization without representation.

B305 "India as a Career," CR:33 (Dec. 1859), 464-77. Debunks ICS life.

B306 "Indian Affairs: Recent Legislation," W:106 (Oct. 1876), 309-64.

B307 "Indian Constitutional Law," CR:89 (July, Oct. 1889), 141-64, 302-41.

B308 "The Indian Crisis," QR:156 (July 1883), 243-69. Anti-Ripon.

B309 "Indian Faults and English Calumnies," CR:31 (Dec. 1858), 443-65. On British criticism of India.

B310 "Indian Legislation and Legislative Councils," CR:90 (Jan. 1890), 28-95.

B311 "Indian Legislation since the Mutiny," CR 51:102 (1870), 193-213.

B312 "The Indian Political Department," CR 63 (1876), 382-92.

B313 "The Indian Post Office," CR:89 (July 1889), 115-29.

B314 "Indian Public Works: the Non-Responsibility of the Indian Government Officials," W:102 (Oct. 1874), 439-56.

B315 "The Interloper in India," CR:31 (Dec. 1858), 303-48. On colonization.

B316 KEENE, H. G. "India in 1880," CR 73:145 (1881), 1-15.

B317 ———. "The Indian Services," CR 74:148 (1882), 203-26. Eulogy of the fine men who served India.

B318 [LAWRENCE]. "Administration of Sir John Lawrence," CR 48:96, 226-53.

B319 ———. "Sir John Lawrence," BM:105 (April-June 1869), 416-37, 576-606, 709-44. Biography and career in India.

B320 "The Legislative Council," CR 55:109 (1872), 119-41.

B321 LEITNER, G. W. "Indians in England and the India Civil Service," AR, Ser. 2: 6 (July 1893), 90-105. Objects to sending Indians to England, where they are "spoiled."

B322 LETHBRIDGE, ROPER. "The Proposed Inquiry into Indian Administration," AR:5 (April 1888), 276-95. Objects to the personnel.

B323 ———. "The Spoliation of the Landlords and the Tenants of Behar: the Cadastral Corvée," AR, Ser. 2:6 (Oct. 1893), 299-312. On exploitation by low officials.

B324 [LYALL]. "Government of the Indian Empire," ER:159 (Jan. 1884), 1-40.

B325 LYALL, A. C. "Twelve Years of Indian Government (1882-94)," ER:181 (Jan. 1895), 1-32.

B326 ———. "Forty-one Years in India; Review of Lord Roberts's Book," ER:185 (Jan. 1897), 1-34.

B327 LYS, F. J. "The India Civil Service and the Universities," FR:59 (Jan.-June 1893), 525-34. Analysis of preparation and results on exams.

B328 [LYTTON]. "Lord Lytton's Administration," BM:166 (Dec. 1899), 852-70.

B329 ———. "The Viceroyalty of Lord Lytton," QJPSS:3 (Aug. 1880), 30-72. An evaluation.

B330 MACLAGAN, MICHAEL. "'Clemency' Canning," HT:9 (1959), 233-42. Summary in HA:5.

B331 MARTIN, BRITON. "The Viceroyalty of Lord Dufferin," HT:10 (Dec. 1960), 821-30; 11 (Jan. 1961), 56-64.

B332 [MAYO]. "The Late Earl of Mayo, Viceroy and Governor-General of India," BM:112 (Aug. 1872), 218-37. On his administration.

B333 ———. "Lord Mayo, Fourth Viceroy of India," CR 62:124 (1876), 414-40.

B334 ———. "Lord Mayo's Administration," ER:143 (April 1876), 387-419. Review of W. W. Hunter's *Life*.

B335 McRAE, MALCOLM. "Sir Charles Trevelyan's Indian Letters, 1859-65," EHR:77 (Oct. 1962), 706-12. Summary of contents; in Bodelian Library.

B336 MORISON, J. L. "Lord Elgin in India, 1862-63," CHJ:1 (1924), 178-96. Based on letters in the Elgin papers.

B337 MOZOOMDAR, PROTAP CHUNDER. "Present Day Progress in India," NC:48 (Dec. 1900), 993-1000.

B338 NAOROJI, DADABHAI. "England's Honour toward India," AR, Ser. 2:4 (Oct. 1892), 311-16.

B339 "A Note on the Re-Organization of District Administration," QJPSS:7 (Jan. 1885), 1-12.

B340 "The Organisation of the Public Works Department," CR 50:100, 48-72.

B341 OSBORN, ROBERT D. "India under Lord Lytton," CoR:36 (Dec. 1879), 553-73. "Under Lord Lytton, British rule in India has become a tawdry and fantastic system of personal rule."

B342 ———. "Representative Government for India," CoR:42 (Dec. 1882), 931-53. Argues forcefully in favor of it.

B343 "Our Future," CR:30 (June 1858), 423-52. On post-mutiny policy.

B344 "Our Position in India," W:103 (April 1875), 346-85.

B345 PAL, DHARM. "A Critical Review of Lord Lawrence's Policy of Masterly Inactivity," JPUHS:10 (April 1947), 35-53.

B346 ———. "Humble Beginnings of Indianization of Civil Services," CR:98 (Feb. 1946), 65-71. Dates it in the late 1860's.

B347 "Parliamentary Committee on Indian Public Works," QJPSS:4 (July 1881), 1st independent section, 1-29. The organization of public works by the government, and Parliamentary recommendations.

B348 PELLY, LEWIS. "British India," FR:2 (Aug. 1865), 31-42.

B349 PERKINS, H. E. "Seven Years of Indian Legislation," CR 65:129 (1877), 143-60.

B350 [PERRY]. "Sir Erskine Perry's Notes on the Deccan Riots Report of 1875," QJPSS:1 (Sept. 1878), 1-12.

B351 PLAYFAIR, LYON. "On the New Plan of Selecting and Training Civil Servants for India," FR:28 (July-Dec. 1877), 115-25. A criticism.

B352 PRASAD, BISHESHWAR. "Non-Officials in the Councils of 1861," IHCP:5 (1941), 533-37. The reasons for the constitutional changes in 1861—a factual and interpretive essay.

B353 PRASAD, BISHESHWAR. "Some Early Post-Mutiny Schemes of Decentralization," IHCP:3 (1939), 1567-80. Indian and British plans to turn local government over to Indians.

B354 "Prospects of the Indian Empire," ER:107 (Jan. 1858), 1-50. On the stability of British rule.

B355 "Provincial Councils," CR 56:111 (1873), 171-201.

B356 "The Public Service Commission of 1886," MR:13 (Jan. 1913), 80-88.

B357 "Recollections of an Indian Civilian," CR:101 (July, Oct. 1895), 44-84, 225-57; 102 (Jan., April 1896), 16-45, 229-57; 103 (July 1896), 11-27.

B358 "Reform by Instalments," CR:30 (June 1858), 395-422. On the need for wide reforms in many administrative fields.

B359 ROBINSON, E. K. "India and the Viceroyalty," FR:64 (Sept. 1895), 439-53.

B360 ROY, PARBATI C. "The Alleged Danger of the Indian Civil Service 'Resolution,'" W:140 (July-Dec. 1893), 495-504. On ICS reform.

B361 "The Royal Proclamation to India," BM:85 (Jan. 1859), 113-26.

B362 SINGH, H. L. "A Plan for the Abolition of the Supreme Council, 1859-1861," BPP:80 (July-Dec. 1961), 86-92. Based on Wood Papers in the India Office Library.

B363 SLAGG, JOHN. "Parliament and the Government of India," CoR:45 (Feb. 1884), 210-23. By an M.P.; proposals for reform in Parliamentary control of the government of India.

B364 SMITH, BRIAN C. "Sir Henry Maine and the Government of India (1862-87)," JIH:41 (Dec. 1963), 565-75. Maine's views as Law Member of the Governor General's Council, as Vice Chancellor of the University of Calcutta, and as member of the Council of the Secretary of State for India.

B365 SMITH, SAMUEL. "India Revisited," CoR:49 (June 1886), 794-819; 50 (July 1886), 60-79. "Reply" by M. E. Grant Duff, CoR:51 (Jan., Feb. 1887), 8-31, 181-95. Comments by Dadabhai Naoroji, "Sir M. E. Grant Duff's Views about India," CoR:52 (Aug., Nov. 1887), 221-35, 694-711. Changes since 1863 noted and disputed.

B366 "Some Observations on Problems of Indian Administration," CR: 98 (April 1894), 278-300.

B367 SOVANI, N. V. "British Impact on India after 1850-57," CHM:2 (1954), 77-105. Concentrates on the period before 1914.

B368 TAYLOR, HERBERT. "The Future of India," CoR:39 (March 1881), 464-77. Critical of policy.

B369 [TEMPLE]. "Sir Richard Temple," CR:104 (Jan. 1897), 139-44.

B370 ———. "Sir Richard Temple's India in 1880," QR:152 (July 1881), 50-79. Economic and political conditions.

B371 TEMPLE, RICHARD. "India during the Jubilee Reign," AR:4 (July 1887), 1-41. The blessings of British rule.

B372 TIGNOR, ROBERT L. "The 'Indianization' of the Egyptian Administration under British Rule," AHR:68 (April 1963), 636-61. The application of Indian experience to Egypt, 1882-92.

B373 TOWNSEND, MEREDITH. "Will England Retain India?" CoR: 53 (June 1888), 795-813. Predicts that the English will be quickly forgotten in India, the railways torn up, etc.

B374 WEDDERBURN, WILLIAM. "Russianized Officialism in India: The Fly in the Ointment," AR, Ser. 2:5 (Jan. 1893), 1-14. Oppression of the villagers by ICS men.

B375 [WOOD]. "Sir Charles Wood's Administration of Indian Affairs," BM:102 (Dec. 1867), 686-701. Secretary of State for India, 1859-66.

6. ADMINISTRATION AND REFORMS, 1898 TO 1919

B376 AGA KHAN. "The Royal Visit—Some Impressions and Reflections," E&W:5 (March 1906), 211-15.

B377 "ANGLO-INDIAN." "Lord Curzon's Services to India," NA:176 (Jan. 1903), 68-79.

B378 ARCHER, W. "Montagu-Chelmsford Report," FR:110 (Aug. 1918), 263-71.

B379 ARUNDEL, A. T. "Decentralisation of Government in India," NC:65 (May 1909), 810-25; 66 (July 1909), 143-57. On Curzon's administration, reforms, and recommendations of the Royal Commission of 1907.

B380 BHATTACHARYA, SUKUMAR. "Lord Curzon's Impressions of the Indian Administration, 1898-1901," IHRC:31 (1955), 50-60.

B381 ———. "The Men Who Ruled India, 1899-1901; a Sketch by Lord Curzon," MR:102 (Aug. 1957), 114-19. Curzon's opinion of men he worked with, from his letters.

B382 CHAKRAVARTI, TRIPURARI. "New Light of the Minto-Morley Reforms of 1909," CR:73 (Dec. 1939), 321-34. Excerpts from Minto's and Morley's opinions on reform.

B383 CHIROL, VALENTINE. "Constitutional Reform in India," QR: 230 (Oct. 1918), 401-21. On the Montford reform scheme.

B384 COTTON, H. E. A. "Constitution-making for India, a Great Achievement," CoR:117 (Jan. 1920), 63-70.

B385 ———. "The Viceroyalty of Lord Chelmsford," CoR:119 (June 1921), 764-70. A survey.

B386 COTTON, HENRY. "The Present Political Situation in India," AR: NS 5 (July 1, 1914), 16-27. An attack on the ICS. Refuted by J. Pollen, "'Divide and Rule'—India's Destruction," AR: NS 5 (Aug. 15, 1914), 137-46.

B387 CURZON, G. N. "The Future of British India," WW:9 (Dec. 1904), 5589-93. "Our work is righteous and it shall endure."

B388 DAS, M. N. "Political Ideologies of Britain vis-à-vis Problems of Indian Empire: 1905-10," QRHS 3:3 (1963-64), 135-41.

B389 "The Durbar and After," RT:2 (June 1912), 395-421. Commentary on the effects of the 1911 Delhi Durbar.

B390 FANSHAWE, ARTHUR. "The Post Office of India: Its Work and Its Romance," BM:182 (Dec. 1907), 789-811. Largely anecdotal.

B391 FORREST, GEORGE W. "The Administration of India," BM:102 (Oct. 1917), 513-32. On the civil service.

B392 ———. "British Democracy and Indian Government," FR:95 (April 1911), 617-28. Analyzes Lord Morley's statements.

B393 ———. "The Government of India," BM:178 (Aug. 1905), 165-91. Constitutional history.

B394 ———. "The Indian Civil Service," BM:188 (Oct. 1910), 510-26. On the recruitment and training of candidates.

B395 FRASER, A. H. LOVAT. "The Montagu-Chelmsford Report," NC:84 (Oct. 1918), 771-84.

B396 ———. "Problems of Indian Administration," ER:227 (Jan. 1918), 166-87.

B397 FULLER, BAMPFYLDE. "The Claims of Sentiment upon Indian Policy," NC:62 (Dec. 1907), 958-68. On the desirability of decentralizing the administration of Bengal.

B398 ———. "The Foundations of Indian Loyalty," NC:66 (Aug. 1909), 181-94. Against the Morley-Minto reforms.

B399 GHOSE, SAILENDRA NATH. "The Montagu-Chelmsford Reform Proposals," D:66 (May 3, 1919), 457-59. Complains of the lack of economic reform.

B400 GOKHALE, G. K. "Constitutional Reforms in India," CoR:95 (March 1909), 284-87. On Morley's statement on Indian reforms Dec. 1908.

B401 ———. "Self-Government for India," AR. Ser. 3:22 (July 1906), 233-49.

B402 "The Government of India," MR:24 (Aug. 1918), 212-16. On Montford reforms.

B403 HILL, CLAUDE H. "Fair Play for India," NC:90 (July 1921), 109-17. On the development of constitutional government.

B404 HORTON, R. F. "What We Are Doing in India," CoR:103 (May 1913), 626-39. A visitor recites the blessings of British rule.

B405 "India: Old Ways and New," RT:3 (Dec. 1912), 52-80. On the change of approach of government in the previous decade.

B406 "India under Lord Hardinge," QR:226 (July 1916), 99-115.

B407 "India under Lord Morley," QR:214 (Jan. 1911), 203-24.

B408 "The Indian Councils at Work," BM:188 (Nov. 1910), 701-16.

B409 "Indians and Higher Government Posts," MR:18 (Dec. 1915), 627-32. Statistics from the "Combined Civil List for India" up to July 1, 1915.

B410 IYER, G. SUBRAMANIA. "Britishers and Indians in Our Public Services," HR:26 (Dec. 1912), 433-41.

B411 ———. "The Royal Commission on Public Services in India," HR:26 (Aug., Sept., Nov. 1912), 107-14, 197-208, 307-16.

B412 JINNAH, M. A. "Reorganizing the Indian Council," FR:102 (Oct. 1914), 612-20. Attacks the rejection of Council of India Bill in House of Lords.

B413 KARKARIA, R. P. "The Law Membership of the Imperial Executive Council," HR:23 (Jan., Feb. 1911), 35-39, 149-55.

B414 ——— and MACDONALD, MIDDLETON. "Lord Curzon," CR: 121 (Oct. 1905), 531-52.

B415 "L.R." "Sir John Rees as an Indian Authority," HR:23 (Jan., Feb., April 1911), 56-62, 186-91, 310-14. Criticism of an Anglo-Indian commentator.

B416 LAJPAT RAI, LALA. "The Debate on the India Council Bill in the House of Lords," MR:16 (Sept. 1914), 299-303. Long excerpts from editorials in British newspapers.

B417 LEE, E. D. "Case for the Rowlatt Act in India," FR:112 (Aug. 1919), 228-38.

B418 "Lord Curzon, Lord Kitchener, and Mr. Brodrick," BM:178 (Sept. 1905), 427-44.

B419 MACDONALD, J. RAMSAY. "India after the War," CoR:112 (Sept. 1917), 280-87. Advocates advance to self-government.

B420 ———. "The Indian Services Report," CoR:111 (March 1917), 327-35. On reform in the selection of Indians for government services.

B421 MALCOLM, IAN. "George Curzon," QR:245 (July 1925), 1-22. Revealing character sketch.

B422 MALLESON, WILFRED. "Curzon and Kitchener; Some Personal Reminiscences," FR:130 (Aug. 1928), 145-56.

B423 MAZUMDAR, VINA. "Sir Herbert Hope Risley and Indian Constitutional Reform: 1906-1909," PU:18 (Jan. 1963), 129-41.

B424 MEHROTRA, S. R. "The Politics behind the Montagu Declaration of 1917," PSI, pp. 71-96. A thorough "interim report" (since many papers were not available) on the political background of the declaration on the "progressive realisation of responsible government in India."

B425 MITRA, S. M. "The House of Lords and the Indian Princes," FR:93 (June 1910), 1090-99. Suggests that a few selected princes be admitted to the House of Lords.

B426 MOOKERJEE, H. C. "The Provisions of the Rowlatt Act and Their Justification," CR:86 (Jan. 1943), 1-11.

B427 ———. "The Rowlatt Bill in the Legislature," CR:85 (Dec. 1942), 173-88. Statements by Indians on the Bill in the legislature and in the press.

B428 ———. "The Rowlatt Report and Its Reception," CR:85 (Nov. 1942), 89-101.

B429 MOONEY, HUGHSON F. "British Opinion on Indian Policy, 1911-1917," Hn:23 (Feb. 1961), 191-210. An overview of official opinion based on parliamentary debates, government documents, newspapers, and RT. Summary in HA:8 (No. 2781).

B430 MORLEY, JOHN. "Signs of the Times in India," ER:206 (Oct. 1907), 265-305. Speech in House of Commons, June 6, 1907.

B431 ———. "Lord Morley and Indian Reform," QR:210 (April 1909), 692-711.

B432 "Outsiders as Public Servants in British India," MR:19 (June 1916), 611-14. On extent to which Indians from British and princely territories should be employed in civil and military posts.

B433 "POLITICUS." "Lord Islington's Commission," MR:12 (Oct. 1912), 365-68. On the Royal Commission on the Civil Services of India.

B434 RATCLIFFE, S. K. "Lord Curzon in India," CoR:134 (Aug. 1928), 161-67. Based on Ronaldshay's *Life of Lord Curzon*.

B435 RAY, PRITHWIS CHANDRA. "India at the Cross-Roads: the Reforms and After," CoR:121 (Feb. 1922), 218-25. Criticism of Montford reforms and dyarchy by the editor of *Bengalee*.

B436 REES, J. D. "Coronation Concessions in India," FR:97 (Jan.-June 1912), 303-15. On reactions to annulment of the partition of Bengal.

B437 ROBERTS, CHARLES. "Indian Reforms, with a Reply to Lord Sydenham," CoR:114 (Sept. 1918), 237-45.

B438 [RONALDSHAY]. "Lord Ronaldshay's Speech at Mymensingh," MR:24 (Sept. 1918), 306-13. On the Defense of India Act.

B439 "The Rowlatt Committee's Report," MR:24 (Aug. 1918), 208-09. On press reactions, based on the *Tribune* and *Kesari*.

B440 "S.K." "The Public Service Commission at Madras," MR:13 (March 1913), 316-18.

B441 SHARMA, JOTEYLAL. "Indians in the State Service," HR:25 (Feb. 1912), 178-84. Figures on government employment and salaries.

B442 SINGH, NIHAL. "British Witnesses before the Joint Parliamentary Committee," MR:27 (Jan. 1920), 50-55.

B443 ———. "India's Constitutional Reforms," CoR:114 (Aug. 1918), 141-50.

B444 ———. "The Indian Deputations and the Joint Parliamentary Committee," MR:26 (Sept., Nov. 1919), 282-88, 486-92; 27 (Jan. 1920), 34-50. Membership lists of deputations and résumé of proceedings.

B445 ———. "The Net Results of the King's Indian Tour," FR:97 (Jan.-June 1912), 523-42. Praises it as wholly beneficial.

B446 SMITH, GOLDWIN. "British Empire in India," NA:183 (Sept. 7, 1906), 338-48. Signs of its demise.

B447 "Some Statistics of Higher Indian Government Posts," MR:12 (Nov. 1912), 533-47.

B448 SYDENHAM OF COMBE. "India and Mr. Charles Roberts, M.P.," CoR:114 (Nov. 1918), 494-502. On reforms.

B449 "The Treatment of Sedition in India," BM:181 (Feb. 1907), 257-65.

B450 TRIPATHI, AMALES. "Morley Minto Reforms," BPP:82 (July-Dec. 1963), 81-87; 83 (1964), 75-81, 144-52; 84 (Jan.-June 1965), 49-62.

B451 WARD, A. "India under Lord Curzon," QR:200 (July 1904), 210-39.

B452 WASTI, S. RAZI. "Sir Mian Muhammad Shafi on the Morley-Minto Reforms," ASP:9 (June 1964), 151-83. Prints letters to Col. Dunlop Smith, Minto's private sec'y.

B453 WEDDERBURN, WILLIAM. "An Indian Catechism for the British Elector," CoR:111 (March 1917), 419-27.

B454 ———. "King George and India," CoR:101 (Feb. 1912), 153-64. Assessment of the Delhi Durbar.

B455 ———. "The Royal Commission on the Indian Public Service; Its Objects and Reasons," CoR:103 (April 1913), 481-90.

B456 ———. "The Vice-Royalty of Lord Hardinge," CoR:109 (March 1916), 298-306.

B457 WHEELER, STEPHEN. "Lord Curzon in India," AC:9 (April 1901), 708-18.

B458 "X." "Some Observations on the Reform Scheme," MR:24 (Oct. 1918), 348-58. With historical background.

B459 YATE, CHARLES E. "India under the Emperor," NC:84 (Nov. 1918), 869-79. On the Montford reforms.

7. ADMINISTRATION AND REFORMS, 1919 TO 1950

B460 ADENWALLA, MINOO. "British Responses to Indian Nationalism—the Irwin Declaration on Dominion Status, 1929," StOA:5 (1964), 121-41. Based on published sources.

B461 ANSARI, A. S. BAZMEE. "Djūnāgarh," EI:2, 597-98. City and former·princely state which ceded to Pakistan but was occupied by Indian troops.

B462 ARCHBOLD. W. A. J. "Federalism in India," CoR:131 (May 1927), 612-16.

B463 ———. "New Indian Constitution," ER:242 (Oct. 1925), 279-90. Discussion of the Commonwealth of India Bill.

B464 ATTLEE, C. R. "The Indian Report: the Labour Minority View," AR: NS 31 (1935), 247-59; discussion pp. 260-70.

B465 BAHADUR, LAL. "The Simon Commission and India," AUJR:8 (Jan. 1960), 13-24.

B466 BANERJEE, D. N. "The Growth of Parliamentary Government in India, 1919-1950," PrlA:9 (Spring 1956), 160-72. Survey of constitutional history.

B467 ———. "The Negotiations and After; the Lahore Resolution of 1940 and Mr. Jinnah," MR:76 (Dec. 1944), 281-86.

B468 ———. "Position of the President of India," MR:87 (June 1950), 450-55. Description of duties.

B469 ———. "The Sapru Committee and Leading Principles of a New Constitution for India," MR:78 (March 1946), 173-76.

B470 ———. "The Wavell Offer," MR:78 (Aug. 1945), 82-87.

B471 BARNES, G. S. "The New Indian Legislatures at Delhi," NC:90 (Aug. 1921), 281-89. On membership and early debates.

B472 BARTON, WILLIAM P. "The Indian Provincial System and the Reforms," CoR:139 (Feb. 1931), 154-62.

B473 ———. "Indian Reform and the Peasant," FR:141 (Feb. 1934), 177-85. On the White Paper and its effects.

B474 ———. "The Viceroy's Council and Indian Politics," FR:158 (Aug. 1942), 109-15. Examines Indian composition and the status of Indians on the Council.

B475 ———. "The Wavell Plan and After," QR:284 (Jan. 1946), 17-29.

B476 BHATTACHARYYA, N. C. and others. "A Critique of the White Paper," MR:53 (June 1933), 674-89; 54 (July 1933), 52-63. By members of the Politics Club of Calcutta: P.N. Sarkar, S. Guha, A. Sen, B.N. Banerjea, H.K. Sanyal, S.K. Lahiri.

B477 BIRDWOOD, C. B. "Indecision in India," NC:139 (March 1946), 107-14. Problems of running the government amidst Indian politics.

B478 BISSON, T. A. "Autonomous India: the Administrative Issues," FPR:7 (Sept. 30, 1931), 277-98.

B479 ———. "Constitutional Developments in India," FPR:9 (Sept. 13, 1933), 150-60.

B480 BORSA, GIORGIO. "Le trattative per l'indipendenza dell'India" [The Negotiations for the Transfer of Power in India], Po:23 (1958), 406-39. Summary in HA:5 (No. 2479): "Based on British and Indian published documents. A bibliography is included."

B481 BRAILSFORD, H. "Princes and Peasants at the Round Table," PoQ:2 (Oct. 1931), 548-63. Discussion of the draft constitution, outlining points of Indian dissatisfaction; especially good on the issue of separate electorates as against reserved seats.

B482 BURMAN, DEBAJYOTI. "Third Partition of Bengal?" MR:79 (May 1946), 369-72. With historical background.

B483 CADOGAN, EDWARD. "The Government of India Bill," QR:264 (April 1935), 347-66.

B484 ———. "Report of the Indian Statutory Commission and Its Critics," QR:255 (Oct. 1930), 260-80. On the Simon Commission report.

B485 CAMPBELL-JOHNSON, ALAN. "Reflections on the Transfer of Power," AR: NS 48 (July 1952), 163-73; discussion pp. 173-82.

B486 CLOKIE, H. McD. "New Constitution for India," APSR:30 (Dec. 1936), 1152-65. A review of it.

B487 COATMAN, JOHN. "India and the New Franchise," NC:115 (June 1934), 655-64. Favors indirect election with wide franchise.

B488 ———. "The Round Table Conference," NC:111 (Jan. 1932), 24-34. Summary of discussions.

B489 "The Constitutional Development of India, 1917-42," RS, pp. 74-86. Reprinted from BIN:19 (April 18, 1942), 329-35, 351-53. A chronology, Aug. 20, 1917 to April 13, 1942.

B490 "Constitutional Proposals of the Sapru Committee," InC:421 (May 1946), 241-69. Summary of the report, with introduction and interim proposals.

B491 CRADDOCK, REGINALD. "Indian Reforms and the Simon Commission," CoR:133 (April 1928), 433-41.

B492 "Cripps Mission to India," InC:381 (June 1942), 305-59. Explanatory introduction by G. Spry; text of the draft declaration; documentary material relating to the negotiations.

B493 DATTA, JATINDRA MOHAN. "The Electorate in Bengal—Its Problems," MR:49 (June 1931), 632-38.

B494 ———. "Vote for Women: How They Use It," LSGI:9 (Jan. 1939), 243-50. Analysis of voting figures.

PART I: ARTICLES

B495 "Documents Concerning the Origin and Purpose of the Indian Statutory Commission," InC:258 (March 1930), 127-89. Documents on the Simon Commission and a bibliography.

B496 FITZGERALD, R. C. "Further Developments in the British Commonwealth of Nations," WA: NS 3 (July 1949), 269-81. On the Attlee Declaration of April 28, 1949.

B497 GHOSAL, AKSHOY KUMAR. "Cabinet Mission and After," MR:81 (Feb., March, May 1947), 109-11, 197-203, 363-66.

B498 GHOSH, S. C. "The British Conservative Party and the Indian Problem, 1929-1934; a Case Study of a Decision and the Actual Operation of Powers," CR:171 (April 1964), 55-71.

B499 ———. "Decision-Making and Power in the British Conservative Party: a Case Study of the Indian Problem 1929-34," PoS:13 (June 1965), 198-212.

B500 GLEDHILL, ALAN, "Dustūr: xiv, Pākistān," EI:2, 668-72. On the Pakistan constitution.

B501 GRIFFITHS, PERCIVAL. "Struggle for Stability," NC:144 (July 1948), 11-19. Factors in the transfer of power.

B502 HAILEY, LORD. "India in the Modern World, a British View," FA:21 (April 1943), 401-11. Suggests that Britain might willingly withdraw from India.

B503 HALIFAX, VISCOUNT. "Political Future of India," FA:13 (April 1935), 420-30. On the Simon Commission report.

B504 HAYWARD, M. H. W. "The Congress Scheme and the Simon Report," NC:108 (Sept. 1930), 355-63.

B505 HOLAND, R. E. "Prospects of Indian Federation," NC:110 (Sept. 1931), 297-314.

B506 HUQ, MAHFUZUL. "From Separate Electorates to a Separate State," ASP:10 (June 1965), 167-201.

B507 "India and the Round Table Conference," RT:22 (Dec. 1931), 100-17.

B508 "India and Pakistan; Pressures External and Internal," RT:54 (June 1964), 228-39. The pressures for partition.

B509 "Indian Statutory Commission," ER:247 (Jan. 1928), 163-77.

B510 ISLAM, ZAFARUL. "Some Parliamentary Papers pertaining to West Pakistan," PHS:12 (Oct. 1964), 291-310. Descriptive summary of 63 papers.

B511   KRISHNA, B. "Mass Migration from West Punjab," CR:113 (Dec. 1949), 182-91. A brief, factual account, anti-Muslim in tone.

B512   KRISHNA MENON, V. K. "The Simon Report: a Study," InAf:1 (Sept. 1930), 125-41.

B513   LINLITHGOW, LORD. "Speech on the Federation of India Delivered before the Indian Legislature, Sept. 21, 1936," InC:324 (Nov. 1936), 533-39.

B514   LYONS, M. D. "India's New Government; Personalities in the New Indian All-Indian Cabinet," C:44 (Sept. 27, 1946), 566-69. Thumbnail sketches.

B515   MAJUMDAR, A. K. "The Cripps Mission," MIF, pp. 358-71. With bibliography of newspaper reports, official reports, and memoirs.

B516   MARRIOTT, J. A. R. "Making a Constitution," FR:135 (May, June 1931), 592-603, 754-65. The problems involved.

B517   MATHUR, RAMESH NARAIN. "Evolution of the Office of the Speaker in India," MR:104 (Oct. 1958), 273-78. Based on Legislative Assembly Debates, 1921-1930.

B518   MESTON, LORD. "India and the Simon Report," CoR:138 (Aug. 1930), 137-46.

B519   ———. "The Indian Commission and Its Tasks," CoR:133 (Jan. 1928), 1-16. On the Simon Commission.

B520   ———. "The White Paper," CoR:143 (May 1933), 513-20.

B521   MITCHELL, KATE L. (ed.). "Cripps Mission to India," Am:6 (May 1942), 107-52. Documents, speeches, and commentary on the mission.

B522   MOLSON, H. "India and the Conservative Party," NC:114 (Aug. 1933), 129-39. Background of the White Paper.

B523   MOOKERJEE, H. C. "British Business in Indian Legislatures," MR:75 (April 1944), 257-66.

B524   ———. "Non-Official Europeans in Indian Legislatures," MR:75 (Jan. 1944), 25-30.

B525   ———. "Our Obligations to the Non-Official European," MR:75 (June 1944), 417-21; 76 (July-Sept. 1944), 23-30, 91-95, 147-52.

B526   MORISON, THEODORE. "The Outlook for India," CoR:139 (April 1931), 409-15. The results of the Round Table Conference.

B527   ———. "The Report of the Simon Commission," CoR:138 (Sept. 1930), 288-95.

B528 [MOUNTBATTEN]. "Lord Mountbatten on His Viceroyalty," AR: NS 44 (Oct. 1948), 345-55. An address at the Imperial Institute.

B529 MUDALIAR, A. RAMASWAMI. "An Indian Federation: Its Constitutional Problems and Possible Solution," MUJ:5 (Supplement, 1933), 104 pp.

B530 NAIR, SANKARAN. "The Indian Commission: a Criticism," CoR:133 (Feb. 1928), 150-58. The Simon Commission.

B531 ———. "The Simon Commission's Report," CoR:138 (Oct. 1930), 429-38.

B532 "AN OBSERVER." "The Indian Provincial Elections," AR: NS 33 (1937), 449-56. Detailed results of 1937 elections: seats won by parties in each province.

B533 O'DWYER, MICHAEL F. "Present Conditions in India," FR:115 (July-Dec. 1921), 177-93. Critical of the working of the Montford reforms.

B534 ———. "Three Years of Reform in India: a Plea for the Indian Masses," FR:120 (Jan.-June 1924), 353-69.

B535 OLIVIER, LORD. "The Disease of Indian Dyarchy," CoR:127 (May 1925), 554-62.

B536 PILCHER, GEORGE. "The British Services in India," FR:119 (Jan.-June 1923), 74-88. On political maneuvers over the Indianization of the civil service.

B537 ———. "Lord Reading's Indian Viceroyalty," ER:243 (April 1926), 224-39. A survey of his term in office.

B538 POLE, D. GRAHAM. "India and the White Paper," MR:53 (May 1933), 497-502. "The Labour Party's standpoint."

B539 "The Proposals of the Simon Commission; Symposium of Opinions," AR: NS 26 (July 1930), 405-20. Mostly British opinion.

B540 "Reactions to the Cabinet Mission Proposals," MR:79 (June 1946), 485-508.

B541 READING, MARQUESS OF. "Progress of Constitutional Reform in India," FA:2 (July 1933), 609-20. Comment on Montford reforms.

B542 REED, STANLEY and CRADDOCK, REGINALD. "The Simon Report; the Report and After," NC:108 (Aug. 1930), 151-68. Summary.

B543 "Rehabilitation of Displaced Persons in India," ILR:58 (Aug. 1948), 187-98. On measures taken by the Indian government; from published statements, newspaper reports.

B544 RHODES, CAMPBELL. "India's First Step," NC:94 (Dec. 1923), 826-35. On the first Indian parliament under Montford reforms.

B545 RICE, STANLEY. "The Passing of the Indian Civil Service," FR: 116 (March 1922), 585-92.

B546 ROY, NARESH CHANDRA. "Indian Civil Service and Provincial Autonomy," CR:74 (Feb. 1940), 151-68. A discussion of the working relations between the civil service and ministerial government at the provincial level under the Government of India Act of 1935.

B547 SAYEED, KHALID BIN. "The Governor-General of Pakistan," PH:8 (1955), 330-39. Summary in HA:1 (No. 3368): "Reviews the powers and functions of the Governor-General, which are largely based on the Government of India Act of 1935."

B548 SCHECHTMAN, JOSEPH B. "Evacuee Property in India and Pakistan," PA:24 (Dec. 1951), 406-13; IQ:9 (Jan.-March 1953), 3-34. The problem and attempts at its solution; documented.

B549 SHIVA RAO, B. "How Cripps' Mission Failed," A:42 (July 1942), 394-97.

B550 "Simon and India," LA:338 (Aug. 1, 1930), 655-63. Editorials from the London Times, New Statesman, Daily Herald.

B551 SINGH, GANDA. "A Diary of the Partition Days," JIH:38 (April, Aug. 1960), 205-32, 241-84. April 1, 1947–Jan. 16, 1948; with references to printed sources.

B552 SINHA, SACHCHIDANANDA. "Dyarchy in Indian Provinces in Theory and Practice," AR: NS 24 (1928), 33-62, discussion pp. 63-84.

B553 SPATE, OSKAR H. K. "The Boundary Award in the Punjab," AR: NS 44 (Jan. 1948), 3-8, discussion pp. 8-15. Discussion of the issues.

B554 ———. "Geographical Aspects of the Pakistan Scheme," GJ:102 (Sept. 1943), 125-36. With maps of percentage of various religions in each district.

B555 ———. "The Partition of the Punjab and Bengal," GJ:110 (1947), 201-22. With very good maps.

B556 SPEAR, PERCIVAL. "Britain's Transfer of Power in India: Review Article," PA:31 (June 1958), 173-80. Discussion of V. P. Menon's book.

B557 ———. "From Colonial to Sovereign Status: Some Problems of Transition with Special Reference to India," JAS:17 (Aug. 1958), 567-77. A "balance sheet" of British policy in the 20th cent.

B558 ———. "Indo-British Relations in the Future," AR: NS 42 (July 1946), 232-37, discussion pp. 238-43. Observations on Indian feelings toward Britain just before Independence.

B559 SPRY, GRAHAM (ed.). "Cripps Mission to India," InC:381 (June 1942), 305-59. With text of draft declaration and documentary material relating to negotiations.

B560 SRIVASTAVA, G. P. "Western Influences on the Constitutional Philosophy of India," UB:10 (April 1963), 61-69. Summary of constitution-makers' assumptions.

B561 SUNDERLAND, J. T. "Testimonies of Competent Englishmen as to the Fitness of India for Self-Rule," MR:42 (Oct. 1927), 420-27.

B562 VENKATARAMANI, M. S. and SHRIVASTAVA, B. K. "The United States and the Cripps Mission," IQ:19 (July 1963), 214-65.

B563 WILLIAMS, L. F. RUSHBROOK. "Indian Constitutional Problems: a Survey of Opinion in British India and the Indian States," NC:125 (March, May 1939), 282-94, 554-66.

B564 WILLSON, W. S. J. "The Simon Report; a Non-Official European View," NC:108 (Sept. 1930), 345-54.

B565 WINTERTON, EARL T. "The Indian Impasse," FR:137 (Jan. 1932), 1-7. On the mixed success of the Round Table Conferences.

B566 ———. "The Solutions of the Simon Report," FR:134 (Aug. 1930), 145-56. Favorable critique.

B567 YOUNGHUSBAND, FRANCIS. "India: the Next Step," CoR:142 (July 1932), 1-9. Next step: keep governing.

B568 ———. "The Indian Round Table Conference," CoR:141 (Jan. 1932), 1-8. Its goals and results.

B569 YUSUF ALI, A. "Indian Reaction to the White Paper," AR: NS 29 (1933), 411-22, discussion pp. 423-34.

B570 ZETLAND, MARQUESS OF. "The Origin of the Round Table and the London Conferences of 1930 and 1931," PI, pp. 281-300. From the government point of view.

B571 ———. "Self-Government for India," FA:9 (Oct. 1930), 1-12. On Montford reforms, Simon Commission.

8. JUDICIAL ADMINISTRATION

B572 ADAM, LEONHARD. "Criminal Law and Procedure in Nepal a Century Ago: Notes Left by Brian H. Hodgson," FEQ:9 (Feb. 1950),

146-68. Based on documents in the India Office Library; reprints notes on punishments and crimes.

B573 "Administration of Criminal Justice in Bengal," CR:6 (1846), 135-89; 87 (Oct. 1888), 323-44; 90 (April 1890), 253-70.

B574 "Administration of Justice in India," ER:73 (July 1841), 425-60. Critical of the administration.

B575 "The Agitation in Regard to the Native Magistrates Jurisdiction Bill," QJPSS:5 (Nov. 1882), 23-41.

B576 AHMAD, BADRUD-DIN. "Old Judicial Records of the Calcutta High Court," IHRC:5 (1923), 70-76.

B577 ALI, HAMID. "The Customary and Statutory Laws of the Muslims in India," IC:11 (July, Oct. 1937), 354-69, 444-54. The laws followed by each group of Muslims.

B578 "The Anglo-Indian Courts of Justice," CR 16:31 (1851), 1-32. Courts for British citizens in Bengal.

B579 BANERJEE, ANIL CHANDRA. "Dewani and Criminal Jurisdiction," IHRC:19 (Dec. 1942), 38-40.

B580 ———. "The Sinha Peerage Case," CR:58 (Feb. 1936), 187-91. Conflict of laws, or at least of customs, in a claim for a seat in House of Lords.

B581 BANERJEE, D. N. "Had the Mayor's Courts (Established in India by the Royal Charter of 24th September 1726) Any Criminal Jurisdiction?" IHRC:18 (Jan. 1942), 76-81.

B582 BANERJEE, INDUBHUSAN. "The Case of Swarup Chand—An Incident in the Quarrel between the Supreme Court and the Supreme Council," IHCP:7 (1944), 478-82.

B583 BANERJEE, PHANINDRA NATH. "Indian Law Officers in Early British Judiciary of Bengal (1772-1793)," QRHS 4:3 (1964/65), 152-58.

B584 BANERJEE, SUKUMAR. " 'The Mayor's Court'—British Indian Judiciary," CR:174 (March 1965), 233-38.

B585 ———. "The Supreme Court—British India Judiciary," CR:176 (Aug. 1965), 117-43.

B586 BARING, EVELYN. "Recent Events in India," NC:14 (Oct. 1883), 569-89. On the Ilbert Bill.

B587 BASU, K. K. "Native Pleaders in an Early District Court in Bengal," IHRC:22 (1945), 43-44. Names and qualities.

B588 BEIGHTON, T. DURANT. "The Modern History of Trial by Jury in India," AR, Ser. 3:17 (Jan. 1904), 17-52.

B589 "The Bengal Penal Code," CR 13:25 (1850), 162-99.

B590 BHANU, DHARMA. "Administration of Justice in the Upper Provinces," OHRJ:5 (April & July 1956), 105-12. Survey of early 19th cent.

B591 BOMPAS, C. H. "The Administration of Civil Justice in Bengal," CR:3 (July 1900), 20-28.

B592 BOSE, PRAMATHA NATH. "The Legal Exploitation of the Indian," MR:21 (Jan. 1917), 30-37. The cost of "the English machinery for the administration of justice."

B593 CANNON, GARLAND H. "Sir William Jones and Edmund Burke," MP:54 (Feb. 1957), 165-86. On their friendship and quarrel, with previously unpublished letters, some on the Indian judicial system.

B594 CHAND, BOOL. "The Working of the Indian Federal Court," IJPS:4 (April 1943), 354-62. Opened Dec. 1937.

B595 CHANDRA, G. N. "Early Penal System in the Bengal Presidency," IHRC:32 (1956), 20-27. 18th cent. system.

B596 CHATTERJI, NANDALAL. "The Administration of Justice in Bihar and Bengal during Verelst's Governorship," JBORS:26 (1940), 40-59. The jurisdiction of the various courts.

B597 CHAUDHURY, BHUPENDRA NARAYA. "Judicial Administration of Assam, 1845-58," GUJ:11 (1960), 1-16.

B598 CHOWDHURY, NANI GOPAL. "Some Excerpts from Unpublished Records Relating to the Trial of Riza Khan Naib Nazim and Naib Deevan of Bengal (1765-72)," IHRC:23 (1946), 24-26.

B599 "Civil Justice in the Santal Pergunnahs," CR:87 (Oct. 1888), 345-53.

B600 "Civil Procedure in the Punjab," CR 42:84 (1865), 259-300.

B601 COHN, BERNARD S. "From Indian Status to British Contract," JEH:21 (Dec. 1961), 613-28. Based on records in the India Office Library and Allahabad Central Records Office. On the operation of British law on land disputes in early courts in the Benares region.

B602 COTTON, EVAN. "An Artist and His Fees. The Story of the Suit Brought by Ozias Humphry against the Governor-General," BPP:34 (July-Dec. 1927), 1-19. In the 1780's.

B603 ———. "Memories of the Supreme Court, 1774-1862," BPP:30 (Oct.-Dec. 1925), 150-98; 32 (July-Dec. 1926), 14-20.

B604 "County Courts and Courts of Small Causes," CR 43:85 (1866), 182-226.

B605 "The Court Amlas in Lower Bengal," CR 22:44 (1854), 415-28. On the Indian personnel of courts.

B606 "Courts of Small Causes in Bengal," CR 50:99, 81-93.

B607 "Crime and Punishment in the Punjab," CR:32 (March 1859), 53-81.

B608 "Criminal Administration in Bengal," CR 28:56 (June 1857), 462-86; 41:82 (1865), 225-96.

B609 "Criminal Law in Bengal," CR 12:24 (1849), 516-68.

B610 DERRETT, J. DUNCAN M. "The Administration of Hindu Law by the British," CSSH:4 (1961-62), 10-52. Examines British presuppositions and practice in extrapolation and interpretation.

B611 ———. "Nandakumar's Forgery," EHR:75 (April 1960), 223-38. A legal dispute placed in its social and personal setting. Conclusion: "Nandakumar was sacrificed . . . to a maxim ['equality before the law'] which, for a moment, was allowed to get out of hand."

B612 DEY, SHUMBHOO CHUNDER. "The Bengal Tichbourne Case," CR:112 (Jan. 1901), 103-24. Detailed account of mid-19th cent. case of identity of Raja Protap Chand.

B613 ———. "A History of the Bengal High Court," CR:114 (Jan., April 1902), 70-108, 312-53; 115 (Oct. 1902), 353-99; 116 (April 1903), 190-229; 117 (Oct. 1903), 159-91.

B614 ———. "Notices of Eminent Judges of the High Court," CR:119 (July 1904), 265-313. Brief biographies.

B615 ———. "Sir Elijah Impey," CR:265 (July 1911), 285-318.

B616 DIGHE, V. G. "Penal Code of the Peshwas," IHCP:10 (1947), 448-53. A summary of crimes and punishments on record.

B617 DOBBIN, CHRISTINE. "The Ilbert Bill: A Study of Anglo-Indian Opinion in India, 1883," HS:12 (Oct. 1965), 87-102.

B618 DUTT, L. P. "Administration of Justice in Bengal in the Last Decades of the 18th Century," IHRC:14 (1937), 27-32; BPP:54 (July-Dec. 1937), 18-25. Rough outline.

B619 FINK, H. R. "Crimes and Punishments under Hindu Law," CR 61:121 (1875), 123-41.

B620 FIRMINGER, W. K. (ed.). "Reprint of a Rare Pamphlet on the Nanda Kumar Trial," BPP:9 (Oct.-Dec. 1914), 259-81. By "A Gentleman Resident in Calcutta," published London, 1776.

B621 "The Fuller Case and Indian Appellate Courts," CR 66:131 (1878), 38-67. On application of criminal law to Eurasians.

B622 FYZEE, ASAF A. A. "Muhammadan Law in India," CSSH:5 (1962-63), 401-15. The sources of law in the pre-British era and modifications by the British.

B623 ———. "Shāh Muhammad Sulaimān (1886-1941)," IC:21 (Jan. 1947), 37-47. Biography of a chief justice of the Allahabad High Court.

B624 GADBOIS, GEORGE H., JR. "Evolution of the Federal Court of India: an Historical Footnote," ILI:5 (Jan.-March 1963), 19-45. Covers 1921-1935.

B625 ———. "The Federal Court of India: 1937-1950," ILI:6 (April 1964), 253-315.

B626 GOLDSMID, JULIAN. "Questions of the Day in India," NC:13 (May 1883), 740-58. Discusses the Ilbert Bill.

B627 HOBHOUSE, ARTHUR. "Last Words on Mr. Ilbert's Bill," CoR: 44 (Sept. 1883), 400-05. Recapitulation of the controversy.

B628 ———. "Native Indian Judges: Mr. Ilbert's Bill," CoR:43 (June 1883), 795-812.

B629 [HODGSON]. "Brian Houghton Hodgson," CR:104 (April 1897), 332-49.

B630 HODGSON, B. H. "On the Administration of Justice in Nepal, with Some Account of the Several Courts, Extent of Their Jurisdiction, and Modes of Procedure," AsR:20 (1836), 94-134.

B631 [IMPEY]. "Sir Elijah Impey," CR 7:14 (1847), 449-523. Review of his memoirs.

B632 "Indian and English Criminal Law," CR 43:86 (1866), 380-426.

B633 "Indian and English Criminal Procedure," CR 44:87 (1866), 105-50.

B634 "Indian Codification," CR:88 (April 1889), 358-78.

B635 "The Indian Contract Law," CR 46:92, 485-504.

B636 "Indian Judges, British and Native," ER:130 (Oct. 1869), 539-55.

B637 "Indian Law Reform," CR 7:14 (1847), 419-48; 43:86 (1866), 293-317.

B638   JARDINE, J. "Indian Official Opinions on Trial by Jury," AR, Ser. 2:5 (April 1893), 293-308.

B639   JOHNSTONE, D. C. "Recent Judicial Developments in India," AR, Ser. 3:12 (Oct. 1901), 260-80.

B640   "JUSTICE." "Administration of Justice in the Presidency of Bengal," MR:23 (June 1918), 605-12. With statistics of cases handed down from the High Court in 1916 and an outline of the court system.

B641   "The Law Courts of the Bengal Presidency," CR:34 (March 1860), 41-79.

B642   "Law in and for India," W:77 (Jan. 1862), 1-30. On the inequitable administration of justice.

B643   "The Law of Evidence in India and in England," CR:45 (May 1867), 126-54.

B644   "Law Reform," CR:6 (1846), 522-68. On British law in Bengal.

B645   LELE, P. R. "The Right to Sue the Secretary of State for India in Council," MR:21 (Jan. 1917), 45-52.

B646   "The Lex Loci; Marriage and Inheritance," CR 3:6 (1845), 323-74.

B647   LINDSAY, BENJAMIN. "Law," MIW, pp. 107-37. Its changes under British rule.

B648   LIPSTEIN, K. "The Reception of Western Law in India," ISSB:9 (1957), 85-95.

B649   MACKARNESS, FREDERIC. "The Law in England and in India Regarding Confessions to the Police," CoR:106 (July 1914), 52-58.

B650   "Macpherson on Procedure in the Company's Civil Courts," CR 15:29 (1851), 76-96.

B651   MACRAE, C. C. "Criminal Jurisdiction over Englishmen in India," FR:40 (Aug. 1883), 203-14. On the Ilbert Bill.

B652   MAINE, HENRY S. "Mr. Fitzjames Stephens' Introduction to the Indian Evidence Act," FR:19 (Jan.-June 1873), 51-67.

B653   MARKBY, WILLIAM. "Indian Law," EB:14, 434-46. On English, Hindu, and Muslim law, with a brief list of authorities.

B654   MATHUR, L. P. "The Origin of the Ilbert Bill," IHRC:30 (1954), 84-86. On the role of Behari Lal Gupta.

B655   MISRA, BANKEY BIHARI. "The Judicial Administration of the East India Company in Bengal 1765-1782," BRS:37 (1951), 153-274, 191-251; 38 (March, June 1952), 6-34, 245-93; 38 (Sept. & Dec. 1952), 377-409; 39 (March & June 1953), 107-84.

B656 MITRA, R. C. "Perjury under the Regulations of the East India Company," IHCP:23 (1961), 108-13. Discusses the effect of the British legal system in furthering the crime of perjury.

B657 ———. "Some Aspects of Judicial Administration for Indians in Chandernagore in 1791-1793," IHCP:9 (1946), 381-84. The effect of the French Revolution on judicial procedures.

B658 MITTER, BROJENDRA. "Lord Sinha," MR:43 (April 1928), 454-57. Biography of an advocate of the Calcutta Court.

B659 MITTER, S. C. "Judiciary in Free India," MR:83 (May 1948), 366-70. Present position and historical background.

B660 MORYNE, J. DAWSON. "Native Law in the Courts of the Madras Presidency," MJLS:23 (1855?), 1-36.

B661 MUKHERJI, TARIT KUMAR. "Aldermen and Attorneys—Mayor's Court, Calcutta, IHQ:26 (March 1950), 51-66. A closely documented narrative of the court's history, 1726-70.

B662 ———. "Dispute between Court Cutcherry and Mayor's Court, Calcutta," IHQ:27 (March 1951), 35-43. A series of clashes over jurisdiction in mid-18th cent.

B663 NELSON, J. H. "The Administration of Justice in Madras," FR:34 (July-Dec. 1880), 300-11.

B664 "Non-Regulation Justice," CR:32 (June 1859), 251-78. On justice in the Punjab.

B665 "Notes on Criminal Justice," CR:87 (Oct. 1888), 278-87.

B666 "On the Administration of Justice in British India, with the State of the King's Courts and Juries There," OH:6 (Aug. 1825), 279-89; 7 (Oct. 1825), 22-34. Critical opinions.

B667 "On the Study of Law in Our Indian Colleges," CR:7 (1847), 105-23.

B668 "Our Judicial System and the Black Acts," CR 13:26 (1850), 345-91.

B669 "The Penal Code," CR 28:55 (March 1857), 47-80.

B670 "POLITICUS." "Separation of Judicial and Executive Functions," MR:21 (June 1917), 700-10.

B671 "The Public Service Commission and Judicial Reform," CR:88 (Jan. 1889), 171-209.

B672 PUGH, LEWIS PUGH. "Idealistic Legislation in India," CoR:44 (July 1883), 32-37. Comments on Hobhouse's comments on the Ilbert Bill.

B673 "PUNJABI." "The Law of Easements in the Panjab and the Formation of Customary Law," CR 69:137 (1879), 128-45.

B674 RAICHOUDHURI, P. C. "Jury System in India," MR:96 (Aug. 1954), 125-29. Its history.

B675 ———. "Warren Hastings and the Adalat System of Bengal," MR:97 (June 1955), 484-87.

B676 RĀM RĀZ. "On the Introduction of Trial by Jury in the Hon. East India Company's Courts of Law. . . ." RAS:3 (1836), 244-57.

B677 RAMSBOTHAM, R. B. "The Munsiffs: an Account of Their Origin under the Judicial Administration of the East India Company," JIH:4 (Jan. 1926), 94-104; IHRC:8 (Nov. 1925), 61-69. A letter dated 1778 from Edward Otto Ives and facts on court reforms behind the origin of munsiffs.

B678 RASHID, SH. ABDUR (tr.). "A Contemporary Account of Judicial Administration in Oudh during the Time of Wajid Ali Shah 1847-56," IHRC:31 (1955), 164-69.

B679 RAY, NARESHCHANDRA. "The Indian Judge (A Comparative Study)," CR:26 (Feb. 1928), 151-79. A learned attack on the judicial system.

B680 RAY, NIKHILRANJAN. "The Press and the Law in Contempt of Court in India (a Critical Study)," CR:101 (Oct. 1946), 41-54.

B681 ———. "The Press and the Law of Contempt of Court of India (Scandalising the Court)," CR:95 (May, June 1945), 43-48, 85-89.

B682 "Reporting in India," CR 46:91, 4-43. On the reporting of law cases and decisions.

B683 [RIPON]. "Lord Ripon's 'Small Measure,' " BM:134 (July 1883), 117-32. Ilbert Bill.

B684 RUNGTA, R. S. "Indian Company Law Problems in 1850," AJLH:6 (1962), 298-308. Summary in HA:9 (No. 412): "Effects of the Indian Companies Act of 1850, . . . the first piece of legislation showing an interest in commercial institutions on the part of the Indian government." Based on published legislative materials and previous studies.

B685 "S." "Penal Code for India," W:31 (Aug. 1838), 393-405.

B686 SHAW, JOHN. "The Predecessors of the High Court of Madras," MJLS (1880), 21-53; (1881), 81-157. The first article covers the period to 1726, the second to 1862.

B687 SINNET, A. P. "Anglo-Indian Complications, and Their Cause," FR:40 (Sept. 1883), 407-21. Anti-Ilbert Bill.

B688 "Some Legal and Constitutional Aspects of the Crawford Case," CR:89 (Oct. 1889), 390-409.

B689 SRINIVASACHARI, C. S. "Early Stages in the Development of the Madras Judiciary," BRS:30 (1944), 211-28; 31 (1945), 8-17, 135-47.

B690 ———. "The Recorder's Court in Madras (1798-1801) and Some of Its Findings," IHRC:27 (1950), 62-72. Summary of some cases.

B691 [STEPHEN]. "Mr. Stephen's Minute on the Administration of Justice in British India," CR 56:112 (1873), 236-62.

B692 STEPHEN, J. FITZJAMES. "Codification in India and England," FR:18 (Dec. 1872), 644-72. State of the law in India and the bearing it may have on the state of law in England.

B693 ———. "Foundations of the Government of India," NC:14 (Oct. 1883), 541-58. On the Ilbert Bill.

B694 SUBRAMANIAN, M. C. "Attempts to Introduce Judicial Reforms in Madras 1763-1800," IHRC:20 (1943), 8-11.

B695 SUTHERLAND, LUCY S. "A Letter from John Stewart, Secretary and Judge Advocate of Bengal, 1773," IA:10 (1956), 1-12.

B696 ———. "New Evidence on the Nandakuma Trial," EHR:72 (July 1957), 438-65. Reprints portions of Vansittart's journal relating to the trial.

B697 SYKES, JNO. G. W. "On Contract: an Essay towards a Popular Introduction to the Indian Contract Act of 1872," CR 61:122 (1875), 245-80.

B698 THAKUR, VASUDEO V. "The Honourable Chief Justice Rama Shastri Prabhune of the Poona Supreme Court," IHRC:16 (1939), 206-10. His decisions on cases.

B699 "Torture in Madras," CR 29:58 (Dec. 1857), 439-66. On justice in Madras.

B700 "Trial by Jury in Bengal," CR:86 (Jan. 1888), 131-69.

B701 "Trial by Jury in India," CR 14:28 (1850), 409-20.

B702 "The Trial of Maharaja Nana Kumar:—a Narrative of a Judicial Murder," CR:82 (Jan., April 1886), 100-92, 303-438.

B703 "The True Foundations of British Rule in India," QJPSS:6 (Nov. 1883), 1-36. On the need to associate Indians in the judicial system.

B704 "Unpaid Native Agency," CR 42:84 (1865), 245-58. On local magistrates.

B705 VAN VOLLENHOVEN, C. "Aspects of the Controversy on Customary Law in India," AR: NS 23 (1927), 113-28. A scholarly historical study.

B706 WEST, RAYMOND. "Mr. Justice Telang," RAS (1894), pp. 103-47. Tribute to Bombay judge, 1850-1893?

B707 WHITE, G. S. "The Judges of the Supreme Court at Madras, (1801-1862), JIH:18 (Aug. 1939), 155-78. "The object of this paper is to give some description of the Judges of the Court, a reference to the practice or procedure of the Court and to quote some of the cases disposed of by them."

9. POLICE AND JAILS

B708 BALIGA, B. S. "Prison Administration in Madras, 1802-1840," IHRC:20 (1943), 3-6.

B709 BASU, K. K. "British Jails in India in the Late 18th Century," PU:2 (Aug. 1945), 23-24.

B710 "The Bengal Police," CR:59 (1874), 113-38, 379-403. History, 1862-1874.

B711 "Bengal Police Reform," CR:92 (April 1891), 282-304.

B712 CHATTERJEE, NANDALAL. "Exclusion of High Caste Hindus from Oudh Police after the Mutiny," IHRC:29 (1953), 13-14. From records at Lucknow.

B713 "The Corruption of the Police—Its Causes and Remedies," CR 3:5 (1845), 147-64.

B714 C[OTTON], H. J. S. "The Bengal Police," CR 56:111 (1873), 87-105.

B715 "Criminal Statistics and Jail Discipline in Bengal," CR:30 (June 1858), 266-304.

B716 DE, S. C. "Cuttack Jail in 1859," OHRJ:3 (June 1954), 45-47. The report of an inspector.

B717 GHOSE, SAILEN. "Stray Notes on Calcutta Police in 1791," IHRC:31 (1955), 161-63.

B718 GILES, A. H. "Detective Experiences in Bengal," CR 80:160 (1885), 280-334. A police officer's comments on the police system.

B719 "Indian Jail Industry," CR 29:57 (Sept. 1857), 18-34.

B720 "Jail Discipline in the N.W.P.," CR 27:53 (Sept. 1856), 17-41.

B721 "Jail Discipline in the Punjab," CR:37 (Dec. 1861), 225-44.

B722 MACAULIFFE, M. "The Panjab Police," CR:79 (1884), 416-39; 80 (1885), 72-96.

B723 "The Madras Constabulary," CR:35 (Dec. 1860), 350-70.

B724 MAJUMDAR, NIHARKANA. "Justice and Police in Bengal in 1765," CR:142 (March 1957), 317-28; 143 (April 1957), 25-39. On the "framework and functioning of the indigenous system of criminal administration of Bengal about 1765."

B725 MATHUR, Y. B. "Jail Administration in the Punjab, 1849-75," JIH:43 (April 1965), 159-82.

B726 "Military Officers in the Indian Police," CR:85 (Oct. 1888), 284-96.

B727 MULVANY, JOHN. "Bengal Jails in Early Days," CR:293 (July 1918), 293-316.

B728 ———. "Two Notable Prison Administrators in Bengal. Frederick J. Mouat and Alfred Swayne Lethbridge," CR:291 (Jan. 1918), 73-104.

B729 "The New Police," CR 42:84 (1865), 329-68.

B730 "Police and Police Courts in British India," CR 79:157 (1884), 21-38.

B731 "The Police in the North West," CR:37 (Dec. 1861), 327-42. Defects in the system in the Northwest Provinces.

B732 "The Police of Bengal," CR 41:81 (1865), 26-68.

B733 "The Police of Calcutta," CR:87 (Oct. 1888), 306-22; 88 (Jan. 1889), 9-28.

B734 "Prison Discipline in Bengal," CR 23:45 (1854), 106-35.

B735 "Prison Discipline in India," CR 6:12 (1846), 449-99.

B736 "Prison Management," CR 53:105 (1871), 29-56.

B737 "Revelations Concerning the Police and Courts," CR 11:22 (1849), 318-96. On scandals in mofussil courts.

B738 ROY, N. B. "Interesting Episode of an Outbreak in Bihar Jails, 1855," IHRC:33 (1958), 130-40. Extracts from judicial proceedings.

B739 SEN, DAKSHINACHARAN. "Bengal Police Administration Report for the Year 1913 and Detection of Penal Code Offences by the Police," MR:17 (June 1915), 705-09.

B740 "The Village Police of Bengal," CR:87 (Oct. 1888), 203-12.

PART I: ARTICLES

10. *THE MILITARY*

B741 ABBASI, MOHAMMAD MADNI. "Nawab Sumroo of Sardhana," PR:4 (April 1956), 37-38. Story of Walter Reinhart, soldier of fortune.

B742 ADYE, JOHN. "Native Armies of India," NC:7 (April 1880), 685-709. On the history of Indian soldiers in British service.

B743 AIYER, P. S. SIVASWAMY. "The Army and Navy in India," AAAPSS:145 (Sept. 1929), suppl. 19-26.

B744 ARCHER, MILDRED. "The Two Worlds of Colonel Skinner 1778-1841," HT:10 (Sept. 1960), 608-15. Biography of Anglo-Indian adventurer, with pictures from his album of paintings. The two worlds are Indian and British.

B745 "The Army in India," QR:116 (Oct. 1864), 413-39.

B746 "The Army of India," ER:161 (April 1885), 388-423. Based on House of Commons papers.

B747 "Army Reform," CR:27 (Sept. 1856), 94-149. Just before the Mutiny.

B748 ARTHUR GEORGE. "Lord Curzon and Lord Kitchener," FR:84 (Aug. 1905), 244-53. On their controversy over military administration.

B749 ATKINSON, C. T. "A Cavalry Regiment of the Mahratta Wars," SAHR:33 (1955), 80-87. History of the 27th Light Dragoons.

B750 ———. "In the Days of John Company; the Early Services of the King's Troops in India," SAHR:32 (1954), 111-17. History of regiments under the Company.

B751 ATKINSON, CHARLES FRANCIS. "Army: Indian Army," EB:2, 615-16. A concise history of the British army's composition and organization.

B752 AUCHINLECK, CLAUDE. "The Armies of India, 1668-1947," RIGB:34 (1951), 587-98. Brief history of organization and activity, and brief account of splitting the armies at Partition.

B753 "AVUNCULUS." "A Subaltern's Prospects in the Indian Army," FR:100 (July 1913), 147-57.

B754 BALFOUR, E. "Number of Soldiers Discharged from the Madras Army," MJLS:15 (1847?), 554-68.

B755 BANERJEA, PRAMATHANATH. "Military Expenditure of the East India Company," CR:23 (June 1927), 410-26. The pay of Indian and British soldiers in different branches of the services.

[124]

B756 BARAT, AMIYA. "The European Officers of the Bengal Native Infantry (1796-1852)," BPP:80 (July-Dec. 1961), 110-23.

B757 "Barrackpore Massacre—Burmese War—and Present State of the Native Army in Bengal," OH:5 (April 1825), 13-33.

B758 BARTON, W. P. "Caste and the Indian Military Problem," CoR: 140 (Dec. 1931), 709-17. Says caste emasculated Hindus.

B759 ———. "The World War and the Problem of the Defence of India," QR:278 (Jan. 1942), 99-114.

B760 BASU, B. D. "Reorganisation of the Indian Army after the Mutiny," MR:40 (Sept. 1926), 268-73.

B761 BEATSON, F. C. "The Recent Military Policy of the Government of India," NC:82 (Aug. 1917), 260-75. Expenses of the Indian Army in Mesopotamia.

B762 "The Bengal Artillery," CR 9:18 (1848), 415-510. Brief history.

B763 "The Bengal Cavalry," CR:26 (June 1856), 549-91.

B764 "The Bengal Commissariat," CR:54 (1872), 144-58, 267-84; 55 (1872), 314-24. On military organization.

B765 BIDDULPH, H. (ed.). "The European Army in India after the Indian Mutiny: Captain R. Biddulph's Memorandum," SAHR:18 (1939), 11-15. A memo on organization, Aug. 31, 1860.

B766 BOULGER, DEMETRIUS. "The Armies of Native India," AR:8 (Oct. 1889), 257-79.

B767 "Broome's History of the Bengal Army," CR 14:28 (1850), 497-540.

B768 [BUCKLE]. "Captain Buckle's History of the Bengal Artillery," CR 12:24 (1849), 329-47.

B769 BULLOCK, H. "Some Soldiers of Fortune," BPP:41 (Jan.-June 1931), 143-48; 42 (July-Dec. 1931), 93-101; 43 (Jan.-June 1932), 30-36; 44 (July-Dec. 1932), 61-69; 49 (Jan.-June 1935), 83-92; 50 (July-Dec. 1935), 5-15, 114-20; 51 (Jan.-June 1936), 7-18. Brief histories.

B770 CADELL, PATRICK (ed.). "The Autobiography of an Indian Soldier," SAHR:37 (1959), 3-11, 49-56. Summary of "From Sepoy to Subadar" by Sitaram Pande, with comments.

B771 ———. "The Beginnings of Khaki," SAHR:31 (1953), 132-33. On the introduction of the khaki uniform c. 1850.

B772 ——— (ed.). "The Indian Mutiny Journal of Private Charles Wickins of the 90th Light Infantry," SAHR:35 (1957), 96-108, 170-74; 36 (1958), 17-24, 80-86, 130-36.

B773 ———. "The Raising of the Indian Army," SAHR:34 (1956), 96-99. Brief history, with principal dates, of army organization.

B774 CARDEW, F. G. "Major-General Sir David Ochterlony, Bart., G.C.B. 1758-1825," SAHR:10 (Jan. 1931), 40-63. A biography.

B775 ———. "Native Army of India," BM:162 (Aug. 1897), 194-206.

B776 "The Career of an Indian General; Sir Charles MacGregor, K.C.B.," BM:144 (Nov. 1888), 664-80.

B777 CHAND, BOOL. "Military Booty in British India," IHRC:25 (Dec. 1948), 131-35.

B778 CHATTERJI, NANDALAL. "Lord Wellesley and the Provincial Battalions," JIH:31 (April 1953), 107-10. The organization, duties, and composition of provincial battalions.

B779 CHAUDHURI, HARIPADO. "The Vellore Mutiny," MR:98 (Aug. 1955), 125-28. A reappraisal.

B780 CHAUDHURI, NIRAD C. "Cost of the Troops in Bengal," MR: 57 (April 1935), 400-03.

B781 ———. "India and Imperial Defence," MR:49 (April 1931), 386-96. Evolution of policy.

B782 ———. "The 'Martial Races' of India," MR:48 (July, Sept. 1930), 41-51, 295-307; 49 (Jan., Feb. 1931), 67-79, 215-28. Based on information in the Simon Report and on the Peel Commission Report (1859) on the Organization of the Indian Army.

B783 [CLYDE]. "The Life of Colin Campbell, Lord Clyde," CR 73:146 (1881), 223-52. Early 19th cent. soldier.

B784 COHEN, STEPHEN P. "Officer Tradition in the Indian Army," USI:94 (Jan. 1964), 32-38.

B785 [COKE]. "Soldier of the Frontier; Coke of Coke's Rifles," BM:163 (June 1798), 765-78.

B786 "Considerations on the Present State of the Native Army of India. By an Indian Officer," OH:7 (Oct. 1825), 121-28.

B787 CREAGH, O'MOORE. "Report of the Army in India Committee of 1919-1920," NC:88 (Nov. 1920), 888-97. A far right point of view on Indian defense.

B788 DATTA, KALIKINKAR. "Parliamentary Enactment for Military Discipline in India, 1754," PU:2 (Aug. 1945), 1-5.

B789 ———. "Recruits for the Company's Troops in Bihar, 1754-57," BRS:31 (1945), 121-23. A note on their number and duration of service.

B790 "The Defence of the Country," CR 29:57 (1857), 97-120. On army reform; written before the Mutiny.

B791 "The Demise of the Indian Army," BM:90 (July 1861), 100-14. On its reorganization.

B792 "Esher Committee Report," MR:29 (March 1921), 369-75. Commission to report on the organization of the army in India, 1919-20.

B793 "The European Soldier in India," CR:30 (March 1858), 121-48.

B794 EWART, J. SPENCER. "Colonel Edward Hamilton of the Honourable East India Company's Service," BM:208 (Dec. 1920), 771-96. Based on a memoir Hamilton dictated to his wife.

B795 FAWCETT, R. H. "The Native Army of Madras," CR 70:139 (1880), 533-42.

B796 [GARDNER]. "A Soldier of Fortune in the East," BM:164 (July 1898), 116-31. Alexander Haughton Gardner.

B797 GODE, P. K. "The Manufacture and Use of Fire-arms in India between A.D. 1450 and 1850," BV:9 (1948), 202-28.

B798 GOLDSMID, F. J. "The Native Armies of India," AR:6 (July 1888), 17-44.

B799 "Great Battles and the E. I. Co's Army," CR 23:45 (1854), 96-105.

B800 GREG, W. R. "Employment of Our Asiatic Forces in European Wars," FR:29 (June 1878), 834-49. Discusses the effect of the militaristically trained Indian on England's ambitions.

B801 GRIER, SYDNEY C. "The Mutiny at Vellore in 1806," BPP:28 (Oct.-Dec. 1924), 166-80. From records and letters.

B802 GUTTERIDGE, WILLIAM. "The Indianisation of the Indian Army, 1918-1945; A Case Study," R:4 (May 1963), 39-48.

B803 HALL, J. T. S. "The Royal Indian Navy," RCAS:32 (Jan. 1945), 68-79. A historical sketch.

B804 HARDEN, F. G. "Uniforms of the Indian Soldier," USI:94 (July 1964), 290-96.

B805 HARRIS, C. "Cardwell System and India," NC:124 (Aug. 1938), 178-86. On British garrison in India.

B806 "Havelock," CR:35 (Sept. 1860), 228-79. On Major General Sir Henry Havelock.

B807 HILL, S. CHARLES. "Major Randfurlie Knox, Dilawar Jang Bahadur: a Memoir," BORS:3 (Mar. 1917), 99-163. The life of an Irish officer.

B808 ———. "The Old Sepoy Officer," EHR:28 (April, July 1913), 260-91, 497-514. History of Indian officers in the Madras army, with narratives about individual officers.

B809 HOBBS, HENRY. "American in India," BPP:66 (1946-47), 19-32. Quotations from other works on the careers of Sir David Ochterlony and Dr. Josiah Harlan.

B810 ———. "Cadets," BPP:55 (Jan.-June 1938), 202-33. Discourse on their life.

B811 "Hodson," BM:165 (March 1899), 522-39. Of Hodson's Horse.

B812 HODSON, V. (ed.). "The Baraset Cadet College, East Indies," SAHR:2 (July 1923), 130-36. Account of insubordination at the Company's military school near Calcutta in 1810.

B813 ———. "The So-Called 'Mutiny' of the Officers of the Bengal Army in 1796," BPP:36 (July-Dec. 1928), 69-80. Prints letters on it.

B814 HOLMES, T. R. E. "Last Words on Hodson of Hodson's Horse," EHR:7 (Jan. 1892), 48-79. On the truth of allegations against Hodson's motives.

B815 "The Horse-Supply in India," BM:141 (Feb. 1887), 265-79. For military purposes.

B816 "The Horse Supply of India," CR 57:113 (1873), 101-29.

B817 HOSTEN, H. (ed.). "Some Old Records of the Madras Army (1757-1759)," ASB:12 (1916), 273-86. Lists of records, ships, French prisoners.

B818 "India and the War," CR 52:103 (1871), 1-21. The Indian military situation.

B819 "The Indian Army," BM:21 (May 1827), 563-74.

B820 "The Indian Army," ER:97 (Jan. 1853), 183-220.

B821 "The Indian Army," CR 26:51 (March 1856), 177-210. On the necessity for reforms. Also see CR:89 (Oct. 1889), 225-50.

B822 JEFFREYS, H. B. "An Indian Problem," CoR:101 (Jan. 1912), 30-38. On native officers.

B823 JHA, ADITYA PRASAD. "The First Mutiny in the Bengal Army, 1764," BRS:42 (March 1956), 24-35.

B824 KAMATH, M. SUBRAYA. "The Real Incidence of Military Expenditure in India," MR:29 (Jan. 1921), 61-62. Background to the Esher Report.

B825 KEENE, H. G. "Indian Military Adventurers of the Last Century," CR 71:141 (1880), 55-85.

B826 KHANNA, D. D. "Supply System of Wellington's Army in India," USI:94 (April 1964), 195-99.

B827 KHERA, P. N. "Impact of India's Foreign Policy on Her Military Policy and the Role of the Army in India, 1899-1921," QRHS 4:4 (1964/65), 195-202.

B828 ———. "Role of the Indian Army, 1900-1939," USI:94 (July 1964), 277-89.

B829 KINCAID, C. A. and W.C.S. "Two Sepoys," BM:206 (Aug. 1919), 204-13. Stories of 2 Indian soldiers who served in Mesopotamia.

B830 [KITCHENER]. "Lord Kitchener in India," BM:186 (Aug. 1909), 153-65. His administration of the army.

B831 KUNZRU, HIRDAY NATH. "Defense of India," AAAPSS:233 (May 1944), 6-11. A survey of the armed forces by the president of the Servants of India Society.

B832 [LAKE]. "Lord Lake," CR 43:85 (1866), 1-56.

B833 ———. "Memoir of the Late Right Hon. Gerard Lake, . . ." AAR:8 (1806), part 2, "Characters," 1-9.

B834 [LAWRENCE]. "Stringer Lawrence," BM:171 (Feb. 1902), 205-21. "The Father of the Indian Army."

B835 LESLIE, J. H. "Materials for a History of the Bombay Army," SAHR:10 (1931), 155-61, 218-22. Lists of regiments and officers.

B836 "Letter of a Bengal Officer, on Certain Grievances of the Indian Army," OH:5 (May 1825), 422-27.

B837 "Low's History of the Indian Navy," ER:148 (Oct. 1878), 343-79.

B838 "M.B." "The Defense of India," BIN:17 (Aug. 10, 1940), 993-1004. Summary of problems.

B839 MACMUNN, GEORGE. "The Indianization of the Indian Army," BM:217 (March 1925), 419-28. The pros and cons.

B840 ———. "A Lost Legion; the Story of the Oudh Irregular Force," SAHR:13 (1934), 74-81.

B841 "The Madras Native Army," CR:33 (Sept. 1859), 127-57.

B842 MARSH, T. A. PERRY. "Our Young Soldiers in India," W:146 (Aug. 1896), 156-68. Their mortality rate.

B843 MAXWELL, E. L. "Umedwars," CM, Ser. 3: 37 (Nov. 1914), 708-18. A popular account of recruiting in the Punjab.

B844 "Military Defence of our Empire in the East," CR:2 (Oct. 1844), 32-72.

B845 "Military Society in India—and Chapters of Indian Experience," CR 22:44 (1854), 429-58.

B846 MIROSHNIKOV, LEV IVANOVICH. "The Role of the Indian Army in Persia, Transcaucasia and Turkestan, 1914-1920: A Soviet Historian's Interpretation," CAR:12 (1964), 156-59; tr. from NAA (1963).

B847 MISRA, G. S. "Napoleon's Egyptian Expedition and Its Repercussions on Wellesley's Policy," UPHS: NS 3 (1955), 62-80. On military policy vis-à-vis the French; from India Office Library documents.

B848 MOJUMDAR, KANCHANMOY. "Recruitment of the Gurkhas in the Indian Army, 1814-1877," USI:93 (April-June 1963), 143-57. From papers at Katmandu, Delhi, Punjab Record Office, Oxford, London, and printed sources.

B849 MOLONY, J. CHARTRES. "The Dusky Legion," BM:239 (May 1936), 707-24. World War I experience with the Madras Volunteer Guards ("The Mudguards").

B850 ———. "A Soldier of Old India," BM:252 (Nov. 1942), 290-99. On Frederick Young, Gurkha officer.

B851 MOOKERJEE, H. C. "Organisation for Recruitment in the Punjab in the Last War," CR:90 (Feb. 1944), 73-80. The regulations during World War I.

B852 ———. "Organisation of the Punjab Recruitment," CR:90 (March 1944), 151-59. In World War I.

B853 ———. "The War of 1914-18 and the Appearance of Discontent," CR:83 (June 1942), 211-34; 84 (July-Sept. 1942), 1-22, 111-21, 203-14. Refers to the Indian section of the Indian Army.

B854 "Mortality of European Soldiers in India," CR 16:31 (1851), 33-76.

B855 "The Native Indian Army," QJPSS:7 (Jan. 1885), 13-43.

B856 [O'BRIEN]. "The Strange and Eventful History of Cormac O'Brien," BM:229 (April 1931), 485-95. Story of a soldier of fortune, early 19th cent.

B857 "On the Existing Discontent in the Indian Army," OH:6 (Aug. 1825), 256-67.

B858 "Origin and State of the Indian Army," QR:18 (Jan. 1818), 388-423.

B859 "Our Military Establishment," CR 10:20 (1848), 369-403.

B860 [PEARSE]. "An Anglo-Indian Worthy," BM:185 (May 1909), 706-19. Col. Thomas Deane Pearse.

B861 "Recent Military Memoirs," CR 14:28 (1850), 265-95.

B862 "Recruiting and Army Reform," CR 43:86 (1866), 461-86.

B863 REID, ROBERT. "The Assam Rifles in Peace and War," BM:261 (May 1947), 414-22.

B864 "The Reorganization of the Army," CR:45 (May 1867), 106-25.

B865 "Reorganization of the Indian Army," CR:33 (Sept. 1859), 186-251.

B866 RITCHIE, C. "A Sepoy Muster Book of 1768," SAHR:32 (1954), 18-23. With miscellaneous information on sepoy units.

B867 ROACH, JOHN. "The 39th Regiment of Foot and the East India Company, 1754-57," JRL:41 (Sept. 1958), 102-38. The first royal regiment to serve in India; a very detailed narrative of their story. Based on papers of Col. Samuel Bagshawe in the John Rylands Library and papers in the India Office Library.

B868 RUSSELL, W. W. "The Story of the Indian Air Force," AR: NS 41 (Jan. 1945), 28-35. Illustrated.

B869 SARKAR, JADUNATH. "Some European Soldiers of Fortune," BPP:65 (1945), 1-6. Names of Europeans in Persian *ākhbārāt*—in hopes some reader will identify them.

B870 "Scheme for the Amalgamation of the Indian and British Armies," CR:36 (March 1861), 144-57.

B871 "Services of Distinguished Military Officers in India," OH:4 (Jan. 1825), 53-62.

B872 "Skinner of Skinner's Horse," BM:170 (Sept. 1901), 374-88.

B873 SRINIVASACHARI, C. S. "The Vellore Mutiny of 1806. A New Study of Its Origin," IHCP:11 (1948), 195-98. Stresses the factor of religion.

B874 STANLEY, ARTHUR. "Gillespie of Vellore," AQ:22 (July 1931), 337-44. Career of officer in command against the mutineers.

B875 STEELE, RUSSELL V. "The Uniform of European and Native Troops in the British Service in India, 1760-1860," SAHR:13 (1934), 189-213. Illustrated.

B876 ———. "Uniforms at Addiscombe," SAHR:33 (1955), 40 and plate. Photograph of cadet uniforms, c. 1855.

B877 STEIN, AUREL. "Notes on the Life and Labours of Captain Anthony Troyer," ASB, Ser. 3 (Letters): 6 (1940), 45-59. Austrian who served with the British in India.

B878 TEMPLE, RICHARD. "The Native Armies of India," CoR:47 (May 1885), 617-26. On British-run and princely forces.

B879 THORBURN, S. S. "Impressment for Transport in India," BM:171 (March 1902), 382-92. On army transport on the North West Frontier.

B880 VAKIL, C. N. "Employment of Indian Troops out of India," MR:32 (Sept. 1922), 301-07. Lists of the more important expeditions in which Indian troops were employed, 1838-1920.

B881 VERNEY, FREDERICK W. "Our Armies in India," NC:17 (June 1885), 1009-1020. The need for reform.

B882 WALLACE, ROBERT. "Object-Lesson for the Indian Government; the Transport Service and Health of Our Army in India," BM:163 (Feb. 1898), 262-72.

B883 "Ways and Means of Meeting the Additional Army Expenditure," QJPSS:7 (Feb. 1885), 1-30.

B884 "Wellington in India," CR 27:54 (Dec. 1856), 376-430.

B885 WILLCOCKS, JAMES. "The Indian Army Corps in France," BM:202 (July 1917), 1-33.

B886 WYNDHAM, HORACE. "When Napier Ruled in India; Iron Hand in Velvet Glove," AQ:44 (April 1942), 133-42. On his military administration.

B887 YATE, A. C. "India 1878-1918: Disraeli Vindicated," NC:84 (Dec. 1918), 1063-77. The role of the Indian Army in 40 years of British wars.

B888 YUSUF ALI, A. "India's Services in the War," CoR:108 (Oct. 1915), 446-56. Brief review of India's services during first year of World War I.

11. LOCAL SELF-GOVERNMENT

B889 "All-India Local Self-Government Statistics 1931-32," LSGI:4 (April 1934), 2-89. Income and expenses of District councils and municipalities throughout India. This is a regular feature in LSGI, which also regularly prints more detailed statistics about local self-government in Bombay State.

B890   BARFIVALA, CHUNILAL D. "The Bombay Village Panchayats Act, 1933, and the Rules Thereunder (as Amended up to March 31, 1944) (A Study)," LSGI:14 (April 1944), 341-434; 15 (July, Oct. 1944, Jan. 1945), 1-18, 19-42, 43-74; 16 (July 1945, Jan. 1946), 75-90, 91-110.

B891   ——. "Rao Bahadur R.R. Kale, B.A., L.L.B., M.L.C., Advocate (O.S.) Satara. President of the Maharashtra Branch of the Local Self-Government Institute; A Biographical Sketch," LSGI:3 (July 1932), 13-17.

B892   BOMAN-BEHRAM, B. K. "The Rise of Municipal Government in the City of Ahmedabad, BUJ:4 (Jan. 1936), 40-63. From records in the Bombay Government Secretariat.

B893   "Bombay Marches On . . . Local Self-Government," LSGI:22 (Oct. 1951), 275-97.

B894   DAR, M. B. L. "Development of Local Self-Government in India (With Special Reference to the United Provinces)," LSGI:20 (July 1949), 1-9. Background in ancient, Mughal, and British times.

B895   "Delhi Municipal Committee Marches On: A Review of 90 Years of Progress," LSGI:24 (Oct. 1953), 104-10.

B896   "District Boards and County Council," CR:95 (Oct. 1892), 267-85.

B897   "The District Municipal Improvement Act," CR 42:83 (1865), 26-56.

B898   FRASER, A. H. L. "Local Self-Government in the Central Provinces of India," FR:45 (Jan.-June 1886), 238-47.

B899   KABIR, ROKEYA RAHMAN. "Local Self-Government in Bengal," ASP:7 (June 1962), 138-90. Legislative history to 1887, and some data on membership to local boards.

B900   KATHIA, N. K. "The Administrative and Financial Control of Municipalities and District Boards in the United Provinces: Control over Local Board Structure," LSGI:25 (July 1954), 93-169.

B901   "Local Self-Government and the Puri Address," CR:94 (April 1892), 406-17.

B902   "Local Self-Government in India," W:121 (Jan. 1884), 63-83.

B903   "Local Self-Government in Orissa," LSGI:21 (July 1950), 1-21. A very short history.

B904   "Local Self-Government in the Bombay Presidency," QJPSS:6 (no. 3, 1883), 27-76; (no. 4, 1883), 23-61.

B905 MALLIK, S. N. "Local Self-Government in India," AAAPSS:145 (Suppl., Sept. 1929), 36-44. Historical survey.

B906 MANGUDKAR, M. P. "The Constitutional Development of Local Self-Government in India during the Last 100 Years," LSGI:25 (Jan. 1955), 629-39.

B907 "Municipal Betterment Act and State Taxation," CR:92 (April 1891), 361-90.

B908 NAIK, S. S. "Village Panchayats in the Mysore State in 1931-32," LSGI:4 (July 1933), 22-28. Summary of annual report.

B909 NAYAK, B. J. "An Analytical Study of the Bombay Local Boards Act, 1923 (Act. VI of 1923)," LSGI:28 (July, Oct. 1957), 128-96, 369-414.

B910 NEELKANTHAN, K. "Growth and Development of Local Bodies in Kerala," LSGI:31 (April 1961), 551-80.

B911 "Observations on Local Self-Government in Bengal," CR 78:155 (1884), 157-65.

B912 PILLAY, K. P. K. "Local Self-Government in Madras Presidency," LSGI:22 (July, Oct. 1951), 85-167, 298-337; 23 (July 1952), 71-148.

B913 "Practical Experience of Local Self-Government in Bengal," CR:87 (Oct. 1888), 234-46.

B914 PRASAD, RAMAYAN. "Local Self-Government in Vindhya Pradesh," LSGI:31 (April 1961), 475-539. Traces development.

B915 RAM, V. S. and LOOMBA, A. L. "Village Panchayats in the United Provinces," LSGI:5 (Jan. 1935), 1-10. Historical account.

B916 ROY, NARESH CHANDRA. "Local Self-Government in Bengal (Evolution of District and Local Boards)," LSGI:5 (Oct. 1934), 49-65.

B917 ———. "Village Self-Government in Bengal (Its Evolution)," LSGI:5 (July 1934), 33-42.

B918 ———. "Village Self-Government in Bengal," LSGI:5 (Jan. 1935), 135-68.

B919 SAMANT, S. V. "Village Panchayats," LSGI:28 (July, Oct. 1957), 1-127, 264-334. History and evolution of the village as an institution in India; last part mostly about present-day finances.

B920 SHAH, RASIKCHANDRA G. "The Growth of Local Self-Government in the Presidency since 1858," LSGI:11 (July, Oct. 1940), 71-138, 267-312. Bombay Presidency.

B921 SHARIB, ZAHURUL HASSAN. "The Development of Town Area Committees in Uttar Pradesh," LSGI:27 (July 1956), 66-88. Gives historical background.

B922 SHARMA, M. P. "The Evolution of Rural Local Self-Government and Administration in U.P.," LSGI:25 (Oct. 1954, Jan., April 1955), 369-429, 431-89, 675-760; 26 (July, Oct. 1955), 34-81, 253-70.

B923 TEMPLE, RICHARD. "Local Self-Government in India: the New Departure," CoR:43 (March 1883), 373-82. Hopes for Ripon's scheme.

B924 THAKORE, J. M. "Development of Local Self-Government in Bombay and Saurashtra," LSGI:27 (Oct. 1956), 159-206.

B925 ———. "A Monograph on Local Self-Government in Saurashtra," LSGI:22 (Jan. 1952), 391-496.

B926 VENKATARANGAIYA, M. "The Constitutional Development of Local Boards in the Madras Presidency," LSGI:3 (Oct. 1932), 25-47.

B927 ———. "Local Self-Government in India," LSGI:31 (Oct. 1960), 329-45. The history of local self-government for 4,000 years; no footnotes.

B928 ———. "The Tax-Revenues of Local Boards in Madras Presidency; A Historical Survey," LSGI:8 (Oct. 1937), 96-115. Figures from 1873 to 1924.

B929 VENKATA RAO, V. "Administration of District Boards in Madras Presidency," LSGI:22 (July, Oct. 1951), 1-83, 201-62; 22 (Jan., April 1952), 343-90, 407-48; 23 (July 1952, Jan. 1953), 1-46, 279-316.

B930 ———. "A Hundred Years of Local Government in Andhra and Madras," LSGI:28 (April 1958), 675-730; 29 (July 1958, Jan., April 1959), 109-73, 319-80, 548-80; 30 (July, Oct. 1959, Jan. 1960), 1-60, 151-204, 325-412; 31 (July 1960), 1-78.

12. BENGAL, BIHAR, AND ORISSA, 1750 TO 1773

B931 ABDUL ALI, A. F. M. "Kedgeree—A Bygone Seaport of the Gangetic Delta," BPP:48 (July-Dec. 1934), 5-11.

B932 ———. "Munny Begum, the 'Mother of the Company,'" BPP:29 (April-June 1925), 148-54.

B933 ———. "Notes on the Early History of the English Factory at Dacca," BPP:32 (July-Dec. 1926), 14-20.

B934 ANSARI, A. S. BAZMEE. "Mīr Dja'far or Mīr Muḥammad Dja'far Khān," EI:2, 371-72. Includes extensive bibliography.

B935 ASKARI, SYED HASAN. "Raja Dhiraj Narain," PU:1 (July 1944). Covers 1752-1773; on the brother of the Naib Nizam of Bihar.

B936 ———. "A Source-Book of Mid-Eighteenth Century Indian History," PU:4 (Jan. 1949), 22-45. Edited translation of a Persian manuscript covering the period from the fall of the Nawab Sarfaraz Khan Haider-Jung to the death of Sirajuddaulah.

B937 ———. "An Unpublished Persian Letter of Mir Qasim," BPP:57 (July-Dec. 1939), 10-23; IHRC:15 (Dec. 1938), 134-46.

B938 BALL, UPENDRANATH. "The Story of the Black Hole Tragedy Re-Examined," CR:76 (Aug. 1940), 137-52. Denies its veracity.

B939 BANERJEE, D. N. "The Accession of Nazm-ud-Dowla to the Throne of Bengal and the Position of the East India Company," IHRC:16 (1939), 62-75.

B940 ———. "The Resident at the Durbar (Moorshedabad), His Position and Functions (1765-1772)," BPP:57 (July-Dec. 1939), 24-35; IHRC: 15 (Dec. 1938), 69-79. Based on records in the Imperial Record Office.

B941 ———. "Studies in the Early Government System of the Company in Bengal (1765-74)," BPP:48 (July-Dec. 1934), 115-23; 55 (Jan.-June 1938), 67-115, 164-201.

B942 BANERJI, BRAJENDRANATH. "The Last Days of Nawab Mir Qasim," BPP:34 (July-Dec. 1927), 88-96.

B943 ———. "The Mother of the Company (Compiled from Original Papers)," BPP:32 (July-Dec. 1926), 37-48, 136-40.

B944 BAYNE, R. R. "Notes on the Remains of Portions of Old Fort William Discovered during the Erection of the East Indian Railway Company's Offices," ASB:52 (1883), part 1, 105-19. "Note on further discoveries. . . ." ASBP (1883), p. 42.

B945 BEAMES, J. "Notes on the History of Orissa under the Mohamedan, Maratha, and English Rule," ASB:52 (1883), part 1, 231-57.

B946 BEVERIDGE, H. "The Patna Massacre," CR 79:158 (1884), 338-78. Of 1763.

B947 BHALLA, P. N. "The Mother of the Company," JIH:22 (Aug.-Dec. 1943), 128-44. The life and activities of Munni Begam, consort of Mir Jafar Khan.

B948 BHATTACHARYA, SUKUMAR. "An Omichand Episode in the Early Nineteenth Century," IHRC:32 (1956), 64-70. Intrigue.

B949 "The Black Hole; Full Proceedings of the Debate," BPP:12 (Jan.-June 1916), 136-71. Proceedings of meeting held March 24, 1916.

B950 BLOCHMANN, HENRY. "Notes on Sirājuddaulah and the Town of Murshidabād Taken from a Persian Manuscript of the Tarikh-i-Mancūrī," ASB:36 (Nov. 1867), 85-104. Persian text and translation.

B951 CHAKRAVARTY, P. C. "The Geography of Calcutta up to the Nineteenth Century," MR:80 (Sept. 1946), 203-11.

B952 CHATTERJI, NANDALAL. "The Abdali Menace to Bengal (1767-9)," BPP:55 (Jan.-June 1938), 151-63.

B953 ———. "Bengal under the Diwani Administration, 1765-1772," JIH:32 (Dec. 1954), 265-81; 33 (April 1955), 47-84.

B954 ———. "Clive and the Company's Gumastahs," IHQ:28 (Sept. 1952), 290-92. Reprints selections from Bengal Select Committee Records, 1766, on the problem of controlling the Company's agents.

B955 ———. "Clive and the Junior Civil Servants," IHRC:17 (1940), 78-79. His attitude toward them.

B956 ———. "Clive's Dispute with Mr. George Gray Regarding the Confinement of Ramnaut Das," JIH:29 (Dec. 1951), 311-15. An incident in 1765 which Chatterji claims "was an essential link in the chain of circumstances . . . [leading to] Clive's absolute control over his own Council."

B957 ———. "Clive's Dispute with Mr. George Gray Regarding the Levy of Tax on Public Woman," IHRC:20 (1943), 33-34.

B958 ———. "The Early Phase of Mir Qasim's Career," CR:44 (Sept. 1932), 299-310.

B959 ———. "The Genesis of Mir Qasim's War with the English," CR: 47 (June 1933), 317-31. Largely from Bengal Public Consultations.

B960 ———. "Mir Qasim and the Revolution of 1760 at Murshidabad," BPP:48 (July-Dec. 1934), 101-14.

B961 ———. "Mir Qasim at Monghyr," IHQ:8 (Sept. 1932), 571-82. Political history, 1762; British and Persian documents.

B962 ———. "Mir Qāsim at Patna, 1761," BORS:18 (1932), 332-52. Political history; Persian texts.

B963 ———. "Mir Qasim's Accession to the Masnad of Murshidabad," CR:43 (April 1932), 99-109.

B964 ———. "Mir Qasim's Army," IHQ:11 (June 1935), 253-64. The organization and training on European lines.

B965 ———. "Mir Qasim's Frontier Policy, 1761-62," BPP:45 (Jan.-June 1933), 23-30. Allahabad Univ. MSS and records.

B966 ———. "The Mission of Messrs. Amyatt and Hay to Mir Qasim (1763)," UPHS:6 (Jan. 1933), 35-55; the same, under the title, "The Deputation . . ." BPP:46 (July-Dec. 1933), 100-111. English records and MSS at Allahabad Univ.

B967 ———. "The Mission of Messrs. Vansittart and Hastings to Mir Qasim," BPP:46 (July-Dec. 1933), 1-13. British records.

B968 ———. "Mr. Vansittart's Mission to Mir Qasim, 1762," AHRS:7 (July 1932), 17-30.

B969 ———. "The Revenue Administration of Mīr Qāsim in Bihar and Bengal (1760-63)," BORS:21 (1935), 61-73. Based largely on British sources; some Persian texts also used.

B970 ———. "The Revolution of 1760 in Murshidabad," UPHS:5 (Jan. 1932), 93-102. English records and MSS at Allahabad Univ.

B971 "Chronicles of the Hutwa Raj," CR:105 (July 1897), 33-44.

B972 CHURCHILL, A. B. N. "Short Notes on the History of Fort William," CR:120 (Jan. 1905), 1-19.

B973 [CLIVE]. "The Death of Clive," BPP:47 (Jan.-June 1934), 36-43. Contemporary reports and other evidence.

B974 ———. "Clive, Robert Clive, Baron," EB:6, 532-36. Laudatory account of "the statesman and general who founded the empire of British India."

B975 COTTON, H. E. A. "Alexander Grant's Account of the Loss of Calcutta in 1756," BPP:34 (July-Dec. 1927), 20-37. Prints a letter.

B976 ———. "Clive and the Strachey Family," IHRC:6 (1924), 7-24. Largely records on Stracheys.

B977 ———. "Patna Massacre of 1763," BPP:41 (Jan.-June 1931), 5-29.

B978 ———. "Patna Massacre of 1763: A Note on the Victims," IHRC: 13 (1930), 10-32.

B979 ———. "An Unpublished Letter of Lord Clive," BPP:51 (Jan.-June 1936), 112-13.

B980 COTTON, JULIAN JAMES. "Survivors of the Black Hole," BPP: 29 (Jan.-March 1925), 68-72. Follows subsequent lives of some of the survivors.

B981 DASGUPTA, A. P. "Nawab Najimuddowla and the English," CR: 61 (Nov. 1936), 183-94.

B982 ———. "The Select Committee in Bengal and Its Conflict with the Council in 1770," BPP:55 (Jan.-June 1938), 34-47.

B983 DAS GUPTA, S. N. "The Revolt of Tilok Chand of Bardwan, 1760—An Episode in the Relations between the East India Company and the Local Chieftains of Bengal," UPHS:7 (Nov. 1934), 34-51. Persian records.

B984 DATTA, KALIKINKAR. " 'Alīvardī as Deputy Governor of Bihar," IHQ:13 (Dec. 1937), 617-23. Political history.

B985 ———. "Bihar Affairs in 1756-58," JIH:40 (Dec. 1962), 781-801. A chronicle.

B986 ———. "Durlabhrām, A Prominent Bengal Officer of the Mid-Eighteenth Century," IHQ:16 (March 1940), 20-39. Biography of a high official.

B987 ———. "Fortification of Calcutta and the Nawabs of Bengal, 1740-57," PU:1 (July 1944), 1-18.

B988 ———. "Recovery of Calcutta by the English," CR:46 (March 1933), 377-98; 49 (Oct. 1933), 40-53.

B989 DISKALKAR, D. B. "An Unpublished Letter of Major James Rennell dated Bengal, August 31, 1765," BPP:46 (July-Dec. 1933), 26-31. Describes Bengal.

B990 DODWELL, H. "Clive in India," QR:232 (July 1919), 38-56. A summary of his career.

B991 DUTT, SUDHINDRA K. "Further Light on the Black Hole," MR:49 (March 1931), 279-86. From contemporary accounts.

B992 "E. C." "Unpublished Letters of Lord Clive (Correspondence with Admiral Watson)," BPP:52 (July-Dec. 1936), 75-86.

B993 FIRMINGER, W. K. "How the English Acquired the Twenty-Four Parganahs," CR:272 (April 1913), 169-94.

B994 FOSTER, WILLIAM. "William Barwell, Governor of Fort William, 1748-49," BPP:27 (Jan.-March 1924), 35-43. Biographical sketch.

B995 FURBER, HOLDEN and GLAMANN, KRISTOF. "Plassey: A New Account from the Danish Archives," JAS:19 (Feb. 1960), 177-87. Danish text and English tr. in facing columns; annotated.

B996 GHOSAL, HARI RANJAN. "Cheap the Magnificent," IHQ:22 (Sept. 1946), 200-06. A detailed account of John Cheap's rise to wealth through trade while in the Bengal civil service, end 18th and early 19th cent.

B997 GUPTA, BRIJEN K. "The Actual Losses in the Fall of Calcutta in 1756," EHR:75 (Jan. 1960), 90-91. Revises figures on financial loss of the East India Company in Sirajaddaullah's raid.

B998 ———. "The Black Hole Incident," JAS:19 (Nov. 1959), 53-63. A detailed discussion of available figures on casualties.

B999 GURNER, C. W. "An Apologia for Conspiracy," BPP:36 (July-Dec. 1928), 8-12. A London pamphlet of 1760 on 1757.

B1000 HODSON, Maj. V. C. P. "The Black Hole of Calcutta; A Footnote on Some of the Victims and Survivors," BPP:47 (Jan.-June 1934), 51-56, 123.

B1001 HUGHES, A. "The Tarikh i Bangala Mahabat Jangi of Nawab Yusufali Khan, Containing a New Account in Persian of the Reign of Nawab Sirajuddaulla," BPP:77 (Jan.-June 1958), 5-19. Photographic facsimile and translation of an MS in the British Museum, previously unnoticed because incorrectly catalogued.

B1002 HYDE, H. B. "List of Black-Hole Victims, 20th-21st June, 1756," ASBP (July 1899), pp. 81-84.

B1003 JAMESON, A. KEITH. "A Forgotten Military Expedition in Bengal," CR: NS 293 (July 1918), 246-61. Took place during the latter part of the 1760's.

B1004 JANG, SAIYID AMIR ALI MIDHAT. "An Account of Muhammad Reza Khan," MsR:2 (July-Sept. 1927), 56-64; 3 (April-June 1929), 25-37. On "the founder of the Chitpore Family and the celebrated Nai-Subhahdar and Naib-Dewab of Bengal, Bihar and Orissa," and on the grant of divani to the British in 1765.

B1005 JHA, JAGDISH CHANDRA. "Early British Penetration into Chotanagpur (1769-73)," BRS:43 (Sept.-Dec. 1957), 329-33. British records and correspondence.

B1006 KHAN, ABDUS SUBHAN. "Yūsuf 'Alī Khān, Author of the Tārīkh-i-Bangāla-i-Mahābatjangī," ASB, Ser. 4:1 (1959), 173-76. Describes a Persian chronicle-biography of 'Alivardi. Two other Persian chronicles of the 1750's and 1760's are also briefly discussed.

B1007 KHAN, IMTIAZ MOHAMAD. "Mohamad Reza Khan and His Trial," CR:17 (Dec. 1925), 386-406; 18 (Feb. 1926), 249-72. During Hastings' administration; from British and Persian records.

B1008 MAITRA, ABSHAY KUMAR. "Plassy (June 23rd, 1757)," MR:2 (July 1907), 40-50. Historiographical résumé.

B1009 MARTINEAU, A. "L'Episode du 'Black Hole': histoire ou légende" [The "Black Hole" Episode: History or Legend], BPP:12 (Jan.-June 1916), 32-42.

B1010 "The Massacre of Patna," CR:84 (Jan. 1887), 44-70.

B1011 NADVI, SAIYED MUZAFFARUDDIN. "An Impartial Study of Nawab Siraj-ud-dawla," PPHC:3 (1953), 190-201. "He was one of the early martyrs who fell in the battle of freedom against the British."

B1012 OLDHAM, C. E. A. W. "A Unique Plan of the Battle of Buxar Found in a Copy of Rennell's 'Bengal Atlas,'" BPP:50 (July-Dec. 1935), 69-74.

B1013 RAGHUVANSHI, V. P. S. "Fall of Sirajuddaula, The Nawab of Bengal," JIH:39 (Aug. 1961), 287-301. From English records and English translations of Persian records.

B1014 ———. "The Treaty of February 1757 between the East India Company and Nawab Sirajuddaula of Bengal," URS:7 (1961/62), 99-114.

B1015 ROY, JYOTIRMAY. "History of Manipur," CR:143 (June 1957), 269-80; 144 (Sept. 1957), 316-26; 145 (Oct.-Dec. 1957), 165-75, 258-61. English and Bengali records and accounts.

B1016 SARKAR, JADUNATH (tr.). "Alivardi Khan in Orissa and Bihar," BPP:66 (1946-47), 63-74; 67 (1948), 1-21; 68 (1949), 1-25. Alivardi's career before he seized the Bengal throne, his reign, and the history of Bengal to 1757. Translated from Persian MS of Karam Ali Khan, *Muzaffar-Namah*.

B1017 ———. "Plassey, 1757," MR:83 (Jan. 1948), 21-27.

B1018 SETH, MESROOB J. "Is the Calcutta Black Hole a Myth?" BPP:29 (April-June 1925), 224-25. Evidence that it was a hoax.

B1019 "The Siege of Calcutta," BM:172 (Dec. 1902), 836-53. In 1756.

B1020 SINHA, A. N. "A Study in Some Early British Sanads Relating to Jungleterry," IHRC:18 (Jan. 1942), 209-45. Persian MS and English translation.

B1021 SINHA, NARENDRAKRISHNA. "Mir Qasim as an Exile from Bengal: 1764-77," CR:55 (May 1935), 193-202.

B1022 ———. "Some Information about Omichand from the Calcutta High Court Records," MR:82 (Nov. 1947), 395-97. His associations with Clive.

B1023 SIRCAR, D. C. "Documents of Rānī Bhavānī of Nātor," ASB, Ser. 4:4, nos. 3&4 (1962), 141-50. 2 plates of the 2 documents, which transfer rent-free lands; carefully analyzed and translated.

B1024 SRIVASTAVA, ASHIRBADI LAL. "Was the Abdali Invasion of 1766-67 a Real Menace to Bengal?" CR:76 (July 1940), 47-61. Disputes account by N. L. Chatterji (in BPP:55) on the basis of Persian and Marathi MSS that Chatterji did not use.

B1025 SUTHERLAND, L. S. "Two Letter-Books of Richard Barwell, 1769-73," IA:7 (July-Dec. 1953), 115-45; 8 (Jan.-June 1954), 14-42.

B1026 TEMPLE, R. C. (ed.). "Alexander Grant's Account of the Loss of Calcutta in 1756," IAn:28 (Nov. 1899), 293-302. Written in 1774.

B1027 WILSON, PROFESSOR. "Documents Illustrative of the Occurrences in Bengal, in the Time of the Nawābs Mīr Jaffier and Kāsim Alī Khān," RAS:13 (1852), 115-45. Persian texts and translations.

B1028 WILSON, C. R. "The Building of the Present Fort William, Calcutta," CR:119 (July 1904), 374-88.

B1029 ———. "The Topography of Old Fort William," ASB:62 (1893), 104-26. Two maps (1753) of Fort William and part of Calcutta.

B1030 ———. "An Unrecorded Governor of Fort William in Bengal," ASB:67 (Aug. 1898), 167-77. Edward Stephenson.

B1031 ———. "A Short History of Old Fort William in Bengal," BPP:1 (July-Oct. 1907), 30-46; 93-111; 2 (Jan. 1908), 1-16.

B1032 WYLIE, DAVID T. (ed.). "A Nabob and His Friends: Major John Grant, M.P.," BPP:38 (July-Dec. 1929), 119-23. Letters written in 1760's.

13. *BENGAL, BIHAR, ORISSA, AND ASSAM, 1773 TO 1950*

B1033 AHMAD, NAFIS. "The Evolution of the Boundaries of East Pakistan," OG:2 (July 1958), 97-106. With maps.

B1034 ———. "The Indo-Pakistan Boundary Disputes Tribunal, 1949-50," GR:43 (July 1953), 329-37. Details of boundary disputes in Bengal.

B1035 AHMAD, QEYAM UDDIN. "Some Unpublished Letters of Raja Shitab Rai Taken from Collections of the Commonwealth Relations Office Library," IHRC:35 (1960), 11-22. In Vansittart's time.

B1036 "Annals of the Bengal Presidency," CR:13 (1850), 86-123; 15 (1851), 202-52; 19 (1853), 156-209.

B1037 "Another Chapter on Assam," CR 21:42 (1853), 382-415. Description of the area.

B1038 APCAR, J. G. "Municipal Administration in Calcutta," CR:124 (Oct. 1907), 480-99. Brief history.

B1039 "Assam since the Expulsion of the Burmese," CR 19:38 (1853), 413-39.

B1040 "Assamese Matters, Past and Present," CR 23:45 (1854), 38-65. Description of the country.

B1041 BALL, UPENDRANATH. "The District Administration in Bengal," MR:79 (March 1946), 198-201.

B1042 BANERJEE, BENOYENDRA NATH. "Working of Provincial Autonomy in Bengal," IJPS:3 (July 1941), 72-82.

B1043 BANERJEE, S. C. "Naib Nazims of Dacca during the Company's Administration," BPP:59 (July-Dec. 1940), 17-29; IHRC:16 (1939), 13-23. From British records, 1778-1843.

B1044 BANERJI, BREJENDRANATH. "Sannyasi Rebellion in Bengal," MR:40 (Sept., Oct. 1926), 286-93, 394-400.

B1045 BARPUJARI, H. K. "Early Judicial Panchayats in Assam," JIH: 42 (Aug. 1964), 343-49. 1820's; based on Bengal records.

B1046 ———. "Papers Relating to the Annexation of Jayanta (1835)," IHRC:30 (1954), 25-29. Based on Bengal records.

B1047 BASU, K. K. "Bhagalpur in the Early 19th Century," IHRC:34 (Dec. 1958), 47-54.

B1048 ———. "The Early Europeans in Bhagalpur," IHRC:15 (Dec. 1938), 90-106. List of residents in late 18th, early 19th cent.

B1049 ———. "The History of Singbhum, 1821-1836," BRS:42 (June 1956), 283-98.

B1050 [BEADON]. "Sir Cecil Beadon's Administration of Bengal," CR: 45 (Aug. 1867), 451-69; 46:91, 118-36.

B1051 "Bengal As It Is," CR:3 (1845), 165-210.

B1052 "The Bengal Civil Service," CR:90 (April 1890), 388-92.

B1053 "Bengal in 1870," CR 52:103 (1871), 128-45.

B1054 BEVERIDGE, H. "The City of Patna," CR 76:152 (1883), 211-33. Brief history.

B1055 BHATTACHARYA, NRIPENDRA C. "John Cheap of Surul," VBQ:21 (Winter 1955-56), 223-31. East India Company's resident in Birbhum, noted for his private fortune.

B1056 BHATTACHARYA, SUKUMAR. "Lord Carmichael in Bengal; Proposal for His Recall," BPP:79 (July-Dec. 1960), 67-70.

B1057 BHATTASALI, NALINI KANTA. "Some Facts about Old Dacca," BPP:51 (Jan.-June 1936), 48-57. With map.

B1058 BISHUI, KALPANA. "The Origin and Evolution of the Scheme for the First Partition of Bengal (1905)," QRHS 5:2 (1965/66), 76-96.

B1059 BLECHYNDEN, KATHLEEN. "Some Old Calcutta Worthies," E&W:6 (Oct. 1907), 1037-43. Some 18th cent. personalities.

B1060 BOSE, BASANTA KUMAR. "An Abandoned Port of the Sunderbuns," BPP:37 (Jan.-June 1929), 43-52. Correspondence in 1859 on building a port near Calcutta.

B1061 BOSE, NIRMAL KUMAR. "East and West in Bengal," MII:38 (Sept. 1958), 157-75. Discusses contact beginning with end of 17th cent., and subsequent reactions, both Bengali and English.

B1062 ————. "Calcutta: A Premature Metropolis," SA:213 (Sept. 1965), 90-102. With maps.

B1063 ————. "Modern Bengal," MII:38 (Dec. 1958), 229-95. On change of all types.

B1064 BOURDILLON, JAMES. "The Partition of Bengal," SOA:54 (Dec. 15, 1905), 102-19; discussion pp. 119-24. Summary of the 1905 scheme, with good map of various proposed divisions.

B1065 BROOMFIELD, J. H. "The Partition of Bengal: A Problem in British Administration, 1830-1912," IHCP:23 (1961), 13-24. History of the failure to decentralize government early in the administration of Bengal; administrative reasons for slowness of administrative reform; the influence of Calcutta business in politics and its decline by 1905.

B1066 BUCHANAN, FRANCIS. "The Journal of Dr. Francis Buchanan (Afterwards Buchanan Hamilton) from the 1st November 1812 to the 26th February 1813, When Carrying Out His Survey of the District of Shahabad: Edited, with Notes and Introduction by C. E. A. W. Oldham, C.S.I." BORS:11 (1925), i-xxi, 201-392.

B1067 ————. "Journal of Francis Buchanan (Patna and Gaya Districts): Edited, with Notes and Introduction, by V. H. Jackson, M.A.," BORS:8 (1922), 145-366. B. Chowdhury says in BPP:76 (1957), 137, that this is better edited than the published version edited by M. Martin, though it omits many appendices.

B1068 BURGESS, JAMES. "Extracts from the Journal of Colonel Colin Mackenzie's Pandit of His Route from Calcutta to Gaya in 1820," IAn:31 (Feb. 1902), 65-75. Reprint from *Oriental Magazine and Calcutta Review*, 1823.

B1069 BURMAN, DEBAJYOTI. "History of Bengal's Shifting Boundary and Population," MR:79 (April 1946), 264-75. With good maps and tables.

B1070 ————. "Municipal Calcutta; Calcutta's Charter of Freedom (The Municipal Act of 1923)," LSGI:10 (Oct. 1939), 205-19.

B1071 BURTON-PAGE, J. "Bihār," EI:1, 1209-10.

B1072 "Calcutta in the Olden Time—Its Localities," CR 18:36 (1852), 275-320.

B1073 "The Census and the Decline of Bengal," CR:97 (Oct. 1893), 308-25.

B1074 "The Census of Bengal," MR:14 (Aug. 1913), 216-21.

B1075 CHAKRAVARTI, P. C. "Genesis of the Partition of Bengal (1905)," MR:105 (April 1959), 296-98. Quotations of policy statements on the need for partition, 1896-1904.

B1076 CHATTERJEE, AMIYA BHUSHAN. "The Hooghly River and Its West Bank: A Study in Historical Geography," GRI:25 (Sept. 1963), 164-82. Pp. 171-82 consider modern history.

B1077 CHATTERJI, NANDALAL. "A Sannyasi Agitator from Lucknow among the Santals of Hazaribagh," IHRC:28 (1951), 11-12. In 1881.

B1078 ———. "Shamsuddaulah's Intrigue against the English," BPP:53 (Jan.-June 1937), 31-34. End of the 18th cent.

B1079 ———. "When Cuttack Had No Public Market," OHRJ:1 (Oct. 1952), 205-07. 1806 improvements of Cuttack.

B1080 CHAUDHURI, BENOY. "The Denajpore Report of Buchanan Hamilton," ISPP:2 (Oct.-Dec. 1960), 19-36. A summary and review of Buchanan's report.

B1081 "The Chronicle of Krishnaghur," CR 25:49 (1855), 104-16. On the chronicle of the family of Raja Krishna Chandra of Navadwipa, Bengal.

B1082 "The City of Calcutta and Its Municipal Constitution," CR 70:139 (1880), 478-98.

B1083 "Correspondence of the Settlement of Khoordah in Pooree," OHRJ:3 (March 1955), i-xxxiv (beginning p. 214); 4 (June & Sept. 1955), xxxv-lxxxv (beginning p. 41); "Appendix: Selections from the Correspondence on the Settlement of Khoordah Estate in the District of Pooree. Dated Calcutta the 13th May 1818," OHRJ:4 (Dec. 1955 & March 1956), lxxxvii-cxxvii (beginning p. 103). Letters from W. Ewer, Commissioner, to W. B. Bayley, Acting Chief Sec'y to the government.

B1084 COTTON, H. E. A. "An Echo from Old Bengal," BM:182 (Sept. 1907), 419-24. On "Begum Johnson," daughter of William Watts of Calcutta.

B1085 ———. "Letters from Bengal: 1788-1795; Unpublished papers from the Correspondence of Ozias Humphry, R.A.," BPP:35 (Jan.-June 1928), 107-34.

B1086 ———. "The Sheriffs of Calcutta, 1727-1930," BPP:38 (July-Dec. 1929), 1-14, 99-118; 39 (Jan.-June 1930), 153-55. Continued by Narendranath Ganguly in BPP:69 (1950), 51-52, covering the years 1931-1950. History and sources discussed in vol. 39.

B1087 "The Covenanted Civil Service and Financial Reform in Bengal," CR:84 (Jan. 1887), 139-53.

B1088 "The Cuttack Tributary Mehals—Recent Operations against Ungool," CR 9:17 (1848), 190-220.

B1089 DALTON, ED. TUITE. "Notes of a Tour Made in 1863-64 in the Tributary Mehals under the Commissioner of Chota-Nagpore, Bonai, Gangpore, Odeypore and Sirgooja," ASB:34 (May 1865), 1-31.

B1090 ———. "Notes on a Tour in Manbhoom in 1864-65," ASB:35 (Nov. 1866), 186-95.

B1091 DANI, A. H. "Dhākā (Dacca)," EI:2, 216-17.

B1092 DAS, G. S. "History of Cuttack," OHRJ:3 (March 1955), 197-214.

B1093 DAS, M. N. "Curzon's Successors and the Partition of Bengal: a Conflict in Conscience," JIH:39 (Dec. 1961), 393-400. Based on the Morley papers.

B1094 DASGUPTA, BHASKAR. "The Memorable Tussle for the Governorship of Bengal," MR:111 (June 1962), 478-80. Between Warren Hastings and Sir John Clavering, 1777.

B1095 DATTA, BHABATOSH. "The Bengal Development Bill, 1935," MR:58 (July 1935), 98-104. Background and interpretation.

B1096 DATTA, JATINDRA MOHAN. "Inaccuracies in Official Statistics in West Bengal," MR:90 (Aug. 1951), 147-50.

B1097 DATTA, KALIKINKAR. "Governors and Deputy-Governors of Bihar in the Eighteenth Century," BPP:81 (Jan.-June 1962), 32-36. From an MS (Persian and Urdu) at Patna University.

B1098 ———. "Santhal Insurrection of 1855-56," BPP:50 (July-Dec. 1935), 29-43; 51 (Jan.-June 1936), 19-35.

B1099 ———. "Some Unpublished Papers Relating to Indo-British History and Administration from 1790-98," IHQ:11 (Sept. 1935), 401-73. Letters received by the District Judge of Patna, arranged by various topics and edited, with notes.

B1100 DAVIDSON, C. J. C. "Dacca in 1840," BPP:42 (July-Dec. 1931), 36-48. Davidson's diary.

B1101 DAVIES, C. COLLIN. "Calcutta as Capital: the Objections of Warren Hastings," AR: NS 29 (1933), 243-48. Prints a minute by Hastings dated June 4, 1782.

B1102 DE, S. C. "British Conquest of Orissa and Early British Administration," OHRJ:3 (June, Sept., Dec. 1954), 48-62, 118-26, 157-62.

B1103 ———. "Cuttack Town in 1814," OHRJ:8 (July 1959), 87-88. From an MS report.

B1104 DESIKACHAR, S. V. "The Assam Company Bill: Its Constitutional Importance," IHRC:31 (1955), 170-73. Dispute in 1844-45.

B1105 "The Diary of Govinda Das," CR:106 (Jan., April 1898), 79-96, 372-83.

B1106 DUTT, K. N. "Assam in 1855," IHCP:14 (1951), 264-75. Survey of political, economic, social conditions, actually for 1835.

B1107 "Eastern Bengal and Assam," EB:8, 830-31. An account of the 1905 partition of Bengal and the events in 1906, told in some detail.

B1108 EUSTIS, F. A., and ZAIDI, Z. H. "King, Viceroy and Cabinet: the Modification of the Partition of Bengal, 1911," H:49 (June 1964), 171-84.

B1109 "Financial and Administrative Reforms in India—Bengal," CR: 84 (Jan., April 1887), 88-111, 299-330.

B1110 FIRMINGER, WALTER KELLY. "Historical Introduction to the Bengal Portion of 'The Fifth Report,'" ISPP:3 (Oct. 1961–Sept. 1962), 149-79, 313-43, 361-514, 519-634. A classic history.

B1111 ———. "Three Biographical Notes," BPP:47 (Jan.-June 1934), 44-47. General Gustavus Ducarel, Hercules Durham, William Hay.

B1112 GHOSE, A. C. "Rural Behar," CR:110 (April 1900), 218-32.

B1113 GHOSE, HEMANDRAPROSAD. "Bengal (1750-1800)," CR:137 (Oct.-Dec. 1955), 81-106, 221-37; 138 (March 1956), 243-64; 139 (April-June 1956), 83-102, 223-37; 141 (Dec. 1956), 221-28; 142 (Jan.-March 1957), 1-8, 109-28.

B1114 GHOSE, SATYENDRA NATH. "Municipal Calcutta; The Mackenzie Bill—How Bengal Fought It," LSGI:10 (July 1939), 71-114.

B1115 GROVER, B. L. "The Rationale of the Partition of Bengal (1905)," BPP:83 (July-Dec. 1964), 90-100. From Curzon papers.

B1116 GUPTA, S. C. "Date of the Acquisition of Darjeeling by the East India Company," IHRC:23 (1946), 44-45.

B1117 HARTWELL, G. "A Report on a List of the Forts in the District of Cuttack," OHRJ:7 (July 1958), 105-24. 1809 list: name of fort, how long present raja had reigned, his age; distance from Cuttack, and remarks. 36 forts listed.

B1118 HEWITT, J. F. "Chota Nagpore: Its People and Resources," AR:3 (April 1887), 396-429.

B1119 HOME, AMAL. "Municipal Calcutta; The Story of Its Evolution," LSGI:10 (July 1939), 53-70. Starts with Job Charnock and ends with the year 1899.

B1120 "Hooghly Past and Present," CR:95 (Oct. 1892), 258-66; 96 (Jan., April 1893), 22-42, 277-88; 97 (July, Oct. 1893), 71-81, 341-66; 98 (Jan. 1894), 152-70; 99 (July 1894), 153-64; 104 (April 1897), 355-73.

B1121 HUMPHRIES, EDITH M. "Bob Pott," BPP:51 (Jan.-June 1936), 69-104. 1756-95.

B1122 "Hunter's *Annals of Rural Bengal*," ER:129 (Jan. 1869), 200-29. A review.

B1123 HUNTER, W. W. "A River of Ruined Capitals," NC:23 (Jan. 1888), 40-53. The Hughli, from the Bay of Bengal to Murshidabad.

B1124 INGLIS, W. A. "Some of the Problems Set Us by the Rivers of Bengal," ASB: NS 5 (1909), 393-405. Economics, navigation, etc.

B1125 "J.B.P." "Rustic Bengal," CR:59 (1874), 180-214, 350-78.

B1126 JHA, ADITYA PRASAD. "Nature of the Santhal Unrest of 1871-75 and Origin of the Sapha Hor Movement," IHRC:35 (Feb. 1960), 103-13.

B1127 ———. "Views of a Contemporary British Official on Civil Administration of Bengal and Bihar in 1855," IHCP:21 (1958), 472-79. The Commissioner of Patna District, William Tayler.

B1128 JHA, JAGDISH CHANDRA. "Early British Contacts with Singhbhum," PU:18 (Jan. 1963), 148-56. To 1821.

B1129 ———. "Ganga Narain and the Bhumij Revolt of 1832-33," MR:112 (Dec. 1962), 481-84.

B1130 ———. "The Hos (Larka Kols) of Singhbhum in the Early 19th Century," CR:168 (July 1963), 71-76. Wars against a tribal people.

B1131 ———. "Patkum (in Manbhum) in the Early British Period," CR:173 (Dec. 1964), 218-22.

B1132 ———. "Some Light on the Origins of the Bhumij Revolt of 1832-33," JIH:43 (Aug. 1965), 593-99.

B1133 ———. "Tribal Unrest in Tamar, 1819-1820," CR:164 (Sept. 1962), 215-19. A pargana in Chota Nagpur.

B1134 JHA, JATA SHANKAR. "History of Darbhanga Raj," BRS:48 (1962), sec. 1, 14-104.

B1135 ———. "Restoration of Indigenous Police in a Tribal Area of Bihar and Bengal, 1800," BRS:49 (1963), 265-75.

B1136 "KRGM." "A Withered Beldame Now. Portrait of a Settlement," USI:86 (1956), 85-91. Summary in HA:4 (No. 2277): "A short historical portrait of Balasore, a town in Orissa, which since 1893 has been the site of an ordnance proving range."

B1137 LAMBERT, RICHARD D. "Religion, Economics, and Violence in Bengal; Background of the Minorities Agreement," MEJ:4 (July 1950), 307-28.

B1138 "M." "Sir Philip Francis—a True Friend of India," MR:17 (April 1915), 504-06. Quotations from 2 contemporary minutes, on the Permanent Settlement and the question of British colonists.

B1139 [MACPHERSON]. "Captain MacPherson and the Khonds," CR 8:15 (1847), 1-51. On relations with Orissa hill tribes.

B1140 ———. "Major Chartres MacPherson," CR 43:85 (1866), 57-67.

B1141 MATHUR, D. B. "Lord Curzon and the Politico-surgery of Bengal (October 16, 1905–December 12, 1911): A Review," MR:114 (Oct. 1963), 270-82.

B1142 McLANE, JOHN R. "The Decision to Partition Bengal in 1905," IESHR:2 (July 1965), 221-37.

B1143 [MESTON]. "The Hon'ble Sir James Meston," HR:25 (March 1912), 310-12. Lt. Governor of Bengal.

B1144 MITRA, KALIPADA. "The Defence of the Frontier of Bihar and Orissa against Maratha and Pindari Incursions (1800-1819)," IHRC:16 (1939), 150-57.

B1145 ———. "Defence of Patna against the Apprehended Pindari Incursion of 1812," IHQ:17 (March 1941), 77-81. Reprints 10 letters in the office of the Bihar and Orissa Research Society, Patna.

B1146 "The Mofussil Records of Bengal," CR 54:108 (1872), 204-22. Their badly kept condition.

B1147 MUKHARJI, BIJAY BEHARI. "Communal Representation in the Services, etc. in Bengal," MR:80 (Nov. 1946), 366-74.

B1148 MUKHERJEE, PRABHAT. "The Commissioners of Orissa: Henry Ricketts," OHRJ:11 (1962), 106-13.

B1149 ———. "Employment of the People of Orissa in Government Service in the 19th Century," OHRJ:8 (July 1959), 110-17. Not statistical; rather impressionistic.

B1150 MUKHERJI, T. K. "The Bengal Council's Relations with the Calcutta Mayor's Court in the Days of Harry Verelst," JIH:29 (Dec. 1951), 253-66.

B1151 MURPHY, RHOADS. "The City in the Swamp: Aspects of the Site and Early Growth of Calcutta," GJ:130 (June 1964), 241-56. With maps and bibliography.

B1152 "Orissa Past and Present," CR 44:87 (1866), 1-34. Under the British.

B1153 PAL, DHARM. "The Bengal Legislature on Its Trial," CR:97 (Oct. 1945), 8-12. Refers to period in the 1860's.

B1154 ———. "An Episode of the Bengal Administration (1867-1868)," CR:96 (July 1945), 1-6.

B1155 PATNAIK, SUDHAKAR. "Orissa in 1867," OHRJ:10 (Oct. 1961), 61-73. Miscellaneous items from newspapers, mostly *Utkal Dipika*.

B1156 ———. "Orissa in 1868," OHRJ:10 (1962), 44-58.

B1157 [PAULL]. "The Story of James Paull," BPP:28 (July-Sept. 1924), 69-109. A commercial adventurer of the late 18th cent., early 19th cent. in Bengal, known in his day "by his persistent efforts to impeach Lord Wellesley."

B1158 "R.N.R." "Manipur, Past and Present," BM:256 (July 1944), 71-76. Description and history.

B1159 RAINEY, H. JAMES. "Jessore," CR:63 (1876), 1-27; 64 (1877), 351-86; 65 (1877), 248-78; 66 (1878), 398-432. History and conditions.

B1160 RAY, BHABANI CHARAN. "British Attempt to Settle Boundary Line between Bengal and Orissa," BRS:43 (Sept.-Dec. 1957), 285-90. Before 1803.

B1161 RAY, SUKUMAR. "Calcutta (Kalikātā)," EI:2, 7.

B1162 RAYCHAUDHURI, M. L. "A Sanad of Captain James Browne, Military Collector of Zilla Jungle Tarai (1776 A.D.)," IHRC:17 (1940), 149-57. The Persian sanad and translation.

B1163 ROWSELL, FRANCIS W. "The Doomsday Book of Bengal," NC:6 (Dec. 1879), 1033-50. Review of W. W. Hunter's "A Statistical Account of Bengal."

B1164 ROY, N. B. "New Aspects of the Santhal Insurrection, 1855-56," IHRC:35 (Feb. 1960), 172-91.

B1165 ROY, NARESH CHANDRA. "The Working of the Public Service Commission in Bengal," IJPS:3 (Oct. 1941), 192-211.

B1166 ROY, SURESH CHANDRA (ed.). "A Young Civilian in Bengal in 1805," BPP:29 (April-June 1925), 110-47. A journal, probably by Henry Roberdeau.

B1167 SANIAL, S. C. "Macaulay in Lower Bengal," CR:123 (April, July 1906), 291-312, 463-81; 124 (Jan. 1907), 77-109.

B1168 ———. "More Echoes from Old Calcutta," CR:135 (July, Oct. 1912), 285-327, 380-424.

B1169 SARKAR, INDIRA. "The Physical Geography of Bengal during the Time of Nabin Sen," CR:153 (Dec. 1959), 218-24. 1850-1905.

B1170 SARKAR, S. C. "Some Notes on the Intercourse of Bengal with the Northern Countries in the Second Half of the Eighteenth Century," IHRC:13 (1930), 99-109. Based on English records.

B1171 SARVADHIKARI, DEVAPRASAD. "Early Public Life in India," BPP:37 (Jan.-June 1929), 125-29. Bengal public activities in 1840's and '50's.

B1172 "Selections from the Calcutta Gazettes," CR 39:77 (1864), 125-42. On book by W. S. Seton-Karr, covering 1784-88.

B1173 SINGH, SURESH. "The Haribaba Movement in Chotanagpur, 1931-32," BRS:49 (1963), 284-96. Tribal unrest led by a self-proclaimed "chela" of Gandhi.

B1174 SINHA, N. K. "New Light on the History of North-East India," CR:86 (Jan. 1934), 50-52. On Bengali letters in the Imperial Records Department.

B1175 SIRCAR, P. K. "River Characteristics and Floods of Southern West Bengal," IG:1 (Aug. 1956), 5-16. Includes historical material on floods and flood control; bibliography of references.

B1176 "The Sonthal Pergunnahs," CR:35 (Dec. 1860), 510-31.

B1177 "The Sonthal Rebellion," CR:26 (March 1856), 223-64.

B1178 SPENCER, DOROTHY M. "The Hunt for Birsa; A Fragment of History," BPP:83 (Jan. 1964), 1-6. Birsa was a Munda leader arrested 1895; his activity led to the Chota Nagpur Tenancy Act of 1908.

B1179 STIRLING, ANDREW. "An Account, Geographical, Statistical, and Historical, of Orissa Proper, or Cuttack," AsR:15 (1825), 163-338.

B1180 STUART, M. M. "Bob Pott in Murshidabad," BPP:45 (Jan.-June 1933), 5-22. Letters of an agent, 1780's.

B1181 SYED, M. HAFIZ. "H. E. Dr. Kailashnath Katju—Governor of West Bengal," HR:83 (Aug. 1948), 138-40. Biographical sketch.

B1182 TEMPLE, RICHARD. "The Manipur Blue-Book," CoR:59 (June 1891), 917-24. Interpretation of a military disaster by a conservative.

B1183 THOMPSON, W. H. "Two Centuries of Growth on the Eastern Side of the Ganges Delta," CR:297 (July 1919), 308-18. A discussion of the shifting watercourse.

B1184 "Tipperah," CR:35 (Dec. 1860), 324-49.

B1185 "The Topography of Govinda Das's Diary," CR:107 (July 1898), 172-84.

B1186 TOYNBEE, G. "A Sketch of the History of Orissa (From 1803 to 1828)," OHRJ:9 (1960), ?; 10 (April & July 1961), Supplement; 10 (Oct. 1961), Supplement.

B1187 "The Tree-Daubing of 1894," CR:106 (Jan. 1898), 135-43.

B1188 "The Village-Watch in Bengal; or a Century of Abortive Reform," CR 80:159 (1885), 97-120.

B1189 "Village Watch in Lower Bengal," CR 44:87 (1866), 253-65.

B1190 WALI, MAULVI ABDUL. "The Kol Rebellions of 1832-33," CR:267 (Jan. 1912), 37-45.

B1191 "Wanderings of a Pilgrim in the East," CR 15:30 (1851), 475-500. On book by Fanny Parks: description of Bengal.

B1192 "The Workings of the Arms' Act (XI of 1878), in the Lower Provinces," CR:88 (Jan. 1889), 1-8.

B1193 ZAIDI, Z. H. "The Political Motive in the Partition of Bengal, 1905," PHS:12 (April 1964), 113-49. Documented from India Office Library, British Museum, National Library of Scotland.

14. BOMBAY PRESIDENCY

B1194 ABDUL ALI, A. F. M. "Phases of Early British Administration in Bombay," BPP:40 (July-Dec. 1930), 18-26; MsR:4 (April-June 1930), 10-20. Administrative history.

B1195 "Administrative Reforms in the Bombay Presidency," QJPSS:4 (July 1881), 1-56, 4th independent section. Figures on revenue and population.

B1196 ARUNACHALAM, B. "Bombay City: Stages of Development," BGM:3 (1955), 34-39.

B1197 "Bombay Domestic Annals, A.D. 1800-1810," CR:96 (Jan. 1893), 175-84; 99 (July 1894), 49-74.

B1198 BURTON-PAGE, J. "Bīdjāpūr," EI:1, 1202-04.

B1199 DA CUNHA, J. GERSON. "The Origin of Bombay," RASB:20 (Extra No., 1900), 1-368, index pp. i-xv. Mainly 16th and 17th cent., but pp. 356-65 touch on post-1750 period.

B1200 DASS, DAYAL. "Some Unpublished Letters about Goa (1835 A.D.)," UPHS: NS 3 (1955), 50-61. Its relations with Bombay.

B1201 [ELPHINSTONE]. "Mountstuart Elphinstone," CR:34 (March 1860), 34-40. Brief biography and appraisal.

B1202 FIRMINGER, WALTER K. "The Letters of a Governor of Bombay, 1839-1841," CR:128 (April 1909), 186-212; 129 (July, Oct. 1909), 309-53, 552-608; 130 (Jan., April 1910), 49-79, 182-226. Letters by Sir James R. Carnac.

B1203 "Five Years' Administration of Sir James Fergusson," QJPSS:7 (Oct. 1884), 44-66. Retiring governor of Bombay.

B1204 "History of Coorg," CR:27 (Sept. 1856), 180-207. In 18th and 19th cent.

B1205 JEEJEEBHOY, J. R. B. "An Account of Some Unfortunate Officials of the Bombay Government," IHCP:10 (1947), 481-95. "History of the dismissal, suspension or removal of Bombay officials" up to 1888; English officials only.

B1206 JOSHI, C. B. "The Historical Geography of the Islands of Bombay," BGM:4 (1956), 5-13.

B1207 KOGEKAR, S. V. "The Bombay Presidency 1937-39: an Interlude," IJPS:2 (Jan. 1941), 324-39. Under Congress ministry.

B1208 MODI, JIVANJI JAMSHEDJI. "Bombay as Seen by Dr. Edward Ives in the Year 1754 A.D.," RASB:22 (1905), 273-97. Excerpts and summarizes Ives' *A Voyage from England to India. . . .* (London 1773).

B1209 "Municipal Corporation of Greater Bombay," LSGI:26 (July 1955), 1-33. Refers to the many departments and their functions, often giving a brief historical background.

B1210 "The Political Department in Bombay," CR 56:112 (1873), 288-302.

B1211 "Present Condition of Coorg," CR:27 (Dec. 1856), 478-95.

B1212 SINGH, RAGHUBIR. "Manuscript Letter-Book of Sir Charles Warre Malet, 1780-1784," IHRC:14 (1937), 19-27; BPP:55 (Jan.-June 1938), 11-19. Description thereof, with list of the letters; Malet was in Cambay.

B1213 SINGH, VJAGIR. "Bombay: A Study in Historical Geography 1667-1900 A.D.," NGJI:6 (March 1960), 19-29. With maps.

B1214 SOLTYKOFF, ALEXIS. "Bombay and Calcutta in 1841," JPUHS:2 (April 1933), 72-84. Tr. & ed. by H. L. O. Garrett.

B1215 SYDENHAM, G. "An Account of Bījapūr in 1811," AsR:13 (1820), 433-55.

15. MADRAS, THE CARNATIC, AND THE CIRCARS

B1216 "Affairs of India," ER:16 (April 1810), 128-57. Reviews 3 sets of papers pertaining to the aftermath of Vellore.

B1217 AIYYAR, K. R. VENKATA RAMAN. "The Rebellion of the Madura Renters (1755-64)," IHRC:18 (Jan. 1942), 363-67. From Persian and English records in Madras.

B1218 ASIRVATHAM, E. "Law and Administration in the Madras Presidency 1937-39," IJPS:2 (July 1940), 92-107. The working of provincial autonomy.

B1219 ———. "Laws and Administration in the Madras Presidency (1937-39)," IJPS:1 (Oct. 1939), 212-22. Same as above.

B1220 BALIGA, B. S. "A Brief Sketch of the Character and Achievements of Thomas Saunders," BPP:57 (July-Dec. 1939), 36-45; IHRC (Dec. 1938), 45-53. Governor of Madras, 1750's. Based on Madras records.

B1221 ———. "Humanitarian Ideas in Madras, 1800-1835," IHRC:18 (Jan. 1942), 34-43. Largely from judicial records.

B1222 BELL, T. L. "Statistics of the Sircar of Yelgunthul," MJLS:17A (1849?), 20-102.

B1223 BRADLEY, DR. "Statistical Report of the Sircar of Pytun," MJLS:16 (1848?), 235-79.

B1224 BUTTERWORTH, A. "Warren Hastings and the Governors of Madras," AR: NS 30 (1934), 362-70.

B1225 "The Carnatic Question Considered," ER:11 (Jan. 1808), 462-84.

B1226 CASSELLS, A. "'A Brave but Unfortunate Officer,' Colonel William Baillie," BPP:47 (Jan.-June 1934), 1-26. Letters from Fort St. George, 1770's.

B1227 "The Ceded Districts, Madras," CR 24:47 (1855), 68-89.

B1228 COTTON, CHARLES W. E. (ed.). "Letters on Vellore Mutiny," MS:6 (1915-16), 150-54.

B1229 COTTON, EVAN. "The Journals of Archibald Swinton," BPP:31 (Jan.-June 1926), 13-38; IHRC:8 (Nov. 1925), 6-32. With Clive in the Carnatic.

B1230 DAS GUPTA, A. P. "A Note on the Personal Relations of Warren Hastings and Sir Thomas Rumbold," CR:41 (Nov.-Dec. 1931), 296-305. From correspondence in the British Museum between Hastings and the Governor of Madras, 1778-1780.

B1231 ———. "Sir Eyre Coote and the Question of Military Command in the Carnatic War (1780-83)," IHQ:6 (June 1930), 229-43.

B1232 DAS GUPTA, J. N. "An Indian Pepys," CR:299 (Jan. 1920), 47-59. Excerpts from the diary of Ananda Ranga Pillai.

B1233 "Disturbances at Madras," ER:16 (Aug. 1810), 399-413. Reviews 3 accounts of army discontent in Madras.

B1234 DUNCAN, JONATHAN. "Historical Remarks on the Coast of Malabar, with Some Description of the Manners of Its Inhabitants," AsR:5 (1798), 1-36.

B1235 "Early Madras History," CR 38:75 (1863), 87-108.

B1236 FRYKENBERG, ROBERT ERIC. "Elite Groups in a South Indian District: 1788-1858," JAS:24 (Feb. 1965), 261-81.

B1237 ———. "Traditional Processes of Power in South India: An Historical Analysis of Local Influence," IESHR:1 (Oct.-Dec. 1963), 122-42. Based on records in the India Office Library, Madras, and Guntur record offices.

B1238 GOODALL, F. "Rural Madras," CR 60:120 (1875), 269-79. Its general condition.

B1239 GOPAL RAO, KANDREGULA JAGANNATHA RAO. "Brief Summary of the Circumstances Connected with the Acquisition of the Northern Circars by the Government and the Part Played by Kandregula Family (Zamindars Residing in Rajahmundry)," IHCP:7 (1944), 422-27. A guide to documents for local history, 1750-1800.

B1240 HARRISON, J. B. "Arcot," EI:1, 624-25.

B1241 "Historical Tables Concerning the Presidency of Fort St. George," MJLS (1879), pp. 103-34. Compiled by a member of the Madras Civil Service: a) Acquisitions of Territory by the British in the Presidency of Fort St. George (with year, territory, how acquired, district now representing it, approximate area, and land revenue); b) Governors of Fort St. George (landed in Madras, assumed charge of office, made over charge, embarked for England, remarks).

B1242 KRISHNAYYA, D. N. "Chikaveerarājendra Wadiar, the Last Rājah of Coorg," MS:50 (1959-60), 46-59.

B1243 ———. "The South Kanara Insurrection of 1837," IHRC:33 (1958), 109-11.

B1244 LOVETT, H. VERNEY. "Warren Hastings and Madras," AR: NS 33 (1937), 442-48.

B1245 "The Madras Commission on Public Works," CR 22:43 (1854), 143-207.

B1246 MENON, P. K. KARUNAKARA. "A Short Account of the Tellicherry Settlement," MUJ:14 (July 1942), 189-250. The chief town of the northern half of Malabar district in the 18th and 19th cent.

B1247 NATARAJAN, S. "A Note on Some Unpublished Letters of Mahfuz Khan Bahadur," IHRC:28 (1951), 71-73. On the social, political, and economic conditions in the Carnatic, 1866-1875.

B1248 NEWBOLD, LIEUT. "Account of the Ceded Districts," MJLS:10 (1843?), 109-31.

B1249 PARUKUTTY, S. "Macaulay in Madras," E&W:6 (Sept., Oct. 1907), 909-14, 1044-49.

B1250 PAWAR, A. G. "Some Documents Bearing upon the History of the Karnatak (1749-1755)," IC:17 (Jan. 1943), 65-76.

B1251 PILLAY, K. K. "The Pānchālamkuṛichi Rebellion (1797-99)," IHCP:21 (1958), 410-20. The career of the South Indian rebel, from Madras records.

B1252 RICE, STANLEY P. "A Unique Trial," CR:112 (Jan. 1901), 136-45. 1779 trial of 4 men for deposing Lord Pigot, Governor of Madras.

B1253 SASTRI, K. N. VENKATASUBBA. "More Light on Sir Thomas Munro," IHRC:14 (1937), 127-37. On his administration and land policies; documents printed without comment.

B1254 SHERWANI, H. K. "Banganapalle," EI:1, 1015. Small state in S. India prior to its merger in Madras state in 1948.

B1255 SIMKINS, ETHEL. "Coast Plains of South India," EG:9 (Jan., April 1933), 19-50, 136-59. Maps of soils, rainfall, crops.

B1256 SINGH, PRITHIPAL. "Raja Sir T. Madhava Rao, K.C.S.I.," E&W:5 (April 1906), 366-73. Madras administrator.

B1257 SRINIVASACHARI, C. S. "The Abolition of the Titular Dignity of the Nawab of the Carnatic," IHRC:23 (1946), 1-3.

B1258 ———. "The Case of Sir Thomas Rumbold (1781-83)," CR:85 (Dec. 1942), 208-17.

B1259 ———. "A Curious Phase of Lord Pigot's Proceedings against Tanjore (1775-76)," IHRC:15 (Dec. 1938), 53-58; BPP:56 (Jan.-June 1939), 42-47.

B1260 ———. "The Early Development of the Government of the Presidency of Fort St. George," MUJ:1 (1928), 227-45.

B1261 ———. "A Fresh Study of Sir John Macpherson, a Madras Civilian," IHRC:25 (Dec. 1948), 34-41. Late 18th cent.

B1262 ———. "Macartney, The Carnatic and Tanjore," IHRC:28 (1951), 90-97. Based on Persian correspondence.

B1263 ———. "Nawab Muhammad Ali and the Siege of Arcot (1751)," IHQ:14 (Sept. 1938), 545-52.

B1264 ———. "Nawab Umdatu'l Umara of the Carnatic (1795-1801), and the English," IHCP:6 (1943), 253-66. Based on English sources.

B1265 ———. "A Sketch of the Nawabs of the Carnatic in Their Relations with the English," MsR:1 (Jan.-June 1927), 45-53, 54-62; 2 (Jan.-March 1928), 16-23; 3 (July-Sept. 1928), 34-43.

B1266 ———. "The Sovereign Status of the Nawabs of the Carnatic Discussed in the Recorders Court and the Supreme Court at Madras in the Years 1798-1811," IHRC:22 (1945), 1-4.

B1267 ———. "Two Madras Correspondents of Governor Robert Palk, Chokappa and Muttikrishna," IHRC:21 (1944), 1-3.

B1268 ———. "Yusuf Khan's Rebellion and the French Attempt at Recovery (1762-64)," IHRC:16 (1939), 24-32. Madura rebellion.

B1269 SUBBA RAO, R. "Correspondence between the East Indian Company and the Kandregula Family in the Eighteenth Century," JAHRS:3 (Oct. 1928 & Jan.-April 1929), 209-22; 4 (July & Oct. 1929), 61-71; 5 (Jan. & April 1930), 125-46; 10 (1936-37), 194-208. Correspondence 1759-1806 of family in Rajahmundry Circar.

B1270 WARD, MAJOR. "Some Account of the Hill Tribes of the Piney Hills in the Madura District. Communicated by Capt. T. J. Taylor," ASB:4 (Dec. 1835), 664-67.

B1271 WIGHT, ROBERT and WARD, CAPT. "Statistical Observations on the Varragherries or Pulney-Mountains," MJLS:5 (1837?), 280-89, 433; 6 (1838?), 280-94.

B1272 ZUNUDDIN, MIR. "A Page from the Auto-Biography of Mir Nur-ud-din Khan Bahadur 'Shuja Jung,' Aide-de-Camp to the Commanders-in-Chief, Madras," IHRC:6 (1924), 142-49.

16. DELHI, AGRA, AND OUDH, 1800 TO 1950

B1273 "The Administration of Oudh," CR:35 (Sept. 1860), 126-63.

B1274 "The Age of Conquest—Is It Past?" CR 25:49 (1855), 117-37. On "Private Life of an Eastern King," the King of Oudh.

B1275 AHMAD, ENAYAT. "Origin and Evolution of the Towns of the Uttar Pradesh," GO:1 (Jan. 1956), 38-58. Maps showing towns founded in various eras of the Mughal and British rule; also map showing "towns less populous in 1941 than 1881."

B1276 AHMAD, SAFI. "Mawlawi Masīh-al-Dīn Khan, 'plenipotentiary' of Wajid 'Ali Shāh in London," JPHS:10 (Jan. 1962), 38-51.

B1277 ANSARI, A. S. BAZMEE. "A'ẓamgarh," EI:1, 809.

B1278 ———. "Bareilly (Barēlī)," EI:1, 1042.

B1279 AWASTHI, D. "Sir Spencer Harcourt Butler and His 'Eastern Oxford,'" ASP:10 (June 1965), 159-66. The "architect" of modern Lucknow.

B1280 AZHAR, MIRZA ALI. "Nawab Saadat Ali Khan and Wellesley's Interference in Awadh," PPHC:2 (1952), 282-97. Largely from Mill's *History of British India.*

B1281 ———. "Wajid Ali Shah of Avadh (Oudh)," PPHC:1 (1951), 312-41. A diatribe against the British.

B1282 BANERJI, B. N. "Some Original Sources for a Biography of Begam Sombre," IHRC:6 (1924), 96-99. Begam of Sardhana (near Meerut).

B1283 BAQIR, MOHAMMAD. "The End of Muslim Rule in Oudh," HFM:2, 1831-1905, part 1, 127-44.

B1284 BHANU, DHARMA. "History and Administration of the Province of Agra, 1803-1858," UB:3 (Aug. 1956), 147-56.

B1285 ———. "The Presidency of Agra, 1834-36," AUJR:5 (Jan. 1957), 49-63. Chapter from Ph.D. thesis at Agra.

B1286 BHATIA, SHYAM SUNDER. "Historical Geography of Delhi," IG:1 (Aug. 1956), 17-43. Deals largely with pre-British Delhi, but touches on modern changes.

B1287 BHATNAGAR, G. D. "The Annexation of Oudh," UB:3 (Aug. 1956), 55-66. Uses British papers and Persian works.

B1288 ———. "Some Aspects of Oudh Administration under Wajid Ali Shah. Police Administration," IHCP:13 (1950), 313-16. Figures on crime before British rule.

B1289 CHATTERJI, NANDALAL. "Disposal of Unclaimed Lands in Post-Mutiny Oudh," UPHS: NS 2 (1954), 16-17.

B1290 ———. "A Forgotten Agitation against the Amalgamation of Oudh with the N.W. Province," IHCP:9 (1946), 351-52. Lucknow agitation in 1877.

B1291 "The Close of the Oudh Controversy," CR 46:92, 435-84. History of British administration and settlement.

B1292 COHN, BERNARD S. "The Initial British Impact on India; a Case Study of the Benares Region," JAS:19 (Aug. 1960), 418-31. "The concern is with the nature of the political system before the establishment of British rule and the changes wrought by that rule." Documents the rise of a new class, the "under civil servants." Based on records in India Office Library, U. P. Central Record Office.

B1293 COTTON, J. J. "William Knighton's Private Life of an Eastern King," IHRC:9 (1926), 25-35. Synopsis of book.

B1294 DAYAL, PRAYAG. "A Farmān of King Wājid 'Alī Shāh of Oudh," UPHS:8 (July 1935), 86-91. Facsimile of Persian MS in Lucknow, dated 1264 A.H. (1847-48).

B1295 "The Dehra Dun," CR:95 (Oct. 1892), 350-86; 96 (Jan., April 1893), 130-51, 372-401; 97 (July, Oct. 1893), 164-75, 245-70; 98 (Jan. 1894), 82-103.

B1296 DEWAR, D. "The Administration of the Ceded Provinces under Henry Wellesley, 1801-3," UPHS:1 (June 1918), 47-108. Prints a number of laws and enactments.

B1297 DIKSHIT, R. K. and MIRZA, MOHAMMAD WAHID. "A Firman of King Muhammad Ali Shah of Oudh of 1253 A.H. [1837-38]," UPHS: NS 2 (1954), 47-50.

B1298 "The District Officer, N.W.P., His Miscellaneous Duties," CR 28:55 (Mar. 1857), 109-28.

B1299 DIVER, M. "Honoria Lawrence in 1843," CM:153 (May 1936), 513-26. Wife of Henry Lawrence; her account of a trip through Oudh to join her husband.

B1300 "Examination of the Oude Papers," OH:7 (Nov. 1825), 311-31.

B1301 GAUR, Y. C. "Metcalfe and Oudh," IHRC:23 (1946), 48-50.

B1302 HALIM, A. "The Aligarh Diary," IHRC:24 (Feb. 1948), 45-46. A running chronology of daily events 1772 to present, in a private collection.

B1303 HASAN, NURUL. "Āgra," EI:1, 252-54.

B1304 ———. "Allāhābād," EI:1, 417-18.

B1305 "History and Statistics of Cawnpore," CR 14:28 (1850), 378-408.

B1306 "The History of Lieutenant-Governor the Honourable Henry Wellesley's Administration of the Ceded Provinces in Oude," AAR:9 (1807), 17-30.

B1307 "The Kingdom of Oude," CR 3:6 (1845), 375-427.

B1308 MACLAGAN, EDWARD. "The Site of the Battle of Delhi, 1803," PHS:3 (1915), 127-43. An attempt to establish the site; 2 colored maps.

B1309 MADGE, E. W. and DHAR, K. N. "The Hessings, Father and Son: Killahdars of Agra," CR:267 (Jan. 1912), 1-18.

B1310 MASALDAN, P. S. "The First Legislative Assembly in the U.P.," IJPS:3 (Oct. 1941), 182-91.

B1311 MAUNSELL, E. B. "The Defence of Delhi by Burn and Ochterlony, October, 1804," AQ:26 (April 1933), 82-92. Military history.

B1312 MUHAMMAD, S. ABU. "Dasturul Amal of Nawab Saadat Ali Khan of Oudh," UPHS:4 (Oct. 1928), 28-90. Rules of the appointment of district officers, and their duties; issued Sept. 30, 1819. From a Persian MS in the collection of R. Burn.

B1313 "Murder of Commissioner Fraser—Delhi, 1835; a Tale of Circumstantial Evidence," BM:123 (Jan. 1878), 32-38.

B1314 NAGAR, R. N. "The Tahsildar in the Ceded and Conquered Provinces (1801-1833)," UPHS: NS 2 (1954), 26-34.

B1315 NARAIN, MAHESH. "Lucknow: a Study in Historical Geography," AUJR:10 (Jan. 1961), 131-41. Brief history, from pre-Mughal period to the present.

B1316 NIGAM, KRISHNA CHARAN. "Notice of a Persian Manuscript on the Nawabs of Oudh," UPHS:13 (Dec. 1940), 58-65. Note on Tarikh-i-Sa'adat, written in time of Sa'adat Ali Khan, Nawab Wazir of Oudh, 1798-1814; list of contents.

B1317 NIGAM, M. N. "Evolution of Lucknow," NGJI:6 (March 1960), 30-46. With maps.

B1318 "Oudh," CR:34 (June 1860), 218-39. Its administration.

B1319 "The Physical Capabilities of Oude," CR:26 (June 1856), 415-44.

B1320 PRASAD, NANDAN. "The Oudh Treaty of 1837," IHCP:13 (1950), 297-302. An assessment of its validity.

B1321 "Public Correspondence in the North Western Provinces," CR 18:36 (1852), 321-39. On public works.

B1322 QANUNGO, S. N. "Wajid Ali Shah: the Last King of Oudh," MR:114 (Nov. 1963), 352-55.

B1323 SEN, S. N. "Lord Auckland on Delhi," CR:74 (March 1940), 255-70. Prints a minute on conditions, dated 7 March 1838.

B1324 SINGH, SHILENDRA K. "Minto and the Begums of Oudh," IHCP:14 (1951), 295-301. Political history based on Oudh Papers.

B1325 SPEAR, T. G. P. "The British Administration of the Delhi Territory (1803-57)," JIH:19 (Aug. 1940), 235-48. A survey of Metcalfe's Delhi system, theory and practice.

B1326 "Stocqueler's Life of Nott," CR 22:44 (1854), 459-80. On envoy at the Court of the King of Oudh.

B1327 [THOMASON]. "The Hon. James Thomason, Late Lieut.-Governor, N.W. Provinces," CR 21:42 (1853), 472-523.

B1328 TRITTON, A. S. "Aligarh," EI:1, 403.

B1329 UPADHYAYA, R. D. "Delhi As It Was 100 Years Ago," MR:117 (March 1965), 199-200.

B1330 VARMA, GANGA PRASAD. "Lucknow: Past and Present," HR: 19 (April 1914), 361-69.

17. THE PUNJAB, 1850 TO 1950

B1331 "The Administration of the Punjab," CR 21:41 (1853), 225-83.

B1332 BARWICK, G. F. "Dhuleep Singh," EB:8, 144. Maharaja of Lahore.

B1333 CANDLER, EDMUND. "Amritsar," BM:186 (Sept. 1909), 346-59. Description of the Sikhs.

B1334 COATMAN, J. "The Punjab Finger-Print Bureau," BM:218 (Aug. 1925), 246-61. Its history and activities.

B1335 GRIFFIN, LEPEL. "Maharaja Duleep Singh," AR, Ser. 2:7 (Jan. 1894), 21-52. Heir of Ranjit Singh.

B1336 HASAN, NURUL. "Amritsar," EI:1, 454.

B1337 KHOSLA, J. N. "The Cost of Administration in the Punjab," IJPS:1 (July 1939), 58-68.

B1338 "Life in the Punjab," CR 26:52 (June 1856), 445-73.

B1339 MATHUR, Y. B. "Police Administration in the Punjab, 1849-75," JIH:41 (Dec. 1963), 731-48; 42 (April 1964), 195-217. On the formal organization.

B1340 NAIDIS, MARK. "John Lawrence and the Origin of the Punjab System, 1849-57," BPP:80 (Jan.-June 1961), 38-46. "The intent here is to suggest that John Lawrence contributed little that was really creative to the Punjab school, and, in fact, the reforming zeal of the Punjab system originated outside the province."

B1341 "The Punjab Government; a Political Study," CR:37 (Sept. 1861), 1-34.

B1342 "A PUNJABI." "Six Years of Punjab Rule," CR 65:129 (1877), 75-91. 1871-76.

B1343 RAY, S. N. "Mahatma Hansraj," MR:65 (Jan. 1939), 89-92. "A Maker of the Modern Punjab."

B1344 RODGERS, CHARLES J. "Amritsar in 1881," CR 74:148 (1882), 306-15. General description.

B1345 SINGH, S. GANDA. "Some Correspondence of Maharaja Duleep Singh," JIH:27 (April 1949), 1-23; IHRC:25 (Dec. 1948), 89-103. Prints correspondence on relations with British.

B1346 STEWART, COSMO. "Jan Nikal Seyn's Man," BM:218 (Dec. 1925), 794-801. Story of a Sikh who served with John Nicholson.

B1347 VERMA, DIPCHAND. "Provincial Autonomy in the Punjab. (April 1937–Oct. 1939)," IJPS:1 (April 1940), 449-63. Its workings.

18. SIND

B1348 "The Ameers of Sindh," CR:1 (May 1844), 217-45.

B1349 "British Administration of Scinde," CR 14:27 (1850), 1-50.

B1350 "CADI." "Hur Outlaws," BM:223 (March 1928), 383-402. Fighting outlaws in Sind in the 1890's.

B1351 CHISHTIE, K. A. "Lord Ellenborough's Policy Regarding Sind," IHCP (1939), pp. 1581-1603. Based on Ellenborough Papers.

B1352 DATTA, JATINDRA MOHAN. "Sind," MR:50 (Oct. 1931), 400-03. Recommendations for the separation of Sind at the first Round Table Conference.

B1353 FORTESCUE, JOHN W. "The Napiers," BM:236 (July 1934), 115-39. The career of three men, one of whom conquered Sind.

B1354 GILES, R. "The Last of the Amirs," NC:86 (Dec. 1919), 1140-50. Briefly describes Sir Ali Murād Khān Tālpur, his people, his land.

B1355 GUPTA, NAGENDRA. "Sind in the Eighties," MR:40 (Aug.-Dec. 1926), 153-56, 332-35, 377-80, 483-87, 582-86; 41 (Jan. 1927), 14-19.

B1356 HUTTENBACK, ROBERT A. "British Relations with Sind during the First Afghan Crisis, 1838-1841: a Study in Imperial Foreign Policy," IHQ:36 (Dec. 1960), 209-26. Based on India Office Library and Punjab documents.

B1357 ———. "The French Threat to India and British Relations with Sind, 1799-1809," EHR:76 (Oct. 1961), 590-99. Based on India Office Library records, Bombay Government records in Elphinstone College, National Archives documents.

B1358 ———. "The Khosa Controversy and the Anglo-Talpur Rivalry over Cutch, 1814-1820—a Foot-Note to the History of Sind," JIH:42 (Aug. 1964), 323-28.

B1359 KAPUR, ANUP CHAND. "The Ministerial Imbroglio in Sind," HR:83 (July 1948), 9-15. Provincial politics in 1948.

B1360 "Karachi (A Bird's-Eye View)," CR:91 (July 1890), 107-26.

B1361 KHERA, P. N. "British Policy towards Sindh, 1834-37," JPUHS:3 (April, Dec. 1934), 42-53, 131-38; 4 (Dec. 1935), 115-25.

B1362 MACMURDO, JAMES. "Account of the Province of Cutch, and of the Countries Lying between Gujarat and the River Indus," LSBT:2 (1820), old ed., 205-41; new ed. 217-55.

B1363 MANGHIRMALANI, THAKURDAS LOKMANDAS. "Hindus under the Talpurs of Sindh," MR:51 (March 1932), 265-72. The Talpurs, a Baluchi tribe, ruled Sind, 1782-1843.

B1364 ———. "Mirza Khusrow Beg," MR:46 (Nov. 1929), 518-24. Sindhi nobleman.

B1365 MARIWALLA, C. L. "Capture of Karachi," MR:78 (Sept. 1945), 162-67. By the British.

B1366 "Mohan Lal in Afghanistan," BM:60 (Nov. 1846), 539-54. Review of book dealing with history of Sind and life of Dost Mohammad Khan.

B1367 POSTANS, J. "Memorandum on the City of Shikarpore, in Upper Sindh," ASB 10:109 (1841), 17-26.

B1368 ———. "Report on Upper Sindh and the Eastern Portion of Cutchee, with a Memorandum on the Beloochee and other Tribes of Upper Sindh and Cutchee, and a Map of Part of the Country Referred to," ASB:12 (Jan.-June 1843), 23-44. With fold-out map.

B1369 RAHIM, A. "The Fall of Sind," HFM:2 (1831-1905), part 1, 47-71.

B1370 "Recent Works on Scinde," CR 16:32 (1851), 383-411.

B1371 SAXENA, S. K. "Seton's Mission to Sind and His Recall," IHRC: 23 (1946), 50-54.

B1372 "Sindh Controversy—Napier and Outram," CR 6:12 (1846), 569-614.

B1373 YOUNGHUSBAND, FRANCIS E. "General Romer Young-husband and Scinde," CM:93 (March 1906), 359-69. On the campaign of conquest.

19. *ANDAMAN AND NICOBAR ISLANDS*

B1374 BIRCH, WM. B. "The Andaman Islands," CR 66:131 (1878), 152-77.

B1375 ———. "The Nicobar Islands," CR 66:133 (1878), 586-615.

B1376 DAS GUPTA, S. N. "Proceedings Relative to a Settlement at the Andamans," IHRC:24 (Feb. 1948), 51-57.

B1377 DYER, A. SAUNDERS. "The Andaman Islands," CR:116 (April 1903), 260-91. Description and social life.

B1378 "The Nicobar Islands," CR 51:102 (1870), 266-88.

B1379 ROUTH, G. M. "The Andaman Islands," FR:158 (July-Dec. 1945), 110-15. On economic problems.

B1380 TARLING, NICHOLAS. "Pirates and Convicts: British Interest in the Andaman and Nicobar Islands in the Mid-Nineteenth Century," JIH:38 (Dec. 1960), 505-26.

B1381 TEMPLE, RICHARD CARNAC (ed.). "Extracts from the Bengal Consultations of the 18th Century Relating to the Andaman Islands," IAn: 29-32 (1900-1903), throughout volumes; see index in volumes for pp. Covers period 1788-1796.

B1382 ——— (ed.). "Miscellaneous Papers Relative to the Settlements in the Andaman Islands in the XVIIIth Century," IAn:28 (Dec. 1899), 323-31.

B1383 ———. "An Unpublished Document about the Nicobars (1771)," IAn:29 (Nov. 1900), 341-47. The observations of John Ritchie, surveyor.

B1384 ———. "An Unpublished XVIIIth Century Document about the Andamans," IAn:30 (1901), 232-38.

20. *1857*

B1385 AHMAD, QUEYAMUDDIN. "Maulvi Ali Karim; A Scholar-Soldier of Bihar during the Movement of 1857-59," IHRC:33 (1958), 9-15.

B1386 ———. "The Unique Trial of 'Arrah Town' for Rebellion against Government during 1857-59," BRS:46 (1960), 155-62. Discusses records of case.

B1387 ———. "The Wahabis and the Movement of 1857-59," BRS:45 (1959), 244-260. Examines why the Bihar Wahhabis did not rise.

B1388 ALI, AMEER. "Origins of the Indian Army," CoR:99 (June 1916), 776-81. Sketch of troops involved in Mutiny.

B1389 ANSARI, A. S. BAZMEE. "'Azīm Allāh Khān," EI:1, 822. Life of a man "said to have been the brain of the political upheaval (known as the Mutiny) of 1857"; in the service of Nānā Ṣāḥib.

B1390 ———. "Bakht Khān," EI:1, 935-54. "Commander-in-Chief of the 'rebel' native forces."

B1391 ASHRAF, K. M. "Ghalib and the Revolt of 1857," Reb., pp. 245-56. Discusses Ghalib's diary, gives excerpts. Bibliography of relevant works by Ghalib.

B1392 BAGLEY, F. R. "1857; A Small Boy in the Indian Mutiny," BM: 227 (March 1930), 427-42. Memories of a 5-year-old in Agra.

B1393 BAJPAI, S. C. "Later Days of Nana Saheb of Bithur," JIH:43 (Aug. 1965), 647-55.

B1394 BANERJEE, BROJENDRA NATH. "The Last Days of Nana Sahib of Bithoor," IHRC:12 (1929), 59-62; BPP:39 (Jan.-June 1930), 150-52. A letter dated 1860.

B1395 BANERJI, S. K. "Bahadur Shah II of Delhi and the Administration of the Mutineers," IHRC:24 (Feb. 1948), 47-50.

B1396 "The Bengal Mutiny," BM:72 (Sept. 1857), 372-92. Blames it on the patronage system.

B1397 BENNETT, AMELIA. "Ten Months' Captivity after the Massacre at Cawnpore," NC:73 (June 1913), 1212-34; 74 (July 1913), 78-91. Graphic description by girl 18 years old at the time.

B1398 BHARGAVA, Y. "Letters about the Mutiny of 1857 in Madhya Bharat," IHRC:33 (1958), 39-43. Description and brief summary of information.

B1399 BHATNAGAR, I. "Rao Tula Ram, Rebel Chief of Rewari," JIH: 42 (Aug. 1964), 471-77.

B1400 BLAKELEY, PHILLIS R. "William Hall, Canada's First Naval V.C.," DR:38 (1957), 250-58. Summary in HA:5 (No. 3080): "A brief biography of a Nova Scotian Negro who won the Victoria Cross for his feats as a seaman during the Sepoy Mutiny in 1857."

B1401 BRYNE, JAMES. "British Opinion and the Indian Revolt," Reb., pp. 291-312. "Concerned particularly with the reaction of the British working class," i.e., of the Chartist, Ernest Jones.

B1402 BUCKLER, F. W. "The Political Theory of the Indian Mutiny," RHS, Ser. 4:5 (1871), 71-100. An ingenious argument based on evidence at the trial of Bahādur Shah II; argues that the E. I. Co. was a Mughal vassal, and *it* was the mutineer.

B1403 BURN, R. and CADELL, PATRICK. "Rani Lakshmi Bai of Jhansi," RAS (1944), pp. 76-78. Questions veracity of Kincaid's sources (RAS, 1943), and his conclusions.

B1404 CADELL, PATRICK. "The Outbreak of the Indian Mutiny," SAHS:33 (1955), 118-20. With letter from John MacNabb, 18 years old, to his mother on the "cartridge question."

B1405 "The Campaign of 1857-58," CR:32 (March 1859), 186-250.

B1406 CHAND, NANAK. "Diary of the Mutiny at Cawnpore," UPHS:3 (Dec. 1927), 3-53. Tr. from Urdu; by agent of a bank.

B1407 CHANDRA, SUDHIR. "The 'Hindu Patriot' and the Revolt of 1857-58," MR:118 (Sept. 1965), 225-27.

B1408 CHATTERJEE, HARAPRASAD. "Sepoy Army—Its Strength, Composition and Recruitment on the Eve of the Mutiny of 1857," CR:139 (May 1956), 164-72; 140 (July, Aug., Sept. 1956), 31-40, 101-10, 191-202 [title varies].

B1409 ———. "The Sepoy Mutiny and the Hindu Muslim Reaction," CR:142 (March 1957), 296-305. Claims Muslims were equally loyal and disloyal as Hindus.

B1410 CHATTERJI, NANDALAL. "Lawless Brigands and Soldiers of Freedom in the Great Revolt of 1857," JIH:34 (Aug. 1956), 209-10. A note on papers in U. P. that "reveal the interesting fact that during the Mutiny days hundreds and thousands of erst-while dacoits suddenly . . . turned into patriotic rebels."

B1411 ———. "Was the Great Revolt of 1857 a Fight for National Freedom?" JIH:33 (Dec. 1955), 341-46.

B1412 CHAUDHARY, V. C. P. "Mutiny and Titles with Special Reference to Bihar," IHRC:35 (Feb. 1960), 69-76.

B1413 CHAUDHRI, MOHAMMED AHSEN. "The Impact of the 'Revolt' of 1857 on British Colonial Policy," PHS:11 (July 1963), 208-19.

B1414 CHI, HSIEN-LIN. "Shih-lun 1857-59 nein yin-tu ta Ch'i-i ti Ch'i-yin hsin-chin ho ying-hsiang" [On the National Uprising of 1857-59 in India; Its Cause, Nature and Effects], LY:5 (1957), 19-34. Summary in HA:3 (No. 1479): "Surveys the Indian Mutiny of 1858 from a Marxist standpoint."

B1415 COLVIN, AUCKLAND. "Agra in 1857; a Reply to Chapter 21 of Lord Roberts' 'Forty-One Years' Reminiscences in India," NC:41 (April 1897), 556-68.

B1416 DAS, MANMATHA NATH. "Western Innovations and the Rising of 1857," BPP:76 (Jubilee, 1957), 71-81. "The purpose of this paper is to show that the scientific and technological innovations as well as the educational or social measures had practically little to do with a predominantly political issue."

B1417 DATTA, KALIKINKAR. "A Contemporary Mutiny Account: Memorial of an Indian Planter," IHRC:28 (1951), 19-25. Prints the memorial.

B1418 ———. "Nature of the Indian Revolt of 1857-59," BPP:73 (1954), 16-24. On the role of zamindars in Bihar, emphasizing how little help they gave the British.

B1419 ———. "Some Contemporary Records Relating to the Movement of 1857-59 in Chotanagpur, Manbhum, Singbhum and Palamau," IHRC: 31 (1955), 12-16. Some letters.

B1420 ———. "Some Original Documents Relating to the Indian Movement of 1857-59," IHRC:30 (1954), 34-42. In Bihar.

B1421 ———. "Some Newly Discovered Records Relating to the Bihar Phase of the Indian Movement of 1857-59," PU:8 (March-June 1954), 1-6. Statement of one Nishan Singh to the Deputy Magistrate on his arrest.

B1422 DEWAR, DOUGLAS and GARRETT, H. L. "A Reply to Mr. F. W. Buckler's *The Political Theory of the Indian Mutiny*," RHS, Ser. 4:7 (1924), 131-59. Buckler's reply, pp. 160-65.

B1423 DURAND, H. M. "Central India in 1857," CR 62:124 (1876), 365-89.

B1424 EDWARDES, S. M. "A Few Reflections on Buckler's Political Theory of the Indian Mutiny," IAn:52 (Aug. 1923), 198-203. A criticism of "special pleading" that the Mutiny was caused by the English treatment of Bahadur Shah.

B1425 "Englishwomen in the Rebellion," CR:33 (Sept. 1859), 108-26.

B1426 "Extracts from Letters Written at Benares during the Mutiny by an Officer of the Indian Civil Service," UPHS:5 (Jan. 1932), 1-17.

B1427 FITCHETT, W. H. "Tale of the Great Mutiny," CM, 3rd Ser.: 10 (Jan.-June 1901), 90-108, 240-57, 391-401, 537-51, 667-87, 801-21; 11 (July-Dec. 1901), 71-83, 249-64, 377-90, 520-42, 651-64, 796-803. A popular account.

B1428 FOURNIAN, CHARLES. "Contemporary French Press," *Reb.*, pp. 313-21. French press reaction to Mutiny.

B1429   FRANZ-WILLING, GEORG. "Der Indische Aufstand 1857-1859" [The Indian Insurrection 1857-1859], WAG:21 (1961), 29-48, 109-30. Based on English-language sources.

B1430   GARRETT, H. L. O. "The Trial of Bahadur Shah II," PUHS:1 (April 1932), 3-18. Based on records in Punjab Records Office and Punjabi Mutiny correspondence.

B1431   GHOSE, BENOY. "The Bengali Intelligentsia and the Revolt," Reb., pp. 103-18. On the social and religious factors in Bengali attitudes toward the events of 1857.

B1432   HAQ, S. MOINUL. "Hakim Ahsanullah Khan's Memoirs," PHS:6 (Jan. 1958), 1-33. Memoirs of the minister and chief confidant of Emperor Bahadur Shah II, in "rough translation" by a British officer; an eyewitness account of the Mutiny.

B1433   ———. Same, with "Appendix: Mutiny Diary of a Clerk of Delhi Gazette Press," PHSM:2 (1958), 57 pp.

B1434   ——— (tr.). "The Story of the War of Independence, 1857-58 by 'Allamah Fadl-i-Haqq of Khayrabad," PHS:5 (Jan. 1957), 23-57. An eyewitness account by an eminent teacher in Delhi; composed while a prisoner in the Andamans.

B1435   ——— (ed.). "Syed Ahmed Khan's Letter to John Kaye," PHS:8 (July 1960), 227-31. A brief note on 1857.

B1436   HASAN, MEHDI. "Bahadur Shah II, His Relations with the British and the Mutiny," IC:33 (Jan. 1959), 95-111. Based on Persian manuscripts.

B1437   HEELEY, SIBYL. "Delhi, 1857. A Man Hunt," BM:228 (Nov. 1930), 682-705. Reminiscences of the author's grandfather.

B1438   HENDERSON, P. A. WRIGHT. "The Story of Cawnpore: By the Warden of Wadham College," BM:175 (May 1904), 628-45.

B1439   [HODSON]. "William Stephen Raikes Hodson (1821-1858)," EB:13, 558-59. Biographical sketch of Hodson of Hodson's Horse, leader of light cavalry in the Mutiny.

B1440   "India," ER:106 (Oct. 1857), 544-94. A review of 8 books and pamphlets on the Mutiny.

B1441   "The India Question—Its Present Aspects and Teachings," CR:30 (June 1858), 355-94. On the aftermath of 1857.

B1442   "India under Lord Canning," ER:117 (April 1863), 444-97. On the Mutiny.

B1443   "The Indian Crisis of 1857," CR:29 (Dec. 1857), 377-438.

B1444 "Indian Heroes," W:70 (Oct. 1858), 350-75. Reviews 7 diaries of the Mutiny.

B1445 "Indian Mutiny," QR:102 (Oct. 1857), 534-70.

B1446 "The Indian Mutiny," W:112 (Oct. 1879), 328-86.

B1447 "The Indian Mutiny," BM:173 (April 1903), 564-82. A summary of events.

B1448 "The Indian Mutiny," EB:14, 446-51. Causes and events.

B1449 "The Indian Mutiny and the Land-Settlement," BM:84 (Dec. 1858), 701-08.

B1450 "The Indian Mutiny in Fiction," BM:161 (Feb. 1897), 218-31.

B1451 JHA, JATA SHANKAR. "Correspondence among the Organisers of the Anti-British Plot of 1857 in Bihar," BRS:41 (Sept. 1955), 340-56. Reprints 16 letters, dated Oct. 11, 1855 to June 19, 1857, all sent and received by Muslims.

B1452 ———. "The Patna Conspiracy of 1857," IHRC:32 (1956), 78-84. From letters and records at Calcutta.

B1453 ———. "Some Unpublished Correspondence Regarding Nana Sahab's Stay in Nepal in the State Archives of Bihar," JIH:42 (Aug. 1964), 525-36.

B1454 JHA, KAMESHWAR. "A Study of Some Mutiny Letters of Sohagpur," IHRC:33 (1958), 105-08. Relates to Madhya Pradesh.

B1455 JOSHI, P. C. "1857 in Our History," Reb., pp. 119-222. A Marxist interpretation of the historiography of 1857.

B1456 KANT, RAMA. "Nepal and Indian Revolt of 1857," PSR:4 (Oct. 1965), 71-80.

B1457 KAUL, IQBAL. "Antecedents of the Jagirdars of Ambapani under Bhopal State and Their Declaration of 'Jihad' during the Mutiny," JIH:40 (April 1962), 179-89. Heavily researched account of the political intrigues of a rebel family on the borders of Bhopal, who tried to use the Mutiny to reinstate the family fortunes.

B1458 "Kaye's History of the Sepoy War," ER:124 (Oct. 1866), 299-340; "Kaye's History of the Sepoy War, Vol. II," ER:133 (Jan. 1871), 90-122.

B1459 "Kaye's Sepoy War," CR 41:81 (1865), 95-113.

B1460 KHALDUN, TALMIZ. "The Great Rebellion," Reb., pp. 1-70. "The primary cause of the revolt was the imperialist exploitation of the Indian people."

B1461 KHAN, A. R. "Hakim Ajmal Khan's Role in the Struggle for Freedom," PPHC:6 (1956), 213-34.

B1462 KINCAID, C. A. "Lakshmibai Rani of Jhansi," RAS (1943), pp. 100-104. Disputes the imputation of revenge as a motive; declares circumstances beyond her control led her to fight the British.

B1463 KOMAROV, E. N. [Economic Causes of the Popular Uprising in India, 1857-1859], SV:4 (1957).

B1464 LAMBRICK, H. T. "The Bengal Army and the Mutiny," L:57 (May 23, 1957), 813-15.

B1465 LESLIE, J. H. and MOLESWORTH, F. C. (eds.). "The Diary and Letters of Arthur Moffatt Lang, 1st Lieutenant, Bengal Engineers. India—1857 to 1859. With Explanatory Notes, Maps, Portraits, Illustrations, etc.," SAHR:9 (Jan., April, Oct. 1930), 1-26, 73-97, 189-213; 10 (1931), 69-108, 129-42, 195-206; 11 (1932), 1-25.

B1466 "The Literature of the Rebellion," CR:32 (March 1859), 106-21.

B1467 "Lord Clyde's Campaign in India, August 1857 to February 1858," BM:84 (Oct. 1858), 480-514.

B1468 MACHWE, P. "1857 and Indian Literature," IL:1 (Oct. 1957), 53-59. Annotated bibliography of literary works on 1857 in Indian languages.

B1469 MACMUNN, GEORGE. "Delhi After the Storming; with Excerpts from the Manuscript of F. C. Maisey," CM, Ser. 3:68 (May 1930), 549-61.

B1470 ———. "Some New Light on the Indian Mutiny," BM:224 (Oct. 1928), 433-46. An attempt to summarize events and interpret them.

B1471 MAJUMDAR, R. C. (ed.). "Some Unpublished Documents Regarding the Mutiny of 1857," BPP:76 (Jubilee Issue, 1957), 45-70. 14 documents from the Kaye collection in the India Office Library on the role of Bahadur Shah and Rani of Jhansi.

B1472 ———. "Some Unpublished Records Regarding the Sepoy Mutiny," IHRC:33 (1958), 115-19.

B1473 MALLICK, A. R. "The Muslims and the Mutiny," L:57 (May 30, 1957), 875-76.

B1474 MARIWALLA, C. L. "Sind and the Indian 'Mutiny' of 1857," MR:81 (March 1947), 227-34. Based on memoirs, biographies, and official files.

B1475 MOJUMDAR, KANCHANMOY. "Later Days of Nana Saheb," BPP:81 (July-Dec. 1962), 96-107. Based on records and newspapers.

B1476 MOORE, K. "At Meerut during the Mutiny," NC:54 (Nov. 1903), 826-38. "A lady's narrative of her experiences during the outbreak."

B1477 MUKHERJEE, HARIDAS and UMA. "The Great Rising of 1857," MR:102 (Sept. 1957), 203-08. Disputes R. C. Majumdar's interpretation that it inspired the later nationalists.

B1478 NAIDIS, MARK. "John Lawrence, Mutiny Hero," BPP:82 (Jan.-June 1963), 1-11. Based on John Lawrence Papers in India Office Library.

B1479 [NICHOLSON]. "John Nicholson of Delhi," BM:163 (Feb. 1898), 207-23.

B1480 NOGARE, LILIANA DALLE. "Echoes of 1857 in Italy," Reb., pp. 322-31.

B1481 NUTT, KATHARINE F. "The Sepoy Mutiny of 1857: the New Look," MQ:1 (Oct. 1959), 41-55. Traces theory of Mutiny as first war of independence to K. M. Panikkar, 1920; claims Nehru relied on him as a source for Discovery of India; discusses centenary films on the Mutiny.

B1482 OSIPOV, A. M. "K Voprosu o roli radzhputskogo krest'ianstva v indiiskom natsional'nom vosstanii 1857-1859 godov" [On the question of the role of Rajput peasants in the Indian national uprising of 1857-59], VIs:6 (1957), 71-83; summary in HA:4 (No. 1286): "An attempt to emphasize the 'progressive nature' of the Mutiny of 1857. . . . Based on recent Indian publications."

B1483 ———. [The Peasantry of the North-Western Provinces on the Eve of the Uprising of 1857-59], PUI.

B1484 PANDYA, G. B. "Vagher Revolt of 1858-59," IHCP:14 (1951), 225-29. The revolt of a backward community in Kathiawad.

B1485 "The Poetry of the Rebellion," CR:31 (Dec. 1858), 349-67.

B1486 "The Poorbeah Mutiny—the Punjab," BM:83 (Jan. 1858), 94-101. A narrative from Lahore.

B1487 "The Post Office in the Mutiny," PHS:4 (1916), 129-40. Two memoranda on Dāk service.

B1488 "The Principles of Our Indian Policy," W:84 (July 1865), 185-219. Discussion of background to the Mutiny.

B1489 "The Punjab in 1857," BM:89 (April 1861), 501-16. On John Lawrence.

B1490 QURESHI, I. H. "The Causes of the War of Independence," HFM:2 (1831-1905), part 1, 230-69.

B1491   RAHIM, M. A. "An Immature Plan of the Abortive Rising of 1857," US:1 (April 1964), 36-45.

B1492   RIZAWI, M. H. "A Glance over the Mutiny Files in the Custody of the Regional Office of the National Archives of India at Bhopal," IA:9 (Jan.-June 1955), 53-54. Lists briefly administrative orders and reports in files.

B1493   SAFA, M. N. "The War of Independence, 1857-59," HFM:2 (1831-1905), part 1, 270-332.

B1494   SALMOND, JOHN A. "The Frantic Roars of the London Times; British Public Opinion and the Indian Mutiny," BPP:82 (July-Dec. 1963), 88-105.

B1495   SARDESAI, G. S. "The Last Days of Nana-saheb of Bithur," MR:60 (Nov. 1936), 508-10.

B1496   SAREEN, TILAK RAJ. "Gwalior under the Mutineers," JIH:43 (Aug. 1965), 625-32.

B1497   SARKAR, JAGADISH NARAYAN. "The Mutiny in Manbhum," IHRC:32 (1956), 36-48.

B1498   ———. "The Mutiny of 1857-58 and the Palamau Jagirdars," BRS:41 (1955), 527-71. A study of the role of jagirdars in one district of Bihar.

B1499   ———. "Restoration of Order in Manbhum after the Mutiny (1857-'58)," BRS:43 (Sept.-Dec. 1957), 341-58. Based on British correspondence, much of which is printed here.

B1500   SATYANARAYANA RAO, S. " '1857' in Karnāṭaka," MS:48 (1957-58), 66-76.

B1501   SCOTT-MONCRIEFF, G. K. "General Sir Alexander Taylor, G.C.B.," BM:195 (Jan. 1914), 117-37. On an engineer in the Punjab in 1850's, with his part in events of 1857.

B1502   SEN, SURENDRA NATH. "The 'Mutiny' Reconsidered," L:57 (May 16, 1957), 783-84.

B1503   ———. "Writings on the Mutiny," HIPC, pp. 373-84.

B1504   SHARMA, GOPAL LAL. "Kuer Singh and Eighteen-fifty-seven," MR:114 (Dec. 1963), 440-42.

B1505   SHASTIKO, P. "Indian Mutiny of 1857-1859 and the Reaction of the Russian Public," UPHS:4 (1956), 84-88. Brief quotations from Russian press reactions in 1857.

B1506   ———. "Russian Press on 1857," Reb., pp. 332-36.

B1507 SHYWALKER, T. S. "The Ancestors of the Rani of Jhansi," IHRC:24 (Feb. 1948), 9-13.

B1508 "The Siege of Cawnpore and Lord Canning's Administration," CR:83 (July 1886), 57-110.

B1509 "Siege of Lucknow," CR:31 (Sept. 1858), 112-49.

B1510 "Sindia and Dhar," CR 40:79 (1864), 102-23. Their history and role in 1857.

B1511 SINGH, SATINDRA. "Political Organisation of the Indian Mutineers; a Study of the History of Political Institutions," IJPS:8 (Jan. 1947), 752-60; CR:104 (July 1947), 37-45. On the government established at Delhi, its formal structure and something of its working. Based on Urdu Mutiny papers in Imperial Record Department.

B1512 ———. "Sociological Interpretation of Indian Mutiny," CR:101 (Nov. 1946), 85-100. Marxian analysis.

B1513 SOLANO, E. JOHN. "The Siege of Arrah; an Incident of the Indian Mutiny," BM:175 (Feb. 1904), 228-42.

B1514 SPEAR, PERCIVAL. "1857 in Delhi," PQ:7 (Summer 1957), 14-17. A fine summary of events in Delhi, illustrated.

B1515 SRIVASTAVA, K. L. "The Contribution of the Press to Development of National Ideas and Dissatisfaction against the British Rule Especially in Central India—Malwa during the Revolt of 1857," IHCP:17 (1954), 318-21. Lists papers publishing "nationalist" views before and during 1857.

B1516 ———. "Influence of the Press on the Outbreak of the Mutiny Especially in Central India—Malwa," IHRC:19 (Dec. 1942), 156-58.

B1517 TAIMURI, M. H. R. "Some Unpublished Documents on the Death of the Rani of Jhansi and the Mutiny in Central India," IHRC:29 (1953), 157-59. Lists documents.

B1518 TEMPLE, RICHARD C. "In the Century before the Mutiny," IAn:52 (Nov. 1923), 307-13. On the causes of the Mutiny.

B1519 "Then and Now:—a Retrospect and an Estimate," CR:86 (April 1888), 308-28. On 5 books on 1857.

B1520 TING, TSE-LIANG. "Kuan-yu 1857 nien yin-tu ta ch'i-i chung ti fung-chien shih-li ho che-tz'u ch'i-i ti hsin-chih wen-t'i" [The Feudal Elements in the Great Uprising of 1857 in India and the Character of the Uprising], LY:5 (1957), 35-54. Summary in HA:3 (No. 2612): "Corrects some of the views expressed in Rajan P. Dutt's *India To-day* on the Indian Mutiny of 1857, noting that the masses were the driving force of the uprising."

B1521 TINKER, HUGH. "1857 and 1957: the Mutiny and Modern India," IAf:34 (Jan. 1958), 57-65. On the Anglo-Indian partnership and the nature of Indians' loyalties to England; interprets 1857 as freezing the modernization of Indian society.

B1522 TWEEDIE, W. "A Memory and a Study of the Indian Mutiny," BM:176 (Aug. 1904), 184-204. By a former ensign at Banaras.

B1523 VIBART, E. "Sepoy Revolt at Delhi, May, 1857," CM, Ser. 3:3 (Sept.-Nov. 1897), 304-22, 447-60, 603-11.

B1524 WELCH, COLIN. "The Indian Mutiny," E:44 (1957), 15-22. Summary in HR:4 (No. 1287): "Suggests that the causes of the Mutiny can be traced in part to the differing social psychologies of the English and Indians. . . . The author's account of the Mutiny itself is based on Sir John Hayes [Kaye's] *History of the Sepoy War in India.*"

B1525 WICKINS, PETER (ed.). "The Indian Mutiny Journal of Private Charles Wickins of the 90th Light Infantry," SAHR:35 (1957), 96-108, 170-74; 36 (1958), 17-24, 80-86, 130-36.

21. RELATIONS WITH PRINCES

B1526 "The Armies of the Native States," QJPSS:1 (Oct.? 1878), 1-23; 7 (Sept. 1884, Feb. 1885), 23-67, 31-72.

B1527 BANERJI, ALBION. "Indian States and the Constitution Bill," CoR:147 (March 1935), 313-20.

B1528 BARTON, W. P. "The Deadlock in India and the Indian States," QR:281 (July 1943), 16-27.

B1529 ———. "The Indian Princes and the Cabinet Mission," QR:285 (Jan. 1947), 126-38.

B1530 BHATTACHARYA, SUKUMAR. "Lord Curzon and the Indian Princes, 1899-1901," IHRC:33 (1958), 44-51. Prints letters.

B1531 CARDEW, F. G. "Indian Imperial Service Troops," BM:160 (July 1896), 5-15. Armies of the princely states.

B1532 "Contrasted Opinions of Lord Hastings and Sir Charles Metcalfe on the Right of Interference with Native Indian Governments," OH:3 (Dec. 1824), 541-53.

B1533 DATTA, KALIKINKAR. "The Malabar Rajahs and the East India Company," BPP:57 (July-Dec. 1939), 1-9. Based on English records.

B1534 FINLEY, MARK. "The Changing Role of the Indian Princes," CoR:176 (Oct. 1949), 230-35.

B1535 FURBER, HOLDEN. "The Unification of India, 1947-1951," PA: 24 (Dec. 1951), 352-71. On accession of the princely states.

B1536 GRIFFIN, LEPEL. "The Native Princes of India and Their Relations with the British Government," AR:8 (July 1889), 209-28.

B1537 GUPTA, D. C. "A Survey of the Present Constitutional Position of the Indian States," MR:60 (Sept. 1936), 268-75.

B1538 "Indian Annexation: British Treatment of Native Princes," W:79 (Jan. 1863), 115-57.

B1539 "Indian Treaties," CR 40:80 (1865), 381-418. With princes.

B1540 "KERALAPUTRA." "The Internal States of India," AAAPSS:145 (Sept. 1929), Supplement 45S-58S. Historical survey of their legal and political position.

B1541 KIBE, M. V. "Constitution and Function of the Indian League," MR:36 (Sept. 1924), 241-44. The Chamber of Princes and its Relationship to the Government of India and the League of Nations.

B1542 KRISHNAMACHARI, V. T. "Indian States and Their Position in Indian Polity," AAAPSS:233 (May 1944), 12-17.

B1543 LEE-WARNER, W. "Native States of India," QR:176 (Jan. 1893), 198-221. History of British relations with them.

B1544 LETHBRIDGE, ROPER. "The New Viceroy and Our Indian Protectorate," AR, Ser. 2:7 (Jan. 1894), 59-70. On relations with princes.

B1545 MACMUNN, G. "Princes of India and the British Crown," EnR: 64 (May 1937), 559-67. Summarizes different classes of princely states.

B1546 MOHSIN-UL-MULK (Mehdi Ali). "The Attack on the Native States of India," NC:26 (Oct. 1889), 545-60. Defense of the Nizam of Hyderabad's rule.

B1547 "Native Thinker." "Lord Curzon and the Native States," CR:121 (July 1905), 398-407.

B1548 "The Nizam's Offer," AR:5 (Jan. 1888), 1-20. On policy towards native states.

B1549 O'DWYER, M. F. "Relations of the Indian States to British India," FR:127 (June 1927), 759-68. In the light of nationalist attitudes towards princes.

B1550 "Our Military Policy Towards the Native States of India," BM: 139 (Feb. 1886), 267-78.

B1551 PAL, DHARM. "British Policy towards the Native States of India (1864-1868)," JIH:25 (Aug. 1947), 217-39. An analytical account.

B1552 PANIKKAR, K. M. "The Position of Indian States," AR: NS 22 (1926), 251-68; discussion 269-77.

B1553 ———. "The Princes and India's Future," FA:21 (April 1943), 571-73. Their rights to self-determination.

B1554 PASHA, COLES. "Indian Principalities and Other Problems," CoR:121 (June 1922), 721-30.

B1555 "Princes' Delegation to the Conference; Biographical Sketches," NEI:38 (Aug. 28–Sept. 4, 1930), 233-34, 259. The Round Table conference.

B1556 RAMAIYA, A. "The Point of View of Indian States' Subjects," CoR:125 (April 1929), 505-08.

B1557 RATCLIFFE, S. K. "The Crown, the Government, and the Indian Princes," CoR:100 (Dec. 1911), 782-91. Relationship over previous 50 years.

B1558 SINGH, BHUPINDER. "Indian Princes and the British Empire," NC:105 (Feb. 1929), 179-89. By the Maharajadhiraj of Patiala.

B1559 ———. "The Present Situation of the Indian Princes," CoR:134 (Nov. 1928), 561-67.

B1560 SYDENHAM OF COMBE. "Future of the Indian Native States," NC:101 (June 1927), 831-41.

B1561 WEDDERBURN, DAVID. "Protected Princes of India," NC:4 (July 1878), 151-73.

22. FOREIGN RELATIONS

B1562 ABIR, M. "Relations between the Government of India and the Sharif of Mecca during the French Invasion of Egypt, 1798-1801," RAS (1965), pp. 33-42.

B1563 ADYE, JOHN. "Central Asia—a Military Problem," CoR:52 (Nov. 1887), 712-23. India not much threatened by Russia.

B1564 ANDRONOV, I. "The Nazi Plan to Conquer India; Documentary Survey," NT:14 (April 7, 1965), 16-20.

B1565 BANERJEE, ANIL CHANDRA. "Side Lights on Anglo-Russian Relations, 1864," IHRC:24 (Feb. 1948), 30-34. Extracts from *The Moscow Gazette.*

B1566 BARTON, WILLIAM P. "India's Foreign Policy," CoR:178 (Nov. 1950), 267-70.

B1567 BASU, B. K. "India's Frontier Problems in the 19th and 20th Centuries with Tibet and China: Historical Background," QRHS 5:1 (1965/66), 30-36.

B1568 CHATTERJEE, NANDALAL (ed.). "Russian Bogey and Lord William Bentinck," BPP:75 (1956), 1-16. Prints sections from Bentinck's minute of March 13, 1835, dealing with Indian preparedness for a Russian attack.

B1569 CRANE, ROBERT I. "Indo-American Relations, 1939-1959," QRHS:2 (1962-63), 163-70. In the context of communications theory.

B1570 DAVIES, ARTHUR. "Swaraj," NC:106 (Oct. 1929), 433-42. "Reply" by Reginald Craddock, NC:106 (Nov. 1929), 607-11. On India's hopes from the League of Nations.

B1571 DAYAL, HARISHWAR. "The Genesis and Organisation of the Indian Foreign Service," IYBIA:1 (1952), 26-34.

B1572 DMITRIEV, G. L. [On Ties between India and (Russian) Central Asia in the Second Half of the 19th Century], IsA:3 (May-June 1962), 198-200. Noted in SPA:2 (March 1963), 29. A review of documents in the Uzbek state archives.

B1573 "England and Russia in the East," ER:142 (July 1875), 264-306. Review of papers by Sir Henry Rawlinson; includes materials on Indian policy on the North West Frontier.

B1574 FONTERA, RICHARD M. "Anti-Colonialism as a Basic Indian Foreign Policy," WPQ:13 (June 1960), 421-32. Compares it to American isolationism.

B1575 "Foreign Policy of Sir John Lawrence," ER:125 (Jan. 1867), 1-47. Largely with Arabs and Afghans.

B1576 FURBER, HOLDEN. "The Letters of Benjamin Joy, First American Consul in India," IA:4 (July-Dec. 1950), 219-27. Prints the letters.

B1577 GOROSHKO, G. B. [Foreign Policy Problems in Indian Historical Literature], NAA:1 (1965), 178-84. Cited in SPA:5 (March 1966), 30-31.

B1578 GUPTA, JYOTI SWARUP. "India and the League of Nations," MR:40 (Aug. 1926), 161-64.

B1579 GUPTA, KARUNAKAR. "A Study of Indo-Soviet Relations, 1946-1955," CR:139 (April 1956), 37-47.

B1580 HUTTON, JAMES. "The Subsidiary System in India," CoR:6 (Sept.-Dec. 1867), 172-185. Subsidiary alliance system in late 18th cent.

B1581 "Imperialism for India," CR:81 (Oct. 1885), 241-70.

B1582 "An Indian Official." "India as a World Power," FA:27 (July 1949), 540-50.

B1583 KAUSHIK, DEVENDRA. "Some Aspects of Relations between the Indian and Central Asian Peoples in the Latter Half of the 19th Century and Early 20th Century," JIH:43 (Dec. 1965), 897-903.

B1584 KHAIR, M. A. "William Phillips' Mission to India, 1942-1943," ASP:9 (Dec. 1964), 65-72. American diplomat, sent as Roosevelt's personal representative.

B1585 KHAN, M. ANWAR. "A Letter from the Amir of Bukhara to the Government of India (1870-71)," PHS:12 (Jan. 1964), 26-30.

B1586 KUMAR, RAVINDER. "The Records of the Government of India on the Berlin-Baghdad Railway Question," HJ:5 (1962), 70-79. The influence of India on British policy toward Russia, Turkey.

B1587 LA FOY, MARGARET. "India's Role in the World Conflict," FPR:18 (May 1, 1942), 38-47. Documented account of Indian attitudes and contributions to the war.

B1588 LALLA, N. N. "Lord Dalhousie and the Faithful Allies of the British," BHS:2 (March 1929), 15-50. From British records, especially *The Nizam's Cession Papers.*

B1589 LANDON, P. "Tibet, China and India," FR:98 (Oct. 1912), 655-62. On India-Tibet treaty arranged by Younghusband.

B1590 LIUSTERNIK, YE. [The Archives Relate. . . .], AAS:10 (Oct. 1962), 52. Abstract in SPA:3 (June 1963), 22.

B1591 LYALL, ALFRED. "Frontiers and Protectorates," NC:30 (Aug. 1891), 312-28. On British policy of buffer-states in India.

B1592 MEHROTRA, S. R. "Imperial Federation and India, 1868-1917," JCPS:1 (1961), 29-40. Place of India within the empire.

B1593 MIROSHNIKOV, L. I. [The "German Threat" to India and English Expansion in Iran in 1914-1920 (An Answer to Opponents)], NAA:6 (1963), 55-72; cited in SPA:4 (Oct. 1964), 17.

B1594 MOJUMDAR, KANCHANMOY. "Nepal-Tibet War, 1855-56," USI:94 (April 1964), 175-94.

B1595 ———. "Nepal's Relations with Indian States (1800-50)," JIH:43 (Aug. 1965), 403-65.

B1596 MOOKERJEA, SOBHANLAL. "Indo-Nepalese Relations," CR:176 (July 1965), 35-50. Largely current, but some historical background.

B1597 MORISON, THEODORE. "A Colony for India," NC:84 (Sept. 1918), 430-41. Proposal that German East Africa be an Indian colony.

B1598 MUKERJI, RADHAKUMUD. "India and League of Nations Minorities Treaties," MR:50 (July 1931), 49-52.

B1599   NABOKOFF, C. "Russia and India," CoR:130 (Oct. 1926), 476-83. On the Russian bogey.

B1600   PRAVADYA, BALRAM SINGH. "Mr. Nehru, the Indian National Congress and India's Membership in the Commonwealth," IS:4 (1962-63), 298-311. Reasons for entering and relations with the Commonwealth, based on speeches and statements.

B1601   PROKHOROV, E. P. "Problemy indii v russkoi pechati 40-kh godov XIX veka" [The Problems of India in the Russian Press of the 1840's], VMU:1 (1959), 105-18. Abstract in HA:8 (No. 1671): Based largely on the writings of V. G. Belinski and the journals *Otechestvennye Zapiski, Biblioteka dlia chteniia* and *Russkii Invalid.*

B1602   RAI, GANPAT. "Lord Mayo's Diplomacy," IHRC:18 (Jan. 1942), 250-57.

B1603   RASU'ZADE, P. "Political Relations between India and Central Asia in the Second Half of the 19th Century," CAR:12 (1964), 219-27. Uses official records to "establish that St. Petersburg had at no stage the slightest inclination to operate militarily beyond her own Central Asian theatre."

B1604   "The Russians in the East," CR 43:85 (1866), 68-100.

B1605   SHAHANI, RANJEE G. "India against Hitler," NC:129 (Feb. 1941), 179-91. Statements and editorials.

B1606   SHNEIDMAN, J. LEE. "The Proposed Invasion of India by Russia and France in 1801," JIH:35 (Aug. 1957), 167-75. Examines and questions the validity of a document on Franco-Russian alliance, and gives a short account of the Cossack invading force cut short by Tsar Paul's murder.

B1607   SINGH, SHILENDRA K. "Minto and Goa," IHRC:29 (1953), 133-41. Based on British records.

B1608   SINGHAL, D. P. "Goa: End of an Epoch," AuQ:34 (March 1962), 77-89. Gives historical background and reactions to the Goa takeover.

B1609   SLAGG, JOHN. "Parliament and the Foreign Policy of India," CoR:46 (July 1884), 115-26. For increased parliamentary control over Indian affairs.

B1610   SOLOV'YEV, O. F. "Russia's Relations with India (1800-1917)," CAR:6 (1958), 448-64. Summary of an article based on "painstaking and original research," in which the propaganda element is "marginal." Based on Russian archival material.

B1611 SUTHERLAND, L. S. "The East India Company and the Peace of Paris," EHR:62 (April 1947), 179-90. Negotiations behind the treaty of 1763, ending the Seven Years War, and its provisions for India.

B1612 SYDENHAM OF COMBE. "India as a Colonising Power," NC:84 (Oct. 1918), 762-70. On a proposal that India be given Mesopotamia as a colony.

B1613 [TURKIN, V. N.]. "Anglo-Nepalese Relations, 1914-1923," CAR 13:2 (1965), 157-63. Tr. of article in KS:75 (1964).

B1614 VAMBERY, A. "Will Russia Conquer India?" NC:17 (Jan., Feb. 1885), 25-42, 297-311.

B1615 VERMA, DINA NATH. "India and Asian Solidarity, 1900-1939," BRS:49 (1963), 316-28.

B1616 VISHNUGUPTA. "Public Opinion and Foreign Policy in India," MR:50 (Oct. 1931), 449-58.

B1617 WATSON, A. "India and Korea," NC:148 (Sept. 1950), 155-61. Examines implications of Nehru's policy.

B1618 YU SHENG-WU and CHANG CHEN-KUN. "China and India in the Mid-19th Century," Reb., pp. 337-52. On Indian and Chinese sympathy with and participation in each other's wars.

B1619 YUSUF ALI, A. "India and the League of Nations," CoR:119 (May 1921), 633-41. The Indian delegation to Geneva.

C. NATIONALISM AND POLITICS

1. *GENERAL*

C1 ASAWA, KHYALI LAL. "Concept of Gram Swarajya in Modern Indian Political Thought (in Hindi)," PSR:1 (1962), 157-66.

C2 BAGAL, JOGESH C. "Mile-stones to Our Freedom Struggle," MR: 94 (Sept., Oct., Nov. 1953), 223-29, 303-09, 389-96.

C3 ———. "Our Freedom Struggle in England," MR:84 (Dec. 1948), 459-66.

C4 BAYLEY, DAVID H. "Violent Public Protest in India: 1900-1960," IJPS:24 (Oct.-Dec. 1963), 309-25. A statistical analysis.

C5 CHANDRA, SUDHIR. "Non-Violence in the Indian National Movement," Q:42 (July 1964), 44-48.

C6 CHATTERJEE, ANNAPURNA. "The Indian Press and Rastraguru Surendra Nath Banerjea," CR:171 (May 1964), 107-11.

C7 ———. "A Phase of India's Struggle for Freedom," CR:173 (Oct. 1964), 77-80.

C8 ———. "Rashtraguru Surendranath Banerjea," CR:171 (April 1964), 47-54; 172 (Aug. 1964), 135-38.

C9 ———. "Women in India's Struggle for Freedom," CR:175 (April 1965), 61-62.

C10 COTTON, EVAN. "Some Outstanding Political Leaders," PI, pp. 185-202. Sketches of Gokhale, Tilak, Banerjea, C. R. Das, Sapru, Malaviya, Nehru father and son, V. S. Srinivasa Sastri, Lajpat Rai, Aga Khan, Ali brothers, Mohammed Shafi, Ambedkar.

C11 DEVDUTT. "The Indian Struggle and Its Legacy: 1885-1947," AAWA:2 (Spring 1965), 68-75.

C12 DEVI, KAMALA. "Surendranath Banerjea," CR:68 (Aug., Sept. 1938), 201-10, 283-93. Biographical essay.

C13 DEVIATKINA, T. F. "Bor'ba Indiiskogo Natsional'nogo Kongressa za vliianie na molodezh'" [The Struggle of the Indian National Congress for Influence on Youth], KS:75 (1964), 92-99.

C14 DUTT, BHUPENDRA LAL. "The Indian National Congress. The Story of Its Foundation," MR:59 (1936), 75-81. With photographs and dates of presidents, 1885-1934; on pp. 81-86, a résumé of Congress activities.

C15 FRANDA, MARCUS F. "The Organizational Development of India's Congress Party," PA:35 (Fall 1962), 248-60. Examines the organization of India's Congress Party since independence.

C16 [From Materials of the Institute of Marxism-Leninism, under the CPSU Central Committee], NAA:5 (1964), 61-64; cited in SPA:5 (Nov. 1965), 22. Documents in Russian and English on ties between India and the International.

C17 GOKHALE, B. G. "Some Aspects of Indian Liberalism," SAQ:62 (1963), 275-87. Noted in HA:9 (No. 3125).

C18 GOL'DBERG, N. M. "Indiiskie zhurnaly Iasnopolianskoi biblioteki kak odin iz istochnikov izucheniia natsional'no-osvoboditel'nogo dvizheniia v Indii" [The Indian periodicals of the library in Yasnaya Polyana as a source for research on the Indian national liberation movement], SV:4 (1955), 116-30. Noted in HA:4 (No. 2977): "An important collection of Indian periodicals and some Indian books of 1896-1910 are housed in the Tolstoi Museum. The author describes the newspaper *Free Hindustan.*"

C19 GOYAL, O. P. "The Idea of the Nation in Extremist Political Thought," MR:111 (March 1962), 211-12. Brief commentary on writings of B. C. Pal and Aurobindo Ghose.

C20 GRAY, R. M. "Women in Indian Politics," PI, pp. 156-65.

C21 GUPTA, NAGENDRANATH. "Lala Lajput Rai," MR:44 (Dec. 1928), 735-40.

C22 GUPTA, SUBODH BHUSHAN. "Annie Besant: a Political Sketch," PSR:3 (May 1965), 89-100.

C23 GWYNN, J. T. "Balance in India," FR:137 (Feb. 1932), 160-72. Discusses Congress leaders, and their changes over the years.

C24 HALDER, GOPAL. "Revolutionary Terrorism," SBR, pp. 224-57. Gives background and traces development through 1946.

C25 "The Indian National Congress," MR:59 (Jan. 1936), 81-86. Survey of 50 years' activities.

C26 KAUSHIK, DEVENDRA. "An Obscure Journal of the Indian Revolutionaries at Baku," FAR:13 (Nov. 1964), 176-78. An Urdu journal at Ali Sher Novai Library, Tashkent: *Azad Hindustan Akhbar.*

C27 KAUSHIK, PITAMBAR DATT. "Non-Gandhian Influences on Pre-Independence Ideology of Indian National Congress," MR:112 (Oct. 1962), 274-80. On currents represented by C. R. Das and Motilal Nehru before 1927 and by Jawharlal Nehru and Subhas Chandra Bose after 1927.

C28 ———. "Sources and Background of Pre-Independence Ideology and Programme of the Indian National Congress," UB:10 (Aug. 1963), 63-76.

C29 KAVIRAJ, NARAHARI. "Peasant Questions," SBR, pp. 517-28. Discusses peasant uprisings against the British and landlords.

C30 KER, J. CAMPBELL. "Subversive Movements: Sedition, Anarchy, Terrorism, Communism, Red Shirt Movement," PI, pp. 226-46. By a former member of the C.I.D.

C31 KUMAR, MAHENDRA. "A Survey of Select Studies on Nehru," GM:8 (July 1964), 265-74.

C32 MAJUMDAR, BIMANBEHARI. "Contribution of the Darbhanga Raj Family to the National Movement in India," BRS:48 (1962), Sec. 2, 33-40.

C33 MAJUMDAR, R. C. "The Growth of Nationalism in India," IAC: 10 (July 1961), 96-113.

C34 McCULLY, BRUCE T. "Bibliographical Article: The Origins of Indian Nationalism According to Native Writers," JMH:7 (Sept. 1935), 295-314. Excellent bibliographic essay, discussing three categories: 1) roots of nationalism in terms of native institutions; 2) contact with Great Britain, seen as beneficent; 3) contact with Great Britain, seen as baneful. Surveys books and articles in English language only.

C35 MEHROTRA, S. R. "The Development of the Indian Outlook on World Affairs before 1947," JDS:1 (April 1965), 269-94.

C36 MEL'NIKOV, A. M. "Antifeodal'naia bor'ba krest'ianstva Indii nakanune vtoroi mirovoi voiny (1937-1939)" [Struggle of the Indian Peasantry against the Feudal System before the Second World War (1937-1939)], UZIV:12 (1955), 196-216. Summary in HA:4 (No. 3190): on "the local peasants' organizations (Kisan sabha) in India, which united in 1936 to form the All-Indian Peasants' Confederation."

C37 MENON, K. RUKMINI. "How National Was the Indian National Congress?" AJPH:11 (April 1965), 70-81.

C38 MOOKERJEE, H. C. "Indian Leadership and the Awakening of the Masses," CR:77 (Oct. 1940), 11-23. On the growing political awareness of the rural population.

C39 MORRIS-JONES, W. H. "The Exploration of Indian Political Life: Review Article," PA:32 (Dec. 1959), 409-20. On a number of contemporary theories of Indian politics.

C40 ———. "India's Political Idioms," PSI, pp. 133-54. Although written about post-independence India, quite suggestive for all nationalist politics and administration; discusses three idioms: modern, traditional, and saintly.

C41 MUKHERJEE, UMA and HARIDAS. "The Alleged Uniqueness of India's Freedom Movement," MR:112 (Aug. 1962), 103-07. A critical discussion of Tara Chand's *History of the Freedom Movement in India* and the thesis that India's struggle for freedom was unique as an ethical and nonviolent phenomenon.

C42 ———. "Satis Mukherjee of the Dawn Society," MR:118 (July 1965), 25-31.

C43 MURDESHWAR, D. R. "The Late Shri G. V. Mavalankar," LSGI: 26 (April 1956), 588-92. Speaker of the Lok Sabha.

C44 NORTH, ROBERT C. "M. N. Roy: The Revolution in Asia," S:31 (1960), 102-08. Noted in HA:8 (No. 2010).

C45 RAO, VASANT D. "The Background of India's Foreign Policy (A Survey of the Various Resolutions Passed by the Indian National Congress between 1885 and 1947)," QRHS:4 (1964/65), 207-19.

C46 ROLNICK, PHYLLIS. "Charity, Trusteeship, and Social Change in India: A Study of a Political Ideology," WP:14 (1962), 439-60. Summary in HA:9 (No. 409).

C47 ROTHERMUND, DIETMAR. "Bewegung und Verfassung. Eine Untersuchung der Politischen Willensbildung in Indien, 1900-1950" [(National) Movement and Constitution. An Inquiry into the Development of Political Objectives in India, 1900-1950], VZ:10 (1962), 126-48. Summary in HA:9 (No. 410): "Based on government and party records, newspapers, and memoirs."

C48 ———. "Constitutional Reforms versus National Agitation in India, 1900-1950," JAS:21 (Aug. 1962), 505-22. Study of the interrelation of structure, function, and aspiration in the nationalist movement; asks, "to what extent does the Indian constitution reflect the aspirations of the Indian freedom movement?"

C49 ———. "Nationsbildung in Indien" [The Creation of an Indian Nation], VZ:11 (1963), 392-403. Summary in HA:10 (Sept. 1964) (No. 156).

C50 SANKHDER, B. N. "V. S. Srinivasa Sastri—the Demosthenes of India," MR:118 (Oct. 1965), 308-11.

C51 SINGH, NIHAL. "Fearless Fighter for Indian Freedom—a Pen Picture of Vithalbhai Jhaverbhai Patel," MR:54 (Dec. 1933), 636-43.

C52 ———. "A Great Muslim Nationalist," MR:52 (Dec. 1932), 616-24. Sir Syed Ali Imam, Muslim nationalist.

C53 ———. "Lala Lajpat Rai," MR:55 (Jan., Feb., March 1934), 1-7, 188-94, 251-59.

C54 SINGHA, S. S. "Christianity and Indian Nationalism," CoR:140 (Aug. 1931), 227-30.

C55 SORABJI, CORNELIA. "A Bengali Woman Revolutionary," NC: 114 (Nov. 1933), 604-11. Name of the woman not given; discusses revolutionary methods.

C56 TAGORE, SOUMYENDRA NATH. "Evolution of Swadeshi Thought," SBR, pp. 203-23.

C57 VARMA, VISHWANATH PRASAD. "Marxism and M. N. Roy," IJPS:22 (1961), 279-92. The evolution of Roy's acceptance and later rejection of Marxism.

C58 ZACHARIAS, H. C. E. "The Road to Indian Autonomy," RP:8 (July 1946), 307-30. Good summary of the nationalist movement and constitutional reforms.

2. NATIONALISM AND POLITICS TO 1919

C59 ADENWALLA, MINOO. "Hindu Concepts and the Gita in Early Indian National Thought," StOA (1961), pp. 16-23. "Our aim here is to examine how . . . Bal Gangadhar Tilak and Aravindo Ghose utilized the Hindu concepts of Karma and dharma . . . to transmit a message of nationalism and political action."

C60 AHLUWALIA, M. M. "Press—and India's Struggle for Freedom, 1858 to 1909," JIH:38 (Dec. 1960), 599-604. Some tidbits of information on press opinions on the nationalist movement.

C61 BAGAL, JOGESH CHANDRA. "Congress in Bengal," SBR, pp. 164-86. Covers period 1885-1920.

C62 ———. "Rajnarain Bose and Indian Nationalism," MR:75 (June 1944), 444-47. Reprints his prospectus for a "Society for the Promotion of National Feeling among the Educated Natives of Bengal," 1861.

C63 BAHADURJI, D. N. "Some Notes on the Indian National Congress of 1906," E&W:6 (Feb. 1907), 143-47.

C64 BAINS, J. S. "The Ghadr Movement: a Golden Chapter of Indian Nationalism," IJPS:23 (Jan.-March 1962), 48-59. From contemporary pamphlets and interviews.

C65 [BANERJEA]. "Sir Surendra Nath Banerjea," MR:38 (Sept. 1925), 373-80. Obituary.

C66 BANERJEE, ANIL CHANDRA. "Political Consciousness before 1857," SBR, pp. 139-51.

C67 BANERJEE, KALYAN KUMAR. "Dadabhai Naoroji: Nestor of Indian Politics," CR:153 (Dec. 1959), 229-41.

C68 ———. "The Gadar Movement and the Hand of Germany," MR: 118 (July 1965), 32-36.

C69 ———. "The Gadar Strategy: Shipping Men and Arms to India; the Story of a Programme That Failed," MR:118 (Aug. 1965), 112-19.

C70 ———. "Har Dayal and Ram Chandra—an Assessment of Two Gadar Leaders," MR:117 (May 1965), 337-43.

C71 ———. "The Indo-German Conspiracy: Beginning of the End," MR:118 (Nov. 1965), 381-86.

C72 ———. "The U.S.A. and the Indian Revolutionary Activity: Early Phase of the Gadar Movement," MR:117 (Feb. 1965), 97-101.

C73 BANERJI, NRIPENDRA CHANDRA. "Swadeshi Days," MR:81 (Jan. 1947), 32-36. On the Dawn Society and Anti-Circular agitation against Sir Bampfylde Fuller's administration.

C74 BASU, NIRMALKUMĀR. "'Bipincandra Pāl' (A Biography of Bipincandra Pāl, the Social Thinker and Leader of Bengal)," BP:15 (1958-59), 169-72.

C75 "BENGAL MAGISTRATE." "The Home Rule Movement in India and in Ireland: A Contrast." CoR:57 (Jan. 1890), 78-97; correction, CoR: 57 (Feb. 1890), 300.

C76 BHATTACHARYA, SACHCHIDANANDA. "The Indian National Congress and Lord Dufferin," BPP:84 (July-Dec. 1965), 161-66.

C77 BHATTACHARYA, SUKUMAR. "An Intercepted Letter of Keir Hardie to Bal Gangadhar Tilak: A Proposal to Hold a Session of the Indian National Congress in London," JIH:37 (April 1959), 81-84. Dated March 31, 1911.

C78 ——— (ed.). "Lord Curzon and the Indian National Congress," CR:131 (April 1954), 39-52. Private correspondence between Curzon and George Hamilton, Secretary of State.

C79 BISHUI, KALPANA. "Lord Dufferin and the Indian National Congress," QRHS:4 (1964-65), 73-79. Based on correspondence.

C80 BOND, BRIAN. "Amritsar, 1919," HT:13 (Oct. 1963), 666-76. Discussion Dec. 1963, p. 873. Illustrated with portraits.

C81 BOSE, ARUN COOMER. "Efforts of the Indian Revolutionaries at Securing German Arms Across the Seas during World War I," CR: 162 (Jan. 1962), 33-43. On Bengali terrorist international plots paralleling Ghadr Party negotiations; from English records and Bengali works.

C82 ———. "India's Fight for Freedom in Europe till 1914," CR:155 (June 1960), 289-302. From contemporary publications; deals with propaganda and conspiracy.

C83 ———. "Indian Nationalist Agitations in the U.S.A. and Canada till the Arrival of Har Dayal in 1911," JIH:43 (April 1965), 227-40.

C84 BOSE, YOTINDRA MOHAN. "India's Awakening: the Swadeshi Movement," Ou:85 (Jan. 19, 1907), 130-35.

C85 BROOMFIELD, J. H. "The Vote and the Transfer of Power, a Study of the Bengal General Election, 1912-1913," JAS:21 (Feb. 1962), 163-81. Analysis of who contested the elections, who voted, the background of the Bengal partition and how it affected the electorate, the effect of other issues, and the use of the vote as a new form of power in long-standing struggles. Based largely on biographical information from varied sources on individual candidates.

C86 BROWN, D. MACKENZIE. "The Philosophy of Bal Gangadhar Tilak: *Karma* vs. *Jñāna* in the *Gītā Rahasya*," JAS:17 (Feb. 1958), 197-206. On Tilak's commentary on the Gita, based on the English translation of the *Rahasya*; stresses it as a background for Gandhi's political use of the Gita.

C87 BROWN, GILES T. "The Hindu Conspiracy, 1914-1917," PHR:17 (Aug. 1948), 299-310. On the Ghadr party, based on American records; condensed from the author's master's thesis.

C88 CHANDRA, BIPAN. "Lord Dufferin and the Character of the Indian Nationalist Leadership," En: NS 2 (Spring 1965), 24-45.

C89 ———. "Two Notes on the Agrarian Policy of Indian Nationalists, 1880-1905," IESHR:1 (April 1964), 143-74.

C90 CHATTERJEE, PROTUL CHANDRA. "Bengal and Political Agitation," HR:28 (Dec. 1913), 863-74.

C91 CHATTERJEE, RAMANANDA. "Keshub Chunder Sen and 'Nation-Building,'" MR:64 (Nov. 1938), 602-06.

C92 ———. "Presidential Address of Mr. Ramananda Chatterjee at the All India Anti-Communal Award Conference, Bombay, 25th October, 1934," MR:56 (Nov. 1934), 591-610.

C93 CHATTERJI, NANDALAL. "The Congress Session of 1907," JIH: 38 (April 1960), 131-37; IHCP:21 (1958), 543-48. A detailed account of the Surat Congress.

C94 ———. "The First Case of *Hartal* in British India," IHRC:33 (1958), 56. A 1790 demonstration in Benares.

C95 CHATTERJI, NANDALAL. "The Forgotten Precursor of the Indian National Congress," MR:86 (Oct. 1949), 282-84; JIH:36 (April 1958), 9-14. The Indian Association of Calcutta, founded 1876.

C96 ———. "The Foundation of the Congress and *Russophobia*," JIH: 36 (Aug. 1958), 171-77; reprinted under the title, "Was the Congress a Child of Russo-phobia?" JIH:37 (Dec. 1959), 367-73. An inquiry into A. O. Hume's motives.

C97 ———. "How the First Split Came in the Indian National Congress," MR:85 (Jan. 1949), 54-55.

C98 CHAUDHURY, V. C. P. "Lytton's Indian Administration and the Birth of Nationalism," QRHS 4:3 (1964/65), 126-37.

C99 CHESNEY, G. T. "India—the Political Outlook," NC:35 (June 1894), 890-904. On signs of unrest.

C100 CHOWDHURY, SASHI BHUSHAN. "Pre-Congress Nationalism," SBR, pp. 152-63. Covers period 1857-1885.

C101 CLARK, T. W. "The Role of Bankimcandra in the Development of Nationalism," HIPC, pp. 429-45.

C102 COTTON, H. E. A. "The Problem of Indian Discontent," CoR:121 (April 1922), 426-33. On economic and political discontent.

C103 "Cow-Killing Riots, Seditious Pamphlets and the Indian Police," AR, Ser. 2:7 (Jan. 1894), 84-95. Anti-police.

C104 CRANE, ROBERT I. "Problems of Divergent Developments within Indian Nationalism, 1895-1905," StOA (1961), pp. 1-15. Discusses the varieties of backgrounds, influences, and developments in nationalism.

C105 CUMPSTON, MARY. "Some Early Indian Nationalists and Their Allies in the British Parliament, 1851-1906," EHR:76 (April 1961), 279-97. Discusses Dadabhai Naoroji and friends, Irish support of Indian political associations before 1885, and early Congress relations with Parliament; most of material pre-1890.

C106 DAS, M. N. "Impact of Liberal Victory in Britain on Indian Politics: 1905-6," JIH:41 (Dec. 1963), 619-29.

C107 ———. "Measures against the Indian Press during the Bande-Mataram Movement," JIH:41 (April 1963), 167-76. From the Morley Papers.

C108 DE, SUSHIL CHANDRA. "An Instance of Organised No-tax Campaign and *Hartal* during the Early British Regime in Orissa," IHRC: 33 (1958), 72-77. In 1810 and 1814.

C109 DUBEY, SATYA NARAYAN. "Individual, Society and State in Indian Extremists' Political Thought, 1905-1920," UB:4 (Dec. 1957), 67-76. Largely on Bipincandra Pal and Aurobindo Ghose.

C110 ———. "Nationalism and Internationalism in Indian Extremists' Political Thought," UB:4 (March 1958), 55-66. Largely on B. C. Pal, Aurobindo Ghose, and Tilak.

C111 DUTT, BHUPENDRA LAL. "The Indian National Congress," MR:59 (Jan. 1936), 75-81. The story of its foundation.

C112 EGERTON, W. E. "Facts from Bihar about the Mud-daubing," NC:36 (Aug. 1894), 279-85. Thought to have political significance by some, religious by others.

C113 "AN ENGLISHWOMAN." "Amritsar," BM:207 (April 1920), 441-46. An eyewitness account of the 1919 riots and massacre; sympathetic to Dyer.

C114 FRASER, ANDREW. "The Situation in India," CoR:96 (Nov. 1909), 562-67. On unrest.

C115 "A FRIEND OF BENGAL." "Bande Mataram," E&W:5 (Nov. 1906), 1077-87. On the writing and spirit of the hymn.

C116 GANGULY, SATYENDRA NATH. "A Glimpse of the Original Revolutionary Societies of Bengal," MR:116 (Nov. 1964), 382-84.

C117 GARVIN, J. L. "Full Light on Indian Unrest," FR:94 (Sept. 1910), 386-403. "Nothing but our own cowardice or sheer incapacity can subvert our dominion in India."

C118 GHOSE, A. M. "Sri Aurobindo: A Political Sketch," PSR:2 (March 1963), 81-90. Sources not indicated, but factual.

C119 GHOSH, SUJATA. "The British Indian Association (1851-1900)," BPP:77 (July-Dec. 1958), 99-119. A history of "the oldest living political organisation in India," based on Association records.

C120 ———. "The British Indian Association and the Indigo Disturbances in Bengal," IHRC:34 (Dec. 1958), 140-45.

C121 GOETZ, HERMANN. "Die Entstehung des Indischen Nationalismus" [The Rise of Indian Nationalism], Sm:6 (1955), 368-96. Summary in HA:4 (No. 127).

C122 GOKHALE, B. G. "Swami Vivekananda and Indian Nationalism," JBR:32 (Jan. 1964), 35-42. Based on his speeches and writings.

C123 [GOL'DBERG, N. M. and SEMENOVA, N. I.]. "Namdhari Rising of 1872 in the Punjab," CAR:9 (1961), 94-101. Analysis of a Russian article on a Sikh uprising, interpreted as part of a general political awakening. Based on British records.

C124 GOPALAKRISHNA, S. "Allan Octavian Hume and the Foundation of the Congress," MR:117 (Feb. 1965), 120-21.

C125 GOYAL, O. P. "Political Ideas of Justice M. G. Ranade," IJPS:23 (July-Sept. 1962), 258-67. With numerous quotations.

C126 GRIFFIN, LEPEL. "The Bengāli in Indian Politics," FR:57 (Jan.-June 1892), 811-19. The Bengali Baboo as a scheming intriguer.

C127 GROVER, B. L. "Allan Octavian Hume's Political Testament: an Appraisal," MR:116 (Oct. 1964), 269-74.

C128 ———. "The Genesis of the Indian National Congress," BPP:82 (July 1963), 131-39; MR:114 (Sept. 1963), 195-200; JIH:41 (Dec. 1963), 607-18. On Hume's role and the motives of others involved.

C129 GUPTA, BRIJEN K. "Connection with Britain as an Issue in Indian Nationalist Politics, 1885-1905," JIH:41 (Aug. 1963), 489-516. Argues that the search for political power, not ideology, shaped the political issues of the times.

C130 HALDAR, AMAL. "Bipin Chandra Pal," MR:113 (Mar. 1963), 221-23. Brief biography.

C131 HAMBLY, G. R. G. (ed.). "Mahratta Nationalism before Tilak; Two Unpublished Letters of Sir Richard Temple on the State of the Bombay Deccan, 1879," RCAS:49 (1962), 144-60.

C132 ———. "Notes on the Soviet Interpretation of the Namdhari Uprising of 1872," CAR:9 (1961), 195-200. Comment on the Gol'dberg-Semenova article above.

C133 ———. "Unrest in Northern India during the Vice-Royalty of Lord Mayo, 1869-72: the Background to Lord Northbrook's Policy of Inactivity," RCAS:48 (Jan. 1961), 37-55. British reaction to income-tax agitation and Wahhabism; based on Mayo and Temple papers.

C134 HAQ, S. MOINUL. "The Rise of Hindu Nationalism," HFM:2 (1831-1906), part 2, 430-50.

C135 HARNETTY, P. "Nationalism and Imperialism in India (The Viceroyalty of Lord Curzon, 1899-1905)," JIH:41 (Aug. 1963), 391-403. Based on India Office documents and newspapers.

C136 HARRISON, H. L. "Representative Councils and the Indian National Congress," AR:5 (Jan. 1888), 105-27. Advocates representative government.

C137 HASHMI, M. M. "Surendranath Banerjee, Syed Ahmad Khan and the British Rule," JPUHS:11 (June 1960), 13-17. Cites the Morley Collections in India Office Library. Compares and contrasts Banerjee and Syed Ahmad Khan.

C138 "Home Rule and India," CR:100 (April 1895), 244-52.

C139 "Home Rule for India," CR:99 (July 1894), 279-89.

C140 HUNTER, W. W. "Popular Movements in India," CoR:59 (Feb. 1891), 153-69. Interpreted as expressions of loyalty.

C141 " 'India for the Indians' or 'India for England,' " CR:91 (July 1890), 32-47.

C142 "The Indian National Congress," W:130 (July 1888), 155-72. With a number of statements by and about Congress.

C143 "The Indian National Congress," CR:88 (April 1889), 385-92.

C144 ISLAM, ZAFARUL. "Oktiabrskaia revoliutsiia i Indiia" [The October Revolution and India], NAA:4 (1964), 71-80. Cited in SPA:5 (June 1965), 24.

C145 ———. "Two Historic Letters," JPUHS:11 (June 1960), 7-12. Mohsin-ul Mulk's letter of Aug. 4, 1906, to Archbold; "Sir Sayyid Ahmad on the Mutiny," 14 Dec. 1864: a letter to Sir John Kaye.

C146 IYENGAR, V. G. K. "The First Andhra Conference," MR:14 (Aug. 1913), 169-73. Report of the conference and its resolutions.

C147 JOSHI, ANANDRAO. "First Indian M.P.—Dadabhai Naoroji," MR:72 (July 1942), 37-39.

C148 JOSHI, V. S. "Tilak and the Revolutionaries," MR:117 (Jan. 1965), 29-33.

C149 KAVIRAJ, N. "The Origin of the Indian National Congress; Bengal's Contributions to It," MR:76 (Oct. 1944), 190-92.

C150 KIPLING, RUDYARD. "The Enlightenments of Paget, M.P.," CoR:58 (Sept. 1890), 333-55. An attack on the Indian National Congress.

C151 KRÜGER, HORST. "Zur Entwicklung der Antiimperialistischen Ideologie in Indien zu Beginn des 20. Jahrhunderts" [On the Adolescence of Anti-Imperialist Ideology in India at the Beginning of the 20th Century], Mi:9 (1963), 263-83.

C152 KUMAR, RAVINDER. "The Deccan Riots of 1875," JAS:24 (Aug. 1965), 613-35. Source: Bombay State Archives.

C153 KUTINA, M. ["From the History of Political Organizations of the Indian National Bourgeoisie, Precursors of the Indian National Congress"], ONU:3 (1961), 62-64. Abstract in SSAB 1:2, 22.

C154 LANDOR, A. HENRY SAVAGE. "Chief Causes of Discontent in India," NA:170 (March 1900), 384-94.

C155 LAW, EDWARD FITZGERALD. "Disaffection in India," BM:182 (Aug. 1907), 287-304. Claims it is caused by poor administration.

C156 LEBRA, JOICE C. "British Official and Non-Official Attitudes and Policies toward the Indian National Congress, 1885-1894," IHQ:31 (June 1955), 134-52. A census of opinions, attempting to discern and define differences between official and non-official opinions; based on books, parliamentary papers, *Calcutta Review*.

C157 MACNICOL, N. "The Future of India," CoR:114 (July 1908), 73-80. Holds that unrest is not an elite phenomenon alone.

C158 [MADHOLKAR]. "The President-Elect of the Indian National Congress," HR:26 (Dec. 1912), 575-78. Sketch of life of Rao Bahadur R. N. Madholkar.

C159 MAJUMDAR, BIMAN BEHARI. "The Inner Circle of the Congress in the Pre-Gandhian Era," QRHS 5:1 (1965/66), 38-51.

C160 ———. "Nationalism in India in Pre-Congress Days," IJPS:19 (April-June 1958), 142-47. Notes on the rise of nationalism after the Mutiny.

C161 MAJUMDAR, RAMESH CHANDRA. "The Genesis of Extremism," SBR, pp. 187-202.

C162 MARKHANDIKAR, R. S. "G. G. Agarkar—a Study in Radical Liberalism, 1856-1896," MR:118 (Dec. 1965), 518-23.

C163 MATHUR, D. B. "Gopal Krishna Gokhale's Concept of Democratic Decentralisation," MR:113 (June 1963), 455-59.

C164 ———. "Public Life in India: The Crisis in Character (A Study of G. K. Gokhale's Ideas and Services)," PSR:2 (Oct. 1963), 22-30. From Gokhale papers in the National Archives, New Delhi.

C165 [MEHTA]. "The Late Sir Pherozeshah Mehta: An Appreciation," HR:32 (Dec. 1915), 472-78. Life and works of the merchant and Congressman.

C166 MISRA, UMA SANKAR. "Lord Dufferin and the Indian Congress," W:132 (July 1889), 92-96. "Reply" by B. N. Dar, W:133 (Jan. 1890), 80-92.

C167 MITRA, S. M. "George Thompson in 1843," CR:128 (Jan. 1909), 108-24. With list of Thompson's speeches in Calcutta.

C168 ———. "India in 1813 and 1913," FR:101 (April 1914), 705-17. "The unrest in India is due to the fact that hardly any attention is being paid by British authorities to Indian psychology."

C169 ———. "Lord Cromer and Orientals," NC:63 (May 1908), 743-50. Applies thoughts expressed in Cromer's *Modern Egypt* to India.

C170 MOOKERJEE, H. C. "The War of 1914-1918 and the Appearance of Discontent," CR:83 (June 1942), 211-34; 84 (Sept. 1942), 203-14.

C171 MORLEY OF B. "British Democracy and Indian Government," NC:69 (Feb. 1911), 189-209. Favorable review of Chirol's *Indian Unrest*.

C172 MUKHERJEE, UMA and HARIDAS. "Sri Aurobindo and Bande Mataram," MR:114 (Aug. 1963), 125-29. Daily paper founded by Bipin Chandra Pal, Aug. 1906–Oct. 1908.

C173 ———. "The Story of Bande Mataram Sedition Trial (1907)," MR:106 (Oct. 1959), 286-88. Includes excerpts from press commentary.

C174 MUSTAFI, ASHOKE. "Thomas Paine and Foreign Rule in India," CR:161 (Dec. 1961), 273-81.

C175 ———. "Thomas Paine and Young Bengal," CR:162 (Feb. 1962), 143-46.

C176 NAIDIS, MARK. "Amritsar Revisited," Hn:21 (Nov. 1958), 1-17. A review of events and effects.

C177 NAIR, T. M. "An Indian's View of the Indian Problem," NC:84 (Sept. 1918), 415-29. Anti-Brahmin.

C178 NAKAMURA, HEIJI. "Bipin-chandora-paru no seijishiso ni tsuite" [A Study of the Political Thought of Bipinchandra Pal], TBKK:20 (1960), 213-60. Summary in HA:7 (1961) (No. 2465).

C179 NANDA, B. R. "Gokhale's Year of Decision," JIH:43 (Aug. 1965), 543-64. 1897.

C180 NATH, D. L. "George Thompson: a Forgotten Political Teacher of Nineteenth Century Bengal," MR:112 (July 1962), 63-65. "Father of political education in India." Includes bibliography of his works and published speeches.

C181 "The National Congress," CR:88 (April 1889), 393-411.

C182 "The National Congress Movement," CR:88 (Jan. 1889), 140-55.

C183 NIVEDITA, SISTER. "The Indian National Congress," HR:26 (Dec. 1912), 429-32.

C184 PAL, BIPIN CHANDRA. "The Forces behind the Unrest in India," CoR:97 (Feb. 1910), 225-36. The British impact and "Hindu Renaissance."

C185   PAL, BIPIN CHANDRA. "The 'Modern Review' on the Situation," MR:113 (June 1963), 448-49. Article by Pal reprinted from *Bande Mataram*, June 6, 1908.

C186   PAL, JNANANJAN. "Bipinchandra Pal," SBR, pp. 556-80.

C187   PAREL, ANTHONY. "Hume, Dufferin, and the Origins of the Indian National Congress," JIH:42 (Dec. 1964), 707-25. The ties with the Theosophical movement; why meetings were held in Calcutta and Bombay simultaneously; refutation of W. C. Bonnerji's Hume-Dufferin conspiracy theory.

C188   PRASAD, BIMLA. "The Indian National Congress and the Problem of Poverty, 1885-90," PU:17 (July 1962), 35-44.

C189   ―――. "The Indian Nationalist Movement and Policy towards Neighbors, 1885-1905," PU:8 (March-June 1954), 100-10. Analysis of Congress' foreign policy attitudes.

C190   PRASAD, RAJENDRA. "The Champaran Agrarian Problem," HR:38 (July 1918), 49-56.

C191   PROTHERO, M. E. D. "Public Opinion in India," QR:182 (Oct. 1895), 429-53. On Congress and others.

C192   RAGHAVENDRA RAO, K. "The Early Phase of Indian Nationalism (1878 to 1897)," KU:5 (June 1961), 49-61; 6 (June 1962), 115-27. "This paper is based on a first-hand inspection of every issue of the Madras newspaper, *The Hindu*, between 1878 and 1897." Important material on the background to Congress and on the "pre-Tilak" phase of its activities as reported in the press; reactions of various sectors of the educated public, especially Muslims. Material on A. O. Hume and Annie Besant.

C193   ―――. "A Nineteenth Century Indian Debate in Political Sociology," KU:8 (1964), 278-85.

C194   RAIKOV, A. V. [On the Question of the Revolutionary Activity of Tilak (1905-1909)], NAA:2 (1965), 53-58. Cited in SPA:5 (March 1966), 32.

C195   ―――. [The Activity of Patriotic Organizations of Indian Immigrants in 1905-1907], NAA:2 (1962), 120-28. Summary in SPA:2 (Oct. 1962), 15.

C196   ―――. "Novye dannye o B. G. Tilake" [New Data on B. G. Tilak], VIs:11 (1956), 132-35. Abstract in HA:3 (No. 542). A report on five articles by Tilak, written for *Kesari*.

C197   RAO, C. SESHAGIRI. "The Andhra Movement," HR:28 (Aug. 1913), 572-77.

C198 RATTRAY, AUSTIN. "The Indian 'National Congress,'" AR:7 (Jan. 1889), 202-24. On signs of unrest.

C199 RAY, PRITHWIS CHANDRA. "The Indian National Congress— a New Chapter," MR:19 (Feb. 1916), 207-13. Résumé of Congress history.

C200 REES, J. D. "Franchise and Functions in India," NC:86 (July 1919), 170-80. Discusses Lord Southborough's reports and anti-Brahmin movement in Madras.

C201 REISNER, I. M. [Peasant Movements among Sikhs in the Second Half of the 18th and Early 19th Centuries], UZIV:3 (1951).

C202 ———. "Pervaia Russkaia Revoliutsiia i probuzhdenie Asii" [The First Russian Revolution and the Awakening of Asia], PIS:5 (1955), 23-33. Summary in HA:4 (No. 1569).

C203 ———. "Russkaia Revoliutsiia 1905-1907 gg. i probuzhdenie Azii" [The Russian Revolution of 1905-1907 and the Awakening of Asia], SV:2 (1955), 14-30; summary in CAR:4 (1956), 218-24 (see esp. "India," pp. 221-24); also noted in HA:4 (No. 2982): "Based on *Novaia istoria stran zarubezhnogo vostoka* (Moscow, 1952); Ivanov, *Ocherk istorii Irana* (Moscow, 1952); Sabotsinskii, *Persiia* (Moscow, 1913), and on Indian Newspapers."

C204 ———. "Vydaiushchiisia indiiskii patriot i demokrat Bal Gangadkhar Tilak (k stoletiu so dnia rozhdeniia)" [The Eminent Indian Patriot and Democrat Bal Gangadhar Tilak (on his Centenary)], SV:4 (1956), 73-89. Abstract in HA:5 (No. 691): "Based on material from the Archive for Russian Foreign Policy and the *Times in India,* 1907-1908."

C205 RISLEY, H. H. "The Race Basis of Indian Political Movements," CoR:57 (May 1890), 742-59. A colorful exposition of racial splits among Indians.

C206 ROW, HANUMANTHA. "The First Andhra Conference," HR:28 (Sept. 1913), 705-08.

C207 ROW, K. S. RAMACHANDRA. "The Andhra Movement," MR:19 (April 1916), 433-38.

C208 RUSTAMOV, U. "Severo-indiiskie kniazhestva i revolutsionnyi pod'em" [The North Indian Principalities and Revolutionary Enthusiasm in the Years 1905 to 1908], SV:2 (1956), 133-36. Summary in HA:5 (No. 693): "Based on material from the Central Military Historical State Archive and on *Turkestanskie Vedomosti* [Turkestan News] (1902, and 1908)."

C209 SAJUNLAL, KASIM ALI. "Mr. Charles Bradlaugh, M.P. and the Indian National Congress," IHCP:21 (1958), 523-35. A draft bill proposed by Bradlaugh for reforming Legislative Councils, 1889, as printed in the *Hyderabad Record,* and other material from this paper and from Bradlaugh's published collection of speeches.

C210 SAPRU, TEJ BAHADUR. "The Late Dr. Satish Chandra Banerji: An Appreciation," HR:32 (July 1915), 87-90. Biography of the lawyer and public figure.

C211 SAREEN, T. R. "The Indian National Congress and the Indian States (1885-1890)," BPP:83 (July-Dec. 1964), 115-17.

C212 SARKAR, BENOY KUMAR. "The Sociology of 'Asia for Asians,'" CR:84 (July 1942), 44-64. Sees 1905 as "the birth of Young Asia."

C213 SARKAR, HEM CHANDRA. "Ananda Mohan Bose," E&W:5 (Oct. 1906), 1001-11. First Secretary of the Indian Association.

C214 SARKAR, SUMIT. "Trends in Bengal's Swadeshi Movement, 1903-1908," BPP:84 (1965), 10-37, 140-60.

C215 SEN, KALYAN. "The Bengal Provincial Conference of 1888," MR:109 (June 1961), 471-73. A note on a congress to protest provincial social and political problems; part of the widening political consciousness accompanying the founding of the Indian National Congress.

C216 SEN, PULINBIHARI. "Works of Bipinchandra Pal: A Bibliography," SBR, pp. 581-604. Lists works in English and Bengali.

C217 SHARROCK, J. A. "Some Misconceptions about the Unrest in India," NC:66 (Sept. 1909), 361-76. On the need to stand firm against Brahmin unrest.

C218 SHETH, PRAVIN N. "Political Awakening in Surat (19th Century)," GRS:27 (Jan. 1965), 40-48. Taken from "Source Material for 'A History of the Freedom Movement in India,'" vol. I.

C219 SINGH, NIHAL. "Bepin Chandra Pal," MR:52 (July 1932), 35-39. On his exile.

C220 ———. "Character Sketch of Colonel Josiah Wedgwood, M.P.," MR:27 (April 1920), 374-79. Biographical sketch of an Indian champion in Parliament.

C221 ———. "Mr. Tilak's Work in England," MR:26 (Oct. 1919), 367-73.

C222 ———. "Unrest in India: Its Genesis and Trend, as an Expatriated East-Indian Sees It," Ar:38 (Dec. 1907), 601-09.

C223 ———. "What Does India Want Politically?" FR:94 (July-Dec. 1910), 425-34.

C224 SINGH, PARDAMAN. "The Indian National Congress–Surat Split," BPP:84 (July-Dec. 1965), 121-39.

C225 SLAGG, JOHN. "The National Indian Congress," NC:19 (May 1886), 710-21.

C226 SPELLMAN, JOHN W. "The International Extensions of Political Conspiracy as Illustrated by the Ghadr Party," JIH:37 (April 1959), 23-45. India as "the first major example of what has now become practically a *sine qua non* of revolutions—international conspiracy." A careful history of the Ghadr Party abroad.

C227 SUBRAHMANYAM, T. V. "The Indian National Congress: An Epitaph," CR:118 (April 1904), 217-25.

C228 SUNDERLAND, JABEZ T. "The New Nationalist Movement in India," AM:102 (Oct. 1908), 526-35. Anti-British.

C229 TEMPLE, RICHARD. "Political Effect of Religious Thought in India," FR:39 (Jan.-June 1883), 132-43. Claims it to be helpful to continuance of British rule.

C230 THAPAR, K. S. "Maharaja Dalip Singh's Return to India," IHCP:4 (1940), 383-92. The background for unrest in Calcutta and the "emergence of a subversive sect [among Sikhs] called the Kookas," with their history in 1860's-1880's.

C231 TRIPATHI, AMALES. "Bankim Chandra and Extremist Thought," BPP:84 (July-Dec. 1965), 167-79. To be continued.

C232 ———. "India Office on the Indian National Congress," IHRC:35 (1960), 203-07. Letters from Kimberley and Cross to Dufferin, 1886-87.

C233 TURHOLLOW, ANTHONY F. "The Letter from Madras to President Wilson," IHCP:23 (1961), 31-38. A letter from Sir S. Subramaniam Iyer asking U. S. support for Indian home rule. Printed, with discussion of background and effect.

C234 "The Unrest in India," QR:209 (July 1908), 216-48. "Our first duty is the maintenance of order."

C235 VARMA, VISHWANATH PRASAD. "The Economic and Social Activities of Lokamanya Tilak," PU:15 (1960), 27-39; M:5 (Aug.-Sept. 1960), 19-32.

C236 ———. "The Genesis of Extremism in Indian Politics, 1897-98," PU:17 (July 1962), 1-24.

C237 ———. "Lokamanya Tilak and Early Indian Nationalism, 1881-1896," PU:16 (1961), 1-35.

C238 ———. "Sri Aurobindo's Theory of Nationalism (A Reconstruction and Critique)," PU:11 (?); 12 (1958), 50-72.

C239 VISHINDAS, HASSARAM. "The Congress and Conferences at Karachi," MR:15 (Feb., March 1914), 223-32, 342-55.

C240 WATSON, ROBERT SPENCE. "Indian National Congresses," CoR:54 (July 1888), 89-104. Who attends, their views.

C241 [WEDDERBURN]. "Sir William Wedderburn and India: A Study," HR:37 (Feb. 1918), 165-69.

C242 WESTBROOK, W. F. "The Religion of Humanity—Sir Henry Cotton," MR:19 (Jan. 1916), 51-57. Biography of president of Congress, 1904; with bibliographical references.

3. NATIONALISM AND POLITICS, 1920 TO 1950

C243 ABBAS, K. A. "Fascism over India," A:39 (June 1939), 323-27. With photo of S. C. Bose.

C244 ABBASI, YUSUF. "A Tussle for the Panjab Leadership," JPUHS: 11 (June 1960), 19-25. Between Sir Fazl-i-Husain and Sir Sikander Hayat Khan, in 1935.

C245 "After the India Report," RT:25 (Mar. 1935), 299-317.

C246 ALEXANDER, H. G. "The Prospect in India," CoR:153 (May 1938), 571-77. Reviews objections of Congressmen to the new constitution.

C247 "The Ambedkar Plan," MR:77 (June 1945), 252-53. Communal adjustments.

C248 ANAND, MULK RAJ. "The Situation in India: a Letter to an Englishman," FR:157 (Jan.-July 1942), 443-49. On attitudes toward the war.

C249 AYER, S. A. and RAO, G. K. "Kher—A Man of Compassion," GM:1 (July 1957), 250-55. Biographical details on the man who was Chief Minister of Bombay in 1937 and 1945.

C250 "B.R.K." "Sardar Vallabhbhai Patel," MR:85 (Jan. 1949), 33-35.

C251 BAHADUR, LAL. "The Simon Commission and India," IHQ:35 (Dec. 1959), 295-311. On the Indian reaction, based on MS material in Congress files.

C252 BANERJEE, NRIPENDRA CHANDRA. "Extracts from My Unpublished Autobiography," CR:101 (Oct. 1946), 1-14.

C253 BENN, WEDGWOOD. "The War and India's Freedom," CoR:156 (Dec. 1939), 652-59. Statements on the demand for freedom.

C254 BLACKETT, BASIL. "The Economics of Indian Unrest," FA:8 (Oct. 1929), 41-51. Argues that unrest is "purely political" and is divorced from the masses.

C255 BRADLEY, B. "Indian Elections," LM:19 (April 1937), 229-40. Discussion of Congress politics, with some details of the vote.

C256 BRAILSFORD, H. N. "India's Other Voice," LA:339 (Jan. 1931), 466-69. Reprinted from *Advance* (Calcutta). Includes Jawaharlal Nehru's speech from the dock before serving two years in jail.

C257 BROWN, F. H. "Political Forces at Work during 1932," PI, pp. 301-18. A fairly detailed account of Indian politics.

C258 BROWN, W. NORMAN. "Religion and Practical Politics in India. Some Religious Movements That Have Furthered Nationalist Endeavor in India," A:26 (March 1926), 242-46, 254-56. Photos of C. R. Das and family, and of the burning of foreign cloth.

C259 ———. "Religion in India's Political Psychology; Three Serious Obstacles with which the Nationalist Leaders Have to Contend," A:26 (Feb. 1926), 149-53, 160-64.

C260 CHATTERJEE, RAMANANDA. "Civil Disobedience in India," A:30 (Aug. 1930), 548-53. Photos of women active in Civil Disobedience Movement.

C261 ———. "Is India Never to Walk Alone?" A:35 (May 1935), 298-305. Attack on new constitution; photo of Chatterjee.

C262 CHATTERJI, NANDALAL. "Netaji Subhas Chandra Bose and India's Struggle for Freedom," JIH:40 (April 1962), 153-57.

C263 CHAUDHURI, NIRAD C. "Subhas Chandra Bose—His Legacy and Legend," PA:26 (Dec. 1953), 349-57. On Bose's influence on politics in 1940's.

C264 COATMAN, JOHN. "India Today and Tomorrow," FA:18 (Jan. 1940), 314-23. Summary of political situation at outbreak of World War II.

C265 ———. "Present Situation in India," NC:107 (June 1930), 741-53. On Gandhi, the Simon Commission, and Nehru report.

C266 COHEN, STEPHEN P. "Subhas Chandra Bose and the Indian National Army," PA:36 (Winter 1963-64), 411-29. Based on printed biographies.

C267 COUSINS, MARGARET E. "Mrs. Rukmini Lakshmipathi, First Congress Woman M.L.C." MR:57 (June 1935), 644-46.

C268 CRADDOCK, REGINALD. "Tragedy in India, Quo Vadimus?" NC:109 (June 1931), 667-80. In favor of "firmness" against the revolutionaries.

C269 DAS, S. R. "An Indian Parent to His Son in England," CoR:126 (Sept. 1924), 342-49. On Indian politics, by the Advocate-General of Bengal.

C270 DASTUR, ALEC J. "Twenty-Five Years of Indian Socialism," IQ: 16 (1960), 105-19. Abstract in HA:8 (No. 2937): "A critical analysis of the policies, activities, and failures of the Indian Socialist parties from the founding in 1934 of the All-India Congress Socialist Party."

C271 "The Delhi Parliament," RT:11 (June 1921), 637-56. Comments on the debates.

C272 "Developments in India," BIN:19 (Aug. 22, 1942), 729-41. Chronological summary of politics, Aug. 4-16, 1942, with summary of comment in the Indian press.

C273 DIVATIA, H. V. "Balasaheb Kher—As I Knew Him," GM:1 (July 1957), 237-40. Chief Minister of Bombay; this article is more about Divatia than Kher.

C274 "The Economic and Social Aspirations of the Indian Nationalists," RT:14 (Sept. 1924), 741-66.

C275 ELLIOTT, W. Y. "Strong Government from Delhi," A:32 (March 1932), 169-73. On nationalist agitation, with photos.

C276 "English Repression and Indian Unity," N:120 (Jan. 21, 1925), 77-78, 80. Texts of emergency ordinance, Calcutta Pact, and All-Parties Resolution.

C277 GARRATT, G. T. "Deadlock in India," A:30 (July 1930), 476-81, 531-33. On nationalism.

C278 ———. "The Third Round Table Conference," NC:113 (Feb. 1933), 129-43. On the issues.

C279 ———. "What India Really Thinks," NC:117 (March 1935), 268-79.

C280 GOPINATH. "The Home Rulers' Technique of Political Propaganda," UB:9 (Dec. 1962), 111-18. Their use of the press, petitions, etc.

C281 GORDON, L. [Glorious Son of the Indian People], AAS:7 (July 1962), 56-58. A review of Ajoi Kumar Ghosh, Stat'i i rechi [Articles and Speeches] (Moscow, 1962, 352 pp.). Summary in SPA:2 (Mar. 1963), 28-29; also SPA:3 (Oct. 1963), 18.

C282 GREEN, JAMES FREDERICK. "India's Struggle for Independence," FPR:16 (June 1, 1940), 70-84. Good summary of nationalism in 1930's.

C283 GWYNN, J. T. "India in 1928," FR:130 (July 1928), 35-43. On political situation.

C284 HAITHCOX, JOHN P. "Nationalism and Communism in India: the Impact of the 1927 Comintern Failure in China," JAS:24 (May 1965), 459-73.

C285 HALDAR, M. K. "Nehru's Foreign Policy," Q:43 (Oct./Dec. 1964), 21-27.

C286 HARDGRAVE, ROBERT L., JR. "The DMK and the Politics of Tamil Nationalism," PA:37 (Winter 1964/65), 396-411. Includes some pre-Independence background.

C287 HARTOG, MABEL. "India and the Cabinet Mission," CoR:169 (April 1946), 193-97. The political situation at the end of the war.

C288 HODSON, H. V. "Responsibilities in India," FA:21 (July 1943), 733-42. The demands and tactics of Congress and the Muslim League.

C289 ———. "Struggle for Power in India," FR:151 (May 1939), 549-58. Survey of political factions.

C290 "India: a Survey of the Situation," RT:15 (Dec. 1924), 137-55. On politics.

C291 "India on the Threshold," BM:209 (Feb. 1921), 137-47. On unrest.

C292 "India: Politics and Religion," RT:16 (Sept. 1926), 771-91.

C293 "India: Swaraj the Phoenix," RT:24 (June 1934), 563-78. On revival of the Swaraj Party.

C294 "India: The Political Chaos," RT:15 (March 1925), 335-52.

C295 "India: The Reaction to the Communal Award," RT:23 (Dec. 1932), 142-61.

C296 "India through Indian Eyes," RT:11 (Dec. 1920), 146-52; (March 1921), 365-81.

C297 "Indian Legislative Council," RT:10 (Dec. 1919), 135-42. On the politics of its Sept. 1919 session.

C298 "Indian Politics," RT:8 (June 1918), 565-99; 9 (March, June 1919), 321-55, 545-64.

C299 "Indian Politics before the Reforms," RT:25 (Dec. 1934), 126-39.

C300 "Indian Rage at MacDonald's Vote Plan," LD:114 (Sept. 3, 1932), 8-9. Brief excerpts from press editorials in England and India, on communal settlement plan.

C301 INGALLS, DANIEL H. H. "The Heritage of a Fallible Saint: Annie Besant's Gifts to India," APS:109 (April 1965), 85-88.

C302 "Interregnum in India," RT:26 (Dec. 1935), 116-27.

C303 KAUTSKY, JOHN H. "Indian Communist Party Strategy since 1947," PA:28 (June 1955), 145-60. Largely deals with 1947-51.

C304 KEMP, TOM. "Leaders and Classes in the Indian National Congress, 1918-1939," SS:28 (Winter 1964), 1-19. Congress as an instrument of the Indian bourgeoisie.

C305 KHANNA, MEHR CHAND. "Hindu Party Calls for Freedom, with Safeguards for All," A:43 (April 1943), 226-29. With resolutions of the Hindu Mahasabha.

C306 KNOX, RAWLE. "The Future of the Sikhs," CoR:172 (Dec. 1947), 332-36.

C307 [KONOW]. "Dr. Sten Konow on India of To-day," MR:37 (June 1925), 654-59. Based on Konow's articles for the *Chicago Daily News.*

C308 LACEY, PATRICK. "Deadlock in India," NC:122 (July 1937), 100-14. Suggests a way out.

C309 ———. "The Indian Assembly," NC:121 (March 1937), 413-20. On politics therein.

C310 "Letters from Ahmedabad," CC:49 (May 11, 1932), 605-07. From an unnamed woman on civil disobedience.

C311 LEVKOVSKY, A. I. [The Swadeshi Movement—the Beginning of a Mass All-India Freedom Movement], NLM (in Russian).

C312 LOVETT, H. VERNEY. "India 1914-40: An Historical Study," QR:276 (Jan. 1941), 9-29.

C313 ———. "Indian Politics, 1940-41," QR:277 (Oct. 1941), 256-73. Excellent political reporting, as are the following articles by Lovett.

C314 ———. "India in 1942: the Cripps Mission and After," QR:279 (Oct. 1942), 125-40.

C315 ———. "India, August to December 1942," QR:280 (April 1943), 125-39.

C316 ———. "India: January to October 1943," QR:282 (Jan. 1944), 31-46.

C317 ———. "India in 1944," QR:283 (Jan. 1945), 57-71.

C318 MASANI, M. R. "The Communist Party in India," PA:24 (March 1951), 18-38. History and position.

C319   MAYNARD, JOHN. "The Sikh Problem in the Punjab, 1920-1923," CoR:124 (Sept. 1923), 292-303. On the Akali unrest.

C320   McCLELLAN, GRANT S. "India's Problems as a Free Nation," FPR:22 (Sept. 7, 1946), 142-55. Intelligent summary of problems.

C321   MEL'NIKOV, A. M. "Krest'ianskoe dvizhenie v Indii v 1934-1936 godakh i obrazovanie vseindiiskogo krest'ianskogo soiuza" [The Peasant Movement in India in the Years 1934-1936 and the Formation of the All India Peasant Union], VIs:6 (1954), 117-27. Noted in HA:1 (No. 805): "Points out the leading role played by the Indian Communist Party and by Communist sympathizers in organizing active peasant movements. . . . The main source cited is the 'All India Kisan Bulletin' as published in the *Indian Labour Journal*."

C322   MISHRA, KIRAN. "International Outlook of Indian Nationalism," AAWA:1 (Summer 1964), 145-62.

C323   MOORE, ARTHUR. "Wishful Thinking about India," NC:141 (Jan. 1947), 10-15. On Congress-League maneuvers.

C324   MORRIS-JONES, W. H. "The Exploration of Indian Political Life: a Review Article," PA:32 (Dec. 1959), 409-20. On a number of contemporary theories of Indian politics.

C325   MUSENBERG. "Unbekannter Passagier auf U 180" [Unknown Passenger Aboard Submarine 180], Fr:19 (1955), 181-82. Abstract in HA:1 (No. 2374): "Describes the transportation of 2 German-trained Indian fascists by a German submarine to a mid-sea rendezvous with a Japanese submarine in April 1943."

C326   NAKAMURA, HEIJI. [On the First Satyagraha Movement in India, 1919-22], RK:225 (1958) (in Japanese).

C327   NATH, PARESH. "M. N. Roy, India's One-man Party," A:43 (March 1943), 151-53.

C328   NEHRU, JAWAHARLAL. "India's Demand and England's Answer," AM:165 (April 1940), 449-55.

C329   ———. "The Unity of India," FA:16 (Jan. 1938), 231-43.

C330   O'DWYER, MICHAEL F. "Anarchy in India," FR:115 (Feb. 1921), 177-91. Claims Gandhi is the cause of it all.

C331   ———. "Gandhi and the Prince's Visit to India," FR:116 (Feb. 1922), 191-203. Gandhi should be in jail.

C332   ———. "India without Mr. Montagu and Gandhi," FR:118 (July-Dec. 1922), 212-29. Then things would settle down.

C333 O'DWYER, MICHAEL F. "Indian Congress Claim for Independence," NC:123 (March 1938), 285-96.

C334 ———. "Indian Politics and Economics," ER:246 (July 1927), 165-78.

C335 ———. "Politics and Religion in India Today," ER:244 (Oct. 1926), 228-48.

C336 ——— and PERCY, E. "India Report," NC:117 (Jan. 1935), 1-23.

C337 OLIVIER, LORD. "The Boycott of the Simon Commission," CoR: 133 (May 1928), 564-71.

C338 ———. "Indian Political Atmosphere," CoR:132 (Aug. 1927), 159-67. On misleading coverage of Indian politics in England.

C339 PARULEKAR, N. B. "Indian Women as Noncooperators," A:31 (Jan. 1931), 22-27. With photographs.

C340 PATEL, VITALBHAI. "Gandhi's Rival Speaks," LA:345 (Oct. 1933), 146-47. On Patel, translated from *Prager Tagblatt* (Prague).

C341 PATRO, A. P. "The Justice Movement in India," AR: NS 28 (1932), 27-40; discussion pp. 41-49.

C342 "Personnel of the 'Round Table' Conference," MR:48 (Oct. 1930), 463-65.

C343 PRAVADYA, BALRAM SINGH. "The Attitude of the Indian National Congress to Dominion Status, 1930-1947," IS:6 (Jan. 1965), 285-309.

C344 RAJAGOPALACHARI, CHAKRAVARTI. "Reconciliation in India," FA:23 (April 1945), 422-34. On the Hindu-Muslim-British triangle in negotiations.

C345 RAO, B. SHIVA. "New Social Forces in India," FA:23 (July 1945), 635-43. On left-wing politics and social discontent.

C346 ———. "Vicious Circle in India," FA:19 (July 1941), 842-51. On the princes, Pakistan, Gandhi, and the British.

C347 RAO, KODANDA. "India and England," AAAPSS:186 (July 1936), 73-80. A moderate's criticism of British rule, by the Secretary of the Servants of India Society.

C348 "The Reception of the Indian White Paper," RT:23 (June 1933), 548-67.

C349 "The Return of the Commission to India," RT:19 (Dec. 1928), 95-112. On reactions to the Simon Commission.

C350 ROSS, COLIN. "Things Seen in India," LA:338 (June 1, 1930), 401-07. Argues that withdrawal of British would mean disaster. Translated from *Vossische Zeitung* (Berlin).

C351 ROTHERMUND, DIETMAR. "The Panjab Press and Non-Co-operation in 1920," IHCP:23 (1961), 39-47. The positions taken by the Sikh, Urdu, and English-language press on non-cooperation and Hindu-Muslim unity.

C352 ROY, BASANTA KOOMAR. "The Crisis in India," OC:40 (Jan. 1926), 14-32. On nationalism.

C353 ROY, M. N. "Indian Bourgeoisie and the National Revolution," LM:11 (March 1929), 163-70.

C354 RUDOLPH, LLOYD I. and RUDOLPH, SUSANNE HOEBER. "The Political Role of India's Caste Associations," PA:33 (March 1960), 5-22. Based on Madras politics.

C355 SAPRU, TEJ BAHADUR. "The Problem of India's Aspirations," CoR:124 (Nov. 1923), 573-83.

C356 ——— and KHAN, ZAFRULLA. "Indian Public Opinion and the White Paper," IAf:12 (Sept. 1933), 611-28. With discussion following.

C357 "Sat Sri Akal," BM:213 (March 1923), 407-13. On the Akali Sikh movement.

C358 SATYARTHI, D. "Congress Goes to a Village," A:37 (May 1937), 344-48. On Congress meeting at Faizpur, with photographs.

C359 SHANKAR, SHYAM. "Political Views of Orthodox Hindus," AR: NS 24 (1928), 85-108; discussion pp. 109-14.

C360 SINGH, GANDA. "The Origin of the Hindu-Sikh Tension in the Panjab," JIH:39 (April 1961), 119-23. Traces tension to the 1880's.

C361 SINGH, HARI KISHORE. "The Rise and Secession of the Congress Socialist Party of India (1934-1948)," SAA:1, 116-40. History of the party and sketches of the principal figures.

C362 SINGH, HARNAM. "American Public Opinion about Indian Politics (1918-1939)," IQ:5 (Oct.-Dec. 1949), 342-49. Brief summary of press comments.

C363 SINGH, NIHAL. "Annie Besant: A Personal Impression," MR:54 (Nov. 1933), 489-96.

C364 ———. "India in Transitional Travail," CoR:123 (April 1923), 464-71. On mood of discontent.

C365 SINGH, NIHAL. "The Sikh's Struggle against Strangulation," FR: 97 (Jan.-June 1912), 82-90. On fostering of communal consciousness.

C366 SORABJI, CORNELIA. "Prospice: the New India," NC:109 (Feb. 1931), 176-83. Anti-Congress.

C367 STRICKLAND, C. F. "Indian Village and Indian Unrest," FA:10 (Oct. 1931), 70-80. Claims unrest is basically economic in origin.

C368 TALBOT, PHILLIPS. "The Independence of India," FPR:23 (June 15, 1947), 74-95. A good account of the events leading up to the transfer of power and of the condition of the country at independence.

C369 "A Thirty-Five Years' Resident in India," BM:229 (May 1931), 725-30. The only way to deal with Congress is to smash it.

C370 VARMA, VISHWANATH PRASAD. "The Political Philosophy of Subhas Chandra Bose," CR:157 (Oct. 1960), 46-62.

C371 VENKATARAMANI, M. S. and SHRIVASTAVA, B. K. "The United States and the 'Quit India' demand," IQ:20 (April-June 1964), 101-39.

C372 VOIGHT, F. A. "The India Revolution during the War," NC:142 (Nov. 1947), 212-18. Summary of activity, with excerpts from statements.

C373 WILLIAMS, L. F. RUSHBROOK. "India between the Conferences," FA:9 (July 1931), 624-37. Communal politics between Round Table Conferences.

C374 ———. "Indian Unrest and American Opinion," AR: NS 26 (1930), 479-96, discussion 497-508. Interesting analysis.

C375 WISER, CHARLOTTE VIALL. " 'Madam President' in the Chair in India. A Woman's Hands and Her Fiery Words Guiding the Indian National Congress," A:26 (July 1926), 634-42. Description of the 40th Congress, with photographs of Sarojini Naidu and Pandit Malaviya.

4. GANDHI

C376 ADENWALLA, MINOO. "Gandhi and Indian Nationalism Reappraised," MA:4 (Winter 1959/60), 69-81. A critical appraisal of Gandhi's political methods.

C377 ALEXANDER, HORACE G. "Mr. Gandhi and the Untouchables," CoR:147 (Feb. 1935), 194-201. From articles in *Harijan*.

C378 ———. "Social and Political Ideas of Mahatma Gandhi," IQ:3 (Oct.-Dec. 1947), 382-91.

C379 ANDREWS, C. F. "Gandhi and Indian Reforms," YR: NS 19 (March 1930), 491-507.

C380 ———. "Heart-beats in India; Gandhi Again Comes to the Fore in India's Struggle for Freedom," A:30 (March 1930), 196-99, 216-17. With photographs.

C381 ———. "Mahatma Gandhi's Birthplace," CoR:153 (Jan. 1938), 35-42.

C382 ASAD, MOHAMMED. "The Jingo Mahatma," LA:344 (Aug. 1933), 489-95. Translated from *Neue Zürcher Zeitung* (Zurich). Interprets two fasts as attempts to keep Hindus and untouchables united against Muslims.

C383 BISSOONDOYAL, B. "Le Mahatma Gandhi et l'Ile Maurice" [Mahatma Gandhi and Mauritius], FrA: NS 18 (Jan. 1962), 19-23. On knowledge of Gandhi in Mauritius.

C384 BLYTH, E. M. E. "Mahatma Gandhi: A Study in Destructiveness," QR:256 (1931), 388-401.

C385 BOSE, NIRMAL KUMAR. "Gandhiji's Ideas on Social Integration," IQ:4 (Oct.-Dec. 1948), 333-41.

C386 CHIGNE, HERVÉ. "Réalisme et prophétisme de Gandhi" [Gandhi's Realism and Propheticism], Es: NS 31 (April 1963), 568-92. By a Franciscan.

C387 COATMAN, J. "Mr. Gandhi," NC:109 (April 1931), 403-13.

C388 DATTA, KALIKINKAR. "Indigo Ryots' Statements at Champaran in 1917," IHRC:33 (1958), 57-64. Prints statements.

C389 D'IAKOV, A. M. and REISNER, I. M. "Rol' Gandi v natsional'no-osvoboditel'noi bor'be narodov Indii" [Gandhi's Role in the National Struggle for Liberation of the Peoples of India], SV:5 (1956), 21-34. Abstract in HA:5 (No. 855): "Corrects the views held previously by Soviet scholars (including the authors of this article) on Gandhi and the Indian national bourgeoisie. . . . Because of the specific conditions which existed in colonial India . . . the national bourgeoisie possessed the right to act in the name of the people. . . . The authors emphasize Gandhi's honesty and self-denial and describe his progressive activities. Based on works of Nehru."

C390 DIWAKER, R. R. "Gandhi and the Uplift of Women," GM:8 (April 1964), 120-26.

C391 EMERSON, GERTRUDE. "Gandhi, Religious Politician," A:22 (1922), 389-95, 405, 407, 408-10, 412. Personal impressions.

C392 EWER, W. N. "An Englishman Views Gandhi in London," A:32 (Feb. 1932), 92-95, 125. With photographs of Gandhi in London.

C393 FLORIS, GEORGE A. " 'Nine Hours to Rama'—The Man Who Killed Gandhi," CR:203 (April 1963), 167-75. An account of Nathuram Vinayak Godse's last days.

C394 FULLER, J. F. C. "Gandhi—Saint or Sinner?" NC:111 (Aug. 1931), 164-78.

C395 GANDHI, MOHANDAS K. "Britain in India," LA:338 (May 1, 1930), 264-70. Gandhi's letter to Irwin, March 2, 1930, before beginning civil disobedience; reprinted from *Young India.*

C396 "The Gandhi Movement," RT:20 (June 1930), 507-23. On non-cooperation.

C397 "Gandhi to Chiang Kai-shek," N:155 (Oct. 24, 1942), 411-12. Hitherto unpublished letter.

C398 "Gandhi-Nehru Correspondence," MR:54 (Oct. 1933), 481-82.

C399 "Gandhi-Tolstoy Correspondence, 1909-1910," GM:5 (Jan. 1961), 65-74. 4 letters by Gandhi, 3 by Tolstoy.

C400 [Gandhi]. "A Pot-Pourri of Gandhi's Letters, 1924," GM:4 (April 1960), 143-50. To Sarojini Naidu, Mohamed Ali, Malaviya, Rajagopalachari, and others.

C401 ———. "Some Letters from Gandhi to Tagore: 1932-1935," GM:3 (July 1959), 197-203.

C402 ———. "The Tagore-Gandhi Debate of 1921," GM:5 (April 1961), 145-66. Reprints the articles written in the course of the debate.

C403 ———. "Three Early Letters from Gandhi to Gokhale," GM:3 (Jan. 1959), 36-39. Dated Jan., Feb., March 1902.

C404 ———. "Two Letters from Gandhi to Richard Gregg," GM:4 (Oct. 1959), 275-81.

C405 "Gandhiji's First Arrest and Its Repercussions," CR:87 (April 1943), 1-12. On the public reaction to 1919 arrest.

C406 GOUR, H. S. "Gandhism—and After," HR:43 (March 1921), 1-15; LA:309 (May 14, 1921), 389-96. Anti-Gandhi.

C407 HANNON, MARK. "Gandhi in the New York Times, 1920-1930," GM:4 (April 1960), 127-33. Brief history of the *Times*'s reporting.

C408 HENDRICK, GEORGE. "Gandhi, 'Indian Opinion,' and Freedom," GM:2 (April 1958), 153-59. Description of the South African paper published by Gandhi.

C409 ———. "Influence of Thoreau and Emerson on Gandhi's Satyagraha," GM:3 (July 1959), 165-78.

C410 "India: Mr. Gandhi Again," RT:23 (Sept. 1933), 807-22.

C411 IYER, RAGHAVAN N. "Gandhi's Interpretation of History," GM: 6 (Oct. 1962), 319-27.

C412 JACK, HOMER A. "Gandhi and the Commissars," GM:2 (April, July 1958), 133-40, 201-10. Gandhi on the Communists and Russia, from his printed works.

C413 KARPOV, IU. D. [Gandhi's Principle of Non-Violence in the Philosophical-Sociological Groundwork of the National Liberation Struggle of the Indian People], VMUE:1 (Jan.-Feb. 1965), 79-88; cited in SPA:5 (Nov. 1965), 21.

C414 KRISHNA, B. "The Defeat of Mahatma Gandhi," EW:16 (Oct. 1962), 20-22. On his inability to exercise power over Muslims.

C415 KUMARAPPA, J. C. "Social and Political Ideas of Mahatma Gandhi," IQ:2 (Oct.-Dec. 1946), 352-60. Analytical summary, without footnotes.

C416 MAHADEVAN, T. M. P. "The Ethical Politics of Mahatma Gandhi," IYBIA:7 (1958), 319-30. Discusses attempts by scholars to systematize his ideas and assess them.

C417 MAHALÉ, M. K. "L'Ahimsa de Gandhi devant l'opinion française" [Gandhi's *ahimsa* before French Opinion], KU:9 (1965), 150-63.

C418 "Mahatma Gandhi on the Jewish Problem," MR:65 (Feb. 1939), 147-48. On Palestine.

C419 MARTYSHIN, O. [Toward a Definition of the Social Ideas of Gandhism], VF:1 (Jan. 1965), 95-106; cited in SPA:5 (Nov. 1965), 21.

C420 MAUDE, AYLMER. "Gandhi and Tolstoy," CoR:137 (June 1930), 701-05. Letter from Tolstoy to Gandhi, Sept. 7, 1910.

C421 McCLAY, DUNCAN. "Truth and Mr. Gandhi," NC:115 (Jan. 1934), 59-71. Anti-Gandhi.

C422 MEHROTRA, S. R. "Gandhi and the British Commonwealth," IQ:17 (Jan.-March 1961), 44-57. History of his desire to see India remain in the Commonwealth. Summary in HA:8 (No. 2939).

C423 MOOKERJEE, H. C. "The First All-India Hartal," CR:86 (March 1943), 167-80. An account of the April 1919 events.

C424 ———. "Suspension of Rowlatt Satyagraha and Its Evaluation," CR:87 (May 1943), 67-76.

C425 MORAES, FRANK. "Gandhi Ten Years After," FA:36 (Jan. 1958), 253-66. The extent to which Gandhism outlived the man.

C426 MORISON, THEODORE. "The Government of India and Civil Disobedience," CoR:141 (Feb. 1932), 137-43.

C427 MORRIS-JONES, W. H. "Mahatma Gandhi—Political Philosopher?" IJPS:21 (July-Sept. 1960), 203-24. A comparison of Gandhi's thought with that of T. H. Green; poses some searching questions to his philosophy of non-cooperation. A postscript of 6 pages comments on Joan Bondurant's *Conquest of Violence*.

C428 "Mr. Gandhi's Jail Experiences," MR:6 (Oct., Nov. 1909), 391-94, 453-58.

C429 "Mr. Gandhi's Second Jail Experience," MR:6 (Dec. 1909), 553-64.

C430 "Mr. Gandhi's Third Jail Experience," MR:7 (Jan. 1910), 26-32.

C431 MUKHERJEE, SUDHANSU BIMAL. "The Indian Problem in South Africa; Cape Town—Success (1927-46)," CR:142 (Jan. 1957), 47-60.

C432 ———. "The Indian Problem in South Africa: Smuts-Gandhi Agreement—the Cape Town Agreement (1914-1927)," CR:141 (Oct. 1956), 59-78.

C433 ———. "The Indian Struggle in South Africa under Mahatma Gandhi: The Birth of Satyagraha (1907-1914)," CR:139 (June 1956), 247-66; 140 (Aug. 1956), 133-48.

C434 NARAIN, IQBAL. "The Gandhi-Smuts Agreement, Its Historical Background and Appraisal," AUJR:5 (July 1957), 211-34. From archival records.

C435 NARAIN, LAXMI. "Mahatma Gandhi as a Journalist," JQ:42 (Spring 1965), 267-70.

C436 NAIR, PYARELAL. "The Gandhi Institutions," EaW:4 (April 1950), 4-6. On the various associations and organizations founded by Gandhi.

C437 POLAK, H. S. L. "Memories of Gandhi," CoR:173 (March 1948), 134-37. Gandhi in South Africa.

C438 PRATT, F. G. "M. K. Gandhi as a Factor in Indian Politics," PI, pp. 203-25. An acute interpretation, stressing his "idealistic intransigence."

C439 RAMANATHAN, P. S. "The Ethical and Religious Ideas of Mahatma Gandhi," IQ:3 (July-Sept. 1947), 274-86.

C440 REYNOLDS, REGINALD. "Jack Hoyland—an English Follower of Gandhi," GM:2 (July 1958), 283-94.

C441 RIVETT, KENNETH. "The Economic Thought of Mahatma Gandhi," BJS:10 (March 1959), 1-15. A sympathetic interpretation.

C442 ROBERTS, W. H. "Review of the Gandhi Movement in India," PSQ:38 (June 1923), 227-48. An early appraisal of Gandhi's politics.

C443 ROLLAND, ROMAIN. "Préface à l'autobiographie de Gandhi" [Preface to Gandhi's Autobiography], Eu:25 (April 15, 1931), 465-90.

C444 ROTHERMUND, INDIRA N. "Mahatma Gandhi and Hindu Tradition," MR:108 (Nov. 1960), 353-60. A substantial article with bibliographical references.

C445 ROY, EVELYN. "Mahatma Gandhi: Revolutionary or Counter-revolutionary? A Reply to Romain Rolland and Henri Barbusse," LM:5 (1923), 158-67.

C446 RUDOLPH, SUSANNE HOEBER. "The New Courage; an Essay on Gandhi's Psychology," WP:16 (Oct. 1963), 98-117. Perceptive study of the psychology of various nationalisms and of Gandhi's personal solutions to cultural problems.

C447 SARKAR, SUBHASH CHANDRA. "Gandhi and Modern Indian Journalism," IAC:13 (Oct. 1964), 97-111. Gandhi's career as an editor.

C448 SINGAM, S. DURAI RAJA. "The Polaks and Gandhiji," IR:63 (May-June 1964), 173-77.

C449 SORABJI, CORNELIA. "The Gandhi Apocrypha," NC:110 (Nov. 1931), 594-601. Collected over the years.

C450 TIDMARSH, KYRIL. "The Soviet Re-assessment of Mahatma Gandhi," SAA:1, 86-115. The shifts in the Soviet line, 1921-56, with numerous quotations from periodical literature and books.

C451 WANG, LIANG-CH'UN. "Lüeh-lun kan-ti ti li-shih tso-yung" [On Gandhi's Role in Indian History], WSC:4 (1958), 51-62. Abstracted in HA:5 (No. 1280): "The author concludes that Gandhi's thought and activities were very backward, and that his understanding of imperialism and Indian feudalism was hardly perfect."

C452 WATSON, FRANCIS. "Gandhi and the Viceroys," HT:8 (Feb. 1958), 88-97. Summary of Gandhi's personal relations with the viceroys; see also letter in HT:8 (March 1958), 206, from a retired Lt.-General who estimates that Gandhi's presence at Partition "was worth two battalions to me," no more.

5. MUSLIM POLITICS AND HINDU-MUSLIM CONFLICT

C453 ABBAS, K. A. "Jinnah, the Enigma of India," A:40 (Aug. 1940), 432-34.

C454 al-AFGHĀNĪ, DJAMĀL al-DĪN. "Lettre sur l'Hindoustan" [Letter on India], Or:9 (3ᵉ trimestre 1965), 213-15. Reprinted from *L'Intransigeant*, 24 Avril 1883.

C455 AHMAD, AZIZ. "Iqbal et la théorie du Pakistan" [Iqbal and the Theory of Pakistan], Or:17 (1ᵉʳ trimestre, 1961), 81-90. Analysis based on Iqbal's Persian writings and letters to Jinnah.

C456 ———. "Les musulmans et le nationalisme indien" [The Muslims and Indian Nationalism], Or:22 (2ᵉ trimestre 1962), 75-94.

C457 ———. "Remarques sur les origines du Pakistan" [Remarks on the Origins of Pakistan], Or:7 (No. 26, 1963), 21-29. Brief history of 20th cent. separatism.

C458 ———. "Sayyid Ahmad Khan, Jamāl al-Din al-Afghānī and Muslim India," SI:13 (1960), 55-78. An important article on the background and importance of the Khilafat movement.

C459 AHMAD, QEYAMUDDIN. "An Early Case of Constitutional Agitation in Bihar (1892-97)," IHRC:32 (1956), 71-77. Shi'i agitation to carry out Alam procession at Gaya.

C460 ———. "A Study of the Attempts for Indo-Turkish Collaboration against the British," IHCP:17 (1957), 346-50. 1876-1880.

C461 AHMAD, RAFIUDDIN. "India: Is British 'Raj' in Danger?" NC: 42 (Sept. 1891), 493-500. An Indian Muslim view of British policy in the Middle East.

C462 AHMAD KHAN, SHAFAAT. "Hindu-Muslim Relations," AR: NS 23 (1927), 585-92. "Some of my best friends are Hindus."

C463 AKHMEDZIANOV, A. and LI, V. [Two Trends in "Muslim Nationalism"], AAS:1 (Jan. 1964), 58-59; cited in SPA:4 (Oct. 1964), 17.

C464 ALI, AMEER. "A Cry from the Indian Mohammedans," NC:12 (Aug. 1882), 193-215. Includes tables of Christian, Muslim, and Hindu employees and gazetted officers in Calcutta and the mofussil.

C465 ———. "India and the New Parliament," NC:60 (Aug. 1906), 254-67. Discusses how minority rights should be upheld.

C466 ———. "Memoirs of the late Rt. Hon'ble Syed Ameer Ali," IC:5 (Oct. 1931), 509-42; 6 (1932), 1-18, 163-82, 333-62, 503-25. Introduction by Ernest H. Griffin.

C467 ———. "The Unrest in India—Its Meaning," NC:61 (June 1907), 873-85. On Hindu-Muslim relations.

C468 ALI, MOHAMMED. "Le mouvement musulman dans l'Inde" [The Muslim Movement in India], RPI:1 (Jan. 1914), 110-19. Translation of speech given in London at banquet of the Islamic Society, Nov. 11, 1913.

C469 ALI, RAHMAT. "Contribution à l'étude du problème hindou-musulman" [Contribution to the study of the Hindu-Muslim Problem], RdE:6 (1932), 269-414. Strong anti-British bias.

C470 ANDREWS, C. F. "The First Days of the Moplah Rising," MR:31 (April 1922), 469-72.

C471 ———. "Hakim Ajmal Khan," MR:31 (June 1922), 681-86. Biography of Muslim nationalist doctor by a friend.

C472 AZIZ, ZARINA. "Muslim Nationalist Movements in India (1857-1947)," PR:4 (Aug. 1956), 9-14; (Sept. 1956); (Oct. 1956), 11-15, 40.

C473 BANERJEE, D. N. "The Negotiations and After—The Two Nations Theory of Mr. Jinnah," MR:77 (Feb.-May 1945), 64-67, 110-13, 162-67, 211-15. Correspondence between Gandhi and Jinnah.

C474 BARTON, WILLIAM. "Hindu and Afghan on the Indian Frontier," CoR:171 (Feb. 1947), 77-79. Hindu-Muslim problems on North-West frontier.

C475 BEG, ABDULLAH ANWAR. "Liaquat Ali Khan: As Leader and Statesman," PR:8 (Nov. 1960), 17-18, 20.

C476 ———. "Liaquat at Oxford," PR:10 (Nov. 1962), 23-25. Liaquat Ali Khan.

C477 BINDER, LEONARD. "Pakistan and Modern Islamic-Nationalist Theory," MEJ:11 (Autumn 1957), 382-96; 12 (Winter 1958), 45-56. On Muslim political history, extensively documented.

C478 BIRNBAUM, ERVIN. "Some Theoretical and Practical Aspects of the Islamic State of Pakistan," PHSM:1 (1956), 70 pp. Good brief history of Muslim separatism and the establishment of Pakistan.

C479 BLUNT, WILFRED SCAWEN. "Ideas about India: III. The Mohammedan Question," FR:42 (July-Dec. 1884), 624-37.

C480 BOLITHO, HECTOR. "Tracking the Quaid's Footprints," PQ:2 (Spring 1952), 6-8, 54-55. Extracts from Bolitho's diary as he began research for biography of Jinnah.

C481 BOULGER, DEMETRIUS C. "The Moplah Warning," CoR:120 (Nov. 1921), 658-64. Urges consideration of Muslim views.

C482 BRIGGS, F. S. "The Indian Hijrat of 1920," MW:20 (April 1930), 164-68. An eyewitness account.

C483 BROWN, JAMES D. "The History of Islam in India, III: From the Mutiny of 1857 to the Establishment of Pakistan, August 15, 1947," MW:39 (July 1949), 179-94. A political history.

C484 BROWN, W. NORMAN. "India's Pakistan Issue," APS:91 (April 1947), 162-80. Summary of the issues.

C485 BUCKLER, F. W. "The Historical Antecedents of the Khilāfat Movement," CoR:121 (May 1922), 603-11. On the relationship between Mughal claims on the caliphate to the Khilafat movement; interesting but unsound.

C486 CALLARD, K. "Djināh (Jinnah), Muḥammad 'Alī," EI:2, 545-46.

C487 CHAPY, ANDRÉ. "L'Islam dans la constitution du Pakistan" [Islam in Pakistan's Constitution], Or:3 (Juillet 1957), 120-27. Concludes that the constitution is a modern one and that the Islamic background is used more to reassure the 'ulama than to force Islamic tradition on a modern society.

C488 CHATTERJEE, ASHOKE. "Are the Musalmans of Bengal Really in an Effective Majority," MR:40 (Aug. 1926), 125-27. With tables of population figures.

C489 CHATTERJEE, RAMANANDA. "The Bengal Hindu Manifesto and Muslim Bengalis," MR:51 (June 1932), 613-18.

C490 ———. "The Communal Award," MR:52 (Sept. 1932), 327-32.

C491 CHIROL, VALENTINE. "The Downfall of the Ottoman Khilafat," RCAS:11 (1924), 229-43; FA:2 (1924), 571-82. Deals with the Indian reaction.

C492 CHOPRA, HIRA LALL. "Maulana Abul Kalam Azad; a Brief Survey of His Eventful Career," II:11 (March 1958), 1-15. With photographs.

C493 CHOUDHARY, LAKSHMI KANT. "The Pan-Islamic Movement: A Significant Factor in Indian Politics," PU:19 (July 1964), 148-55. Based on materials gathered for a Ph.D. at Patna.

C494 CHUGHTAI, MUNIR UD-DIN. "The Central National Muhammadan Association: the First All-Muslim Political Organization," JPUHS: 14 (June 1962), 61-66.

C495 COATMAN, J. "Hindu-Mohammedan Problem in India," AM:138 (July 1926), 121-31. Good survey of the political problem.

C496 CROSTHWAITE, CHARLES. "The Tangle in India," BM:185 (Feb. 1909), 286-99. On Hindu-Muslim difficulties.

C497 "Development of the Non-Cooperation Movement," RT:11 (Sept. 1921), 868-81. Largely on Hindu-Muslim politics.

C498 DUTT, JATINDRA MOHAN. "Communalism in the Bengal Administration," MR:49 (Jan. 1931), 45-49.

C499 ———. "The Real Nature of the Muhammadan Majority in Bengal," MR:49 (Feb. 1931), 211-15.

C500 "An F. R. S. S. and F. R. ECON. S. (Lond.)." "Further Notes on Partition of Bengal," MR:81 (March 1947), 221-26. With statistical tables on the distribution of Muslims and Hindus.

C501 FAULKNER, P. LEO. "Wilfred Scawan Blunt and Indian Affairs," CR:8 (Sept. 1923), 387-94. Biographical sketch.

C502 "Fitness for Predominant Influence," MR:49 (Jan. 1931), 110-16. On Muslim–non-Muslim population ratios in Bengal.

C503 GANKOVSKIĬ, IU. V. "Azad Kashmir, 1947-1958 gg. (k istorii kashmirskogo voprosa)" [Azad Kashmir, 1947-1958 (on the History of the Kashmirian Question)], KS:51 (1962), 167-82.

C504 GHULAM-US-SAQLAIN. "The Mussalmans of India and the Armenian Question," NC:37 (Jan.-June 1895), 926-39. On the interest in Pan-Islam.

C505 [GORDON-POLONSKAYA, L. R.]. "Muslim Nationalism in the Indian Subcontinent: Lyudmila Gordon-Polonskaya and Her Critics," CAR:13 (1965), 131-48. Summary of *Musul'manskiye techeniya v obshchestvennoy mysli Indii i Pakistana (kritika musul'manskogo natsionalizma)*, Moscow, 1963, and of two reviews of it in NAA and VF.

C506 GREGORY, W. H. "Loyalty of the Indian Mohammedans," NC:20 (Dec. 1886), 886-900.

C507 GUPTA, SISIR K. "Islam as a Factor in Pakistani Foreign Relations," IQ:18 (July-Sept. 1962), 230-53. Deals with Muslim League attitudes before Independence as well as Pakistani policy.

C508 ———. "Moslems in Indian Politics, 1947-60," IQ:18 (Oct.-Dec. 1962), 355-81. On the effects of Partition and two general elections.

C509 HAMID, ABDUL. "The Aligarh Movement (Political and Social)," HFM:2 (1831-1905), part 2, 503-32.

C510 ———. "Nehru Report and Quaid-i-Azam," JPUHS:12 (June 1961), 13-15.

C511 ———. "The Simla Deputation," PPHC:6 (1956), 153-58. Denies the 1906 deputation was a "command performance."

C512 [HAQ]. "Mr. Mazharul Haque's Presidential Address," MR:19 (Feb. 1916), 249-52. Notes from presidential address to the Bombay session of the Muslim League.

C513 [———]. "Syed Mazhar-ul-Haq," MR:19 (Jan. 1916), 86-87. Member of Supreme Legislative Council 1910-12; president of Muslim League, 1915.

C514 HOSSAIN, SYUD. "England, Turkey, and the Indian Mahomedans," AR: NS 6 (Feb. 15, 1915), 143-55. The importance of the caliphate to Indian Muslims.

C515 "India: The Musalman Panic," W:97 (April 1872), 359-80. Review of Hunter's *Our Indian Musalmans*.

C516 ISLAM, ZAFARUL. "Documents on Indo-Muslim Politics (1857-1947); The Aligarh Political Activities (1883-93)," PHS:12 (Jan. 1964), 14-25. 1. Constitution of Syed Ahmed Khan's United Indian Patriotic Association; 2. Muslim Petition to the House of Commons (against the principle of elections); 3. Constitution of the Muhammadan Anglo-Oriental Defence Association of Upper India.

C517 ———. "Jinnah and Muslim Political Separation," PPHC:6 (1956), 171-96. With many quotations from Jinnah's writings and speeches.

C518 ——— and WOLDMAN, JOEL M. "Indian Muslims and the Ilbert Bill: 1883-1884," ASP:8 (Dec. 1963), 131-54. Based on microfilms of India Office material at Michigan University.

C519 JAIN, MAMRAJ SINGH. "The Aligarh Movement—Its Origin and Development (a Summary)," UB:9 (April 1962), 125-30.

C520 ———. "The Genesis of Muslim Opposition to Indian National Congress in 1887," UB:9 (Aug. 1962); summary in QRHS:2 (1962-63), 98-99.

C521 "Jinnah-Viceroy Correspondence," MR:80 (Nov. 1946), 325-26.

C522 KARUNAKARAN, K. P. "Interrelation between Religion and Politics in Pakistan," IQ:14 (Jan.-Mar. 1958), 43-62. Brief history of the interplay between religion and politics in Muslim history.

C523 KHALID, ANWAR-UL-HAQ. "Nawab Muhsin-ul-Mulk: One of the Makers of Pakistan," PR:2 (Oct. 1954), 41-42.

C524 KIDWAI, MOHAMMAD HASHIM. "Theocracy in Modern Politics—a New Political Testament," IJPS:6 (Oct. 1944), 108-14.

C525 KRIPALANI, J. B. "The Voice of Reason," MAKA, pp. 30-36. A thoughtful essay on Azad.

C526   LACEY, PATRICK. "Two Indias," CoR:157 (June 1940), 703-09. On the Pakistan scheme.

C527   LAMBERT, RICHARD D. "Religion, Economics and Violence in Bengal: Background of Minorities Agreement," MEJ:4 (July 1950), 307-28. On disturbances after Partition.

C528   LANG, EDWARD. "The All-India Moslem League," CoR:92 (Sept. 1907), 344-52. Contains excerpts from Nawab of Dacca's speech proposing its formation.

C529   MACCOLL, MALCOLM. "The Musalmans of India and the Sultan," CoR:71 (Feb. 1897), 280-94. Argues that Indian Muslim discontent is the expression of a small minority.

C530   MACKINNON, A. C. B. "The Moplah Rebellion, 1921-1922," ArQ:7 (Jan. 1924), 260-77. Account of the military operations, with map and diagrams.

C531   MAHMUD, SYED. "A Resplendent Personality," MAKA, pp. 37-51. Includes a long excerpt from Maulana Azad's speech to the Court, 1922.

C532   MAJUMDAR, BIMAN BEHARI. "The Congress and the Moslems," QRHS 5:2 (1965/66), 65-77.

C533   MALIK, HAFEEZ. "Abu'l Kalām Āzād's Theory of Nationalism," MW:53 (Jan. 1963), 33-44. Deals with early 1920's.

C534   MANDELBAUM, DAVID GOODMAN. "Hindu-Moslem Conflict in India," MEJ:1 (Oct. 1947), 369-85. A summary of causes and landmarks.

C535   MASSIGNON, LOUIS. "My Meetings with Maulana Azad," MAKA, pp. 27-29. Mentions a teacher in Baghdad they both learned from.

C536   MATHEWS, MAXINE. "Pakistan, History and Prospects," CH: NS 10 (March, April 1946), 244-52, 328-34. A summary of Muslim separatist history.

C537   McPHERSON, HUGH. "The Origin and Growth of Communal Antagonism, Especially between Hindus and Muhammadans, and the Communal Award," PI, pp. 106-23.

C538   MITRA, S. M. "England, India, and the Balkan War," NC:72 (Nov. 1912), 1077-84. Effect of Britain's Middle-East policy on Indian Muslims, in 1870's as well as 1912.

C539   MOAZZAM, ANWAR. "Jamāl al-Dīn al-Afghānī in India," AIIS:4 (1960), 84-95. Contains original material on the pan-Islamic leader.

C540 MORISON, THEODORE. "The Hindu-Moslem Problem of India," CoR:139 (June 1931), 710-17. On the relevance of Balkan political settlements to Hindu-Muslim problems.

C541 ———. "Muhammedan Movements," PI, pp. 86-105. Largely a summary and review.

C542 al-MUJAHID, SHARIF. "The Ideology of Pakistan," US:2 (April 1965), 39-58.

C543 ———. "Maulana Muhammad Ali: A Political Study," PQ:5 (Winter 1955), 54-59.

C544 "The Moslem League," MR:25 (Feb. 1919), 210-11. Speeches at the Delhi session of the All-India Moslem League by M. A. Ansari and Fazlul Huq.

C545 MUJEEB, M. "The Tadhkirah: A Biography in Symbols," MAKA, pp. 134-52. On Azad's spiritual autobiography, with long excerpts.

C546 O'DWYER, MICHAEL. "The Mohammedans of India and India's Mohammedan Neighbors," RCAS:8 (1921), 194-213; discussion pp. 213-18. On conspiracies during and after World War I.

C547 PANIKKAR, K. M. "The Psychology of the Hindu-Moslem Riots," CoR:131 (Feb. 1927), 230-36. An intelligent analysis.

C548 PUCKLE, FREDERICK. "Gandhi-Jinnah Conversations," FA:23 (Jan. 1945), 318-23. Summary of their debate.

C549 ———. "The Pakistan Doctrine: Its Origins and Power," FA:24 (April 1946), 526-38. A history of the Muslims in India with discussion of their "psychology of inferiority."

C550 QURESHI, I. H. "The Development of Pakistan," CHM:4 (1958), 1009-30; bibliography p. 1030. Emphasizes the separate identity of Hindus and Muslims in 18th and 19th cent.

C551 "Resolution re Outbreak of Lawlessness at Dacca," MR:48 (Oct. 1930), 412-29. Reprinted from the Official Report of Legislative Assembly Debates, July 16, 1930.

C552 SEN, SACHIN. "Muslim Political Thought since 1858," IJPS:6 (Oct. 1944), 97-108. Implications of the Pakistan movement.

C553 SHAH, IKBAL ALI. "Economic Justification of Pakistan," CoR:164 (Oct. 1943), 231-34. Claims Pakistan could be self-supporting.

C554 SINGH, ODAY PERTAP. "The Cow Agitation or the Mutiny-Plasm in India," NC:35 (April 1894), 667-72. A confused attack on Hindu and English faddists.

C555 SMITH, W. CANTWELL. "Amīr 'Alī, Sayyid (1849-1928)," EI:1, 442-43. Jurist and writer, Shi'ite.

C556 ———. "The 'Ulamā' in Indian Politics," PSI, pp. 39-51. Thoughtful discussion of the development of the 'ulama as a class and political force in the 18th and 19th cent.

C557 SPEAR, PERCIVAL. "Review of *Jinnah, the Creator of Pakistan,* by Hector Bolitho," TwC:157 (April 1955), 384-88. With an assessment of Jinnah.

C558 SUHRAWARDY, HASSAN. "The Indian Crisis: Muslim Viewpoints," RCAS:30 (Jan. 1943), 53-70.

C559 SULERI, Z. A. "Mr. Jinnah," CoR:170 (July 1946), 42-45. A portrait.

C560 SUNDERLAND, J. T. "Hindu and Mohammedan Riots," MR:43 (Jan. 1928), 1-7.

C561 "Support for Bengal Partition," MR:81 (April 1947), 259. List of supporting organizations and individuals.

C562 SYED, M. HAFIZ. "Liaquat Ali Khan—A Brief Life Sketch," MR: 90 (Dec. 1951), 461-62.

C563 TALBOT, PHILLIPS. "The Rise of Pakistan," MEJ:2 (Oct. 1948), 381-98.

C564 TEMPLE, RICHARD. "The Mahdi and British India," CoR:47 (Mar. 1885), 305-14. On the effect of British policy in the Sudan on the "Oriental mind."

C565 THORPE, C. LLOYD. "Education and the Development of Muslim Nationalism in Pre-Partition India," PHS:13 (Jan., April, July 1965), 1-26, 131-53, 244-64. Based on secondary sources.

C566 WALTER, HOWARD A. "Lahore as a Moslem Centre," MW:8 (1918), 235-41. Some information on Muslim organizations.

C567 WASTI, S. RAZI. "Early Years of the All India Muslim League (1906-10)," PHS:9 (Oct. 1961), 240-60. Uses contemporary journals and British records.

C568 ———. "The Simla Deputation, 1906," PHS:10 (April 1962), 161-82. Based on Minto-Morley correspondence.

C569 "YAMADATTA." "Islam in Danger," MR:70 (Nov. 1941), 491-93. Figures on Muslim population and occupations in Bengal.

C570 ZETLAND, MARQUESS OF. "After the Indian Conference," FA:10 (April 1932), 369-81. Hindu-Muslim affairs since the Second Round Table Conference.

D. ECONOMIC HISTORY

1. BIBLIOGRAPHIES

NOTE: the five-volume *Index of Economic Journals* (Homewood, Illinois: Richard D. Irwin, Inc., 1961-62) is the best source of articles on economic history that appear in economic journals. The articles listed in this *Guide* are primarily from other journals, although the major articles from economic journals have been included.

D1 BALKRISHNA, DR. "The Economic History of India, Materials for Research at Bombay," BHS:1 (March 1928), 43-64. A summary of official sources.

D2 KOMAROV, E. N. "Survey of Russian Pre-Revolutionary and Soviet Studies on the Economic History of India in the Modern Age," CIEH:1, 95-102.

D3 MAAS, WALTHER. "Sammel Bericht. Zur Indischen Wirtschaftsgeschichte" [Summary Report. On Indian Economic History], VSW:43 (1956), 368-72. Summary in HA:3 (No. 2096): "A bibliographical essay on Indian historiography from the 14th to the 20th centuries, mainly listing economic and social histories, and monographs by Indian authors which have been published in English."

D4 MORRIS, MORRIS D. and STEIN, BURTON. "The Economic History of India: A Bibliographic Essay," JEH:21 (June 1961), 179-207. "Only English language materials are included, but almost all significant work in the field has been in English." Includes a helpful discussion on problems of periodization and "middle-range" generalizations.

D5 RAYCHAUDHURI, TAPAN. "Some Recent Writing on the Economic History of British India: an Essay in Bibliography," CIEH:1, 115-49.

D6 TRAGER, FRANK N. "A Selected and Annotated Bibliography on Economic Development, 1953-1957," EDCC:6 (Dec. 1957), 257-329. 409 entries.

2. GENERAL ECONOMIC HISTORY

D7 AMBIRAJAN, S. "McCulloch on India," MSESS:33 (May 1965), 125-40. John Ramsey McCulloch, 1789-1864, economist and statistician associated with ER.

D8 ANSTEY, VERA. "Economic Development," MIW, pp. 258-304. Under British rule.

D9 ANTONOVA, K. A. "O genezise kapitalizma v Indii" [On the Genesis of Capitalism in India], GKSV, pp. 179-95; SV:6 (1957).

D10 BADEN-POWELL, GEORGE. "Fifty Years of Colonial Development," FR:43 (June 1883), 928-38.

D11 BANERJEE, MRITYUNJOY. "Indian Economy under Independence," MR:89 (March 1951), 206-09.

D12 BASU, K. K. "Weights and Measures in Bhagalpur, Monghyr, and Rajmahal under the Hon'ble Company," PU:1 (Jan. 1945), 1-6.

D13 BHAIJI, M. MOHSIN. "The Functional Distribution of Muhammedan Population in Bombay City," BUJ:6 (Jan. 1938), 163-74. On their economic position.

D14 BHANU, DHARMA. "Economic Life in the Agra Province (1830-1860)," AUJR:5 (July 1957), 185-97. Largely from gazetteers.

D15 BHATTACHARYA, SABYASACHI. "Laissez Faire in India," IESHR:2 (Jan. 1965), 1-22. A survey of the policy, heavily documented.

D16 "British India," QR:113 (April 1863), 289-322. Largely on its economic condition.

D17 CHACKO, GEORGE K. "The Context of Indian Economic Development—I: British Balance of Payments and Evolution of Indian Economic Policy," IJE:38 (Jan. 1958), 249-73. Tables on imports, home charges, and balance of payments; discusses interrelation of economic theories and practice.

D18 CHANDA, A. K. "Public Enterprises in India," MUJ:32 (July 1960), 199-230. Traces development in 20th cent.

D19 CHANDRA, BIPAN. "The Problem of Poverty and Indian National Leadership, 1880-1905," En: NS 1 (Monsoon 1964), 54-106. Extensively documented.

D20 CHATTERJEA, S. C. "The Damodar Valley Project," IQ:3 (Jan.-March 1947), 19-31.

D21 CHATTERJI, KEDAR NATH. "The Damodar Valley Project," MR:89 (April 1951), 309-13.

D22 COHN, BERNARD. "The Role of the Gosains in the Economy of Eighteenth and Nineteenth Century Upper India," IESHR:1 (April 1964), 175-82.

D23 "The Commerce, Resources, and Prospects of India," CR:28 (June 1857), 364-461.

D24 DANVERS, JULAND. "The Public Works and Progress of India," AR:1 (April 1886), 327-53. Irrigation and railway development.

D25 DATTA, BHABATOSH. "Rameścandra Datta o Bhāratbarsher ārthik itihās" [Rameścandra Datta and the Economic History of India], BP:11 (1952-53), 199-209. Critique of Datta's work on Indian economic history.

[221]

D26 "The Department of Revenue, Agriculture, and Commerce," CR 53:105 (1871), 1-28. Brief history of its organization.

D27 DHAR, KIRAN NATH. "Some Indian Economists," CR:126 (July 1908), 418-35. Biographies of British economists of India: James Wilson, Samual Laing, John Strachey, Robert Knight, Robert Hollingbery, George Kellner.

D28 DIGBY, WILLIAM. "The 'Indian Phantom' No Phantom, But a Grievous Reality," AR, Ser. 3:15 (April 1903), 339-66. On the economic condition of India. "Reply" by A. R. Bonus, AR, Ser. 3:16 (July 1903), 15-29. See R. E. Forrest, below.

D29 DRAVID, N. A. "The Growth of Indian Expenditure," HR:23 (Feb. 1911), 139-48. Figures from 1898-99 to 1908-09.

D30 "The East India Question," BM:33 (May 1833), 776-803. On the economic situation.

D31 "The Economic and Financial Condition of India," RT:14 (Dec. 1923), 94-113. A survey.

D32 "The Economics of Public Works," CR:32 (June 1859), 344-79.

D33 FORREST, R. E. "The Indian Phantom," AR, Ser. 3:14 (Oct. 1902), 233-51. See William Digby, above.

D34 GADGIL, D. R. "The Economic Prospect for India," PA:22 (June 1949), 115-29.

D35 GHOSAL, HARI RANJAN. "Tirhut at the End of the Eighteenth and the Beginning of the Nineteenth Century (1790-1820) (An Economic Survey Based on Unpublished Records)," BRS:19 (Dec. 1953), 365-76. A survey of agriculture, industry, trade, prices.

D36 GHOSH, D. "The Bombay Plan of Economic Development of India," CR:91 (April 1944), 1-8.

D37 "The Government of India: Its Liabilities and Resources," W:72 (July 1859), 112-64.

D38 HAMIDULLAH, MUHAMMAD. "Haidarabad's Contribution to Islamic Economic Thought and Practice," WI: NS 4 (1955), 73-78. On 20th cent. financial administration.

D39 HARINGTON, ARTHUR. "Economic Reform in Rural India," CR: 74 (1882), 138-74, 382-418; 76:151 (1883), 153-81; 80 (April 1885), 435-59; 81 (Oct. 1885), 346-75.

D40 HATE, C. A. "The Economic Conditions of Educated Women in Bombay City," BUJ:3 (Jan. 1935), 1-43. Results of a personal survey.

D41 "India: Its Products and Improvement," CR:30 (March 1858), 33-65.

D42 JOSEPH, TERESA. "Poor Relief in the City of Madras; with Special References to the Problem of Professional Begging," MUJ:5, part 2 (July 1933?), 195-232.

D43 KALE, V. G. "The Economic Creed of the Late Mr. Ranade," HR: 26 (July 1912), 9-14.

D44 KALIAGIN, B. A. [Economic Structure and Forms of Property among the Naga Tribes], NAA:1 (1965), 87-92. Cited in SPA:5 (March 1966), 32. Covers end of the 19th cent. to 1939.

D45 KEYNES, J. M. "Recent Economic Events in India," EJ:19 (March 1909), 51-67.

D46 KOMAROV, E. N. "Colonial Exploitation and Economic Development (Some Problems of the Economic History of India under Colonial Rule)," DCI, pp. 731-49. With a Select Bibliography of Works by Soviet Authors on Economic History of India from the 17th Century to Independence (Pub'd in Russian), pp. 746-49.

D47 ———— and PAVLOV, V. I. "Rynochnye sviazii i ekonomicheskaia organizatsiia remesla v Indii na rubezhe.XVIII i XIX vekov" [The Market Relations and the Economic Organization of Handicraft in India in the Late 18th and Early 19th Centuries], GKSV, pp. 138-63.

D48 LEVKOVSKII, A. I. "Osobennosti razvitiia krupnogo kapitalist-icheskogo predprinimatel'stva v Indii" [Special Features of the Development of Big Capitalistic Enterprise in India], SV:2 (1955), 107-24. Summary in HA:4 (No. 2280): "Deals with British capital investment, trends in the development of Indian industry, and the activity of banks in the period from 1870 to 1945. Based on works by Indian authors."

D49 LINDSAY, H. A. F. "India's Trade and Industrial Statistics, Past, Present, and Future," RSS:97, part 3 (1934), 399-422. On published sources of statistics, with discussion.

D50 LOKANATHAN, P. S. "The Bombay Plan," FA:23 (July 1945), 680-86. Summary of the plan for economic development and its implications.

D51 MAHAPATRA, MONORAMA. "General Economic Condition of Orissa," OHRJ:1 (July 1952), 171-77.

D52 MAITRA, PRIYATOSH. "Nineteenth Century Charter Acts and Economic Transition in India," CR:141 (Oct. 1956), 79-92.

D53 MANDAL, GOBINDA CHANDRA. "The Economic Problem of Burdwan Division," MR:82 (Aug. 1947), 113-16. With statistical data from 1911.

D54 MARU, A. H. "Development of Employers' Organisations in India," ILR:27 (Feb. 1933), 220-36. Summary history of chambers of commerce and employers associations.

D55 MATSUI, TŌRU. "Indo kindai shi ni okeru 'kōshinsei' ni tsuite" [On the Modern History of India and the Problem of 'Underdevelopment'], RK:262 (1962), 7-15. Abstract in HA:9 (No. 407): "Criticizes the traditional views of Indian rural society as being 'super-historical stagnation'. . ."

D56 METCALF, THOMAS R. "The British and the Moneylender in Nineteenth-Century India," JMH:34 (Dec. 1962), 390-97. Based on India Office records and National Archives records. Discusses the rise to power of the moneylender class and the influence of British rule on this power.

D57 MILLS, LENNOX A. "Some Aspects of British Native Policy in India," QQ:40 (Aug. 1933), 365-74. A survey of public works programs.

D58 MITRA, R. C. "Economic Condition of India in 1774-77 (From the Journal of Modave)," IHQ:27 (March 1951), 44-51. Material from the diary of a French adventurer.

D59 "MOFUSSILITE." "Village Uplift; an Interlude," BM:224 (Aug. 1928), 179-86. On an agricultural and industrial exhibition.

D60 MORELAND, W. H. "The Study of Indian Poverty," AR: NS 16 (Oct. 1920), 616-30; discussion, 631-39.

D61 MORRIS, MORRIS D. "Toward a Reinterpretation of Nineteenth Century Indian Economic History," JEH:23 (1963), 606-18. An iconoclastic and stimulating article.

D62 MUKERJEE, RADHAKAMAL. "The Economic History of India: 1600-1800," UPHS:14 (Dec. 1941), 41-96; 15 (July, Dec. 1942), 65-111, 102-24. Many tables of figures.

D63 MUZUMDAR, S. M. "India's Struggle with the Great Depression (1929-33)," BUJ:8 (July 1939), 52-70.

D64 NAIDIS, MARK. "The Standard of Living of the British in India," Hn:12 (Nov. 1959), 42-62. A general survey, 1700 to about 1900.

D65 "A Note on Economic Reform," QJPSS:7 (Nov. 1884), independent section, 1-17.

D66 "Oudh and Optimism," CR 58:116 (1874), 313-40. On economic conditions.

D67 PANANDIKAR, S. G. "Money-lenders," A:37 (May 1937), 358-61. With photographs of itinerant money-lenders.

D68 PANI, P. K. and SIVASUBRAMANIAN, N. S. "Study of Some Aspects of Economic Growth of India (During Pre-War and Post-War Periods)," CSA:8 (Oct. 1958), 49-64. A technical discussion of the problems in estimating growth rates; 2 tables of index numbers of business activity.

D69 PATEL, SURENDRA J. "Long-term Changes in Output and Income in India: 1896-1960," IEJ:5 (Jan. 1958), 233-46. Charts.

D70 PAVLOV, V. I. [Economic Changes in Maharashtrian Towns in the Second Half of the 19th Century], NLM.

D71 PRASAD, BANARSI. "A Page from the Account Book of Nawab Mubariz'ud-Daulah," IHRC:33 (1958), 26-35. 1835 accounts.

D72 "The Progress of India," ER:119 (Jan. 1864), 95-136. On agricultural development, communications, and public works.

D73 RAO, V. K. R. V. "National Income of India," AAAPSS:233 (May 1944), 99-105. Tables based on 1931 census.

D74 SANYAL, NALINAKSHA. "Economic Planning for Bengal," MR: 54 (Oct. 1933), 423-30.

D75 SEN, SUNIL KUMAR. "Economic Enterprise," SBR, pp. 543-55. Covers period 1833-1914.

D76 SHAH, A. M., SHROFF, R. G. and SHAH, A. R. "Early 19th Century Village Records in Gujarat," GRS:25 (April 1963), 126-34; CIEH:2 (1963), 89-100. Lists kinds of economic records available in some villages.

D77 SHAH, IKBAL ALI. "Three Post-War Plans for India," FR:162 (July-Dec. 1944), 172-78. On plans for economic development.

D78 SHERWANI, LATIF AHMAD. "The Basis of Economic Development in Pakistan," PA:22 (Dec. 1949), 381-87. Resources and industrial development to date.

D79 SINGH, VIR BAHADUR. "Colonialism and Economic Stagnation," WZHUB:9 (1959-60), 551-60. Summary in HA:8 (No. 2370).

D80 ———. "Pseudo-development under British Rule," WZHUB:9 (1959-60), 561-72. Summary in HA:8 (No. 2371).

D81 SINHA, BIMALCHANDRA. "Two Recent Indications of West Bengal's Economic Decay," MR:93 (Jan. 1953), 33-37.

D82 SINHA, J. C. "Economic Condition of the Ceded Districts (1800-07)," IHRC:17 (1940), 56-61. The Madras ceded districts; records in the Alienation Office, Poona.

D83 SINHA, J. C. "Economic Theorists among the Servants of John Company (1766-1806)," EJ:35 (March 1925), 47-59. Based on East India Company records in Calcutta.

D84 SINHA, NARENDRA KRISHNA. "Economic Background of the Century," SBR, pp. 1-7. 1790-1900.

D85 "The Southern Ghats," CR 38:76 (1863), 286-320. Agriculture and industry south of Goa.

D86 SOVANI, N. V. "Ranade's Model of the Indian Economy," AV:4 (March 1962), 10-20. Theory and specific ideas on the Indian economy.

D87 SRINIVASACHARI, C. S. "The Economic Condition of the Madras Presidency on the Eve of the British Conquest," MUJ:2 (1929), 68-81; 3 (Dec. 1930), 61-76. District by district.

D88 SWAMINATHAN, V. S. "Pakistan Problems and Prospects," MEJ: 4 (Oct. 1950), 447-66. Largely on economic resources and trade.

D89 [TENNANT]. "Dr. Tennant's *Indian Recreations*," ER:4 (July 1804), 303-29. On the improvement of agriculture and commerce in India.

D90 THAKUR, K. P. "Stock Exchange Stinks," MR:81 (April 1947), 314-18. With statistical tables showing instability of prices.

D91 THAVARAJ, K. "Pattern of Public Investment in India, 1900-1939," IESHR:1 (July-Sept. 1963), 36-56. Tables on investment in irrigation, roads, railroads in the largest provinces.

D92 THOMAS, P. J. "Population and Production (1920-31)," IJE:15 (April 1935), 736-47; MUJ:7 (1935), 93-102. On correlations between population, agriculture, and industrial production.

D93 ——— and PILLAI, B. NATARAJA. "Economic Depression in the Madras Presidency (1820-1854)," MUJ:6 (July 1934?), 219-41.

D94 THORNER, ALICE. "The Secular Trend in the Indian Economy, 1881-1951," EW (Special No. 14, July 1962), 1156-57, 1159-61, 1163-65.

D95 "War against Poverty in India," RT:19 (March 1929), 342-62. On the general economic situation.

D96 WAUGH, A. "India and Pakistan: the Economic Effects of Partition," AR: NS 44 (April 1948), 113-27. With discussion.

D97 WRIGHT, H. R. C. "The East India Company and the Native Economy in India: The Madras Investment, 1795-1800," DCI, pp. 761-80.

3. *LAND SETTLEMENT AND LAND REVENUE ADMINISTRATION*

D98 AHMED, Q. "An Old Survey Report of Historical Importance," IHRC:30 (1954), 9-14. 1825 report of land in Patna Division.

D99   AIYANGER, S. KRISHNASWAMI. "Ananda Ranga Pillai's Diary and the Revenue Administration of Tirupati," IHRC:16 (1939), 5-12.

D100   ALAEV, L. B. "Nekotorye voprosy razvitiia indiiskoi obshchiny v kontse XVIII-nachale XIX veka" [Certain Problems in the Development of the Indian Commune at the End of the Eighteenth and the Beginning of the Nineteenth Centuries], VI:8 (Aug. 1962), 85-96.

D101   ALEXANDER, JAMES. "On the Tenures and Fiscal Relations of the Owners and Occupants of the Soil in Bengal, Behar, and Orissa," ASB:14 (July-Dec. 1845), 527-45.

D102   ALI, AMEER. "The Life Problem of Bengal," NC:14 (Sept. 1883), 421-40. On land settlement.

D103   "An Amended Rent Law," CR 41:81 (1865), 159-68.

D104   ANTONOVA, K. A. [On the Introduction of the Ryotwari Settlement], KS:10 (1953); German tr. in OSEI.

D105   BADEN-POWELL, B. H. "The Permanent Settlement of Bengal," EHR:10 (April 1895), 276-92. Brief history of the policy and its effects.

D106   BALIGA, B. S. "The Amani System of Land Revenue Administration in Madras," IHRC:17 (1940), 10-17. Late 18th cent., early 19th cent.

D107   ———. "Village Settlements of Land Revenue in Madras, 1807-22," IHRC:21 (1944), 4-6. Brief summary.

D108   BANERJEE, D. N. "Some Aspects of the Post-Diwani Land Revenue System in Bengal and Bihar," IJE:14 (Jan. 1934), 321-38 for 1765-69; 16 (April 1936), 643-57 for 1772.

D109   BARRIER, NORMAN G. "The Formulation and Enactment of the Punjab Alienation of Land Bill," IESHR:2 (April 1965), 145-65. Background to the 1900 bill.

D110   "The Bengal Tenancy Act," CR:83 (July 1886), 111-43.

D111   BHANU, DHARMA. "Early Land Settlements in the Upper Provinces," UB:2 (July 1955), 17-25. Up to 1833.

D112   BOSE, C. N. "The Duke of Argyll on the Permanent Settlement of Bengal," CR 52:104 (1871), 171-203.

D113   BROWN, F. H. "Tenancy Law in North-Western India," W:156 (July 1901), 61-67.

D114   BURMAN, DEBAJYOTI. "History of Land Revenue Settlement in Bengal," MR:78 (Nov., Dec. 1945), 304-08, 359-66.

D115 "C.S.B." "Landed Proprietorship, Land-Tenures, and the Vestiges of Local Self-Government under Native Rule in Orissa," CR 77:154 (1883), 236-63.

D116 CAMPBELL, R. "Lord Ripon's Indian Land Legislation," FR:41 (Jan.-June 1884), 625-36.

D117 "Canal Rent vs. Land Revenue," CR 49:97, 1-36.

D118 "Canara-Madras Land Revenue," CR 21:42 (1853), 356-81.

D119 "Capital and Land," CR 38:76 (1863), 321-46. On land settlement in the North-west Provinces and Punjab.

D120 CARNEGY, PATRICK. "Our Land Revenue Policy in Northern India," CR 64:127 (1877), 160-79.

D121 CHAKRABARTTI, B. B. "Relics of Shah Hamid Danishmund at Mangalkot," IHRC:20 (1943), 19-22. Grants of the 1780's in Bengal.

D122 CHANDRA, PRAKASH. "The Permanent Settlement of Bengal," CR:56 (July 1936), 47-50. A discussion of who was responsible for the legislation.

D123 CHATTERJI, J. L. "Early Revenue Authorities of Bengal," CR: 124 (Oct. 1908), 584-614.

D124 CHATTERJI, NANDLAL. "The Settlement of Waste Lands in Oudh after the Mutiny," IHCP:11 (1948), 208-09. Summary of 1870 regulations on lease and sale of waste land.

D125 CHAUDHURI, S. B. "Pattani (Putnee) Tenures," CR 62:124 (1876), 330-64.

D126 COHN, BERNARD S. "Comments on Papers on Land Tenure," IESHR:1 (Oct.-Dec. 1963), 177-83. Comments on papers by Hauser, McLane and Metcalf.

D127 "The Collector of Revenue in the North West Provinces of India," CR 23:45 (1845), 136-61.

D128 CONNELL, CHARLES JAMES. "Our Land Revenue Administration in Upper India," CR 66:131 (1878), 87-124.

D129 ———. "Our Land Revenue Policy in Northern India," CR 63:126 (1876), 331-54.

D130 CROSTHWAITE, C. H. T. "A Land Policy for Northern India," CR 56:112 (1873), 203-35.

D131 DACOSTA, J. and NIGHTINGALE, FLORENCE. "The Bengal Tenancy Bill," CoR:44 (Oct. 1883), 577-602. Comments on bill being considered by Indian legislature.

D132 DANTAZAGI, VISHESHWAR DAYAL. "Permanent Settlement in the Upper Provinces," JIH:1 (Feb. 1922), 312-26. A well-written account.

D133 DAS GUPTA, AMARPRASAD. "The Committee of Circuit at Krishnagar," IHRC:16 (1939), 91-96.

D134 ———. "The Settlement of Dacca, Sylhet and Tipperah in 1772," IHRC:17 (1940), 73-77.

D135 ———. "Settlement of Rajshahi by the Committee of Circuit in 1772," IHCP:3 (1939), 1508-19. The methods and procedures of a British land-settlement committee in Bengal.

D136 DATTA, KALIKINKAR. "An Old Village Survey Report," IHRC: 29 (1953), 15-18. A survey in 1825 at Patna.

D137 "A Deed of Permanent Property Granted by Sir W. Bentinck Governor-in-Council of Fort St. George, to Camadana Sobhanadry Rao, Zamindar of Charmahal," AHRS:16 (1945-46), 84-90. Text of a grant dated Nov. 14, 1806.

D138 "A DISTRICT OFFICER." "Policy of the New Rent Law for Bengal and Behar," CR 72:143 (1881), 161-95.

D139 DUTT, ROMESH. "The Peasant Proprietors of India," AR, Ser. 3: 16 (Oct. 1903), 231-44. Against settlement in Bombay, Madras.

D140 "Enhancement of Rents," CR 39:77 (1864), 97-124.

D141 FISCHER, J. F. "Indian Revenue and Land Systems," AR, Ser. 3: 16 (Oct. 1903), 245-91. Favors extension of system established by A. Cotton in Madras.

D142 FUKAZAWA, HIROSHI. "Lands and Peasants in the Eighteenth Century Marāthā Kingdom," HJE:6 (June 1965), 32-61. Based on Marathi records.

D143 GHOSAL, HARI RANJAN. "The Problem of Effecting Permanent Settlements in Tirhut," IHRC:35 (Feb. 1960), 91-95.

D144 ———. "Resumption of Rent-Free Tenures for Assessment by the Company's Government (1819-1850)," IHCP:13 (1950), 316-19. Figures on resumption in Bengal.

D145 ———. "A Study of the Land Revenue Records of Tirhut (1783-1838)," IHRC:30 (1954), 43-47. Based on papers at Muzaffarpur.

D146 GHOSH, J. C. "Immediate Effects of the Permanent Settlement in Bengal," IJE:10 (April 1930), 828-45.

D147 ———. "Rent and Land-Revenue in Bengal," IJE:10 (July 1929), 59-80.

D148 GORDON, L. R. "Polozhenie krest'ian Vostochnogo Pakistana" [The Situation of the Peasants in East Pakistan], UZIV:12 (1955), 217-56. Summary in HA:4 (No. 2273): "Shows the changes which took place in the life of the Bengali peasants from the end of the 18th century to 1950 and explains the reasons for them."

D149 ———. [The Relation of Landlord and Tenant in the Northwestern Frontier Province 1918-1929], UZIV:5 (1953); German tr. in OSEI.

D150 GOSWAMI, KUNJA GOVINDA. "The Satak Copper Plate Grant of King Rāma Siṃha II, of Jaintia of 1809 A.D.," ASB: NS 25 (1929), 165-69. A land grant.

D151 "Government of British India—Revenue Systems," ER:55 (April 1832), 79-108.

D152 "The Great Indian Question," BM:95 (May 1864), 597-614. The land revenue question.

D153 "The Great Rent Case," CR 41:82 (1865), 398-418. An 1865 decision giving Bengali ryots some rights to the land.

D154 GUPTA, HIRA LAL. "Land System in Northern India under the East India Company," JIH:42 (April 1964), 169-93. A summary; no references.

D155 GUPTA, SULEKH CHANDRA. "British Land Policy in U.P. in the First Quarter of the Nineteenth Century," AV:1 (Dec. 1959), 327-39. In Hindi, with English summary pp. 338-39: "The contemporary impact of the evolution of economic theory in Britain on the land policies of the British rulers in India."

D156 ———. "Land Market in the North Western Provinces (Uttar Pradesh) in the First Half of the Nineteenth Century," IER:4 (Aug. 1958), 51-70. Figures on sales and mortgages, 1847 to 1862, and figures on inherited vs. purchased land in Cawnpore in 1840 and 1872.

D157 GURNER, C. W. "The Merchant Zemindars," BPP:29 (1925), 56-67, 155-63. The position of the East India Company as zamindars in Bengal.

D158 ———. "The Zemindars of the Twenty-four Pargannahs; Their Re-instatement by Warren Hastings," BPP:33 (Jan.-June 1927), 85-91.

D159 HAMBLY, G. R. G. "Richard Temple and the Punjab Tenancy Act of 1868," EHR:79 (Jan. 1964), 47-66. An opponent of the "reaction in favour of aristocratic land-tenures" after the Mutiny.

D160 HAUSER, WALTER. "The Indian National Congress and Land Policy in the Twentieth Century," IESHR:1 (July-Sept. 1963), 57-65. Based on records at Patna and on printed works.

D161 "ICH DIEN." "The Land Laws of Bengal," CR:110 (Jan., April 1900), 105-29, 273-303.

D162 "Indian Land Revenue," CR:53 (1871), 267-94.

D163 "Indian Land Tenure Considered as an Economic Question," CR 47:94, 68-106.

D164 "Indian Taxation: Lord Cornwallis's Land Settlement," W:94 (July 1870), 24-35.

D165 "J.C.G." "The Rent Question," CR 65:129 (1877), 161-66.

D166 ———. "The Rent Question in Bengal," CR 63:125 (1876), 88-124.

D167 "J.S.M." "N.-W.P. Settlements," CR 75:149 (1882), 106-14.

D168 JAMESON, A. KEITH. "The Permanent Settlement in Midnapur," CR:291 (Jan. 1918), 44-57.

D169 JHA, ADITYA PRASAD. "Tenants' Rights in Bengal and Bihar after Permanent Settlement (1793-1819)," IHCP:23 (1961), 78-90. The customs Cornwallis counted on to protect the ryots and the regulations supplementing them.

D170 "K.N.R." "The Khudkasht Ryot of Bengal," CR 77:153 (1883), 9-57. On rights of occupation.

D171 KERR, J. H. "Selected Paras Concerning Survey and Settlement Operation in Darbhanga District (1896 to 1903)," BRS:48 (1962), Sec. 1. Paragraphs on the district from an unidentified source.

D172 "Khas-Mehals," CR 25:49 (1855), 1-19. On land revenue in Bengal.

D173 KOMAROV, E. N. "K voprosu ob ustanovlenii postoiannogo oblozheniia po sisteme zamindari v Bengalii" [On the Question of Introducing a System for Permanent Tax Assessment on the Basis of the Zamindar System in Bengal], UZIV:12 (1955), 3-60. Summary in HA:4 (No. 2278): "Discusses the motives of British colonizers, and their objectives, in introducing the 'Permanent Settlement' in Bengal in 1793."

D174 KOTOVSKII, G. G. "Arenda i arendnye otnosheniia v Tamilnade (Iuzhnaia Indiia) v 1917-1939 gg" [Rent and Land Tenure in Tamilnad (South India), 1917-1939], UZIV:12 (1955), 161-95. Summary in HA:4 (No. 3188): "The author describes how the capitalist system of land tenure developed. Based on British and Indian publications." German translation in OSEI.

D175 KUZMIN, S. A. [Landholding and Land Revenue Policy in Sind in the Second Half of the 19th Century], IAEH.

D176 "The Land Acquisition Act, and the Law of Compensation," CR: 88 (Jan. 1889), 42-54.

D177 "The Land Revenue of India," BM:92 (Nov. 1862), 598-606.

D178 "The Land Revenue of Madras," CR 17:34 (1852), 282-339; 32 (March 1859), 82-105.

D179 "The Land System of India," CR 38:75 (1863), 109-58.

D180 "Land Tenure in the North-West Provinces," CR 41:82 (1865), 350-64.

D181 "The Land Tenures of British India," W:89 (Jan. 1868), 197-223.

D182 "The Land-Tenures of Upper India," CR 42:84 (1865), 369-83.

D183 "The Law of Land Sale in British India," QJPSS:3 (No. 3, 1880), 1-29.

D184 MADGE, W. C. "Principles of British Land Legislation in India," CR 79:157 (1884), 39-55.

D185 "Manual of Surveying, and the Revenue Survey," CR 16:31 (1851), 321-38. On the system of surveying in Bengal and North-West Provinces.

D186 MATHUR, L. P. "Land Revenue Settlement Policy in North-West Provinces 1801-80," IHRC:31 (1955), 130-37. Material from National Archives.

D187 MATHUR, Y. B. "Land Revenue Administration of the Punjab (1849-75)," BPP:82 (Jan.-June 1963), 44-56.

D188 McLANE, JOHN R. "Peasants, Money-Lenders and Nationalists at the End of the 19th Century," IESHR:1 (July-Sept. 1963), 66-73. Examines "the validity of the British claim, made at the end of the 19th Century, that they protected the peasants from the upper classes."

D189 METCALF, THOMAS R. "The Impact of the Mutiny on British Attitudes to India," IHCP:23, part 2 (1961), 24-31; also, under title "The Influence of the Mutiny of 1857 on Land Policy in India," HJ:4 (1961), 152-63. Examines behavior of Oudh peasantry and the consequent British determination that the peasant could not be trusted.

D190 ———. "Laissez-faire and Tenant Right in Mid-Nineteenth Century India," IESHR:1 (July-Sept. 1963), 74-81. Based on India Office records.

D191 ———. "The Struggle Over Land Tenure in India, 1860-1868," JAS:21 (May 1962), 295-307. Discusses issues, arguments, and legislative developments in Bengal, Oudh and the Punjab.

D192 MISRA, B. R. "Early Land Revenue History of the Agra Province: Permanent vs. Temporary Settlement," IJE:15 (July 1934, April 1935), 79-96, 489-504.

D193 MITRA, K. P. "The Office of the Qanungo in Bihar," IHRC:21 (1944), 17-19.

D194 MITRA, RAJENDRALALA. "The Bisen Talukdars of Northern Oudh," CR 74:148 (1882), 382-418.

D195 MOOKERJEA, ASHUTOSH. "The Proposed New Rent Law for Bengal and Behar," CR 71:142 (1880), 345-98; 76:152 (1883), 324-47.

D196 MUKHERJI, NILMANI. "The Ryotwari System and Mirasi Rights in the Madras Presidency (1792-1827)," IHCP:23 (1961), 91-95.

D197 MUKHERJI, SAUGATA. "A Note on Lakhiraj Lands," IHCP:21 (1958), 426-30. An examination of the various meanings of "rent-free" land in the 18th cent. Draws largely on the work of Tapan Kumar Raychoudhuri & Ranajit Guha.

D198 [MUNRO]. "Sir Thomas Munro, and the Land Tax," CR 15:30 (1851), 351-74.

D199 NAGAR, R. N. "The Kanungo in the North Western Provinces (1801-1833)," IHRC:18 (Jan. 1942), 116-20.

D200 ———. "The Mofussil Special Commission in the North Western Provinces (1801 to 1810)," IHRC:17 (1940), 82-86.

D201 ———. "The Patwari in the Ceded and Conquered Provinces under the East India Company (1801-1833)," UPHS: NS 8 (1960), 5-10. The position of the village record-keeper.

D202 ———. "A Report on the Rent-free Estates in the Ceded and Conquered Provinces," IHRC:33 (1958), 120-24. Extracted from 1820 report.

D203 ———. "Some Details of the Revenue Administration of the Ceded Province (1801-1833)," IHRC:16 (1939), 116-22.

D204 ———. "The Tahsildar in the Ceded and Conquered Provinces (1801-1833)," UPHS: NS 2 (1954), 26-34. Regulations on his powers and duties.

D205 NARENDRANATH, RAJA. "Punjab Agrarian Laws and Their Economic and Constitutional Bearings," MR:65 (Jan. 1939), 29-36. With historical survey.

D206 NATARAJAN, B. "Economic Ideas behind the Permanent Settlement," IJE:22 (Jan. 1942), 708-23. Dispatches of the Court of Directors and 18th cent. printed works are the source.

D207 NEILL, J. W. "The Ryots of the Dekhan, and the Legislation for Their Relief," AR, Ser. 2: 7 (April 1894), 396-419.

D208 O'DONNELL, C. J. "The Core of the Rent Bill," CR 80:159 (1885), 207-18.

D209 "On the Revenue System of India, and Its Two Principal Divisions of Zumeendarry and Ryotwarry Settlements," OH:6 (Aug. 1825), 211-24.

D210 "The Owner of the Soil," CR:32 (June 1859), 308-341. On revenue administration.

D211 "P.N." "The Rent Enhancement Bill," CR 65:130 (1877), 322-55.

D212 PATRO, A. P. "Land Revenue Policy in Madras," HR:28 (Sept. 1913), 701-04. Brief historical review.

D213 "Permanent Assessment of Land Revenue in Bengal," MR:23 (Feb. 1918), 122-29. Historical résumé, 1757-1793.

D214 "Permanent Settlement in Its Present Aspect," CR 51:101 (1870), 157-76.

D215 PILLAI, T. SANKARAN. "Reforms in Land-Holdings in India," MUJ:25A (July 1953 & Jan. 1954), Suppl. 1-68; 26A (July 1954 & Jan. 1955), Suppl. 69-141. History and proposals, based on secondary sources.

D216 "The Principle of Assessments," CR 42:84 (1865), 419-23.

D217 "Proposed Reforms in the Re-settlement of Land Assessments," QJPSS:6 (Oct. 1883), 1-22.

D218 RAJ, JAGDISH. "The Introduction of the Taluqdari System in Oudh," CIEH:1, 46-79. Good study of the effects of the Mutiny on settlement policy and practice in Oudh.

D219 ———. "Sir John Lawrence and Oudh Cultivators," IHRC:35 (Feb. 1960), 122-28.

D220 RAMSBOTHAM, R. B. "The Kanungo: Some Aspects of His Office in Bengal during the Early Days of the Company," JIH:3 (Sept. 1924), 205-17.

D221 ———. "Some Suggestions for Stabilizing the Settlement of the Land Revenue in Bengal Made Previous to 1786," JIH:4 (Sept. 1925), 94-99; IHRC:7 (Jan. 1925), 50-54. Suggestions pre-dating Philip Francis's; gives extracts from records.

D222 RAVINDRAN, T. K. "Land Tenures of Malabar," BRAS:34/35 (1959-60), 91-101. Different types in current practice.

D223 RAY CHAUDHURI, TAPAN KUMAR. "An Old Custom of Estate Division in Bihar. An Interesting Record of the Sadr Diwani Adalat," IHRC:26 (1949), 21-22.

D224 ————. "Rent-Evasion in Bengal in the Seventeen Nineties," IHCP:12 (1949), 224-27. Based on a letter from the Judge of Burdwan to the Sadr Diwani Adalat in 1800.

D225 "The Revenue Survey," CR:33 (Sept. 1859), 1-28.

D226 "The Revenue System of Bombay," CR:44 (Feb. 1867), 355-68.

D227 "The Revision of the N.W.P. Settlements," CR 54:107 (1872), 35-53.

D228 ROBINSON, PHIL. "Auction Sales in the Benares Province," CR 58:116 (1874), 356-88.

D229 ROGERS, A. "The Land Revenue Administration of Poona," AR:7 (Jan. 1889), 134-89. With figures on revenue. "A Rejoinder" by H. P. Malet, AR:8 (July 1889), 105-16.

D230 ————. "A Quarter of a Century of Land Revenue Administration in Madras," CR:118 (Jan. 1904), 64-75.

D231 ROY, SARAT CHANDRA. "The Administrative History and Land Tenures of the Ranchi District under British Rules," CR:266 (Oct. 1911), 414-71. Reprinted in MIA:41 (Oct.-Dec. 1961), 276-323.

D232 "Saugor and Nerbudda Territories," CR:37 (Sept. 1861), 125-48. On land revenue.

D233 SAYANNA, V. V. "Land Values in the Madras Province," BUJ:16 (Jan. 1948), 29-39. On changes in land values.

D234 SEMYENOVA, N. I. [British Land Revenue Policy in Punjab in the Middle of the 19th Century], IAEH.

D235 ————. [Village Community and Feudal Land Tenure in Punjab in the First Half of the 19th Century], UZIV:12 (1955); German tr. in OSEI.

D236 SEN, S. P. "Pattas or Title Deeds of the Villages Comprising the French Colony of Chandernagore," IHCP:9 (1946), 393-99. Prints English translations of 18th cent. French pattas.

D237 "The Settlement of the N.W. Provinces," CR 12:24 (1849), 413-67.

D238 SRINIVASACHARI, C. S. "The Origins of Ryotwar Settlement in the Madras Presidency," BV:10 (1949), 285-95.

D239 SUNDARAM, LANKA. "Revenue Administration of the Northern Circars," AHRS:13 (?); 14 (1943-44), 22-58; 15 (1944-45), 1-118. A scholarly account of the revenue settlement in the last half of the 18th cent.; reprints documents in 8 appendices, vol. 15. Source: Madras Revenue Dispatches.

D240 "The Talookdaree Tenure of Upper India," CR 43:85 (1866), 137-60.

D241 "The Tenure of Land," CR 42:83 (1865), 94-105.

D242 THOMAS, JOHN F. "Notes on Ryotwar," MJLS:9 (1841?), 53-78.

D243 "Travancore and Its Land Tenures," CR:112 (Jan. 1901), 125-35.

D244 [TUCKER]. "A Few Cursory Notes of Mr. Tucker's Work on the Finances of the East India Company," OH:7 (Oct. 1825), 89-97. On land settlement.

D245 VAKIL, MANEKLAL. "Land Taxation in India," MR:61 (Jan.-April, 1937), 72-75, 164-70, 281-86, 418-21.

D246 [WEDDERBURN]. "Mr. Wedderburn and His Critics on a Permanent Settlement for the Deccan," QJPSS:3 (Oct. 1880), 17-36.

D247 WRIGHT, H. R. C. "Some Aspects of the Permanent Settlement in Bengal," EcHR: NS 7:2 (1954), 204-15. The thinking behind land policy and motives of the Permanent Settlement; examines cliché that the aim was to create an Indian landed gentry.

D248 "The Zemindar and the Ryot," CR:6 (1846), 305-53. On agriculture in Bengal.

4. OTHER AND GENERAL REVENUE

D249 "The Abkari Mehal," CR 29:58 (Dec. 1857), 280-304. On revenue administration in North-West Provinces.

D250 ADAMS, GEORGE. "India: A Remediable Grievance," NC:42 (Sept. 1897), 486-92. On the collection of revenue.

D251 ALI, AMEER. "Some Indian Suggestions for India," NC:7 (June 1880), 963-78. Largely on taxation.

D252 BANERJEA, PRAMATHANATH. "Income-Tax in India," MR: 65 (Jan. 1939), 102-06. Historical résumé.

D253 ———. "Financial Resources of the East India Company," CR:24 (Aug. 1927), 191-237.

D254 BANERJEE, TARASANKAR. "Withering Away of the Sayer Duties in the Bengal Presidency," CR:175 (April 1965), 47-56.

D255 BHATNAGAR, G. D. "Revenue Administration of Wajid Ali Shah," UPHS:4 (1956), 43-52. Facts and figures on Oudh revenue administration in the 1840's and '50's, from British and Persian records.

D256 CHANDRA, G. N. "Revenue Records in the Early Days of the Company," IA:8 (July-Dec. 1954), 110-20.

D257 C[OTTON], H. J. S. "The Road Cess Act, 1871," CR 53:106 (1871), 295-320.

D258 CROMER, E. B. "Indian Progress and Taxation," QR:219 (Oct. 1913), 483-92.

D259 DEWAR, DOUGLAS. "The Inland Customs Revenue of the Province of Agra," UPHS:3 (May 1922), 1-24. Regulations and annual income, 1824-54.

D260 HAMBLY, G. R. G. "The Income Tax Controversy in India," CIEH:2 (1963), 1-20. 1869-73 debate; based on Parliamentary papers and correspondence in India Office Library.

D261 "The Income-Tax in India," CR 54:107 (1872), 92-117.

D262 "Indian Prosperity," BM:94 (Aug. 1863), 198-216. On the revenue system.

D263 "Indian Stamp Act," QR:38 (Oct. 1828), 489-503. On East India Company revenues.

D264 "Indian Taxation of Englishmen," ER:47 (Jan. 1828), 134-84. On a pamphlet against "the new Indian Stamp Act."

D265 NAGAR, R. N. "Early Revenue Policy of the East India Company in the Ceded and Conquered Provinces (1801-1815)," UPHS:12 (Dec. 1939), 52-59.

D266 ———. "Employment of Indians in the Revenue Administration of the North-Western Provinces (1801-33)," UPHS:13 (Dec. 1940), 66-73. General policy; no figures given.

D267 ———. "The Subordinate Services in the Revenue Administration of the North-Western Provinces: 1801-1833," UPHS:15 (Dec. 1942), 125-34.

D268 NAIDIS, MARK. "A Note on Sir John Lawrence and the Income Tax," BPP:79 (July-Dec. 1960), 77-82. A new view into the character of a man usually portrayed as a "granite, monolithic personality."

D269 "On Certain Indian Taxes—a Symposium," CR 70:139 (1880), 403-23.

D270 PAGAR, S. M. "The Indian Income Tax: Its History, Theory, and Practice," IJE:2 (Dec. 1918), 305-28.

D271 PATWARDHAN, R. P. "A Problem about Revenue Accounts in the 18th Century," IHRC:30 (1954), 94-97.

D272 RAMSBOTHAM, R. B. "Letters Received by the Chief of Chittagong during 1774 from the Committee of Revenue at Fort William, Calcutta," BPP:40 (July-Dec. 1930), 7-17. Prints the letters.

D273 RAMSBOTHAM, R. B. "Some Aspects of the Revenue Collection in Bengal Immediately after the Assumption of the Diwani," IHRC:5 (1923), 35-44.

D274 "The Revenues of India," QR:130 (Jan. 1871), 93-122.

D275 ROY CHOWDHURY, BIRENDRA KISHORE. "The Bengal Agricultural Income-Tax Bill," MR:71 (Jan. 1942), 65-68.

D276 SINHA, R. M. "Revenue Administration of Nagpur State under the British Management (1818-1830)," JIH:43 (Aug. 1965), 633-45.

D277 SOHONI, S. V. "Notes on the Revenue History of Darbhanga Raj," BRS:48 (1962), sec. 1, 105-41. Covers 1558-1808.

D278 "Sources of Revenue in British India," OH:6 (July 1825), 21-30. Comments on Tucker's "Financial Situation of the East India Company," advocating land-tax.

D279 SUBBA RAO, R. "Fourteen Persian Firmans of the Period 1172-1179 A.H. (1760-67 A.D.)," AHRS:8 (April 1934), 245-54. Relating to revenue administration in the Northern Circars.

D280 "Taxation in India," CR:88 (Jan., April 1889), 55-77, 305-32; 89 (July 1889), 75-98.

D281 "The Taxation of India," QR:149 (April 1880), 486-518.

D282 "The Use of Torture in India," ER:103 (Jan. 1956), 153-80. Comment on report from Madras on torture used in collection of revenue.

D283 VAKIL, C. N. "Incidence of Taxation in India," MR:32 (Nov. 1922), 545-50. With tables from 1871-1922.

5. AGRICULTURE AND RURAL POVERTY

D284 "Agricultural History in Madras and What It Teaches," CR:96 (Jan. 1893), 75-97.

D285 BARTON, WILLIAM P. "The Indian Peasant, the Peasant Soldier, and Economic Planning," QR:283 (April 1945), 165-76. On economic development after World War II.

D286 "The Bengal Ryot," BM:113 (Feb. 1873), 147-63. Account of his daily life.

D287 BHAT, SHRIDHAR BHASKAR. "Letter of National Importance about 80 Years Old," IHRC:35 (1960), 44-48. Letter dated March 3, 1880, from Florence Nightingale to S. H. Chiplonkar on improving the conditions of Indian agriculturalists.

D288 BHATIA, B. M. "An Enquiry into the Conditions of the Agricultural Classes in India, 1888," CIEH:1, 80-94. Based on papers connected with the secret enquiry ordered by Lord Dufferin in 1888, excerpts of which were used by Digby for *Prosperous British India.* Reproduces family budgets.

D289 BHOUMICK, N. P. "Food Problem in India," MR:88 (Aug. 1950), 105-16. Production of food crops and area under cultivation, 1941-46.

D290 BLUNT, WILFRED SCAWEN. "Ideas about India:—I. The Agricultural Danger," FR:42 (July-Dec. 1884), 164-78. On financial problems.

D291 BURMAN, DEBAJYOTI. "Early History of Agriculture in Bengal," MR:78 (Sept. 1945), 157-61. Through 19th cent.

D292 "C.R.M." "Notes on the Ryot of Behar," CR 69:138 (1879), 332-47.

D293 CHAKRABARTI, R. "Milk Production in India (1920-21 to 1959-60)," AV:7 (Sept. 1965), 220-31.

D294 CHATTERJI, NILANANDA. "The Cattle-Problem of India," MR:29 (March 1921), 342-48. With government statistics.

D295 CHOWDHURY, BENOY. "Growth of Commercial Agriculture in Bengal (1757-1900)," ISPP:4 (April-June 1963), 227-97 ("The Cultivation of Poppy under Monopoly Control"); 4 (July-Sept. 1963), 461-508; 5 (Oct.-Dec. 1963), 5-87 ("The Problems of Indigo Cultivation").

D296 ————. "Some Aspects of Peasant-Economy of Bengal after the Permanent Settlement," BPP:76 (Jubilee 1957), 137-49. An economic analysis based mainly on Buchanan Reports.

D297 ————. "Some Problems of the Peasantry of Bengal before the Permanent Settlement," BPP:75 (1956), 134-51. Discusses farming systems, taxes, rents, economic differentiation of the peasantry; based on Board of Revenue records.

D298 COATS, THOMAS. "Account of the Present State of the Township of Lony; in Illustration of the Institutions, Resources, etc. of the Marratta Cultivators," LSBT:3 (1823), Old ed., 172-264; New ed., 183-280.

D299 "Colebrooke's Remarks on Bengal," ER:10 (April 1807), 27-40. Review applauds work on improving cultivation and agriculture.

D300 DAS, RAJANI KANTA. "Economics of Indian Agriculture," MR: 69 (Jan. 1941), 32-38. With statistical tables from 1925.

D301 DATTA, KALIKINKAR. "State of Agriculture in Bengal during the Mid-Eighteenth Century," CR:55 (June 1935), 297-302. Fully annotated summary of crops.

D302 "EROPMAR." "Reis and Ryot in Upper India," CR:111 (July 1900), 64-78.

D303 FRANKS, H. GEORGE. "Village Debt Settlement: a New Account of Elphinstone's Policy in the Territories Conquered from the Peshwa in 1817," IJE:9 (July 1928), 45-66. From records in Poona Residency Records.

D304 "G." "Is Behar Rack-Rented? An Enquiry into the Condition of the Behar Ryots," CR 78:155 (1884), 179-207. With tables.

D305 GHATGE, M. B. "The Family Budgets of Farmers in the Charotar Tract of Kaira District in the Bombay Province," BUJ:10 (Jan. 1942), 32-56. With tables.

D306 GHOSE, HEMENDRA PROSAD. "Decay of Villages in Bengal," CR:124 (July 1907), 394-408. Causes.

D307 GHOSH, INDU BHUSAN. "Agricultural Resources of East and West Bengal," MR:83 (April 1948), 277-82. Comparisons made from statistical reports.

D308 ———. "Food Economy of West Bengal," MR:85 (May 1949), 366-72. With crop statistics.

D309 GUPTA, SULEKH CHANDRA. "Agrarian Structure in U.P. in the Late 18th and Early 19th Century," CIEH:1, 21-45. "This paper examines certain general features of the village communities in the Ceded and Conquered Provinces. . . . It analyses their composition, the web of economic relations which held together their members and the integral character of the relationships between the Indian revenue system and all aspects of economic life in the village communities."

D310 "Indian Agricultural Exhibitions," CR 41-82 (1865), 365-97.

D311 JOSHI, C. B. "Indapur Village—A Study in Economic History," IHRC:15 (Dec. 1938), 175-81. 18th & 19th cent. from Peshwa Dafter records.

D312 KAMATH, S. "Scarcity of Cattle in India," HR:28 (Nov. 1913), 810-13. With tables of figures.

D313 KLEIN, I. "Utilitarianism and Agrarian Progress in Western India," EcHR:18 (Dec. 1965), 576-97. Based on Elphinstone papers.

D314 KOMAROV, E. N. [Village and Farming in Bengal in the Second Half of the 18th Century], UZIV:18 (1957).

D315 KOTOVSKY, G. G. [Agrarian Policy of British Rulers in India in the 1860's], PUI.

D316 ———. [Agrarian Relations in Maharashtra in the Late 19th and Early 20th Centuries], NLM.

D317 KUMAR, DHARMA. "Agricultural Wages in the 19th Century in Madras," CIEH:2 (1963), 63-88. A district-by-district analysis that "suggests modification of the generally accepted thesis identifying the pressure of population on land as a decisive influence in the growth of a proletariat."

D318 KUMAR, RAVINDER. "Rural Life in Western India on the Eve of the British Conquest," IESHR:2 (July 1965), 201-20. Social and economic structure.

D319 "The Land and Labour of India," CR:45 (Aug. 1867), 397-413.

D320 "Land Improvement in the North-West," CR 52:104 (1871), 217-26.

D321 "Land Law Reform and Agricultural Banks," QJPSS:4 (July 1881), 32-57, 2nd independent sec. Figures on agricultural poverty.

D322 LAUD, D. S. "Food Supplies of Bombay," LSGI:7 (Jan. 1937), 89-100. Gives sources and seasons of food.

D323 "Life in the Rice Fields," CR 29:57 (Sept. 1857), 121-56. On rural life.

D324 MAMORIA, CHATURBHUJ. "Problems of Indian Agriculture," MR:87 (March 1950), 192-200. With gov't. statistics.

D325 MINOCHA, V. S. "Ranade on the Agrarian Problem," IESHR:2 (Oct. 1965), 357-66.

D326 MOHILE, V. G. "Agricultural Holdings in India with Special Reference to the Bombay Presidency," BUJ:1 (July 1932), 65-82. On legislation in Bombay.

D327 MROZEK, BOGUSLAW. "Powstanie systemów zamindari i rajjatwari w rolnictwie indyjskim na przelomie XVIII i XIX wieku" [The Rise of the System of Zamindari and Ryotwari in Indian Agriculture at the Turn of the 19th Century], PO:25 (1958), 45-60.

D328 MUKHERJEE, KARUNAMOY. "The Basic Problems of Rural Indebtedness in Bengal," MR:83 (May 1948), 391-94. With historical background.

D329 MUKHERJEE, N. "The Ryotwari System and Rural Society of the Madras Presidency (1792-1827)," BPP:78 (July-Dec. 1959), 111-22. Based on Madras records.

D330 MUKHERJEE, RADHAKAMAL. "Agricultural and Agrarian Problems in Bengal," MR:38 (Nov. 1925), 538-47. Lecture delivered before the Bengal Economic Society, Calcutta University, July 1925.

D331 O'BRIEN, AUBREY. "The Welfare of the Indian Agriculturist," NC:104 (Sept. 1928), 322-31.

D332 O'DONNELL, C. J. "The Wants of Behar," CR 69:137 (1879), 146-66. Largely agricultural.

D333 "The Peasants of Our Indian Empire," W:110 (July 1878), 135-50. On rural poverty.

D334 RAGHAVA RAO, G. "The Growth of Agricultural Production in the Bombay Presidency," BUJ:7 (Jan. 1939), 98-117. Growth of agricultural production in British districts, 1901-31.

D335 RASTYANNIKOV, V. G. [Forms of Feudal Exploitation of Peasantry in Punjab During Colonial Period], KS:21 (1956).

D336 ———. [On the Character of Commodity Production in Grain Cultivation in Punjab], KS:23 (1957).

D337 ———. "Torgovoe skotovodstvo v pendzhabe (obzor dannykh za 70-e gody XIX B.—40-e gody XX B.)" [Commercial Cattle Breeding in the Punjab (A Survey of Data Between the 1870's and the 1940's)], KS:42 (1961), 65-77.

D338 REID, DONALD N. "The Disaffection in Behar," FR:61 (Jan.-June 1894), 808-16. On agricultural problems.

D339 "Rice in East Bengal," CR 48:95, 48-61.

D340 "Rural Economy of India in Ancient and Modern Times," CR 40:79 (1864), 32-60.

D341 "The Ryot in Bengal," CR:34 (June 1860), 240-50.

D342 SHARMA, GOPAL LAL. "Reflections on the Liabilities of the Ryots of Gaya District in 1820," BRS:47 (1961), 441-48.

D343 "Some Agrarian Questions in the Punjab," CR:88 (April 1889), 266-82.

D344 SRINIVASACHARIAR, C. S. "Agristic Serfs in South India at the Advent of British Rule," IJE:14 (Jan. 1934), 464-73. On their living conditions, from contemporary reports.

D345 STEBBING, E. P. "The Royal Commission on Agriculture in India and the Indian Forests," NC:105 (March 1929), 327-39.

D346 STRICKLAND, C. F. "Agriculture in India," QR:252 (Jan. 1929), 118-33. On current problems.

D347 TAKAHATAKE, MINORU. [On the Peasantry of Bengal in the Late 18th Century], SZ 68:10 (1959).

D348 ———. [On the Zamindars of Bengal Before the Permanent Settlement], TG 42:2&3 (1959).

D349 THOTAPALI, S. "An Examination of Indian Crop Statistics," BUJ:11 (Jan. 1943), 117-24. Evaluation of statistics.

D350 TRIVEDI, A. B. "Agriculture in Kathiawar," BUJ:10 (July 1941), 89-123. With tables.

D351 VIJAYARAGHAVACHARYA, T. "Measures for Improvement of Agriculture," AAAPSS:233 (May 1944), 92-98. Survey of Linlithgow Commission's recommendations and results.

D352 ZACHARIAS, C. W. B. "Cereal Production in Madras," MUJ:16 (1945), 113-24. 1919-43.

6. IRRIGATION

D353 "Canals of Irrigation in the N.W. Provinces," CR 12:23 (1849), 79-183.

D354 DACOSTA, J. "Irrigation Works and the Permanent Settlement in India," CoR:27 (March 1876), 549-58. Believes that permanent settlement of the land tax could finance huge projects.

D355 DILKE, CHARLES W. "An Australian View of India," FR:58 (Dec. 1892), 704-12. View of India's irrigation system by Mr. Deakins, Australian Minister of Water Supply.

D356 "English Capital and Indian Irrigation," CR:32 (March 1859), 172-85.

D357 INGLIS, W. A. "Life and Work of General Sir Arthur Cotton, R.E., K.C.S.I.," CR:112 (April 1901), 248-63. He worked on irrigation systems.

D358 "The Irrigation Movement in Bankura," MR:37 (Jan. 1925), 18-27.

D359 JACOB, LIONEL. "Irrigation in India," CoR:105 (June 1914), 800-08. History of British works.

D360 KANETKAR, B. D. "Pricing of Irrigation Service in India (1854-1959)," AV:2 (June 1960), 158-68.

D361 KURIYAN, GEORGE. "Irrigation in India," MUJ:15 (July 1943, Jan. 1944), 46-58, 161-85. A survey of types and irrigation and problems thereof, with maps.

D362 MAMORIA, C. B. "Irrigation in India, Its Past and Present," MR:90 (Dec. 1951), 448-58.

D363 OLIVIER, E. E. "The Financial Aspects of Indian Irrigation," CR:72 (1881), 90-112, 404-23.

D364 "PENSYL." "Early Irrigation in the Punjab," BM:258 (Sept. 1945), 158-61.

D365 RAO, S. V. S. "Irrigation Development in India," MR:89 (Feb. 1951), 144-46. From 1938 to date.

D366 WEDDERBURN, WILLIAM. "Florence Nightingale on India," CoR:105 (April 1914), 509-17. Summary of a book on irrigation, never published: "The Zemindar, the Sun, and the Watering Pot, as Affecting Life and Death in India."

7. FAMINES

D367 AITKEN, BENJAMIN. "The Coming Famine in India," CoR:93 (Jan. 1908), 6-16.

D368 ALEXANDER, HORACE. "Famine Returns to India," CoR:165 (Jan. 1944), 20-23. On the 1943 famine.

D369 ARCHIBALD, E. D. "The Cycle of Drought and Famine in Southern India," CR 66:131 (1878), 125-51. With statistics.

D370 ARNOLD, EDWIN. "The Famine in India," NA:164 (March 1897), 257-72. On the generosity of the sympathetic Britons.

D371 BEST, CAPT. "Effects of the Famine of 1833," MJLS:13 (1845?), 186-95.

D372 BHATIA, B. M. "Famines, Food Shortage and Food Policy in India (1860-1909)," En:5 (Dec. 1961?), 67-82. Maintains there was a food shortage in India throughout the period, aggravated by bad food policy of the government.

D373 BROUGH, WILLIAM. "India's Famine and Its Cause," Ar:24 (Sept. 1900), 299-312. Attributes it to fiscal mis-management.

D374 CAMPBELL, W. HOWARD. "Famine Relief in South India," W:151 (March 1899), 259-68.

D375 CARNAC, JAMES RIVETT. "Some Account of the Famine in Gujarat, in the Years 1812 and 1813," LSBT:1 (1819), Old ed., 296-303, New ed., 321-29. With extensive bibliography of sources.

D376 CHARI, S. V. "Famine Relief in Madras 150 Years Ago," IHRC:6 (1924), 78-84.

D377 CHAUDHURI, NANI GOPAL. "An Eye-Witness's Account of the Famine of 1770 in Calcutta," MR:76 (July 1944), 30-33.

D378 ———. "Monopoly of Grain during the Bengal and Bihar Famine of 1770," IHQ:21 (June 1945), 124-34. On British government investigations and their findings.

D379 ———. "Some of the Results of the Great Bengal and Bihar Famine of 1770," IHCP:12 (1949), 239-49. Effects on population, land, silk and cotton industries.

D380 CHENEVIX-TRENCH, C. G. "Famine in India: A retrospect and a Plea," BM:254 (Oct. 1943), 295-300.

D381 CHESNEY, GEORGE M. "Famines and Controversy," NC:51 (March 1902), 478-92. Defense of British famine relief.

D382 ———. "Indian Famines," NC:2 (Nov. 1877), 603-20. How the improvement of irrigation could alleviate future famines.

D383 CLINE, G. W. "Indian Finance and Famine Taxation," CR 66:134 (1878), 839-65.

D384 COLVIN, AUCKLAND. "The Indian Famine and the Press," FR:21 (Jan.-June 1874), 484-95. Defense of British famine policy, with map of Bengal and Bihar famine area and statistics on prices.

D385 CROSTHWAITE, C. H. T. "Thakur Pertāb Singh: A Tale of an Indian Famine," BM:162 (July 1897), 28-54.

D386 DAS, G. C. "A Note on the Famines of India," OHRJ:8 (Oct. 1959 & Jan. 1960), 209-17. A survey of famines, especially in Bengal and Orissa.

D387 DEVADHAR, GOPAL KRISHNA. "The Famine of 1908 in India and the Work Done by Non-Official Agencies," MR:6 (Sept. 1909), 250-64.

D388 DUFFERIN and AVA, MARQUESS of. "How India Fights the Famine," NA:164 (April 1897), 385-403.

D389 DUTT, ROMESH C. "Famines in India and Their Remedy," FR: 68 (Aug. 1897), 198-214. Includes brief review of famines in the past.

D390 ELLIOTT, CHARLES. "The Famine in India, 1899-1900," AR, Ser. 3:11 (April 1901), 225-42; 12 (Oct. 1901), 229-59. With tables.

D391 ———. "The Recent Famine in India and the Reports of the Second Famine Commission," AR Ser. 3:8 (July 1899), 1-41. With map and tables.

D392 FAGAN, HENRY STUART. "Orissa," CoR:4 (Jan.-April 1867), 73-89. Critical of famine relief and prevention measures.

D393 "Famine: Famines in India," EB:10, 167-68. History and British policy.

D394 FURRELL, JAMES W. "Famines in India and the Duty of Government in Connection with Them," CR:58 (1874), 144-70, 303-12.

D395 GHOSH, KALI CHARAN. "Famine's Toll in 1943," MR:75 (May 1944), 346-48.

D396 ———. "Indian Famine Relief Measures—Old and New," MR:74 (Nov. 1943), 372-76.

D397 HAYTHORNTHWAITE, J. P. "A Brief Account of the Famine of 1897 in the North-West Provinces of India," IEvR:26 (Oct. 1899), 201-17.

D398 HOCKING, WILLIAM ERNEST. "Famine over Bengal," A:44 (Aug. 1944), 345-49. Gives background.

D399 HOPKINS, E. WASHBURN. "England and the Famine in India," Fo:24 (Nov. 1897), 342-49. The famine was the fault of the villagers.

D400 "The Indian Famine: How Dealt with in Western India," W:109 (Jan. 1878), 139-58.

D401 "The Indian Famine Reports," BM:128 (Dec. 1880), 726-41.

D402 "Indian Famines," ER:146 (July 1877), 68-101. Based on Parliamentary papers.

D403 "Indian Famines and Their Remedies," QR:195 (Jan. 1902), 54-78. Review of 4 works.

D404 IRWIN, H. C. "Famine and State Duty," CR 60:120 (1875), 211-32.

D405 ———. "The Famine Commission on Tenant Right in Upper India," CR 72:144 (1881), 372-82.

D406 KIRKWOOD, T. M. "The Impending Famine," FR:66 (July-Dec. 1896), 856-68.

D407 "The Lesson of the Famine," CR 46:91, 188-216.

D408 MADGE, W. C. "Famine Taxation," CR 66:133 (1878), 551-60.

D409 MAHALANOBIS, P. C. "The Bengal Famine: the Background and Basic Facts," AR: NS 42 (Oct. 1946), 310-15; discussion pp. 315-18. By a statistician.

D410 MAMORIA, C. B. "Problem of Population and Food Supply in India," MR:89 (Jan. 1951), 39-49.

D411 MEHTA, V. N. "Famines and Standards of Living," AAAPSS:145, Supplement (Sept. 1929), 82-89.

D412 MITRA, K. P. "Scarcity in Bihar (1783 and 1792)," IHRC:17 (1940), 113-22. From British records.

D413 MUKHERHEE, KARUNAMOY. "The Bengal Famine of 1943 and Problems of Agricultural Rehabilitation," CR:100 (Sept. 1946), 145-50.

D414 ———. "Bengal Famine of 1943 and Problems of Rehabilitation of Artisans," CR:102 (Jan. 1947), 21-28. Gives figures and argues that Government did not do enough.

D415 ———. "The Famine of 1943 and the Nature of Land Transfer in a Village of Bengal," MR:81 (April 1947), 309-12.

D416 ———. "Some Aspects of Socio-Economic Consequences of the Bengal Famine of 1943," MR:80 (Aug. 1946), 142-44. With tables.

D417 MUKHERJEE, P. "The Orissa Famine of 1866," OHRJ:6 (April 1957), 69-95.

D418 "The Mysore Famine of 1876-78," CR:87 (Oct. 1888), 261-77.

D419 NEOGY, K. C. "Some Aspects of the Food Muddle," MR:74 (Sept. 1943), 201-08. On the 1943 famine.

D420 "Operation of the Laisser-faire Principle in Times of Scarcity," CR 46:91, 102-17. On famine policy.

D421 OSBORN, ROBERT D. "The Truth about the Indian Famine of 1877-78," CoR:37 (Feb. 1880), 227-46. Accounts of eyewitnesses.

D422 PAL, DHARM. "The Bengal and Orissa Famine (1865-66)," CR:99 (May 1946), 49-59.

D423 PEDDER, W. G. "Famine and Debt in India," NC:2 (Sept. 1877), 175-97. Reviews government reports, examines causes.

D424 "Political Economy and Famine Relief in Bengal," CR 60:120 (1875), 375-99.

D425 POTTER, J. G. "Report on Famine Industrial Relief Work in Agra," IEvR:26 (Oct. 1899), 221-28.

D426 RAINEY, H. JAMES. "Famines in Bengal, and the Reclamation of the Sundarban as a Means of Mitigating Them," CR 59:118 (1874), 332-49.

D427 ROGERS, A. "Report of the Indian Famine Commission, 1901," W:158 (July 1902), 55-75. A summary.

D428 SAMARTH, V. M. "Famines in India (Some Facts and Suggestions)," CR:115 (July 1902), 76-100.

D429 SINHA, BIMAL CHANDRA. "The Recent Bengal Famine: the Ultimate Background—an Irish Parallel," MR:76 (July 1944), 35-40.

D430 SINHA, N. K. "The Famine of 1769-70 (B.S. 1176-1177)," BPP: 77 (July-Dec. 1958), 120-31. Its extent and effect on the population of Bengal.

D431 SRIVASTAVA, HARI SHANKER. "The Indian Famine of 1868-70," UB:9 (April 1962), 27-40. From British records.

D432 SUTHERLAND, J. T. "Causes of Indian Famines," NEM: NS 23 (Sept. 1900), 56-64. Chief cause: British exploitation.

D433 VENKATARAMANI, M. S. "The Roosevelt Administration and the Great Indian Famine," IS:4 (1962-63), 241-64. On the 1943 famine; based on newspaper sources.

8. CO-OPERATIVE MOVEMENTS

D434 BANNERJEA, DEVENDRA NATH. "Indian Agriculture and the Cooperative Movement," CoR:130 (Sept. 1926), 352-60.

D435 CATANACH, I. J. "Democracy and the Rural Co-operative Movement: Some Reflections on the Indian Experience," DCI, pp. 353-61. Materials from Bombay.

D436 "A CO-OPERATOR." "Co-operative Progress in India," MR:15 (March 1914), 300-03. Statistical information about cooperative societies from 1906.

D437 EWBANK, R. B. "The Co-operative Movement in India," QR:225 (April 1916), 368-82.

D438 MAMORIA, C. B. "History and Growth of Co-operative Movement in India," MR:94 (Aug., Sept. 1953), 109-12, 192-97.

D439 MUKERJEA, RAICHARAN. "The Co-operative Movement in India," MR:19 (Jan. 1916), 106-10.

D440 NAIDU, B. V. NARYANASWAMI. "The Co-operative Movement in the Madras Presidency," IJE:14 (Jan. 1934), 418-47. With tables.

D441 NAMBIAR, O. T. GOVINDAN. "Co-operation in Madras," MR: 16 (Oct. 1914), 355-62. With statistics 1905-13.

D442 SANYAL, ABANI NATH. "System of Working of the Ghee Society," MR:64 (July 1938), 60-65. Case history of a cooperative, 1929-37.

9. INDUSTRY, GENERAL

D443 BOYLE, J. A. "The Fisheries of Southern India," CR 62:124 (1876), 239-55.

D444 BURMAN, DEBAJYOTI. "Early History of Sugar in Bengal," MR:75 (Feb. 1944), 106-11.

D445 "Cement Industry in India: 1914-1964," EE:44 (Jan. 29, 1965), 241-46. Tables of finances.

D446 CHANDRA, SUSHIL. "History of Oil Industry in Agra," AUJR: 10 (Jan. 1962), 125-29. On vegetable oil mills.

D447 CHETTY, SHANMUKHAM. "India's Fighting Strength," FA:20 (April 1942), 410-20. Largely on industrial production in World War II.

D448 CHICHEROV, A. I. "Podchinenie remesla torgovym kapitalom v serevo-vostochnykh i iugo-vostochnykh raĭonakh Indii v XVII v" [The Subordination of Handicraft by Commercial Capital in the North-Eastern and South-Eastern Districts of India in the 17th Century], KS:51 (1962), 111-32.

D449 "Cinchona Cultivation in India," CR 42:84 (1865), 369-83. The source of quinine.

D450 DAS, RAJANI KANTA. "Causes of India's Industrial Inefficiency," MR:48 (July 1930), 8-18.

D451 GHOSH, INDU BHUSAN. "Vegetable Oilseeds and Oils in West Bengal's Economy," MR:87 (May 1950), 364-67. Statistics, 1939-49.

D452 GINWALA, PADAMJI P. "Industrial Development in Relation to Natural Resources," AAAPSS:233 (May 1944), 113-20.

D453 GODE, P. K. "The History of Tobacco in India and Europe— Between A.D. 1500 and 1900," BV:16 (1956), 65-74. Excerpts from early references in writings and pictures.

D454 ———. "Studies in the Regional History of Indian Paper Industry (Paper-Manufacture at Behar and Arwal in A.D. 1811-1812 as Described by Francis Buchanan)," BV:6 (1945), 126-30.

D455 ———. "Studies in the Regional History of Indian Paper Industry: Harihar on the Bank of the Tungabhadrā in A.D. 1790 as Described by Capt. Edward Moor," BV:5 (1944), 87-95.

D456 "India; the Commercial and Economic Situation," RT:13 (March 1923), 366-87. On industry in general.

D457 JOSHI, P. C. "The Decline of Indigenous Handicrafts in Uttar Pradesh," IESHR:1 (July-Sept. 1963), 24-35. Largely based on census reports.

D458 KANJILAL, KAILAS CHUNDRA. "The Development of Local Industries in India," CR:111 (July 1900), 101-111.

D459 KEIR, ARCHIBALD. "Of the Method of Distilling as Practised by the Natives at Chatra in Ramgur and in the Other Provinces, Perhaps, with But Little Variation," AsR:1 (1788), 309-19.

D460 KOTOVSKY, G. G. [Handicraft Industry and Disintegration of Peasantry in Southern India], KS:15 (1955); German tr. in OSEI.

D461 LEVKOVSKY, A. I. [Development of Indian Capitalistic Enterprise in Sugar Industry 1920-1940], UZIV:18 (1957).

D462 ———. [Lower Forms of Capitalistic Enterprise in Indian Industry: A Brief Outline], KS:15 (1955); German tr. in OSEI.

D463 MAMORIA, CHATURBHUJ. "Fisheries Resources of India," MR:89 (Feb. 1951), 113-19.

D464 MOOKERJEE, H. C. "India's Hemp Drug Policy under British Rule," MR:84 (Dec. 1948), 446-54.

D465 ———. "Management and Control of British Industries in India," CR:93 (Oct.-Dec. 1944), 1-4, 29-32, 59-63.

D466 ———. "A Review of Cottage Industries in Congress Provinces," CR:74 (Jan. 1940), 14-24.

D467 MOOKERJEE, H. K. "Fisheries in India," CR:95 (June 1945), 97-101.

D468 MORELAND, W. H. "The Industrial Movement in India," QR: 227 (April 1917), 297-313.

D469 NATH, LALA BAIJ. "Ghazipur—the Land of Roses," E&W:4 (July 1905), 703-08. On the attar of rose industry.

D470 PAVLOV, V. I. [A Brief Outline of the Rise of Big Industrial Capitalists in India under Colonial Rule], UZIV:10 (1954).

D471 POLIER, LIEUT.-COL. "The Process of Making Attar, or Essential Oil of Roses," AsR:1 (1788), 332-35.

D472 RAJARATNAM, S. S. "The Industrial Development of India, 1918-1944," CE:3 (Sept. 1954), 27-37. Summary review.

D473 REISNER, L. I. [Role of "Manufacture" in the Development of Some Branches of Factory Industry in the United Provinces of India in the Late 19th and the First Quarter of the 20th Centuries], IAEH.

D474 ——— and SHIROKOV, G. K. [The Industry of India at the End of the Colonial Period], NAA:4 (1961), 50-67. Abstract in SSAB:1 (1962), 38.

D475 SAMALDAS, LALUBHIA. "Industry and Commerce," AAAPSS: 145 suppl. (1929), 90-100. Pre-war and 1926 figures given.

D476 SEN, AMARTYA KUMAR. "The Commodity Pattern of British Enterprise in Early Indian Industrialization, 1854-1914," DCI, pp. 781-808.

D477 SHIROKOV, G. K. "K voprosu o deiatel'nosti otraslevykh obedineii v indiiskoi promyshlennosti" [On the Question of Activity of Branch

Unions (specialized associations) in Indian Industry], NI:51 (1962). Abridged and translated, "Specialized Associations in Indian Industry," CAR:11 (1963), 297-307. On business associations in tea, jute, coal, sugar, cement industries.

D478 SIRCAR, NILUATAN. "The Industrial Situation," MR:21 (Jan. 1917), 77-86. Written evidence before the Industrial Commission.

D479 SOM, KANIKA. "Industrial Relations in West Bengal, 1948-1952," MR:95 (Jan. 1954), 33-35.

D480 TALATI, B. G. "The Paper Industry in India," BUJ:16 (July 1947), 25-33.

D481 UZAIR, MD. "Industry in East Bengal during British Industrial Revolution," PEJ:4 (Aug. 1954), 282-95. Based on published 18th cent. sources.

D482 VENKATARAMAN, K. S. "Coir Industry and Trade on the Malabar Coast," BUJ:8 (Jan. 1940), 52-87; 9 (July 1940), 154-83; 10 (July 1941), 61-88.

D483 "Work and Wages in the East," CR:37 (Sept. 1861), 149-59. On industrial development.

a. Cotton and Textiles

D484 ABDUL ALI, A. F. M. "The Silk Industry in Bengal in the Days of John Company," IHRC:7 (Jan. 1925), 87-97; BPP:29 (Jan.-March 1925), 30-43. From English records.

D485 ALAYEV, L. B. "Razvitie indiiskogo tkachestva do pronikoveniia v Indiuu evropeĭtsev" [The Development of the Indian Weaving Industry before the European Penetration], GKSV, pp. 164-78.

D486 BASU, SATISHCHANDRA. "The Present Situation in the Bombay Cotton Mill Industry and Its Problems," MR:11 (March 1912), 243-47.

D487 "Bombay Cotton, and Indian Railways," CR 13:26 (1850), 328-44.

D488 BRANDIS, ROYALL. "Cotton Competition—U.S. and India—1929-1948," SEJ:17 (Jan. 1951), 270-87. With tables.

D489 BURMAN, DEBAJYOTI. "Bengal's Cotton Manufactures: Two Centuries of Struggle," MR:74 (Oct. 1943), 289-96.

D490 ———. "Early History of Silk in Bengal," MR:76 (Aug.-Oct. 1944), 107-11, 160-62, 207-08.

D491 BURNETT-HURST, A. R. "Lancashire and the Indian Market," RSS:95 (1932), 395-454. Tables of imports and exports of cotton yarn and yard goods, 1913-39; with discussion.

D492   CHAKRABARTY, SARADA CHARAN. "Cotton Cultivation in West Bengal," MR:88 (Aug. 1950), 151-53. Production expenses.

D493   "Cotton Cultivation in India," CR:37 (Sept. 1861), 87-107.

D494   CHOUDHURY, SUKUMAR RAY. "The Present War and the Problem of Cotton Piece Goods in India," CR:88 (July 1943), 42-47. Figures on supply and demand.

D495   DAS, TARAKNATH. "Anglo-Japanese Rivalry in Cotton Industry and India," MR:55 (Jan. 1934), 8-10.

D496   DATTA, K. K. "Impact of the Industrial Revolution on India's Economy," CR:118 (Jan. 1951), 33-38. Deals largely with textile industry.

D497   DE, BARUN. "An Account of the Cultivation of Cotton in Bengal," IHRC:34 (Dec. 1958), 197-207.

D498   DHOLAKIA, H. L. "The Cotton Textile Control," BUJ:14 (July 1945), 14-28. Effect of wartime controls on industry and trade.

D499   DODWELL, H. "The Madras Weavers under the Company," IHRC:4 (1922), 41-46. Their condition at the end of the 18th cent.

D500   GARG, HAR CHARAN LAL. "100 Years of Cotton Textile Industry in India," MR:95 (June 1954), 461-64.

D501   GHOSAL, HARI RANJAN. "Cotton Industry in Bengal, Bihar and Orissa during the Early Nineteenth Century," JIH:18 (Aug. 1939), 195-214. Based on government records.

D502   GUJRAL, LALIT. "Sir Louis Mallet's Mission to Lord Northbrook on the Question of the Cotton Duties," JIH:39 (Dec. 1961), 473-87. From British records.

D503   JAGTAP, M. B. " 'Ghongdi' (Woolen Hand-Woven Blanket) Industry in a Village during 1943-58," AV:2 (Mar. 1960), 15-27. In Marathi; summary in English, pp. 26-27.

D504   JHA, J. S. "East India Company's Cloth Investment in Bihar (1770-1778)," BRS:46 (1960), 177-92.

D505   KHAITAN, D. P. "The Indian Cotton Textile Industry," MR:64 (Aug. 1938), 185-88.

D506   KOUL, SODARSHUN. "The Development of Silk Industry in Kashmir," HR:25 (May-June 1912), 413-19. History of sericulture under the British.

D507   LOGAN, FRENISE A. "The American Civil War: an Incentive to Western India's Experiments with Foreign Cotton Seeds?" AH:30 (1956),

35-40. Account of the history of experimentation after outbreak of American Civil War.

D508 ———. "Factors Influencing India's Ability to Maintain Its Monopoly of the Cotton Export Trade after 1865," IHCP:23 (1961), 48-55. Figures and opinions on the poorer quality and higher price of Indian cotton.

D509 ———. "India—Britain's Substitute for American Cotton, 1861-1865," JSH:24 (Nov. 1958), 472-80. A survey of the Indian cotton boom, based on records in Bombay.

D510 ———. "India's Loss of the British Cotton Market after 1865," JSH:31 (Feb. 1965), 40-50.

D511 MARSHMAN, J. C. "Notes on the Cultivation of Cotton in the District of Dharwar; Past, Present, and Future," RAS:19 (1862), 351-60.

D512 McLEOD, C. C. "Indian Jute Industry: Its History, Cultivation, and Manufacture," SA:82, Supplement (Sept. 30, 1916), 218-19.

D513 MEHTA, N. C. "The Indian Cotton Industry," MR:18 (Sept. 1915), 262-67. Historical survey, with statistics 1913-14.

D514 MOOKERJEE, H. C. "The Indian View of the Jute Industry," CR: 93 (July, Aug. 1944), 1-11, 76-92. Views of Chambers of Commerce.

D515 MUKERJI, B. B. "The East India Company and the Silk Industry (1800-1840)," IJE:15 (Apr. 1935), 459-75.

D516 MUNSHI, M. C. "The Surat Weaving Industry," BUJ:12 (July 1943), 17-30. Economic and sociological study.

D517 NARAYANAN, T. K. "Some Salient Features of Indo-Japanese Trade," MUJ:10 (July 1938), 200-17. Largely on textile and yarn trade.

D518 PILLAI, P. P. "The Indian Cotton-Mill Industry 1853-1922," IJE: 5 (1924-25), 127-51. With a number of tables.

D519 "Resources of India," W:79 (April 1863), 396-428. Largely on cotton-growing.

D520 SARKAR, P. B. "The Jute Crisis," MR:62 (Nov. 1937), 505-09. 1913-1934.

D521 SHAH, P. G. "History of the Indian Cotton Industry during the Nineteenth Century," MR:11 (April 1912), 382-95. A substantial article.

D522 ———. "History of the Silk, Wool, and Jute Industries of India during the Last Century," MR:12 (Oct. 1912), 369-80.

D523 SINGH, S. B. "Bengal's Cotton Trade with China (1800-1833)," BRS:46 (1960), 233-40. Based on proceedings of the Bengal Board of Trade.

D524 SINHA, BIMAL CHANDRA. "The Present Cloth Situation and Cloth Rationing in Bengal," MR:78 (July 1945), 23-26. With tables 1937-1943.

D525 SINHA, J. C. "The Beginning of Jute Export to England. Based on Manuscript Records of English East India Company in London and in Calcutta," IHRC:13 (1930), 93-98. In the 1790's.

D526 ———. "The Dacca Muslin Industry," MR:37 (April 1925), 400-08. History of the industry; a public lecture given at Dacca University, Feb. 26, 1925.

D527 ———. "Jute in Early British Days," ASB: NS 27 (1931), 149-56.

D528 SIRCAR, J. K. "Sisal Hemp in India," MR:63 (Jan. 1938), 45-48.

D529 SUMMERS, T. "Development of Cotton in India: Sind, a Second Egypt," AR: NS 5 (Oct. 1, 1914), 298-351; discussion pp. 352-64.

D530 SUNDARARAMA SASTRI, N. "Localisation of Cotton Textile Industry in India," MUJ:10 (July 1938), 226-37. With 20th cent. production figures for Bombay, Ahmedabad, "Rest of Bombay Presidency," "Rest of India."

D531 TRIVEDI, A. B. "The Gold Thread Industry of Surat," BUJ:9 (July 1940), 184-210.

D532 ———. "The Silk Weaving Industry of Surat," BUJ:10 (Jan. 1942), 105-19.

D533 VENKATARAMAN, K. S. "The Economic Condition of Handloom Weavers," BUJ:10 (Jan. 1942), 74-104; 11 (July 1942), 108-43. With tables.

D534 ———. "The Hand-loom Industry in South India," MUJ Supplement, bound in vols. 7-8, 290 pp. Numerous tables of statistics.

D535 ZOLLINGER, MELLY and RAO, W. LAKSHMANA. "Prices, Wages and Profits in the Khadi Industry," MR:55 (Jan. 1934), 89-94.

b. *Indigo*

D536 BASU, K. K. "An Account of the Early Indigo Planters in Bhagalpur," IHRC:14 (1937), 71-75; BPP:54 (July-Dec. 1937), 69-74. Names of early 19th cent. planters and their holdings.

D537 DE, AMALENDU. "Growth of the Indigo Plantation in Bengal," CR:173 (Dec. 1964), 207-17.

D538 ———. "Indigo Plantation—A Source of Oppression," BPP:82 (July-Dec. 1963), 154-60; 83 (Jan.-June 1964), 56-68.

D539 "Indigo and Indigo Planting," CR:30 (March 1858), 189-230.

D540 "The Indigo Blue Book," CR:34 (June 1860), 355-77.

D541 "Indigo in Lower Bengal," CR 7:13 (1847), 186-219.

D542 "J.H." "About Indigo Planting and Indigo Planters," CR 77:153 (1883), 148-57.

D543 MATSUI, TŌRU. "Jūkyūseiki indo no aisan gijutsu ni tsuite" [On the Methods of Indigo Production in 19th Century India], AKR:10 (1958), 63-90. Summary in HA:5 (No. 134).

c. *Iron, Steel, Coal, and Other Minerals*

D544 BARPUJARI, H. K. "The Surveys and Operations at the Petroleum Springs and Coal-beds in Assam (1826-58)," IHRC:34 (Dec. 1958), 69-73.

D545 BARRACLOUGH, L. J. "The Indian Coal Mining Industry with Particular Reference to Management," CR:100 (July 1946), 1-7.

D546 BEHRE, CHARLES H., JR. "India's Mineral Wealth and political Future," FA:22 (Oct. 1943), 78-93. On the geographical distribution of minerals, with a fold-out map.

D547 BRUSH, JOHN E. "The Iron and Steel Industry in India," GR:42 (Jan. 1952), 37-55. Includes maps of iron and steel centers, and graphs of historical growth.

D548 CHATTERJEE, RAMANANDA. "The Origin of the Tata Works at Jamshedpur," MR:69 (Feb. 1941), 234-37.

D549 CHICHEROV, A. I. "O sotsial'no-ekonomicheskoĭ kharakteristike zhelezodelatel'nykh masterskikh v Maĭsure v kontse XVIII veka" [On the Social-Economic Character of Iron Production in Mysore at the End of the 18th Century], GKSV, pp. 212-27.

D550 DANIEL, HAWTHORNE. "Tata, Indian Industrial Genius," A:25 (June 1925), 494-99, 541-43. Photographs of family, and first steel plant.

D551 DATTA, KALI KINKAR. "Notes on the Saltpetre Trade of the English at Patna (1739-48). Based on Unpublished Records in the Imperial Record Department, Calcutta," IHRC:13 (1930), 67-73.

D552 DEY, H. L. "The Progress of the Steel Industry, 1924-27: How Far the Growth Was Due to Protection," IJE:9 (July 1928), 1-24.

D553 GHOSAL, H. R. "Documents Relating to Saltpetre Manufacture in Bihar in the Early Nineteenth Century," IHRC:23 (1946), 40-42. Extracts from records.

D554 JAMES, FREDERICK. "The House of Tata—Sixty Years of Industrial Development in India," AR:44 (July 1948), 251-60; discussion pp. 261-63. A eulogistic account of Tata enterprise.

D555 MATHUR, JAMSHED. "The Indian Iron and Steel Industry," MR:89 (June 1961), 487-89.

D556 MITRA, SUNIL KUMAR. "Aluminum Industry in India," MR:87 (Jan. 1950), 63-66. With production statistics.

D557 MITTER, B. L. "The Discoverer of Iron-Ores for the Tata Iron and Steel Works," MR:13 (May 1913), 555-57. P. N. Bose.

D558 SARKAR, ANIL KUMAR. "History of Indian Iron and Steel Industry," CR:168 (Aug. 1963), 133-55.

D559 SHAH, P. G. "Aluminum Industry in India," MR:13 (Jan., Feb. 1913), 21-26, 204-10.

D560 SINGH, SHYAM BIHARI. "Saltpetre Industry of Zillah Tirhoot during the First Quarter of the 19th Century," BRS:37 (Sept. & Dec., 1951), 48-64. The center of India's saltpeter industry.

D561 STEVENSON, J. "On the Manufacture of Saltpetre as Practiced by the Natives of Tirhūt," ASB:2 (Jan. 1833), 23-27.

d. *Opium*

D562 ARBUTHNOT, ALEXANDER J. "The Opium Controversy," NC:11 (March 1882), 403-13.

D563 BUTLER, D. "On the Preparation of Opium for the China Market: Written in March 1835, and then Communicated to the Benares and Behār Agencies," ASB:5 (March 1836), 165-79.

D564 CHANDRA, G. N. "Some Facts about Opium Monopoly in Bengal Presidency," BPP:76 (Jubilee 1957), 123-36. From the East India Company point of view.

D565 CUST, ROBERT. "The Opium Question or 'Is India to Be Sacrificed to China?'" CR 80:159 (1885), 168-88.

D566 "D.W.K.B." "The Indian Opium Revenue," CR 63:126 (1876), 365-81.

D567 DANE, RICHARD M. "Opium in China and India," AS: NS 23 (1927), 49-71; discussion pp. 72-78. History of the trade.

D568 DUNNICLIFF, H. B. "The Indian Opium Trade: An Historical Review," AR: NS 34 (1938), 349-59. By a chemist; factual and informative.

D569 GHATAK, K. K. "The Origins of the British Opium Monopoly," CR:162 (March 1962), 243-46.

D570 "The Historical Aspects of the Opium Question," CR:102 (April 1896), 258-72.

D571 "The Indo-Chinese Opium Question as It Stands in 1893," CR:97 (July 1893), 119-36.

D572 MOOKERJEE, H. C. "British Opium Policy," CR:101 (Nov., Dec. 1946), 75-84, 197-208; 102 (Feb., March 1947), 101-08, 181-86; 103 (May 1947), 71-82. Title varies.

D573 ———. "India's International Opium Policy," MR:81 (March-June 1947), 193-96, 283-87, 359-63, 452-56; 82 (July, Aug. 1947), 25-28, 109-12.

D574 PATON, W. "The Opium Situation in India," CoR:132 (July 1927), 75-83.

D575 WRIGHT, H. R. C. "The Abolition by Cornwallis of the Forced Cultivation of Opium in Bihar," EcHR: NS 12 (1959), 112-19. Study of economic conditions under which opium was grown and of the contracts to grow it; based on Bengal Board of Revenue Proceedings.

D576 ———. "The Emancipation of the Opium Cultivators in Benares," IRSH 4:3 (1959), 446-60. History of exploitation of the ryots in late 18th cent. and later partial protection of them.

D577 ———. "James Augustus Grant and the Gorakhpur Opium, 1789-1796," RAS (April 1960), pp. 1-16.

e. Salt

D578 BANERJEE, TARASANKAR. "Dwarkanath Tagore—the Salt Dewan," CR:169 (Nov. 1963), 207-12. On his service under the East India Company; based on records.

D579 CHATTERJI, NANDALAL. "Mr. A. O. Hume and the Question of Salt Tax in Oudh," UPHS: NS 2 (1954), 9-15. A report dated Sept. 4, 1867, supporting the tax.

D580 ———. "Oudh and the Question of Salt Tax in 1867," IHRC:27 (1950), 54-55. Arguments in favor of imposing it.

D581 DASGUPTA, BINAYBHUSHAN. "A Picture of the Salt Industry in Bengal during the Days of the Prosperity in the Nineteenth Century," CR:40 (July 1931), 13-27.

D582 DE, S. C. "Salt Monopoly in Orissa and Its Effects during the Early British Rule," IHRC:29 (1953), 19-24.

D583 GHOSAL, HARI RANJAN. "The Company's Salt Campaign in Bihar in the Early Nineteenth Century," BRS 34:3&4 (1948), 1-7. Extracts from records on the attempt to enforce the monopoly.

D584 GHOSE, HEMENDRA PRASAD. "Salt in Bengal," MR:50 (Aug. 1931), 139-42.

D585 HAKSAR, KAILAS NARAIN. "The Salt Revenue and the Indian States," AR: NS 25 (1929), 7-16. British control of the manufacture and trade in the states.

D586 HUQ, M. "The Salt Trade in Bengal during the Second Half of the 18th Century," ASP:3 (1958), 104-24. Appendixes give figures on the Company's receipts from salt, 1766-84, and information on production and prices.

D587 NAG, JITENDRA KUMAR. "History of Bengal's Salt Industry," MR:66 (Sept. 1939), 300-03.

D588 ———. "The Salt Agencies of the East India Company and the Present Revival," MR:77 (March 1945), 116-19.

D589 RAY, PARIMAL. "History of Taxation of Salt under the Rule of the East India Company," CR:33 (Nov. & Dec. 1929), 175-94; 34 (Jan., Feb., March 1930), 35-43, 215-24, 347-54; 35 (April, May, June 1930), 17-21, 193-200, 321-25; 36 (July, Aug., Sept. 1930), 29-34, 184-87, 340-44; 37 (Oct., Nov. & Dec. 1930), 64-67, 265-79. On the salt industry as a whole; based on parliamentary papers and contemporary publications, well-documented.

D590 SAHA, RADHAMADHAB. "Saltworkers of Nadia (1785-1795)," BPP:83 (Jan.-July 1964), 25-31.

D591 "The Salt Monopoly," CR 24:48 (1855), 387-406.

D592 "The Salt Revenue of Bengal," CR 7:14 (1847), 524-70.

D593 STRICKLAND, C. F. "Salt Making in India," SA:144 (April 1931), 260-61. With photographs.

f. Tea

D594 BRUCE, C. A. "Report on the Manufacture of Tea, and on the Extent and Produce of the Tea Plantations in Assam," ASB:8 (June 1839), 497-526; MJLS:10 (1843?), 169-98.

D595 CHAKRABARTI, B. B. "Introduction of Tea-Plantation in India," IHRC:18 (Jan. 1942), 44-52.

D596 CLERKE, E. M. "Assam and the Indian Tea Trade," AR:5 (April 1888), 362-83.

D597 DATTA, DEBABRATA. "Tea Industry in Cachar—Its Origin," BPP:84 (Jan.-June 1965), 1-9.

D598 GHOSH, INDU BHUSAN. "Expansion of the Calcutta Tea Market," MR:88 (July 1950), 57-61. 1939-1949.

D599 [LEES]. "Major Lees' Memorandum on the Tea Districts of Assam," CR:45 (May 1867), 155-77.

D600 MARSHMAN, J. C. "Notes on the Production of Tea in Assam, and in India Generally," RAS:19 (1862), 315-20.

D601 "Our Tea Gardens in Assam and Cachar," CR:35 (Sept. 1860), 38-63.

D602 PHOOKAN, L. N. "Early Days of the Assam Tea Industry," MR:58 (July 1935), 24-28.

D603 ROY CHOWDHURY, N. C. "Tea Industry in India and Pakistan," MR:87 (Feb. 1950), 118-21. Production and export statistics for 1948.

D604 ROYLE, J. FORBES. "Report on the Progress of the Culture of the China Tea Plant in the Himalayas, from 1835 to 1847," RAS:12 (1850), 125-52.

D605 SHARMA, SUNIL K. "Origin and Growth of the Tea Industry in Assam," CIEH:2 (1963), 119-43. History, statistical data.

D606 "Tea Cultivation in India," CR 40:80 (1865), 295-344.

10. LABOR

D607 BAGCHI, NIRMALYA. "The First Beginnings of the Unemployment Problem in the Bengali Middle Class," CR:118 (March 1951), 208-12. In the 3rd quarter of the 19th cent.

D608 BOSE, BELA. "The Extent of Unemployment in India," MR:94 (Nov. 1953), 374-76. From census reports.

D609 ———. "Unemployment in India; a Historical Analysis," MR: 107 (April 1960), 274-88. A survey of the patterns of industrial growth and their relation to employment.

D610 BOSE, SANAT KUMAR. "Labour Conditions," SBR, pp. 529-42. 1850-1914.

D611 CHOLIA, R. P. "Dock Labourers in Bombay," BUJ:6 (Jan. 1938), 175-89.

D612 DAS, RAJANI KANTA. "The Background of the Labor Problem," MR:31 (June 1922), 700-05.

D613 DAS, RAJANI KANTA. "Employment and Working Conditions in India," MLR:57 (Sept. 1943), 452-69. On wartime labor conditions, with tables.

D614 ———. "Factory Legislation in India," MR:29 (Jan. 1921), 35-39.

D615 ———. "Rise of Factory Labor in India," MLR:14 (March 1922), 417-37. Based on Imperial Gazetteer of India and other printed sources.

D616 ———. "The Royal Commission on Labour in India," MR:51 (Jan. 1932), 68-74. Analysis of its report.

D617 ———. "Wages, Hours, and Living Standards in India," MLR:57 (Oct. 1943), 689-99.

D618 DAS, TARAKNATH. "India in the Eighth International Labour Conference," MR:40 (Aug. 1926), 137-49.

D619 DATAR, B. N. and PATEL, I. G. "Employment during the Second World War," IER:3 (Feb. 1956), 13-27. An analysis of expansion in agriculture and industry, and figures on employment.

D620 FREMANTLE, S. H. "Indian Factory Legislation," IJE:1 (Jan. 1916), 67-94. History of its development in England and India.

D621 GHOSAL, HARI RANJAN. "Labour in Early Nineteenth Century, Bihar," BRS:32 (1946), 98-105. On the scarcity of labor, some figures on wages, and existence of slavery.

D622 ———. "Trade Union Spirit among the Weavers of Bengal towards the Close of the 18th Century," IHRC:28 (1951), 42-43. Based on Bengal records.

D623 GORDON, L. A. [Economic Condition of Working Class in Bombay in the Early 20th Century], NLM.

D624 ——— and VAFA, A. KH. [Study in the USSR of the History of the Indian Workers' Movement (Historiographic Review)], VI:4 (1962), 174-85. Abstract in SPA:3 (June 1963), 22.

D625 GUPTA, LAKSHMI NARAIN. "Labour Conditions in India during the War," MR:83 (Jan. 1948), 57-60.

D626 JAMES, RALPH C. "Labor Mobility, Unemployment, and Economic Change: An Indian Case," JPE:67 (1959), 545-59. Summary in HA:9 (No. 413). On labor in 55 cotton textile mills of Bombay.

D627 KOMAROV, E. N. [Economic Condition and Formation of an Industrial Proletariat in Bengal, 1917-1950], UZIV:5 (1953).

D628 KOTOVSKY, G. G. [Forms of Exploitation of Plantation Workers in Southern India], UZIV:10 (1954).

D629 KRISHNA, BAL. "Labour Conditions in India," MR:28 (Sept. 1920), 269-77. Statistical tables based on *Prices & Wages* Report, 1919.

D630 KRISHNAMURTY, J. "Secular Changes in the Occupational Structure of the Indian Union 1901-1961," IESHR:2 (Jan. 1965), 42-51.

D631 KUREISHY, K. U. "An Analysis of the Civilian Labour Force in Its Bearing on the Growth of Urban Population, West Pakistan, 1901-1951," PGR:13 (1958), 89-99. With tables.

D632 KYDD, J. C. "The First Indian Factories Act (Act XV of 1881)," CR:293 (July 1918), 279-92.

D633 "The Labour Difficulty in Bengal," CR 47:94, 156-93.

D634 LEVKOVSKY, A. I. [Economic Situation and Conditions of Working Class in India in 1923-1927], UZIV:18 (1957).

D635 LOGSDAIL, A. "The Assam Tea Garden Labour Question," CR:116 (April 1903), 255-59.

D636 LOKANATHAN, P. S. "Report of the Royal Commission on Labour," MUJ:3 (July 1931), 196-210. A critique.

D637 MAKSIMOV, M. A. and RASTYANNIKOV, V. G. [Some Specific Features of Formation and Exploitation of Agricultural Labour in India under Colonial Rule], SV:6 (1956).

D638 MAMORIA, C. B. "Unemployment in India," MR:95 (April 1954), 276-85. With statistical tables, 1937-53.

D639 MATHUR, JIVAN NARAIN. "Trade Unionism in India," UB:3 (Feb. 1957), 21-30. Origin, growth and obstacles thereto, function and organization.

D640 MORRIS, MORRIS DAVID. "Caste and the Evolution of the Industrial Workforce in India," APS:104 (April 1960), 124-33. Discusses what is known and (mostly) not known about the influence of caste on various aspects of industrial workers' lives in modern Indian history; challenges most traditional assumptions. Bibliography and bib. footnotes.

D641 ———. "The Recruitment of an Industrial Labor Force in India, with British and American Comparisons," CSSH:2 (April 1960), 305-28. Aspects of labor mobilization in Bombay cotton mills 1855-1914, compared with earlier recruitment in Great Britain and New England.

D642 ———. "Some Comments on the Supply of Labour to the Bombay Cotton Textile Industry, 1854-1951," IEJ:1 (Oct. 1953), 138-52.

D643 MUKHERJEE, PRABHATKUMAR. "The Labour Problem in Bengal," MR:23 (April 1918), 358-63.

D644 PRASADA, RAI SAHEB CHANDRIKA. "The Condition of Indian Railwaymen," MR:39 (April 1926), 429-37. Edited version of a speech.

D645 PROTHERO, MICHAEL. "Industrial Conditions and Trade Unions in India," ER:236 (Oct. 1922), 364-81.

D646 RAO, B. SHIVA. "Industrial Labor in India," FA:14 (July 1936), 675-84. On labor conditions.

D647 ――――. "Labor in India," AAAPSS:233 (May 1944), 127-33. Social and economic background of labor problems.

D648 RASTYANNIKOV, V. G. [Hired Agricultural Labour in Punjab], UZIV:18 (1957).

D649 SARKAR, T. P. "Tea Garden Labour," MR:52 (Sept. 1932), 281-84. Labor recruitment by the Tea Districts Labour Association.

D650 SHAPOSHNIKOVA, L. V. "Bor'ba indiiskogo proletariata za edinstvo deistvii (1934-39 GG.)" [The Struggle of the Indian Proletariat for Solidarity], VIs:2 (1957), 97-108. Abstract in HA:4 (No. 3192): "The author describes how the individual trade unions combined under the leadership of the All-Indian Trade Union Congress, thus enabling the workers to fight against imperialism and war and to use strikes not only as an economic weapon but for political ends as well."

D651 ――――. "The Workers' Movement in India in 1934-6," CAR:9 (1961), 314-18. Summary of an article on the period of a "soft" communist line in India and developments in trade unionism vis-à-vis Congress. Based on British records.

D652 SHIROKOV, G. K. [Forms of Recruitment of Labour Force for Tea Gardens of North-Eastern India in Colonial Period], KS:23 (1957).

D653 SINGH, NIHAL. "Conditions of Wage-workers in Mysore State," MR:50 (Oct., Nov. 1931), 369-76, 496-502.

D654 SUNDARAM, LANKA. "India and the International Labour Organization," AR: NS 27 (1931), 609-14; 28 (1932), 268-70, 614-23.

D655 ――――. "Royal Commission on Labour in India," CoR:137 (June 1930), 753-59. The problems facing it.

D656 TRANT, W. "Trades Unionism in India," FR:32 (July-Dec. 1879), 261-77. On the sources of its weakness.

11. TRADE

D657 ABDUL ALI, A. F. M. "Patna—Her Relations with John Company Bahadur," BPP:41 (Jan.-June 1931), 30-40.

D658 ALEXANDROWICZ-ALEXANDER, CHARLES HENRY. "The Discriminatory Clause in South Asian Treaties in the Seventeenth and Eighteenth Centuries," IYBIA:6 (1957), 126-42. They provided trade monopolies.

D659 BAGAL, JOGESH C. "Rustomji Cowasji," MR:54 (July 1933), 21-29. Parsi merchant and philanthropist of Calcutta.

D660 BALKRISHNA, DR. "The English Monopoly in Indian Spices," IHRC:14 (1937), 32-39. Brief history to end of 18th cent.

D661 BANERJEE, ANIL CHANDRA. "India's Trade with Turkestan (1873)," IHRC:25 (Dec. 1948), 66-72.

D662 BHOWNAGREE, MANCHERJEE MERWANJEE. "Sir Jamsetjee Jeejeebhoy, Bart. (1783-1859)," EB:15, 300. Parsi merchant and philanthropist.

D663 BHUYAN, S. K. "The Baillie Brothers," IHRC:24 (Feb. 1948), 85-89. Career of Hugh Baillie, pioneer of East India Company's commerce with Assam in late 18th cent., and his brothers.

D664 BOSE, S. C. "Fifty Years of Indo-British Trade (1875-1925)," MR:49 (Feb. 1931), 162-67.

D665 ———. "A Study of Indo-American Trade since 1875," BUJ:1 (July 1932), 58-64.

D666 CHATTERJI, NANDALAL. "Mir Qasim's Attitude toward the Private Inland Trade of the English," CR:45 (Oct. 1932), 69-84.

D667 "Commercial Morality and Commercial Prospects in Bengal," CR 9:17 (1848), 163-89.

D668 "Considerations on the Trade with India," ER:10 (July 1807), 334-68.

D669 COTTON, EVAN. "A Famous Calcutta Firm; the History of Thacker Spink and Co.," BPP:41 (Jan.-June 1931), 157-64.

D670 COTTON, H. J. S. "The Rice Trade in Bengal," CR 58:115 (1874), 171-88.

D671 CRADDOCK, REGINALD. "British Industries and the Indian Market," NC:99 (Jan. 1926), 1-19. "Reply" by George Pilcher, NC:99 (March 1926), 338-48. "Rejoinder," NC:99 (April 1926), 502-07.

D672 DAS, N. "The Old Agency Houses of Calcutta," CR:46 (March 1933), 317-26. An attempt to sort out important factors in the economic history of Bengal in the early 19th cent.

D673 DAS GUPTA, ASHIN. "Malabar in 1740," BPP:79 (July-Dec. 1960), 90-117. Commercial history of Dutch trade; largely from archives in Algemeen Rijksarchief, The Hague.

D674 ———. "The Makings of Travancore," BPP:80 (July-Dec. 1961), 124-48. From Dutch records.

D675 DATTA, KALI KINKAR. "Asiatic and Inter-Provincial Trade of Bengal in the Mid-Eighteenth Century," CR:34 (March 1930), 406-15.

D676 ———. "History of the British East India Company's Trade in Bengal in the Time of Alivardi (1740-1756)," CR:40 (Aug. 1931), 199-225. Diplomatic history; from Company records.

D677 ———. "History of the East India Company's Trade in Bengal (1757-1765)," CR:46 (Jan. 1933), 71-110.

D678 ———. "India's Trade with Europe and America in the Eighteenth Century," JESHO:2 (1959), 313-23. A summary of goods, ports, and trends in trade.

D679 "The Economic Results of Free Trade and Railway Extension," QJPSS:7 (Sept. 1884), 1-4.

D680 FISCHEL, WALTER J. "The Activities of a Jewish Merchant House in Bengal, 1786-1798," REJ, Ser. 4:3 (July-Dec. 1964), 433-98.

D681 FURBER, HOLDEN. "The Beginnings of American Trade with India, 1784-1812," NEQ:11 (June 1938), 235-65.

D682 GADGIL, D. R. "Immigrant Traders in Poona in the 18th Century," AV:1 (March 1959), 8-16. In Marathi; English summary p. 16. On Gujarati Banias in Poona.

D683 GANGULI, B. N. "Indo-American Trade," IQ:6 (July-Sept. 1950), 234-47. Survey of 20th cent. trends.

D684 GEDDES, JAMES. "Our Commercial Exploitation of the Indian Population," CR:55 (1872), 340-81; 56 (1873), 139-70, 352-82.

D685 GHOSAL, HARI RANJAN. "The Americans in East India Trade (1794-1819)," IHRC:32 (1956), 58-63. Summary of extent of trade.

D686 ———. "Charter Act of 1793 and the Outlines of British Commercial Policy in India During the Next Twenty Years," CR:73 (Nov. 1939), 171-81. Figures on freight rates and cargos.

D687 ———. "Indo-American Trade during the French Revolutionary and Napoleonic Wars," JIH:41 (Aug. 1963), 421-29. Largely from Bengal Board of Trade Records.

D688 ———. "Indo-South African Trade (1797-1819)," IHRC:25 (Dec. 1948), 116-20.

D689 ———. "Records Relating to Company's Commercial Residencies in the Bengal Presidency," IHRC:31 (1955), 121-29.

D690 ———. "Some Aspects of Malabar's Trade during 1793-1813," JIH:40 (Aug. 1962), 293-99.

D691 GLAMANN, KRISTOF. "Bengal and the World Trade about 1700," BPP:76 (Jubilee, 1957), 30-39. On Dutch trade in silk, sugar, and other commodities; based on Dutch archival materials.

D692 GOLDSMID, F. J. "Karachi and Its Future," AR:5 (April 1888), 440-61. History, with trade figures.

D693 HAJELA, G. L. "Changing Pattern of India's Foreign Trade since the First World War," UB:2 (July 1955), 63-68.

D694 HARNETTY, PETER. "The Imperialism of Free Trade: Lancashire and the Indian Cotton Duties, 1859-1862," EcHR:18 (Aug. 1965), 333-49.

D695 HUQ, MAZHARUL. "East India Company's 'Investment' Policy and External Trade in Bengal in the 18th Century," PEJ:4 (Aug. 1954), 201-24. No footnotes.

D696 "Indian Financial Statement for 1883-84," QJPSS:6 (Aug.? 1883), 40-61. On trade balance and duties; tables given.

D697 "Indo-Pakistan Trade Pact," MR:89 (March 1951), 173-77.

D698 JONES, M. E. MONCKTON. "Free and Open Trade in Bengal," EHR:30 (Jan. 1915), 28-41. History of the growth of free trade, with documents printed from the 1770's.

D699 KAKITSUBO, M. "Trade Relation between India and Japan," CR:59 (June 1936), 267-74. Brief analysis of the textile trade, with figures.

D700 KARIM, ABDUL (ed.). "An Account of the District of Dacca, Dated 1800," ASP:7 (Dec. 1962), 289-341. Many details on trade and on cotton industry.

D701 LEVIN, S. F. "Reformatorskoe dvizhenie v indiĭskoĭ torgovoĭ obshchine ismailitov-khodzha v 1829-1866 gg" [The Reform Movement in the Indian Trade Society of the Ismaili-Khoja in 1829-1866], KS:51 (1962), 151-66.

D702 LEVKOVSKY, A. I. [Managing Agencies—An Instrument of Exploitation of Indian People by British Imperialism], UZIV:10 (1954).

D703 LITTLE, J. H. "The House of Jagatseth," BPP:20 (Jan.-June 1920), 111-200; 22 (Jan.-June 1921), 1-119. The history of the Bengali business house in the 18th cent.

PART I: ARTICLES

D704 LYUSTERNIK, Y. Y. and SHAPOT, Y. G. "Russian-Indian Trade in the Eighteenth Century," CAR:8 (1960), 416-34. A "slightly abridged translation" of an article published in Russia. "A detailed and well-documented account of a number of schemes . . . not one of which . . . was ever put into practice. . . . The main aim of the article is . . . to stress the alleged difference between Russian and British intentions towards India at that time and to demonstrate that Russia's intentions have not changed."

D705 MADAN, B. K. "Trade of India," AAAPSS:233 (May 1944), 171-79. Figures, 1927-42.

D706 "The Market for British Goods in India a Century Ago," MR:2 (Dec. 1907), 540-46. Testimony on the renewal of the Company charter, 1813.

D707 MEHTA, G. L. "Commercial Organization in India," AAAPSS:233 (May 1944), 180-86. History of Chambers of Commerce.

D708 MISRA, PANCHANAND. "Indo-American Trade Relations: the Period of Growth—1784-1850," JIH:42 (Dec. 1964), 833-46. American archival sources and Indian consular dispatches.

D709 ———. "Indo-American Trade Relations, 1866-1880," JIH:43 (Dec. 1965), 763-69.

D710 MITRA, R. C. "A French Account of Commerce in India in 1774," IHRC:27 (1950), 22-25. On Pondicherry.

D711 MITTRA, PEARY CHAND. "Notes on Early Commerce in Bengal," CR:72 (1881), 113-28.

D712 MOLSON, H. "British Trade and the New Indian Constitution," NC:110 (July 1931), 31-40. Discusses economic problems to be faced at the resumed Round Table Conference.

D713 "The Monopolies of the East India Company," MR:4 (July 1908), 95-100. Historical review.

D714 MOOKERJEE, RADHA KAMAL. "The Transition in the Internal Trade of India," MR:15 (April 1914), 454-57. With statistical tables.

D715 MOORE, R. J. "Imperialism and 'Free Trade' Policy in India, 1853-4," EcHR:17 (Aug. 1964), 135-45.

D716 NARAIN, V. A. "Anglo-Nepalese Commercial Treaty of 1792," BRS:43 (Sept.-Dec. 1957), 334-40. From British records on its negotiation.

D717 "On Tabular Returns of the N.W. Frontier Trade with Afghanistan," ASB:10 (1841), 251-65, 476-77.

D718 "P.B.P." "Evils to British Commerce, Produced by the East India Company's Monopoly," OH:5 (April 1825), 65-68.

D719 PAVLOV, V. I. "Ocherk deiatel'nosti torgovtsev i rostovshchikov v kolonial'noi Indii" [On the Activities of Merchants and Money-lenders in Colonial India], UZIV:12 (1955), 99-160. Summary in HA:4 (No. 2282): "Discusses the methods employed by the merchants and usurers of the Marwar caste in Rajputana . . . 1750-1940."

D720 RAY, PARIMAL. "The Indian Wheat Trade," AR: NS 28 (1932), 298-302, 486-90, 595-613. Figures from 1870's to 1910's.

D721 ROORBACH, GEORGE B. "International Competition in the Trade of India," InC:268 (March 1931), 93-203. A number of good tables on foreign trade.

D722 "Russian Trade with India," CR:53 (1871), 204-26.

D723 SACHSE, F. M. "Thackeray's Apologia," BPP:41 (Jan.-June 1931), 41-50. On private trade, by the grandfather of the novelist.

D724 SALETORE, G. N. "Aspects of Maratha Trade in the 18th Century," BUJ:24 (July 1955), 1-8. Summary in HA:2 (No. 1064). Based on records at the National Archives and in Central Record Office, Allahabad; quotes trade agreements of the 1780's.

D725 SARKAR, BENOY KUMAR. "The Strength and Limitations of Economic Japan vis-à-vis Young Bengal," CR:49 (Nov. 1933), 132-39. On Japanese dumping of goods in Bengal.

D726 SARKAR, U. N. "The Merchandise of Peshawar and of the Neighboring Markets in 1838," IHRC:22 (1945), 59-62. Items and prices.

D727 SEN, MANKUMAR. "India's Foreign Trade," MR:86 (July 1949), 30-33.

D728 SEN, S. N. "The Story of a Trading Boat, 1793," IHQ:20 (Dec. 1944), 301-18. Based on 12 Portuguese letters in the Cochin Records Office, translated in the appendix. Shows the interrelationship of trade and diplomacy.

D729 SHARMA, KRISHNA KUMAR. "The Indo-British Trade Agreement," MR:52 (Nov. 1932), 552-56.

D730 SINGH, NIHAL. "India's Contribution to Japanese Prosperity," MR:42 (Aug. 1927), 129-35. "An estimation of the movements of Indo-Japanese trade."

D731 SINHA, H. "Boycott Movement and Its Effect on Trade," MR:49 (March 1931), 328-30; 50 (Sept. 1931), 308-10. With tables.

D732 SINHA, J. C. "The Company's Trade in Bengal in the Days of Cornwallis (Based Mainly on Manuscript Records in the Imperial Record Office, Calcutta)," IHRC:9 (1926), 62-68; BPP (Jan.-June 1927), 123-29.

D733 ———. "Indo-American Trade, Past and Present," ASB: NS 25 (1929), 201-21. With tables, mostly from Home Misc. Records.

D734 ———. "The Trade Depression, Its Causes and Remedies," MR: 53 (April 1933), 404-09.

D735 SINHA, N. K. "East India Company's 'Investment' Policy in the 18th Century," BPP:73 (Jan.-June 1954), 25-44. Facts and figures on trade.

D736 ———. "French Commerce in Bengal, 1757-1793," BPP:73 (July-Dec. 1954), 104-15. A close, factual account of trade and British-French friction. Based on English records.

D737 "The Swedish East India Company," BPP:42 (July-Dec. 1931), 144-45.

D738 "Tenasserim Teak Timber Traffic," CR 21:41 (1853), 98-169.

D739 TRIPATHI, AMALES. "The Agency Houses in Bengal," BPP:73 (July-Dec. 1954), 119-26; 74 (1955), 22-27. The struggle for free trade in Calcutta in the late 18th cent., early 19th cent.

D740 ———. "Some Reflections on the East India Company's Charter of 1813," IHCP:12 (1949), 227-39. A Marxist, fact-filled discussion of the decision to end the Company's trade monopoly and a vigorous summary of its effects.

D741 "The Value of India to England," QR:120 (July 1866), 198-220. On trade.

12. TARIFFS

D742 ADAMS, WALTER. "A Political Force in Indian Economic Development," IJE:30 (July 1949), 1-18. Tariff policy as prejudicial to Indian industrial development.

D743 ADARKAR, B. P. "Tariffs and Fiscal Policy," AAAPSS:233 (May 1944), 141-45. Historical survey.

D744 BANERJEE, TARA SANKAR. "Transit and Town Duties in Bombay and Madras in the First Half of the Nineteenth Century," BPP: 82 (Jan.-June 1963), 31-43.

D745 ———. "Transit and Town Duties in the Bengal Presidency (1765-1810)," VBQ:30 (1964), 24-61.

D746 BANERJI, PRAMATHANATH. "India and Imperial Preferences," MR:32 (Oct. 1922), 481-88. A review of the history of tariffs in India as related to British colonial policy.

D747 DATTA, KALI KINKAR. "Nawab Alivardi's Perwanah for Regulating the Custom Duties on the Company's Trade in Bengal," BPP:46 (July-Dec. 1933), 122-24.

D748 HARNETTY, P. "The Indian Cotton Duties Controversy, 1894-1896," EHR:77 (Oct. 1962), 684-702. On British parliamentary politics.

D749 HASAN, SAIYID NURUL. "Some Facts Regarding Customs Administration in the Ceded and Conquered Provinces, 1810-25," IHRC:21 (1944), 36-38. Extracts from letters.

D750 JACKSON, R. RAYNSFORD. "India and Lancashire," FR:25 (Jan.-June 1876), 877-96. Justification of the cotton duty, with a number of statistics.

D751 LEE-WARNER, W. "India's Peril from Protection," FR:100 (Oct. 1913), 625-36. On tariffs and taxes.

D752 LETHBRIDGE, ROPER. "The Late Mr. Justice Ranade as a Tariff Reformer," AR, Ser. 3:27 (April 1909), 252-57.

D753 MISRA, UMEY SHANKAR. "Pereat India; Floreat Manchester—The Indian Cotton Duties," AR, Ser. 2:8 (July 1894), 50-57.

D754 SARKAR, NALINI RANJAN. "The Jute Export Duty," MR:42 (Dec. 1927), 729-34.

D755 SYDENHAM OF COMBE. "Indian Cotton Duties," QR:227 (April 1917), 528-41.

D756 WEBB, M. DE P. "India's New Policy—Protection," NC:94 (July 1923), 112-20.

13. TRANSPORTATION AND COMMUNICATION

D757 AGARWAL, SHRI NARAYAN. "Indian Shipping—Past and Present," MR:79 (Jan. 1946), 30-32.

D758 ANDERSON, D. Y. "Communications—Railways," AAAPSS:145 Supplement (Sept. 1929), 59-67.

D759 BADHEKA, K. O. "Transport Problems of Kathiawar," BUJ:1 (Jan. 1933), 308-22. On railroad and port development.

D760 BAWA, VASANT KUMAR. "Salar Jang and the Nizam's State Railway 1860-1883," IESHR:2 (Oct. 1965), 307-40.

D761 BELL, HORACE. "Indian Railways," AR:3 (April 1887), 331-55. On rates and expenses.

D762 BHANDARKAR, D. R. "Shipping in Bombay in 1795-96," IHRC: 13 (1930), 73-84; BPP:41 (Jan.-June 1931), 129-33. With appendix of arrivals and departures of vessels, 1795-96.

D763 BOULGER, DEMETRIUS. "The P. and O. Company," AR:7 (April 1889), 241-58. Its history.

D764 BUSHBY, FRANK E. "Old-Time Conveyances in Calcutta," BPP: 41 (Jan.-June 1931), 138-40. With drawings.

D765 CLARKE, GEOFFREY R. "Post and Telegraph Work in India," AR: NS 23 (1927), 79-98; discussion pp. 99-108. A history of the system.

D766 COTTON, H. J. S. "Has India Food for Its People?" FR:28 (July-Dec. 1877), 863-77. Largely on problems of transporting food.

D767 DAS GUPTA, ARUN KUMAR. "Notes on Communications in the Early 19th Century," IHRC:27 (1950), 35-37.

D768 DE, A. C. "Indian Railways a Century Ago," MR:81 (Feb. 1947), 126-33.

D769 DORIASWAMI, S. V. "The Indian Public Debt and the Railway Programme," MR:16 (July 1914), 40-45. Sir William Meyer's commitment to a heavy railway program discussed, with reference to the public debt, 1839-1912.

D770 "The East India Railway," CR:31 (Sept. 1858), 230-46.

D771 "Eastern Bengal and Its Railways," CR:36 (Mar. 1861), 158-84.

D772 "The Electric Telegraph," CR:28 (Mar. 1857), 24-46.

D773 FAWCETT, R. H. "Railways of India from a Military Point of View," CR 66:133 (1878), 616-36.

D774 FIRMINGER, WALTER K. (ed.). "Bishop Wilson and the Second Earl of Clare," BPP:2 (Jan., April 1908), 17-46, 131-42. Correspondence in the 1830's on steam transportation between England and India.

D775 ———. "The Early Days of Steam Navigation in Indian Waters," CR:121 (July 1905), 422-42.

D776 FOWLER, WILLIAM. "India, Her Wheat, and Her Railways," NC:15 (Feb. 1884), 274-92. The economic importance of the railways.

D777 "G.H." "The Opening of the East Indian Railway," BPP:2 (Jan. 1908), 55-61. Some contemporary reactions to the opening of the East India Railway in 1854.

D778 GHOSAL, HARI RANJAN. "India's Ship-Building Industry in the Past," PU:2 (Dec. 1945-May 1946), 58-65. With facts and figures on some 19th cent. ships.

D779   GRAHAM, GERALD S. "By Steam to India," HT:14 (May 1964), 301-12. With illustrations.

D780   "A Guide up the River Ganges from Calcutta to Cawnpore, Futteh Chur, Meerat, &c; with the Correct Distances of Every Station," BPP:31 (Jan.-June 1926), 1-9. Distances given in terms of hours of travel.

D781   HARNETTY, PETER. " 'India's Mississippi': The River Godavari Navigation Scheme, 1853-71," JIH:43 (Dec. 1965), 699-732.

D782   [HEAD]. "Captain Head's Steam Navigation to India," ER:57 (1833), 313-29. On the itinerary to India, and on the advantages of emigration.

D783   HOSKINS, H. L. "The Growth of British Interest in the Route to India," JIH:2 (May 1923), 165-77. The problem of communication with India up to 1839.

D784   HURD, ARCHIBALD. "The High Road to India: 1829-1929," NC:106 (Aug. 1929), 243-52. On Lt. ("Steam") Johnston.

D785   "Indian Guaranteed Railways," CR:44 (Feb. 1867), 281-308.

D786   "Indian Railway Reform," W:92 (July 1869), 1-36.

D787   "Indian Railways," QR:125 (July 1868), 48-78.

D788   KAUSHIK, R. S. "Three Decades of Air Transport in India," MR: 114 (Aug. 1963), 110-13. With figures on mileage flown.

D789   LEHMANN, FREDERICK. "Great Britain and the Supply of Railway Locomotives of India: A Case Study of 'Economic Imperialism,' " IESHR:2 (Oct. 1965), 297-306.

D790   LOGAN, FRENISE A. "The American Civil War: A Major Factor in the Improvement of the Transportation System of Western India?" JIH:33 (April 1955), 91-102. The role of the cotton boom in instigating road building and improvement.

D791   MacPHERSON, W. J. "Investment in Indian Railways, 1845-1875," EcHR: NS 8 (1955), 177-86. "An analysis of the reasons behind this investment, and . . . the motives of the three main groups interested in the enterprise."

D792   MALIK, M. B. K. "The Origin and Growth of Pakistan Railways," PQ:11 (Summer 1962), 22-27. Illustrated.

D793   MAMORIA, C. B. "Air Transport in India," MR:95 (Jan. 1954), 25-31. Its history.

D794   MARSHMAN, J. C. "On the Cost and Construction of the Railways in India," RAS:20 (1863), 397-405.

D795 MUKERJEA, RAICHARAN. "Nationalisation of Indian Railways," MR:15 (Jan. 1914), 36-40. Advocates state ownership and management of railways.

D796 OLDHAM, C. E. A. W. "Routes, Old and New, from Lower Bengal 'Up the Country,'" BPP:28 (July-Sept. 1924), 21-36; 30 (July-Sept. 1925), 18-34. Description of routes, with maps.

D797 O'MALLEY, L. S. S. "Mechanism and Transport," MIW, pp. 221-57. History under the British.

D798 "Our Indian Railways," CR:5 (1846), 221-42; 7 (1847), 321-71.

D799 PHILLIMORE, R. H. "Visual Telegraph, Calcutta to Chunai, 1816-28," IHRC:27 (1950), 78-85.

D800 PRASAD, AMBA. "Indianization of Superior Railway Services," MR:71 (Feb. 1942), 161-64. Statistics 1929-39.

D801 ———. "The Proposal of a Federal Railway Authority in the Government of India Act, 1935," JIH:38 (Aug. 1960), 327-63. Administrative history.

D802 "Railway Fuel in the Punjab," CR:46, 262-327.

D803 "Railways in India," MR:5 (June 1909), 487-93. Historical review from 1858, with debate before Select Committee on East Indian Railways, 1858.

D804 RAJA, SUNDARA. "The First Indian Aviator," MR:12 (July 1912), 50-53. S. V. Setti.

D805 RAMSBOTHAM, R. B. "A Proposal for the Establishment of an Improved System of Telegraphic Communication by Lt.-Col. John Macdonald of the East India Company's Military Service," IHRC:11 (1928), 14-20; BPP:37 (Jan.-June 1929), 57-63.

D806 ROBERTSON, MURRAY. "Railways of India, Their Policy and Finance," NC:70 (July 1911), 84-103.

D807 ROSENTHAL, ETHEL. "By Rail Direct from Madras to Delhi," AR: NS 26 (1930), 345-52. Description of the route, with map.

D808 ———. "His Exalted Highness the Nizam's Guaranteed State Railways, Hyderabad, Deccan, India," AR: NS 22 (1926), 578-88. Three pictures and a map.

D809 ROY, P. C. "William Boyce and the Indian Telegraph, 1805-1817," CR:146 (Jan. 1958), 49-54.

D810 SAIGAL, BRIJ. "Lord Elgin I and the Indian Railways," IHCP:14 (1951), 279-84. Progress in railway building in the 1860's.

D811 SANYAL, NALINAKSHA. "Indian Railways, 1925-1928," CR:33 (Oct., Nov. & Dec. 1929), 9-20, 122-48. Tables of information on freight and passengers, rates, volume, etc.

D812 ———. "Statutory Railway Authority," MR:57 (Jan. 1935), 8-13.

D813 SARKAR, S. C. "Some Notes on the Intercourse of Bengal with the Northern Countries in the Second Half of the Eighteenth Century," BPP:41 (Jan.-June 1931), 119-28.

D814 SEN, S. N. "'Steam' Johnston," BPP:60 (Jan.-June 1941), 6-18; IHRC:16 (1939), 232-43. An entrepreneur who established a steam navigation company in Bengal; with figures on navigation.

D815 THORNER, DANIEL. "The Pattern of Railway Development in India," FEQ:14 (Feb. 1955), 201-16.

D816 TIWARI, RAMSWARUP D. "Indian Salt Industry: The Transport Problem," BUJ:5 (Jan. 1937), 131-64. Gives freight rates, 1916 and 1937.

D817 ———. "Leather Industry: Its Transport Problem," BUJ:6 (Jan. 1938), 73-124.

D818 "The Voyage to India in the Eighteenth Century," CR:89 (Oct. 1889), 342-51.

14. PRICES AND WAGES

D819 ADYANTHAYA, N. K. "A Statistical Study of the Prices of Food-grains in the Madras Presidency from 1874 to 1930," MUJ:5 (July 1933?), 233-38; 6 (Jan. 1934?), 87-109.

D820 ALI, AMEER. "Rupee and the Ruin of India," NC:33 (March 1893), 515-24. Wages and prices involved in the price of the rupee.

D821 ATKINSON, F. J. "Rupee Prices in India, 1870 to 1908: With an Examination of the Causes Leading to the Present High Level of Prices," RSS:72 (Sept. 1909), 496-573. With tables of prices, wages, and trade.

D822 BEOHAR, R. "High Prices in India," MR:29 (June 1921), 702-07. With price tables.

D823 BHATTACHARYA, D. "Trend of Wages in India (1873-1900)," AV:7 (Sept. 1965), 202-12.

D824 CHATTOPADHYAY, ANILKUMAR. "Wages and Standard of Living of Jute Workers in Bengal," CR:107 (June 1948), 147-57. Figures since 1927.

D825 DATTA, KALI KINKAR. "Markets and Prices of Articles in Bengal (1740-1765)," IJE:11 (April 1931), 669-82. From Bengal records.

D826 DESAI, R. C. "Consumer Expenditure in India, 1931-2 to 1940-1," RSS: Series A, 111 (part 4, 1948), 261-307.

D827 GHOSAL, H. R. "Price Changes and Price Control in India during the Last Two Hundred Years," BRS 32:3&4 (1946), 297-307. Figures on food prices, 1753-1813, with some discussion of trends after that.

D828 GHURYE, G. S. "Salary and Other Conditions of Work of Clerks in Bombay City," BUJ:9 (Jan. 1941), 106-36.

D829 GUHA, RANAJIT. "Evidence on Some Correlations of Rents and Prices in Bihar under Early British Rule," IHRC:34 (1958), 55-68.

D830 MANDAL, GOBINDA CHANDRA. "Agriculture vs. Industrial Prices in India," MR:85 (June 1949), 453-55. With statistics from 1921.

D831 ———. "The Movement of Profits and Wages in India during the War," MR:80 (Aug. 1946), 116-18. With tables.

D832 MATHUR, S. C. "Variation in Cost of Living of Agricultural Labour (Since 1939)," AUJR:5 (July 1957), 253-61.

D833 MORISON, T. "The Instability of Prices in India before 1861," RSS:65 (Sept. 1902), 513-25. With tables and graphs; based on settlement reports in the U. P. area.

D834 MUKERJI, KSHITIMOHAN. "An Index for Bombay Working Class Cost of Living," AV:1 (June 1959), 138-47. In Bengali (Devanagari script), English summary p. 147. Tables cover 1900-1951.

D835 ———. "Price Movements in India between 1823 and 1871," AV:5 (Dec. 1963), 326-36. In Bengali (Devanagari script), English summary p. 336.

D836 ———. "Trend in Real Wages in Cotton Textile Industrial in Ahmedabad from 1900 to 1951," AV:3 (June 1961), 124-34.

D837 ———. "Trend in Real Wages in Cotton Textile Mills in Bombay City and Island, From 1900 to 1951," AV:1 (March 1959), 82-96.

D838 ———. "Trend in Textile Mill Wages in Western India: 1900 to 1951," AV:4 (June 1962), 156-66.

D839 ———. "Trends in Real Wages in the Jute Textile Industry from 1900 to 1951," AV:2 (March 1960), 57-69.

D840 MUKHERJEE, KARUNAMOY. "The Income and Standard of Living of the Rural Population in Bengal," MR:82 (Dec. 1947), 453-55.

D841 MYLES, W. H. "Sixty Years of Panjab Food Prices 1861-1920; a Statistical Survey," IJE:6 (1925-26), 1-52. With tables and graphs.

D842 NARAIN, BRIJ. "Eighty Years of Punjab Food Prices, 1841-1920," IJE:6 (1925-26), 397-460.

D843 NARAIN, SURAJDEV. "Prices of Food-stuffs in Tirhoot since the Last Decade of the Eighteenth Century," BRS:37 (Sept. & Dec. 1951), 144-67. Wages of English and Indian government employees and detailed figures on price of rice and maize, 1888-1937; discussion of causes of rise in price.

D844 PALEKAR, SHREEKANT A. "Real Wages and Profits in India, 1939-50," IER:3 (Aug. 1957), 34-45; EW:9 (Annual No. Jan. 1957), 151-60. Work done for a Ph.D. dissertation at Harvard, showing ratio of real wages to industrial profits.

D845 PATEL, SURENDRA J. "Long-term Changes in Output and Income in India: 1896-1960," IEJ:5 (Jan. 1958), 233-46. An attempt to estimate figures.

D846 SHIROKOV, G. K. [Forms of Wages at Tea Gardens in Assam and Bengal in Colonial Period], IAEH.

D847 SINGH, D. BRIGHT. "Price Trends in India since 1939," MUJ: 26A (July 1954 & Jan. 1955), 33-55, 149-80.

D848 STIRLING, EDWARD. "Price of Grain at Allygurh, near Delhi, from the Year 1804 to 1832 Inclusive," ASB:3 (Dec. 1834), 620-21. Average prices for wheat and gram.

D849 THOMAS, P. J. "The Problem of Rural Indebtedness," MUJ:6 (Jan. 1934?), 29-64. With tables on mortgages and prices.

D850 ——— and SASTRY, N. SUNDARARAMA. "Commodity Prices in South India, 1918-35," MUJ:11 (1939), 144-66.

15. CURRENCY, BANKING, AND FINANCE

D851 AHMAD, QEYAMUDDIN. "An Historical Account of the Banaras Mint in the Later Mughal Period, 1732-1776," NSI:23 (1961), 198-215.

D852 AMBIRAJAN, S. "Laissez-Faire in Madras," IESHR:2 (July 1965), 238-44. On the formation of the Government Bank early 19th cent.

D853 ANDREWS, A. PIATT. "Indian Currency Problems of the Last Decade," QJE:15 (Aug. 1901), 483-516. With tables and charts.

D854 AYYANGAR, M. S. SESHA. "Gold and Indian Currency," MR:21 (May 1917), 571-77.

D855 BANERJEA, PRAMATHANATH. "Banking in the Days of John Company," CR:25 (Nov. 1927), 133-40.

D856 BANERJEE, MRITYUNJOY. "The Balance of Payments in India," MR:88 (July 1950), 26-31. With statistics from 1923-24.

D857 BANERJEE, P. N. "Deficits and Surpluses in the Accounts of the East Indian Company," IJE:8 (July 1927), 1-26.

D858 "Banking in the Mufassal," CR:93 (Oct. 1891), 316-41. "Reply," CR:94 (Jan. 1892), 203-08.

D859 BASU, K. K. "Currency and Coinage in Bihar under the Hon'ble Company," BRS:30 (1944), 237-43. Local specie and relative values.

D860 BHATNAGAR, NARENDRA KUMAR. "Public Debt of India since 1930," UB:7 (Dec. 1960), 115-28. Deals mainly with the period 1948-58, with 4 pp. on 1792-1947.

D861 BHATTACHARYA, SABYASACHI. "Trevelyan, Wilson, Canning and the Foundation of Indian Financial Policy," BPP:80 (Jan.-June 1961), 65-73. From government records.

D862 CAMPBELL, G. "The Finances of India," FR:25 (Jan.-June 1876), 514-35. Summary of sources of revenue, expenditures.

D863 CARDEW, A. G. "The Financial Aspects of the White Paper," CoR:144 (Nov. 1933), 541-49. On the Scheme for Constitutional Reforms.

D864 CHAUDHURI, NALINI R. "The Indian Banking Companies Act of 1949," MR:86 (July 1949), 65-68.

D865 CHESNEY, GEORGE. "The Depreciation of Silver and the Indian Finances," NC:5 (Jan. 1879), 97-111.

D866 ————. "The Indian Finances," FR:31 (Jan.-June 1879), 842-65.

D867 COYAJEE, J. C. "Money Reconstruction in India (1925-27)," AAAPSS:145 (Sept. 1929), Supplement 101-14.

D868 CUNNINGHAM, HENRY STEWART. "The Finances of India," AR:5 (April 1888), 241-75.

D869 ————. "Indian Finance Troubles," AR, Ser. 2:7 (April 1894), 251-70.

D870 DANIELL, CLARMONT. "The Gold-Supply of England and India," BM:149 (March 1891), 394-405.

D871 ————. "India's Demand for a Gold Currency," BM:152 (Oct. 1892), 597-614.

D872 DASS, DAYAL. "First Uniform Currency for India," IHRC:33 (1958), 65-71. Hastings' reforms.

D873   DATTA, P. "Rise of the Calcutta Money Market in Relation to Public Borrowing and Public Credit (1772 to 1833)," CR:46 (Feb. 1933), 171-203. Based on British records.

D874   DE, AMALENDU. "Some Facts on the Early History of Savings Banks in Bengal," MR:117 (Mar. 1965), 195-98.

D875   DE, S. C. "Cowry Currency in Orissa," OHRJ:1 (July 1952), 10-21 [= 106-17]. Early 19th cent.

D876   DODWELL, H. "The Substitution of Silver for Gold in the Currency of South India," IJE:3 (Jan. 1921), 183-204. Based on 18th cent. records.

D877   DORIASWAMI, S. V. "The Economic Progress of India and the Fiscal Question," MR:18 (Dec. 1915), 648-56.

D878   ———. "Fifty Years of British and Indian Finance, 1865-1915: A Study," HR:34 (July 1916), 28-39.

D879   ———. "Indian Currency and Finance," MR:15 (Feb. 1914), 189-95. From 1898 to 1913.

D880   ———. "Indian Finance and the Chamberlain Commission," HR: 32 (July, Aug. 1915), 31-39, 125-34.

D881   ———. "Indian Financial Reform and Messrs. Samuel Montagu & Co.'s Anti-Gold Crusade," MR:19 (May 1916), 502-06.

D882   ———. "A State Bank for India," MR:15 (March, April 1914), 333-37, 413-21.

D883   EZEKIEL, HANNAM and ROACH, NEVILLE. "The Debt of Bombay Port Trust, 1914-1957," BUJ: NS 27 (July 1958), 25-60. With tables.

D884   FAWCETT, HENRY. "The Financial Condition of India," NC: 5 (Feb. 1879), 193-218.

D885   ———. "The New Departure in Indian Finance," NC:6 (Oct. 1879), 639-63.

D886   ———. "The Proposed Loans to India," NC:5 (May 1879), 872-89.

D887   "The Finances of India under Lord Lytton," QJPSS:2 (Feb.? 1880), 2-39.

D888   "Financial State of the East India Company," OH:5 (June 1825), 539-49.

D889   FURRELL, JAMES W. "The Indian Exchange and Currency Question," CR 63:125 (1876), 69-87.

D890 GHOSAL, HARI RANJAN. "Currency Situation in Bengal at the End of the Eighteenth Century," BRS:33 (1947), 170-74. Extracts from records showing the effects of Company investments and the weavers' position in relation to the scarcity of silver.

D891 GHOSH, A. S. "The Financial Relation between England and India," W:148 (Oct. 1897), 401-12.

D892 GODE, P. K. "Keshavbhat Karve, a Poona Banker of the Peshwa Period and His Relations with the Peshwa and Damāji Gaikwad," BUJ:6 (July 1937), 87-91. Descriptions of letters from 1754, 1767, 1768.

D893 "A Gold Standard for India," CR:106 (Jan. 1898), 63-70.

D894 GRIFFIN, LEPEL. "The House of Commons and Indian Finance," FR:20 (Oct. 1873), 488-504.

D895 GRODKO, N. D. "Iz istorii gosudarstvennogo dolga Indii" [On the History of the Indian Public Debt], UZIV:12 (1955), 257-305. Abstract in HA:4 (No. 2274).

D896 HARRISON, F. C. "An Attempt to Estimate the Circulation of the Rupee," EJ:1 (Dec. 1891), 721-51; 2 (June 1892), 256-79.

D897 ———. "Indian Finance and Currency," QR:220 (April 1914), 465-82.

D898 "How Far British Capital in India Is British," MR:23 (Jan. 1918), 52-56.

D899 "India and Its Finance," W:60 (July 1853), 177-99.

D900 "Indian Accounts," CR 40:80 (1865), 419-51. On financial scandal.

D901 "Indian Administration and Finance," ER:156 (July 1882), 60-94.

D902 "The Indian Currency Commission," BM:154 (Aug. 1893), 293-309. The problems it faced.

D903 "Indian Currency, Finance, and Legislation," QR:109 (April 1861), 566-607.

D904 "Indian Finance," CR:27 (Sept. 1856), 208-33.

D905 KHAN, YUSUF HUSSAIN. "Nawab Muhammad Ali Walajah's Petition to the Court of Directors of the East India Company," IHRC:14 (Dec. 1937), 124-26. 18th cent. financial claim.

D906 KOTOVSKY, G. G. [Moneylending and Expropriation of Peasantry in Madras. A Brief Outline], KS:10 (1953).

D907 KULKARNI, G. B. "Population and Supplies of Cereals in India with Special Reference to Her Balances of International Payments since 1920," IJAE:10 (March 1955), 88-104. With figures and tables.

D908 LAHIRI, A. N. "Indo-British Coins since 1835," NSI:23 (1961), 90-114.

D909 LAING, S. "The Crisis in Indian Finance," NC:7 (June 1880), 1065-77.

D910 LAWSON, W. R. "India on a Gold Basis," CoR:73 (April 1898), 491-99. Describes the gradual working toward a gold standard.

D911 ———. "The Indian Currency Muddle," BM:155 (March 1894), 440-55.

D912 LEVKOVSKII, A. I. "Vozniknovenie i kharakter deiatel'nosti angliiskikh i indiiskikh bankov v kolonial'noi Indii" [The Origin and Character of the Activity of British and Indian Banks in Colonial India], SV:4 (1956), 57-72. Abstract in HA:5 (No. 132): "Describes the origin of English banks in India since 1770 and the particular development of Indian capitalism from the end of the 19th cent. to 1939. . . . Based on the findings of the Indian Central Banking Enquiry Commission (1931), and of the Indian Industrial Commission 1916-1918 (1918), and on works by A. Baster (1929), D. S. Savkar (1938), and B. R. Rau (1930)."

D913 MACLEAN, J. M. "Boycotted Silver," AR:1 (April 1886), 432-49. On the price of gold and the rupee.

D914 MARRIOTT, EDWARD FRERE. "Indian Currency Policy," FR: 70 (July-Dec. 1898), 595-604.

D915 MATEER, S. "Coinage of Travancore," MJLS (1889-94), 49-67. Contemporary coinage, described and illustrated.

D916 MENON, P. K. K. "Malabar Coinage in the Eighteenth Century," IHCP:21 (1958), 633-39. A study of their relative values.

D917 MITRA, K. P. "Currency in Orissa," IHRC:15 (Dec. 1938), 114-23; BPP:57 (July-Dec. 1939), 66-76. In early 19th cent.

D918 "Moreau's Finances of the East India Company," OH:6 (Aug. 1825), 316-18. With table of revenue and expenditures from the Company's possessions, 1792-1822.

D919 MUKERJEE, KARUNAMOY. "The Problems of Agricultural Finance in Bengal: Past and Present," CR:12 (July 1949), 41-51. Figures on credit and credit societies since 1930.

D920 MUKERJI, B. "Indian Finance in 1916-17," HR:34 (Sept. 1916), 234-41.

D921 MUKHERJEE, B. "Federal Finance and the Case for Bengal," MR:59 (May 1936), 508-16. Historical background and tables.

D922 NANAVATI, MANILAL B. "Banking in India," AAAPSS:233 (May 1944), 152-60. Historical survey.

D923 NATARAJAN, B. "Influence of Classical Theories on Interest Regulation in India (1800-55)," EcHR:9 (May 1939), 186-92. From District Records of Madras.

D924 NICHOLSON, J. SHIELD. "The Indian Currency Experiment," CoR:64 (Sept. 1893), 339-50. On closure of Indian mints for coining silver.

D925 PANDIT, V. S. "Foreign Borrowings, Barter Terms of Trade and Price-Level in India: 1898-1913," BUJ:2 (July 1933), 97-100. Based on a master's thesis at Bombay.

D926 PARDASANI, N. S. "Causes of Indian Gold Exports," BUJ:7 (July 1938), 120-30.

D927 PERROTT, H. R. "The Rupee and Indian Prices," ASB:6 (1910), 109-29.

D928 RANADE, M. G. "Currencies and Mints under Mahratta Rule," RASB:20 (1902), 191-200. Classifies and compares coins minted up to 1835.

D929 RANGA CHARI, T. M. and DESIKA CHARI, T. "Indo-Danish Coins," MJLS (1888-89), 69-82. Descriptions and drawings, 17th cent. through 19th cent. coins.

D930 RAU, B. RAMCHANDRA. "The Early History of the Presidency Bank of Bombay (Based on Manuscript Records of the Government of Bombay)," CR:42 (Jan., Feb. 1932), 89-107, 177-200.

D931 ———. "Organized Banking in the Days of John Company," BPP:37 (Jan.-June 1929), 145-57; 38 (July-Dec. 1929), 60-80. History, with tables.

D932 ———. "Some Specific Services of the Indigenous Bankers of Bombay," IHRC:12 (1929), 54-59. A note on "ant currency" or Anka Chulur.

D933 "Revenue and Commerce of India," ER:45 (March 1827), 340-68. On East India Company finances.

D934 ROBERTSON, J. BARR. "Bimetallism and the Finances of India," W:114 (Jan. 1881), 200-38.

D935 ———. "East Indian Currency and Exchange," W:114 (Oct. 1880), 459-88.

D936 ROY, PARIMAL. "The Bengal Money-Lenders Act, 1933," MR: 56 (Aug. 1934), 157-60. Historical résumé.

D937 SACHSE, F. M. "Financial Stringency in the 18th Century," BPP:43 (Jan.-June 1932), 121-25. Company finances in the 1770's.

D938 SAHAI, ISHWAR. "The Financial Administration of Lord William Bentinck," IHQ:11 (Dec. 1935), 652-85. History of his reforms.

D939 SALETORE, B. A. "A Forgotten Gujarati Brahman Banker," IHRC:30 (1954), 155-60. Arjunji Nathaji Trivedi.

D940 SARKAR, BIMALA KANTA. "Development of Rural Finance in Bengal," MR:47 (Feb. 1930), 204-09.

D941 ———. "Rural Finance in British India; Lines of Development in Relation to Provincial and Central Governments up to 1930," LSGI:17 (Oct. 1946), 135-222. Historical background and development, with figures.

D942 SARMA, S. K. "The Sterling Debt of India," HR:32 (Aug. 1915), 147-55.

D943 SHARMA, K. K. "Trends in Indian Finance since 1938-39," UB:2 (Dec. 1955), 67-84.

D944 SHIRRAS, GEORGE FINDLAY. "Public Finance in India," AAAPSS:144 (Sept. 1929), Supplement 115-23.

D945 SINGH, HIRA LAL. "The Indian Currency Problem, 1885-1900," BPP:80 (Jan. 1961), 16-37.

D946 SINHA, BIMAL CHANDRA. "Bengal's Post-War Finances: A Study of the Bengal Budget, 1946-47," CR:100 (Sept. 1946), 129-39.

D947 ———. "Rack and Ruin—a Study of Bengal Finances, 1937-1947," MR:80 (Aug. 1946), 110-16.

D948 SINHA, J. C. "Currency in Early British Days," IJE:7 (1926-27), 166-75.

D949 ———. "The Earliest Currency Committee in India (1787)," IHRC:8 (Nov. 1925), 183-90; MR:38 (Dec. 1925), 654-58. Called Sept. 25, 1787, by Cornwallis to enquire into the scarcity of silver coin.

D950 ———. "Some Currency Reforms of Hastings," IHRC:6 (1924), 74-78.

D951 SMITH, I. T. "East Indian Currency and Exchange," W:114 (April 1881), 506-26.

D952 STAGG, H. "A Brief History and Description of His Majesty's Mint, Calcutta," ASB:NS 26 (Numismatic Supplement 43, 1930), 15N-22N.

D953 STRACHEY, RICHARD. "The Indian Budget Estimates," NC:7 (June 1880), 1078-88.

D954 TAYLOR, GEORGE P. "The Coins of Aḥmedābād," RASB:20 (1902), 409-47. Pp. 437-42 deal with 18th and early 19th cent. coins.

D955 ———. "The Coins of Surat," ASB:22 (1905), 245-72. Pp. 266-72 deal with 1750-1835; 3 plates.

D956 THAKUR, K. P. "War-Time Banking in India," MR:78 (Nov. 1945), 284-87. With tables.

D957 THAKURDAS, PURSHOTAMDAS. "Currency and Exchange," AAAPSS:233 (May 1944), 146-51. Survey of the fate of the rupee under British rule.

D958 THAVARAJ, M. J. K. "Rate of Public Investment in India, 1898-1938," CIEH:2 (1963), 41-62. With tables.

D959 THAVARAJ, M. K. "Public Investment in India, 1898-1914: Some Features," IER:2 (Aug. 1955), 37-52. An analysis of government investment in railways, irrigation, etc., showing that the money came almost entirely from internal sources.

D960 THOMAS, P. J. "Indian Finances in Depression," MUJ:10 (July 1938), 179-99. Tables on many facets of the economy.

D961 THORNTON, W. T. "A New View of the Indian Exchange Difficulty," W:114 (July 1880), 173-92.

D962 THURSTON, EDGAR. "Note on the History of the East India Company's Coinage, from 1753-1835," ASB:62 (1893), 52-84. Details for each area.

D963 VAKIL, C. N. "Government Finance," AAAPSS:233 (May 1944), 134-40.

D964 WODAK, E. "Indian Rupees dated 1862," SANJ:8 (April 1957), 12-13. Plate with portrait of Queen Victoria.

D965 WOOD, J. S. "Exchange with India," BM:147 (March, April 1890), 384-407, 557-82. Discussion by W. I. Gray and Clarmont Daniell BM:148 (July 1890), 127-44. Currency problems.

16. "THE DRAIN"

D966 ANDREWS, C. F. "India and England: the Economic Relation," CoR:126 (July 1924), 38-44.

D967 ATKINSON, F. J. "A Statistical Review of the Income and Wealth of British India," RSS:65 (June 1902), 209-83. An attempt to base an answer to the Drain question on facts and figures.

D968 CHANDRA, BIPAN. "Indian Nationalists and the Drain, 1880-1905," IESHR:2 (April 1965), 103-44.

D969 CHESNEY, GEORGE. "Value of India to England," NC:3 (Feb. 1878), 227-38.

D970 COLVIN, ELLIOT G. "Effects of British Rule in India," NC:66 (Sept. 1909), 527-41. Criticism of William Digby's *Prosperous British India*.

D971 DATTA, KALI KINKAR. "Economic Drain on India during the Second Half of the Eighteenth Century," BRS:45 (1959), 77-88. Figures on private remittance of bullion to England, and Bengali assistance to Madras.

D972 ———. "The First Two Anglo-Mysore Wars and Economic Drain on Bengal," JIH:20 (April 1941), 12-21.

D973 GANGULI, B. N. "Dadabhai Naoroji and the Mechanism of 'External Drain,'" IESHR:2 (April 1965), 85-102.

D974 HYNDMAN, H. M. "The Bankruptcy of India," NC:4 (Oct. 1878), 585-608; 5 (March 1879), 443-62.

D975 ———. "Bleeding to Death," NC:8 (July 1880), 157-76.

D976 KEAY, J. SEYMOUR. "The Spoliation of India," NC:14 (July 1883), 1-22; 15 (April, May 1884), 559-82, 721-40; 16 (Oct. 1884), 611-18.

D977 McLANE, JOHN. "The Drain of Wealth and Indian Nationalism at the Turn of the Century," CIEH:2 (1963), 21-40. A review of arguments and an examination of the figures involved; based on contemporary writings and correspondence in the India Office Library. Conclusion: charges of "Drain" contributed importantly to the causes of the 1905 disorders.

D978 McMINN, CHARLES. "The Wealth and Progress of India: Facts and Fictions," AR, Ser. 3:27 (Jan. 1909), 31-76.

D979 MORELAND, W. H. "Some Thoughts about the 'Drain' in India," AR:NS 16 (Jan. 1920), 33-40. Discusses the drain as a "sentimental drain" on "national self-respect" and offers a program to bring the debt home.

D980 [MORLEY, JOHN]. "Impoverishment of India Not Proven," FR: 30 (Dec. 1878), 867-81. On drain theory and the cost of the military stationed there.

D981 SEN, SUNIL K. "Government Purchase of Stores for India (1858-1914)," BPP:80 (Jan.-June 1961), 47-64. Annual expenditure for various items.

D982 SINHA, N. K. "Drain of Wealth from Bengal in the Second Half of the Eighteenth Century," BPP:71 (1952), 34-43. Company trading policy and practice.

D983 THOMAS, P. J. "India's Gold Exports," MUJ:4 (Jan. 1932).

D984 TRIPATHI, AMALES. "Controversy on the Nature of Indian Debt," IHCP:13 (1950), 281-85. A debate on the drain: evidence given before a select committee of Parliament, 1830 and 1831.

D985 WALKER, G. H. W. "The 'Economical Drain' Economically Examined, or a Plea for the 'Tribute,'" CR:69 (1879), 213-25.

D986 WOOD, W. MARTIN. "The 'Home Charges' of the Government of India: Their Nature and Incidence," AR, Ser. 2:6 (July 1893), 75-89.

E. SOCIAL HISTORY

1. GENERAL

E1 AHMAD KHAN, MUIN-UD-DIN. "A Police Report of the Zilah Dacca-Jalalpur Dealing with the Manners and Morals of the People (Dated A.D. 1799)," PHS:7 (Jan. 1959), 24-35. Annotated.

E2 ANDREWS, C. F. "The Untouchable Problem," CoR:144 (Aug. 1933), 152-60.

E3 AROKIASWAMI, M. "Charitable Institutions under the E. I. Company in Madras," MUJ:31 (July 1959), 131-36.

E4 ———. "Public Lotteries in Madras under the East India Company (1787-1845)," MUJ:A 30 (July 1958), 171-77.

E5 BANERJEE, RAMESH CHANDRA. "Hindu and Muslim Public Spirit in Bengal," MR:55 (March 1934), 312-16. With tables showing numbers of Hindus and Muslims in educational institutions and engaged in charity works.

E6 BANERJI, PORESH NATH. "The Remarriage of Hindu Widows," CR:115 (July 1902), 101-10.

E7 BARNETT, SAMUEL A. "The Poor of the World: India, Japan, and the United States," FR:60 (Aug. 1893), 207-22. Section on India, 207-17. Mentions voluntary relief agencies, and those provided by the state.

E8 BASU, B. K. "Notes on Slave Trade and Slavery in India during the Early Days of John Company," MsR:4 (April-June 1930), 21-34.

E9 BASU, K. K. "The Early Europeans in Bhagalpur," BPP:56 (Jan.-June 1939), 81-97. List of 412 residents, gathered from district records and a cemetery; gives name, occupation, details of land held.

E10 "The Behar Ryot at Home," CR:91 (Oct. 1890), 274-305.

E11 "The Bengal Military Orphan Society," CR:44 (1866), 151-82; 45 (Aug. 1867), 296-316.

E12 "Bengal Village Biographies," CR:31 (Sept. 1858), 193-229. Portrait of a village through character sketches.

E13 "A Bengali Brahman." "The So-called Superiority of the Brahmans," MR:14 (Dec. 1913), 611-17.

E14 BHAGAT, M. G. "The Untouchable Classes of Maharashtra," BUJ:4 (July 1935), 130-74. With tables.

E15 BHATIA, B. M. "Growth and Composition of Middle Class in South India in Nineteenth Century," IESHR:2 (Oct. 1965), 341-56.

E16 BIRNEY, WILLIAM S. "Notable Clubs in Bengal," BPP:65 (1945), 70-73. The history of the Bengal Club and the United Service Club.

E17 BOSE, ASHISH. "Six Decades of Urbanization in India, 1901-1961," IESHR:2 (Jan. 1965), 23-41. With tables.

E18 BOSE, BASANTA KUMAR. "Vignettes from Social Life in the 18th Century Calcutta," BPP:43 (Jan.-June 1932), 126-32. From British records.

E19 BOSE, NIRMAL KUMAR. "Social and Cultural Life of Calcutta," GRI:20 (Dec. 1958), 1-46. An historical review.

E20 ———. "Some Aspects of Caste in Bengal," MII:38 (June 1958), 73-97. Reviews the changes therein during the last 50 years.

E21 "Burning of Hindoo Widows," OH:1 (March 1824), 551-60; 2 (June 1824), 173-86. Extracts from "Directions . . . to District Police Officers."

E22 "Calcutta Domestic Life," CR 12:24 (1849), 494-515.

E23 "Calcutta in the Olden Time—Its People," CR:35 (Sept. 1860), 164-227.

E24 CAMPBELL, A. D. "Slavery in S.-India," MJLS:1 (1833), 243-55.

E25 CHANDRA, SUDHIR. "Evolution of the Social Policy of the Company's Government in India," Q:47 (Oct.-Dec. 1965), 35-40.

E26 [CHISHOLM]. "Mrs. Chisholm," C&AR:10 (April 1853), 284-90. The social-service-minded wife of an officer of the Company.

E27 CODRINGTON, K. DE B. "A Bombay Diary of 1838," AR: NS 35 (1939), 112-22.

E28 COHN, BERNARD S. "The British in Benares: a Nineteenth Century Colonial Society," CSSH:4 (1961-62), 169-99. An analysis of "social origins and kin ramifications," the residents' training, life, and work in India; points out their sense of "moral exile" and remoteness from Indians. Based on records in London and U.P. Central Record Office.

E29 ———. "The Pasts of an Indian Village," CSSH:3 (1961), 241-49. On the peasants' world-view.

E30 ———. "Some Notes on Law and Change in North India," EDCC: 8 (Oct. 1959), 79-93. Based on field work in U.P.

E31 "Cowell's Tagore Law Lectures—The Hindu Family," CR 52:104 (1871), 243-70.

E32 DAS, SUDHIR RANJAN. "Some Aspects of the Nineteenth Century Bengali Society," JNB, pp. 271-83.

E33 DATTA, JATINDRA MOHAN. "Some Sociological Facts about 'Suttees,'" MR:71 (May 1942), 439-41. Statistics 1815-28.

E34 DATTA, KALI KINKAR. "Position of Women in Bengal in the Mid-Eighteenth Century," CR:37 (Oct. 1930), 17-32. From contemporary Indian literature and British observations.

E35 DODWELL, H. "Madras Nabobs," CR:296 (April 1919), 224-40. A "social history of Madras in the 18th century" based on court records.

E36 "The Edinburgh Academy in India," CR:99 (July, Oct. 1894), 137-52, 225-48; 100 (Jan. 1895), 173-86.

E37 "The English in India—Our Social Morality," CR:1 (Aug. 1844), 290-336.

E38 "English Life in Bengal," CR:33 (Dec. 1859), 306-45.

E39 "An English-Woman in India." "English-Women in India," CR 80: 159 (1885), 137-52. On the dreariness of life in India.

E40 "English Women in Hindustan," CR:4 (1845), 96-127.

E41 FAGAN, P. J. "Grave Problem of India Today," NC:94 (1923), 413-23. Against the Indian elite.

E42 FAWCETT, MILLICENT GARRETT. "Infant Marriage in India," CoR:58 (Oct. 1890), 712-20. Traces life history of a Hindu girl from birth; advocates legislation.

E43 "Female Infanticide in Central and Western India," CR:1 (Aug. 1844), 372-448.

E44 "Female Infanticide in the Punjab," CR:104 (Jan. 1897), 145-76.

E45 FINK, H. R. "The Hindu Custom of 'Sitting Dharna,'" CR:62 (1876), 37-52. On the right of a creditor to sit on debtor's doorstep.

E46 FOOT, ISAAC. "Round Table Conference, the Future, and the Depressed Classes," CoR:139 (March 1931), 282-90. Excerpts from speeches on social problems.

E47 FUKAZAWA, HIROSHI. [On the Forced Labour in the 18th Century Maratha Kingdom], HiR:48, no. 3 (1962).

E48 ———. [On the Slavery in the 18th Century Maratha Kingdom], HiR:45, no. 6 (1961).

E49 "The Functions of Modern Brahmans in Upper India," CR:84 (April 1887), 257-98.

E50 FURBER, HOLDEN. "In the Footsteps of a German 'Nabob': William Bolts in the Swedish Archives," IAr:12 (1958), 7-18. The attempts of a German adventurer to recoup his fortune.

E51 "G.P.S." "The Aristocracy of Behar," CR 76:151 (1883), 80-101.

E52 GANGULY, NARENDRANATH. "The Calcutta Cricket Club: Its Origin and Development," BPP:52 (July-Dec. 1936), 22-37, 113-31.

E53 ————. "A Note on Sati," BPP:70 (1951), 55-57. A statistical account, 1815-1828, and a Frenchman's observations from the Calcutta Journal, 1828.

E54 GHOSAL, HARI RANJAN. "Some Unpublished Documents Relating to Gang Robbery and Thuggee in the Company's Lower Provinces in Bengal during the Early 19th Century," IHRC:21 (1949), 55-57. Summarizes 10 letters.

E55 GHOSH, JOGENDRA CHANDRA. "The Village Community of Bengal and Upper India," CR 74:148 (1882), 227-70.

E56 GHOSH, PRAPHULLA CHANDRA. "Housing Problems in Calcutta," MR:30 (July 1921), 27-33.

E57 "A Girl's Life in India, a Hundred Years Ago," CR:95 (July 1892), 51-66.

E58 GRANT, CHARLES. "The Poor of India," NC:2 (Dec. 1877), 868-83. Discusses possible relief to the poor.

E59 GRAY, H. "The Progress of Women," MIW, pp. 445-83. Under the British.

E60 GUPTA, HIRALAL. "A Critical Study of the *Thugs* and Their Activities," JIH:37 (Aug. 1959), 167-77. Thuggee as a function of social disorder accompanying British rule.

E61 "H.G.K." "Rural Life in Northern India," CR 68:135 (1875), 113-36.

E62 "Hindu Women," CR 40:79 (1864), 80-101. Their social condition.

E63 "Human Sacrifices and Infanticide in India," ER:119 (April 1864), 389-412.

E64 HUNTER, WILLIAM WILSON. "Annals of Rural Bengal," ISPP: 6 (Oct. 1964, Jan.-March, April 1965), 1-51, 71-97, 107-62, 207-61. Reprints first three chapters.

E65 HUTTON, J. H. "Primitive Tribes," MIW, pp. 417-44. The impact of British sovereignty.

E66 "Illustrations of Anglo-Indian Society," CR 8:16 (1847), 548-68.

E67 "Indian Ennui," CR 27:53 (Sept. 1856), 42-54. On English attitudes toward India.

E68 "Indian Society," ER:48 (Sept. 1828), 32-47. Review of R. Richards' book on character and condition of the natives.

E69 "Indian Volunteer Organization," CR:89 (Oct. 1889), 352-61.

E70 "Indigo Planters and Missionaries," CR:34 (March 1860), 113-41. Defends the planters as a class.

E71 KEENE, H. G. "Anglo-Indian Mufasal Life in the Last Generation," CR 66:134 (1878), 712-28.

E72 KHAN, M. SIDDIQ. "Life in Old Dacca," PQ:9 (Summer 1959), 20-27. Manners and customs in the 19th cent.; illustrated.

E73 KHUNDKAR, HENRY. "Duelling Days in Old Calcutta," CR:267 (Jan. 1912), 19-36.

E74 "Kulinism amongst the Brahmins in Bengal," CR:93 (July 1891), 127-33.

E75 LAMB, HELEN B. "The Indian Business Communities and the Evolution of an Industrialist Class," PA:28 (June 1955), 101-15. An outline of the social background of business communities.

E76 "Life in Bombay," CR 17:33 (1852), 97-113.

E77 LISTON, D. "Translation of a Servitude-Bond," ASB:6 (Jan.-June 1837), 950-52.

E78 LOKHANDWALLA, SHAMOON T. "'Ãda: India," EI:1, 172-73. On modifications of Muslim custom under the British; useful bibliography.

E79 [MACKENZIE]. "Journal of Six Years in India," CR 21:42 (1853), 524-44. Mrs. Colin Mackenzie's journal.

E80 "Married Life in India," CR 4:8 (1845), 394-417. On British marriage customs in India.

E81 MITRA, R. C. "Dhurna and Brahmanical Immunities in Bengal under Early British Rule," IHCP:21 (1958), 421-25. A note on the moral duress practiced by Brahmans on their debtors in the form of threats of self-immolation.

E82 MOLONY, J. CHARTRES. "An Indian Hill Station," BM:247 (May 1940), 625-39. Description of Nilgiri Hills.

E83 MUKERJEE, RADHAKAMAL. "From the Village to the City; Ways of Dwelling in the Communities of India," A:40 (Aug. 1940), 439-42.

E84 MUKHERJEE, AMITABHA. "Slavery in Bengal in the Early Nineteenth Century," CR:176 (July 1965), 51-57.

E85 MUKHOPADHYAY, AMITABHA. "Sati as a Social Institution in Bengal," BPP:76 (Jubilee 1957), 99-115. Break-down of figures on incidence of sati, and an attempt to explain the custom in social and psychological terms.

E86 MÜLLER, F. MAX. "The Story of an Indian Child-Wife," CoR:60 (Aug. 1891), 183-87. On Soudamini Ray, wife of Babu Kedar Nath Ray, 1858-1890's; became a Brahmo.

E87 "The Nations of India and Their Manners," ER:98 (July 1953), 33-61. On English law and language in India.

E88 NIGHTINGALE, FLORENCE. "The People of India," NC:4 (Aug. 1878), 193-221. On their social condition.

E89 "AN OLD INDIAN." "Letters on the Present State of India," BM: 17 (May, June 1825), 574-91, 701-12; 18 (Aug.-Oct. 1825), 183-94, 303-15, 401-17. Social history.

E90 "AN OLD INDIAN." "Social Life in Bengal Fifty Years Ago," CR 73:146 (1881), 378-400; 74:147 (1882), 183-92.

E91 O'MALLEY, L. S. S. "The Hindu Social System," MIW, pp. 354-88. Its changes in the 19th and 20th cent.

E92 "Passages from the Autobiography of a Bengalee Gentleman of Sixty Years Ago," CR:95 (July 1892), 148-68.

E93 PATELL, BOMANJI BYRAMJI. "The First Year Funeral Expenses of a Parsee of the Last Century (1763)," AnSB 3:3 (1892-94), 144-57. Prints and translates a Gujarati MS.

E94 ———. "Suicides among the Parsees of Bombay during the Last Twelve Years," AnSB 4:1 (1895-99), 14-22. An analysis of causes.

E95 PAVLOV, V. I. [Some Features of the Rise of the Bourgeoisie in Bengal (Before the World War II)], KS:23 (1957).

E96 PRADHAN, R. GOPINATH. "Bombay Workers of Untouchable Classes," BUJ:4 (Jan. 1936), 134-61. A sociological study.

E97 "The Races, Religions and Languages of India as Disclosed by the Census for 1881," CR:83 (July 1886), 164-91.

E98 RAGHUVANSHI, V. P. S. "Social Morality in India in the 18th Century," QRHS 4:1/2 (1964/65), 80-85. Based on European sources.

E99 RATCLIFFE, S. K. "The Cooch Behar Marriage," FR:139 (Jan.-June 1933), 159-72. On the marriage of Keshub Chunder Sen's daughter to the Raja of Cooch Behar.

E100 RAWLINSON, H. G. "The Englishwoman in India," EaW:4 (Jan. 1950), 10-12. On Mrs. William Hawkins in the 17th cent. and Eliza Draper, who in the 1760's became involved with Lawrence Sterne.

E101 RAZZEL, P. E. "Social Origins of Officers in the Indian and British Home Armies: 1758-1962," BJS:14 (1963), 248-60. Summary in HA:10 (Sept. 1964), 132.

E102 REHATSEK, E. "Statistics of Suicides Committed in the City of Bombay during the Year 1886 [1887, 1888, 1889, 1890]," AnSB:1, 330-40, 442-48; 2, 65-71, 255-60, 294-300 [continues].

E103 REISNER, I. M. [Process of Disintegration of Village Community in Maharashtra in the 17th, 18th and Early 19th Centuries], UZIV:5 (1953).

E104 ROY, N. B. "A Note on the Household Effects of an Ordinary Noble Man of the 18th Century A.D.," BPP:74 (1955), 147-50. A list of the effects at his death in 1764 of a courtier of Raja Ramnarain, Gov. of Bihar.

E105 "The Rural Population of Bengal," CR:1 (May 1844), 189-216. Review of a police report.

E106 "Selections from Indian Records," CR 55:110 (1872), 275-82. On social conditions in Bengal, 1748-67.

E107 SEN, S. N. "Lord Cornwallis and Slave Trade in Bengal," CR:89 (Dec. 1943), 152-60.

E108 SETHI, D. P. "Social Work in India: A Historical Perspective," MR:117 (Mar. 1965), 182-88.

E109 SINGH, HARBANS. "A Nineteenth Century Marriage in Northern India," MR:93 (Jan. 1953), 60-63. The marriage of Prince Nan Nihal Singh, grandson of Ranjit Singh.

E110 SINGH, NIHAL. "India's 'Untouchables,'" CoR:103 (March 1913), 376-85. Their condition.

E111 SINGH, O. P. "Decay of the Landed Aristocracy in India," NC: 31 (May 1892), 830-38.

E112 SINHA, N. K. "Mayor's Court Records (1749-74) and Supreme Court Records of the 18th Century in the Calcutta High Court," BPP:69 (1950), 22-36. Social and commercial history.

E113 SINHA, PRADIP. "The Suburban Village in Bengal in the Second Half of the 19th Century—a Study in Social History," BPP:82 (July-Dec. 1963), 140-53. Based on English and Bengali material, including fiction.

E114 SKRINE, FRANCIS H. "Anglo-Indian Life before the Mutiny," AR:NS 5 (July 1, 1914), 1-15. British customs.

E115 SRINIVAS, M. N. "A Note on Sanskritization and Westernization," FEQ:15 (Aug. 1956), 481-96. A classic attempt to find concepts by which the modernization of Indian society can be explained.

E116 STAAL, J. F. "Sanskrit and Sanskritization," JAS:22 (May 1963), 261-75. Critical comment on Srinivas's theory.

E117 "Suttee," CR:46, 221-61.

E118 SWAMINATHAN, V. S. "Women's Movement in India," CoR:174 (July 1948), 26-30.

E119 TURNBULL, H. G. "Miss Mayo and Her Critics," FR:131 (March 1929), 355-69.

E120 TYABJI, F. B. "Social Life in 1804 and 1929 amongst Muslims in Bombay," RASB:6 (1930), 286-300. Mostly reminiscences of social life within his Khoja family, a reforming one.

E121 UMAR, MUHAMMAD. "Life of the Mughal Royalty in India during the 18th Century," MIQ:4 (1961), 137-53.

E122 ———. "Mughal Aristocracy during the 18th Century," MIQ:5 (1963), 88-112.

E123 "Voyages in the P. and O.; Reminiscences of an Old Fogey," BM: 128 (Nov. 1880), 593-627. On Anglo-Indian society.

E124 WEEKS, EDWIN LORD. "Recent Impression of Anglo-Indian Life," HM:91 (Nov. 1895), 903-22. With a number of drawings.

E125 "Woman in India: Her Influence and Position; The English-woman in India: Her Influence and Responsibilities," CR:83 (Oct. 1886), 347-70.

E126 WOODHOUSE, T. "Indigo Days in India; a Plantation 'Sahib's' Experiment in Friendliness to the Unfriendly," A:26 (Jan. 1926), 32-37, 76-79. Interesting photographs.

E127 "Young Civilians and Mofussil Courts," CR:33 (Sept. 1859), 49-73. Their life in the mofussil.

2. POPULATION

E128 ANDREWS, C. F. "India's Greatest Problem: Overcrowding on the Land," CoR:155 (Feb. 1939), 179-85. On the possibility of birth control.

E129 BAYLEY, WILLIAM BUTTERWORTH. "Statistical View of the Population of Burdwan, etc.," AsR:12 (1816), 547-65. Tables of houses and population, by caste.

E130 BEVERLEY, H. "Remarks on the Recent Census of the Town of Calcutta," ASBP (1876), pp. 111-13. Preliminary survey of the results, compared with 1866 and 1872 censuses.

E131 "Births and Deaths in British India," MR:28 (July 1920), 86-87. Table compiled from statistics in the Supplement to the Gazette of India, June 5, 1920.

E132 BOGUE, D. J. and ZACHARIAH, K. C. "Urbanization and Migration in India," IUF, pp. 27-54. District-by-district figures of "urbanward migration 1941-51" and on other parameters of the migrant population.

E133 BOSE, ASHISH. "A Note on the Definition of 'Town' in the Indian Census: 1901-1961," IESHR:1 (Jan. 1964), 84-94.

E134 CHAND, GYAN. "The Frozen Manpower of India," AAAPSS:233 (May 1944), 55-61. On population.

E135 [CHANDRASEKHAR]. "A Bibliography of Professor S. Chandrasekhar's Books and Select Papers and Articles on Population and Related Subjects: 1937-1962," PoR:6 (July 1962), 191-97.

E136 CHANDRASEKHAR, S. "Growth of Population in Madras City 1639-1961," PoR:8 (Jan. 1964), 17-45.

E137 ———. "India's Human Resources," AAAPSS:233 (May 1944), 62-77. Analysis of census figures.

E138 DAS, RAJANI KANTA. "Differential Fertility in India," MR:62 (Sept. 1937), 248-54.

E139 DAS, TARAKNATH. "Some Aspects of the Population Problem in India," MR:38 (Oct. 1925), 403-15. Based on *Statistical Abstract for British India*, 1911-12 to 1920-21.

E140 DATTA, JATINDRA MOHAN. "Variation in Sex-Ratio in Bengal during 150 Years," MII:37 (April-June 1957), 133-48.

E141 DATTA, THAKUR. "Mortality in India," MR:27 (March 1920), 314-18. Mortality rate by province, 1881-1900, 1898-1917; in India as a whole, 1885-1917.

E142 DAVIS, KINGSLEY. "India and Pakistan: the Demography of Partition," PA:22 (Sept. 1949), 254-64.

E143 ———. "Urbanization in India: Past and Future," IUF, pp. 1-26. Figures and trends in the 20th cent.

E144 DUTTA, BHUPENDRA NATH. "Population of Bengal—a Sociological Enquiry," MR:62 (Aug. 1937), 201-07.

E145 "The First Census of the Panjab, 1855," JPUHS:4 (Dec. 1935), 159-62.

E146 GEDDES, ARTHUR. "The Social and Psychological Significance of Variability in Population Change, with Examples from India, 1871-1941," HuR:1 (1947), 181-205. Interesting maps and charts.

E147 GHOSH, A. "A Study of Demographic Trends in West Bengal during 1901-1950," PS:9 (March 1956), 217-36. With tables.

E148 ———. "The Trend of the Birth Rate in India, 1911-1950," PS:10 (July 1956), 53-68. With tables.

E149 HATHORN, H. V. "Census of the Population of the City and District of Murshedabad, Taken in 1829," ASB:2 (Nov. 1833), 567-69. Hindu and Muslim households and population in thanas of the city and district.

E150 KARVE, D. G. "Population Problem in India: a Regional Approach," BUJ:11 (Jan. 1943), 48-54. Regional analysis of increase, 1881-1931.

E151 MACDONALD, K. S. "Baroda Census Report, 1901," CR:116 (Jan. 1903), 46-67.

E152 MOLONY, J. CHARTRES. "A Numbering of the People," BM:245 (Feb. 1939), 217-31. Experiences in taking census in Madras, 1911.

E153 MUKHERJEE, BHUJANGA BHUSHAN. "Trends of Population in India," MR:60 (July 1936), 8-13.

E154 "Population Mortality in Calcutta," ASB:7 (Oct. 1838), 888-91. "Mortality among all classes in Calcutta for 20 years, but for the Native Population only 5 years."

E155 "Population of Allahabad," ASB (1832), pp. 34-35. Estimates by area in 1824: Hindus, Muslims, and houses.

E156 PRINSEP, H. T. "Estimate of the Risk of Life to Civil Servants of the Bengal Presidency, in Each Year of their Residence in India," ASB:1 (July 1832), 277-88. "Corrected Estimate. . . ." ASB:6, part 1, 341-46.

E157 ———. "Table of Mortality for Ages from Birth to Twenty Years, Framed from the Registers of the Lower Orphan School, Calcutta," ASB:7 (Sept. 1838), 818-28.

E158 PRINSEP, JAMES. "Census of the Population of the City of Benares," AsR:17 (1832), 470-98. Census taken in 1800 by Zulficar Ali, Kotwar, under the Resident, Mr. Deane, re-examined by the author. Detailed by area of city and by caste, also price of grain.

E159 RAGHAVA RAO, G. "The Nature of the Growth of Population in the British Districts of the Bombay Presidency," BUJ:6 (Jan. 1938), 125-62. With tables.

E160 RAYCHAUDHURI, T. C. "The Population Problem in Bengal," CR:94 (Feb. 1945), 36-39.

E161 SARKAR, BENOY KUMAR. "The Population Trend in India with Reference to Food and Nutrition," IJE:20 (Jan. 1940), 271-302.

E162 SHEJWALKAR, T. S. "Material for Population Estimates in the Peshwa Dafter," IHRC:26 (1949), 16-18.

E163 TEMPLE, RICHARD. "The Rapid Growth of the Population in India," FR:57 (March 1892), 426-36. As a sign of prosperity.

E164 WALTERS, HENRY. "Census of the City of Dacca," AsR:17 (1832), 535-58. Population by thanah, caste, profession; also the price of muslins.

3. FAMILIES, CLANS, AND ETHNIC GROUPS

E165 ABDUL WADUD, KAZI. "The Mussalmans of Bengal," SBR, pp. 460-78. Brief history.

E166 "Among Mahommedans in the Punjab," BM:204 (Oct. 1918), 486-94. Local social and political life.

E167 ANSARI, A. S. BAZMEE. "Djāt," EI:2, 488-89. On the Jats.

E168 "Armenians in India," CR:98 (Jan. 1894), 132-51.

E169 "Bengali Barbers," CR:32 (June 1859), 335-43. On life and customs.

E170 "Biographies (with Portraits) of their Highnesses, the Present and the Two Preceding 'Aga Sahibs' of Bombay, the Chiefs of the Khojas and other Ismailians, . . ." AR, Ser. 2:8 (July 1894), 150-63. On the Aga Khans.

E171 BOSE, BASANTA KUMAR. "A Bygone Chinese Colony in Bengal," BPP:47 (Jan.-June 1934), 120-22. On a Chinese soldier of fortune, 18th cent.

E172 BULLOCK, H. "Four Free-Lance Families," JPUHS:2 (Dec. 1933), 156-65. Genealogies of 18th cent. and early 19th cent. military adventurers, all connected by blood or marriage.

E173 CARR, HUBERT. "Minority Communities: The British Commercial Community," PI, pp. 140-47. Their political organization and outlook.

E174 CHAND, NĀNAK. "Index to 'Hindu Tribes and Castes as Represented in Benares,'" ASB:65, part 3 (Special No., 1896), 112 pp.

E175 CHETTUR, K. N. "The Nambudri-Brahmins of Kerala," CR:113 (July 1901), 121-36. Customs.

E176 "The Chinese Colony in Calcutta," CR:31 (Dec. 1858), 368-84.

E177 CHOWDHURY, D. A. "Islam in Bengal," MW:18 (April 1928), 147-54. On the rise in number of Muslims, 1881-1921.

E178 CROOKE, WILLIAM. "The Moplahs of Malabar," ER:235 (Jan. 1922), 181-93.

E179 DAMISHKY, PAUL J. E. "The Moslem Population of Bombay," MW:1 (1911), 117-29. Description of different sects.

E180 DATTA, JATINDRA MOHAN. "Who the Bengali Muhammadans Are?" MR:49 (March 1931), 303-09.

E181 DIGBY, WILLIAM. "Eurasians as Leaven in India and Ceylon," CR 64:127 (1877), 180-208.

E182 "The East Indian Community," CR 11:21 (1849), 73-90. On Anglo-Indians.

E183 EDWARDS, THOMAS. "The Eurasian Movement of 1829-30," CR 76:151 (1883), 102-33. On the rights of Anglo-Indians.

E184 ———. "Eurasians and Poor Europeans in India," CR 72:143 (1881), 38-56.

E185 FAGAN, PATRICK. "Minority Communities: The Sikhs," PI, pp. 124-32. Their political role.

E186 FISCHEL, WALTER J. "The Jewish Merchant-Colony in Madras (Fort St. George) during the 17th and 18th Centuries. A Contribution to the Economic and Social History of the Jews in India," JESHO:3 (1960), 78-107, 175-95. Based on publications of the Madras Record Office and documents in the India Office Library.

E187 FRYKENBERG, ROBERT ERIC. "British Society in Guntur during the Early Nineteenth Century," CSSH:4 (1961-62), 200-08.

E188 FYZEE, A. A. A. "Bohorās," EI:1, 1254-55. Shi'is of the Ismaili sect.

E189 GHOSH, BENOY. "Some Old Family-Founders in 18th Century Calcutta; The Setts of Sutanuti," BPP:79 (Jan.-June 1960), 42-55.

E190 HALIM, A. "French-Indian Families of Aligarh," JIH:30 (Aug. 1952), 155-80. Three family histories and some generalizations on their culture.

E191 HEDIN, ELMER L. "The Anglo-Indian Community," AJS:40 (Sept. 1934), 165-79. History of their social position.

E192 HURWITZ, JOACHIM. "Marginal Men of India: an Enquiry into the History of the Anglo-Indians," In:8 (April 1955), 129-47.

E193 KIRKPATRICK, W. "The British Community of India," EnR:56 (April 1933), 431-42. Urges Anglo-Indians to organize to get their share of government patronage.

E194 "KOMMA." "The Sikh Situation in the Punjab," FR:NS 113 (1923), 238-51. On the preservation of the community.

E195 "The Kulin Brahmins of Bengal," CR:2 (Oct. 1844), 1-31.

E196 "The Lindsays in India," CR 13:26 (1850), 221-56. An English family history in India.

E197 LOKHANDWALLA, SH. T. "The Bohras: A Muslim Community of Gujarat," SI:3 (1955), 117-35. Ethnology and 20th cent. social and religious history.

E198 MANDELBAUM, DAVID GOODMAN. "The Jewish Way of Life in Cochin," JSS:1 (1939), 423-60. Covers 13th cent. to 20th cent.

E199 MOLONY, J. CHARTRES. "Minority Communities: the Depressed Classes," PI, pp. 132-40. Their political status.

E200 MONIER-WILLIAMS. "The Pārsīs," NC:9 (March 1881), 500-16. Description of society and religion.

E201 MORENO, H. W. B. "Anglo-Indian Women of the Past," BPP: 39 (Jan.-June 1930), 53-58. 19th cent. women.

E202 ———. "Ethnology of the Eurasian or Anglo-Indians," MsR:4 (April-June 1930), 47-67.

E203 ———. "Status of Women in Anglo-Indian (Eurasian) Community," MsR:4 (July-Sept. 1929), 38-45.

E204 NAHAR, P. C. "The Genealogy of the Jagat Seths of Murshidabad," IHRC:5 (1923), 18-27.

E205 NAIDIS, MARK. "British Attitudes toward the Anglo-Indians," SAQ:62 (Summer 1963), 407-22. History of the Anglo-Indian community's relations with the British official and non-official communities.

E206 NATESA SASTRI, T. M. "The Criminal Classes of the Bellary District," CR:121 (Oct. 1905), 498-508.

E207 OLIVIER, LORD. "Anglo-Indians and Their Communal Claims," CoR:127 (April 1925), 423-31. On their dissatisfaction with their rights after the Government of India Act.

E208 "P.K." "The Anglo-Indian Question," CR:69 (1879), 382-91.

E209 "The Panjāb Rājās," CR 53:106 (1871), 244-66.

E210 PATON, WILLIAM. "Minority Communities: The Indian Christians," PI:152-55.

E211 POOL, WILLIAM C. "Late Eighteenth Century Calcutta and Life in Its European Colony," CR:109 (Dec. 1948), 175-89; 110 (Jan. 1949), 27-34. Miscellaneous excerpts from contemporary accounts.

E212 "The Portuguese East Indians of Malabar," CR:107 (July 1898), 79-87.

E213 RAHMAN, A. F. K. "Origin of the Rohillas," IHCP:6 (1944), 293-97. Source of the name in the 18th cent. and change in referent.

E214 RHODES, CAMPBELL. "Minority Communities: The Anglo-Indians," PI, pp. 147-52. Their political status.

E215 RICKETTS, MRS. "English Society in India," CoR:101 (May 1912), 681-88. Glowing picture of Anglo-Indian society.

E216 SALETORE, B. A. "Some Prominent Parsis in the 18th Century," IHRC:29 (1953), 164-67.

E217 SANDBERG, GRAHAM. "Our Outcast Cousins in India," CoR: 61 (June 1892), 880-99. On Eurasian community.

E218 SETH, M. J. "Armenians at Agra and Gwalior," MsR:4 (Oct.-Dec. 1929), 41-62.

E219 SRINIVASACHARI, C. S. "Right and Left Hand Castes Disputes in Madras in the Early Part of the 18th Century," IHRC:12 (1929), 68-76. Disputes among sepoys.

E220 STANTON, H. V. WEITBRECHT. "The Untouchables of India and Their Enumeration," AR:NS 16 (1920), 171-84. Two tables: "Aboriginal Tribes of India and Burma before Domiciled," "Castes Included among Domiciled Untouchables"; both give name, locality, occupation, number.

E221 STRIZOWER, SCHIFRA. "Jews as an Indian Caste," JJS:1 (April 1959), 43-57. Traces history and notes examples of assimilation to Indian culture.

E222 TAKLE, JOHN. "Islam in Bengal," MW:4 (1914), 3-19. Map of districts with per cent of Muslims in each; information on population growth in the 20th cent., literacy and religious tendencies.

E223 "The Territorial Aristocracy of Bengal; 1. The Bardwān Rāj," CR 54:108 (1872), 171-94; "2. The Nadiyā Rāj," CR 55:109 (1872), 85-118; "3. The Dinagepoor Rāj," by E. Vesey Westmacott, CR 55:110 (1872), 205-24; "4. The Rājās of Rājshāhi," CR 56:111 (1873) 1-42; "5. The Kasimbazar Rāj," CR 57:113 (1873), 88-100; "6. The Kāndi Family," CR 58:115 (1874), 95-120.

E224 TITUS, MURRAY T. "Notes on Islam in India," MW:18 (April 1928), 199-203. Muslim population according to 1921 census.

E225 VANSITTART, EDEN. "The Tribes, Clans, and Castes of Nepāl," ASB:63 (1894), 213-49. By a captain of the 5th Gurkhas.

E226 WADIA, P. A. "The Parsis of Bombay and Parsi Charities," BUJ:4 (July 1935), 88-104.

E227 WARREN, W. PRESTON. "Islam in Southern India," MW:21 (Oct. 1931), 352-67. Describes various groups.

E228 WISE, JAMES. "The Muhammadans of Eastern Bengal," ASB:63 (May 1894), 28-63.

E229 WOOD, W. H. ARDEN. "The Problem of the Domiciled Community in India," AR:NS 24 (1928), 417-35. Discussion pp. 436-46. On the Anglo-Indian community.

E230 YAPP, M. E. "Durrānī," EI:2, 628-29.

4. BRITISH-INDIAN SOCIAL RELATIONS

E231 BLUNT, WILFRED SCAWEN. "Ideas about India:—II. Race Hatred," FR:42 (July-Dec. 1884), 445-59. On Indian-English relations.

E232 CATON, ANNE R. "Fraternisation in India," CoR:169 (May 1946), 292-95. On contact of British soldiers with Indians in war.

E233 CHAUDHARY, V. C. P. "Title and Its Implications (1871-75)," BRS:45 (1959), 435-44. The qualifications necessary to receive the titles Rai Bahadur, Maharajah, Rajah, Ranee, and Khan Bahadur.

E234 DAS, M. N. "Indo-British Racial Antipathy during the Morley-Minto Era," BPP:79 (July-Dec. 1960), 71-76. From the Morley Papers.

E235 ———. "Lord Curzon and the Problem of European Racialism in India," JIH:39 (April 1961), 163-68. Based on Curzon correspondence.

E236 GHOSH, SUJATA. "The Racial Question and Liberal English Opinion as Reflected in the Friend of India, from the Mutiny to the Ilbert Bill," BPP:81 (Jan.-June 1962), 57-63. From editorials.

E237 GOKHALE, B. G. "Indians and the British: a Study in Attitudes," HT:13 (April 1963), 230-38. Places turning point at Ilbert Bill agitation; illustrated with drawings.

E238 "INDICUS." "Indian Reforms and the Station Club," CoR:116 (Sept. 1919), 321-26. On the expulsion of Indians from the club before 1919.

E239 MESTON, LORD. "Quo Vadis in India," CoR:118 (Oct. 1920), 457-65. On the discovery by Englishmen of their own unpopularity after World War I.

E240 NAIDIS, MARK. "British Attitudes toward the Anglo-Indians," SAQ:112 (Summer 1963), 407-22.

E241 POLAK, HENRY S. L. "Wasted Opportunities in India," CoR:145 (May 1934), 540-47. On the gap in sympathy between England and India.

E242 RAHMAN, K. "An Anglo-Indian Novelist of the Thirties: a Study in Race Relations," US:1 (Aug. 1964), 63-80.

5. SOCIAL REFORMS

E243 AGARWALA, A. N. "The Social Security Movement in India," EJ:56 (Dec. 1946), 568-82. History of social security legislation in India.

E244 BALL, UPENDRA NATH. "The Uplift Movement in India," MR: 40 (Sept. 1926), 246-52.

E245 BANERJEE, D. N. "Warren Hastings and the Suppression of Dacoity in Bengal: Purwana of Instructions to Fouzdars," IHRC:22 (1945), 12-14. Prints instructions.

E246 BANERJI, AMIYA CHARAN. "Brahmananda Keshu Bhandra Sen," SBR, pp. 79-93. Bengali social reformer.

E247 BANNERJI, BRAJENDRANATH. "Raja Radhakanta Deb's Services to the Company," BPP:33 (Jan.-June 1927), 130-33. Extracts from tributes to the opponent of Ram Mohun Roy's campaign to prohibit sati.

E248 BARTON, W. P. "Indian Federation and the Untouchable," QR:268 (Jan. 1937), 18-28. Efforts at reform.

E249 BRAYNE, F. L. "Village Uplift in the Punjab," AR:NS 25 (1929), 115-30. Discussion 131-40.

E250 [CARPENTER]. "Miss Mary Carpenter's First Visit in Calcutta," CR:129 (July 1909), 257-66. Activities of a social reformer, 1866.

E251 DAS, MANMATHA NATH. "Movement to Suppress the Custom of Female Infanticide in the Punjab and Kashmir," MII:37 (Dec. 1957), 280-93. Movement began in mid-19th cent.

E252 DATTA, KALIKINKAR. "Suppression of Thugi in Bihar," PU:6 (Jan.-April 1952), 17-19. Extracts from records in the library of the Bihar Research Society, Patna.

E253 "Documents sur la situation sociale dans l'Inde et les projets de réforme" [Documents on the Social Situation in India and the Reform

Projects], RMM:44-45 (April-June 1921), 53-204; 46 (Aug. 1921), 102-60; 47 (Oct. 1921), 157-205. Reprints some of Gandhi's writings, Command Papers, Congress documents.

E254 "The First Series of Government Measures for the Abolition of Human Sacrifices among the Khonds," CR:6 (1846), 45-108.

E255 FRERE, H. BARTLE E. "Abolition of Slavery in India and Egypt," FR:39 (Jan.-June 1883), 349-68.

E256 [GOKHALE]. "Mr. Gokhale's Servants of India Society and Its Work," MR:25 (June 1919), 623-25.

E257 HARTOG, MABEL. "Indian Village Uplift: A Visit to Gurgaon," CoR:124 (Sept. 1928), 337-44. Brayne's project.

E258 HEIMSATH, CHARLES H. "The Origin and Enactment of the Indian Age of Consent Bill, 1891," JAS:21 (Aug. 1962), 491-504. Sources: Records of the Government of India, Reports of the Native Press, Dayaram Gidumal's *The Status of Women in India* (Bombay 1889).

E259 HUTTON, JAMES. "India Pacified and Purified," AR:3 (Jan. 1887), 93-128. On suppression of thagi, sati, etc.

E260 "The Indian Christian Marriage Act, 1872," CR 60:119 (1875), 1-20.

E261 "An Indian Reformer," CR:83 (July 1886), 20-35.

E262 JAMES, C. CARKEET. "Forty Years' Sanitary Progress in Bombay," AR:NS 12 (Oct. 1, 1917), 282-92. Discussion pp. 293-300.

E263 JOSHI, C. V. "Social Reform under Maharaja Anandrao Gaikwad (1800-1820 A.D.)," IHRC:16 (1939), 202-03. From Baroda records.

E264 KARVE, D. K. "Professor Karve's Work in the Cause of Indian Women as Described by Himself," MR:18 (Nov. 1915), 537-46.

E265 "The Khonds—Abolition of Human Sacrifice and Female Infanticide," CR 10:20 (1848), 273-341.

E266 MAJUMDAR, LILA. "The World of Women," SBR, pp. 509-16. The work of reformers advocating the enlightenment of women in the 19th cent.

E267 "Marriage of Hindu Widows," CR 25:50 (1855), 351-68. On Hindu law and proposed reform.

E268 "Means of Improving the Condition of the Natives of India," OH:2 (June 1824), 195-205. Critical of British policy.

E269 MITTRA, KALIPADA. "Suppression of the Suttee in the Garhjat State of Orissa," BPP:43 (Jan.-June 1932), 133-36. Regulations.

E270 MITTRA, KALIPADA. "Suppression of Suttee in the Province of Cuttack," BPP:46 (July-Dec. 1933), 125-31.

E271 MUKHERJEE, S. N. "A Note on Sir William Jones and the Slave Trade in Bengal," BPP:82 (July-Dec. 1963), 106-11.

E272 MUKHOPADHYAY, AMITABHA. "Movement for the Abolition of Sati in Bengal," BPP:77 (Jan.-June 1958), 20-41. British and Bengali opinion and actions. Based on Parliamentary papers, Bengali materials on Rammohun Roy, and contemporary press.

E273 NAIDU, MUTHYALAYYA. "Beginning of Widow Remarriage Movement in India," MR:118 (Dec. 1965), 490-92.

E274 NAIR, C. SANKARAN. "Indian Law and English Legislation," CoR:100 (Aug., Sept. 1911), 213-26, 349-64. Much on marriage laws.

E275 NATARAJAN, K. "The Working Faith of the Indian Reformer," HR:23 (Jan. 1911), 9-14. By the editor of the Indian Social Reformer.

E276 O'DWYER, MICHAEL F. "Mother India, Swaraj, and Social Reform," FR:129 (Feb. 1928), 171-82. Says that public opinion may do more for reform than laws would.

E277 REES, J. D. "Meddling with Hindu Marriages," NC:27 (Oct. 1890), 660-76. A number of opinions, English and Indian, on reform of Hindu marriage laws.

E278 SAIGAL, BRIJ. "Lord Elgin I and the Social Reforms," UPHS: NS 3 (1955), 81-88. General survey of policy.

E279 SARMA, JYOTIRMOYEE. "Social Change in Bengal in the Latter Half of the Nineteenth Century," MII:33 (1953), 104-26. A general account of institutions, advocating social reforms.

E280 SEED, GEOFFREY. "The Abolition of Suttee in Bengal," H:NS 40 (1955), 286-99. Summary in HA:3, 390.

E281 SEN, M. "Swami Vivekananda and Social Reform," CR:170 (Feb. 1964), 187-89.

E282 "Social Improvements, Past and Future," CR:88 (April 1889), 283-90.

E283 SORABJI, CORNELIA. "Stray Thoughts of an Indian Girl," NC: 30 (Oct. 1891), 638-42. Against reform of marriage laws.

E284 ———. "Temple-Entry and Untouchability," NC:113 (June 1933), 689-702. A conservative view.

E285 SRINIVASACHARI, C. S. "The India Reform Society and Its Impact on the Indian Administration in the Decade 1853-62," IJPS:8 (July 1946), 648-61. A London society founded by John Dickinson, Jr.

E286 "The Suppression of Thuggee and Dacoity," CR:35 (Dec. 1860), 371-95.

E287 THAPAR, SAVITRI. "Family Planning in India," PS:17 (1963), 4-19. Summary in HA:10 (Sept. 1964), 156-57; includes history.

E288 THOMPSON, EDWARD. "The Suppression of Suttee in Native States," ER.245 (April 1927), 274-86. Covers 1833-62 in Rajputana.

E289 VENKATARAMAN, S. R. "Thakkar Bapa," MR:89 (March 1951), 224-25. Biography of a member of the Servants of India Society.

E290 WALTERS, H. CRAWFORD. "New India and Temperance Reform," CoR:124 (Aug. 1923), 223-27.

6. TRAVEL ACCOUNTS

E291 "A.B.C." "A French Traveller in India in the Last Century," MR:12 (July 1912), 28-41. Victor Jacquemont.

E292 BAGCHI, PRABODHCHANDRA. "Victor Jacquemont in India," CR:56 (July 1936), 51-60. Summary and excerpts from his diary.

E293 BAKTAY, ERVIN. "New Data Concerning the Life of Alexander Csoma de Koros," ASB, 3rd Ser., 23:2 (1957), 11-19. De Koros was in India and the Himalayas 1822-42.

E294 "BIBLIOPHILE." "Bishop Heber's Journal (1824-25)," MR:32 (Aug. 1922), 155-63.

E295 BISSOONDOYAL, B. "India as Seen by French Travellers," IAC: 11 (April 1962), 434-43. Brief summary of French accounts, 18th & 19th cent.

E296 BULLOCK, H. "General Ventura's Family and Travels," IA:1 (Jan.-Oct. 1947), 18-25. Attempts to unravel the journeys around India 1822-55.

E297 CAIRD, JAMES. "Notes by the Way in India: the Land and the People," NC:6 (July-Oct. 1879), 119-40, 244-63, 529-50, 705-27. A travelogue.

E298 DUFF, M. E. GRANT. "A Month in Southern India," CoR:60 (Sept. 1891), 313-32. Good travelogue.

E299 ———. "Notes on an Indian Journey," CoR:25 (May 1875), 895-917; 26 (June-Nov. 1875), 44-62, 311-25, 518-44, 590-613, 785-808. Observations and thoughts in 1874.

E300 "European Adventurers in India," ER:134 (Oct. 1871), 361-90. On memoirs of George Thomas and James Skinner, with long excerpts.

E301 FORSTER, E. M. "Indian Entries from a Diary," HM:224 (Feb. 1962), 46-56. From his trip to India, 1912-13.

E302 "A Frenchman's View of India, 1829-32," BPP:47 (Jan.-June 1934), 81-89. Victor Jacquemont.

E303 [HEBER]. "Bishop Heber's Indian Journals, etc.," QR:37 (Jan. 1828), 100-47.

E304 "India," ER:48 (Dec. 1828), 312-34. On Bishop Heber's narrative.

E305 "Jacquemont's Letters from India," W:22 (April 1835), 304-13.

E306 KRISHNAMURTI, S. "Sir Robert Chambers: a Johnsonian in India," BUJ:18 (Sept. 1949), 1-5. A visitor to India in the 1790's.

E307 MALLESON, G. B. "Foreign Adventurers in India," CR:65 (1877), 1-50. In late 18th cent.

E308 QUIN, EVA WYNDHAM. "Trip to Travancore," NC:31 (Feb. 1892), 255-62.

E309 "Recent Travels in Upper India," ER:57 (1833), 358-70. Review of books by Skinner, Mundy, and Archer.

E310 "Romance and Reality of Indian Life," CR:2 (Dec. 1844), 377-442. Reviews a number of travellers' accounts and early histories.

E311 "Rousselet's Travels in India," W:105 (April 1876), 386-423. A French traveler among princely states.

E312 SEN, SAMAR N. "Joseph Tieffenthaler and His Geography of Hindustan," ASB, Ser. 4:4, 3&4 (1962), 75-99. With plates and map. Jesuit missionary, traveled in north India 1743-70; published a careful description of his journey.

E313 SLUSZKIEWICZ, EUGENIUSZ. "India as Seen by Polish Travellers of the XIX Century," IAC:11 (Jan. 1962), 336-39. Very brief note on travelers' accounts.

E314 ———. "India as Seen by Polish Travellers up to the 19th Century," IAC:9 (April 1961), 385-403. Largely on Maksymilian Wikliński; based on Polish accounts, but not documented.

E315 SOLTYKOFF, ALEXIS. "Lucknow in 1841," JPUHS:1 (Dec. 1932), 148-54. Translated and edited by H. L. O. Garrett. From a diary by a Russian visitor.

F. CULTURAL HISTORY

1. *GENERAL*

F1   ALI, M. MOHAR. "Religious Toleration in British India and the Genesis of the Lex-Loci Act, 1850," ASP:9 (Dec. 1964), 45-63.

F2   ANTONOVA, K. A. "K istorii Russko-Indiiskikh kul'turnykh sviasei. Iz tetradei G. S. Lebedeva (1795-1797 gg.)" [On the History of Cultural Relations Between Russia and India. From the Diaries of G. S. Lebedev (1795-1797)], IsA:1 (1956), 156-95. Abstract in HA:4 (No. 2459): "The musician Gerasim Stepanovich Lebedev (1749-1818) lived in India from 1785 to 1797. He translated two English comedies into Bengali and founded the first Bengali theater in Calcutta in 1795. Based on twenty documents."

F3   AROKIASWAMI, M. "French Influence on South Indian Culture," JIH:40 (April 1962), 191-99.

F4   ARTE, S. B. "Mr. D. G. Phalke and His 'Hindusthan Cinema Films,'" MR:23 (May 1918), 516-19.

F5   AWASTHI, R. K. "Materialism and Epistemology in M. N. Roy's New-Humanism (Critique)," UB:9 (April 1962), 95-115.

F6   ———. "Theory of Social Dynamics in M. N. Roy's New-Humanism (Critique)," UB:9 (Dec. 1962), 87-109.

F7   AYYUB, ABU SAYEED. "Jawaharlal Nehru on Religion," Q:43 (Oct.-Dec. 1964), 9-20; 47 (Oct.-Dec. 1965), 27-34.

F8   BAGAL, JOGESH C. "Henry Derozio: the Teacher-Patriot," MR:55 (June 1934), 644-47.

F9   BANERJEE, ROMESH CHANDRA. "State Patronage to Hindu and Muslim Religions during the East India Company's Rule," BPP:56 (Jan.-June 1939), 23-36. Based on Parliamentary papers, with extracts from memorials and government memos.

F10   BAUSANI, ALESSANDRO. "Storia e attività della 'Angŭman-i Taraqqī-i Urdŭ' di Karaci" [History and Activities of the Anjuman-i Taraqqi-i Urdu of Karachi], OM:35 (June, Nov. 1955), 331-45, 536-48. A society organized for the promotion of Urdu learning.

F11   BEARCE, GEORGE D. "Intellectual and Cultural Characteristics of India in a Changing Era, 1740-1800," JAS:25 (Nov. 1965), 3-17.

F12   ———. "John Stuart Mill and India," BRAS:29 (Dec. 1954), 67-80. Examines the effect of India on J. S. Mill's thought and vice versa.

F13   "Bengali Festivals and Holidays," CR:18 (1852), 49-71.

F14 "The Bethune Society," CR:16 (1851), 483-500. On its aims and activities.

F15 BHARATI, AGEHANANDA. "Hindu Scholars, Germany, and the Third Reich," Q:44 (Jan.-March 1965), 74-77.

F16 BHATTACHARYA, K. K. "Sarojini Naidu, the Greatest Woman of Our Time," MR:85 (April 1949), 289-91. Biography.

F17 BRUSH, JOHN E. "Distribution of Religious Communities in India," AAAG:39 (June 1949), 81-98. Based on 1941 census; with maps.

F18 [CHATTERJYA]. "Ram Kisto Chatterjya," CR:19 (1853), 81-104.

F19 COTTON, EVAN. "Antonio Angelo Tremamondo," BPP:35 (Jan.-June 1928), 151-55. Founder of a riding academy in 1770's in Calcutta.

F20 COTTON, H. J. S. "Prospects of Moral Progress in India," FR:30 (Sept. 1878), 387-98. On government policy, especially toward education.

F21 DAS, HARIHAR. "The Rev. Krishna Mohan Banerjee, D.L., C.I.E., Brahmin, Christian, Scholar and Patriot (1813-1885)," BPP:37 (Jan.-June 1929), 133-44; 38 (July-Dec. 1929), 48-59, 139-55.

F22 DAS, MANMATHA NATH. "The Spirit of 'Young Bengal' and Its Influence on Bethune," CR:139 (June 1956), 275-82.

F23 ———. "Transmission of Koh-i-noor from Lahore to London," JIH:42 (Dec. 1964), 699-706. Papers on its seizure and transmission, 1849.

F24 DATTA, BHABATOSH. "Baṅkimcandra o pāshcātya manīshā" [Bankimchandra and the Genius of the West], BP:16 (1959-61), 45-58. A review of Bankimchandra Chatterjee's life and thought, showing his advocacy of European rationalism and empiricism in religion and other matters. Cites his own writings and other Bengali works.

F25 DATTA, KALI KINKAR. "Relations between the Hindus and the Muhammadans of Bengal in the Middle of the Eighteenth Century (1740-1765)," JIH:8 (1929), 328-35. Material on cultural assimilation.

F26 ———. "Trends of Religious Thought in Pre-Nineteenth Century India," IAC:1 (Oct. 1952), 153-64. On sects in the 18th cent.

F27 DATTA, SURENDRA KUMAR. "Causes of the Expansion or Retrogression of Religions in India; a Study of the Census of 1911," IRM: 3 (1914), 639-58.

F28 DE LA VALETTE, JOHN. "The Encouragement of Art and Archaeology in the Indian States," IAL:NS 5 (1931), 111-27.

F29 [DEB]. "Radhakant Deb," CR:45 (Aug. 1867), 317-26.

F30 DEY, SHUMBHOO CHUNDER. "Ramaprosad Roy," CR:129 (July 1909), 287-308; 131 (July, Oct. 1910), 334-51, 460-77. The youngest son of Rammohun Roy.

F31 DIGHE, V. G. "The Renaissance in Maharashtra: the First Phase (1818-1870)," RASB:NS 36/37 (1961/1962), 23-31.

F32 DOBIE, MARRYAT R. "Dr. John Leyden and Sir William Burrough," BPP:52 (July-Dec. 1936), 67-74.

F33 DUTT, ROMESH. "Notes on Govin Chunder Dutt," CR:115 (Oct. 1902), 400-02. Literary and cultural figure, father of Toru Dutt.

F34 EDWARDES, MICHAEL. "Rudyard Kipling and the Imperial Imagination," TwC:153 (June 1953), 443-54. Kipling as an interpreter of the British in India.

F35 ELLIOT, R. H. "Indian Conjuring," BM:233 (April 1933), 475-94. On how the tricks are done.

F36 ——. "Indian Magic," BM:233 (June 1933), 819-34. How it's done.

F37 "English Ideas, Indian Adaptation," CR:30 (March 1858), 1-32. On educated Indians.

F38 ERSKINE, WILLIAM. "Diaries of Sir William Erskine," RASB 25:72 (1918-19), 373-409. First secretary of the Royal Asiatic Society, Bombay Branch. I. Journey to Ellora, 1820; II. Journey to Gujrat, 1822-23.

F39 FIRMINGER, W. K. and COTTON, EVAN. "The Company's Vendu Master," BPP:43 (Jan.-June 1932), 88-91. George Williamson, auctioneer in 1770's in Calcutta.

F40 "Genesis of 'The Calcutta Review,'" CR:117 (July 1903), 111-15.

F41 GLASENAPP, HELMUTH VON. "The Influence of Indian Thought on German Science, Philosophy and Literature," ASB, 3rd Ser., 23:2 (1957), 1-10. A brief survey.

F42 GODE, P. K. "My Reminiscences of the Late R. D. Ranade," POr: 21, nos. 3&4, 1-11. Marathi translation in *Navabhārata* (Oct. 1957), pp. 16-24; Hindi translation in *Dārśanika*, Allahabad.

F43 GRIERSON, G. A. "The Early Publications of the Serampore Missionaries (A Contribution to Indian Bibliography)," IAn:32 (June 1903), 241-54. Includes most of the bibliographical information from *Memoirs of the Serampore Baptist Mission*, covering publications 1801-1832.

F44 GUHACHAUDHURI, DVIJENDRA NATH. "Memoirs of a Polyhistor," CR:145 (Nov. 1957), 189-209. Memoirs of Avināś Chandra Guha.

F45 HAQ, S. MOINUL. "Sami'-ullah Khan, Mohsin-ul-Mulk and Hali (Sami'-ullah Khan and Mohsin-ul-Mulk)," HFI:2, 1831-1905, Part 2, 533-43.

F46 HAVELL, E. B. "Indian Administration and 'Swadeshi,'" NC:61 (June 1907), 892-901. A plea for the encouragement of Indian creativity.

F47 HAWARD, E. "Kipling Myths and Traditions in India," NC:125 (Feb. 1939), 194-202.

F48 "Hindu and Mahomedan Religious Endowments," QJPSS:3 (Oct.? 1880), 1-16.

F49 HOSTEN, H. "The Three First Type-Printed Bengali Books," BPP:9 (July-Sept. 1914), 40-63; 13 (July-Sept. 1916), 67-68. On 3 books printed in Lisbon in 1743 (in Roman characters).

F50 HOYLAND, J. S. "Plato, the Idea of Progress, and India," NC:101 (April 1927), 519-31. Feels that the idea of progress can be most effectively communicated by the sort of education offered by missionaries.

F51 "ICH DIEN." "Religious and Charitable Endowments of Bengal Zemindars," CR:111 (July, Oct. 1900), 79-100, 223-49; 112 (Jan. 1901), 50-77.

F52 INAMDAR, N. R. "Political Thought of Balshastri Jambhekar (1812-1846), The Pioneer of Renaissance in Maharashtra," IJPS:21 (Oct.-Dec. 1960), 321-30. Editor of *The Bombay Durpan*, 1832-40, professor of math at Elphinstone College, 1842-44; biographical sketch included.

F53 "India in England," CR:28 (June 1857), 335-63. On British knowledge of India.

F54 IYER, RAGHAVAN N. "La puissance britannique comme véhicule de la civilisation européenne en Inde" [British Power as a Vehicle of European Civilization in India], Co:13/14 (1955), 71-80. Translated from the English by G. Meyer.

F55 ———. "Utilitarianism and All That (The Political Theory of British Imperialism in India)," SAA:1, 9-71. A critique of the utilitarian justifications for imperialism, analyzed in 4 strands: Burke's "Moral code," Bentham's "Programme," Plato's "Attitude of mind," and Wilberforce's "Transcendental sanction and belief in oneself"; also the ideas and methods of Indian nationalism as shaped by reaction to these ideas.

F56 ———. "Utilitarianism and Empire in India," L:63 (March 24, 1960), 526-27. Intellectual history.

F57 JAY, EDWARD JOAQUIM. "Revitalization Movements in India," AT:5 (1956), 46-74. A history of revivalist, reformist, and messianic movements among the Munda tribes of Central India.

F58 "K. N." "Ramananda Chatterjee: a Biographical Assessment," MR: 117 (May 1965), 36-75. Founder of MR.

F59 KABIR, HUMAYUN. "Indian Muslims," CHM:2 (1954), 476-84. Ruminations on the Hindu-Muslim synthesis and the British impact on it.

F60 KEDROVA, S. M. "O sotsiologicheskoi i filosofskoi mysli Indii vtoroi poloviny 19. veka" [On the Sociological and Philosophical Thought in India in the Second Half of the 19th Century], VIMK:5 (1959), 110-22. Summary in HA:6 (1960) (No. 370).

F61 KEENE, H. G. "Conflict of Civilizations in India," NC:63 (June 1908), 1022-30. Against the "occidentalizing tendency" of English education.

F62 KENNEDY, VANS. "Remarks on the 6th and 7th Chapters of Mill's 'History of British India,' Respecting the Religion and Manners of the Hindus," LSBT:3 (1823), Old ed., 117-71; New ed., 125-82.

F63 KETKAR, VENKATESH BAPUJI. "Indian and Foreign Chronology," RASB (Extra No., 1923), pp. 1-214. 40 tables on pp. 171-212, to be used in calculations for B.C. 3102 to 2100 A.D. Bibliography of 10 useful items, pp. 166-68.

F64 KHAN, M. SIDDIQ. "The Early History of Bengali Printing," LQ: 32 (Jan. 1962), 51-61. Good study on printing in Bengali before the Serampore enterprise; uses Bengali sources.

F65 KNIGHTON, W. "Young Bengal at Home," CoR:38 (Dec. 1880), 888-97. Describes them as "the Athenians of India."

F66 KRISHNAMURTI. "Dr. Johnson and India," BUJ:17 (Sept. 1948), 65-71. On Johnson's interest in India; from letters and Boswell's *Life*.

F67 LYALL, A. C. "The Religious Situation in India," FR:18 (Aug. 1872), 151-65. A view of the number and varieties of religion and the British impact thereon.

F68 MADGE, E. W. and DHAR, K. N. "Some Illustrated Works on India," CR:270 (Oct. 1912), 355-79.

F69 MITRA, S. C. "[Auto-]Biographical Sketch," MR:112 (July 1962), 67-70. A psychologist; gives outline of growth of psychology as a subject in Indian universities.

F70 [MITTRA], S. "Kissory Chand Mittra," CR:124 (April 1907), 229-52.

F71 ———. "Peary Chand Mittra," CR:120 (April 1905), 237-60.

F72 "Modern Progress in India," CR:100 (Jan. 1895), 121-31. Review of P. N. Bose, *History of Hindu Civilization During British Rule*.

F73 MORAES, FRANCIS. "Dr. Swaminatha Aiyar, Editor and Writer," TC:4 (Jan. 1955), 40-52. D. 1942.

F74 MUKERJI, D. P. "The Intellectuals in India," Con:4 (Jan. 1956), 443-55. Their psychology.

F75 MUKERJI, K. "The Renaissance in Bengal and Maharashtrian Thought from 1850 to 1920," AV:4 (Dec. 1962), 331-42. An economic-class interpretation.

F76 MUKHERJEA, SISIR KUMAR. "India in Russian Literature," IAL: NS 19 (1945), 24-32.

F77 MUKHERJEE, HARIDAS. "The Dawn Society of Calcutta (1902-1907)," MR:93 (May 1953), 399-403. A society to supplement the religious and moral instruction of college students and to counter their passivity.

F78 MUKHERJEE, PRABHAT. "The Konarak Temple in the Nineteenth Century," OHRJ:7 (April 1958), 56-60. Snatches of descriptions of it.

F79 MUKHERJEE, S. N. "Sir William Jones and the British Attitudes towards India," RAS (April 1964), pp. 37-47.

F80 MUKHERJEE, SUJIT. "Early American Images of India," IQ:20 (Jan.-March 1964), 43-50. 19th cent.

F81 NAIDIS, MARK. "Evolution of the Sahib," Hn:19 (Aug. 1957), 425-35. A survey of the Anglo-Indian cultural outlook.

F82 ———. "Henty's Idea of India," VS:8 (Sept. 1964), 49-58. George Alfred Henty wrote adventure stories.

F83 PARULEKAR, R. V. "Literacy of India in Pre-British Days," LSGI: 11 (Oct. 1940), 195-226.

F84 PHILLIMORE, R. H. "The Indian Postage Stamps of 1854-55," IA:8 (July-Dec. 1954), 100-09. The trials and tribulations of Captain Thullier, Deputy Surveyor General, when he undertook the printing of the first postage stamps in India.

F85 POCOCK, D. F. "Notes on the Interaction of English and Indian Thought in the 19th Century," CHM:4 (1958), 833-48.

F86 PRASAD, BENI. "Influence of Modern Thought on India," AAAPSS:233 (May 1944), 46-54.

F87 PURNAIYA, P. N. "The Calendar of Tipu Sultan," IAn:2 (April 1873), 112-15. His own invention.

F88 RANGANATHAN, A. "Ananda K. Coomaraswamy—an Essay in Interpretation," FrA:19 (Oct.-Dec. 1963), 993-999. Intellectual biography.

F89 RASHID, AISHA. "Shibli Numani: A Life Sketch," PR:10 (Sept. 1962), 25-26.

F90 RAWLINSON, H. G. "Indian Influence on the West," MIW, pp. 535-75.

F91 ———. "Indian Influences on Western Culture," RAS (1947), 142-50. A sketch of references in and influence on poetry from Chaucer to Yeats, and a brief survey of influence on Western art.

F92 RAY, SIBNARAYAN. "Decline of the Indian Intellectuals: A Note," Q:19 (Oct.-Dec. 1958), 23-31. A discussion of 20th cent. forces for escape into collectivist ideologies.

F93 ROY, NARESH CHANDRA. "Early Indian Contributors to the Calcutta Review," CR:91 (Cent. No., 1944), 55-68.

F94 SANIAL, S. C. "Captain David Lester Richardson," CR:123 (Jan. 1906), 70-89. Editor and literary figure in Calcutta; principal of Hindu College in mid-19th cent.

F95 SARATH-ROY, A. R. "Kipling Seen through Hindu Eyes," NA:199 (Feb. 1914), 271-81.

F96 SARKAR, JADUNATH. "V. Khare," MR:42 (July 1927), 65-67. Maratha poet, dramatist and historian.

F97 SARKAR, SUSOBHAN CHANDRA. "Derozio and Young Bengal," SBR, pp. 16-32. Lists members of "Young Bengal." Based on Hindu College records.

F98 SARVADHIKARY, DEVAPRASAD. "Kissory Chand Mittra," CR: 42 (March 1932), 327-58. Largely from newspaper and CR files.

F99 SAVYASACHI. "Acharya Kakasaheb Kalekar—Literateur, Educationist, Parliamentarian; Fifty-five Years of Public Service," MR:115 (May 1964), 360-64. Brief biography.

F100 SEN, PRIYARANJAN. "Public Movements in Bengal as Channels of Western Influence," CR:23 (April 1927), 73-91.

F101 ———. "Some Channels of Western Influence in Bengal," CR:20 (Sept. 1926), 428-39. On the law courts and the press.

F102 SENA, VINOD. "The Dilemmas of the Indian Intellectual; a Counter-Statement," Q:26 (July-Sept. 1960), 73-83. Rebuttal of Edward Shils (below).

F103 SHASTRI, HARAPRASAD. "Mm. Haraprasad Shastri," MR:85 (Feb., March 1949), 130-33, 216-19. Autobiographical sketch of Sanskrit and Pali scholar.

F104 SHILS, EDWARD. "The Culture of the Indian Intellectual," SR: 67 (Spring-Summer 1959), 239-61, 401-21; also Q:24 (Jan.-Mar. 1960), 36-49; 25 (April-June 1960), 41-53.

F105 SINHA, MIHIR. "Dwarkanath Tagore, the 'Prince' of the Indian Renaissance," Q:41 (April 1964), 38-45.

F106 SINHA, PRADIP. "The Bengal Victorians: Some Ideas and Attitudes," Q:37 (April 1963), 26-30.

F107 SMITH, GEORGE. "The First Twenty Years of the 'Calcutta Review,'" CR:59 (1874), 215-33.

F108 SMITH, VINCENT A. "James Prinsep," E&W:5 (July 1906), 635-39. A "tribute of affectionate respect."

F109 SPEAR, PERCIVAL. "Bentinck and the Taj," RAS (Oct. 1949), pp. 180-87. On the source of the story that he wished to demolish it.

F110 SUHRAWARDY, ABDULLA AL-MAMUN. "An Indian on Tolstoy," CR:60 (July 1936), 82-83. Translated from the Russian; a "bit of ecstatic prose" written in 1908.

F111 SUTHERLAND, WALTER. "The Founders of the *Calcutta Review*," CR:91 (Cent. No., 1944), 44-54.

F112 THAPAR, ROMILA. "Seminar on Ideas in the 18th and 19th Centuries: a Report," En:NS 1 (Winter 1964), 114-30. "Seminar on Ideas Motivating Social and Religious Movements and Politics and Economic Policy during the 18th and 19th Centuries in India held by the History Department of the Delhi University in November 1963."

F113 TOWNDROW, KENNETH ROMNEY. "Sir William Rothenstein and His Indian Correspondence," IAL:NS 25 (1951), 12-32. Correspondence with E. B. Havell, Ananda K. Coomaraswamy, Rabindranath Tagore.

F114 VON DÖLLINGER, J. "The British Empire in India: a Review of the Life and Works of Garcin de Tassy," CoR:35 (June 1879), 385-403. Address delivered before the Royal Bavarian Academy of Science.

F115 "Young Bengal," BM:75 (June 1854), 648-57. On the grievances of Bengali intellectuals, especially Shoshee Chunder Dutt.

2. *HISTORIOGRAPHY AND ORIENTAL STUDIES*

F116 ABDUL LATIF, SYED. "An Unfinished Masterpiece," MAKA, pp. 116-33. On Maulana Azad's writing the commentary on the Quran, three times; the first two manuscripts were confiscated by the government.

F117 ACHARYA, P. "Short Sketch of Life and Work of Manomohan Chakravarti," OHRJ:6 (July & Oct. 1957), 115-23. Historian of Orissa.

PART I: ARTICLES

F118 ALAEV, L. B. "Izuchenie istorii Indii v SSSR v 1917-1934" [Soviet Studies of the History of India for the Years 1917-1934], NAA:2 (1963), 160-72. Tr. in CAR:12 (1964), 59-66.

F119 ALLCHIN, F. R. "Ideas of History in Indian Archaeological Writing: A Preliminary Study," HIPC, pp. 241-59.

F120 ALSDORF, LUDWIG. "Indian Studies in Germany," IAC:10 (Jan., April 1962), 296-314, 456-61.

F121 ALUR, V. B. "The Necessity of an All-India Historical Association," MR:28 (Dec. 1920), 645-46.

F122 ANSARI, A. S. BAZMEE. "G̲h̲ulām Ḥusayn 'Salim' Zaydpuri," EI:2, 1092. Wrote a history of Bengal, "Riyād al-salāṭīn," completed 1787/88.

F123 ANTONOVA, K. A. [N.M. Gol'dberg. (On his 70th Birthday)], NAA:4 (1961), 253-54. Abstract in SSAB 1:3/4 (1962), 42. On a noted Russian scholar of India.

F124 ARBERRY, A. J. "The Jones Tradition in British Orientalism," IAL:NS 20 (1946), 1-15.

F125 ———. "New Light on Sir William Jones," BSOAS:11 (1946), 673-85. Excerpts from Jones's correspondence, especially on his political views.

F126 ARCHER, MILDRED. "India and Archaeology: The Rôle of the East India Company, 1785-1858," HT:12 (April 1962), 272-79. An illustrated account of early interest in Indian relics.

F127 BAGAL, JOGESH C. "Raja Radhakanta Deb on the Reactionary Attitude of the Europeans in India and the Revival of Sanskrit Learning," MR:72 (Aug. 1942), 157-62. With correspondence printed.

F128 BAL, SARAJIT SINGH. "Cunningham's History of the Sikhs," BPP:82 (July-Dec. 1963), 112-30. Account of the author and background to the manuscript's writing.

F129 BALLHATCHET, K. A. "Some Aspects of Historical Writing on India by Protestant Christian Missionaries during the Nineteenth and Twentieth Centuries," HIPC, pp. 344-53.

F130 BĂNĂṬEANU, VLAD. "First Indianists of the XIX Century in Rumania," IAC:7 (Jan. 1959), 275-82.

F131 ———. "Indian Studies in Rumania in the Past and in the Present," VBQ:27 (1961-62), 239-59.

F132 BAPAT, P. V. "Prof. Dharmanand Kosambi," MR:83 (Feb. 1948), 134-37. Obituary of Pali scholar with bibliography of his works.

F133   BASHAM, A. L. "Modern Historians of Ancient India," HIPC, pp. 260-93.

F134   BASU, P. "The Indian Historical Records Commission," IHRB:21 (1946-48), 27-32. Survey of its work.

F135   BEVERIDGE, H. "The Khurshīd Jahān Numā of Sayyad Ilāhī Bakhsh al Husainī Angrēzābādī," ASB:64 (1895), 194-236. Includes a short biography of the Sayyad, who wrote a Persian history of the world.

F136   "Biographical Sketches of Indian Antiquarians," CR:94 (April 1892), 311-21; 95 (July 1892), 126-47; 96 (Jan. 1893), 98-129.

F137   BISWAS, HARI CHARAN. "Some English Orientalists," CR:128 (Jan. 1909), 64-98. Halhed, Colebrooke, Jones.

F138   CANNON, GARLAND. "The Literary Place of Sir William Jones (1746-94)," ASB, Ser. 4:2 (1960), 47-61. An assessment of his influence on English and European literature.

F139   CASE, MARGARET H. "The Historical Craftsmanship of W. H. Moreland (1868-1938)," IESHR:2 (July 1965), 245-58. With bibliography of his works.

F140   CHAKRAVARTI, CHINTAHARAN. "Mahamahopadhyaya Haraprasad Sastri," MR:50 (Dec. 1931), 686-89. Biography of a pioneer in Indology.

F141   CHAKRAVARTY, SURATH. "Prof. Max Muller and the Contemporary Indian Savants," MR:96 (July 1954), 56-59. Their relationship.

F142   CHATTERJEE, RAMANANDA. "Baman Das Basu," MR:48 (Dec. 1930), 667-75. Author of *Rise of the Christian Power in India.*

F143   CHATTERJI, SUNITI KUMAR., "Sir William Jones: 1746-1794," SWJ, pp. 81-96. Biography and appreciation of his work.

F144   [COLEBROOKE]. "Notices of the Life of Henry Thomas Colebrooke, Esq., by his Son," RAS:5 (1839), 1-60. Biography, with letters and list of works.

F145   CUTTS, ELMER H. "Early Nineteenth Century Chinese Studies in Bengal," IHQ:20 (June 1944), 114-31. On the establishment on Chinese studies as an early part of studies in Fort William College and at Serampore.

F146   ———. "Political Implications in Chinese Studies in Bengal 1800-1823," IHQ:34 (June 1958), 152-63.

F147   DAS, G. N. "John Marshall, 1876-1958," AA:61 (Dec. 1959), 1071-74. Biographical sketch.

F148   DAS GUPTA, N. N. "D. R. Bhandarkar (Eminent Indian Historians Series), QRHS 5:1 (1965/66), 37.

F149   DAS GUPTA, R. K. "Macaulay's Writings on India," HIPC, pp. 230-40.

F150   "The Dawn of Indian Research," CR:100 (Jan. 1895), 1-24.

F151   [DAY]. "Lal Behari Day (1824-1894)," F:3 (July 1962), 322-32. Biography of him as a folklorist.

F152   DE, BARUN. "A Preliminary Note on the Writing of the History of Modern India," QRHS:3 (No. 1/2, 1963-1964), 39-46. Historiography of 18th and early 19th cent.

F153   ———. "Sardar K. M. Panikkar," BPP:83 (Jan. 1964), 69-74. Brief biography.

F154   [DE]. "Chandrakumar De (1881-1946)," F:3 (Nov. 1962), 540-44. Folklorist.

F155   DEJONG, J. W. "Sanskrit Studies in the Netherlands," IAC:5 (April 1957), 421-27. Brief historical account.

F156   DERRETT, J. D. M. "J. H. Nelson: A Forgotten Administrator-Historian of India," HIPC, pp. 354-72.

F157   DEY, SHUMBHOO CHUNDER. "Dwarka Nath Mitter: A Biography," CR:263 (Jan. 1911), 65-111; 264 (April 1911), 212-50.

F158   DIGHE, V. G. "Modern Historical Writing in Marathi," HIPC, pp. 473-80.

F159   DOVER, CEDRIC. "The Cultural Significance of Col. James Skinner," CR:134 (Jan. 1955), 18-24. On Skinner's manuscript materials on Indian manners and history, with illustrations of the illuminations.

F160   [DU PERRON]. "Anquetil du Perron," CR:103 (Oct. 1896), 284-305.

F161   [DUTT]. "Gurusaday Dutt (1882-1941)," F:3 (Sept. 1962), 424-32. Folklorist.

F162   FILLIOZAT, JEAN. "France and Indology," IAC:5 (Jan. 1957), 296-313. Brief account of French Indologists.

F163   FORREST, GEORGE. "Sir Alfred Lyall," BM:193 (May 1913), 698-715. Biographical sketch of ICS man and scholar.

F164 FURBER, HOLDEN. "The Theme of Imperialism and Colonialism in Modern Historical Writing on India," HIPC, pp. 332-43.

F165 GAMAYUNOV, L. S. "Gerasim Lebedev: 'The Founder of Russian Indology,'" CAR:11 (1963), 288-96. Abridged translation of article on the 18th cent. Russian.

F166 GERMANUS, GYULA. "Hungarian Orientalists—Past and Present," IAC:6 (Jan. 1958), 291-98.

F167 GHOSH, DEVA PRASAD. "Indian Historical Art and Archaeological Studies in the Calcutta University," CR:93 (July 1944), 31-37. Summary of work being done in the university and museums.

F168 GLAMANN, K. "Danish Historical Writing on Colonial Activities in Asia, 1616-1845," HIPC, pp. 209-17.

F169 GOKHALE, D. N. "Dr. S. V. Ketkar: A Study," JUP:1 (1953), 167-71. Outline of a Ph.D. dissertation on the life and work of a writer on caste.

F170 GRIERSON, G. A. "On the Early Study of Indian Vernaculars in Europe," ASB:62 (1893), 41-52. Cites mostly 18th cent. scholars.

F171 HABIBULLAH, A. B. M. "Historical Writing in Urdu: a Survey of Tendencies," HIPC, pp. 481-96.

F172 HARDY, P. "Modern Muslim Historical Writing on Medieval Muslim India," HIPC, pp. 294-309.

F173 HARRISON, J. B. "Notes on W. H. Moreland as Historian," HIPC, pp. 310-18.

F174 HARTOG, P. J. "The Origins of the School of Oriental Studies," BSOS:1 (1917), 5-22.

F175 HASAN, NAZIR. "Garcin de Tassy (a French devotee of Urdu)," PR:10 (April 1962), 21-22. A brief but useful account of his work.

F176 HEIN, NORVIN J. (comp.). "A Bibliography of the Writings of John Clark Archer," MW:50 (1960), 207-12. On Islamic and Indian subjects.

F177 "Historiography: India and the West (a seminar)," ITC:2 (1962), 253-308. Paper by N. Subrahmanian, followed by discussion.

F178 [HODGSON]. "Brian Houghton Hodgson (1800-1894)," EB:13, 557. Biographical sketch of soldier and Orientalist.

F179 IMAM, ABU. "Sir Alexander Cunningham (1814-1893): The First Phase of Indian Archaeology," RAS (Oct. 1963), 194-207.

F180   INAYATULLAH, DR. " 'Amelie Sedillot' (1808-1875 A.D.)," PHS: 9 (Jan. 1961), 30-35. Brief biography of French Orientalist.

F181   "The Indian Museum and the Asiatic Society of Bengal," CR 43:86 (1866), 427-60.

F182   "The International Congress of Orientalists, London, 1874," CR 60:120 (1875), 233-68.

F183   ISLAM, ZAFAR UL-. "Historical Research in the Punjab," PPHC: 5 (1955), 111-21. 1849-1947.

F184   JONES, WILLIAM. "Discourse on the Institution of a Society for Enquiring into the History, Civil and Natural, and Antiquities, Arts, Sciences and Literature of Asia," AsR:1 (1788), ix-xvi.

F185   [JONES]. "Sir William Jones—His Life and Writings," CR:6 (1846), 190-240.

F186   "K.S.M." "Two Distinguished Sanskrit Scholars of Cochin," CR:132 (Jan., April 1911), 112-22, 134-40. On B. K. N. N. N. Avergal and M. R. R. V. G. R. Avergal.

F187   KARMAKAR, KALI CHARAN. "Anquetil Duperron and India," BPP:77 (July-Dec. 1958), 83-98. The life, travels, and studies in India of an eminent French Orientalist of the 18th cent.

F188   KOTVICH, M. V. "Oriental Studies in Petrograd between 1918 and 1922," BSOS:3 (1925), 643-57. Lists organizations concerned with oriental studies, with their membership and publications; schools, libraries, museums, monuments, and list of Petrograd Orientalists with their birth dates and specialty; also list of Petrograd Orientalists residing elsewhere and list of deceased Orientalists.

F189   KUNST, ARNOLD. "Indian Studies in Poland: Stanislaw Schayer," IAC:7 (Oct. 1958), 148-64. A few biographical details.

F190   LEHMANN, ARNO. "Karl Graul, the Nineteenth Century Dravidologist," TC:11 (July 1964), 209-25.

F191   [MACKENSIE]. [Biography of Col. Mackensie], MJLS:2 (1834), 262-90, 354-69.

F192   [MAINE]. "Life and Speeches of Sir Henry Maine," QR:176 (April 1893), 288-316.

F193   MAJUMDAR, A. K. "William Carey and Pandit Vaidyanath," ASB, Ser. 4:1 (1959), 233-44. Letters about Vaidyanath, Marathi scholar and translator at Ft. William College.

F194   [MAJUMDAR]. "Kedarnath Majumdar (1277-1333 B.S.)," F:3 (June 1962), 282-88. Folklorist.

F195 MAJUMDAR, R. C. "Nationalist Historians," HIPC, pp. 416-28.

F196 MALLICK, A. R. "Modern Historical Writing in Bengali," HIPC, pp. 446-60.

F197 MARRIOTT, J. A. R. "A Great Anglo-Indian: Sir William Wilson Hunter and His Work," FR:73 (Jan.-June 1900), 1033-44. Analysis of his methods and approach to Indian studies.

F198 MASHTAKOVA, K. A. "Books on India in the Office and Apartment of V. I. Lenin in the Kremlin," NAA:5 (1963), 159-61. Cited in SPA:4 (June 1964), 126. On Lenin's interest in India and vice versa.

F199 MASTER, ALFRED. "The Influence of Sir William Jones upon Sanskrit Studies," BSOAS:11 (1946), 798-806.

F200 MITRA, RAJENDRALAL. "Raja Rajendralal Mitra and Archaeological Survey of Orissa," CR:17 (Nov. 1925), 302-04. A short letter to the Lt.-Governor of Bengal, dated April 16, 1868.

F201 [MITRA]. "Saratchandra Mitra (1863-1938)," F:2 (April 1962), 185-89. Folklorist, anthropologist.

F202 MITRA, SARAT CHANDRA. "Biographical Sketches of Indian Antiquarians: Professor Rāmkrishna Gopāl Bhāndārkar," CR:129 (July 1909), 354-79.

F203 [MITRA-MAJUMDAR]. "Dakshinaranjan Mitra-Majumdar (1877-1957)," F:3 (May 1962), 235-40. Folklorist.

F204 MODI, JIVANJI JAMSHEDJI. "Anquetil du Perron of Paris and Dastur Durab of Surat," RASB 24:69 (1915-16), 385-456.

F205 ———. "Anquetil du Perron of Paris—India as Seen by Him (1755-60)," RASB 24:69 (1915-16), 313-81. A useful study of Anquetil's account and related sources.

F206 ———. "A Few Notes on Broach from an Antiquarian Point of View," RASB:22 (1905), 298-323. Pp. 309-23 deal with the period after the English reconquest of 1772.

F207 MOOKERJEE, ASUTOSH. "The History of the Indian Museum," CR:275 (Jan. 1914), 1-21. In Calcutta.

F208 MUKHERJEE, HARIDAS. "Benoy Sarkar as a Pioneer in Neo-Indology," MR:87 (Feb. 1950), 134-38.

F209 MUKHERJEE, NILMANI. "Romesh Chunder Dutt (1848-1909)," QRHS 3:4 (1963-64), 183-88. As an historian.

F210 MÜLLER, MAX. "Classical Studies in India," CoR:18 (Sept. 1871), 141-51. Survey of the revival in classical studies.

F211 NADEL', KH. S. "Indologiia v KHar'kovskom universitete za poltora veka (istoriko-bibliograficheskii ocherk)" [Indology at Kharkov University for a Century and a Half (a Historico-Bibliographical Sketch)], NAA:2 (1964), 169-73.

F212 NAG, KALIDAS. "The Asiatic Society of Bengal. A Survey of 150 Years' Work," AP:4 (Oct. 1933), 668-74. A very brief survey.

F213 NAKAMURA, HAJIME. "Indian Studies in Japan," IAC:4 (April 1956), 425-39.

F214 NOBEL, JOH. "The Study of Indian Philology at the German Universities," MR:33 (Feb. 1923), 167-72.

F215 "The Oriental Congresses," CR:68 (1879), 221-50. On conferences at St. Petersburg, 1876, and Florence, 1878.

F216 [ORME]. "An Authentic Account of the Life and Character of the Late Robert Orme, Esq., F.A.S. Historiographer to the Honorable the East India Company," AAR:4 (1802), "Characters" 45-55.

F217 PANIKKAR, K. M. "The Understanding of Indian History," TC:5 (July 1956), 35-54. On approaches to Indian history.

F218 "Past and Present: A Symposium on the Attitudes and Approaches to a Study of Our History," Se:39 (Nov. 1962), 10-52.

F219 PHILIPS, C. H. "James Mill, Mountstuart Elphinstone, and the History of India," HIPC, pp. 217-29.

F220 PINTO, V. DE SOLA. "Sir William Jones and English Literature," BSOAS:11 (1946), 686-94. His influence on English literature.

F221 POBOZNIAK, TADEUSZ. "Indian Studies in a Polish University," IL:6 (1963), 14-26. History of teaching on India at Cracow (Jagellonian) University.

F222 [POLIER]. "An Early Orientalist, Colonel Anthony Polier," BPP:39 (Jan.-June 1930), 59-61. French orientalist.

F223 POLLOCK, FREDERICK. "Sir Henry James Sumner Maine (1822-1888)," EB:17, 432-33. Life and works of comparative jurist and historian.

F224 POTTS, E. DANIEL. "British Missionary Archives and the Asian Historian," JAS:24 (Aug. 1965), 645-51. On some materials in the Baptist Missionary Society archives.

F225 RAHIM, M. A. "Historian Ghulām Ḥusain Ṭabātabāi," ASP:8 (Dec. 1963), 117-29. Wrote bad history covering 1707-81.

F226 RAO, P. SUBBA. "Rao Bahadur Rangacharya, M. A.—Scholar, Scientist, Educator," HR:31 (Feb. 1915), 186-96. A Sanskritist.

F227 [RAYCHAUDHURI]. "Upendrakisor Raychaudhuri (1863-1915),"
F:3 (Dec. 1962), 585-88. Folklorist, grandfather of Satyajit Ray.

F228 REICHMAN, JAN. "Wspólczesna historiografia burzuazyjna w
zakresie banań nad wschodem" [Contemporary Bourgeois Historiography
and Oriental Studies], PO:4 (1955), 373-86. Summary in HA:4 (No.
808): "On the basis of an examination of such works as Graisset's
History of China, Toynbee's *A Study of History*, Fitzgerald's *China, a
Short Cultural History*, and Heimann's *Indian and Western Philosophy*,
notes the following characteristics of bourgeois Oriental historiography:
1) The rejection of Marxist research methods; 2) ideography; 3) emphasis on the deterministic effect of geography, race and ideology (religion); and 4) stress on the importance of the role of outstanding personalities."

F229 ROSU, ARION. "India in Rumanian Culture," IAC:8 (Jan.
1960), 276-91. Largely on 19th cent. contacts.

F230 [ROY]. "Obituary of Rai Bahadur Sarat Chandra Roy," BORS:28
(1942), 214-16. Founder of "Man in India."

F231 ROY CHOUDHURY, P. C. "The Story of the Gazetteers," MR:114
(Dec. 1963), 448-51.

F232 "The Royal Asiatic Society," CR 60:119 (1875), 37-58. Brief
history.

F233 "The Royal Asiatic Society of Bengal," MR:65 (Feb. 1939), 194-
200.

F234 RUBEN, W. "Indological Studies in the German Democratic Republic," VBQ:27 (1961-62), 197-211.

F235 SANDESARA, B. J. "Shri C. D. Dalal, First Editor and Principal Organiser of the Gaekwad's Oriental Series," MSUB:12 (Dec. 1962),
184-86.

F236 SARANA, GOPALA. "Dhirendra Nath Majumdar (1903-1960),"
EA:14 (May-Aug. 1961), 105-21. Founder of EA; bibliography of his
works.

F237 SARDESI, G. S. "Historian's Story," MR:118 (July 1965), 62-64.
Autobiographical.

F238 SARKAR, KSHITISH CHANDRA. "A Forgotten Historian and
Antiquarian: The Late Akshay Kumar Maitra," MR:113 (Feb. 1963),
159-62. In Bengali archaeology and literature.

F239 [SEN]. "Deneschandra Sen (1866-1939)," F:3 (Aug. 1962), 371-
84. Folklorist.

F240 SEN, PRIYARANJAN. "Rama Raja," MR:49 (Feb. 1931), 156-57. Pioneer in the history of ancient Indian architecture.

F241 SEN, S. N. "Why Tod Resigned?" IHRC:21 (1944), 94-96. Prints a letter by him, dated Feb. 18, 1822.

F242 SEN, S. P. "French Historical Writing on European Activities in India," HIPC, pp. 183-208.

F243 SHAFI, MOHAMMAD. "'Abd al-Karīm Kashmīri," EI:1, 71-72, Indo-Persian historian; wrote history of Nadir Shah's invasion.

F244 ———. "'Abd al-Karīm Munshi," EI:1, 72. Mid-19th cent. Indo-Persian historian from Lucknow or Cawnpur.

F245 ———. "Bahr al-'Ulūm ('Ocean of the Sciences')," EI:1, 936-37. Honorific title of Lucknow savant (1731/32-1810), who spent his last 15 years in Madras. List of his works given.

F246 SHARMA, RAM SHARAN. "Ideological Basis of Research on Ancient Indian Polity up to 1930," PU:8 (March-June 1954), 81-90. Analysis of 19th and 20th cent. Indian and Western scholars' conceptions of the Indian past.

F247 SINGH, H. L. "Modern Historical Writing in Hindi," HIPC, pp. 461-72.

F248 SLUSZKIEWICZ, EUGENIUSZ. "Indic Studies in Poland," IAC: 7 (April 1959), 412-22.

F249 SMITH, W. CANTWELL. "Modern Muslim Historical Writing in English," HIPC, pp. 319-31.

F250 SPEAR, T. G. P. "British Historical Writing in the Era of the Nationalist Movements," HIPC, pp. 404-15.

F251 SRINIVASACHARIAR, C. S. "European Pioneer Studies in South Indian Languages," BV:5 (1944), 71-86. Writers and their works are mentioned.

F252 ———. "The Promotion of Dravidian Linguistic Studies in the Company's Days," IAn:56 (1927), 1-9.

F253 ———. "Robert Orme and Colin Mackenzie—Two Early Collectors of Manuscripts and Records," IHRC:6 (1924), 84-96. Biographical sketches.

F254 SRIVASTAVA, A. L. "The Historian Sir Jadunath Sarkar," UB:5 (July 1958), 1-7. Biography and appreciation.

F255 STOKES, E. T. "The Administrators and Historical Writing on India," HIPC, pp. 385-403.

F256   TAYLOR, W. "Reports on the Mackenzie MSS," MJLS:7 (1839), 1-51, 277-378; 8 (1840), 1-86, 215-305; 9 (1841), 1-52, 313-76, 452; 10 (1842), 1-42, 388-442; 11 (1843), 86-125; 13 (1845), a57-115; 14 (1846), b112-59; 15 (1847), 173-90; 16 (1848), 55-101; 17 (1849), 277.

F257   TEMPLE, R. C. "Dr. William Crooke, C.I.E., D.S.C., Litt.D., F.B.A.," IAn:53 (Feb. 1924), 21-22. Editor of many books.

F258   TIKEKAR, R. S. (Collector). "Autobiographical Notes: Sir Jadunath Sarkar," MR:113 (March 1963), 218-20.

F259   VESEY-FITZGERALD, S. G. "Sir William Jones, the Jurist," BSOAS:11 (1946), 807-17. Credits him with being the forerunner of the historical and comparative school of English legal philosophy.

F260   WADIA, D. N. "Sir Jeevanjee Jamshedji Modi (1854-1933)," ASBP (1933), cxxviii-cxxxi. Obituary notice of Parsi orientalist, with list of works.

F261   WAGLE, N. B. "Bhau Daji (Ramkrishna Vithal)," EB:3, 845. Hindu physician of Bombay, Sanskrit scholar, and antiquarian.

F262   WHITE, EDITH M. (ed.). "Bibliography of the Published Writings of Dr. L. D. Barnett," BSOAS:12 (1948), 497-523. Librarian of the School of Oriental and African Studies, 1940-1947.

F263   WHYNANT, NEVILLE. "School of Oriental and African Studies," EaW:6 (July 1952), 36. Brief history of the school.

F264   "X." "Sanskritic Studies in Russia," MR:40 (July 1926), 74-75.

3. LIBRARIES

F265   ASADULLAH, K. M. "The Imperial Library, Calcutta," MR:49 (June 1931), 690-93.

F266   BANERJEE, B. N. "Beginnings of Public Libraries in Bengal," CR:84 (July 1942), 65-74.

F267   BOSE, BANI. "A Short History of the National Library," MR:93 (Feb., March 1953), 128-32, 207-10.

F268   BOSE, PRAMIL CHANDRA. "School and College Libraries in the Evolution of Education in Modern India," CR:174 (Jan. 1965), 71-86.

F269   CASSIDY, JAMES. "A Little Known and Remarkable Library," E&W:4 (April 1905), 473-85. On the India Office Library.

F270   "Catalogue of Tipoo's Library," ER:12 (July 1809), 322-32. On a book by Charles Stewart.

F271 DAS, SATYAJIT. "The Press and Registration of Books Act, 1867," ILA:4 (July-Dec. 1962), 96-107. On regulations for depositing books in the National Library.

F272 "Descriptive Notes on Libraries," ASB:NS 13 (1917), lxxx-lxxxviii. On libraries in Lucknow, Benares, Madras, Hyderabad, Deccan, Rampur.

F273 DHAR, K. N. "The Imperial Library, Calcutta," CR:299 (Jan. 1920), 67-80. A brief history.

F274 HOSAIN, HIDAYAT. "The Founders of the Buhar Library," IC:7 (Jan. 1933), 125-46. An account of the founders, the Mir Munshi of Warren Hastings and his great grandson, together with a description of some of the Persian manuscripts in the collection.

F275 "The Library of Tīpū Sultān," IC:14 (Jan. 1940), 139-64. Description of contents.

F276 PRABHU, R. K. "The Baroda Central Library," MR:10 (Dec. 1911), 571-80. History.

F277 PRIOLKAR, A. K. "The Origin and Development of the Library Movement in the Bombay Presidency," IHCP:10 (1947), 500-16. Includes correspondence.

F278 "S.T." "Library Movement in India," MR:91 (April 1952), 309-10.

F279 SHARMA, O. P. "History of the Development of the University Libraries in India—an Appraisal," ILn:19 (Dec. 1964), 128-43. Author on staff of Library of Congress.

4. EDUCATION: GENERAL, ELEMENTARY, AND SECONDARY

F280 ABDUL ALI, A. F. M. "Haji Mohammed Mohsin," MsR:2 (July-Sept. 1927), 34-37. 1730-c.1806; his bequest supported Hughli College and Muslim education.

F281 ALI, S. WAJID. "Pathsala," CR:18 (Feb. 1926), 331-41. Memories of school in a Bengali village.

F282 ANDREWS, C. F. "Munshi Zaka Ullah: A Great Educationist," MR:9 (April 1911), 351-57.

F283 BAGAL, JOGESH CHANDRA. "The Bethune School," MR:85 (June 1949), 468-72. Pioneer women's educational institution of Calcutta, founded May 7, 1849.

F284 ———. "David Hare and the Beginnings of English Education in India," MR:53 (Jan. 1933), 34-36.

F285 ———. "David Hare as a Promoter of Education in India," MR: 55 (Jan. 1934), 46-49.

F286 BAGAL, JOGESH CHANDRA. "Steering through the Storm (1928-35)," MR:88 (Sept. 1950), 227-31. History of Bethune Vidyalaya, 1928-1935.

F287 ———. "Three Pioneer Free Institutions in Calcutta," MR:90 (Sept. 1951), 229-35. The Anglo-Hindu School, Union School, Hare's School.

F288 ———. "Primary Education in Calcutta. Mainly Based on the Manuscript Proceedings of the Calcutta School Society," BPP:81 (July-Dec. 1962), 83-95.

F289 BAIJNATH, LALA. "The Problem of Indian Education," MR:16 (Dec. 1914), 544-56. Statistics from a government publication of 1911-12.

F290 BALIGA, B. S. "Some Aspects of Education in Madras in the Early Nineteenth Century," IHRC:25 (Dec. 1948), 42-47.

F291 [BALLANTYNE]. "Dr. Ballantyne and Government Education," CR 25:50 (1855), 305-22.

F292 BALLHATCHET, KENNETH A. "The Home Government and Bentinck's Educational Policy," CHJ:10 (1951), 224-29; also note, "John Stuart Mill and Indian Education," CHJ:11 (1954), 228. Argues that educational policy was made in India, not England.

F293 BANERJI, BRAJENDRANATH. "Ishwarchandra Vidyasagar as a Promoter of Female Education in Bengal. Based on Unpublished State Records," ASB:NS 23 (1927), 381-97.

F294 ———. "Ishwarchandra Vidyasagar as an Educationist," MR:42 (Sept., Oct. 1927), 256-62, 399-406. Based on unpublished records.

F295 ———. "Ishwar Chandra Vidyasagar as an Unofficial Adviser of the Government," MR:48 (Sept. 1930), 267-71.

F296 ———. "Rammohun Roy as an Educational Pioneer (Based on State Records)," BORS 16:2 (1930), 154-75. Reprints letter of Sir Hyde East, 1816, describing the foundation of Hindu College; also contemporary reports of the English school at Suripara.

F297 ———. "Vidyasagar and Vernacular Education," MR:43 (May, June 1928), 537-41, 650-57.

F298 BANERJI, ROMESH CHANDRA. "Caste Distinction in Educational Reports," MR:52 (July 1932), 60-66.

F299 ———. "The Muhammadans and the Education Policy of the Government," MR:50 (Nov. 1931), 544-47. With statistics.

F300 BASAK, N. L. "Origin and Role of the Calcutta School Book Society in Promoting the Cause of Education in India, Especially Vernacular Education in Bengal (1817-1835)," BPP:78 (Jan.-June 1959), 30-69. Appendixes with lists of donors and subscribers, list of books delivered 1821-35, lists of books printed and distributed; brief discussion of society's impact.

F301 BASU, ANATHNATH. "Education in the Early Pages of the *Calcutta Review* (Old Series)," CR:91 (Cent. No., 1944), 92-98. List of articles and some remarks on missionary attitudes.

F302 ———. "Hundred Years of Western Education in India," CR:56 (July 1935), 1-14, 57 (Oct. 1935), 15-24.

F303 ———. "Literacy in Bengal in the Early British Period," MR:66 (Aug. 1939), 157-60.

F304 ———. "Women's Education in India in the 19th and 20th Centuries," CR:60 (July 1936), 67-80.

F305 BOSE, JOGINDRANATH. "History of English Education in Bengal," MR:10 (Nov. 1911), 459-68.

F306 BOWEN, JOHN. "The East India Company's Education of Its Own Servants," RAS (1955), pp. 105-23. Debates over education up to 1830, and standards set therein.

F307 BROWNING, C. H. "Secondary Education in Bengal," CR:123 (Jan. 1906), 91-113.

F308 ———. "Student Life in India," CR:121 (July 1905), 319-37.

F309 CAMPBELL, A. D., BALFOUR, E. and others. "Education of Natives in India," MJLS:1 (1833), 350-59; 3 (1835), 101-15; 16 (1848?), 380-400.

F310 CHAR, S. RAMA. "Education in Hyderabad," MR:66 (Aug. 1939), 177-81. Statistical analysis.

F311 CHATTOPADHYAY, S. K. "Prof. Zachariah: The Teacher and the Man," CR:161 (Nov. 1961), 167-72. Biographical sketch and recollections by a student.

F312 CHAUDHARY, V. C. P. "The Government of India and Its Educational Policy (1876-80)," BRS:46 (1960), 193-211. Lytton's policy.

F313 "Corporation of Madras Education," LSGI:23 (Oct. 1952), 149-88. A very short history.

F314 "The Council of Education and Lord Hardinge's Minute," CR:15 (1851), 299-319.

F315 COVERNTON, A. L. "The Educational Policy of Mountstuart Elphinstone," BRAS:NS 2 (Aug. 1926), 53-73. Based on government records.

F316 CUNNINGHAM, J. R. "Education," MIW, pp. 138-87. Its history under the British.

F317 CUTTS, E. H. "The Background of Macaulay's Minute," AHR:58 (1953), 824-53. Largely on the missionary background.

F318 DAS, TARAKNATH. "Education of Indians in Foreign Countries," CR:97 (Nov. 1945), 41-47.

F319 DATTA, JATINDRA MOHAN. "The Moslems' Educational 'Disabilities' and the Resumption Proceedings of 1828," MR:54 (Oct. 1933), 451-53.

F320 DATTA, V. N. "Evidence of Unpublished Documents on C. E. Trevelyan's Ideas on Education," IHRC:35 (Feb. 1960), 77-81.

F321 DE, B. "The Educational Systems Adopted and the Results Achieved in the More Important Native States in India," MR:9 (Jan. 1911), 61-71.

F322 DE, S. K. "Ninety-five years of Secondary Education under the University of Calcutta," CR:156 (Aug.-Sept. 1960), 193-213.

F323 ———. "Women's Education in Bengal from the Battle of Plassey to Sepoy Mutiny," CR:161 (Dec. 1961), 255-65.

F324 DESAI, DHANWANT M. "Comparative Primary Education in the Province of Bombay (1893-1947)," LSGI:19 (April 1949), 262-314; 20 (July 1949), 49-80. Traces development in Bombay and other parts of India.

F325 "The Early or Exclusively Oriental Period of Government Education in Bengal," CR:3 (1845), 211-63.

F326 "East Indian Education, and the 'Doveton Colleges,'" CR:24 (1855), 288-330. On education for Indians.

F327 "Education and Hinduism in Bengal," CR:87 (July 1888), 20-36.

F328 "The Education Despatch of 1854," MR:11 (April 1912), 345-51.

F329 "Education in Bengal," CR 40:79 (1864), 138-62; 51:102 (1870), 364-80; 96 (Jan. 1893), 152-63.

F330 "Education in Madras," CR:27 (Sept. 1856), 234-76; 56:112 (1873), 326-51.

F331 "Education in the Punjab," CR:37 (Sept. 1861), 66-86.

F332 "Education of Indians (1833-1853)," MR:7 (Feb. 1910), 174-85; 11 (March 1912), 257-67.

F333 "Education of the Poor," ER:17 (Nov. 1910), 58-88. Cites Bell's school in Madras which was based on Charles Lancaster's system.

F334 "The Educational Establishment of Calcutta, Past and Present," CR:13 (1850), 442-67.

F335 "Educational Reform in Bengal," CR:86 (Jan. 1888), 67-76.

F336 "Elementary Education in Madras," CR 54:107 (1872), 54-65.

F337 EMMOTT, D. H. "Alexander Duff and the Foundation of Modern Education in India," BJES:13 (May 1965), 160-69.

F338 FISHER, THOMAS. "Memoir on Education of Indians," BPP:18 (Jan.-June 1919), 73-156; 19 (July-Dec. 1919), 99-202. Reprint of a memoir compiled in 1827 and 1832.

F339 FRASER, ANDREW H. L. "The Educational Policy of the Government of India," CoR:103 (April 1913), 519-24. On a resolution of the Government of India, Feb. 21, 1913.

F340 ———. "European Education in India," CoR:100 (Oct. 1911), 493-500. Education of Anglo-Indians.

F341 GHOSAL, HARI RANJAN. "An Interesting Chapter in the History of the Company's Educational Policy," IHCP:14 (1951), 229-32. Discussion in the 1830's about the education of zamindar sons.

F342 GHOSE, BENOY. "Iswar Chandra Vidyasagar," SBR, pp. 47-55.

F343 GHOSE, HEMENDRA PRASAD. "The Moslems' Educational 'Disabilities' and the Resumption Proceedings of 1828," MR:54 (Sept. 1933), 297-99.

F344 GHOSE, N. N. "English Education in India from a Native Point of View," CR 78:156 (1884), 327-44.

F345 GHOSH, J. C. "The Educational Leader," MAKA, pp. 101-15. On Maulana Azad's work as Minister of Education.

F346 GHURYE, G. S. "The Financing of Primary Education in Bombay City," BUJ:5 (July 1936), 71-90. Historical survey.

F347 GOVER, CHARLES E. "Pyal Schools in Madras," IAn:2 (Feb. 1873), 52-56. The village schools.

F348 "Government Education," CR:37 (Dec. 1861), 194-224.

F349 GROWSE, F. S. "Hindi School-Literature in the North-Western Provinces," CR 59:118 (1874), 259-72.

F350 GUPTA, HIRALAL. "Gleanings from the Personal Correspondence of Rai Rao Krishna Rao," JIH:30 (April 1952), 9-16. The activities, primarily educational, of a Maratha Brahmin in Saugor, 1820's and 1830's.

F351 GUPTA, S. C. "Some Views on Moral Education Culled from the Records of the Government of India," IHRC:30 (1954), 67-72. 20th cent. views.

F352 HARRISON, H. L. "The Midnapore System of Primary Education," CR 63:125 (1876), 125-72.

F353 "History of Education in India under the Rule of the East India Company, 1813-1833," MR:6 (Oct., Nov. 1909), 348-56, 412-17.

F354 "History of Native Education in Bengal," CR 17:34 (1852), 340-86.

F355 HUSSAIN, S. M. "Islamic Education in Bengal," IC:8 (July 1934), 439-47. 19th and 20th cent.

F356 "Indian Questions," CoR:1 (Jan. 1866), 123-41. On missionary work in education.

F357 JHA, JATA SHANKAR. "The Darbhanga Raj Records Office with a Particular Reference to the Educational Records," IHRC:34 (1958), 33-41. Education in north Bihar, 1860-80.

F358 ———. "An Early Enquiry into the State of Native Education," IHRC:33 (1958), 100-04. 1783 enquiry in Bengal *re* Bhagalpur Madrassa.

F359 ———. "Education in the Darbhanga Raj (1880-1900)," IHRC:35 (Feb. 1960), 114-21.

F360 ———."Sanskrit Education in Bihar (1860-1937)," BRS:47 (1961), 89-105.

F361 ———. "State of Sanskrit Education in Bihar (1813-1859)," BRS: 45 (1959), 265-96. From British records.

F362 KALE, B. M. "A Brief History of the Growth of Primary Education in the City of Bombay," LSGI:7 (April 1937), 18a-18k.

F363 KHAN, IMTIAZ MOHAMAD. "Some Educational Experiments in the Punjab," CR:45 (Oct. 1932), 23-32. Factors in the great increase in school enrollment, 1917-27.

F364 KINGSCOTE, GEORGIANA. "A Brahmin School-Girl," NC:25 (Jan. 1889), 133-39. Discusses Maharani of Mysore's Girls' School, est. 1881.

F365 KOYAL, BIMALENDU. "Professional Studies before the Foundation of the Calcutta University," CR:137 (Dec. 1955), 247-51. Brief account of medical, engineering, and legal education.

F366 LAW, NARENDRA NATH. "Notes on the Educational History of India," MR:13 (May, June 1913), 493-501, 644-47.

F367 LOVETT, VERNEY. "Education in India," QR:252 (Jan. 1929), 134-46. Survey history of the British education system in India.

F368 MADGE, E. W. and DHAR, K. N. "Old Calcutta: Its School-masters," CR:273 (July 1913), 338-50. Brief biographies.

F369 MALICK, A. R. "British Educational Policy," HFR:2, 1831-1905, part 1, 194-229.

F370 MANGUDKAR, M. P. "Public Instruction by the Poona Munici-pality (1884-1952)," JUP:3 (1954), 139-51. Tables of figures on expenditure, number of pupils, their religion, training of teachers.

F371 MATHUR, H. N. "Education of European and Eurasian Children in India, 1860-84," IHRC:31 (1955), 113-20. Government's arrangements therefor.

F372 [MENON]. "The Hon'ble Sir K. Ramunni Menon," MUJ:6, part 2 (July 1934?), 275-77. Biography on the occasion of his retirement as Vice-Chancellor of Madras University.

F373 "Missionary Schools in India," CR 43:86 (1866), 273-97.

F374 MITRA, RAJENDRALAL. "Raja Rajendralal Mitra and Ele-mentary Education in Bengal," CR:17 (Oct. 1925), 127-38. A letter to the magistrate of the 24 Pargannahs, dated April 29, 1868.

F375 [MONTEATH]. "Mr. Monteath's Educational Minute," CR:45 (Aug. 1867), 414-50.

F376 MONTGOMERY, WALTER A. "Progress of Education in India," USOE:49 (1919), 63-93. A summary survey of the education system.

F377 MOOKERJEE, SYAMA PRASAD. "Education in British India," AAAPSS:233 (May 1944), 30-38. A survey.

F378 MOORE, R. J. "The Composition of 'Wood's Education Des-patch,'" EHR:80 (Jan. 1965), 70-85. In 1854.

F379 MORRISON, J. "Educational Mission Work in India: 1837-1897," IEvR:24 (Jan. 1898), 257-66. Summary history.

F380 MUKHERJEE, AMITABHA. "Missionaries and the New Educa-tion in Bengal, 1757-1823," CR:173 (Oct. 1964), 60-72.

F381 MUKHERJEE, UMA and HARIDAS. "Attempts at National Edu-cation," SBR, pp. 410-22. Discusses events of 1905-06 and concludes with the establishment of the National Council of Education, 1906.

F382 MURANJAN, S. K. "Education and Educational Finance in Bombay Presidency," IJE:11 (July 1930), 1-40. With figures for the 1920's.

F383 NAIK, J. P. "Administration and Finance of Primary Education in the Province of Bombay, 1870-1902," LSGI:19 (July, Oct. 1948), 56-76, 77-135.

F384 ———. "The Finance of Primary Education in Municipal Areas of the Province of Bombay," LSGI:13 (Jan.-April 1943), 563-78. 1850-1884.

F385 ———. "History of Local Fund Cess," LSGI:13 (July, Oct. 1942), [?], 435-522. Deals with history of educational funds in rural and urban areas.

F386 ———. "Studies in Primary Education," LSGI:12 (Jan., April 1942), 267-81, 303-37. Bombay, 1823-41.

F387 NARAWANE, V. N. "Primary Education in India in 1931-41 (A Comparative Study)," LSGI:18 (Oct. 1947, Jan. 1948), 251-98, 323-442. Development in various areas.

F388 "Native Female Education," CR 25:49 (1855), 61-103.

F389 NESFIELD, J. C. "Indigenous Schools in Oudh and North-West Provinces," CR 75:150 (1882), 293-316.

F390 ———. "Results of Primary Education in the North-West and Oudh," CR:76 (1883), 348-71; 77 (1883), 72-128.

F391 NEWTON, E. A. "Practical Problems of English Public School Life in India," CR:116 (April 1903), 161-67.

F392 NICHOLSON, EDWARD. "The Education of Indian Women," CR:70 (1880), 517-32.

F393 "Number of Scholars in India According to Race or Creed on the 31st March for the Five Years 1891-92 to 1895-96," IEvR:24 (Oct. 1897), 186. Table, province by province; definition of scholar not given: total each year is about 4 million.

F394 PAL, DHARM. "The Bengal Educational System and Its Critics (in the Post-Mutiny Era)," CR:97 (Dec. 1945), 99-104.

F395 PANIKKAR, K. M. "The Educational Problem of Indian Nationalism," MR:23 (Jan. 1918), 7-17.

F396 PEARSON, C. "Primary Education in India," CR 69:138 (1879), 207-12.

F397 PHILLIMORE, R. H. "Stokes' School, Mussoorie," IA:9 (July-Dec. 1955), 101-12. Based on records and letters.

F398 "Primary Education and Indigenous Schools," QJPSS:5 (Aug.? 1882), 21-50.

F399 "The Problem of Scientific Education in India," CR:108 (April 1899), 347-55.

F400 QANUNGO, BHUPEN. "The Promotion of Education under Canning (1856-1862)," JIH:42 (1964), 493-513. Based on official papers and newspapers.

F401 RAGHUNATHJI, K. "Marathi Schools and Schoolmasters," IAn:8 (Sept. 1879), 246-49. Village schools.

F402 "Reports on Colleges and Schools in India," CR 42:83 (1865), 57-93.

F403 SAHAI, ISHWAR. "The Educational Reform of Lord William Bentinck," JIH:15 (1936), 71-83, 237-54.

F404 SAIGAL, BRIJ. "Progress of Education in the North-West Provinces of Agra and Oudh in the Time of Lord Elgin I," UPHS: NS 2 (1954), 18-25.

F405 SANIAL, S. C. "History of the Calcutta Madrassa," BPP:8 (Jan.-June 1914), 83-111, 225-50.

F406 SEED, GEOFFREY. "Lord William Bentinck and the Reform of Education," RAS (1952), pp. 66-77. Asks why Bentinck failed to act before 1835, and on the basis of detailed examination of the action he did take, attributes it to his fear of a second humiliating dismissal like that from Madras in 1807.

F407 SEN, AMIYAKUMAR. "The Introduction of Western Education in India," CR:170 (March 1964), 225-45; S&C:30 (March 1964), 109-22.

F408 SEN, PRIYARANJAN. "The Cuttack English School: A Chapter in the History of Education in Orissa," CR:129 (Oct. 1963), 21-30. The school in 1840-41.

F409 ———. "Education as a Channel of Western Influence in Bengal," CR:18 (Jan. 1926), 118-34. A survey of major institutions and individuals in early 19th cent.

F410 ———. "Educational and Cultural Societies in Nineteenth Century Bengal," CR:19 (April 1926), 125-36. Brief account of the societies.

F411 ———. "Pooree English School (1835-40)," BORS:27 (1941), 473-84.

F412 ———. "Western Education," SBR, pp. 400-09.

F413 SESHADRI, P. "The Beginnings of English Education in India," E&W:13 (Dec. 1914), 1149-58.

F414   SHAH, MADHURI. "The Administration of Bombay Education in the Province of Bombay," LSGI:20 (July 1949), 196-279. Begins with 1923.

F415   SINGH, JOGENDRA. "The Second Sikh Educational Conference (Being the Full and Revised Text of the Presidential Address Delivered in April 1909)," E&W:8 (June 1909), 564-78.

F416   SINGH, NIHAL. "Recent Educational Progress in India," CoR:113 (Jan. 1918), 63-69. On the foundation of the U. of Mysore, Indian Women's U. at Poona, Hindu U. at Benares.

F417   SINHA, NIRMAL CHANDRA. "Education under Auckland: 1836-42," CR:78 (Feb. 1941), 125-36.

F418   SPEAR, PERCIVAL. "Bentinck and Education," CHJ:6 (1938), 78-101. Summary of Orientalist-Anglicist dispute; p. 101, bibliog. on Macaulay's Minute on Education.

F419   STARK, HERBERT A. "Some Principals of the Calcutta Madrassah in By-Gone Days," MsR:2 (April-June 1928), 32-38. On Aloys Sprenger, William Nassau Lees, and Henry F. Blochmann; covers 1850-78.

F420   ———. "Vernacular Education in Bengal from 1813 to 1912," CR: 283 (Jan. 1916), 25-75; 284 (April 1916), 136-90; 285 (July 1916), 239-81; 286 (Oct. 1916), 362-414. Based on Company records and reports.

F421   "The State of Indigenous Education in Bengal and Behar," CR:2 (Dec. 1844), 301-76.

F422   SUHRAWARDY, HASSAN. "Muhammedan Education," CR:8 (Aug. 1923), 329-38. Presidential Address at Mahomedan Education Conference, April 14, 1923.

F423   SURBADHICHARY, PROSANNOCOOMAR. "Young Bengal's Plea for Science Education Eighty Years Ago," CR:49 (Dec. 1933), 299-310. Reprints a speech given at a meeting of the Bethune Society, Nov. 11, 1852.

F424   TANGRI, SHANTI S. "Intellectuals and Society in Nineteenth-Century India," CSSH:3 (1960-61), 368-94. Discusses "the landmarks of Western education in India, the content of this education, the nature of social and political changes which resulted, . . . the groups that imparted and the groups that received this education, and finally it compares the Indian with the Chinese and to some extent with the Japanese experience." Tables of hours spent on various subjects, of successful candidates in exams; figures on books published, numbers of pupils, changes in population and literacy.

F425 [TREMENHEERE]. "General Tremenheere on Missions," CR 64: 128 (1877), 266-88. On mission schools.

F426 VAIDYA, B. N. "History of Primary Education in the Province of Bombay," LSGI:13 (Jan.-April 1943), 539-61; 14 (April 1943; Jan., April 1944), [?], 223-62; 285-340. Substantial bibliog. in last portion.

F427 VAKIL, K. S. "Adult Education in India, 1937," MR:63 (March 1938), 278-80.

F428 ———. "Education in Bombay City (1804 to 1929)," RASB:6 (1930), 301-12. Based on official records.

F429 "Vernacular Education for Bengal," CR 22:44 (1854), 291-340.

F430 "Vernacular Education in Orissa," CR 38:75 (1863), 63-86.

F431 "Vernacular Education in the Days of the East India Company," MR:11 (Feb. 1912), 184-90.

F432 "Village Schools and Peasant Proprietors in the N.W. Provinces," CR 14:27 (1850), 138-208.

F433 WASTI, S. RAZI. "Sir Harcourt Butler on the Indian Educational and Political Situation in the Early 20th Century," ASP:7 (Dec. 1962), 349-55. Largely from Butler's correspondence with Minto on Hindu-Muslim relations; he was minister in charge of Education on the Viceroy's Council, 1911.

F434 WESTON, A. T. "Technical and Vocational Education," AAAPSS: 145 (Supplement, Sept. 1929), 151-60.

F435 YUSUF ALI, A. "Education in India: The New Outlook," NC:54 (Dec. 1928), 754-56.

5. EDUCATION: UNIVERSITIES AND COLLEGES

F436 "Addiscombe," CR:2 (Oct. 1844), 121-52.

F437 ALI, MOHAMED. "The Mohamedan College at Aligarh," E&W:5 (July 1906), 696-700. A tribute from an "old boy."

F438 ALI, S. WAJID. "Aligarh Memories," MsR:1 (Oct.-Dec. 1926), 37-50.

F439 ANSARI, A. S. BAZMEE. "Dār al-'Ulūm," EI:2, 132. On Farangī Mahall at Lucknow and Nadwat al-'Ulamā' at Lucknow; the latter, under Shibli, "became the first institution in India to adopt modern methods of critical research."

F440 ———. "Dar al-Ulum," PR:9 (May 1961), 31-32, 35.

F441   AWASTHY, D. "Sir Spencer Harcourt Butler and the University Education in India," JIH:43 (Dec. 1965), 855-65.

F442   BAGAL, JOGESH C. "The Hindu College, Predecessor of the Presidency College," MR:98 (July, Sept., Dec. 1955), 55-60, 229-34, 461-67.

F443   BANERJEE, ANILCHANDRA. "Years of Consolidation: 1883-1904," HYUC, pp. 129-78. Describes developments in the U. of Calcutta and various commissions established to study it and to make recommendations for its future.

F444   BANERJEE, NRIPENDRACHANDRA. "Eight Years at Rajshahi (1909-17)," CR:102 (Feb. 1947), 109-24. Extracts from his autobiography: description of college years.

F445   BANERJEE, PRAMATHANATH. "Reform and Re-organization: 1904-1924," HYUC, pp. 211-318. On the U. of Calcutta.

F446   BANERJEE, TRIGUNANATH. "Serampore College," MR:91 (March 1952), 224-27.

F447   BANERJI, BRAJENDRANATH. "The College of Fort William," MR:41 (Feb. 1927), 177-84.

F448   BELL, G. L. "Islam in India—a Study at Aligarh," NC:60 (Dec. 1906), 900-08. Discusses rise and growth of Mahommedan Anglo-Oriental College at Aligarh, est. 1875.

F449   BHATTACHARYYA, SUKUMAR. "Professor Manohar Lal, the First Minto Professor of Economics, Calcutta University—the Story of His Resignation," CR:155 (April 1960), 54-58. University politics, 1910-12.

F450   BOSE, ATINDRANATH. "Recent Activities," HYUC, pp. 365-418. On U. of Calcutta, c. 1934-57.

F451   BOSE, D. M. "Asutosh Mookerjee 1864-1964," S&C:30 (July 1964), 299-311. His activities at Calcutta University.

F452   BROADFOOT, W. "Addiscombe: The East India Company's Military College," BM:153 (May 1893), 647-57. History and customs.

F453   BRUCE, J. F. "A Brief History of the University of the Panjab," JPUHS:2 (Dec. 1933), 97-116.

F454   "The Calcutta University," CR:35 (Dec. 1860), 396-426.

F455   CHAKRABARTI, TRIPURARI. "Foundation of the University of Calcutta," CR:58 (March 1936), 307-14.

F456   ———. "The University and the Government: 1904-1924," HYUC, pp. 179-210. Discusses the Indian Universities Act (1904) and the new policies it engendered.

F457   CHANDAVARKAR, G. A. "The Dayanand Anglo-Vedic College, Lahore," HR:31 (May-June 1915), 516-21.

F458   CHANDRA, PRAKASH. "The Establishment of the Fort William College," CR:51 (May 1934), 160-71. The relations between the Government of India and London with respect to the establishment of the college.

F459   CHATTERJEE, P. N. "History of the Calcutta University Examinations and Curricula (1857-1906)," MR:23 (Jan. 1918), 92-98.

F460   CHATTOPADHYAY, K. P., BOSE, P. K. and CHATTERJI, A. "Undergraduate Students in Calcutta: How They Live and Work," CR: 132 (July 1954), 1-42. Tables of figures on health, habits, expenses, background, plans.

F461   CHOWDHURY, R. N. "A Glimpse of Jaipur College a Century Ago," IHCP:14 (1951), 363-66. Undocumented description of college in existence 1861-67.

F462   "The College of Fort William," CR:5 (1846), 86-123.

F463   COLVIN, AUCKLAND. "Memorials of Old Haileybury," BM:156 (July 1894), 107-17.

F464   CRAWFORD, D. G. "The Centenary of the Calcutta Medical College," BPP:48 (July-Dec. 1934), 71-77. A history.

F465   DAS, M. N. "Attitude of Sir Charles Wood and Lord Dalhousie towards Higher Education in Calcutta," BPP:74 (1955), 151-58. From papers in India Office Library and Edinburgh.

F466   DASGUPTA, AMARPRASAD. "Early Annals of the Calcutta University," CR:63 (June 1937), 306-10; 67 (June 1938), 291-99; 68 (July, Aug. 1938), 6-14, 143-50; 90 (March 1944), 178-87.

F467   ———. "The Post-Graduate and Other Problems: 1924-34," HYUC, pp. 319-64. Other problems of the U. of Calcutta include: revision of matriculation regulations and proposals for a secondary education board, General Medical Council dispute.

F468   DHAR, GOKULNATH. "The Presidency College, Calcutta," CR: 288 (April 1917), 128-36. A brief history.

F469   DOBSON, J. O. "A Madras Centenary," CoR:152 (Sept. 1937), 342-48. On Madras Christian College.

F470   DODWELL, MARCIA. "The New University of Travancore," AR: NS 34 (1938), 192-95.

F471   "East India College," QR:17 (April 1817), 107-54.

F472 "The East India College, Haileybury," CR:4 (1845), 1-42.

F473 "AN EDUCATIONIST." "Sir Asutosh and the Indian Universities Bill of 1904," CR:25 (Nov. 1927), 225-34. Excerpts from speeches of Asutosh Mukherji.

F474 "The Establishment of the Presidency Universities," MR:11 (April 1912), 358-60.

F475 "The Foundation of a College at Calcutta," AAR:2 (1800), "Supplement to the chronicle," 104-11. "Exact copy of the regulation for the college" of Fort William.

F476 FRASER, ANDREW. "Higher Education in India," CoR:97 (Jan. 1910), 33-41. On difficulties of providing it.

F477 GUPTA, PRATULCHANDRA. "Foundation of the University," HYUC, pp. 43-70. Describes initial program of the U. of Calcutta and recommendations for its establishment in 1835; traces early phases of its development, through 1850's.

F478 "H.R.J." "The Calcutta University," CR:113 (Oct. 1901), 346-59.

F479 HAQ, S. MOINUL. "The Aligarh Movement (Educational)," HFM:2, 1831-1905, part 2, 479-502.

F480 HARTOG, P. J. "The Indian Universities," AAAPSS:145 (Sept. 1929), Suppl. 138-50. Table of name, date of founding, whether affiliating or teaching, number of colleges, place of HQ.

F481 "Higher Education—Its Claims on State Support," QJPSS:5 (Aug.? 1882), 51-70.

F482 HUSAIN, MAHDI. "The Local Records and MSS. about the Agra College," IC:22 (Oct. 1948), 355-58.

F483 "Indian Universities—Ideal and Actual," CR:100 (April 1895), 383-401.

F484 "Indian Vernaculars and University Reform," QJPSS:4 (July? 1881), 2nd independent section, 1-31. Advocates reform.

F485 KARR, W. SETON. "Note on the Course of Study Pursued by Students in the Sanskrit College, Calcutta," ASB:14 (Jan.-June 1845), 135-36.

F486 KIBE, M. V. "Mahdaji Scindia and the Agra College. A Peep into the Records of the Family of Gandadhar Shastri," IHRC:23 (1946), 59-63.

F487 KOYAL, BIMALENDU. "How Calcutta University Came Into Being," CR:138 (Feb. 1956), 162-65. With names of the members of the first faculties.

F488 ———. "Plan of a University for Calcutta," CR:138 (Jan. 1956), 59-62. The 1845 plan.

F489 LACEY, PATRICK. "The Medium of Instruction in Indian Universities," AR: NS 34 (1938), 534-42. Largely on Osmania University.

F490 LATIF, 'ABDUL. "The Moslem University Movement," IR:17 (May 1916), 332-35.

F491 LONG, EDWARD G. "A Mahomedan University for India," HR:23 (June 1911), 441-50. On the founding of Aligarh, and statements on its goals.

F492 MACLEOD, D. F. "On the Establishment of a College for Oriental Languages (at Lahore). With Remarks by R. L. Mitra, Mr. Grote, C. Campbell, Major Lees, W. L. Heeley, Mr. Norman, G. M. Tagore, Rev. J. Long, Rev. K. M. Banerjea, Blochmann, Blanford, J. Anderson, and D. Waldie," ASBP (1866), pp. 103-09, 118-33, 141-80. Comments made in meetings.

F493 MACNAGHTEN, CHESTER. "Rājkumār Colleges," CR 68:136 (1879), 267-81. College for princes.

F494 [Madras University]. "History of the Departments (Humanities)," MUJ:28A (Jan. 1957), 277-362. History of the departments and lists of works of the faculties.

F495 MAJUMDAR, R. C. "The Fort William College and the Historical and Geographical Studies in Bengal," BPP:67 (1948), 40-45.

F496 ———. "The Hindu College," ASB:21, Ser. 3, Letters (1955), 39-51. On its establishment.

F497 MALTHUS, T. R. "Statements Respecting the East India College, with an Appeal to Facts, in Refutation of the Charges Lately Brought against it, in the Court of the Proprietors," P:9 (1817), 469-523.

F498 MORISON, THEODORE. "An Indian Renaissance," QR:204 (April 1906), 553-70. On Aligarh.

F499 MUKHOPADHYAYA, CHARU CHANDRA. "High Education in Bengal," CR 70:140 (1880), 708-25.

F500 NIZAMI, K. A. "Deoband," EI:2, 205. On the Dār al-'Ulūm.

F501 "Old Haileybury," CR:112 (Jan. 1901), 78-89.

F502 "AN OLD PANJABEE." "Government College, Lahore," MR:17 (Feb. 1915), 141-46. A brief history.

F503 PAL, BIPINCHANDRA. "Calcutta Student Life Fifty Years Ago," CR:23 (June 1927), 376-93. Reminiscences.

F504   PAL, DHARM. "Calcutta University and Its Critics (in the Post-Mutiny Era)," CR:98 (March 1946), 109-16.

F505   "Paragraphs from the Calcutta University Commission Report," MR:26 (Dec. 1919), 616-29.

F506   PEARSON, C. "The Panjab University College," CR 58:115 (1874), 74-94.

F507   PRICE, BRYNMOR F. "Carey and Serampore—Then and Now," BQ:19 (1961), 101-17. Summary in HA:9 (No. 1691). History of the college.

F508   RANKING, G. S. A. "History of the College of Fort William from Its First Foundation," BPP:7 (Jan.-June 1911), 1-29; 21 (July-Dec. 1920), 160-200; 22 (Jan.-June 1921), 120-58; 23 (July-Dec. 1921), 1-37, 84-153; 24 (1922), 112-38. Includes biographical notes on students.

F509   RASHID, 'ABD-UR. "The Punjab University," AR:6 (July 1888), 63-101. On university finances.

F510   RAY, NIHARRANJAN. "The Formative Years: 1857-82," HYUC, pp. 71-128. Facts and figures on the U. of Calcutta.

F511   SANIAL, S. C. "The Itimad-ud-Daulah Institution at Delhi," IC:4 (April 1930), 310-23. On Delhi College; entirely on the financial arrangements.

F512   SARKAR, JAGADISH NARAYAN. "The Early History of the Patna College," BPP:62 (1942), 92-115; 63 (1943), 31-43; 64 (1944), 68-83. Facts and analysis, 1863–c.1910.

F513   SARKAR, JADUNATH. "Present Condition of the Calcutta University," MR:31 (April 1922), 461-68. A criticism of the policies of Sir Ashutosh Mukerji.

F514   SENGUPTA, GOURANGA GOPAL. "Acharya Brajendra Nath Seal (1864-1938)," MR:116 (Dec. 1964), 421-24. Biography of scholar, Vice-Chancellor of Mysore University.

F515   SINHA, NARENDRAKRISHNA. "Beginning of Western Education," HYUC, pp. 1-42. Briefly describes education in India prior to 1813, then describes developments in medicine, law, engineering, and education for women up to 1840's.

F516   "Studies of the Calcutta University," CR 41:82 (1865), 297-317.

F517   SYDENHAM OF COMBE. "The Danger in India," NC:80 (Dec. 1916), 1113-27. Discusses failure of Western-type university training.

F518   TARAPOREWALA, IRACH J. S. "The Deccan College: Its Past History and Its Future Hopes," DCRI:2 (Nov. 1940), 1-8.

F519 THOMAS, P. J. "The Growth of Higher Education in Southern India (With Documents Relating Thereto)," MUJ:3 (July 1931), 211-45.

F520 "University Reform in India," QR:197 (Jan. 1903), 234-51.

F521 "W." "The Education of the Indian Civil Service," CR 62:123 (1876), 141-47. "Note on the Preceding Article," pp. 148-52. On a proposal to found an Indian Institute at Oxford.

F522 "W.H.M." "The Proposed College for the Civil Service," CR 56:112 (1873), 263-87.

F523 WILKINS, CHARLES. "On the Sikhs and Their College at Patna," AsR:1 (1788), 288-94.

F524 WODEHOUSE, C. "The Keatinge Rajkumar College, Kathiawār," CR 60:119 (1875), 59-68.

6. LANGUAGE AND SCRIPT

F525 ABDULLAH, SYED MUHAMMAD. "The Persian Language during the East India Company's Rule," JPUHS:3 (Dec. 1934), 139-49.

F526 BABU, MOTI. "The Bengali Language under the Bengal Regulations of 1793," MR:118 (Dec. 1965), 469-71.

F527 "Bengali Language," CR:98 (Jan. 1894), 104-31.

F528 CHATTERJI, NANDALAL. "Bengal and the Hindi-Urdu Question in 1875," BPP:74 (1955), 5-21. A controversy among administrators as to the language to be used in Oudh courts. Here the correspondence is reproduced.

F529 ———. "The East India Company's Military Staff and Instruction in the Hindustani Language," UPHS:NS 4 (1956), 1-10. The debate in 1826 on whether to teach Hindustani to soldiers before going to India.

F530 ———. "A Forgotten Official Inquiry on the Hindi-Urdu Controversy," IHRC:30 (1954), 30-33.

F531 ———. "A Forgotten Plea for the 'Kaithi' Script in Uttar Pradesh," IHRC:31 (1955), 75-76. In 1875.

F532 ———. "The Government's Attitude to Hindi-Urdu-Hindusthani in the Post-Mutiny Period," UPHS: NS 3 (1955), 10-34. Prints documents.

F533 ———. "A Nineteenth Century Controversy on the Teaching of Hindustani," JIH:42 (April 1964), 77-87. On whether to teach officers, 1810's and 1820's.

F534 CHATTERJI, NANDALAL. "The Problem of Court Language in British India," JIH:31 (Dec. 1953), 213-16. The arguments of the Hindi-Urdu controversy of 1875-76 in Lucknow.

F535 CLARK, T. W. "The Languages of Calcutta, 1760-1840," BSOAS: 18 (1956), 453-74. History of Arabic, Bengali, English, Hindustani, Persian, Portuguese, Sanskrit, in the light of British policies, missionary activities, and the history of education.

F536 DASS, DAYAL. "Language Controversy a Century Ago," IHRC:32 (1956), 103-06. Persian vs. Hindustani.

F537 GANGULI, SYMACHARAN. "The Behar Dialects—a Rejoinder," CR 76:152 (1883), 260-84.

F538 ———. "The Language Question in the Punjab," CR 75:150 (1882), 344-51.

F539 ———. "Hindi, Hindustani and the Behar Dialects," CR 75:149 (1882), 24-40. See also G. A. Grierson, "In Self-Defence," CR 75:150 (1882), 256-63.

F540 "The Geographical Distribution and Mutual Affinities of the Indo-Aryan Vernaculars," CR:101 (Oct. 1895), 258-74.

F541 GRIERSON, GEORGE A. "A Plea for the People's Tongue," CR 71:141 (1880), 151-68. Against Hindi as a standard language, in favor of varied vernaculars.

F542 MAJUMDAR, J. K. "The Abolition of Persian as Court Language in British India," BUJ:16 (Sept. 1947), 130-42. Prints letters in which issue was debated.

F543 RAJA, K. KUNJUNNI. "The Indian Influence on Linguistics," MUJ (Humanities):30 (July 1958), 93-111. Historical account of the development of Indian linguistics.

F544 RIZVI, S. A. A. "A Farewell Address in Urdu Presented to John Panton Gubbins by the Citizens of Delhi in 1852," BSOAS:27 (1964), 397-407. "The earliest known farewell address written in Urdu"; Gubbins, 27 years in India, the last 7 as Sessions Judge at Delhi; Syed Ahmed Khan was his subordinate. Plates and translation.

F545 [ROY, RAMMOHUN]. "A Proposal to Romanise Indian Scripts about 1832 (ed. by Sir Richard C. Temple)," IAn:58 (Oct. 1929), 192-94. A dialogue, from papers of Rammohun Roy in England, between Babu Mast Hathi (Mr. Mad Elephant) and Babu Dana (Mr. Wiseman).

F546 SEN, PRIYARANJAN. "Hindi in the College of Fort William," CR:59 (May 1936), 140-50. An important account of work in the early 19th cent.

[340]

F547 ———. "Pushtoo in the College of Fort William," CR:74 (Jan. 1940), 75-77. A letter by John Leyden.

F548 ———. "South Indian Languages in the College of Fort William," CR:83 (May 1942), 163-64. A note on the teachers of Tamil and Kanarese on the staff briefly at the beginning of the 19th cent.

F549 SINHA, R. M. "An Old Document Dealing with Hindi-Urdu Controversy," IHRC:34 (1958), 91-93. Summary of proceedings of a meeting in 1871 at Jabalpur.

F550 ZVELEBIL, KAMIL. "A Czech Missionary of the 18th Century as Author of a Tamil Grammar," TC:4 (Oct. 1955), 337-40. A grammar written c. 1755.

7. LITERATURE

F551 AFAQ, S. S. "A Preliminary Survey of the Arabic Literature Produced in Oudh," DCRI:11 (March 1951), 331-60. Brief biographies and list of works of 58 authors: 18th, 19th & 20th cents.

F552 AFZAL, QAISER. "Mohammad Hussain Azad; A Pioneer of Modern Urdu Poetry," PR:11 (June 1963), 9-10.

F553 AHMAD, AZIZ. "Influence de la littérature française sur la littérature ourdoue" [Influence of French Literature on Urdu Literature], Or:11 (3ᵉ trimestre, 1959), 125-35.

F554 ———. "La littérature de langue ourdou" [Literature of the Urdu Language], Or:7 (3ᵉ trimestre 1958), 97-111. Briefly discusses the major figures.

F555 ANAND, MULK RAJ. "English Novels of the Twentieth Century on India," AR: NS 39 (1943), 244-51. Discussion pp. 251-57.

F556 "ANDAL." "Tamil Literature after Gandhi," GM:2 (July 1958), 306-15.

F557 "An Anglo-Indian Soldier and Novelist," BM:122 (Nov. 1877), 575-91. On Col. Meadows Taylor, author of "Confessions of a Thug" and other stories.

F558 ANSARI, A. S. BAZMEE. "Āzurda, Ṣadr al-Dīn Khān b. Luṭf Allāh," EI:1, 827-28. Last grand mufti of imperial Delhi, authority on Urdu language; teacher of Abul Kalam Azad's father. Extensive bibliography.

F559 ———. "Dard," EI:2, 137-38. Urdu poet.

F560 ———. "Djawān, Mirzā Kāẓim 'Alī," EI:2, 490-91. Urdu prose writer and munshī at Fort William College.

F561. ANSARI, A. S. BAZMEE. "Djur'at," EI:2, 602. Urdu poet Ḳalandar Bak̲h̲s̲h̲.

F562 BANERJEE, SRIKUMAR. "The Short Story," SBR, pp. 332-51.

F563 BASU, RAWES. "Recent Bengali Literature," MR:49 (June 1931), 694-96.

F564 BAUSANI, A. "Faḳīr Muḥammad K̲h̲ān," EI:2 758. Urdu writer and poet.

F565 ———. "Mīrzā Asad Allāh K̲h̲ān G̲h̲ālib," EI:2, 1000-01. Urdu poet.

F566 "The Bengali Language and Literature," CR 11:22 (1849), 493-522; 105 (Oct. 1897), 300-13.

F567 "Bengali Literature," CR 52:104 (1871), 294-316.

F568 "Bengali Poetry," CR 17:33 (1852), 1-18.

F569 BHARATI, S. S. "Literature and Drama; Tamil," MIW, pp. 505-13.

F570 BLUMHARDT, J. F. and INAYATULLAH, SH. "Afsūs (Afsōs)," EI:1, 241-42. Urdu poet, in 1800 appointed Head Munshi in Hindustani department, College of Fort William.

F571 BUSHNELL, NELSON S. "Kipling's Ken of India," UTQ:27 (1956), 62-78. Summary in HA:8 (No. 2778): "An essay on the biases and prejudices in Rudyard Kipling's writings about India. . . . Based on extensive literary research."

F572 "Chatterji, Bankim Chandra," EB:6, 9-10. Bengali novelist. Article deals largely with his novel, Ananda Math.

F573 CHELYSHEV, YE. P. "Some Questions of Periodization of the History of Hindi Literature," NAA:5 (1962), 117-32. Abstract in SPA:3 (June 1963), 22.

F574 DA GAMA, F. C. "Narayan Waman Tilak, Poet, Patriot and Preacher," MR:112 (Sept. 1962), 230-34. Bibliography of works.

F575 DANDEKAR, V. P. "Literature and Drama; Marathi," MIW, pp. 498-505.

F576 DAS, OMEO KUMAR. "Impact of Gandhi on Assamese Literature," GM:3 (Jan. 1959), 56-62.

F577 DASGUPTA, JAYANTA KUMAR. "Western Influence on the Poetry of Madhusūdan Datta," BSOS:7 (1933), 117-31. On parallels between his verse and classic Western epics.

F578 DAS GUPTA, SASHI BHUSHAN. "Poetry," SBR, pp. 258-73.

F579 DAYARAM, BULCHAND. "A Modern Hindustani Poet," E&W:4 (Aug. 1905), 884-91. On Hali; translates some of his verse.

F580 DEY, BISHNU. "Michael Madhusudan Datta," SBR, pp. 56-67. Bengali poet.

F581 ———. "A Note on Michael Madhusudan Datta," Q:17 (April-June 1958), 13-18. Life and work of the poet.

F582 DUNN, T. O. D. "Bengali Writers of English Verse," CR:293 (July 1918), 262-78. Mostly 19th cent.

F583 ———. "English Verse in Old Calcutta; with a Digression upon the Origins of Anglo-Indian Literature," BPP:24 (1922), 53-65.

F584 ———. "Meadows Taylor, His Autobiography and Novels," CR: 291 (Jan. 1918), 1-29.

F585 [DUTT]. "Life of Michael M. S. Dutt, in Bengali," CR:98 (Jan. 1894), 171-79.

F586 "Early Bengali Literature and Newspapers," CR 13:25 (1850), 124-61.

F587 EDWARDS, THOMAS. "Henry Louis Vivian Derozio," CR:72 (1881), 283-310; 73 (1881), 35-77.

F588 ———. "The Poetry of Derozio," CR:73 (1881), 301-20.

F589 ———. "Selections from the Inedited Prose and Poetry of Derozio," CR:75 (1882), 214-32.

F590 "English Influence on Bengali Literature," CR:81 (Oct. 1885), 330-45.

F591 FARUQI, KHWAJA AHMAD. "Maulana Azad as a Man of Letters," IL:1 (April-Sept. 1958), 6-13.

F592 GHOSE, LOTIKA. "Manmohan Ghose—His Life and Poetry," CR:113 (Nov. 1949), 93-112. Brief biography and excerpts from poetry.

F593 GHOSH, J. C. "Literature and Drama; Bengali," MIW, pp. 484-92.

F594 GRIBBLE, JAMES D. B. "Tamil Poetry," CR 60:119 (1875), 69-77.

F595 GRIERSON, GEORGE. "A Bibliography of the Panjabi Language," IAn:35 (March 1906), 65-72. Works on Punjabi language and literature.

F596 ———. "A Bibliography of Western Hindi, Including Hindostani," IAn:32 (Jan., Feb., April, June 1903), 16-25, 59-76, 160-79, 262-65. Detailed history of the study of Hindi and Urdu, with bibliography of books about these languages (including a complete bibliography of Garcin de Tassy's works), and of translations from them.

F597 GUPTA, AMARA NATHA. "Study of Anglo-Indian Literature in India," CR:71 (May 1939), 125-33. A discussion of English writing in and on India, and of critical essays thereon.

F598 GUPTA, NAGENDRANATH. "Bankim Chandra Chatterji," MR: 47 (June 1930), 706-12.

F599 GUPTA, P. C. "1857 and Hindi Literature," Reb., pp. 225-35. Numerous quotations from Hindi poetry translated, but cited without dates. Main theme is the humiliation of India.

F600 GUPTA, PRAKASH CHANDRA. "The Impact of Gandhi on Hindi Literature," GM:3 (Jan. 1959), 40-49.

F601 HALDAR, GOPAL. "Bengali Literature before and after 1857 (1856-85)," Reb., pp. 257-70.

F602 HAQ, MD. ENAMUL. "Bengali," EI:1, 1167-69. Brief history of language and literature.

F603 HASAN, NAZIR. "Garcin de Tassy (A French Devotee of Urdu)," PR:10 (April 1962), 21-22.

F604 HASAN, REYĀZUL. "Il poeta musulmano indiano Mohammed Iqbal 1873-1938" [The Indian Muslim Poet Mohammed Iqbal 1873-1938], OM:20 (1940), 605-23. His life and Italian translations of his poetry.

F605 HOWE, SUZANNE. "The Burden of the Mystery: India and Indo-China," NE, pp. 32-81. Weak analysis of about 40 authors who wrote novels incorporating India. Bibliography of 36 books on British India.

F606 HUSAIN, M. HIDĀYAT. "Translation of an Historical Poem of the Emperor Shāh 'Alam II," ASB: NS 7 (1911), 471-73.

F607 HUSAIN, S. EHTESHAM. "Urdu Literature and the Revolt," Reb., pp. 236-41. Mentions works written during the Mutiny.

F608 INAYATULLAH, SH. "Akbar, Sayyid Ḥusayn Allāhābādī," EI:1, 317. Indian Muslim poet.

F609 ———. "Amān, Mīr," EI:1, 430. Urdu writer active at Fort William College.

F610 ———. "Anīs," EI:1, 508-09. Mīr Babar 'Alī, Urdu poet of Lucknow.

F611 ———. "Āzād, Muḥammad Ḥusayn," EI:1, 807-08. Urdu poet and writer.

F612 "India in English Literature," CR:33 (Sept. 1859), 29-48.

F613 JAYASWAL, K. P. "Puran Singh the Sikh Poet," MR:50 (Aug. 1931), 175-78.

F614 LAHIRI, K. "The Equipment and Recognition of the Bengalee Writers of English Verse and the Range of Their Poetry," CR:162 (Feb. 1962), 109-30. Literary history and criticism.

F615 LAMSHUKOV, V. K. [On the Periodization of Marathi Literature], NAA:2 (1965), 111-18. Cited in SPA:5 (March 1966), 32.

F616 LYALL, CHARLES JAMES. "Hindōstānī Literature: 4. Modern Period," EB:13, 489-91. A brief account of Urdu and Hindi works.

F617 MACMUNN, GEORGE. "Some Kipling Origins," BM:222 (Aug. 1927), 145-54. On people and places in Kipling's stories.

F618 MAREK, JAN. "The Date of Muhammad Iqbāl's Birth," AO:26 (1958), 617-20. An attempt to establish the exact date.

F619 MAY, LINI S. "Iqbal," I:6 (Jan. 1958), 28-60. Brief biography and summary of his philosophy.

F620 MISRA, SHYAM BEHARI and SUKHDEO BEHARI. "Literature and Drama; Hindi," MIW, pp. 492-98.

F621 MOHYEDDIN, K. "A Brief Survey of the History of Urdu Literature," PR:2 (Dec. 1954), 28-35.

F622 MOJUMDAR, KANCHANMOY. "Bengali Literature in the First Half of the Nineteenth Century: a Brief Survey," MR:115 (Feb. 1964), 135-48.

F623 MOLONY, J. CHARTRES. "A Tamil Novelist," CoR:171 (April 1947), 240-43. Madhaviah's life and works.

F624 MUKHERJEE, HARIDAS. "The Place of Benoy Sarkar in Bengali Literature," MR:93 (Feb. 1953), 149-52.

F625 MUKHERJEE, SUJIT. "India's Entry into English Fiction," Q:47 (Oct.-Dec. 1965), 51-55. On *Kim* and *Passage to India*.

F626 MUNSON, ARLEY. "Kipling's India," B:39 (March-May 1914), 30-45, 153-71, 255-68. With photographs of locations mentioned in Kipling's works.

F627 PAUL, H. C. "Mirzā Ghālib: His Life and Philosophy," CR:173 (Nov. 1964), 105-24.

F628 "PERISCOPE." "Anglo-Indian Fiction," ER:242 (Oct. 1925), 324-38. Life as seen in fiction.

F629 ———. "Anglo-Indian Poetry," BM:213 (June 1923), 753-66.

F630 PILLAI, G. KUMARA. "Impact of Gandhi on Malayalam Literature," GM:4 (Jan. 1960), 75-81. His impact was slight.

F631 "The Poetry of Anglo-Indian Life," CR 55:109 (1872), 58-71.

F632 "Popular Literature of Bengal," CR 13:26 (1850), 257-84.

F633 QADIR, ABDUL. "Literature and Drama; Urdu," MIW, pp. 522-34.

F634 QURESHI, MUHAMMAD ABDULLA. "Some Aspects of Iqbal's Biography," I:7 (July 1958), 63-71.

F635 RAGHAVAN, R. "Sanskrit Literature, c. 1700-1900," MUJ:28A (Jan. 1957), 175-204.

F636 RAHBAR, DAUD. "Ghālib and the Conversion of Ḥāli," MW:55 (Oct. 1965), 304-10.

F637 RAHMAN, MIZANUR. "Nazrul Islam—A Rebel," PQ:6 (Special Issue, August 1951), 26-27, 50. Brief account of Bengali poet.

F638 RANADE, M. G. "A Note on the Growth of Marathi Literature," RASB:20 (1902), 78-105. A survey of Marathi Literature, 1865-1897; continues Ranade's catalogue covering 1818-1864.

F639 "Recent Anglo-Indian Poetry," CR 29:57 (Sept. 1857), 1-17.

F640 ROBERTSON, LEO C. "A Survey of Anglo-Indian Poetry," MR: 47 (June 1930), 730-38.

F641 RUSSELL, RALPH. "An Eighteenth-Century Urdu Satirist (Sauda, c. 1713-1780)," IL:2 (Oct. 1958–March 1959), 36-45.

F642 SARANGAPANI, M. P. "Mrs. Sarojini Naidu," MR:39 (Jan. 1926), 98-107. Biography.

F643 SARKAR, JADUNATH. "Movements in Indian Literature since 1850," MR:26 (Aug. 1919), 140-44.

F644 SAZANOVA, N. M. "Notes on the Periodization of Hindi Literature," NAA:5 (1963), 141-44. Noted in SPA:4 (June 1964), 21.

F645 SEN, SUKUMAR. "Essays and Essay Writers," SBR, pp. 352-59. Deals with 1850-1914.

F646 SEN GUPTA, SUBODH CHANDRA. "Bankimchandra Chatterji," SBR, pp. 67-78.

F647   SHAFI, AHMAD. "A Poet of Islam—Sir Muhammad Iqbal," MR: 54 (Dec. 1933), 619-24.

F648   SHAHANE, V. A. "B. S. Mardhekar, A Modern Marathi Poet," IIJ:6 (1902), 141-50. Includes a brief history of Marathi poetry since 1885.

F649   SHAUKAT, SAMEENA. "Emperor Shāh 'Ālam II and His Literary Gatherings of the Dīwān-i-Khās," II:14 (Dec. 1961), 54-60.

F650   SHIKHARE, D. N. "Impact of Gandhism on Marathi Literature," GM:4 (July, Oct. 1960), 253-57, 337-42.

F651   SIDDIQUI, ABUL LAIS. "Sami'-ullah Khan, Mohsin-ul-Mulk and Hali (Hali)," HFM:2, 1831-1905, part 2, 543-55.

F652   SINGH, BHUPAL. "Kipling's Tales; an Indian Estimate," A:36 (March 1936), 187-91.

F653   SOMAYAJI, VIDWAN G. J. "Literature and Drama; Telugu," MIW, pp. 513-22.

F654   "The Tamil Language and Literature," CR 25:49 (1855), 158-96.

F655   THANI, NAGAYAM. "Regional Nationalism in Twentieth Century Tamil Literature," TC:10 (Jan. 1963), 1-23.

F656   "The Urdu Language and Literature," CR:4 (1845), 318-54. Discusses contemporary knowledge of Urdu language and literature.

F657   "Vernacular Literature in the North-West Provinces," CR:115 (July 1902), 67-75. On publications of the previous year.

F658   YAMUNACHARYA, M. "Gandhi in Kannada Literature," GM:3 (July 1959), 208-14.

F659   ZVELEBIL, KAMIL. "Bharati's Youth (1882-1904)," TC:4 (April 1955), 140-57. Biography of the poet.

8. FINE ARTS

F660   ARCHER, W. G. "Sir William Rothenstein and Indian Art," IAL: NS 25 (1951), 1-7.

F661   CHUGHTAI, M. ABDULLA. "A Few Hindu Miniature-Painters of the 18th and 19th Centuries," IC:8 (July 1934), 393-412; 4 plates.

F662   COTTON, H. E. A. "The Daniells in India," BPP:37 (Jan.-March 1929), 1-8; IHRC:11 (1928), 39-47. Engravers.

F663   ———. "The Daniells in India: An Unpublished Account of Their Journey from Calcutta to Garhwal in 1788-1789," BPP:25 (Jan.-March 1923), 1-70.

F664 COTTON, H. E. A. "Robert Home," BPP:35 (Jan.-June 1928), 1-24. 19th cent. painter.

F665 ———. "Thomas Hickey: Portrait Painter," BPP:28 (Oct.-Dec. 1924), 142-65.

F666 ———. "Tilley Kettle and His Portraits," BPP:29 (Jan.-March 1925), 44-55. Late 18th cent. portraitist in Calcutta.

F667 COTTON, JULIAN JAMES. "George Chinnery, Artist (1774-1852)," BPP:27 (April-June 1924), 113-26; IHRC:6 (1924), 42-56.

F668 FOSTER, WILLIAM. "British Artists in India, 1760-1840," WSM: 19 (1930-31), 1-88. "Additional Notes," WSM:21 (1932-33), 108-09. Includes a chronological list of artists and their period of residence in India.

F669 ———. "British Painters in Bengal," BPP:29 (Jan.-March 1925), 1-6. Who was there, when.

F670 ———. "George Duncan Beechy," BPP:41 (Jan.-June 1931), 101-04. 19th cent. painter.

F671 ———. "James Augustus Hicky: Some New Facts," BPP:30 (Oct.-Dec. 1925), 123-30.

F672 ———. "Some Foreign European Artists in India," BPP:40 (July-Dec. 1930), 79-98. Brief notes on a number of artists.

F673 ———. "William Hodges, R. A., in India," BPP:30 (July-Sept. 1925), 1-8. Artist in 1780's.

F674 GUPTA, SAMARENDRANATH. "Indian Portraits," MR:24 (Nov. 1918), 482-92. The development of portrait painting in India.

F675 OLDHAM, C. A. "Some Foreign European Artists in India," BPP: 41 (Jan.-June 1931), 68-70. Short notes.

F676 PAVIÈRE, SYDNEY H. "Biographical Notes on the Davis Family of Painters," WSM:25 (1936-37), 115-53. With plates of paintings done in India by Arthur William Davis.

F677 SARASWATI, SARASI KUMAR. "Fine Arts," SBR, pp. 319-31.

F678 SOLOMON, W. E. GLADSTONE. "Bombay and the Revival of Indian Art," IAL:1 (May 1925), 11-22.

9. MUSIC AND DRAMA

F679 ANDERSON, LILY STRICKLAND. "Nautch-girls and Old Rhythms of India," A:25 (Aug. 1925), 676-81, 700-01. Good photographs.

F680 CHOWDHURI, AHINDRA. "The Theatre," SBR, pp. 292-305. Covers 1858-1919.

F681 CLARK, C. B. "Bengali Music," CR 58:116 (1874), 243-66.

F682 DASGUPTA, JAYANTA KUMAR. "Some Early Dramas in Bengali," BSOS:8 (1935), 113-15. Brief discussion of early 19th cent. plays.

F683 DAS GUPTA, R. K. "G. S. Lebedev: The Founder of the Bengali Theatre," IL:6 (1963), 38-50. Based on contemporary journals and documents received from Moscow through the Cultural Department of the Soviet Embassy.

F684 ———. "The Political Background of the Dramatic Performances Control Act of 1876," IHCP:21 (1958), 510-14. Predating the Vernacular Press Act by 2 years, this act was to suppress political plays that came into fashion in 1874.

F685 GHOSHA, SARADA PRASADA. "The Music of Hindustan," CR 69:137 (1879), 18-42.

F686 "Hindu Drama," CR 15:29 (1851), 97-114.

F687 JOSHI, P. C. "Folk Songs on 1857," Reb., pp. 271-87. Numerous excerpts.

F688 MITTRA, KISSORY CHAND. "The Modern Hindu Drama," CR 57:114 (1873), 245-73.

F689 MOOKERJEE, SYAMA PRASAD. "The Bengali Theatre," CR:10 (Jan. 1924), 109-36. Historical account.

F690 MUKHOPADHYAY, MOHINI MOHAN. "Early History of the Bengali Stage," CR:9 (Dec. 1923), 380-87.

F691 MUSTAFA, M. N. "Origins and Development of Bengali Drama," PR:11 (May 1963), 26-27. Brief sketch.

F692 SANYAL, AMIYA NATH. "Music and Song," SBR, pp. 306-18.

F693 SEN GUPTA, SACHIN. "Drama," SBR, pp. 274-91.

10. JOURNALISM

F694 ABDUL ALI, A. F. M. "Persian Newspapers in the Hon. John Company's Days," MsR:1 (Jan.-March 1927), 54-57; BPP:33 (Jan.-June 1927), 34-36. A note on 18th and 19th cent. news sheets.

F695 "ANGLO-INDIAN." "The Native Press of India," AR, Ser. 2:10 (July 1895), 16-28. History and condition.

F696 "Appeal of a Governor General to Public Opinion in India," OH:1 (Jan.-April 1824), 8-77. On the "Banishment of Mr. Buckingham from India"—former editor of the Calcutta Journal, who founded OH.

F697 BAGAL, JOGESH CHANDRA. "Indian Journalism and Our Freedom Movement," MR:84 (Nov. 1948), 373-78. Historical.

F698 ———. "Seynger patra-patrikā o āmāder yātiyatā" [The Journals and Newspapers of That Era and Our Nationality], BP:10 (1951-52), 91-103. Review of the part played by the newspapers and periodicals of 18th and 19th cent. Bengal in political and social history; mentions 23 newspapers and journals.

F699 BANERJI, BRAJENDRA NATH. "Early Persian Newspapers in Calcutta," MsR:3 (April-June 1929), 18-22. Based on state records.

F700 ———. "The First Bengali Newspaper," MR:47 (Feb. 1930), 224-25. Discusses which was first, *Bengal Gazette* or *Samachar Darpan*.

F701 ———. "The First Bengali Newspaper," BPP:50 (July-Dec. 1935), 121-23. *Bengal Gazette*, 1816.

F702 ———. "Rammohan Roy and Freedom of the Press in India," MsR:4 (Jan.-March, 1930), 24-38.

F703 ———. "Rammohun Roy as a Journalist," MR:49 (April, May 1931), 408-15, 507-15; 50 (Aug. 1931), 138-39.

F704 BHOWNAGGREE, M. M. "The Present Agitation in India and the Vernacular Press," FR:62 (Aug. 1897), 304-13.

F705 BISHUI, KALPANA. "Lord Dufferin and the Indian Press," BPP: 84 (Jan. 1965), 38-48.

F706 CHAND, BOOL. "Urdu Journalism in the Panjab," JPUHS:2 (April 1933), 29-42.

F707 CHATTERJEE, ASHOKE. "Kedarnath Chatterjee," MR:118 (July 1965), 20-24. Son of Ramananda Chatterjee; journalist.

F708 CHATTERJEE, RAMANANDA. "Nagendranath Gupta," MR:69 (Feb. 1941), 238-40. Biography of an Indian journalist.

F709 ———. "Origin and Growth of Journalism among Indians," AAAPSS:145 (Supplement, Sept. 1929), 161-68.

F710 DESHPANDE, Y. K. "Century Old Files of Marathi Newspapers," IHRC:25 (1948), 121-24. Describes the *Dyanasindhu* (Bombay), *Prabhakur* (Bombay), *Mitrodaya* (Poona).

F711 DIGBY, WILLIAM. "The Native Newspapers of India and Ceylon," CR 65:130 (1877), 356-94. Includes lists of vernacular papers in each province as of 1877, with place of publication.

F712 ———. "The 'Struggle for Existence' of the English Press in India," CR 62:124 (1876), 256-74. Early history of the press.

F713 EDWARDS, THOMAS. "The Press of Calcutta," CR 77:153 (1883), 58-71. Good source.

F714 "The English Press in India, 1910-11," HR:23 (May, June 1911), 398-410, 499-518. Reviews the editorial policy and achievements of a number of papers.

F715 "Examination of the Arguments against a Free Press in India," OH:1 (Feb. 1824), 197-224.

F716 FEROZE, S. M. A. "The English Press in Pakistan," PQ:7 (Winter, 1957), 8-13. With facsimile illustrations of pre-independence papers published in areas now in Pakistan.

F717 ———. "The Evolution of Urdu Press," PQ:4 (Autumn 1954), 18-23, 62-63.

F718 "Further Acts of Folly and Despotism in India. Suppression of the Calcutta Journal," OH:2 (May 1824), 78-95. See "Appeal . . ." above.

F719 "Further Disclosures of 'Falsehood and Iniquity' Connected with the Suppression of the Calcutta Journal," OH:3 (Sept. 1824), 50-57.

F720 "Further Oppressive Treatment of Mr. Arnot in India," OH:2 (June 1824), 229-47. The Editor of the *Calcutta Journal.*

F721 GOLDSACK, WILLIAM. "The Moslem Press of Bengal," MW:7 (1917), 182-84. Account of one issue each of *al-Islam* and *Muhammad.*

F722 GUPTA, ANIRUDHA. "Indian Newspaper Press and National Movement till 1920," VBQ:27 (1961), 150-62.

F723 GUPTA, HARI RAM. "Delhi Diary of 1825," IHRC:25 (1948), 162-68. On *Jam-i-Jahan Numa,* Persian Calcutta weekly with news on Delhi.

F724 HOSSAIN, SYUD. "Sources of American News on India," NRp:64 (Oct. 22, 1930), 260. Brief account of British domination of news.

F725 "Interest Excited in England on the Subject of the Indian Press," OH:3 (Dec. 1824), 555-62. With extracts from the press.

F726 LAKSHMANAN CHETTIAR, SM. L. "A Brief Survey of the Tamil Press," TC:4 (April 1955), 158-68.

F727 LETHBRIDGE, ROPER. "The Vernacular Press in India," CoR: 37 (March 1880), 459-73. By a former editor of CR; on growth of the press and press laws.

F728 ———. "Government Relations with the Press: an Indian Precedent," NC:83 (Feb. 1918), 403-11.

F729 "Letters to Sir Charles Forbes, Bart., M.P. on the Benefits of a Free Press to the Natives of India," OH:2 (Aug. 1824), 518-52.

F730 LOVETT, PATRICK. "Journalism in India," CR:20 (Sept. 1926), 359-76; 21 (Oct. 1926), 78-90. Memories of a journalist.

F731 MITRA, S. M. "Press in India, 1780-1908," NC:64 (Aug. 1908), 186-206.

F732 MITRA, SUKUMAR. "The Newspaper Press," SBR, pp. 423-38.

F733 MOITRA, MOHIT. "Hindoo Patriot: India's First 'National' Newspaper," CR:169 (Oct. 1963), 135-44. Founded by Harish Chandra Mukherjee, 1853.

F734 MOOKERJEE, H. C. "The Grand Old Man of Bihar," CR:88 (Sept. 1943), 148-56. On Sachchidananda Sinha, ed. HR.

F735 MULVANY, JOHN. "The Story of the Alipore Jail Press," CR:289 (July 1917), 228-46. History of a press operated by prisoners.

F736 NARAIN, SHEO. "The 'Kohinoor' of 1851," JPHS:4 (1916), 51-61. "The earliest Urdu newspaper in Lahore."

F737 "The Native Press of Bengal," CR 43:86 (1866), 357-79. On restrictions thereon.

F738 "The Oldest Paper in India: the Bombay Samachar," CR:106 (April 1898), 218-36.

F739 PILLAI, G. PARAMASWARAN. "The Press in India: Its Origin and Growth," AR, Ser. 3:7 (Jan. 1899), 16-38.

F740 PRADHAN, R. G. "History of the Press Legislation in India," MR: 14 (1913), 131-40, 256-62. From its beginning to 1910.

F741 "The Press and the Indian States' People's Conference," MR:50 (July 1931), 75-82.

F742 "The Press in India in 1913-14," HR:29 (April 1914), 457-64. Reviews English language papers briefly; passes judgment on regional language papers.

F743 QURESHI, I. H. "Two Newspapers of Pre-Mutiny Delhi," IHRC: 18 (Jan. 1942), 258-60. The *Akhbār-i-Dehlī* and *Nūr-i-Mashriqī*.

F744 RATCLIFFE, S. K. "The Press in India," AR:NS 5 (Aug. 15, 1914), 181-207; discussion pp. 208-21.

F745 RAY, NIKHIL RANJAN. "The Press and the Publication of Legislative Proceedings in India," CR:90 (Feb. 1944), 96-107. Considers "to what extent the Press in India is privileged to publish the legislative proceedings of this country."

F746 REES, J. D. "The Native Indian Press," NC:49 (May 1901), 817-28. Describes views of "native" as opposed to English press.

F747 "Remarks on the Influence of the Press, and the Character of Civil Servants in India," OH:2 (July 1824), 373-81.

F748 "The Revival of the Native Press of Western India—the Rast Goftar," CR:107 (July 1898), 226-43.

F749 ROY, PARIMAL. "Legislative Proceedings and Privilege of the Press," MR:55 (May 1934), 500-04.

F750 [ROY]. "Ram Mohun Roy and His Persian Paper," MR:44 (Oct. 1928), 487-88.

F751 "S.L." "Ramananda's Childhood in Bankura," MR:118 (Aug. 1965), 105-11. A free translation from Santa Devi's Bengali biography of Ramananda Chatterjee.

F752 SACHDEVA, KRISHAN LAL. "Delhi Diary of 1828," IHRC:30 (1954), 109-14. On *Jam-i-Jahan Numa*, Persian weekly with Urdu news supplement, Calcutta, 1824-28.

F753 SAJAN LAL, KASIM ALI. "The Akhbar-ul-Haqaiq-wa-Talim-ul-Khalaiq," IHRC:22 (1945), 68-69. A bi-weekly of 1851.

F754 ———. "The Akhbar-i-Malwa," IHRC:20 (1943), 53-56.

F755 ———. "The Amir-ul-Akhbar," IHRC:25 (1948), 172-76. Describes 1856-57 volume of the paper and lists 34 contemporary Urdu and Persian newspapers.

F756 ———. "Azam-ul-Akhbar," IHRC:29 (1953), 83-87. Earliest Urdu newspaper of Madras, 1848-c.1852.

F757 ———. "The Delhi Urdu Akhbār and Its Importance," IC:24 (Jan. 1950), 16-44.

F758 ———. "A Few News-papers of Pre-Mutiny Periods," IHRC:19 (Dec. 1942), 128-32. On the *Jami-ul-Akhbar, Fawaid-un-Nazirin, Qiran-us-sadain, Delhi Urdu Akhbar.*

F759 ———. "The Karnamah," IHRC:26 (1949), 33-36. On a Lucknow weekly, begun 1865; description of its contents in 1870.

F760 ———. "The Omdat-ul-Akhbar of Bareilly," IHRC:24 (Feb. 1948), 100-05. Urdu newspaper begun 1846; description of 1854-56 copies.

F761 ———. "The Panjabi Akhbar," IHRC:28 (1951), 56-61. An Urdu weekly, 1864-90. Summary of reporting and editorial policy.

F762 SAJAN LAL, KASIM ALI. "Professor Ramchandar as an Urdu Journalist," IC:23 (Jan. & April 1949), 22-36. Founded *Fawā'id-un-Nāzirīn* in 1845 in Delhi.

F763 ———. "Sadiq-ul-Akhbar of Delhi," IHCP:17 (1954), 327-31. An Urdu paper of Delhi, 1857.

F764 ———. "Two Urdu Newspapers of Madras in Pre-Mutiny Days," IC:18 (July 1944), 313-22. *A'zam-ul-Akhbar* and *Taisir-ul-Akhbar*.

F765 SANIAL, S. C. "The Father of Indian Journalism Robert Knight— His Life-Work," CR:19 (May-June 1926), 287-325; 20 (July, Aug. 1926), 28-63, 305-49. Although the article begins with a page-long poem, it contains much useful information on the history of the Indian press and the editor of the *Bombay Times* in the third quarter of the 19th cent.

F766 ———. "The First Persian Newspapers of India; a Peep into Their Contents," IC:8 (Jan. 1934), 105-14. On *Jam-i-Jehan Numa* and *Miratu'l-Akhbar*.

F767 ———. "The History of the Indian Press," MsR:2 (Jan.-March 1928), 39-47; 3 (July-Sept. 1928), 16-33. First article treats the growth of the Calcutta press from 1780 to 1799; 2nd deals with the establishment of the first censorship.

F768 ———. "The History of Journalism in India. I. Bengal," CR:124 (July, Oct. 1907), 350-93, 500-62; 125 (Jan., April, July, Oct. 1908), 92-144, 195-247, 351-403, 485-560; "II. Bombay," CR:129 (Oct. 1909), 429-509; 130 (Jan., April 1910), 80-118, 264-94; 131 (July 1910), 352-80; 132 (Jan., April 1911), 1-47, 141-200.

F769 ———. "Struggle over the First Liberation of the Indian Press— Board of Control *vs.* Court of Directors," HR:23 (April, May 1911), 245-52, 360-65.

F770 SANKHDHER, B. M. "Oodunt Martund; the First Hindi Newspaper of India," MR:118 (Sept. 1965), 231-34. Published in Calcutta, 1826-27.

F771 SARKAR, JADUNATH. "Ramananda Chatterjee: India's Ambassador to the Nations," MR:116 (July 1964), 17-21. Founder of MR.

F772 SETON-KARR, W. S. "The Native Press of India," AR:8 (July 1889), 48-63. On its seditiousness.

F773 SHARMA, SRI RAM. "Newspapers as a Source of Modern Indian History," IHRC:29 (1953), 130-32. On *Gnan Prakash*, Poona weekly c. 1849.

F774 SIDDIQI, ASLAM. "The First Urdu Newspaper," IC:21 (April 1947), 160-66.

F775 ———. "Persian Press in India," II:2 (Oct. 1947), 15-26. On Rammohun Roy's *Mirat-ul-Akhbar* and the *Jam-i-Jahan Numa*.

F776 SINGH, D. N. (ed.). "The Indian Press and the War," AR: NS 5 (Oct. 1, 1914), 396-402. Excerpts from editorials.

F777 SINHA, SACHCHIDANANDA. "The Calcutta Press under the East India Company (1780-1858)," CR:91 (Cent. No., 1944), 26-43.

F778 ———. "Recollections and Reminiscences of a Long Life," HR:80 (July 1946)—85 (Dec. 1949), published regularly in installments. Autobiography of the editor of HR.

F779 SINHA, SURENDRA PRASAD. "The Calcutta Press Reaction on Bir Sa Rising (1899-1900)," CR:157 (Nov. 1960), 157-62.

F780 "Sixty Years of the 'Times of India,'" CR:108 (Jan. 1899), 86-104.

F781 "TRUTH." "Why the Native Press Should Be Licensed," CR:110 (Jan. 1900), 130-50.

F782 TYRRELL, F. H. "The 'Fauji Akhbār' or Army Newspaper of India," AR:NS 2 (Oct. 1913), 290-301.

F783 WORDSWORTH, W. C. "The Press," MIW, pp. 188-220.

F784 ZVELEBIL, KAMIL. "Baradi Novinář: z historie tamilske žurnalistiky" [Baradi News: From the History of Tamil Journalism], NO:4 cislo 16 (1961), 156-57.

11. RAMMOHUN ROY

F785 BALL, UPENDRANATH. "Rammohun Roy—Some Facts Connected with His Early Life," CR:61 (Dec. 1936), 297-320.

F786 BANJERJI, BRAJENDRA NATH. "A Chapter in the Personal History of Raja Rammohun Roy; Was He Persecuted in Lawcourts for His Religious Views?" CR:40 (Aug. 1931), 156-79. "Mainly based on state records."

F787 ———. "English Impressions of Rammohun Roy before His Visit to England," MR:51 (March 1932), 279-84. Based on correspondence.

F788 ———. "Hariharananda-Nath Tirthasurami Kulahadhuta," MR:56 (Oct. 1934), 392-93. The spiritual guide of Rammohun Roy.

F789 ———. "The Last Days of Rajah Rammohun Roy," MR:46 (Oct. 1929), 381-88.

F790 ———. "Rammohun Roy and an English Official," MR:45 (June 1929), 682-85. A letter to Lord Minto, April 12, 1809. The first known English composition of Roy.

F791 BANJERJI, BRAJENDRA NATH. "Rammohun Roy (From New and Unpublished Sources)," CR:50 (Jan. 1934), 60-72. His relations with Digby and with his family.

F792 ———. "Rammohun Roy in the Service of the East India Company," MR:47 (May 1930), 570-76.

F793 ———. "Rammohun Roy on Religious Freedom and Social Equality," MR:46 (July 1929), 27-29.

F794 ———. "Rammohun Roy's Embassy to England," MR:55 (Jan. 1934), 49-61.

F795 ———. "Rajah Rammohun Roy's Mission to England," MR:39 (April, May 1926), 391-97, 561-65.

F796 ———. "Rammohun Roy's Political Mission to England," MR:45 (Jan., Feb. 1929), 18-21, 160-65.

F797 ———. "Rammohun Roy: The First Phase (From New and Unpublished Sources)," CR:49 (Dec. 1933), 233-56. Goes up to 1804. See also A. P. Das Gupta, "A Note on 'Rammohun Roy: The First Phase," CR: 50 (Jan. 1934), 86-90; he disputes Banerji's reasoning and conclusions. B. N. Banerji, "Rejoinder," CR:50 (March 1934), 365-71.

F798 ———. "Societies Founded by Rammohun Roy for Religious Reform," MR:57 (April 1935), 415-19.

F799 ——— (ed.). "Sutherland's Reminiscences of Rammohun Roy," CR:57 (Oct. 1935), 58-70. Reproduced from *India Gazette*, Feb. 18, 1834; an account of the voyage to England and the stay there.

F800 ———. "Three Tracts by Rammohun Roy," MR:54 (Dec. 1933), 624.

F801 BASU, K. K. "An Unknown Chapter in the Life of Raja Ram Mohan Roy," IHRC:21 (1944), 50-51. His stay at Bhagalpur, 1809.

F802 BIŚBAS, DILĪPKUMĀR. "Rāmmohan Rāyer dharmamat o tantra-śastra" [The Religious Views of Rammohan and 'Tantrism'], BP:16 (1959-61), 225-48.

F803 BOSE, CHUNILAL. "A Lock of Hair of Rajah Ram Mohan Roy," CR:30 (Feb. 1929), 208-17. Brief biography of Babu Rakhal Das Haldar, who preserved a lock of Roy's hair; with a picture of this lock.

F804 BRADEN, CHARLES S. "Rammohun Roy—Father of New India," OC:48 (July 1934), 147-55.

F805 "A Contemporary Writer on Ram Mohun Roy," MR:24 (Sept. 1918), 296-97. Notice of *Considerations on the State of British India* by Lt. A. White, 1822.

F806 DAS GUPTA, JYOTIRMOY. "Raja Ram Mohun Roy at Rangpur," MR:44 (Sept. 1928), 274-78. With correspondence between Digby and J. Thackeray, Sec'y to the Board of Revenue, Fort William.

F807 DATTA, S. K. "Further Aspects of Raja Rammohun Roy's Work," JPUHS:3 (April 1934), 1-19.

F808 DEY, SHAMBHOO CHUNDER. "The Labours of Raja Ram Mohan Roy," HR:26 (Nov. 1912), 349-61. An appreciation of his efforts for reform.

F809 ———. "Raja Ram Mohan Roy in England," E & W:5 (May 1906), 483-89.

F810 ———. "Raja Ram Mohan Roy in Europe," HR:30 (Sept. 1914), 192-99.

F811 GANGULI, PRABHAT CHANDRA. "Raja Rammohan Roy," SBR, pp. 8-15.

F812 GOSWAMI, C. R. "Ram Mohun and Modern Education in India," MR:114 (Aug. 1963), 129-32.

F813 HAY, STEPHEN N. "Western and Indigenous Elements in Modern Indian Thought: the Case of Rammohun Roy," CJA, pp. 311-28.

F814 [JACQUEMONT]. "A Portrait of Rajah Ram Mohan Roy," MR:39 (June 1926), 689-92. Contemporary account by Victor Jacquemont, written in Calcutta June 25, 1829; tr. from *Voyage dans l'Inde*.

F815 MOORE, ELSA ADRIENNE. "Rammohun Roy; His Possible Influence on American Thought with Special Emphasis upon Periodicals," MR:60 (Sept., Oct. 1936), 281-87, 405-12.

F816 PRASAD, BIMLA. "Rammohan's World Outlook," BRS:37 (March & June 1951), 275-82. Quotations show Roy's sympathy with enlightenment anywhere in the world.

F817 "RAMMOHUN ROY," CR:4 (1845), 355-93; 44 (1866), 219-33.

F818 "Ram Mohun Roy on International Fellowship," MR:44 (Oct. 1928), 466-68. Correspondence with T. Hyde Villiers, Foreign Minister of France.

F819 RAY, NISITH RANJAN. "Bishop Middleton (The First Lord-Bishop of Calcutta) and Raja Rammohan Roy," BPP:83 (July-Dec. 1964), 83-89.

F820 RAY, P. C. (tr.). "Victor Jacquemont on Ram Mohan Ray," CR: 61 (Oct. 1936), 1-6.

F821 RAY, S. N. "Rammohun Roy and English Intellectuals," MR:62 (Aug. 1937), 160-64.

F822 ROY, RAMMOHUN. "The Padishah of Delhi to King George the Fourth of England," MR:39 (April 1926), 373-77. The petition framed by Roy.

F823 ——. "Tuḥfatu'l-Muwaḥḥidīn," II:4 (July 1950), 20 pp. Printed in Persian, with a biographical sketch by M. Ishaque in Persian and one in English by Kalidas Nag.

F824 SEN, AMIYA KUMAR. "A Forgotten Episode in the Life of Raja Rammuhun Roy," MR:115 (Jan. 1964), 29-39.

F825 ——. "Settlement of Europeans in India: The First Phase (1766-1833)," CR:169 (Oct., Dec. 1963), 17-29, 298-308. Much material from Roy's writings.

F826 SEN, KSHITIMOHAN. "Yugaguru Rammohan" [Rammohan, the Teacher to an Age], BP:10 (1951-52), 19-36.

F827 SEN, SIVA NARAYANA. "Some New Light on Raja Rammohun Roy," MR:66 (Oct. 1939), 466-71. Letters.

F828 SEN-GUPTA, NARESCHANDRA. "Raja Rammohun and Law," CR:50 (Jan. 1934), 16-25. An undocumented study of Roy's knowledge of law.

12. RABINDRANATH TAGORE

F829 ALI, HASHIM AMIR. "Rural Research in Tagore's Sriniketan," MR:56 (July 1934), 39-44.

F830 ANDREWS, C. F. "Tagore and the Renaissance in Bengal," CoR:103 (June 1913), 809-17. A pre-Nobel appreciation.

F831 BANERJEE, KALYAN KUMAR. "Rabindranath Tagore and the San Francisco Trial," MR:116 (July 1964), 27-30.

F832 BANERJEE, SUDHANSU MOHAN. "Tagore and the Reaction in the West," MR:106 (July 1959), 21-28. Includes excerpts of press reaction to Tagore and vice versa.

F833 BISWAS, USHA. "The Boyhood Days of Tagore (Rabindranath)," MR:112 (Aug. 1962), 119-26. Review of "Chhelebela" with outline of historical environment into which Tagore was born in 1861.

F834 BOROVIK, E. [Rabindranath Tagore in Russia], AAS:3 (March 1961), 38-40.

F835 CAMPBELL, A. "Tagore's Abode of Peace," A:33 (April 1933), 230-35. On Santiniketan, but includes a photo of Tagore in Germany.

F836 CHATTOPADHYAY, K. P. "Tagore's Survey and Study of Rural Economics and Society and Its Background," MR:111 (June 1962), 451-55.

F837 CHELYSHEV, E. P. "Rabindranat Tagor: k stoletiiu so dnia rozhdeniia" [Rabindranath Tagore: on the Centenary of His Birth], VIMK:27 (1961), 3-21. Summary in HA:8 (No. 1188).

F838 "Chronological Bibliography of Tagore's Works, 1878 to 1941," ILn:16 (June 1961), 14-18. "Courtesy of the Librarian, Visva-Bharati University, Santiniketan."

F839 DHAR, SOMNATH. "Tagore in Singapore and Malaya in 1927," IAC:10 (July 1961), 49-61.

F840 ELMHURST, LEONARD K. "Early Days at Sriniketan," MR:65 (Feb. 1939), 156-58. Reminiscences.

F841 ———. "Rabindranath Tagore and Sriniketan," VBQ:24 (Autumn 1958), 124-44.

F842 GANGULY, N. C. "Dr. Tsemon Hsu at Santiniketan," MR:44 (Dec. 1928), 666-69.

F843 GOKAK, V. K. "Tagore's Influence on Modern Indian Poetry," IL:4 (1961), 99-115.

F844 HALLSTRÖM, PER. "Tagore and the Nobel Prize," IL:4 (1961), 11-19. Text of the report to the Nobel Committee of the Swedish Academy, Oct. 29, 1913.

F845 HAY, STEPHEN N. "The Origins of Tagore's Message to the World," Q (Special Issue, May 1961), pp. 50-54. On "the evolution of . . . 'the prophetic consciousness' of Rabindranath Tagore." See also "Discussion" by V. Romanov and S. N. Hay, Q:30 (Summer 1961), 91-93.

F846 ———. "Rabindranath Tagore in America," AQ:14 (Autumn, 1962), 439-63.

F847 HERDT, GISELA. "Rabindranath Tagore in German Literature," VBQ:27 (1961-62), 260-74.

F848 HURWITZ, HAROLD M. "Ezra Pound and Rabindranath Tagore," AL:36 (March 1964), 53-63. Largely on Pound's reactions to Tagore.

F849 ———. "Tagore in Urbana, Illinois," IL:4 (1961), 27-36. Based on the Daily Illini and interviews.

F850 ———. "Yeats and Tagore," CL:16 (Winter 1964), 55-64. History of their association.

F851 KOWALSKA, AGNIESZKA. "Z dziejow recepcji Rabindranatha Tagore w Polsce" [From the History of the Reception of Rabindranath Tagore in Poland], PO:39 (1961), 265-81. Bibliog. of writings on Tagore in Polish (1913-59), pp. 275-81.

F852 LAGO, MARY M. "The Parting of the Ways: a Comparative Study of Yeats and Tagore," IL:6 (No. 2, 1963), 1-34. Perceptive study of the differences in their views of man and art.

F853 "LITERATUS." "Rabindranath Tagore in America," MR:21 (May, June 1917), 549-53, 659-66. Reprints comments from various American newspapers.

F854 MACHWE, PRABHAKAR. "Articles on and by Tagore in American Journals (March 1913 to February 1960)," IL:4 (1961), 200-06. Arranged chronologically.

F855 MAHALANOBIS, PRASANTA CHANDRA. "The Growth of the Visva-Bharati 1901-1921," VBB:8 (April 1928), 16 pp.

F856 ———. "Rabindranath Tagore's Visit to Canada and Japan," VBQ:7 (April-July 1929), 114-64. Chronicle of his trip in 1929, with excerpts from newspaper articles on him.

F857 MOOKERJEE, GIRIJA K. "Rabindranath Tagore and Romain Rolland—Villeneuve Meeting," Sh:2 (March 1965), 39-44.

F858 MUKHERJI, PRAFULLA C. "Rabindranath Tagore in America," MR:110 (Nov. 1961), 383-92.

F859 "The Myriad-Minded Poet," IL:4 (1961), 20-21. English text of the citation read at conferment of honorary D.Litt. to Tagore by Oxford, Aug. 7, 1940.

F860 NADEL', KH. S. [Review of L. A. Strizhevskaia, ed., *Rabindranath Tagore. Bio-bibliograficheskii ukazatel'*. (Bio-bibliographical index) (Moscow 1961, 174 pp.)], NAA:2 (1962), 230-36. Summary in SPA:2 (Oct. 1962), 16. "Four pages of Soviet titles suggested as additions are given, although the book pretends to be complete."

F861 PETROV, A. K. [Pedagogical Views and Activity of Rabindranath Tagore], SP:5 (May 1961), 88-100. Abstract in SSAB:1, 23.

F862 PETROV, F. [Several Days with a Poet], AAS:5 (May 1961), 39-40. Abstract in SSAB:1 (1962), 42.

F863 "Rabindranath Tagore in Russia," MR:48 (Dec. 1930), 605-11; MR:49 (Jan. 1931), 4-13.

F864 "Rabindranath Tagore's Visit to China; a Narrative Record of the Visva-Bharati Deputation to China," VBB:1.

F865 RAU, HEIMO. "Tagore in Germany," IL:4 (1961), 116-20.

F866 RAY, SIBNARAYAN. "Rabindranath Tagore and Modern Bengal," Q (Special Issue, May 1961), 58-66. A discussion of Tagore's isolation and alienation from "the people" as part of Bengali intellectual history.

F867 ROY, KSHITIS. "Tagore in Hungary," IL:3 (Oct. 1959–March 1960), 28-34. His 1926 trip, based on letters at Santiniketan.

F868 SANYAL, HIRAN KUMAR. "Rabindranath Tagore," SBR, pp. 122-38.

F869 SARKAR, S. C. "Rabindranath Tagore and the Renaissance in Bengal," En:5 (c. Dec. 1961), 1-35. Tr. from the Bengali by Sumit Sarkar.

F870 SEN, PULINBIHARI and MUKHOPADHYAY, SUBHENDU SEKHAR. "Rabindranath Tagore: Contributions and Translations Published in Periodicals," VBN (1961), 55 pp. Arranged by journal and newspaper; many entries annotated.

F871 ———. "Short Stories and Novels of Rabindranath Tagore: a Bibliography of English Translations," IL:4 (1961), 207-17.

F872 SEN, PULINBIHARI and GANGULI, SOBHANLAL. "Tagore-ana; Contributions and Translations Published in the Modern Review," MR:109 (June 1961), 488-93; 110 (Aug. 1961), 154-56.

F873 SEN, SUKUMAR. "Some Early Influences in Tagore's Life," IAC:10 (July 1961), 147-52.

F874 SENGUPTA, BENOYENDRA. "U.S.A.'s Interest in Rabindranath," MR:102 (Aug.-Oct. 1957), 148-54, 235-38, 316-19. A bibliography of Tagoreana in U. S. and European journals.

F875 SEN GUPTA, SANKAR. "Rabindranath Tagore's Role in Bengal's Folk Lore Movement," F:4 (April 1963), 137-52.

F876 SUHRAWARDY, SHAHEED. "Tagore at Oxford," ORLD:2 (Feb.-March 1956), 111-19. Reprinted from Calcutta Municipal Gazette, Special Tagore Number, 1941; personal reminiscences.

F877 TAGORE, RABINDRANATH. "Genesis of English Gitanjali," IL:2 (Oct. 1958–March 1959), 3-4. Translated excerpt from Tagore's Bengali letter to his niece Indiradevi Chaudhurani, dated May 6, 1913.

F878 ———. "The History and Ideals of Sriniketan," MR:70 (Nov. 1941), 433-36. Translation of an address given in 1939.

F879 ———. "Message from India," LA:338 (July 1, 1930), 518-20. Reprinted from Manchester Guardian.

F880 ———. "The Spirit of Japan," MR:21 (June 1917), 611-19.

F881 ——— and SARKAR, JADUNATH. "My Interpretation of Indian History," MR:14 (Aug., Sept. 1913), 113-18, 231-36.

F882 TAGORE, RABINDRANATH and NOGUCHI, YONE. "Poet to Poet (Full Text of Correspondence between Yone Noguchi and Rabindranath Tagore on the Sino-Japanese Conflict)," VBQ: NS 4 (Nov. 1938–Jan. 1939), 199-212.

F883 VASIL'EV, D. [On Tagore's Plan to Visit the USSR (1926)], NAA:2 (1965), 125-27. Cited in SPA:5 (March 1966), 31: "Stressing Rabindranath Tagore's admiration for the Soviet Union."

F884 VDOVIN, V. A. and GAMAIUNOV, L. S. [On the Hundredth Anniversary of the Birth of Rabindranath Tagore], NAA:2 (Feb. 1961), 122-30. "From materials on the visit of Tagore to the Soviet Union": SSAB:1, 24.

F885 ZBAVITEL, DUSHAN. "Rabindranath Tagore and Czechoslovakia," VBQ:22 (Spring 1956-57), 274-82. On translations of his work into Czech and correspondence with professors.

F886 ————. "Rabindranath Tagore in 1887-1891," AO:24 (1956), 581-90. Bengali sources used.

F887 ————. "Rabindranath Tagore in 1891-1905," AO:25 (1957), 405-25.

F888 ————. "Rabindranath Tagore in 1905-1913," AO:26 (1958), 101-13.

F889 ————. "Rabindranath Tagore in 1913-1930," AO:26 (1958), 366-84.

F890 ————. "Winternitz and Tagore," VBQ:24 (Summer 1958), 1-21. Winternitz was Professor of Indo-Aryan Philology at Prague; their correspondence and bibliography of Winternitz's writings on Tagore.

13. HINDU RELIGIOUS MOVEMENTS

F891 "A.C.L." "Christianity and the Brahma Samaj," CR 52:104 (1871), 205-16.

F892 ABDUL ALI, A. F. M. "Glimpses of the Durga Pooja—a Hundred Years Ago," BPP:44 (July-Dec. 1932), 86-88.

F893 "The Arya Samāj," RT:3 (Sept. 1913), 614-36.

F894 BISWAS, DILIP KUMAR. "Maharshi Debendranath Tagore and the Tattvabodhini Sabha," SBR, pp. 33-46. Covers 1839-59; precursor of Brahmo Samaj.

F895 ————. "Tattabodhini Sabha and Debendranath Tagore," IT:5 (1954), 31-49. Abstracted in HA:1 (No. 504): "Based on contemporary Bengali literature and journals. Sketches the history of the Bengali intelligentsia during the first half of the 19th century."

F896 BOSE, ATINDRA NATH. "Swami Vivekananda," SBR, pp. 108-21.

F897 [BOSE]. "Some Interesting Letters; Letters to and from Rajnarain Bose," MR:117 (April 1965), 257-59. Secretary of Tattvabodhini Sabha.

F898 BOSE, SURESH CHUNDER. "Protap Chunder Mozoomdar," E&W:5 (June 1906), 583-94. Brahmo Samaj leader.

F899 "Brahma Samaj," EB:4, 388-89. A convenient summary of beliefs and history.

F900 "The Brahma Samaj and the Native Marriage Act," CR 54:108 (1872), 285-313.

F901 BURKE, MARIE LOUISE. "Swami Vivekananda in New York, December 6 to December 24, 1895," PB:68 (April 1963), 129-51.

F902 CHATTERJEE, RAMANANDA. "Presidential Address at the Twelfth Session of the All India Hindu Mahasabha, Held at Surat, 1929," MR:45 (April 1929), 466-84.

F903 CHATTERJEE, S. P. "Vivekananda Letters," MR:89 (May 1951), 361-64. To an English girl at the turn of the century.

F904 COLLET, SOPHIA DOBSON. "The Brahmo Somaj versus the 'New Dispensation,'" CoR:40 (Nov. 1881), 726-36. Outlines the disagreement; long excerpts from Brahmo publications.

F905 ———. "Indian Theism and Its Relation to Christianity," CoR: 13 (Jan.-March 1870), 230-45. Discusses development and leaders of Brahmo Samaj; Indian Mirror is a source.

F906 CURRAN, JEAN A., JR. "RSS: Militant Hinduism," FES:19 (May 17, 1950), 93-98. The history of its organization.

F907 DAS, JOGANANDA. "The Brahmo Samaj," SBR, pp. 479-508.

F908 DASS, DAYAL. "Tax on Pilgrims," IHRC:31 (1955), 102-05. Developments, 1835-39.

F909 DATTA, RAMA. "Keshub Chunder Sen," MR:84 (Dec. 1948), 477-78.

F910 FREEMANTLE, W. H. "The Brahmo Somaj and the Religious Future of India," CoR:15 (Aug. 1870), 67-80. Evaluation by a Unitarian.

F911 GAJENDRAGADKAR, K. V. "The Mystical Life and Teachings of the Late Sri Gurudeva Dr. R. D. Ranade," KU:4 (June 1960), 14-25. Biographical sketch.

F912 GANGULI, ANIL CHANDRA. "Christianity and Hindu Renaissance," CR:80 (Aug. 1941), 139-44.

F913 GANGULY, N. C. "Foundation of the Brahmo Samaj," MR:44 (Sept. 1928), 282.

F914 GLASENAPP, HELMUTH VON. "Alt-indische und Modern-abendländische Elemente im Heutigen Hindutum" [Old Indian and Modern Occidental Elements in Modern Hinduism], Sm:6 (1955), 307-28. Abstract in HA:1 (No. 2678).

F915 "Government Connection with Idolatry in India," CR 17:33 (1852), 114-77.

F916 GUHA ROY, S. N. "Sri Ramakrishna and the Gospel of Service," MR:59 (1936), 250-54. As it was understood and preached by Vivekananda.

F917 HALIM, A. "Hindu Reformist and Revivalist Movements," HFM: 2, 1831-1905, part 2, 390-414.

F918 "A Hindu Admirer," "Swami Vivekananda," MR:25 (May, June 1919), 491-501, 578-87. From several standard works.

F919 "The Hindus of Puri in Orissa and Their Religion," CR:93 (July 1891), 108-14.

F920 INGHAM, KENNETH. "The English Evangelicals and the Pilgrim Tax in India, 1800-1862," JEIH:3 (July-Oct. 1952), 191-200. From the missionary point of view.

F921 "J." "The Brahma Samaj," CR 60:120 (1875), 356-74.

F922 KNIGHTON, W. "The New Development of the Brahmo Somaj," CoR:40 (Oct. 1881), 570-84. On K. C. Sen's New Dispensation, with long excerpts from speeches.

F923 MAZUMDAR, AMIYA KUMAR. "Sri Ramakrishna Paramahansa," SBR, pp. 94-107.

F924 MONIER-WILLIAMS, MONIER. "Indian Theistic Reformers," RAS: NS 13 (1881), 1-41, 281-90. On the Brahmo Samaj and New Dispensation.

F925 NARAYAN, JAYAPRAKASH. "The Bhoodan Movement in India," AR:54 (Oct. 1958), 265-78, discussion pp. 278-80.

F926 NUNDY, ALFRED. "Religious Aspirations of the Educated Hindu," CR:116 (April 1903), 313-28.

F927 PRASAD, BIMLA. "Vivekananda—An Avowed Internationalist," BRS:37 (Sept. & Dec. 1951), 168-77. Quotations on his belief in spreading his ideas all over the world.

F928 ———. "Vivekananda on India's Mission in the World," BRS:38 (March 1952), 135-46. Many quotations.

F929 "The Present Situation in the Bramho Somaj," CR:101 (Oct. 1895), 391-401.

F930 "Puranism; or, the Popular Religion of India," CR 24:48 (1855), 189-233.

F931 PURI, RAM NATH. "A New Light in India," Ov: NS 52 (July 1908), 26-29. On the Arya Samaj, with photos of the Gurukula Academy at Hardwar.

F932 RADHAKRISHNAN, S. "Hinduism and the West," MIW, pp. 338-53.

F933 RAI, LAJPAT. "The Arya Samaj: Its Aims and Teachings," CoR: 97 (May 1910), 608-20.

F934 "Religion and Character of the Hindus," ER:29 (Feb. 1818), 377-403.

F935 "The Religion of the Brahmo Samaj," CR 64:128 (1877), 332-50.

F936 ROLLAND, ROMAIN. "Un grand mystique indien: Ramakrishna (1836-1886)" [A Great Indian Mystic: Ramakrishna (1836-1886)], Eu: 19 (Feb. 15, 1929), 153-81. His life and ideas.

F937 ———. "Un héros de l'Inde nouvelle: Vivekananda (1863-1902)" [A Hero of the New India: Vivekananda (1863-1902)], Eu:19 (March 15, 1929), 305-36; 19 (April 15, 1929), 465-500; 20 (May 15, 1929), 31-63; 20 (Aug. 15, 1929), 497-537.

F938 ROY, B. K. "Mirovozzrenie Svami Vivekanandy" [Ideology of Swami Vivekananda], VIMK:22 (1960), 83-96. Summary in HA:8 (No. 703): "Lengthy discussion of the Weltanschauung of Swami Vivekananda and the Swami's impact."

F939 SARKAR, JADUNATH. "Raj Narain Bose (1826-1899)," MR:5 (April 1909), 311-319. His role in the Brahmo Samaj.

F940 ———. "Shivanath Shastri," MR:26 (Nov. 1919), 530-34. 1847-1919; a founder of the Sadharan Brahmo Samaj, 1879.

F941 SASTRI, K. S. RAMASWAMI. "The Life and Teachings of Swami Ram Tirath," HR:19 (May-June 1914), 515-25.

F942 SEAL, BRAJENDRANATH. "Paramahansa Ramakrishna, Saint, Mystic, and Seer—with a Brief View of Religious Development from Rammohun to Ramakrishna, and After," MR:61 (April 1937), 398-402.

F943 SEN, MONONIT. "Brahmo Samaj and Swami Vivekananda's Chicago Lectures," MR:114 (Dec. 1963), 443-48. Excerpts from Chicago lectures, coupled with similar quotes from Brahmo leaders.

F944 "The Shaktas—Their Characteristics, and Practical Influence in Society," CR 24:47 (1855), 31-67.

F945 SHARADA. "The English Disciples of Swami Vivekananda," PB: 66 (April 1961), 193-95. A very brief account.

F946 SIRCAR, NIL RALAN. "The Indian Theistic Movement and Its Problems," MR:19 (Jan. 1916), 57-69.

F947 SORABJI, CORNELIA. "Hindu Swamis and Women of the West," NC:112 (Sept. 1932), 365-73. A piece of muck-raking.

F948 THAKUR, V. V. "A Short Note on the Charities of Devi Shri Ahilya Bai Holkar," IHRC:13 (1930), 139-44. Religious charities in the 18th cent.

F949 WILSON, H. H. "A Sketch of the Religious Sects of the Hindus," AsR:16 (1828), 1-136.

14. MUSLIM RELIGION AND CULTURE

F950 ABBOTT, FREELAND K. "The Jihād of Sayyid Aḥmad Shahīd," MW:52 (1962), 216-22. Based on secondary sources.

F951 ———. "Maulānā Maudūdī on Quranic Interpretation," MW:48 (1958), 6-19.

F952 AGA KHAN. "The Indian Moslem Outlook," ER:219 (Jan. 1914), 1-13.

F953 AHMAD, AZIZ. "Djamʿiyya: India and Pakistan," EI:2, 437. With extensive bibliography on Muslim religious and religio-political organizations.

F954 ———. "El Islam español y la India musulmana moderna" [Spanish Islam and Modern Muslim India], FI:1 (1961), 560-70. Deals with the influence of the Moors on Muslims in India from medieval to modern times.

F955 ———. "Le mouvement des mujahidin dans l'Inde au XIXe siècle" [The Movement of the Mujahidin in India in the 19th Century], Or:15 (3e trimestre 1960), 105-16. On Shah Waliullah's movement.

F956 ———. "Political and Religious Ideas of Shāh Walī-Ullāh of Delhi," MW:52 (1962), 22-30. Based on his writings.

F957 AHMAD KHAN, MUIN UD-DIN. "A Bibliographical Introduction to Modern Islamic Development in India and Pakistan 1700-1955,"

Appendix to ASP:4 (1959), 170 pp. In its original form, an MA thesis at McGill University. Arabic, Persian, and Urdu titles transliterated and sometimes translated. Works arranged in chronological and topical sections, most entries annotated critically; each chapter has introduction summarizing the period covered. Includes books and articles; index of authors.

F958 ———. "Chronology of the Farāidī Movement," PHS:13 (Oct. 1965), 314-21. Discussion of the difficulties in establishing chronology.

F959 ———. "Muhsin al-din Ahmad *alias* Dudu Miyān," PHS:11 (July 1963), 234-58. Based on English and Bengali sources.

F960 ———. "Religious Doctrines of the Farā'idīs," PHS:12 (Jan. 1964), 31-59.

F961 ———. "Shah Wali-allah's Conception of *ijtihad*," PHS:7 (July 1959), 165-94.

F962 ———. "Social Organization of the Farā'idīs," PHS:12 (July 1964), 195-206.

F963 ———. "Successors of Dudu Miyān," PHS:11 (Oct. 1963), 278-89. Based on Bengali sources and tradition in the family of Dudu Miyan.

F964 ———. "Ta'aiyyunī Opposition to the Farā'idī Movement," PHS: 12 (April 1964), 150-64.

F965 AHMED, ZIAUDDIN. "Sayid Ahmad Brelvi," PR:11 (Sept. 1963), 8-10. Brief biography.

F966 ALI, S. AMJAD. "A Crusader for Freedom (Sayyed Ahmad Shaheed)," PQ:5 (Independence Anniversary No., 1955), 36-39, 65-66.

F967 ĀLĪ, SAIYAD MURTAJA. "Bānlāya Muslim dharmīya āndolan" [The Islamic Religious Unrest in Bengal], IAP:1 (July-Sept. 1963), 75-94. On the 19th cent.

F968 ANSARI, A. S. BAZMEE. "Al-Dihlawī, Shāh Walī Allāh," EI:2, 254-55.

F969 ———. "Shah Ismail Shaheed," PR:11 (Oct. 1963), 4-9.

F970 ———. "Shah Waliullah," PR:9 (Aug. 1961), 21-24, 28.

F971 ANSARI, ZAFAR AHMAD. "Deoband and Nadwah," HFM:2, 1831-1905, part 2, 415-24.

F972 ASHRAF, K. M. "Muslim Revivalists and the Revolt of 1857," *Reb.*, pp. 71-102. Includes an extensive bibliography of Urdu sources. A Marxist interpretation of Wahhabi politics.

F973 ASIRI, FAZL-E-MAHMUD. "Shah Wali Allah," VBA:4 (1951), 1-50. His life and teachings, from Arabic, Persian, and Urdu sources.

F974 ———. "Shah Wali Allah as a Politician," IsL:7 (March 1955), 35-41. Based on Waliullah's writings.

F975 ASKARI, S. H. "Political Significance of the Movement of Syed Ahmed Brailvi (Based on His Correspondence)," IHRC:31 (1955), 174-80.

F976 BALJON, J. M. S., JR. "Aḥmad Khān," EI:1, 287-88. 1817-98.

F977 ———. "A Modern Urdu Tafsīr," WI: NS 2 (1953), 95-107. On the modernism of Abul Kalam Azad.

F978 ———. "Pakistani Views of Hadith," WI:NS 5 (1956), 219-27. On Islamic modernism.

F979 BARI, MOHAMMAD ABDUL. "The Fara'idi Movement," PPHC: 5 (1955), 197-208. From Bengal records and Persian books.

F980 BAUSANI, A. "Farā'iḍiyya," EI:2, 783-84. Good account of the 19th cent. sect in Bengal.

F981 BHOWNAGREE, MANCHERJEE MERWANJEE. "Aga Khan," EB:1, 362-63.

F982 BRUSH, S. E. "Aḥmadiyyat in Pakistan; Rabwah and the Aḥmadis," MW:45 (1955), 145-71.

F983 CHOPRA, P. N. "Character of the Wahabi Movement," IHRC:35 (Feb. 1960), 66-68.

F984 DIN, R. S. "Mirza Gulam Ahmad, a False Messiah of India," MRW:30 (Oct. 1907), 749-56. With a portrait.

F985 DOUGLAS, R. B. "The Ahmadiya Movement," GUOS:4 (1913-22), 61-68.

F986 FISHER, HUMPHREY. "The Concept of Evolution in Ahmadiyyah Thought," MW:49 (1959), 275-86.

F987 FYZEE, ASAF A. A. "Islamic Law and Theology in India; Proposals for a Fresh Approach," MEJ:8 (Spring 1954), 163-83. Account of modernizers of Islamic thought from Waliullah to Abul Kalam Azad.

F988 GIBB, H. A. R. "Agha Khān," EI:1, 246. On the spiritual head of the Nizari Isma'ilis in India and elsewhere.

F989 GRAEFE, J. E. "Islam and Christianity in Guntur," MW:14 (April 1925), 119-34. A study and survey made in 1923 of the organization of Muslim religious leaders; asks, is Islam becoming Hinduized?

F990 GRISWOLD, H. D. "The Ahmadiya Movement," MW:2 (1912), 373-79.

F991 ———. "Mirza Ghulam Ahmad, the Mahdi Messiah of Qadian," IEvR:29 (Jan. 1903), 322-54.

F992 GUIMBRETIÈRE, ANDRÉ. "Le réformisme musulman en Inde" [Muslim Reformism in India], Or:16 (4ᵉ trimestre 1960), 15-41; 18 (2ᵉ trimestre 1961), 33-55. Many bibliographical footnotes.

F993 HABIB, MOHAMMED. "The Revolutionary Maulana," MAKA, pp. 79-100. Includes material from Qazi Abdul Ghaffar's *Asar-i Abul Kalam Azad*, Azad's *Tarjuman-al-Quran*. On Azad's religious views.

F994 ———. "The Persian Autobiography of Shāh Walīullāh bin 'Abd al-Rahīm al-Dihlavī: Its English Translation and a List of his Works," ASB: NS 8 (April 1912), 161-75.

F995 HAQ, S. MOINUL. "Syed Ahmed Khan," HFM:2, 1831-1905, part 2, 451-78.

F996 HOSAIN, M. HIDĀYAT. "The Life and Works of Bahr-ul-'Ulūm," ASB: NS 7 (Nov. 1911), 693-95. Wrote on Muslim law, logic.

F997 HUSAIN, MAHMUD. "The Successors of Sayyid Ahmad Shahid: Jihad on the North-Western Frontier," HFM:2, 1831-1905, part 1, 145-69.

F998 ———. "The Successors of Sayyid Ahmad Shahid: Trials and Persecution," HFM:2, 1831-1905, part 2, 366-89.

F999 INAYATULLAH, SH. "'Abd al-Hayy, Abu'l-Hasanāt Muhammad," EI:1, 66. Teacher at Farangi Mahal, Lucknow.

F1000 ———. "'Abd al-Kadir Dihlawī," EI:1, 68-69. Third son of Shah Waliullah; translated the Quran into Urdu.

F1001 ———. "Ahl-i Hadīth," EI:1, 259-60. A 20th cent. sect of Indian Muslims, active in purifying the faith and countering the Arya Samaj and Christian missionaries. Useful bibliography.

F1002 ———. "Sayyid Ahmad Brēlwī," EI:1, 282-83. 1786-1831.

F1003 ———. "Shāh 'Abd al-'Azīz al-Dihlawī," EI:1, 59. A son of Shah Waliullah.

F1004 "The Indian Conspiracy, 1864," CR 40:79 (1864), 124-37. On the Wahhabis.

F1005 IVANOV, W. "The Sect of Imam Shah in Gujrat," RASB: NS 12 (1936), 19-70. History and beliefs of a Shi'i Muslim sect.

F1006 "Jamiat-i-dawlat-o-tabligh-i-Islam," MW:14 (April 1925), 182-87. A Muslim missionary society founded in 1920, based in Poona; its plans and purposes.

F1007 KARIM, MOHAMMED NURUL. "Part Played by Haji Shari'atullah and His Son in the Socio-Political History of East Bengal," PPHC:5 (1955), 175-81. Dudu Miyan and his father.

F1008 KHAJA KHAN. "Sufi Orders in the Deccan," MW:18 (July 1928), 280-85. Abbreviated from *The Islamic World* (Lahore), Jan. 1928.

F1009 KHALID, TASADDUQ HUSSAIN. "The Reaction of Muslim India to Western Culture in the 19th Century with Particular Reference to the Wahabi Movement," SIS, pp. 63-84.

F1010 KOPF, DAVID. "Bibliographical Notes on Early, Medieval and Modern Sufism with Special Reference to Its Bengali-Indian Development," F:3 (Feb., March 1962), 69-84, 113-22. Pp. 120-22 deal with post-1750 developments.

F1011 KRAEMER, M. "Islam in India Today," MW:21 (April 1931), 151-76. "The substance of a Report after a three months' visit to India and a careful study of the present situation." An interesting survey.

F1012 MAHOMMED, ISMAIL MOULVI. "Notice of the Peculiar Tenets Held by the Followers of Syed Ahmed, Taken Chiefly from the 'Sirāt-ul-Mūstaqīm,' a Principal Treatise of that Sect, Written by Moulavi Mahommed Ismail," ASB:1 (Nov. 1832), 479-98.

F1013 AL-MAJAHID, SHARIF. "Nineteenth Century Bengali Mujahidin; in the Struggle for Independence," PQ:7 (Summer 1957), 18-23. Emphasizes the role of Bengal in the Wahhabi movement.

F1014 MALIK, HAFEEZ. "The Religious Liberalism of Sir Sayyid Ahmad Khan," MW:54 (July 1964), 160-69.

F1015 "Mappilla Faith and Fanaticism," CR:105 (Oct. 1897), 212-20.

F1016 MODUD, ĀBDUL. "Bhārate ohābī āndolan" [The Wahhabi Unrest in India], IAP:2 (Oct.-Dec. 1963), 178-92; 3 (Jan.-March 1964), 284-302.

F1017 "A MUSSALMAN." "Sir Syed Ahmed Khan: A Study of His Life and Work," IR:10 (Oct. 1909), 753-60.

F1018 MYLREA, C. G. "Lucknow as a Moslem Centre," MW:3 (1913), 31-36. Some information on Shi'a organization and the Arabic revival.

F1019 NADWI, ABDUL QAYYUM. "Deoband and Nadwah," HFM:2, 1831-1905, part 2, 424-29.

F1020 NIZĀMĪ, K. A. "Shah Waliullah Dihlavi and Indian Politics in the Eighteenth Century," IC:25 (1951), 133-45.

F1021 QANUNGO, K. R. "How Local Custom Modifies Scripture (Personal Observation among Villagers of Chittagong Half a Century Ago)," BPP:70 (1951), 23-33. Customs and attitudes of rural Bengali Muslims.

F1022 RAHBAR, MUHAMMAD DAŪD (tr.). "Shāh Walī Ullāh and Ijtihād; A Translation of Selected Passages from His 'Iqd al-jīd fī ahkām al-ijtihād wa-l-taqlīd." MW:45 (1955), 346-58.

F1023 RAHMAN, FAZLUR. "Andjuman (India and Pakistan)," EI:1, 505-06. On the Andjuman-i Tarakki-i Urdū, founded in 1913 by Sir Thomas Arnold and Shibli, and on the Andjuman-i Himāyat-i Islām, founded in 1884 under Saiyid Ahmed Khan's inspiration.

F1024 ———. "Modern Muslim Thought," MW:45 (Jan. 1955), 16-25. Largely on Iqbal.

F1025 ———. "Muslim Modernism in the Indo-Pakistan Sub-Continent," BSOAS:21 (1958), 82-99. A survey of intellectual history from Saiyid Ahmed Khan to the present; distinguishes 4 phases or modes: Westernism, Modernism, Revivalism, Conservatism; includes summary of current thought in Pakistan.

F1026 ———. "The Thinker of Crisis: Shah Waliy-Ullah," PQ:6 (Summer 1956), 44-48. Good summary.

F1027 RAWLINSON, H. G. "Sir Saiyid Ahmed Khan," IC:4 (July 1930), 389-96.

F1028 ROBINSON, PHIL. "The Benares Riots of 1809-1811," CR 65:129 (1877), 92-119. Hindu-Muslim riots.

F1029 ROY, N. B. "An Agitation over Some Prison Regulations, 1856, and the Faraizis," IHRC:34 (Dec. 1958), 146-52.

F1030 ROY CHOUDHURY, P. C. "A Rebel Magistrate of Bihar," MR: 93 (June 1953), 460-63. The career of Maulvi Ahmedullah in the Wahhabi Movement at Patna.

F1031 SAYEED, KHALID B. "The Jama'at-i-Islami Movement in Pakistan," PA:30 (March 1957), 59-68. Good discussion of Syed Abul 'Ala Maudoodi and his Muslim revivalist movement.

F1032 SELL, EDWARD. "New Islam," CoR:44 (Aug. 1893), 282-93. Appreciation of Amīr 'Alī and Chirāgh 'Alī.

F1033 SHABNAM, ALIF. "The Story of Syed Ahmed, Moss-trooper, Freebooter, Saint, and Crescentader," RCAS:14 (1927), 369-72.

F1034   SHERWANI, H. K. "The Political Thought of Sir Syed Ahmad Khan," IC:18 (July 1944), 236-53.

F1035   SIDDIQI, ASLAM. "Syed Aḥmad Shahīd," IC:19 (Jan. 1945), 123-39. A biography.

F1036   ———. "Sayyid Ahmed S̲h̲ahīd's End," IC:22 (Oct. 1948), 383-86.

F1037   SMITH, WILFRED CANTWELL. "Aḥmadiyya," EI:1, 301-03. A 19th & 20th cent. Indian Muslim religious movement.

F1038   TITUS, MURRAY T. "A Hindu Apologist for Islam," MW:14 (Jan. 1925), 37-39. On a 1921 book by T. L. Vaswani entitled "The Spiritual Struggle of Islam."

F1039   TOPA, I. "Sir Syyed Ahmed Khan: A Study in Social Thought," IC:27 (April 1953), 225-41. Source: *Intikhab-e-mazameen-e-sir syyed* (Aligarh, 1920).

F1040   TUFAIL, S. M. "The Late Maulana Muhammad 'Ali (1874-1951)," IsR:39 (Dec. 1951), 12-17. Biography of the Ahmadiyya leader of Lahore.

F1041   VUJICA, STANKO M. "The Ahmadiyya Movement in Islam," EaW:15 (Dec. 1961), 16-20. Its history in India.

F1042   "The Wahhabis in India down to the Death of Sayyid Ahmad," CR 50:100, 73-104; 51 (1870), 177-92, 381-99.

F1043   WALTER, HOWARD ARNOLD. "The Ahmadiya Movement To-day," MW:6 (1916), 66-78. On internal developments, 1913-16, with list of periodical publications.

F1044   YUSUF ALI, A. "Muslim Culture and Religious Thought," MIW, pp. 389-416. Under British rule.

F1045   ZWEMER, S. M. "The Diversity of Islam in India," MW:18 (April 1928), 111-23.

15. *CHRISTIANITY AND CHRISTIAN MISSIONS*

F1046   AITKEN, BENJAMIN. "John Murdoch, LLD," CR:128 (Jan. 1909), 55-63. Madras missionary.

F1047   "The Anglican Establishment in the Diocese of Calcutta," CR 43:85 (1866), 101-36.

F1048   ASHTON, J. P. "The History of the Calcutta Missionary Conference," IEvR:24 (Oct. 1897), 129-41. A chronicle.

F1049   BALLHATCHET, K. A. "Asian Nationalism and Christian Missions," IRM:46 (April 1957), 201-04. A brief account of the history of missionary attitudes toward Hinduism, in criticism of K. M. Panikkar.

F1050 "BIOGRAPHICUS." "Biographical Sketch of an Old Indian Chaplain," OH:2 (July 1824), 404-08. Rev. W. Hirst, F.R.S. 18th cent.

F1051 "Carey, Marshman and Ward," CR:32 (June 1859), 437-69.

F1052 CHESTERMAN, A. DE M. "The Journals of David Brainerd and of William Carey," BQ:19 (1961), 147-56. Summary in HA:9 (No. 1582). A discussion of Carey's journal, which covers June 1793–June 1795.

F1053 "Christian Missionaries in India," CR 48:96, 125-40.

F1054 "Christian Orientalism," CR:32 (June 1859), 279-307. On missionaries and their goals.

F1055 "Christianity in India," CR:34 (June 1860), 198-217.

F1056 COBB, HENRY S. "Records Relating to India in the Archives of the Church Missionary Society," IA:12 (1958), 19-23. General description.

F1057 "Cockburn's Prize Dissertation on India," ER:6 (July 1805), 462-77. About a prize given by Claudius Buchanan for an essay on the best way of "civilizing and evangelizing" India.

F1058 "Corrie and His Contemporaries—the Ante-Episcopal Period," CR 9:18 (1848), 267-313. On the first bishop of Madras.

F1059 CULSHAW, J. "The Mission Press in India," IEvR:27 (Oct. 1900), 200-07. With dates of establishment.

F1060 DATTA, KALIKINKAR. "Some Unpublished Letters Relating to the Roman Catholic Church at Patna," BPP:59 (July-Dec. 1940), 54-64. Trivial, but includes list of Roman Catholic inhabitants c. 1822.

F1061 "The Diocese of Calcutta: Its Subdivision an Urgent and Practical Necessity," CR:87 (July 1888), 74-88.

F1062 "Ecclesiastical Grants in India," CR:92 (April 1891), 345-50.

F1063 EDWARDS, THOMAS. "Christian Effort in India," CR 70:140 (1880), 762-74.

F1064 "The Establishment of the Indian Episcopate—Bishop Middleton," CR 13:25 (1850), 1-39.

F1065 FALLON, PIERRE, S. J. "Christianity in Bengal," SBR, pp. 448-59. Brief history from early 16th cent. onwards.

F1066 FIRMINGER, WALTER K. "Reginald Heber," CR:118 (Jan. 1904), 34-58. Brief biography of the bishop.

F1067 "The First Protestant Missionary to Bengal," CR:7 (1847), 124-85.

F1068 GORDON, ARTHUR N. "The Salvation Army and the Criminal Tribes in India," E&W:13 (Sept. 1914), 821-30.

F1069 "The Honorable Company's Ecclesiastical Establishment," CR 18:35 (1852), 116-36.

F1070 HOSTEN, H. "List of Jesuit Missionaries in 'Mogor' (1580-1803)," ASB: NS 6 (1910), 527-42.

F1071 [HOSTEN]. "Fr. Hosten's Manuscripts on Bengal," BORS:27 (1941), 373-83. Letters, manuscripts, and works of Jesuit missions covering 17th cent. to 19th cent. listed.

F1072 HUNTER, W. W. "Our Missionaries," NC:24 (July 1888), 14-29. Assessment of their role.

F1073 HYDE, H. B. "Recollections of Retired Chaplains of the Hon. E. I. Co.," CR:121 (Oct. 1905), 553-601.

F1074 "Indian Missions," ER:12 (April 1808), 151-81. Reviews pamphlets and tracts relating to the evangelization of India, blames Christian missionaries for troubles such as the Vellore massacre.

F1075 "Indian Missions," QR:138 (April 1875), 345-78.

F1076 "Islam and Christianity in India," CoR:53 (Feb. 1888), 161-80. Reasons for differences in success in conversion.

F1077 JERSEY, M. E. "The Hindu at Home," NC:25 (May 1889), 653-66. Discusses whether Christianity has had any effect on India.

F1078 KAMOJI, D. C. "American Christian Missions in India in the Nineteenth Century," MR:116 (July 1964), 43-52.

F1079 KEESS, A. "History of the Church Missionary Society," CR:110 (Jan. 1900), 74-79.

F1080 "LAYMAN." "The Bishops of Calcutta," CR:114 (Jan. 1902), 130-35. Brief accounts of each.

F1081 "Literary Fruits of Missionary Labors," CR:3 (1845), 36-70.

F1082 LOEHLIN, C. H. "Sikhs and Christians in the Punjab; Past, Present & Future," IRM:51 (Oct. 1962), 451-60. Missions in the Punjab.

F1083 LYALL, A. C. "Missionary Religions," FR:22 (July 1874), 52-67. Doubts that religions will destroy "Brahmanism"; response to article by Max Müller, pp. 68-75.

F1084 ———. "Our Religious Policy in India," FR:11 (Jan.-June 1872), 387-407. Regrets the new policy of separation of church and state in India.

F1085 MACFADYEN, DUGALD. "Duff, Alexander," EB:8, 643-44. Scottish missionary in Bengal.

F1086 "The Mahomedan Controversy," CR:4 (1845), 418-75. On Christian-Muslim conflict in India.

F1087 MAYHEW, A. I. "The Christian Ethic and India," MIW, pp. 305-37.

F1088 [MILMAN]. "Bishop Milman," CR 64:127 (1877), 1-23. Of Calcutta.

F1089 "Missionary Labour in the East," CR 51:101 (1870), 42-62.

F1090 "Missionary Labours of Chaplains in Northern India," CR:3 (1845), 299-322.

F1091 NAIDIS, MARK. "British Nationalism and European Religion in India," WA:30 (April 1959), 19-33. "In British India Christianity was a vehicle of European solidarity as well as a mode of cultural penetration. And an understanding of the former will go far toward explaining the attitude of the infant Indian Republic toward the Christian West." Summary in HA:5 (No. 1279).

F1092 "On The Inefficacy of the Means Now in Use for the Propagation of Christianity in India," OH:5 (June 1825), 586-603. Memoir to the Baptist Missionary Society in England.

F1093 "Our Earliest Protestant Mission to India," CR:1 (May 1844), 94-151.

F1094 PAREKH, MANILAL C. "Reverend Alexander Duff's Imperialism," MR:61 (May 1937), 529-32.

F1095 POTTS, E. DANIEL. "The Baptist Missionaries of Serampore and the Government of India, 1792-1813," JEcH:15 (Oct. 1964), 229-46. Uses records in the Baptist Missionary Society.

F1096 "Pratt, Weitbrecht, and the Church Missionary Society," CR 23:46 (1854), 354-412. On Rev. John James Weitbrecht and Rev. Josiah Pratt.

F1097 "Protestant Missions in India," CR 62:123 (1876), 83-105.

F1098 RAY, NISITH RANJAN. "The Foundation of the Indian Bishopric," MR:114 (Oct. 1963), 295-98.

F1099 RAY, SARAT CHANDRA. "The Agrarian Discontent and the Protestant Missions in Chotanagpur," MR:8 (Dec. 1910), 615-28. History of Christian missions.

F1100 "Results of Missionary Labour in India," CR 16:31 (1851), 231-88.

F1101 "Review of the State of Missions in India and of the Serampore Establishment," OMRR (Sept. 1824).

F1102 ROBINSON, VEN. ARCH. "Malabar Coast Christians," MJLS:1 (1833), 7-13, 94-104, 257-69, 342-50.

F1103 "St. Thomas' the Cathedral Church of Bombay," CR:108 (April 1899), 199-215.

F1104 SALMON, EDWARD (ed.). "The Journals of Dr. Turner, Bishop of Calcutta," AR:6 (July, Oct. 1888), 126-55, 343-73; 7 (Jan. 1889), 74-103. 1829-1830.

F1105 SANIAL, S. C. "The Rev. William Adam," BPP:8 (April-June 1914), 251-72. Biography and letters from the Serampore College Library; Unitarian friend of Ram Mohun Roy.

F1106 SEN, PRIYARANJAN. "William Carey (1761-1834)," CR:52 (Aug. 1934), 225-30. A centenary lecture, quite informative.

F1107 SIDDIQ KHAN, M. "William Carey and the Serampore Books (1800-1834)," Li:11 (1961), 197-280. Account of early printing in India, Carey and the founding of Serampore, the printing and publishing program, and "A Selective and Annotated Bibliography of Serampore Books." Serampore publications listed by year, most entries annotated with comments describing the publication and commenting on its importance. 222 entries.

F1108 SILVA, SEVERINE. "Father Francis Xavier of St. Anne," QJMS: 51 (1960-61), 129-33. 1771-1844.

F1109 "State of the Christian Establishments in Southern India," OH:3 (Sept. 1824), 12-22. Figures of membership.

F1110 [STYLES]. "John Styles on *Methodists and Missions*," ER:14 (April 1809), 40-50.

F1111 VAN DER SCHUEREN, T. "Uplift of the Aboriginals of Chota Nagpur," AR: NS 25 (1929), 65-82. Discussion, pp. 83-88. The work of Belgian Jesuits.

F1112 WALKER, MARY. "The Archives of the American Board for Foreign Missions," HL:6 (Winter 1952), 52-68. Describes the archives, which include correspondence from India, 1813-date.

F1113 WARNE, FRANK W. "India's Mass Movements in the Methodist Episcopal Church," IRM:6 (1917), 193-208. Methods and figures on conversions.

F1114 WEITBRECHT, H. H. "The Revision of the Urdu New Testament," IER:26 (April 1900), 415-46. With history of Urdu versions of the scriptures.

F1115 [WILSON]. "Life and Remains of Bishop Wilson," CR:35 (Sept. 1860), 89-125. On the bishop of Calcutta.

F1116 WILSON, C. E. "The Lay Work of Missionary Societies in India," AR: NS 22 (1926), 436-45. Discussion, pp. 446-53.

F1117 XAVIER, P. F. FRANCIS. "Yearly Record of the Mission of Caruar (Fathers of the Discalced Carmelites). Tr. by Severine Silva," QJMS:45 (1954-55), 105-12, 187-91, 253-57; 46 (1956), 49-55, 127-33; 47 (1956-57), 18-27, 159-64, 228-32, 302-09; 49 (1958-59), 52-58, 135-40, 187-94; 50 (1959-60), 37-45, 101-08, 145-53, 174-78; 51 (1960-61), 26-32, 70-75, 112-19. Written c. 1832, covers 18th cent.; with critical notes.

16. SCIENCE AND MEDICINE

F1118 AGHARKAR, S. P. "The Relations between the Scientific Departments of the Government of India and the Post-Graduate Departments of the Indian Universities," MR:29 (Feb. 1921), 164-66.

F1119 APTE, G. D. "Heerji Eduljee, First Indian Medical Historian," IJHM:4 (Dec. 1959), 43-45. Practiced medicine in Bombay 1865.

F1120 ARCHER, MILDRED. "India and Natural History: the Rôle of the East India Company 1785-1858," HT:9 (Nov. 1959), 736-43. Illustrated account of collectors and painters of Indian wild life.

F1121 BAGAL, JOGESH C. "Early Years of the Calcutta Medical College," MR:82 (Sept., Oct. 1947), 210-15. Based on educational records.

F1122 ———. "Radhanath Sikdar," MR:70 (July 1941), 47-50. Biography of a mathematician and scientist.

F1123 BASU, NARENDRA NATH. "Dr. Mahendra Lal Sircar," MR:95 (April 1954), 308-11. Founder of the Indian Association for the Cultivation of Science.

F1124 BASU, S. K. "Srinivas Ramanujan—the Remarkable Mathematical Genius," CR:171 (April 1964), 1-5.

F1125 BERNDORFER, A. "Tivadar Duka, a Hungarian Physician in India in the Middle of the 19th Century," IJHM 3:2 (1958), 1-7.

F1126 BHATNAGAR, O. P. "Small Pox Vaccine—Its Introduction under Wellesley," IHQ:28 (June 1952), 186-89. Based on records in National Archives.

F1127 "Bombay Medical and Physical Transactions," CR 17:33 (1852), 215-40.

F1128 BOSE, D. M. "Acharya Prafullachandra Ray: a Study," S&C:28 (Nov. 1962), 493-500. Biography of Gandhian chemist.

F1129 BUCHANAN, W. J. "The Introduction and Spread of Western Medical Science in India," CR:278 (Oct. 1914), 419-54.

F1130 "The Central Medical Research Institute," MR:48 (Nov. 1930), 505-16. A report.

F1131 CHATTERJEE, RAMANANDA. "Professor C. V. Raman Wins Nobel Prize," MR:48 (Dec. 1930), 675-78. Physicist, with bibliography of his works.

F1132 DATTA, SUSOBHAN. "India's Contribution to Modern Science," MR:74 (Dec. 1943), 422-27.

F1133 "A Decade of Sanitation in India," CR 55:109 (1872), 72-84.

F1134 "Dr. Dhanakoti Raju, the First Indian M.B. and M.D. of Madras University," IJHM:2 (1957), 130.

F1135 DUFFERIN, HARRIOT. "The National Association for Supplying Female Medical Aid to the Women of India," AR:1 (April 1886), 257-74.

F1136 EDWARDES, M. "Miss Nightingale and the Imperial Cloaca," TwC:154 (Dec. 1953), 452-59. On mortality and health in 19th cent. India, and its effect on the Indian Empire.

F1137 FILLIOZAT, JEAN. "A Hygienist at Pondichery in the 19th Century," IJHM:5 (June 1960), 19-20. On Dr. Huillet, author of several works on the subject.

F1138 "The First Indian Medical Congress," CR:101 (Oct. 1895), 413-22.

F1139 FORREST, G. W. "Plague in India," BM:182 (Oct. 1907), 575-88. History and present state.

F1140 "Hindu Medicine and Medical Education," CR 42:83 (1865), 106-25.

F1141 HOPKINSON, ALFRED. "Science in India," CoR:117 (July 1920), 43-50. Review of progress made in previous few years.

F1142 HUNTER, W. W. "A Female Medical Profession for India," CoR:56 (Aug. 1889), 207-15. Its growth under Lady Dufferin's sponsorship.

F1143 HYDE, H. MONTGOMERY. "Dr. George Govan and the Saharanpur Botanical Gardens," RCAS:49 (Jan. 1962), 47-57. On early botany; illustrated.

F1144 "Indian Epidemics and Mofussil Sanatory Reform," CR 16:31 (1851), 156-230.

F1145 JOSHI, R. M. "Diseases, Medicines and Physicians during the Peshwa Regime (1713-1818)," IJHM:3 (June 1958), 25-32. Based on chapter 9 in V. K. Bhave, *Peshwa Kaleena Maharashtra* (Maharashtra during the Peshwa Regime).

F1146 "The Jubilee Session of the Indian Science Congress," MR:63 (Feb. 1938), 191-202.

F1147 KAR, PRAVASH CHANDRA. "In Memoriam: Radhanath Sickdar (1813-1890)," MR:113 (Feb. 1963), 150-55. A mathematician.

F1148 LARWOOD, H. J. C. "Science in India before 1850," BJES:7 (1958), 36-49. The teaching of Western science in India, compared with teaching in England and Scotland; based on reports and records.

F1149 ———. "Western Science in India before 1850," RAS (April 1962), pp. 62-76. On European collectors and naturalists. Based on contemporary published works.

F1150 [LEYDEN]. "John Leyden," CR:31 (Sept. 1858), 1-53. Early 19th cent. surgeon.

F1151 LIUSTERNIK, E. IA. "Iz istorii russko-indiiskikh nauchnykh sviazei v. 70-90-kh godakh XIX v. Leningrad universitet" [From the History of Russian-Indian Scientific Relations in the 70's to the 90's of the 19th Century], VLU:4 (1964), 39-44; cited in SPA:4 (June 1964), 126.

F1152 LOBB, S. "Physical Science in the Calcutta University," CR 53:106 (1871), 321-43.

F1153 "Lunatic Asylums in Bengal," CR:26 (June 1856), 592-608.

F1154 MAHALANOBIS, P. C. "Subhendu Sekhar Bose: 1906-1938," Sa:4 (part 3, 1939), 313-36. Senior statistician in Statistical Laboratory, Calcutta, 1931-1938.

F1155 "Medical Jurisprudence in India," CR 52:103 (1871), 22-54.

F1156 "Natural Science in India," CR:26 (March 1856), 211-22.

F1157 NEELAMEGHAN, A. (comp.). "Recent Indian Medical Historiography," IJHM:2 (Dec. 1957), 111-20; 4 (June 1959), 37-51; 5 (June 1960), 35-41; 6 (June, Dec. 1961), 40-53, 20-37. Gives works on development of medicine, and on many individuals and institutions, past and present.

F1158 "Nursing in Madras in XIX Century; Extracts from Reports of the General Hospital, Madras, for 1895," IJHM:2 (June 1957), 43-48.

F1159 "AN ONLOOKER." "The First Indian Statistical Conference," MR:63 (Feb. 1938), 203-06.

F1160 "Peeps into the Past of the Madras Medical College (Extracts from the Old Records). Correspondence in 1852-1859, Relating to the Bodies for Dissection," IJHM:4 (Dec. 1959), 35-40.

F1161 "POLITICUS." "Life and Work of Sir J. C. Bose," MR:28 (Sept. 1926), 324-30. Jagadis Chandra Bose; based on printed works.

F1162 "The Public Health of India," CR:105 (Oct. 1897), 363-74.

F1163 "Quarantine and Cholera," CR 48:95, 118-66.

F1164 RAMAN, C. V. "Scientific Researches," AAAPSS:233 (May 1944), 39-45. An historical survey.

F1165 "Reminiscences of the First Woman Student of Madras Medical College," IJHM:2 (June 1957), 63-66. Mrs. Mary Scharlieb, late 19th cent.

F1166 "A Review of the Progress of Sanitation in India," CR 50:100, 1-47.

F1167 ROGERS, LEONARD. "A Short Historical Note on Medical Societies and Medical Journals in Calcutta," ASB: NS 2 (1906), 393-97.

F1168 "The Sanatory Condition of Calcutta," CR:5 (1846), 373-95. On public health.

F1169 "The Sanatory Condition of Peshawur," CR:30 (June 1858), 342-54.

F1170 "Sanitary Reform," CR:27 (Sept. 1856), 1-16.

F1171 "Sanitary Reform in India," CR 50:99, 94-159.

F1172 SARKAR, JADUNATH. "A Twentieth Century Rishi," MR:76 (July 1944), 49-52. Prafulla Chandra Ray, the chemist.

F1173 SEN, BOSISWAR. "The Bose Research Institute," MR:54 (Dec. 1933), 676-78.

F1174 SEN, SAMARENDRA NATH. "Science," SBR, pp. 386-99.

F1175 "The Sick Room in India," CR:3 (1845), 71-101. On illness in India.

F1176 "Some Pioneers of Medical Education in Bengal," MR:46 (Oct. 1929), 454-56.

F1177 "Surgeons in India—Past and Present," CR 23:45 (1854), 217-54. On the medical officers of the Indian Army.

F1178 "T.H.S." "Fighting the Cholera Devil," BM:225 (June 1929), 815-22. In South Travancore.

F1179 THIN, GEORGE. "The Report of the Leprosy Commission in India," FR:61 (Jan.-June 1894), 93-102.

F1180 WATERS, G. "Plague in Bombay," AnSB:5 (1901), 382-96. Figures on mortality in 1896-97, with a description of the course of the disease.

F1181 WILLIAMS, DONOVAN. "Clements Markham and the Introduction of the Cinchona Tree into British India, 1861," GJ:128 (Dec. 1962), 431-42. From India Office records.

PART II · DISSERTATIONS

INDEXES OF DISSERTATIONS

AMERICAN ECONOMIC REVIEW. "List of Doctoral Dissertations in Political Economy in American Universities and Colleges." Annual (September).

AMERICAN HISTORICAL ASSOCIATION. *List of Doctoral Dissertations in History in Progress or Completed at Colleges and Universities in the United States.* Published every 3 years.

ASLIB. *Index to Theses Accepted for Higher Degrees in the Universities of Great Britain and Ireland, 1950/51—.* Annual (1963/64 pub. in 1966).

BOMBAY UNIVERSITY, *Journal.* Lists degrees received and abstracts some dissertations.

CHICAGO, UNIVERSITY LIBRARY. Far East Library. *The University of Chicago Doctoral Dissertations and Masters' Theses on Asia 1894-1962.* Chicago, 1962.

COLUMBIA UNIVERSITY, EAST ASIATIC LIBRARY. *Columbia University Masters' Essays and Doctoral Dissertations on Asia, 1875-1956.* New York, 1957.

DISSERTATION ABSTRACTS. Ann Arbor, Michigan, monthly. Vol. 1-11 called *Microfilm Abstracts.*

FRANCE. Direction des bibliothèques de France. *Catalogue des thèses de doctorat soutenues les universités françaises.* Nouvelle série, 1959–.

GAUTAM, BRIJENDRA PRATAP. *Researches in Political Science in India (A Detailed Bibliography).* Kanpur: Oriental Publishing House, 1966?

GUPTA, G. P. *Economic Investigations in India (A Bibliography of Researches in Commerce and Economics Approved by Indian Universities).* With Supplement 1962. Agra: Ram Prasad & Sons, n.d.

INDIA (REPUBLIC). National Archives. *Bulletin of Research Theses and Dissertations.* Nos. 1-3 (Jan. 1955, Jan. 1956, Jan. 1960).

INDIA (REPUBLIC). National Council of Educational Research and Training. *Educational Investigations in Indian Universities (1939-1961): A List of Theses and Dissertations Approved for the Doctorate and Master's Degree in Education.* New Delhi, 1963. Mimeographed.

INTER-UNIVERSITY BOARD (India). *Bibliography of Doctorate Theses in Science and Arts Accepted by Indian Universities.* Bangalore, 1935, 1946.

KAUL, J. N. "Dissertations in the Social Sciences by Indian Doctoral Scholars, 1933-1953," Ph.D. thesis, University of Michigan, 1955.

LONDON UNIVERSITY. *Historical Research for University Degrees in the United Kingdom.*
For 1911-1928 in *History*, NS 4-13 (1919/20-1928/29);
For 1928/29-1930/31 and 1940-1943 in *Bulletin of the Institute of Historical Research*, Vol. 7, 8, 9, 18, 19.
For other years, in annual *Thesis Supplement* to the *Bulletin.*

MOSCOW, MINISTERSTVO KUL'TURY RSFSR. *Katalog kanditat-skikh i doktorskikh dissertatsii, postupivshikh v biblioteky imeni V.I. Leninq. . . .* Quarterly.

PANJAB UNIVERSITY. Extension Library. *Panjab University Doctoral Dissertations, 1948-1964.* Ludhiana, 1965. 22 pp.

PERSON, LAURA. *Cumulative List of Doctoral Dissertations and Masters' Theses in Foreign Missions and Related Subjects as Reported by the Missionary Research Library in the* Occasional Bulletin, *1950-1960.* New York: Missionary Research Library, 1961. 46 pp.

POONA, UNIVERSITY. *Journal.* Occasionally lists dissertations.

QUARTERLY REVIEW OF HISTORICAL STUDIES. Frequently lists dissertations from Indian universities.

SCHMIDT, EARL R. *Preliminary List of Ph.D. Dissertations on South Asia 1933-1960 (Unedited).* Wisconsin, dittographed.

STUCKI, CURTIS W. *American Doctoral Dissertations on Asia, 1933-1958.* Ithaca, N.Y.: Cornell University, Southeast Asia Program Data Paper No. 37, 1959.

UNESCO. *Theses in the Social Sciences, an International Analytical Catalogue of Unpublished Doctorate Theses, 1940-1950.* Paris: UNESCO, 1952.

UNITED STATES DEPARTMENT OF STATE, Office of External Research. *External Research: Asia; a List of Current Social Science Research by Private Scholars and Academic Centers.* Annual.

UTTARA BHARATI. Lists dissertations accepted at universities in Uttar Pradesh.

G. AREAS NOT PRIMARILY UNDER BRITISH CONTROL

1. *THE FRENCH AND PORTUGUESE*

G1   NENTIN, S. A. "Relations between Tipu and the French," Bombay. Abstract in BUJ:1 (1932), 208-21.

G2   SRIVASTAVA, K. C. "Portuguese in India—1500-1961," Lucknow, after 1950. Under G. S. Misra.

2. *THE MARATHAS*

G3   DEODHAR, YASHWANT NARAYAN. "Nana Phadnis and the External Affairs of the Maratha Empire, 1740-1800," Bombay, 1956. 386 pp. Summary in QRHS:1 (April-June 1961), 34-35.

G4   GUNE, V. T. "Judicial System of the Marathas (A Detailed Study of Judicial Institution from A.D. 1600 to 1818 Based Chiefly on Original Decisions)," Poona, 1949. 205 & 326 pp. Abstract in BUJ:17 (Jan. 1950), 101-04.

G5   GUPTA, B. D. "Bundelkhand under the Maratha Domination—1730-1805," Lucknow, after 1950. Under B. Kishore.

G6   GUPTA, BENI. "The Marathas and the States of Kota and Bundi (1682 to 1818 A.D.)," Rajasthan. Under V. P. S. Raghuvanshi.

G7   HATALKAR, V. G. "The Relations between the French and the Marathas," Bombay (St. Xavier), 1950.

G8   "Maratha Expansion in South India (A.D. 1707-1761)," Madras, 1945.

G9   MEHTA, PRITHVI SINGH. "Relations between the Mewar and the Marathas (1707-1818)," Agra, 1956. Summary in QRHS 2:2 (1962-63), 30-31.

G10   MERCHANT, K. D. "British Relations with Surat—1600 A.D. to 1802 A.D. (Foundation of the British Empire in Western India)," Bombay (St. Xavier), 1948.

G11   NITSURE, K. G. "Critical Study of the Provision for Welfare Activities in the Maratha Empire," Poona. Under D. K. Garde.

G12   SAJANLAL, KASIM ALI. "Nizam Ali's Relations with the Marathas," Bombay. Summary in BUJ:1 (Jan. 1933), 403-08.

G13   SEN, S. N. "Anglo-Maratha Relations during the Administration of Warren Hastings, 1772-1785," Calcutta.

G14 VERMA, SHANTI PRASAD. "Anglo-Maratha Relations, 1772-1783 A.D. (A Study in Indian Diplomacy of the Late Eighteenth Century)," Agra, 1955.

3. OUDH, 1750-1800

G15 AHMAD, SAFI. "Two Kings of Avadh, Mohammad Ali Shah and Amjad Ali Shah (1837-47)," Lucknow, after 1958. Under R. N. Nagar. [Title also cited as, "Four Kings of Avadh."]

G16 BASU, P. "The Relations between Oudh and the East India Company, from 1785 to 1801," London, 1939. Under Dodwell. Summary in IHRB:17 (1939-40), 42-45.

G17 BHATNAGAR, GAURISHWAR DAYAL. "Oudh under Wajid Ali Shah," Lucknow, 1955. Under N. L. Chatterji.

G18 RAHMAN, A. F. M. K. "Rise and Fall of the Rohilla Power in Hindustan, 1707-74 A.D.," London, 1935. Under C. C. Davies.

G19 SHUKLA, B. "Administration of Avadh, 1856-77," Lucknow, after 1957. Under B. Kishore.

G20 SRIVASTAVA, ASHIRBADI LAL. "The First Two Nawab Wazirs of Oudh," Lucknow, 1932.

4. CENTRAL PROVINCES AND BERAR

G21 AGASKAR, M. S. "Mahadji Sindhia—a Political Career in India, i.e. 1730 to 1794," Bombay, before 1955.

G22 BHARGAVA, S. P. "Some Aspects of the Administration of the Central Provinces and Berar (1861-1920)," Nagpur.

G23 CHAVDA, V. K. "Gaekwads and the British: a Study of Their Problems, 1875-1920," Baroda, 1958.

G24 DAS, BHAGWAN. "The Bundela War of Independence and Maharaja Chhatra Sal Bundela," Lucknow, 1955. Under K. R. Qanungo.

G25 GHOSH, B. "British Policy towards the Pathans and the Pindaris in Central India, 1805-1818," London (School of Oriental and African Studies), 1963-64.

G26 JOSHI, SHYAM SUNDER. "The Political and Constitutional Evolution of Central India (Agency) States Constituting the State of Madhya Bharat (1858-1948)," Agra, 1958.

G27 KRISHNA, UMA. "Administrative Organisation of Bhopal State," Agra. Summary in QRHS:3 (1963-64), 144-49.

G28 MOOKERJEE, S. "The Growth of Nagpur, India," Indiana, 1955. 221 pp.

PART II: DISSERTATIONS

G29 QANUNGO, S. "Life and Times of Daulat Rao Sindhia," Lucknow, after 1950. Under B. Kishore.

G30 QANUNGO, S. N. "Jaswant Rao Holkar and His Times," Lucknow.

G31 ROY, M. P. "Pindaris—Their Origin, Growth and Suppression," Rajasthan. Under V. P. S. Raghuvanshi.

G32 ROY, P. C. "Raghoji Bhonsle I of Nagpur," Lucknow, after 1958. Under B. Kishore.

G33 SHARMA, INDRA DUTT. "The Government and Administration at Baroda (1881-1938)," Lucknow, 1949.

G34 SINGH, R. B. "Malhar Rao Holkar," Lucknow, after 1958. Under B. Kishore.

G35 SINHA, B. K. "The Pindaris (1798-1818)," Patna.

G36 SINHA, RAM MOHAN. "Nagpur State in the 19th Century: a Study in Some Aspects of Its Administrative System, 1818-1854," Nagpur.

G37 SRIVASTAVA, PRAFULLA KUMAR. "The Office of the Collector with Particular Reference to the State of Old Madhya Pradesh," Saugar, 1962.

G38 VERMA, D. C. "Kingdom of Bijapur," Lucknow, after 1958. Under B. Kishore.

5. MYSORE

G39 ABHAYAMBAL, UDAYAM. "State Policy and Economic Development in Mysore State since 1881," London, 1930. Under Vera Anstey.

G40 BANU, SYEDA MALLIKA. "Administrative Policy of Tipu Sultan," Mysore, after 1956. Under B. Sheik Ali.

G41 CHARI, B. MUDDA. "Mysore-Maratha Relations in the 18th Century," Mysore, after 1956. Under B. Sheik Ali.

G42 DATTA, SUSILKUMAR. "The Downfall of Tipu Sultan, 1793-99," London, 1924. Under Dodwell.

G43 KASYMOV, A. M. "Bor'ba naroda Maĭsura protiv angliĭskikh kolonizatorov v 1782-1799 gg" [The Struggle of the Mysore People against the English Colonialists, 1782-1799], Moscow (Institute of the Peoples of Asia of the Academy of Sciences of the USSR), 1962. 248 pp.

G44 MASCARENHAS, WILLIAM X. "Hyder Ali and Tipu Sultan in Canara," Bombay. Abstract in BUJ:1 (July 1932), 195-204.

G45 McCORMACK, WILLIAM CHARLES. "Changing Leadership of a Mysore Village," Chicago, 1956.

G46 SASTRI, K. N. V. "The Administration of Mysore under Sir Mark Cubbon, 1834-1861," London, 1930. Under Dodwell.

G47 SHEIK ALI, B. "English Relations with Haidar Ali, 1760-1782," London (School of Oriental and African Studies), 1960. Under Ballhatchet.

G48 VAN LOHUIZEN, J. "The Dutch East India Company and Mysore, 1762-1790," Cambridge (Catherine's), 1957. Under T. G. P. Spear.

6. HYDERABAD

G49 KISHORE, B. "History of Nizam-Maratha Relations," Lucknow, after 1950. Under K. R. Qanungo.

G50 MUTTALIB, M. A. "The Administration of Justice under the Nizams, 1724-1947," Osmania, 1958.

G51 REGANI, SAROJINI. "Nizam-British Relations (1724-1857)," Osmania, after 1956. Under K. Sajanlal.

7. SIKHS AND THE PUNJAB, 1750-1850

G52 CHOPRA, BARKAT RAI. "Kingdom of the Punjab, 1839-1845," Punjab, 1960.

G53 GUPTA, HARI RAM. "History of the Sikhs from 1769 to 1798," Punjab, 1944.

G54 HASRAT, B. J. "Anglo-Sikh Relations 1799-1849," Oxford (St. Catherine's), 1957.

G55 KHANNA, KAHAN C. "Anglo-Sikh Relations, 1839-1849," London, 1931-32. Under Dodwell.

G56 LALL, GULSHAN. "The Punjab as a Sovereign State, 1799-1839," London, 1923. Under Dodwell.

G57 MEHTA, S. D. "George Thomas, Rāja of Hansi," Bombay, 1932. Abstract in BUJ:1 (1932).

G58 PRAKASH, VED. "History of the Sikhs in Bihar," Patna.

G59 RAO, SURAJ NARAIN. "Cis-Sutlej Sikh States, 1800-1849," Punjab, 1953.

G60 SINGH, FAUJA. "Military System of the Sikhs during the Period 1719-1849," Delhi.

G61 SINGH, JOGINDER. "From the First Sikh War to the Annexation of the Punjab," Punjab, 1953.

8. *RAJPUT STATES*

G62 ACHARYA, N. K. "Administration of Jodhpur State from 1800 to 1947," Rajasthan, 1962. Under M. L. Sharma.

G63 BATRA, H. C. "The Relations of Jaipur State with the East India Company," Rajasthan, 1955.

G64 CHOWDHRY, P. S. "Rajasthan between the Two World Wars (1919 to 1939 A.D.)," Rajasthan. Under M. L. Sharma.

G65 GUPTA, B. P. "Administration of Bikaner State," Rajasthan, 1961. Under M. L. Sharma.

G66 GUPTA, KUNJ BEHARI LAL. "The Evolution of Administration of the Former Bharatpur State, 1722-1947," Rajasthan, 1960.

G67 JOSHI, SAROJ. "The Relations of the East India Company with Mewar," Lucknow, 1953-54. Under N. L. Chatterji.

G68 KASLIWAL, R. R. "Administrative System of Jaipur State since 1800 A.D.," Rajasthan, 1951.

G69 MAHESHWARY, S. C. "British Relations with the States of Rajputana (1815 to 1835 A.D.)," Rajasthan, after 1956. Under V. P. S. Raghuvanshi. Summary in QRHS 3:4 (1963-64), 207-08.

G70 MATHUR, R. M. "Relations of the States of Jodhpur, Bikaner and Jaisalmer with the English East India Company," Rajasthan. Under A. L. Srivastava.

G71 PALIWAL, D. L. "Udaipur and the British (1857 to 1919 A.D.)," Rajasthan. Under M. L. Sharma.

G72 PARIHAR, G. R. "Marwar and the Marathas (1724 to 1843 A.D.)," Rajasthan. Under G. N. Sharma.

G73 SHARMA, B. D. "Udaipur and the East India Company (1817 to 1857 A.D.)," Rajasthan. Under M. L. Sharma.

G74 TIKKIWAR, H. C. "Jaipur and Later Mughals (1707 to 1803 A.D.)," Rajasthan. Under M. L. Sharma.

9. *NORTHWEST FRONTIER AND AFGHANISTAN*

G75 DAVIES, C. C. "The North-West Frontier of India, 1890-1908, with a Survey of Policy since 1849," Cambridge, 1926.

G76 HARRIS, L. "British Policy on the North-West Frontier of India, 1889-1901," London (School of Oriental and African Studies), 1959. Under Ballhatchet.

G77 KAPUR, A. C. "The Problem of the North West Frontier of India," Punjab, 1945.

G78 PRABHAKAR, K. R. "North-West Frontier Policy of the Government of India (1849-1899)," Punjab, 1951.

G79 RASTOGI, DAYA PRAKASH. "Indo-British Relations with the North-West Frontier Tribes of India (1864-1901)," Agra, 1960.

G80 RASTOGI, R. S. "North West Frontier Policy of the Indian Government, 1890-1914," Lucknow, after 1950. Under R. N. Nagar. [Title also cited as, "Indo-Afghan Relations."]

G81 SARKAR, K. M. "The Frontier Policy of British India during the Governor-Generalship of Lord Minto, 1807-13," Cambridge, 1936.

G82 SINGH, GANDA. "Ahamad Shah Durrani," Punjab.

G83 TRIPATHI, GANGA PRASAD. "Indo-Afghan Relations 1882-1907," Delhi.

G84 VERMA, BIRENDRA. "The Afghans and the East India Company (1755-1800)," Patna.

10. HIMALAYA AND NORTHEAST FRONTIER

G85 ANAND, A. S. "The Development of the Constitution of Jammu and Kashmir," London (University College), 1962-63.

G86 BAROOAH, N. K. "David Scott on the North-east Frontier of India and in Assam," London (School of Oriental and African Studies), 1963-64. Summary in IHRB:37 (Nov. 1964), 262-64.

G87 BRECHER, MICHAEL. "The Kashmir Impasse," Yale, 1953.

G88 GHOSE, D. K. "British Relations with Kashmir, 1885-1893," London (School of Oriental and African Studies), 1963-64.

G89 GUPTA, S. "British Policy on the North-east Frontier of India," Oxford (Balliol), 1948. Under C. C. Davies.

G90 HOAR, J. C. "Contemporary Nepal: a Historical Study," Georgetown, 1959.

G91 KUMAR, SATISH. "Political System of Nepal Under the Ranas, 1846-1901," Indian School of International Studies.

G92 MIKOIAN, S. A. "Britanskiĭ imperializm v Indii i Kashmirskaĭa problema" [British Imperialism in India and the Kashmir Problem], Moscow (State Institute of International Relations), 1958. 330 pp.

G93 RED'KO, I. B. "Antifeodal'noe i antiimperialisticheskoe dvizhenie v Nepale posle vtoroĭ mirovoĭ voĭny (1945-1956 gg.)" [The Anti-feudal and Anti-imperialist Movement in Nepal after the Second World War (1945-1956)], Moscow (Oriental Institute of the Academy of Sciences of the USSR), 1959. 369 pp.

G94 SETH, S. K. "Indo-Sikkim Relations in the 19th Century," Lucknow, after 1958. Under G. S. Misra.

G95 SINGH, HARNAM. "The Government and Administration of the Jammu and Kashmir State," Lucknow, 1943.

G96 SINGH, RANJEET. "Kashmir under the Sikhs," Lucknow, 1953-54. Under N. L. Chatterji.

G97 TENG, MOHAN KRISHAN. "Social Legislation in Kashmir since 1900," Lucknow, 1963.

11. *OTHER PRINCELY STATES*

G98 PERUMAL, C. A. "Some Aspects of the Administration of the Travancore-Cochin States," Lucknow, 1961.

G99 RAJKUMAR, NAGOJI VASUDEV. "The Government and Administration of Travancore," Lucknow, 1944.

12. *INDIANS OVERSEAS*

G100 ABDUL-HADI, HAFEZ. "La question des Hindous en Afrique du Sud" [The Question of Hindus in South Africa], Paris, 1950. 110 pp.

G101 CUMPSTON, INA M. "The Problem of the Indian Immigrant in British Colonial Policy after 1834," Oxford (Lady Margaret), 1950. Under A. F. Madden.

G102 DUBE, S. P. "Immigration in Africa," Lucknow, 1953-54. Under G. S. Misra.

G103 GUPTA, B. L. "The Political and Civic Status of Indians in Ceylon," Agra, 1953.

G104 KIELL, NORMAN. "A Study of Attitudes of Indian and Pakistani Students in the United States toward America and American Democracy and the Responsibility of American Educational Institutions toward Exchange Students," Columbia, 1949. 189 pp.

G105 MOHAN, RADHA. "The Civic and Political Status of Indians in Burma," Agra, 1958.

G106 SRIVASTAVA, IQBAL NARAIN. "The Civic and Political Status of Indians in South Africa up to the Gandhi-Smuts Agreement: A Survey and Assessment," Agra, 1956.

H. AREAS PRIMARILY UNDER BRITISH RULE

1. ADMINISTRATION AND CONSTITUTIONAL LAW, GENERAL

H1   CHAKRAVARTY, S. "The Evolution of Representative Government in India, 1884-1909, with Reference to Central and Provincial Legislative Councils," London (School of Oriental and African Studies), 1953. Under Philips.

H2   CHAND, B. "Discretionary Powers in the Indian Government, with Special Reference to District Administration," London, 1938. Under Laski.

H3   DIVATIA, K. V. "Nature of Inter-relations of Governments in India in the Twentieth Century," Bombay, 1955.

H4   IQBAL, H. M. "Preventive Detention, with Special Reference to India and Pakistan," London (School of Oriental and African Studies), 1952.

H5   JAIN, RANBIR SINGH. "The Growth and Development of Governor General's Executive Council (1858-1919)," Agra, 1958.

H6   JOSHI, P. L. "The Evolution of Franchise and Electoral System in India," Saugar, 1961.

H7   KADEER, AHMED ABDUL. "Les Rapports entre le gouvernement central et les états dans l'Inde" [The Relations between the Central Government and the States in India], Paris (Droit), 1958. 190 pp.

H8   KEMAL, R. "The Legal and Constitutional Implications of the Evolution of Indian Independence," Glasgow, 1951.

H9   MATHUR, RAMESH NARAIN. "Presidentship of the Indian Legislative Assembly," Delhi. Summary in QRHS:1 (April-June 1961), 32.

H10   MEHROTRA, S. R. "The Growth of the Idea of Commonwealth in India, 1900-1929," London (School of Oriental and African Studies), 1960. Under Philips.

H11   NAIR, P. N. NARAYANAN. "The Role of the District Collector in Indian Administration with Special Reference to Madras," Cornell, 1957.

H12   NATHAN, BHALERAO CHANDRASEN. "The Working of Public Service Commission in India," Baroda, 1963.

H13   OCHS, GEORGE MILTON. "The Labor Party and Constitutional Reform for India," Illinois, 1960. 273 pp. Abstract in DA:21 (April 1961), 3080-81: "The role of the British Labor Party in constitutional reform for India from 1900 . . . to 1939." '

[394]

H14 PRASHAD, G. "Influence of European Political Doctrines upon the Evolution of the Indian Governmental Institutions and Practice, 1858-1938," London, 1941. Under H. Finer.

H15 RAO, R. V. "The Evolution of Representative Institutions in Modern India, 1858-1919," Nagpur, before 1950.

H16 SARAN, PARMATMA. "The Imperial Legislative Council of India (1861-1920)," Agra, 1959.

H17 SINGH, S. "The Council of India, 1858-1919," London (School of Oriental and African Studies), 1955.

H18 SRIVASTAVA, GUR PRASAD. "The Indian Civil Service, 1600-1947," Lucknow, 1952.

H19 THAKUR, RUDRA NATH. "The All India Services—A Study of their Origin and Growth," Bihar, 1963.

H20 VERMA, R. C. "Provincial Administration in India," Allahabad, 1951.

2. ADMINISTRATION TO 1857

H21 BEARCE, GEORGE D. "British Attitudes toward India: 1813-1858," Wisconsin, 1952. 145 pp.

H22 CHANDRA, PRAKASH. "The Relations between the Court of Directors and the Board of Commissioners for the Affairs of India, 1784-1813," London. Summary in IHRB:11 (Nov. 1933), 127-29.

H23 CROWE, A. L. "Sir Josiah Child and the East India Company," London (School of Oriental and African Studies), 1956.

H24 DAS GUPTA, A. "Relations of the Governor-General and Council with the Governor and Council of Madras under the Regulating Act of 1773," London, 1930. Under Dodwell. Summary in IHRB:8 (1930-31), 178-79.

H25 DASS, DAYAL. "Administration of Sir Charles Metcalfe," Lucknow.

H26 DE, BARUN. "Henry Dundas and the Government of India, 1773-1801," Oxford 1961. Under C. C. Davies.

H27 DESIKACHAR, S. V. "Legislative Centralisation in the Government of India, 1833-1861," Delhi. Summary in QRHS:1 (April-June 1961), 31-32.

H28 EYLES, D. "The Abolition of the East India Company's Monopoly, 1833," Edinburgh, 1956. Under R. Pares.

H29 GHOSAL, A. K. "An Administrative Study of the Development of Civil Service in India during the Company's Regime," London (London School of Economics), 1940. Under H. Finer.

H30 GROVER, BASANT LAL. "Development of the Postal System in Northern India under the East India Company (1757-1858)," Punjab, 1959.

H31 INK, JOSEPH. "The Marquis of Hastings and the Non-Intervention Policy in India, 1813-1823," Western Reserve.

H32 JONES, E. B. "The Imperial Ideas of Henry Dundas and British Expansion in the East, 1783-1801," Duke, 1963.

H33 KUMAR, VIRENDRA. "Indian Administration under Lord Hardinge (23 July 1844 to January 1848)," Allahabad, 1945.

H34 MEHTA, B. N. "Sir George Barlow in India," Agra, 1949.

H35 MISRA, GIRJA SHANKAR. "Influence of British Foreign Policy on the Politics of the East India Company (1783-1815)," Lucknow, 1955. Under S. N. Das Gupta.

H36 PRASAD, SRI NANDAN. "Paramountcy under Lord Dalhousie," Allahabad, 1948. [Title also cited as: "The Policy of Dalhousie toward the Protected Indian States."]

H37 SAIGAL, B. "Administration of Lord Elgin I," Lucknow.

H38 SHUKLA, V. S. "Sir John Malcolm in India," Lucknow, after 1955. Under N. L. Chatterji.

H39 SINHA, D. P. "The Internal Policy of Lord Auckland in British India from 1836 to 1842, with Special Reference to Education," London (School of Oriental and African Studies), 1952. Under Philips.

H40 SPRINGER, WILLIAM H. "The Military Apprenticeship of Arthur Wellesley in India, 1797-1805," Yale, 1963.

H41 STOKES, E. T. "Utilitarian Influence and the Formation of Indian Policy, 1820-1840," Cambridge (Christ's), 1952-53.

H42 SULOCHANA, R. "Genesis of the Legislative Machinery in India (1773-1861)," Bombay, 1961. 642 pp.

3. WARREN HASTINGS

H43 KLEIN, RALPH J. "The Impeachment and Trial of Warren Hastings," Western Reserve, 1951.

H44 MARSHALL, P. J. "Impeachment of Warren Hastings," Oxford, 1962. Under Lucy S. Sutherland.

PART II: DISSERTATIONS

4. *ADMINISTRATION AND REFORMS, 1858 TO 1898*

H45 ABRAHAM, BABY. "Central Administration between 1858-1906," Saugar, 1961.

H46 CHAUDHARY, V. C. P. "Politics and Administration in India (1876-1880)," Patna, after 1956. Summary in QRHS 2:2 (1962-63), 78.

H47 GOPAL, S. "The Viceroyalty of Lord Ripon, 1880-4," Oxford (Balliol), 1951-52.

H48 GUJRAL, L. M. "The Internal Administration of Lord Lytton, with Special Reference to Social and Economic Policy, 1876-1880," London (School of Oriental and African Studies), 1958. Under Ballhatchet.

H49 GUPTA, H. L. "India under Lord Amherst," Allahabad, 1946.

H50 HAMBLY, G. R. G. "Sir Richard Temple and the Government of India, 1868 to 1880; Some Trends in Indian Administrative Policy," Cambridge, 1961. Under T. G. P. Spear.

H51 McAREE, JAMES GREGORY. "The Passage of the Government of India Bill of 1858," Minnesota, 1961. Abstract in DA:22 (Aug. 1961), 556.

H52 MOULTON, S. C. "Lord Northbrook's Indian Administration, 1872-1876," London (School of Oriental and African Studies), 1963-64.

H53 NATH, TRILOKI. "Post-Mutiny Settlement in India," Agra, 1958.

H54 PAL, DHARM. "Indian Administration of Sir John Lawrence (Viceroy of India, 1864-1869)," Punjab, 1948.

H55 QANUNGO, BHUPEN. "Lord Canning's Administration and the Modernization of India, 1856-62," Indiana, 1962. 205 pp. Abstract in DA: 23 (Jan. 1963), 2508.

H56 SHARMA, M. "Administration of Lord Lansdowne," Lucknow.

H57 SINGH, H. L. "The Internal Policy of the Indian Government, 1885-1898," London (School of Oriental and African Studies), 1952. Under Philips.

H58 SINGH, V. P. "Administration of India under Lord Northbrook," Delhi.

H59 SRIVASTAVA, KRISHNA SWARUP. "The Administration of India under Lord Mayo," Allahabad, 1949.

H60 WILLIAMS, D. "The Formation of Policy in the India Office, 1858-66, with Special Reference to the Political, Judicial, Revenue, Public and Public Works Departments," Oxford, 1962. Under C. C. Davies.

[397]

H61 ZOBERI, Z. H. "The Relations between the Home and Indian Governments, 1858-1870," London (School of Oriental and African Studies), 1951. Under Philips.

5. ADMINISTRATION AND REFORMS, 1898 TO 1919

H62 MAZUMDAR, V. "Imperial Policy in India, 1905-10," Oxford (St. Hugh's), 1962-63.

H63 MOONEY, H. F. "The British Policy of Devolution in India, 1911-1919," Stanford, 1952.

H64 STUART, FRANK CARPENTER. "The British Nation and India: 1906-1914," New Mexico, 1964. Abstract in DA:26 (April 1966), 6010-11.

6. ADMINISTRATION AND REFORMS, 1919 TO 1950

H65 DESHPANDE, NARAYAN RAGHUNATH. "Constitution-Making in India," Columbia, 1951. 309 pp.

H66 DEVADANAM, CHEBROLU. "The Development of Provincial Autonomy in India, 1919-1949," New York, 1964. Abstract in DA:25 (Sept. 1964), 1873-74.

H67 FOLEY, RUDOLPH X. "The Origins of the Indian Reorganization Act of 1934," Fordham, 1937.

H68 FONTERA, RICHARD M. "Cultural Pluralism and Communism: the Development of the Government of India Act of 1935," New York, 1964.

H69 FRIEDMAN, H. J. "Consolidation of India since Independence: a Comparison and Analysis of Four Territorial Possessions, the French Areas, Hyderabad, and Kashmir," Pittsburgh, 1956. 182 pp.

H70 GAHRANA, GIRRAJ KISHORE. "Growth of Legislative Procedure at the Centre in India, 1919-1952," Agra, 1953.

H71 GHOSH, S. C. "The British Conservative Party and Indian Problems, 1927-1935," Manchester, 1963-64.

H72 INAMDAR, N. R. "Study of the System of Representation in India," Poona. Under S. V. Kogekar. Abstract in JUP:3 (1954), 162-67.

H73 LINDBLAD, G. M. "The Background and Immediate Effects of the Cripps Mission to India," Southern California, 1948. 155 pp.

H74 MATHUR, PRAKASH NARAIN. "Political and Administrative Set Up of Part C States," Agra, 1957.

H75 MEHROTRA, PRATAP NARAIN. "The Provisional Parliament of India," Agra, 1960.

H76 MISRA, R. N. "Distribution of Powers between the Federal Government and the States of India," Lucknow, 1949.

H77 MUKHERJEE, AMIYA. "The Constitutional Developments in India from 1939-1947," Calcutta, 1959.

H78 NAYAR, V. K. SUKUMARAN. "An Analysis of the Major Influences in the Drafting of the Constitution of India," Yale, 1957.

H79 PRASAD, RAMESH. "The Constituent Assembly of India," Agra, 1960.

H80 PUNNAIAH, H. B. "Federalism in the Government of India Act, 1935," Andhra, 1960.

H81 RASHIDUZZAMAN, M. "The Central Legislature in British India 1921-1947," Durham.

H82 RETZLAFF, RALPH HERBERT. "The Constituent Assembly of India and the Problem of Indian Unity: A Study of the Actions Taken by the Constituent Assembly of India to Overcome the Divisive Forces in Indian Social and Political Life during the Drafting of the Indian Constitution," Cornell, 1960. Summary in DA:20 (April 1960), 4155-56.

H83 SHARMA, B. M. "Indian Federation," Lucknow, 1939.

H84 SHREENIVASAN, M. "Problems of Civil Liberties in India, 1918-1939," Aligarh, 1955.

H85 SHUKLA, BISHESHWAR DAYAL. "The Liberal Party as a Factor in Indian Politics and Statesmanship in the Contemporary Social and Political History of India," Agra, 1955.

H86 SINGH, KRISHAN PRATAP. "Indian Constitution in the Making," Saugar, 1963.

H87 SINHA, S. K. "Growth of Federal Ideas and Institutions in India since 1919," Lucknow, 1957.

H88 SURI, P. "The Growth of the Committee System in the Legislature of India, 1920-1947," Allahabad, 1963.

H89 WATSON, VINCENT C. "The Indian Constitution and the Hindu Tradition: Compatibility and Conflict of Basic Political Ideas," Northwestern, 1957.

H90 ZAFAR KHAN, MOIMUZ. "The Council of State (1919-1947)—Its Organization and Working," Aligarh, 1961.

7. JUDICIAL ADMINISTRATION

H91 BANERJEE, T. K. "The Administration of Criminal Justice in Bengal from 1773 to 1861," London (London School of Economics), 1955. Under S. A. de Smith and A. Gledhill.

H92   CHANDRA, RAMESH. "Development of Judicial System in India, 1833-1858," Lucknow, before 1956.

H93   JHA, A. P. "Criminal Administration in Bihar (1793-1835)," Patna.

H94   MISRA, B. B. "The Judicial Administration of the East India Company in Bengal, 1765-1782," London (School of Oriental and African Studies), 1947.

H95   MISRA, K. P. "Role of Federal Court in India under the Constitution Act, 1935," Lucknow, 1954.

H96   NAHALE, KASHINATH JANARDAN. "La Cour suprême de l'Inde" [The Supreme Court of India], Paris (Droit), 1959.

H97   YUSUF, NUR JEHAN MOHAMMED. "Hastings' Experiment in the Judicial System," London, 1929-30. Under Laski.

8. *POLICE AND JAILS*

H98   SAXENA, G. D. "Police and Jails in Bengal Presidency (1757-1857)," Lucknow, 1953-54. Under N. L. Chatterji.

9. *THE MILITARY*

H99   AGARWAL, S. K. "Indian Marine from 1800 to 1858," Lucknow, after 1955. Under N. L. Chatterji.

H100   BARAT, AMIYA. "The Bengal Native Infantry; Its Organisation and Discipline, 1786-1852," London.

H101   GUPTA, J. P. "Armies of the East India Company in the Presidency of Bengal (1757-1857)," Agra, 1954.

H102   MYERS, MARGARET ANN. "Bibliography of Indian Regimental Histories," London (Diploma in Academic Post-Graduate Librarianship).

H103   NARAIN, IQBAL. "The Army in British India," Lucknow, 1953-54. Under R. N. Nagar.

H104   SINGH, NARENDRA. "Army of British India—1658 to 1900," Lucknow, after 1955. Under N. L. Chatterji.

10. *LOCAL SELF-GOVERNMENT*

H105   BANERJI, A. N. "Financing of Local Authorities in British India," London (London School of Economics), 1941.

H106   BORKAKOTY, A. K. "The Growth of Local Self-Government in Assam, 1874-1919," London, 1950. Under Philips and Hall.

H107   MANGUDKAR, M. P. "Municipal Government in Poona, 1882-1947: a Case Study," Poona. Under N. R. Deshpande. Summary in JUP:7 (1956), 177-83.

H108 RAY, NARESCHANDRA. "Rural Self-Government in Bengal," Calcutta, 1936.

H109 SRIVASTAVA, NIRANKAR PRASAD. "Development of Local Government in India," Lucknow, 1962.

H110 VENKATA RAO, V. "A Hundred Years of Local Self-Government in Assam," Allahabad, 1964?.

11. BENGAL, BIHAR, AND ORISSA, 1750 TO 1773

H111 CHATTERJI, NANDA LAL. "Mir Qasim's Rule in Bengal," Lucknow, 1934.

H112 DHAR, NIRANJAN. "The Administrative System of the East India Company in Bengal, 1714-1786," Calcutta.

H113 GUPTA, B. K. "The Relations between Nawab Sirajuddaullah and the East India Company, 1756-1757," Chicago, 1958. 264 pp.

H114 KARIM, A. "Murshid Qulī Khān and His Times," London, 1962. Under J. B. Harrison.

H115 MISHRA, SHREE GOVIND. "History of Bihar (1740 to 1772)," Patna. Summary in QRHS:1 (July-Sept. 1961), 78.

H116 ROY, A. C. (or RAY, A.). "The Career of Mir Jafar Khan, 1757-65," London, 1952. Under Philips.

H117 ROY, B. K. "Maharaja Nanda Kumar," Ranchi. Under K. K. Datta.

H118 ROY CHAUDHURY, P. "North West Frontier Policy of the East India Company in Bengal from 1757 to 1803," Lucknow, after 1958. Under R. N. Nagar.

H119 VIROTTAMA, BALMUKUND. "Political History of Chotanagpur from 1658 to 1858 A.D.," Ranchi. Under P. N. Ojha.

12. BENGAL, BIHAR, ORISSA, AND ASSAM, 1773 TO 1950

H120 BALIGA, B. S. "The Influence of the Home Government on Land Revenue and Judicial Administration in the Presidency of Fort William in Bengal, from 1807 to 1822," London, 1934-35. Under Dodwell. Summary in IHRB:12 (1934-35), 195-99.

H121 BARPUJARI, H. "British Administration in Assam (1825-45), with Special Reference to the Hill-Tribes on the Frontier," London (School of Oriental and African Studies), 1949.

H122 BARRETT, CYNTHIA E. "Lord William Bentinck in Bengal, 1828-1835," Oxford (St. Hilda's), 1953. Under C. C. Davies.

PART II: DISSERTATIONS

H123 BHUYAN, S. K. "The East India Company's Relation with Assam, 1771-1826," London, 1938. Under Dodwell.

H124 CHAUDHURI, B. "British Rule in Assam, 1845-1858," London (School of Oriental and African Studies), 1956.

H125 CHAUDHURI, NANIGOPAL. "A Glimpse into the East India Company's Administration in Bengal," Calcutta, before 1950.

H126 DRUMMOND, J. G. "The Working of the Bengal Legislative Council under the India Act, 1919," Cambridge, 1939. Under E. Barker.

H127 GUHA, MEERA. "The Development of Calcutta: a Study in Urban Geography," London, 1951. Under L. D. Stamp and O. H. K. Spate.

H128 JHA, J. C. "Tribal Unrest on the South-west Frontier of the Bengal Presidency, 1831-1833," London (School of Oriental and African Studies), 1960. Summary in IHRB:35 (1962), 100-01.

H129 MAJUMDAR, NIHAR KANA. "The Nizamat in the British Period in Bengal, 1765-1793," Calcutta.

H130 MUKHERJEE, BINAPANI. "The Hooghly and Its Region," London, 1948. Under Stamp and Spate.

H131 PANDEY, B. N. "Sir Elijah Impey in India, 1774-1783," London (School of Oriental and African Studies), 1957. Under Philips.

H132 PRASAD, RAMESHWAR. "Origin and Development of Public Bodies in Bengal (1828-1875)," Patna.

H133 RAWAT, J. S. "The Relation between the Supreme Court and the Governor General and Council and the Courts of the Company in Bengal between 1774-1803," Agra, 1945. 518 pp.

H134 RAY, B. C. "The British Conquest and Administration of Orissa, 1803-1819," London (School of Oriental and African Studies), 1956.

H135 SINGH, SURESH. "Birsa Munda and His Movement in Chotanagpur (1874-1901)," Patna.

H136 WEITZMAN, SOPHIA. "The Administration of Bengal under Warren Hastings," Manchester, 1922. Under Muir.

13. BOMBAY PRESIDENCY

H137 BHEDWAR, P. S. "Development of Bombay, 1797-1827," Bombay, before 1955.

H138 PATEL, FRENY K. "Poona: A Sociological Study," Poona. Summary in JUP:5 (1955), 184-88.

H139 SINGH, GOVIND S. "An Evaluation of the State of Maharashtra, Its Historical Development and Factors of Unity and Disunity," Clark, 1961-62.

H140 WILSON, L. B. "The Bombay Legislature (1946-52), a Study in Structure, Composition and Work," Bombay, 1953. Under K. P. Mukerji.

14. MADRAS, THE CARNATIC, AND THE CIRCARS

H141 BEAGLEHOLE, T. H. "Thomas Munro and the Development of Administrative Policy in Madras, 1792-1818: the Origins of 'the Munro System,'" Cambridge (King's), 1960. Under Ballhatchet.

H142 BERI, KAILASH K. "Influence of Home Government on Madras Administration, 1800-1825," Punjab, 1963.

H143 FRYKENBERG, ROBERT ERIC. "The Administration of Guntur District, with Special Reference to Local Influences on Revenue Policy, 1837-1848," London (School of Oriental and African Studies), 1960.

H144 PILLAY, K. K. "Local Self-Government in the Madras Presidency, 1850-1919," Oxford (St. Catherine's), 1948. Under C. C. Davies.

H145 RAJU, B. BHIM. "Provincial Autonomy in Madras," Lucknow, 1949.

H146 VENKATA RAO. "District Boards in Madras State," Madras, 1949.

H147 VIJAYALAKSHMI. "Madras Legislature till 1935," Madras, 1959.

H148 VISALAKSHI, N. R. "Growth of Public Services in Madras State," Madras, 1962.

15. DELHI, AGRA, AND OUDH, 1800 TO 1950

H149 BHANU, DHARMA. "History and Administration of the Province of Agra Named Subsequently North-Western Province (1834-1858)," Agra, 1955. Summary in UB:3 (Aug. 1956), 147-56.

H150 CHATURVEDI, KAILASH CHANDRA. "The Annexation of Avadh," Agra, 1960. Summary in QRHS 2:2 (1962-63), 40-42.

H151 DAS, RAMESHWAR BAKSH. "Municipal Administration in the U.P.," Lucknow, 1944.

H152 GUPTA, R. G. "Growth and Functioning of the Kanpur Municipality, 1861-1960," Agra, 1961.

H153 GURBAX, G. R. "Oudh under Wellesley. The Study of the Political Intercourse between Marquess Wellesley and Nawabsaheb Ali Khan of Oudh," Bombay, 1944. 437 pp.

H154 HASAN, ZAHURUL. "Rural Government in U.P.," Lucknow, 1943.

H156 HIRT, H. F. "Aligarh, U.P., India: A Geographic Study of Urban Growth," Syracuse, 1955. 348 pp.

H157 HOLMES, JESSIE. "The Administration of the Delhi Territory, 1803 to 1832," London (School of Oriental and African Studies), 1955. Under C. H. Philips.

H158 JOSHI, INDIRA. "East India Company's Relations with Garhwal," Lucknow, after 1955. Under N. L. Chatterji.

H159 JOSHI, M. P. "Some Aspects of the History of Kumaun Division in the 19th Century," Lucknow, after 1955. Under N. L. Chatterji.

H160 MARKANDAN, K. C. "Administration of the North-Western Provinces between 1835 and 1837," Allahabad, 1950. [Title also cited as: Administration of the North West Frontier Provinces.]

H161 MASALDAN, P. N. "Provincial Autonomy and Its Working in the United Provinces," Lucknow, 1942.

H162 MUKERJEE, ANSUMAN. "The History of Oudh (1801-1856)," Patna.

H163 PANIKKAR, K. N. "Delhi Residency—a Political Study (1803 to 1856 A.D.)," Rajasthan, after 1956. Under V. P. S. Raghuvanshi. Summary in QRHS 3:4 (1963-64), 208-10.

H164 SHARMA, MAHADEO PRASAD. "District Boards in the United Province of Agra and Oudh, Their Evolution, Constitution and Functions," Allahabad, 1941.

H165 SINGH, D. P. "U.P. Civil Service (Executive): Its Growth, Organisation and Functions," Lucknow, 1956.

H166 TEWARI, J. P. "Administration of North West Provinces in 1858," Lucknow, after 1955. Under R. N. Nagar.

H167 THAKORE, M. P. "Aspects of the Urban Geography of New Delhi," London, 1962. Under A. E. Smailes.

16. THE PUNJAB, 1850-1950

H168 BAL, S. S. "British Policy toward the Panjab, 1844-1849," London (School of Oriental and African Studies), 1962-63.

H169 CHHABRA, GURBAKHSH SINGH. "Social and Economic History of Panjab (1849-1901)," Punjab, 1955.

H170 FOWLER, F. J. "A Geographical Analysis of the Development of the Canal Colonies of the Punjab," Leeds, 1939. Under A. V. Williamson.

H171 KHILNANI, N. M. "The Punjab under the Lawrences, 1846-1858," Bombay, 1948. 163 pp.

H172 LAI, R. C. "Reorganization of the Punjab Government, 1847-57," London, 1937. Under H. H. Dodwell.

H173 LAKHANPAUL, NARINDRA KUMAR. "Governor of the Punjab, 1937-1947," Punjab, 1961.

H174 MATHUR, YADUVANSH. "Changes in the Administrative System of the Punjab (1849-75)," Delhi. Summary in QRHS:1 (April-June 1961), 32-33.

H175 MEHTA, SATYA. "Partition of the Punjab—A Study of Its Effects on Administration and Politics of the Punjab, 1947-1957," Indian School of International Studies.

H176 SINGH, BAKHTAVAR. "Social and Economic Policy of the Panjab under the British (1901-1939)," Punjab, 1962.

H177 UPPAL, RAM MURTI. "Punjab Legislature, 1909-1937," Punjab, 1964.

17. *SIND*

H178 HUTTENBACK, R. A. "British Relations with Sind, 1799-1843," California (Los Angeles), 1959.

18. *ANDAMAN AND NICOBAR ISLANDS*

H179 MATHUR, L. P. "History of the Andaman and Nicobar Islands (1756-1947)," Punjab, 1960.

19. *1857*

H180 MUKHERJEE, PARESH NATH. "The War of Indian Independence of 1857-58 in Ganga-Jamuna Doab," Agra, 1960. Summary in QRHS: 2 (1962-63), 83-86.

H181 SRIVASTAVA, K. L. "Mutiny in Central India—Malwa," Agra, 1948.

H182 TEWARI, RAMA SHANKAR. "The War of Independence in Awadh (1857-58)," Agra, 1960. Summary in QRHS:2 (1962-63), 79-83.

PART II: DISSERTATIONS

20. *RELATIONS WITH PRINCES*

H183 BHARGAVA, RAJESHWAR PRASAD. "The Chamber of Princes," Lucknow, 1944.

H184 BUTT, I. A. "Lord Curzon and the Indian States, 1899-1905," London (School of Oriental and African Studies), 1963-64.

H185 "History of the Council of States in India," Madras, 1957.

H186 MEHTA, M. S. "The Relations of the British Government in India with the Indian States, 1813-1823," London. Summary in IHRB:6 (1928-29), 116-17.

H187 PANDEY, K. N. "Lord William Bentinck and the Indian States, 1828-1835," London (School of Oriental and African Studies), 1956.

H188 SHARMA, KUNDAN LAL. "Political Relations of the English East India Company with the Indian States in the Time of Sir John Shore," Agra, 1957. Summary in QRHS 2:1 (1962-63), 43-44.

21. *FOREIGN RELATIONS*

H189 BANERJI, BANI. "The Evolution of British Commonwealth with Special Reference to India," Saugar, 1959.

H190 BILGRAMI, ASGHAR HUSAIN. "Indo-Afghan Relations in the 19th Century," Aligarh, 1955.

H191 BOLAND, GERTRUDE CATHERINE. "India and the United Nations: India's Role in the General Assembly, 1946-1957," Claremont, 1961. 183 pp. Summary in DA:22 (March 1962), 3247-48.

H192 BUDHRAJ, VIJAY SEN. "The Soviet Image of India," American, 1958. 198 pp.

H193 CHAVDA, V. K. "India, Britain and Russia (1838-78): a Study of British Opinion," Leeds, 1961. Under A. Briggs.

H194 CHAWLA, SUDERSHAN. "India and the Communist Bloc," Ohio State, 1959.

H195 DHILLON, A. S. "India in the League of Nations and the International Labor Organization," Harvard, 1935.

H196 DOLE, N. Y. "India in the United Nations: with Special Reference to Special and Economic Matters," Poona. Under N. R. Deshpande.

H197 GATES, ROSALIE P. "The Tibetan Policy of George Nathaniel Curzon Viceroy of India, January 1899–April 1904, December 1904–November 1905," Duke, 1965.

H198 GUPTA, S. S. "British Relations with Bhutan up to 1880," Allahabad, 1946.

H199 KANT, RAMA. "Indo-Nepalese Relations, 1816-1877," Allahabad, 1960.

H200 KHAIR, MOHAMMED ABUL. "United States Foreign Policy in the Indo-Pakistan Subcontinent, 1940-1955," California (Berkeley), 1962. Summary in DA:24 (March 1964), 3710-11.

H201 KOZICKI, RICHARD J. "India and Burma, 1937-1957: a Study in International Relations," Pennsylvania, 1959. 513 pp. Summary in DA: 20 (November 1959), 1850.

H202 KSHIRSAGAR, SHIWARAM K. "Development of Relations between India and the United States, 1941-1952," American, 1957. 293 pp.

H203 KUMAR, RAVINDER. "India and the Persian Gulf Region, 1858-1905," Punjab, 1962.

H204 LAMB, H. A. "The Commercial and Diplomatic Relations between India and Tibet in the Nineteenth Century," Cambridge (Trinity), 1958. Under J. M. K. Vyvyan.

H205 MACKETT, W. C. "Some Aspects of the Development of American Opinion on India, 1918-1947," Southern California, 1957. 219 pp.

H206 MAJUMDAR, A. "Lord Minto's Administration in India (1807-13), with Special Reference to His Foreign Policy," Oxford (Lady Margaret), 1962-63.

H207 MEHRISH, B. N. "Recognition Policy of Government of India towards New States and Governments in Asia from the Period 1947-57," Delhi, 1964.

H208 MOZUMDAR, KANCHAN MOY. "Indo-Nepal Relations, 1837-1877," Indian School of International Studies.

H209 OSBORN, GEORGE KNOX III. "Sino-Indian Border Conflicts: Historical Background and Recent Developments," Stanford, 1963. Summary in DA:24 (July 1963), 269-70.

H210 PHIBBS, PHILIP MONFORD. "Nehru's Philosophy of International Relations," Chicago, 1957. 296 pp.

H211 POWER, PAUL F. "International Relations in the Thought of M. K. Gandhi," New York, 1960.

H212 PRASAD, BIMLA. "The Origins of Indian Foreign Policy: the Indian National Congress and World Affairs, 1885-1947," Columbia, 1948. 256 pp.

PART II: DISSERTATIONS

H213 ROSE, LEO E. "The Role of Nepal and Tibet in Sino-Indian Relations," California (Berkeley), 1960.

H214 SAMRA, CHATTAR SINGH. "India in Communist Perspective," California (Berkeley), 1954.

H215 SAXENA, N. C. "Indo-Burmese Relations," Lucknow, after 1958. Under R. N. Nagar.

H216 SCHMIDT, EARL ROBERT. "American Relations with South Asia, 1900-1940," Pennsylvania, 1955. 427 pp. Abstract in DA:15 (May 1955), 2281.

H217 SETH, U. D. "Indo-American Relations, 1757-1900," Lucknow, after 1958. Under G. S. Misra.

H218 SINGH, BHAG. "Anglo-Russian Relations in the Middle East since 1907, with Special Reference to India," California (Berkeley), 1936.

H219 SINGH, HARNAM. "American Press Opinion on Indian Government and Politics, 1918-1935," Georgetown, 1949.

H220 SINGHAL, D. P. "Indian External Policy, with Special Reference to the North-Western and Eastern Frontiers (1876-1898)," London (School of Oriental and African Studies), 1954. Under Philips.

H221 STERN, BERNARD S. "American Views of India and Indians, 1857-1900," Pennsylvania, 1956. 291 pp.

H222 SURI, MRIDULA. "India's Relations with Frontier States, with Particular Reference to Afghanistan, Persia, Russia, Bhutan, Nepal, Tibet and Burma (1863-1875)," Allahabad, 1965.

H223 TALBOT, PHILLIPS. "Aspects of India-Pakistan Relations, 1947-1952," Chicago, 1954.

H224 TRIPATHI, DWIJENDRA. "The United States and India: Economic Links, 1860-1900," Wisconsin, 1963. 165 pp. Summary in DA: 24 (Jan. 1964), 2884.

H225 TYAGI, SHRI RAM. "Influence of European Foreign Politics on India," Agra, 1954.

H226 WOHLERS, LESTER P. "The Policy of India in Relation to the Tension between the Soviet Union and the United States, with Special Reference to the United Nations," Chicago, 1951.

I. NATIONALISM AND POLITICS

1. GENERAL

I1 ADENWALLA, MINOO D. "From Ram Mohum Roy to Gandhi: a Study of the Role of Political Ideology in the Indian National Movement," Northwestern, 1956. 455 pp. Summary in DA:16 (June 1956), 2497.

I2 BARTARYA, SATISH CHANDRA. "The Indian Nationalist Movement from 1885-1947," Lucknow, 1955. Under B. M. Sharma.

I3 BAYLEY, DAVID H. "Violent Agitation and the Democratic Process in India," Princeton, 1961. 393 pp. Abstract in DA:22 (Jan. 1962), 2444-45. Based on 1950-59 data, but suggestive for earlier periods.

I4 BOCK, ROBERT LEROY. "Subhas Chandra Bose, Bengali Revolutionary Nationalist, 1897-1945," American, 1960. 286 pp. Abstract in DA: 21 (Nov. 1960), 1236-37.

I5 BRAISTED, PAUL JUDSON. "Indian Nationalism and the Christian College," Columbia, 1935. 171 pp.

I6 BROOMFIELD, JOHN H. "Politics and the Bengal Legislative Council, 1912-1926," Australian National, 1964. 482 pp.

I7 CHERIAN, M. E. "Critical Study of the Political Ideas of Some Leading Indian Christians, 1858-1960," Poona. Under D. K. Garde.

I8 GANGOPADHYAY, NALINCHANDRA. "Indian Political Philosophy," Calcutta, 1940.

I9 GOONERATNE, C. D. S. "The Development of Political Consciousness in India, 1757-1931," Chicago, 1933. 265 pp.

I10 GUNG CHUN-YIEN. "A Comparative Study of Indian and Chinese Nationalism," Allahabad, 1945.

I11 HASSAAN, M. R. "Indian Politics and the British Right, 1914-1922," London (School of Oriental and African Studies), 1963-64.

I12 IRSCHICK, EUGENE A. "Politics and Social Conflict in South India: the Non-Brahmin Movement and Tamil Separatism, 1916-1929," Chicago, 1964.

I13 KAUR, MAN MOHAN. "Role of Women in the Freedom Movement, 1857-1947," Punjab, 1964.

I14 KOCHANEK, STANLEY A. "The Organization of Power within the Indian National Congress," Pennsylvania, 1963. Abstract in DA:25 (July 1964), 596.

I15 KRISHNA, G. "The Indian National Congress, 1918-23," Oxford (St. Antony's), 1960-61.

I16 KRISHNA, PURUSNOTMAN M. "The Political Philosophy of Sri Aurobindo. An Exposition and Assessment of the Integral System of a Leading Indian Thinker," New School for Social Research, 1963.

I17 NAIR, M. P. SREEKUMARAN. "The Role of Constitutionalism in the Indian Struggle for Freedom, 1885-1947," Kerala, 1964.

I18 NATH, GOPI. "The Home Rule Movement in India," Agra, 1962. Summary in QRHS:3 (1963-64), 142-43.

I19 ORR, CHARLES A. "A Study of Indian Boycotts," Michigan, 1940. 568 pp. Abstract in DA:18 (1958), 1679-80.

I20 PARK, RICHARD LEONARD. "The Rise of Militant Nationalism in Bengal: a Regional Study of Indian Nationalism," Harvard, 1950.

I21 PAVADYA, BALRAM SINGH. "Attitudes of the Indian Political Parties towards India's Membership of the Commonwealth (1917-1957) with Reference to the Attitude of the Indian National Congress," Indian School of International Studies.

I22 PUROHIT, B. R. "The Influence of Hindu Revivalism on the Indian Nationalist Movement," Saugar, 1959.

I23 SAUNDERS, A. J. "Nationalism in India," Chicago, 1925. Summary in MUJ 1:2 (1928), 152-216; 2:1 (1929), 17-67.

I24 SEAL, A. "The Emergence of Indian Nationalism," Cambridge, 1962. Under Gallagher.

I25 SHAH, L. K. "Education and National Consciousness in India," Chicago, 1928.

I26 SHARMA, I. D. "Influence of Western Ideas on Nationalist Movement in India," Lucknow, 1957.

I27 SHAY, THEODORE L. "Tilak, Gandhi, and Arthaśāstra," Northwestern, 1955. 465 pp. Abstract in DA:15 (March 1955), 2277-78.

I28 SINGH, DIWAKAR PRASAD. "American Official Attitudes towards the Indian Nationalist Movement 1905-1929," Hawaii, 1964. Abstract in DA:25 (Nov. 1964), 2954.

I29 SMITH, DONALD E. "Jawaharlal Nehru's Thought on the Democratic State," Pennsylvania, 1956. 351 pp.

I30 TRIKHA, SANTOSH. "Political Parties in India," Saugar, 1955.

I31 VASIL, R. K. "The Rise of Indian Nationalism," Lucknow, 1957.

PART II: DISSERTATIONS

2. NATIONALISM AND POLITICS TO 1919

132 AHLUWALIA, MADAN MOHAN. "Freedom Movement in India from 1858 to 1909," Punjab, 1960.

133 ARGOV, D. "The Ideological Differences between Moderates and Extremists in the Indian National Movement, with Special Reference to Surendranath Banerjea and Lajpat Rai, 1883-1919," London (School of Oriental and African Studies), 1963-64.

134 BHATTACHARYA, B. C. "Development of Social and Political Ideas in Bengal, 1858-85," London, 1934. Summary in IHRB:15 (1937-38), 46-47.

135 DUBEY, SATYA NARAIN. "Development of Political Thought in India (1885-1919), (A Study in Main Currents)," Agra, 1957. Summary in QRHS:2 (1962-63), 86-89.

136 GHOSH, PANSY C. "The Development of the Indian National Congress, 1892-1909," London (School of Oriental and African Studies), 1958-59.

137 GHOSH, S. K. "The Influence of Western, Particularly English, Political Ideas on Indian Political Thought, with Special Reference to the Political Ideas of the Indian National Congress (1885-1919)," London (School of Oriental and African Studies), 1950. Under Philips.

138 GOYAL, OM PRAKASH. "Political Thought of Gokhale," Delhi, 1962.

139 HARNETTY, PETER. "British Policy and the Development of the National Movement in India: 1885-1905," Harvard, 1958.

140 KLING, BLAIR BERNARD. "The Bengal Indigo Disturbances, 1859-1862: a Study in the Origins of Political Activity in Modern Bengal," Pennsylvania, 1960. 506 pp. Abstract in DA:21 (Oct. 1960), 862-63.

141 KRISHNASWAMI, S. "The 1893 Riots in Bombay," Chicago, 1965.

142 KUTINA, M. M. "Burzhuazno-natsional'nye organizatsii Indii vtoroĭ poloviny XIX veka" [Bourgeois-National Organizations in India in the Second Half of the 19th Century], Tashkent (Academy of Sciences of the Uzbek), 1961. 290 pp.

143 LOASBY, ROLAND. "Lokamanya Bala Gangadhara Tilak, 1856-1920: His Reorientation of the Gita Tradition: a Factor in the Rise of Indian Nationalism," American, 1942.

144 MAITRA, K. K. "History of the Terrorist Movement in India from the Beginning to 1919 (with Special Reference to Bengal)," Rajasthan. Under M. L. Sharma.

145 MARTIN, BRITON, JR. "New India, 1885: a Study of British Official Policy and the Emergence of the Indian National Congress," Pennsylvania, 1964. Abstract in DA:25 (March 1965), 5241-42.

146 McLANE, JOHN R. "The Development of Nationalist Ideas and Tactics and the Policies of the Government of India, 1897-1905," London (School of Oriental and African Studies). Under Ballhatchet.

147 NAIDIS, MARK. "The Punjab Disturbances of 1919: a Study in Indian Nationalism," Stanford, 1950.

148 PAREL, ANTHONY. "The Search for the Indian Political Community: Theory and Practice in the Nineteenth Century," Harvard, 1963.

149 PAUSTIAN, CORNELIA MUNZ. "The Development of Nationalism in India, 1885-1920," Missouri, 1942. 313 pp. Abstract in DA:5 (1944), 80-82.

150 RATHORE, NAEEM GUL. "Indian Nationalist Agitation in the United States: a Study of Lala Lajpat Rai and the India Home Rule League of America, 1914-1920," Columbia, 1965. Abstract in DA:26 (March 1966), 5535.

151 SAMUEL, VAIRANAPILLAI M. "Nationalism in India before 1905," Illinois, 1936.

152 SINGH, SANGAT. "Freedom Movement in Delhi, 1858-1919," Punjab, 1964.

153 SINGH, YUVA RAJ KARAN. "The Political Thought of Sri Aurobindo Ghosh, 1893-1910," Delhi, 1962.

154 TYAGI, OM PRAKASH. "Genesis of Nationalism in India (1857-1919)," Agra, 1960.

155 VERMA, KEDAR NATH. "Sri Aurobindo's Philosophy of History and of Political Evolution: A Comparative Study," Saugar, 1963.

156 WOLPERT, STANLEY A. "Tilak and Gokhale: a Comparative Analysis of Their Social and Political Philosophies," Pennsylvania, 1959.

3. NATIONALISM AND POLITICS, 1920 TO 1950

157 AUSTIN, G. S. "The Indian Constituent Assembly and the Framing of the Indian Constitution," Oxford (St. Antony's), 1963-64.

158 AVASTHI, RAM KUMAR. "Social and Political Ideas of M. N. Roy," Agra, 1960.

159 BAHADUR, LAL. "The Swaraj Party," Agra, 1958.

160 BRASS, PAUL R. "The Congress Party Organization in Uttar Pradesh: the Transformation from Movement to Party in an Indian State," Chicago, 1964.

161 CHANDRA, PRAKASH. "The Political Philosophy of M. N. Roy," Lucknow, 1957.

162 CRANE, ROBERT I. "The Indian National Congress and the Indian Agrarian Problem, 1919-1939. An Historical Study," Yale, 1952. Abstract in DA:26 (July 1965), 333.

163 GURHA, LAKSHMI. "The Growth of Socialism in India," Allahabad, 1954.

164 HAITHCOX, JOHN P. "Nationalism, Communism, and Twentieth Century Jacobism: Royist Tactics in India, 1927-40," California (Berkeley), 1965.

165 HAUSER, WALTER. "The Bihar Provincial Kisan Sabha, 1929-1942: a Study of an Indian Peasant Movement," Chicago, 1961. 214 pp.

166 KAUSHIK, PITAMBAR DATT. "The Congress Ideology and Programme, 1920-47; Ideological Foundations of Indian Nationalism during the Gandhian Era," Saugar, 1963.

167 KOROBKOV, A. F. "Politika Indiiskogo natsional'nogo kongressa i kongressistskie provintsial'nye pravitel'stva nakanune II mirovoĭ voĭny" ["The Policy of the Indian National Congress and Congress Provincial Governments on the Eve of the Second World War"], Moscow (State Institute of International Relations), 1958. 389 pp.

168 NAYAR, BALDEV RAJ. "Contemporary Political Leadership in the Punjab," Chicago, 1963.

169 OVERSTREET, GENE DONALD. "Soviet and Indian Communist Policy in India, 1935-1952," Columbia. Abstract in DA:20 (April 1960), 4155.

170 RAJURKAR, NARSINHA GOVIND. "Jawaharlal Nehru—Nationalism in Theory and Practice," Osmania, 1963.

171 REEVES, PETER D. "The Landlords' Response to Political Change in the United Provinces of Agra and Oudh, India, 1921-1937," Australian National, 1964.

172 RUDOLPH, SUSANNE HOEBER. "Congress in Power: Party in the Context of Asian Democracy," Radcliffe, 1955.

173 RUSCH, THOMAS ALVIN. "Role of the Congress Socialist Party in the Indian National Congress, 1931-1942," Chicago, 1955. 546 pp.

174 SADASIVAN, S. N. "Party and Democracy in India, 1947-1958," Poona. Under D. K. Garde.

I75 SINHA, L. P. "The Origin and Development of Left Wing Movements and Ideas in India, 1919-1947," London (London School of Economics), 1954. Under R. Miliband and W. H. Morris-Jones.

I76 SMITH, RAY THOMAS, JR. " 'Liberals' in the Indian Nationalist Movement, 1918-1947: Their Role as Intermediaries," California (Berkeley), 1964.

I77 WEINER, MYRON. "Indian Political Behavior: a Study of the Development of a Multi-Party System," Princeton, 1955. Abstract in DA: 15 (Nov. 1955), 1643.

I78 WINDMILLER, MARSHALL LOUIS. "Communism in India," California (Berkeley), 1964. Abstract in DA:26 (Nov. 1965), 2855.

4. GANDHI

I79 AVASTHI, R. N. "Techniques of Resolving Tensions with Special Reference to Gandhiji," Lucknow, 1957.

I80 BHATTACHARYA, P. K. "Gandhian Philosophy and Technique of Satyagraha," Saugar, 1957.

I81 BONDURANT, JOAN V. "Gandhian Satyagraha and Political Theory: an Interpretation," California (Berkeley), 1952.

I82 DEVANESEN, CHANDRAN D. "The Making of the Mahatma: an Interpretive Study of M. K. Gandhi's First Forty Years," Harvard, 1962. 605 pp.

I83 DHAWAN, G. N. "The Political Philosophy of Mahatma Gandhi," Lucknow, 1942.

I84 GAMBHIRE, GOVIND GAJANAN. "1. L'Opinion de Mahatma Gandhi sur le varnashrama et le système des castes. 2. L'Opinion de Gandhi sur certaines exceptions à la doctrine de la non-violence" [Mahatma Gandhi's Opinion on Varnashrama and the Caste System. 2. Gandhi's Opinion on Certain Exceptions to the Doctrine of Non-Violence], Strasbourg (Lettres), 1959.

I85 GORDON, ROBERT L. "Mohandas Gandhi: Politician and Statesman, a Political Biography till 1922," Wisconsin, 1951.

I86 HENDRICK, GEORGE. "Thoreau and Gandhi: a Study of the Development of 'Civil Disobedience' and Satyagraha," Texas, 1954.

I87 HOBLITZELLE, H. "The War against War in the 19th Century: a Study of the Western Backgrounds of Gandhian Thought," Columbia, 1959. 210 pp.

I88 JHA, SHIVA NAND. "A Critical Study of Gandhian Economic Thought," Agra, 1960.

189 MATHEWS, JAMES K. "The Techniques of M. K. Gandhi as Religious," Columbia, 1957. 213 pp.

190 MEHTA, USHA. "The Social and Political Thought of Mahatma Gandhi," Bombay. Abstract in BUJ:21 (July 1952), 86-87.

191 MENON, AMMU K. "Mahatma Gandhi's Contribution to Social Welfare in India—a Study of Three Major Programs," Columbia, 1960. 295 pp. Abstract in DA:21 (January 1961), 1988-89.

192 ROTHERMUND, INDIRA N. "Gandhi's Impact on India's International Relations," Pennsylvania, 1959.

193 SHAH, M. V. "Social Philosophy of Gandhiji," Bombay, 1953.

194 SHARMA, B. S. "The Political Philosophy of Mahatma Gandhi in Relation to the English Liberal Tradition," London (London School of Economics), 1954.

195 SHARMA, J. S. "Mahatma Gandhi: a Descriptive Bibliography," Michigan, 1954. 560 pp.

196 SHRIDHARANI, KRISHNALAL J. "War without Violence, the Sociology of Gandhi's *Satyagraha*," Columbia, 1940.

197 SHRIMALI, KALULAL. "The Wardha Scheme; the Gandhian Plan of Education in Mysore, India," Columbia.

198 TEWARI, AMBIKA PRASAD. "Gandhian Methodology of Non-Violence," Allahabad, 1960.

5. MUSLIM POLITICS AND HINDU-MUSLIM CONFLICT

199 AHMED, MANZOORUDDIN. "Concept of Divine Sovereignty in Pakistan," Columbia, 1960. 335 pp. Abstract in DA:21 (Oct. 1960), 949.

1100 ANSARI, MOHAMMED ABDUS SALEM. "An Evaluation of the Quran and of Western Sociology as Guides for Implementing the Goals of the Pakistani Constitution, with Special Reference to Problems of Conflict," Pennsylvania State, 1958. Abstract in DA:19 (Dec. 1958), 1462.

1101 ATWELL, D. S. "East Pakistan: a Study in Political Geography," Clark, 1959.

1102 BAHADUR, LAL. "All India Muslim League, Its History, Activities and Achievements," Agra, 1953.

1103 BECKER, MARY L. "The All-India Muslim League, 1906-1947: a Study of Leadership in the Evolution of a Nation," Radcliffe, 1957.

1104 BINDER, LEONARD. "Islamic Constitutional Theory and Politics in Pakistan," Harvard, 1956.

PART II: DISSERTATIONS

I105   BLUE, FREDERICK I. "Some Factors of the Hindu-Moslem Tension in India," Southern California, 1941.

I106   CHOUDHURY, GOLAM W. "The First Constituent Assembly of Pakistan (1947-1954)," Columbia, 1956.

I107   CHUGHTAI, M. "Muslim Politics in the Indo-Pakistan Sub-Continent, 1858-1916," Oxford (Magdalen), 1960.

I108   EVANS, WALTER B. "The Genesis of the Pakistan Idea: a Study of Hindu-Muslim Relations," Southern California, 1955. 158 pp.

I109   KARAMAT, S. K. "The Western Frontier of Western Pakistan: a Study of Political Geography," Michigan, 1958. 257 pp.

I110   KHAN, M. H. "Muslims in India after 1947: a Study in Political Geography," Clark, 1957. 141 pp.

I111   KRISHNA, KATRAGADDA B. "Communal Representation in India: Its Origin and History," Harvard, 1938. 358 pp.

I112   LAMBERT, RICHARD D. "Hindu-Muslim Riots in India," Pennsylvania, 1952.

I113   MALIK, HAFEEZ. "The Growth of Pakistani Nationalism, 800 A.D.–1947 A.D.," Syracuse, 1961. 797 pp. Abstract in DA:22 (April 1962), 3729.

I114   MAY, LINI S. "Muslim Thought and Politics in India after 1857," Columbia, 1963.

I115   MEKHRI, G. M. "Social Background of Hindu-Muslim Relationships," Bombay, 1947, 527 pp.

I116   METZ, WILLIAM S. "The Political Career of Mohammed Ali Jinnah," Pennsylvania, 1952.

I117   MOHAMMED, SHAN. "The Political Ideas of Sir Syed Ahmad Khan," Allahabad, 1963.

I118   SAYEED, KHALID B. "Central Government of Pakistan, 1947-1951," McGill, 1956.

I119   SETH, SATISH CHANDRA. "The Growth of Communalism in India and the Problem of Hindu-Muslim Relations," Agra, 1959.

I120   SHIKOH, MIRZA MUZAFFAR. "The Constitution of the Islamic Republic of Pakistan: Its Historical Determinants, Constitutional Antecedents, Evolution and Major Problems," New York, 1960. 585 pp. Abstract in DA:21 (May 1961), 3508-09.

I121   TAUNK, BENGALI MAL. "The Role of Khilafat Movement in Indian Politics (Detailed Study of the Indian Khilafat Movement of 1919-1924)," Agra, 1963.

I122 WASTI, S. R. "Lord Minto and the Indian Nationalist Move-ment, with Special Reference to the Political Activities of the Indian Muslims, 1905-10," London, 1962. Under Ballhatchet.

I123 WHEELER, RICHARD S. "Government and Constitution-Making in Pakistan," California (Berkeley), 1957.

I124 WILCOX, WAYNE AYRES. "The Political Assimilation of the Princely States of Pakistan," Columbia, 1960. 277 pp. Abstract in DA:21 (Sept. 1960), 666-67.

I125 ZAKARIA, RAFIQ AHMED. "The Muslims in India: a Political Analysis (from 1885-1906)," London (School of Oriental and African Studies), 1948.

J. ECONOMIC HISTORY

1. *GENERAL ECONOMIC HISTORY*

J1 AHLUWALIA, S. S. "Economic Conditions of the Sikhs," Poona. Under D. R. Gadgil.

J2 AHMAD, N. "An Economic Geography of East Bengal (East Pakistan)," London (London School of Economics), 1951-52.

J3 AMBIRAJAN, S. "Economic Ideas and Indian Economic Policies in the Nineteenth Century," Manchester, 1963-64.

J4 BARSS, LAWRENCE. "Political Change and Economic Growth: a Methodology Applied to Japan, Turkey, and India," Massachusetts Institute of Technology, 1961.

J5 BYKOSKI, LOUIS M. "Economic Development of India and Pakistan, 1945-60," Western Reserve, 1965.

J6 CHABLANI, S. P. "Economic Conditions in Sind, 1592-1843," Bombay, 1946. 300 pp.

J7 CHAND, JAGDISH. "The Economic Consequences of the Government of India Act, 1935," Punjab, 1944.

J8 CHANDRA, BIPIN. "Economic Policies of Indian National Leadership, 1880 to 1905," Delhi.

J9 CHARLES, KOILPILLAI J. "Indian Economic Development: a Study in Economic History and Theory," McGill, 1958. 370 pp.

J10 CHOKSEY, RUSTOM DINSHAIR. "The Economic History of the Bombay Deccan and Karnatak, 1818-1868," Poona (Gokhale Institute), 1941-42.

J11 DAS, M. N. "Studies in the Economic and Social Development of India, 1848-1856," London (School of Oriental and African Studies), 1956.

J12 GHOSAL, HARI RANJAN. "Economic Transition in Bengal Presidency, 1793-1833," Patna.

J13 GREWAL, J. KAUR. "The Financing of Economic Development in India (Practices, Methods, and Problems)," Fordham, 1951. 298 pp.

J14 KENNEY, NANCY J. "The Gandhian Economy and Indian Economic Planning," Fletcher, 1956.

J15 KRISHNASWAMI, A. "Capital Development of India, 1860-1913," London, 1941. Under Vera Anstey.

J16 KUNTE, B. G. "Economic Prosperity of Bombay Province and Sind, 1919-39," Bombay. Abstract in BUJ:28 (July 1959), 60-64.

J17 MISHRA, B. B. "Hinduism and Economic Growth: a Study of the Nature of the Impact of Hinduism on India's Economic Growth with Special Emphasis on the Period since the Mid-Eighteenth Century," London (London School of Economics), 1956.

J18 MISRA, LAKSHMI N. "Indian Commodity Market Speculation," London, 1931-32. Under Coatman.

J19 NAVAMPALLI, KRISHNA S. "Economic Effects of the British on India (1857-1900)," Bombay, 1954. Abstract in BUJ:23 (July 1954), 89-90.

J20 PANDE, V. P. "The Origin, Development and Problems of Village ('Community') Projects in India," London (London School of Economics), 1962-63.

J21 RAMAN RAO, A. V. "An Economic History of the Andhra Districts (1766-1865)," Poona (Gokhale Institute), 1947.

J22 RAY, MANMOHAN. "Foreign Investments in British India from 1857-58 to 1927-28," Calcutta, 1932.

J23 SETH, MANOHAR LAL. "Punjab Money-lender—His Growth and Decline (Under British Rule)," Punjab, 1954.

J24 SINHA, JOGIS CHANDRA. "Economic Annals of Bengal," Calcutta, 1927.

J25 SINHA, NIRMAL CHANDRA. "Indo-British Economy One Hundred Years Ago (Studies in Capital and Labour)," Calcutta, after 1940.

J26 TIWARI, SHRI GOPAL. "The Economic Prosperity of the United Provinces—1921-39," Banaras Hindu, 1949.

J27 ZAIDA, R. H. "The Economic Geography of Madhya Pradesh (Formerly Central Provinces and Berar)," Edinburgh, 1957-58.

2. LAND SETTLEMENT AND LAND REVENUE ADMINISTRATION

J28 AHMAD, ZULIEDA P. "Land Tenure Reforms in India," Radcliffe, 1949. 263 pp.

J29 ANJANAIAH, NALABALA. "Reform of the Raiyatwari Land Revenue System in India with Special Reference to Madras and Bombay," Poona. Under T. M. Joshi.

J30 CHAUDHURI, BENOY. "Agrarian Relations in Bengal after the Permanent Settlement (1793-1819)," Calcutta. Summary in QRHS:1 (April-June 1961), 28-29.

J31 HUQ, MAZHARUL. "East India Company's Land Policy and Management in Bengal from 1698 to 1784," London (London School of Economics), 1963. Under Anstey.

J32 HUSAIN, M. I. "The Formation of British Land-Revenue Policy in the Ceded and Conquered Provinces of Northern India, 1801-1833," London (School of Oriental and African Studies), 1963-64.

J33 JAIN, ROOP CHANDRA. "The Origin and Growth of Peasant Proprietorship in India," Agra, 1960.

J34 KAHLON, SADHU SINGH. "Land Taxation in the Punjab, 1919-1960," Punjab, 1964.

J35 NAGAR, R. N. "Land Revenue Administration of the Ceded and Conquered Provinces," Lucknow.

J36 PATEL, G. D. "The Land Settlement in Gujarat under the British," Poona (Gokhale Institute), 1947-48.

J37 RAJ, J. "British Land Policy in Oudh, 1856-1868," London (School of Oriental and African Studies), 1956.

J38 SAYANNA, V. V. "Land System of the Madras Province," Bombay, 1947? Abstract in BUJ:17 (July 1948), 92.

J39 SENGUPTA, SACHINDRAMOHAN. "An Historical Introduction to the Permanent Settlement of Bengal," Calcutta, 1944.

J40 SHEA, THOMAS WILLIAM, JR. "The Land Tenure Structure of Malabar and Its Influence upon Capital Formation in Agriculture," Pennsylvania, 1959. Summary in DA:20 (July 1959), 126-27.

J41 SIDDIQI, A. "The Land Revenue System in the Ceded and Conquered Provinces and Its Economic Background," Oxford (Somerville), 1962-63.

J42 ———. "Origin and Development of Land Tenures in U.P., 1800-1930," Aligarh, 1957.

J43 SIDHU, KASHMIR S. "An Institutional and Historical Study of Property in Land in Relation to Punjab Customary Law," Cornell, 1957.

J44 SINGH, BISHAMBAR. "The State and the Land and Revenue Reforms in Uttar Pradesh since 1901 to the Present Day," Lucknow, 1955. Under B. M. Sharma.

3. *OTHER AND GENERAL REVENUE*

J45 MANDAL, GOBINDA CHANDRA. "Developments in the Indian Income Tax, 1930-1951," Calcutta, 1955.

J46 NIYOGI, J. "The Evolution of the Indian Income Tax, 1860-1922; a Historical, Critical, and Comparative Study," London, 1930. Under H. Dalton and G. Slater.

J47 SERAJUDDIN, A. M. "The Revenue Administration of Chittagong from 1761-1785," London (School of Oriental and African Studies), 1963-64.

J48 SUNDARAM, LANKA. "Revenue Administration of the Northern Sarkars, 1759-86," London, 1929-30. Under Dodwell. Summary in IHRB: 8 (1930-31), 98-100. Printed in AHRS:6 (Oct. 1931), 87-120; 7 (July, Oct. 1932), 33-48, 67-82; 7 (Jan. 1933), 135-45; 11 (Jan. & April 1938), 160-72; 12 (July, Oct. 1938), 1-8, 77-107; 13 (July 1940), 69-90; 13 (1942), 159-72; 14 (July 1943), 17-26.

4. *AGRICULTURE AND RURAL POVERTY*

J49 BLYN, GEORGE. "Agricultural Trends in India, 1891-1947: Output, Welfare, and Productivity," Pennsylvania, 1961. 338 pp. Abstract in DA:22 (Oct. 1961), 1038-39.

J50 GANGOPADHYAY, BIRENDRANATH. "Trends of Agriculture and Population in the Ganges Valley: A Study in Agricultural Economics," Calcutta, 1937.

J51 KUMAR, DHARMA. "The Growth of Agricultural Labour in the Madras Presidency in the Nineteenth Century," Cambridge, 1962. Under Gallagher.

J52 MAHABAL, S. B. "A Study in Fluctuations in Cropped Area in British India and in Production of Organized Industries in India 1914-1939," Bombay (Gokhale Institute), 1953. Under D. R. Gadgil.

J53 MENEZES, ORLANDO J. "Agricultural Stagnation as an Obstacle to Industrial Growth in India, 1920-1950," Princeton, 1958. 164 pp.

J54 MOSHER, ARTHUR THEODORE. "The Economic Effects of Hindu Religious and Social Traditions on Agricultural Production by Christians in North India," Chicago, 1946.

J55 PANIKAR, P. G. KESAVA. "An Essay on Rural Savings in India," Vanderbilt, 1960. Abstract in DA:20 (June 1960), 4549-50.

J56 SINGH, BALJIT. "Agriculture in Depression," Lucknow, 1941.

J57 SINGH, R. P. "An Enquiry in the Causes of the Depressed Conditions of Agriculture in Rajputana," Agra, 1949.

J58 SINGH, VIR BAHADUR. "The Changing Patterns of Rural Economy in the U.P.," Lucknow, 1951.

5. FAMINES

J59 BHATIA, B. M. "Indian Famines," Delhi.

J60 MUKHERJI, KARUNAMOY. "The Bengal Famine of 1943 and the Problems of Rehabilitation," Calcutta, after 1940.

J61 SRIVASTAVA, HARI SHANKER. "Famines and Famine Policy of the Government of India (1858-1918)," Agra, 1956. Summary in QRHS 2:1 (1962-63), 35-39.

J62 ZAMAN KHAN, SHAH. "The Famine Policy under British Administration in India," Lucknow, after 1955. Under N. L. Chatterji.

6. CO-OPERATIVE MOVEMENTS

J63 CATANACH, I. J. "The State and the Co-operative Movement in the Bombay Presidency, 1880-1930," London (School of Oriental and African Studies), 1960. Under Ballhatchet.

7. INDUSTRY, GENERAL

J64 AGARWALA, R. K. "Industrial Finance in India during World War II," Allahabad, 1955.

J65 BALKRISHNA, R. "Industrial Development of Mysore," London, 1939. Under V. Anstey.

J66 CHAUDHURY, ROHINMOHAN. "The Evolution of Indian Industries," Calcutta, 1932.

J67 EDDISON, JOHN C. "Case Study in Industrial Development—The Growth of the Pulp and Paper Industry in India," Massachusetts Institute of Technology, 1954.

J68 GOWDA, G. VARADE. "Growth of Some Mysore Industries and their Productivities—A Historical and Statistical Study," Delhi.

J69 KAUSUKUTTY, CHANOLIAN K. "Rural Industries in India, a Study in Rural Economic Development with Special Reference to Madras," London, 1951. Under Anstey.

J70 RASTOGI, B. P. S. "A History of Development of the Cottage Industry in U.P. under the British," Lucknow, after 1958. Under R. N. Nagar.

J71 SEN, SUNIL KUMAR. "Aspects of Industrial Policy and Development," Calcutta. Summary in QRHS:1 (1961-62), 174-75.

a. Cotton and Textiles

J72 BHALLA, A. S. "The Industrial Growth and Technological Pluralism in India, with Special Reference to the Cotton Textile Industry," Manchester, 1963-64.

J73 BHARUCHA, K. B. "The History of Cotton-Mill Industry in Western India," London, 1928. Under G. Slater.

J74 GUNDERSON, DORA J. "The Development of the Cotton Industry in India," Wisconsin, 1936.

b. Iron, Steel, Coal, and Other Minerals

J75 DE, N. "The Iron and Steel Industry of India: a Study in Industrial Geography," London (London School of Economics), 1953.

J76 JOHNSTON, WILLIAM A. "India's Iron and Steel Industry: a Study of Planned Industrial Growth," Harvard, 1964.

J77 SPIEGELMAN, ROBERT GERALD. "Protection in India during the Interwar Period: with Special Reference to the Steel Industry," Columbia, 1960. 461 pp. Abstract in DA:21 (July 1960), 92-93.

c. Opium

J78 NIGAM, SALIG RAM. "Opium—India and the League of Nations," Lucknow, 1942.

d. Salt

J79 GHOSH, B. "The Indian Salt Industry, Trade, and Taxation, 1756-1932," London, 1932-33. Under V. Anstey.

e. Tea

J80 AKHTAR, S. M. "The Growth and Development of the Indian Tea Industry and Trade," London, 1931-32. Under V. Anstey.

8. LABOR

J81 KANNAPPAN, SUBBIAH. "The Indian Trade Union Movement: an Account and an Analysis," Fletcher, 1956.

J82 MORRIS, MORRIS DAVID. "A History of the Creation of a Disciplined Labor Force in the Cotton Textile Industry of Bombay City, 1851-1951," California (Berkeley), 1954.

J83 SINHA, SASADHAR. "Post-war Labour Legislation in India—a Comparison with Japan," London, 1931-32. Under V. Anstey.

J84 VARMA, R. "The Evolution of the Trade Union Movement in India," New School for Social Research, 1957.

J85 VIDHYARTHI, RAM DALAREY. "Growth of Labour Legislation in India since 1939 and Its Impact on the Economic Development," Agra, 1960.

9. TRADE

J86 BANERJEE, TARASANKAR. "Internal Market of India (1834-1900)," Calcutta. Summary in QRHS:1 (April-June 1961), 29.

J87 BEVER, V. M. "The Trade in East India Commodities to the American Colonies, 1775-1890," Iowa, 1941.

J88 BHAGAT, GOBERDHAN. "America's Commercial and Consular Relations with India, 1784-1860," Yale, 1963.

J89 MATHUR, O. P. "India's Foreign Trade since 1900," Allahabad, 1951.

J90 PARSHAD, I. D. "Some Aspects of Indian Foreign Trade, 1757-1893," London. Summary in IHRB:7 (1929-30), 183-84.

J91 RAY, PARIMAL. "Indian Foreign Trade, 1870-1930," London, 1931-32. Under Sargent.

J92 SINGH, S. B. "European Agency Houses in Bengal (1783-1833)," Bihar. Summary in QRHS:1 (1961-62), 130-31.

J93 TALWAR, OMPRAKASH. "Pattern of Foreign Trade and Economic Development of an Underdeveloped Economy: India before and after Independence," Cornell, 1955. 472 pp.

J94 TRIPATHI, AMALES. "Trade and Finance in the Bengal Presidency, 1793-1833," London (School of Oriental and African Studies), 1953. Under Philips.

J95 VARSHNEY, ROSHAN LAL. "India's Foreign Trade during and after the Second World War," Lucknow, 1951.

10. TRANSPORTATION AND COMMUNICATION

J96 ASTHANA, B. N. "Railway Finances in India in the Twentieth Century," Allahabad, 1954.

J97 BERNSTEIN, H. T. "Steamboats on the Ganges: 1828-1840," Yale, 1955.

J98 MACPHERSON, W. J. "British Investment in Indian Guaranteed Railways, 1845-1875," Cambridge (Peterhouse), 1954.

J99 SANYAL, N. "Development of Indian Railways," London, 1930. Under Foxwell and Slater.

J100 THORNER, DANIEL. "Investment in Empire: British Railways and Steam Shipping Enterprise in India, 1825-1949," Columbia, 1950.

J101 VERGHESE, K. E. "The Development and Significance of Transport in India (1834-82)," Oxford (Balliol), 1963-64.

11. *PRICES AND WAGES*

J102 AGARWAL, RAM CHARAN. "A Study of Prices and Wages in U.P. since 1857, Based on the Records of Indigenous Bankers and Business Men," Allahabad, 1951.

J103 GOSH, A. K. "An Analysis of Indian Price Structure from 1861," London, 1950. Under R. D. G. Allen and Barna.

J104 NARAIN, LAXMI. "Price Movements in India, 1929," Agra, 1956.

J105 PALEKAR, S. A. "An Analysis of Real Wages in India, 1939-1950," Harvard, 1954.

12. *CURRENCY, BANKING, AND FINANCE*

J106 ALMAULA, NALIN I. "Operations of the Reserve Bank of India (1935-1954)," Pennsylvania, 1956. 246 pp.

J107 BHOURASKAR, D. M. "Public Debt in India, 1929-30 to 1950-51," Bombay, 1957. Abstract in BUJ:25 (Jan. 1957), 109-10.

J108 DATTA, P. "The Origin and Early History of Public Debt in India," London, 1930. Under Coatman.

J109 DESAI, T. M. "The Finance of the Bombay Government, 1936-1951," Bombay, 1951. Abstract in BUJ:20 (July 1951), 70-72.

J110 DHUNJEEBHOY, H. D. "Influence of the Bankers in the Baroda State (1802-1854)," Bombay (St. Xavier), 1946.

J111 GAUR, A. P. "U.P. Finance since 1935 (with Special Reference to Budgets)," Agra, 1953. Summary in UB:1 (Dec. 1954), 83-90.

J112 GHOSH, D. K. "Problems of the Indian Foreign Exchanges since 1927 [or 1937?]," London (London School of Economics), 1951. Under Sayers.

J113 GHOSH, S. "Inflation in India, 1939-1952: a Study of Inflation in an Underdeveloped Economy," London (London School of Economics), 1957.

J114 GOPAL, M. H. "The Financial History of Mysore, 1799-1831," London. Summary in IHRB:8 (1930-31), 179-82.

J115 GUPTA, BHANUBHUSAN DAS. "Paper Currency in India— A Historical and Critical Study," Calcutta, 1925.

J116 GURTOO, DUKH HARAN NATH. "India's Balance of Payments, 1920-1953," Princeton, 1956. Summary in DA:20 (April 1960), 3986-87.

J117 MANOHARAN, T. "Some Aspects of India's Balance of Payments (1919-39)," Bombay. Abstract in BUJ:24 (July 1955), 51-54.

J118 MATHEWS, V. T. "Pattern of Indian Public Expenditure, 1937-52," Bombay, 1958.

J119 MISRA, B. R. "Indian Provincial Finance, 1919-37, with Special Reference to the United Provinces," London, 1939. Under V. Anstey and F. C. Benham.

J120 PATEL, M. H. "Provincial Finance, 1921-1936," Bombay, 1941.

J121 RAM, MALI. "Flight of Foreign Capital from India since 1942," Rajasthan, 1954.

J122 RAMANA, DUVVURI V. "Money, Investment, and Income of India: 1914-1950," Chicago, 1956.

J123 RAMKRISHNA REDDY, G. "Mysore Finances since 1929," Mysore, 1954.

J124 RAO, B. S. "A Study of India's Balance of Payments during 1901-1913 and 1924-1936," Cambridge (St. John's), 1955.

J125 RAU, B. RAMCHANDRA. "Early Banking Institutions in Bombay and their Lesson, 1720-1857," Calcutta, 1931.

J126 ROY, MANOMOHAN. "Foreign Investments in British India from 1857-1858 to 1927-1928," Calcutta, 1932.

J127 SEED, G. "Financial Administration of British India under Lord William Bentinck," St. Andrews, 1949. Under Sir Charles Ogilvie.

J128 SINGH, D. BRIGHT. "Financial Developments in Travancore from 1800 to 1940," Travancore, 1945.

J129 SINHA, HARISCHANDRA. "Early European Banking in India," Calcutta, 1927.

J130 THAVARAJ, M. JOHN KERSOME. "Trends in Public Investment in India, 1898-1938," Delhi.

J131 VARMA, GYAN C. "Local Finance in India," London, 1931-32. Under Coatman.

K. SOCIAL HISTORY

1. GENERAL

K1 BALLHATCHET, KENNETH A. "Social Policy and Social Change in Western India, 1817-1830," London (School of Oriental and African Studies), 1953-54.

K2 BANAJI, D. R. "Slavery in British India," Bombay, before 1933.

K3 CHATTOPADHYAY, A. K. "Slavery in the Bengal Presidency under East India Company Rule, 1772-1843," London (School of Oriental and African Studies), 1962-63.

K4 DESAI, NEERA. "The Impact of British Rule on the Position of Indian Women," Bombay. Abstract in BUJ:20 (Jan. 1952), 81-83.

K5 DUA, SHIVA. "Social Conditions in the Second Half of the 19th Century with Special Reference to the Position of the Women," Delhi.

K6 GUMPERZ, ELLEN McDONALD. "English Education and Social Change in Late Nineteenth Century Bombay, 1858-1958," California (Berkeley), 1965.

K7 GUPTA, ANIMA SEN. "The Role of Women in Indian Public Life in Modern Times," American, 1958. Abstract in DA:19 (April 1959), 2679.

K8 KIDWAI, M. A. "Protection of Minorities in India," Lucknow, 1947.

K9 KUMAR, R. "State and Society in Maharashtra in the Nineteenth Century," Australian National, 1965.

K10 PANT, S. D. "The Social Economy of the Himalayas," Lucknow, 1934.

K11 PATEL, T. N. "The Social Status of Indian Women during the Last Fifty Years (1900-1950)," London (Bedford), 1953.

K12 PURANDARE, S. "Woman as Depicted in Marathi Social Novel (1850 to 1950)," Poona. Summary in JUP:3 (1954), 173-75.

K13 RAGHUVANSHI, V. P. S. "Indian Social Life, 1750-1818, with Special Reference to the Company's Territories as Drawn from European Sources," Allahabad, 1949.

K14 ROY, SUBODH CHANDRA. "Culture Contact as a Dynamic of Social Change: a Study of the Treatment of the Blind in India," New York, 1961. 345 pp. Abstract in DA:22 (Aug. 1961), 466-67.

K15 SCOTT, ROLAND W. "Social Ethics in Modern Hindu Thought," Columbia, 1951. 349 pp.

K16 SINGH, MOHINDER. "Social and Economic Condition of the Depressed Class in Northern India," Lucknow, before 1950.

K17 SINGH, R. L. "Banaras and Its Um Land: a Study in the Development of Human Settlements," London (London School of Economics), 1952.

K18 SPEAR, T. G. P. "English Social Life in India in the Eighteenth Century," Cambridge, 1931-32. Under M. Archbold.

K19 VERMA, ADITYA KISHORE. "The Problem of Minorities in India, 1900-1950," Allahabad, 1954.

2. POPULATION

K20 CHANDRASEKHAR, S. "The Population Problem in India," New York, 1944. 402 pp.

K21 LEARMONTH, A. T. A. "A Regional Study of Survival, Mortality and Disease in British India in Relation to the Geographic Factors, 1921-1940," Edinburgh, 1953.

K22 MATHUR, PRAKASH. "Internal Migration in India, 1941-1951," Chicago, 1961-62.

K23 ZACHARIAH, KUNNIPARAMPIL C. "Historical Study of Internal Migration in the Indian Subcontinent, 1901-1931," Pennsylvania, 1961-62.

3. FAMILIES, CLANS, AND ETHNIC GROUPS

K24 AHMED, SUFIA. "Some Aspects of the History of the Muslim Community in Bengal, 1884-1912," London (School of Oriental and African Studies), 1960. Under Philips.

K25 GOODRICH, D. W. "The Making of an Ethnic Group: the Eurasian Community in India," California (Berkeley), 1952.

K26 HITCHCOCK, JOHN T. "The Rajputs of Khaalaapur: a Study of Kinship, Social Stratification, and Politics," Cornell, 1956.

K27 RAJ, HILDA. "Persistence of Caste in South India: an Analytical Study of the Hindu and Christian Nadars," American, 1958. Abstract in DA:19 (April 1959), 2679.

4. SOCIAL REFORMS

K28 BADHE, G. S. "History of Social Legislation in India," Bombay, 1954.

K29 FRITZ, HENRY E. "The Humanitarian Background of Indian Reform, 1860-1890," Minnesota, 1957.

K30 HJEJLE, BENEDICTE. "The Social Policy of the East India Company with Regard to Sati, Slavery, Thagi, and Infanticide, 1772-1858," Oxford (Lady Margaret Hall), 1958. Under C. C. Davies.

K31 MILLER, MARION C. "The Antislavery Movement in India," Michigan, 1938.

K32 NATH, IQBAL. "Social Legislation in Punjab since 1849," Punjab, 1959.

K33 SHARMA, JAGDISH CHANDRA. "State in Relation to Prohibition in India with Special Reference to the United Provinces," Lucknow, 1950.

K34 SINGH, SITARAM. "Nationalism and Social Reform (1885-1920)," Patna.

K35 VIMLESH. "Development of Social Legislation in India," Allahabad, 1959.

L. CULTURAL HISTORY

1. GENERAL

L1 AHMED, A. F. S. "The Development of Public Opinion in Bengal, 1818-1835," London (School of Oriental and African Studies), 1960. Under Ballhatchet.

L2 BOSTROM, IRENE. "India in English Fiction: 1770-1860," Wisconsin, 1956. 525 pp.

L3 DATTA, V. "The Influence of Western Thought on the Social, Educational, Political and Cultural Development of India, 1818-1840," Cambridge (Fitzwilliam House), 1953.

L4 DEODHAR, S. "The Treatment of India in American Social Studies Textbooks, 1921-1952," Michigan, 1954. 284 pp.

L5 DIKSHIT, HIRA LAL. "A Study of Keshav Das," Lucknow, 1950.

L6 EAPEN, KARIPPACHERIL CHAKKO. "E. M. Forster and India," Colorado, 1962. 211 pp. Abstract in DA:23 (April 1963), 3897.

L7 HANSON, H. A. "The Democratic Ideal in the Thought of India," Boston, 1945.

L8 KOPF, DAVID. "Orientalism and the Genesis of the Bengal Renaissance, 1800-1830," Chicago, 1964.

L9 RAO, KANATUR B. "Rudyard Kipling's India," Iowa, 1957. 293 pp.

L10 SARDESSAI, MANOHAR. "L'Image de l'Inde en France au XVIIIe siècle" [The Image of India in France in the 18th Century], Paris (Lettres), 1958.

L11 SCHRAMM, RICHARD HOWARD. "The Image of India in Selected American Literary Periodicals: 1870-1900," Duke, 1964. Abstract in DA:25 (Nov. 1964), 2987.

L12 SINGH, M. M. "Emerson and India," Pennsylvania, 1947.

L13 SINGH, RAM. "The Impact of Industrialization on Indian Culture," North Carolina, 1953. 313 pp.

L14 VIDYARTHI, MOHAN LAL. "Main Trends of Indian Culture (1772-1856)," Agra, 1958.

L15 VYAS, K. C. "Renascent India," Bombay, 1948. 636 pp. Abstract in BUJ:17 (Jan. 1949), 81-82.

L16 WILKINSON, THEODORE S. "The Impact of Euro-American Culture on India from 1498 onward with Special Reference to Culture Lag," Duke, 1956.

L17 WILLSON, AMOS L., JR. "The Mythical Image of India in Early German Romanticism," Yale, 1954.

2. HISTORIOGRAPHY AND ORIENTAL STUDIES

L18 GREWAL, J. S. "British Historical Writing from Alexander Dow to Mountstuart Elphinstone on Muslim India," London. Summary in IHRB:36 (Nov. 1963), 217-18.

L19 MARATHEY, RAM MAHADEO. "Maurice Magre—a Work of Criticism on a Contemporary French Author Who Has Written Many Books on India, and Who is a Great Orientalist," Bombay, 1941.

L20 MUKHERJEE, S. "Sir William Jones and the Beginnings of Indology," London (School of Oriental and African Studies), 1962-63.

3. LIBRARIES

L21 SHUKLA, L. S. "Growth and Development of University Libraries in U.P. (1858-1960)," Lucknow, after 1958. Under R. N. Nagar.

4. EDUCATION

L22 AHUJA, R. L. "Indigenous Education in the Punjab until Annexation," Punjab, before 1956.

L23 BAHADUR, ROY SHIVENDRA. "History of Education and Social Policy in India in First Half of the 19th Century," Patna.

L24 BHARGAVA, M. L. "History of Secondary Education in U.P. from 1904 to 1947 with Special Reference to Policy and Finance," Allahabad, 1955.

L25 CHINNAPPA, SHANPAPPA PAUL. "The British System of Education in India," Columbia, 1915.

L26 COELHO, E. P. "Four Centuries of Christian Education in Bassein, with a Special Reference to the Educational Contribution Made by the Arch-Bishop T. Roberts," Bombay, 1959.

L27 CUTTS, ELMER H. "British Educational Policy in India under the East India Company," Harvard, 1940.

L28 ELLIOT, V. C. "The Education of Hindu Women from Ancient Days to the Present," Hartford, 1947. 436 pp.

L29 FIROZUDDIN-SAYYID. "Shah Waliullah's Philosophy of Education," Bombay, 1952.

L30 JHA, JATA SHANKAR. "Education in Bihar in the 19th Century (1813-1859)," Patna. Summary in QRHS:2 (July-Sept. 1961), 76-77.

L31 KANUNGO, GOSTHA BEHARI. "The Language Controversy in Indian Education: a Historical Study," Chicago, 1959.

L32 MALLICK, A. R. "The Development of the Muslims of Bengal and Bihar, 1813-1856, with Special Reference to Their Education," London (School of Oriental and African Studies), 1952. Under Philips.

L33 MISRA, B. D. "History of Development of Primary and Secondary Education in U.P. under the British," Lucknow, after 1958. Under R. N. Nagar.

L34 MISRA, MADHURI. "Education in U.P. from 1858 to 1900," Lucknow, after 1955. Under N. L. Chatterji.

L35 MISRA, RAM HARI. "Secondary Education in British India— 1800-1900," Lucknow, 1953-54. Under N. L. Chatterji.

L36 NAIK, C. H. "Education of Women in the Province of Bombay— a Retrospect and a Prospect (1818-1947)," Bombay, 1949. 683 pp.

L37 NARAIN, V. A. "The Life and Career of Jonathan Duncan, 1756-1795," London (School of Oriental and African Studies), 1957. Under Ballhatchet. Founder of Sanskrit College, Benares.

L38 PARASNIS, N. R. "The History and Survey of Education in the Thana District (Bombay State)," Bombay, 1958.

L39 PATEL, H. P. "Basic Education and Its Working in the State of Bombay (a Historical Review)," Bombay, 1958.

L40 SAHAI, GEORGE SYLVESTER. "Christian Missions and Indian Education, 1600-1857," Lucknow, 1952.

L41 SCHAEFER, HERBERT GEORGE. "Basic National Education in India from 1937-1959," Ohio State, 1961-62.

L42 SHRIDEVI, SRIPATI. "The Development of Women's Higher Education in India," Columbia, 1954. Summary in DA:14 (May 1954), 1989.

L43 SHUKLA, DEVENDRA NATH. "History of Indian Educational Policy 1854-1904," Allahabad, 1943.

L44 SHUKLA, S. C. "Educational Development in British India (1854-1904)," Delhi, 1958.

L45 SRIVASTAVA, R. C. "History of Education in India from 1904 to 1937," Allahabad, 1954.

L46 SUBRAHMANYAM, R. S. "The Educational Ideas of Mahatma Gandhi and Rabindranath Tagore—a Comparative Study with relevance to Modern India," Madras, 1958.

L47 VINCENT, ANTONIO M. "A Comparative Study of Secondary Education in India and the United States of America from 1900 to 1956," Texas, 1957.

L48 ZELLNER, AUBREY A. "A History of Education in the Lower Ganges River Area of India from 1858 to 1948," Iowa, 1949. 353 pp.

5. *LANGUAGE AND SCRIPT*

L49 KULKARNI, K. B. "Text Books in Marathi in the 19th Century, Their Authors and Their Effects on the Structure of the Marathi Language," Bombay, 1953.

6. *LITERATURE*

L50 CORNELL, L. L. "Kipling in India," Columbia, 1963. Abstract in DA:24 (May 1964), 4695-96.

L51 HASAN, MOHAMMAD. "Contribution of Lucknow to Urdu Language and Literature," Lucknow, 1952.

L52 HAWKES, CAROL A. "Anglo-Indian Fiction: a Conflict of Cultures as Seen by the Novelist," Columbia, 1953.

L53 JAMALUDDIN, KHWAJA. "The Indian Background of Kipling's Fiction and Poetry," Lucknow, 1952.

L54 LAL, LAKSHMI NARAIN. "Evolution and Technique of Hindi Short Story and Its Sources," Allahabad, 1952.

L55 MATHUR, KAILASH CHANDRA. "The English Romantic Poets and the Chhayavad School of Hindi Poetry," Lucknow, 1952.

L56 MINOCHERHOMJI, ROSHEN N. "Indian Writers of Fiction in English," Bombay, 1945.

L57 MISRA, VISHWANATH. "Influence of English on Hindi Language and Literature," Allahabad, 1950.

L58 NATH, BHOLA. "Studies in Modern Hindi Literature (1926-47) and Its Background," Allahabad, 1952.

L59 PANDIA, M. N. "The Indio-Anglian Novel as a Social Document," Bombay, 1950.

L60 PINGE, S. M. "Study of and Contribution to Marathi Language and Literature by Europeans," Bombay, 1953.

L61 SADIQ, MUHAMMAD. "Muhammad Husayn Azad, His Life, Work and Influence," Punjab, 1939.

L62 SANT, D. K. "Women in Marathi Literature of the British Period (1818-1947)," Bombay, 1953.

L63 SHAIKH, A. U. "The Development of Anglo-Indian Biographical Literature," Bombay, 1944.

L64 SIDDIQUI, GHALIB IQBAL. "Bibliography of Iqbal," Karachi (School of Special Librarianship and Bibliography), 1960.

L65 SINGH, BHUPAL. "A Survey of Anglo-Indian Fiction," Punjab, 1934.

L66 TOMAR, TIKAM SINGH. "Studies in Hindi Bardic Literature from 1600 A.D. to 1900 A.D.," Allahabad, 1952.

L67 VEDALANKAR, S. "The Development of Hindi Prose Literature in the Early Nineteenth Century, 1800-1856," London (School of Oriental and African Studies), 1954.

7. JOURNALISM

L68 AGARWAL, SUSHILA. "The Relation of the Press to the Government and Public Opinion in India, 1900-1935," Allahabad, 1956.

L69 BHURANEY, P. H. "Anglo-Indian Journalism in Bombay up to 1900," Bombay, 1956.

L70 SINGH, SUKHBIR. "Growth of Freedom of Press in India, 1780-1947," Agra, 1962.

8. RABINDRANATH TAGORE

L71 BHATTACHARYA, SEMANTI. "Tagore's Concept of Nationalism and Internationalism: a Historical and Critical Analysis," Columbia, 1953.

L72 HAY, STEPHEN N. "India's Prophet in East Asia: Tagore's Message of Pan-Asian Spiritual Revival and Its Reception in Japan and China, 1916-1929," Harvard, 1957. 281 pp.

L73 MUKHERJEE, SUJIT K. "Passage to America: the Reception of Rabindranath Tagore in the United States, 1912-1941," Pennsylvania, 1963.

9. HINDU RELIGIOUS MOVEMENTS

L74 CHATTERJEE, CHANDRA M. "Relationship of Hindu Festivals to Rural Life in the United Provinces, India," Cornell, 1949. 568 pp.

L75 ENO, ENOLA. "A Critical Evaluation of the Modernist Trends in Hinduism," Chicago, 1925.

L76 GRAHAM, J. REID. "The Arya Samaj as a Reformation in Hinduism, with Special Reference to Caste," Yale, 1942. 2 vols.

L77 MAGEE, JOHN B., JR. "Sri Ramakrishna and John Woolman: a Study in the Sociology of Sanctity," Harvard, 1950.

L78 ROY, ANJALI. "Development of Mysticism in Bengal during the 18th and 19th Centuries," Allahabad, 1951.

10. MUSLIM RELIGION AND CULTURE

L79 AHMAD, QEYAMUDDIN. "The Wahabi Movement in Bihar," Patna. Summary in QRHS:1 (July-Sept. 1961), 77-78.

L80 BARI, M. A. "A Comparative Study of the Early Wahhabi Doctrines and Contemporary Reform Movements in Indian Islam," Oxford, 1954. Under H. A. R. Gibb.

L81 HASSAAN, M. R. "The Educational Movement of Sir Syed Ahmed Khan, 1858-1898," London (School of Oriental and African Studies), 1959. Under Basham.

L82 HOLLISTER, JOHN N. "The Shi'a of India," Hartford, 1946.

L83 JAIN, MAMRAJ SINGH. "The Aligarh Movement—Its Origin and Development," Agra, after 1956. Summary in QRHS:2 (1962-63), 89-93. Under A. L. Srivastava.

L84 KAMALI, S. A. "The Concept of Human Nature in Hujjat Allah al-Baligah and Its Relation to Shah Waliullah's Doctrine of Fiqh," McGill, 1959. 478 pp.

L85 SINGH, H. J. "The Contribution of Sir Muhammad Iqbal to Modern Islamic Thought," Chicago, 1953.

11. CHRISTIANITY AND CHRISTIAN MISSIONS

L86 ALI, MUHAMMAD MOHAR. "The Bengali Reaction to Christian Missionary Activities, 1833-1857," London (School of Oriental and African Studies), 1962.

L87 CORREIA-AFONSO, JOHN. "Jesuit Letters and Indian History," Bombay. Abstract in BUJ:23 (July 1954), 82-83.

L88 DAVIS, WALTER BRUCE STARK. "A Study of Missionary Methods in Bengal from 1793-1905," Edinburgh, 1942. Under Hugh Watt and J. H. S. Burleigh.

L89 DOLBEER, MARTIN LUTHER, JR. "A History of Lutheranism in the Andhra Desa (The Telugu Territory of India) 1842-1920," Hartford, 1957. 481 pp. Abstract in DA:20 (July 1959), 278.

L90 EBRIGHT, DONALD FOSSETT. "The National Missionary Society of India, 1905-1942; an Expression of the Movement toward Indigenization within the Indian Christian Community," Chicago, 1944. 290 pp.

L91 FRANKLIN, C. S. "Missionary Activities in the Time of the East India Company," Lucknow.

L92 HESS, WELDON ROBERT. "The Religious Policy of the British East India Company, 1806-1843," Pennsylvania, 1964.

L93 HUNKER, CARL. "The Influence of William Carey in the Principles of Subsequent Missions," Southern Baptist, 1946. 219 pp.

L94 INGHAM, K. "The Achievements of Christian Missionaries in India, 1793-1833," Oxford, 1949. Under Jenkins.

L95 JOARDAR, N. G. D. "The Indian Christians of Lucknow," Yale, 1949.

L96 MAHTO, SARJU. "Hundred Years of Christian Missions in Chotanagpur since 1845 A.D.," Ranchi. Under P. N. Ojha.

L97 ODDIE, G. A. "The Rev. James Long and Protestant Missionary Policy in Bengal, 1840-1872," London (School of Oriental and African Studies), 1963-64.

L98 PARKER, K. L. "The Development of the United Church of Northern India," Chicago, 1935.

L99 PATHAK, SUSHIL M. "American Protestant Missionaries in India: a Study of Their Activities and Influence, 1813-1910," Hawaii, 1964.

L100 PHILLIPS, C. J. "Protestant America and the Pagan World: the First Half Century of the American Board for Foreign Missions, 1810-1860," Harvard, 1953.

L101 POTTS, E. D. "British Baptist Missions and Missionaries in India, 1793-1837," Oxford (Regent's Park), 1962-63.

L102 SWORD, VICTOR H. "History of the Baptists in Assam," Northern Baptist, 1953.

L103 TEN BRINK, EUGENE L. "The C.M.S. Mission of Help to the Syrian Church in Malabar, 1816-1840: a Study in Protestant-Eastern Orthodox Encounter," Hartford, 1960.

L104 THOMAS, C. CHACKO. "The Work and Thought of Eli Stanley Jones with Special Reference to India," Iowa State, 1955. 337 pp. Abstract in DA:15 (May 1955), 2323.

PART III • NEWSPAPERS

ABBREVIATIONS

ASB	Asiatic Society of India, Bombay Branch
BM	British Museum, London
CaOONL	Ottawa Public Library, Ottawa, Ontario
CaQMMIIS	Institute of Islamic Studies, McGill University, Montreal, Quebec
CLSU	University of Southern California Library, Los Angeles, California
CLU	University of California at Los Angeles, California
CSt	Stanford University Libraries, Stanford, California
CtY	Yale University Library, New Haven, Connecticut
CU	University of California Library, Berkeley
DLC	Library of Congress, Washington, D.C.
EC	Secretariat Record Office of Maharashtra, Elphinstone College, Bombay
GAU	Atlanta University, Atlanta, Georgia
HEW	East-West Center Library, Honolulu, Hawaii
IaU	State University of Iowa Libraries, Iowa City, Iowa
ICU	University of Chicago Library, Chicago, Illinois
IDC	International Documentation Centre, Tumba, Sweden
IEN	Northwestern University Library, Evanston, Illinois
IOL	India Office Library (Commonwealth Relations Library), London
InU	Indiana University Library, Bloomington, Indiana
IU	University of Illinois Library, Urbana, Illinois
MH	Harvard University Library, Cambridge, Massachusetts
MicroM	Micro Methods, Ltd., 17 Denbigh St., London S.W. 1
MicroP	Micro Photo Division, Bell and Howell Company, 1700 Shaw Avenue, Cleveland 12, Ohio
MILC	Midwest Inter-Library Center (center for Research Libraries), Chicago, Illinois
MnU	University of Minnesota Library, Minneapolis, Minnesota
NcD	Duke University Library, Durham, North Carolina
NcU	University of North Carolina Library, Chapel Hill, North Carolina
NjP	Princeton University Library, Princeton, New Jersey
NL	National Library, Calcutta
NN	New York Public Library, New York City
NNC	Columbia University Library, New York City
OBod	Bodleian Library, Oxford University, Oxford
OII	Indian Institute, Catte Street, Oxford
OU	Ohio State University Library, Columbus, Ohio
PP	Free Library of Philadelphia, Philadelphia, Pennsylvania

PU	University of Pennsylvania Library, Philadelphia, Pennsylvania
TNJ	Joint University Libraries, Nashville, Tennessee
ViU	University of Virginia Library, Charlottesville, Virginia
WaU	University of Washington Library, Seattle, Washington
WU	University of Wisconsin Library, Madison, Wisconsin
c.	newspaper existed at this date
n.	negative microfilm
p.	positive microfilm
inc.	holdings incomplete

INDEXES AND GUIDES TO NEWSPAPERS AND SOURCES OF INFORMATION ON LIBRARY HOLDINGS

CHICAGO UNIVERSITY. Libraries. Document Section. *Newspapers in Libraries of Chicago: A Joint Check List.* Chicago, 1936. 257 pp., mimeographed.

HEWITT, A. R. *Union List of Commonwealth Newspapers in London, Oxford and Cambridge.* London: Athlone Press, 1960. 101 pp. India, pp. 37-43; Pakistan, pp. 55-56.

HOOLE, WILLIAM STANLEY. *Foreign Newspapers in Southeastern Libraries.* Tuscaloosa, Alabama: University of Alabama, 1963. 64 pp.

ILLINOIS UNIVERSITY. *Newspapers in the University of Illinois Library.* Urbana, Illinois: March 1942. 43 pp. photographed from typescript.

LIBRARY OF CONGRESS. *Postwar Foreign Newspapers, a Union List.* Washington, D.C.: Library of Congress, Reference Department, 1953. 231 pp.

NATIONAL LIBRARY, INDIA. *Catalogue of Periodicals, Newspapers and Gazettes.* Calcutta: Government of India Press, 1956. 285 pp.

PARSONS, HENRY S. *A Check List of Foreign Newspapers in the Library of Congress.* Washington, D.C.: U.S. Government Printing Office, 1929. 209 pp. India, pp. 109-10.

SCHWEGMANN, G. A. *Newspapers on Microfilm.* 5th ed., Washington, D.C.: Library of Congress, 1963. 305 pp.

YALE UNIVERSITY LIBRARY. *A List of Newspapers in the Yale University Library.* New Haven, Connecticut: Yale University Press, 1916. 216 pp.

Holdings of the following libraries were checked by the editor, assistants, or correspondents: ASB, CaQMMIIS, CU, DLC, EC, HEW, ICU, IEN, MH, MILC, MnU, NN.

NEWSPAPERS

Adyar (Madras)

CONSCIENCE
MnU Ja 16, 1941—Je 1, 1945

Agra (U.P.)

AGRA AKHBAR
2x/wk, then weekly; 1832-44, new ser. 1844-
BM Je 30–D 15, 1838; F 21–O 12, 1839
DLC p. 1947
NL F–D 1844; Ja–Mr 1845; 1846

THE CHRONICLE
2x/wk
EC Ap–O 1846

THE MOFUSSILITE
See *Meerut*, THE MOFUSSILITE

Ahmadabad (Gujarat)

HARIJAN
weekly, F 11, 1933–F 1956?; closed Ag 1942 by the government, all
files destroyed; reopened F 10, 1946
pub. Harijan Sevak Sangh
ed. R. V. Sastri, Mahadev Desai, Pyarelal Nair, Kishorilal Mashru-
wala, Maganbhai Desai
ICU vol. 3, 5, 7-10, 16, 18, 19
NN F 2, 1948

YOUNG INDIA
O 8, 1919–1932 (previously published in Bombay under the manage-
ment of BOMBAY CHRONICLE); weekly (briefly, in 1919, 2/wk)
ed. M. K. Gandhi, O 8, 1919–
EC N 1915–O 1919; 1921-1932
ICU 1921-1931 (vol. 3-13)
NN 1919-1932 (inc.)
NNC Ja 1, 1925–Ja 14, 1932 (inc.)

Ajmer (Rajasthan)

DARBARA
Hindi weekly
DLC p. Ap 1944–D 1953; Ja 1957–D 1960; Ja 1962–
ICU 1962–

Aligarh (U.P.)

ALIGARH INSTITUTE GAZETTE
Urdu weekly
ed. Sir Syed Ahmed Khan
IOL 1875-1878

Allahabad (U.P.)

AMRITA BAZAR PATRIKA
daily, D 12, 1943–
DLC O 16, 1944–D 31, 1946 (few issues missing)

BHARATA
Hindi daily, 1928–
DLC p. S 3, 1946–
HEW film Ja 1946–D 1960; Ja 1962–D 1963
ICU 1962–

THE COCHRANE
BM Mr 1–O 15, 1897; F 1, 1905

DESHDOOT
Hindi weekly, 1938–
DLC p. O 1948–Je 1950

INDEPENDENT
daily, F 5, 1919–1923
founder: Motilal Nehru
ed. Syed Hossain, 1919; Bipin Chandra Pal, My 1920
NL complete files

INDIAN HERALD
daily
IOL 1880-1882

THE INDIAN PEOPLE
2x/wk, 1907-1909; absorbed by THE LEADER in 1909
NL 1908, Ja–O 1909

THE INDIAN UNION
absorbed by THE ADVOCATE, *Lucknow*

THE LEADER
daily, also semi-weekly edition; 1909–
founded by Pandit Malaviya and friends, with N. Gupta and C. Y.
Chintamani as joint editors
DLC O 1, 1942–D 31, 1961 (2 or 3 issues missing each month);
n. & p. 1962–
HEW film Ja 1962–D 1963
ICU 1962–
IOL 1929– (inc.)
NL Jl–S 1923; Jl–D 1953; 1954
NN Ja 18, 1920–Je 1922 (2x/wk ed.)

THE PIONEER
see THE PIONEER, *Lucknow*

PIONEER MAIL AND INDIAN WEEKLY NEWS
    1874–Mr 27, 1931
    BM Ja 17, 1874–Mr 27, 1931

    DLC Ag 17–N 30, 1923
    IOL 1875–1914
    MicroP 1911–1922; Ap 1924–1930
    NN 1914–Mr 1931

THE STAR
    BM Ag 26, 1929–S 29, 1930

THE WEEK'S NEWS
    Ja 7, 1888–
    NN Ja 7, 1888

Ambala (Punjab)

THE TRIBUNE
    weekly, F 2, 1881–; 2x/wk O 16, 1886–; 3x/wk Ja 1, 1898–; daily
        Ja 1, 1906–
    publication began in Lahore; due to communal rioting staff fled
        from Lahore on afternoon of Ag 15, 1947; publication resumed in
        Simla S 25, 1947. Ambala became place of publication My 13, 1948
    CU My 1922–(few issues missing)
    DLC S 9, 1942; O 1, 1942–Ag 14, 1947 (some issues missing)
    HEW film 1962-1963
    ICU 1962-
    IOL 1883-1899; 1948
    MnU Jl 31, 1925–Ja 1, 1926; F 18, 1926–Ja 24, 1930; My 1931–1938;
        Mr 1939–O 1940; 1941-42; F 1943-1950
    NL 1955–
    NN scattered issues in 1920
    NNC complete files
    Tribune office: complete files

Amritsar (Punjab)

AKĀLĪ PATRIKĀ
    Punjabi daily, 1920–
    DLC My 2–S 22, 1938 (inc.); Mr 8, 1950–

THE ONWARD
    BM F 11, 1924

Banaras (Benares, Varanasi) (U.P.)

AJ
    Hindi daily, 1920–
    DLC p. Mr 1947–
    HEW film Mr 1947–D 1959

ICU 1962–

PU 1948–(fairly complete)

ĀZĀD

Urdu daily

DLC p. scattered issues in 1950, 1952, 1953

BENARES RECORDER

c. 1840's, 2x/wk

BHOODAN

weekly, 1956–

ed. S. Dhadda

pub. for Akhil Bharat Sarva Seva Sangh; organ of the Bhoodan
movement

ICU vol. 1–

SANMARG (Akhilia Bharatiya Dharmasangha)

Hindi daily

DLC p. Ag 1950–N 1952; Ja 1953–

HEW film Ag 1950–D 12, 1951; 1952-1960

ICU 1962–

YUGĀVANĪ

Nepali weekly

DLC Je 7–S 13, 1951 (inc.)

Bangalore (Mysore)

AL-KALĀM

Urdu daily, 1924–

DLC p. S 28, 1946–D 1953; Ja 1957–D 1962; Je 1963–

ICU 1962–

BANGALORE DAILY POST

IOL 1887-1888(?)

BANGALORE EXAMINER

3x/wk

IOL 1877-1888

BANGALORE HERALD

absorbed by BANGALORE SPECTATOR in 1868

BM Ag 20, 1861

BANGALORE SPECTATOR

daily, 1868–

IOL 1877–Mr 1895

DECCAN HERALD

daily

DLC Mr 13, 1949 (vol. 2, no. 71)–D 31, 1961 (2 or 3 issues missing each month)

HEW film 1963
ICU 1962–

EVENING MAIL
daily
Andhra Pradesh State Central Library (Asafia Library), Hyderabad,
A.P., vol. 18, 20 (1903, 1905)

PRAJAVANI
Kannada
DLC p. 1962–
HEW film 1963
ICU 1962–

Bankipore (Bihar)

THE BEHAREE. WEEKLY MAIL AND MOFUSSIL
BM Jl 20, 1916–Ag 30, 1917 (inc.)

THE BEHAR HERALD
weekly 1874–
NL Jl–D, 1898; 1899; 1903-1904; 1908-1910

THE BEHAR TIMES
weekly 1894–
founder and ed. Sachchidananda Sinha
NL 1897-1902

Baroda (Gujarat)

NAVA GUJARĀTA
Gujarati weekly
DLC p. Ap 1944–D 1949

Berhampore (Bengal)

See *Murshidabad*

Bhopal (M.P.)

MADHYA PRADESH CHRONICLE
daily
DLC n. & p. 1962–
HEW film 1962; Jl–D 1963
ICU 1962–

Bijnor (U.P.)

MADINA
Urdu, weekly 1920–; then 2x/wk
ed. Abu Saeed Bazmi, Badrul Hasan Jalāli *et al.*
DLC n. & p. 1912-1925; 1927-1961; 1963-
HEW film 1912-1925; 1927-1960
IAU 1921-1923, 1937-1940
MnU p. of n. at DLC

[446]

Bombay

ADVOCATE OF INDIA
after 1925 incorp. with INDIAN NATIONAL HERALD
BM Je 13, 1887; Mr 18, 1911–Mr 29, 1912; O 12, 1912—S 11, 1914;
Ja 9, 1915–Ja 9, 1925 (inc.)

AMERIKANA SAMDESA
Gujarati weekly, 1951–
DLC p. Ap 7, 1951–D 1952

AMERIKANA VĀRTĀHARA
Marathi weekly, 1951–
DLC p. Ap 28, 1951–D 1952

ANGLO-INDIAN EMPIRE
BM Ap 3–O 30, 1909

ANGLO-INDIAN REVIEW
BM Ja–Je, Ag, 1916

ARGUS
weekly
IOL 1872-73

BHARAT
daily, Ag 8, 1949–
DLC N 23, 1949—D 31, 1952 (few issues missing)

BHARAT JYOTI
Sunday edition of FREE PRESS JOURNAL, 1938–
DLC Ap 2, 1944 (vol. 6, no. 25)—D 31, 1961 (few issues missing)

BOMBAY CHRONICLE
weekly
EC 1825–Ja 1826; S–O 1832

THE BOMBAY CHRONICLE
daily, 1913–Ap 4, 1959
founder: Ferozshah Mehta
ed. B. G. Horniman (until deported in 1919)
ASB Mr 1913–Ap 1959; Sunday ed., F 10, 1935–Mr 1939; Jl 1940–
Mr 1959
BM Mr 3, 1913–Jl 13, 1918; D 9, 1918–Mr 9, 1923 (inc.)
DLC Mr 16, 1930—Je 28, 1931 (Town & Dak ed. bound together;
14 issues missing)
Dak ed. (reprints features of Town ed. of previous day): S 9,
O 15-24, N 2-20, 25, 1942; Ja 18, 1943–Ap 4, 1959; Town ed.: Ag
17–D 31, 1942 (missing S 21-26); Ja 1-16, Jl 17, D 1, 2, 4-8, 1943;
Ag 22, S 12, 1944

EC Ap 1913–1940; 1948-1959

IEN N–D 1925; Ja–O 1926; F–D 1927; 1928-1933 (some few gaps)

InU D 1946–

MILC Ag 29–S 11, 1931; O 29, 1932—F 12, 1933; Ap–Ag, O 9, 1933—
My 6, 1934; Je–Ag 1934; Ja–Ag 1935

NL Mr–S 1923

BOMBAY COURIER

English & Gujarati; 2x/wk, 3x/wk, weekly; 1790-1847

founder: Luke Ashburner; see Chart II, TIMES OF INDIA

ASB Ag 1812–1826; 1831; 1833-37; 1839; 1842

BM Ja 1–D 4, 1803; Ja 4–D 27, 1806; Ja 9, 1819–D 25, 1830; Mr 4,
1845—Mr 13, 1846 (imp.)

DLC Ap 19, 1800 (vol. 2, no. 395); Ja 31–Ap 25, 1818 (Ap 11
missing); Suppl. Ja 31–Ap 25, 1818

EC 1797–F 1798; 1800, 1803–Ap 1813; 1814-1846

IOL 1793-1847

NL Jl 1793–Ap 1794; My 1797–Ap 1798; My 1799; 1800; 1826-1827

BOMBAY DARPAN

English and Marathi, 1832-1840; fortnightly through Ap 1832,
weekly thereafter

EC 1832, 1834

BOMBAY EXAMINER

weekly

EC D 1835–My 1837

BOMBAY GAZETTE

weekly 1791–; 3x/wk; daily, Ja 1850–

O 1791: recognized as an official gov't paper

1792: merged with BOMBAY HERALD

1842: ed. Mr. Fair, deported for criticizing the gov't

1849: incorp. THE GENTLEMAN'S GAZETTE(?)

1850: known as BOMBAY GAZETTE AND INDIAN MAIL

1859: ed. J. M. Maclean

ASB 1814; 1816-1820; 1822-1830; 1832; 1835; 1840-1841; 1862-1864;
Ja–Je 1866; Ja–Je 1867; 1868; Jl 1869–1882; Jl 1883–Je 1887; O
1887–1894; Jl 1895–My 1897; Jl–S 1897; Jl 1898–Je 1903; Ja–S
1904; 1905-1913

BM Ap 6, 1814—D 29, 1830; Mr 28, 1839; D 2, 20, 30, 1841; My 22,
1911—Mr 7, 1914 (inc.)

DLC My 6, 1812; Ja 28–Ap 8, Ap 22, 1818; Ja 13–F 17, F 24, 1819;
Suppl. Ja 28–Mr 18, Ap 1-22, 1818; Ja 13-27, F 10-24, 1819
Ap 17, My 7, 1909 bound with BOMBAY GAZETTE OVERLAND
SUMMARY, in place of numbers missing from that ed.

EC Ja–Je 1809; Ja–Je 1810; Ja–Je 1818; 1813-1817; 1819–S 1842; 1850-1858; 1860-1862; Jl 1863–Je 1865; 1866–Mr 1914
IOL 1813-1914

BOMBAY GAZETTE OVERLAND SUMMARY
BM F 29, 1868—Ag 30, 1872 (inc.); N 17, 1906–Mr 25, 1911
DLC D 30, 1899—Je 19, 1909. 14 vol.
IOL 1875-1911
OBod 1900-1904

BOMBAY GUARDIAN
weekly Mr 7, 1851–
ASB Mr 7, 1851–1853; 1866–1884; 1886–1889
BM Mr 7–D 26, 1851; Ja 4, 1890–D 26, 1891
CtY N 8, 1873–Ja 20, 1894
DLC D 2, 1882
EC My 1856–1859; 1863; 1874; 1878; 1880–Jl 1905

BOMBAY HALKARU AND VARTMAN
English and Gujarati weekly
EC 1833–Ap 1835

BOMBAY HERALD
1789 or 1791-1792
Bombay's first English weekly, incorp. into BOMBAY GAZETTE in 1792

BOMBAY MESSENGER
Portuguese weekly
EC Mr–D 1831

BOMBAY MONTHLY TIMES
see BOMBAY TIMES

BOMBAY NATIVE OBSERVER
weekly
EC Ja–Jl 1833

BOMBAY REVIEW AND INDIAN ADVERTISER
weekly
ASB D 7, 1878—D 18, 1880

BOMBAY SAMACHAR
English and Gujarati; 1819 or 1822–, weekly; 1833–, 2x/wk; 1860–, daily
founder: Fardoonjii Marzban (Murzaban)
originally entitled MUMBAI-NA-SAMA-CHAR; first "native" newspaper in Bombay
DLC p. Ap 1944–D 1962; Ja 1964–

HEW film Ja 1944–D 1953; Ap 1954–D 1960
ICU 1962–

BOMBAY SATURDAY REVIEW
weekly (Sat.)
ASB Ap 1861–Ap 1868

THE BOMBAY SENTINEL
daily
DLC Mr 6, 1945—Je 29, 1946; Jl 10, 1947—My 11, 1948 (fairly complete)

BOMBAY STANDARD AND CHRONICLE OF WESTERN INDIA
daily, early 1858–1859
absorbed by BOMBAY TIMES, JOURNAL OF COMMERCE in 1859 to form BOMBAY TIMES AND STANDARD; see Chart II, TIMES OF INDIA
EC 1858-59
IOL 1858-59

BOMBAY TELEGRAPH AND COURIER
daily, 1847-1861; see Chart II, TIMES OF INDIA
EC 1847–S 1856; Je 1860–My 1861
IOL 1847-1856
NL Jl–D 1860

BOMBAY TELEGRAPH AND COURIER. OVERLAND SUMMARY
fortnightly
IOL 1857

BOMBAY TIMES
Ja 1–My 23, 1842, known as BOMBAY TIMES; Je 18, 1842—Ag 27, 1845, known as BOMBAY MONTHLY TIMES; S 15, 1845—Ja 1, 1848, known as BOMBAY TIMES. BI-MONTHLY OVERLAND SUMMARY OF INTELLIGENCE
monthly, Ja 1–S 1842; 2x/mo, O 1-15, 1842; monthly, N 1, 1842–Ag 27, 1845; 2x/mo, S 15, 1845–Ja 1, 1848
See Chart II, TIMES OF INDIA
BM N 1, 1842–Ag 1845; S 15, 1845–D 29, 1857
DLC Ja 1, 1842–Ja 1, 1848 (missing: F 1842, Jl 1843)

BOMBAY TIMES. JOURNAL OF COMMERCE
2x/wk, N 3, 1838–; daily 1850–
absorbed BOMBAY STANDARD to form BOMBAY TIMES AND STANDARD, 1859; see Chart II, TIMES OF INDIA
ed. J. E. Brennan (d. of cholera Jl 1839); 1840–, G. Buist; c. 1859–, Robert Knight
ASB 1841, 1845

BM Mr 31, N 6, 1841
EC 1838-1846, 1848-1859

BOMBAY TIMES AND STANDARD
daily, 1859-1861; continued as TIMES OF INDIA My 18, 1861
IOL 1860-1861

BOMBAY TIMES. MONTHLY SUMMARY
BM Ap 1, My 22, 1841

BOMBAY WEEKLY GUIDE
pub. under the auspices of Bombay commercial interests
EC O 1832–Ap 1833

BOMBAY WITNESS
weekly
EC Jl 1844-1846

BRITISH INDIA GENTLEMEN'S LITERARY GAZETTE
daily
EC Mr 1843-1850

COMMERCIAL INDIA
weekly
DLC Mr 10, 1945–D 28, 1946 (5 issues missing)

COMMUNIST
CU n. S 7, 1947–Ja 1948

CONGRESS SOCIALIST. ORGAN OF THE CONGRESS SOCIALIST
PARTY (sub-title varies)
weekly, D 21, 1935–Je 25, 1939
ed. Asoka Mehta; contains socialist opinion and articles on USSR
CU p. of NN volumes
NN (vol. 1, no. 1–vol. 4, no. 26 (D 21, 1935–Je 25, 1939) (inc.)

ECONOMIC TIMES
daily
DLC My 30, 1961 (vol. 1, no. 87)–D 31, 1961; n. & p. 1962–
HEW film Ja 1962–D 1963

FINANCIAL EXPRESS
daily
DLC Ag 17, 1961 (vol. 1, no. 154)–D 31, 1961 (6 issues missing);
n. & p. 1962–
ICU 1962–

FREE PRESS JOURNAL
Sunday ed. entitled BHARAT JYOTI, *q.v.*
daily, Je 1930–

CU Ag 1951–
DLC Ap 3, 1944–D 30, 1961 (some issues missing); n. & p. 1962–
(inc. Sunday ed.)
ICU 1962–
MILC Jl 1933–Je 1935, 9 vols. (inc.)
PU 1948–(fairly complete)

GENTLEMAN'S GAZETTE
1847–; see BOMBAY GAZETTE

GUJARAT SAMACHAR
Gujarati
DLC p. Ja–D 1958

HINDI PUNCH
English and Gujarati weekly
IOL 1907-1931

HINDUSTAN
Sindhi
DLC p. 1962–
ICU 1962–

ILLUSTRATED WEEKLY OF INDIA
weekly, F 3, 1929–; formerly TIMES OF INDIA ILLUSTRATED
WEEKLY
DLC F 3, 1929–D 1940
ICU Jl 1957–
IOL 1937–
MILC 1955–

INDEPENDENT INDIA
weekly, Ap 4, 1937–1945
ed. M. N. Roy; numbering continued by the Calcutta periodical,
RADICAL HUMANIST
HEW film Ap 1937–N 1938; Ja 1939–Je 1940; 1945–Mr 1949
NN n. & p. Ap 4, 1937–N 27, 1938; Ja–Ag 27, 1939; D 17, 1939–Ja
23, 1940

INDIAN DAILY MAIL
daily
NN My 8, 9, 11-14, 1931

INDIAN MIRROR
DLC O 6, 1935 (vol. 3, no. 38)

INDIAN NATIONAL HERALD
BM N 13, 1926—Ap 4, 1929 (including Sunday ed.)

INDIAN NATIONALIST

sub-title on some issues: "The One-Anna Congress Weekly"
weekly, 1923-1924; pub. Indian Nationalist Syndicate; ed. L. G.
Khare
NN vol. 1-2

INDIAN SOCIAL REFORMER

weekly, 1890-1952 (vol. 63); founded in Madras, moved to Bombay
S 1901; ed. 1934-1938: K. Natarajan
ICU S 1923–1952 (scattered issues missing)
IOL 1899-1909
MicroM 1899-1909

INDIAN SPECTATOR

See Chart I, p. 454

INDIAN STATESMAN

daily, 1872–; see INDIAN STATESMAN AND GAZETTE OF ASIA
IOL 1872-1876

INDIAN STATESMAN AND GAZETTE OF ASIA

daily, –1872; cont. as INDIAN STATESMAN
IOL Ja–Ap 1872

INDU PRAKASH

English and Marathi weekly, c. 1877
ASB 1883-1895

THE IRIS

weekly
EC Jl–D 1827

ISMĀĪLĪ

Gujarati weekly
DLC p. Ja 1936–D 1937; Mr 1938–Je 1939; Ap 4, 1948–D 1958

JAM-E-JAMSHED (Jami-Jamshed)

Gujarati, 1832-1857 (suppressed when regulations of "Gagging Act"
were ignored)
DLC p. Ja 1947–D 1956; 1958–
HEW film Ja 1947–1956; 1958-1960; 1963

JANATA

weekly
CU film 1946-1951 (almost complete); Ja 6, 1952; Jl 20–D 28, 1952;
Ja 4-18, 1953

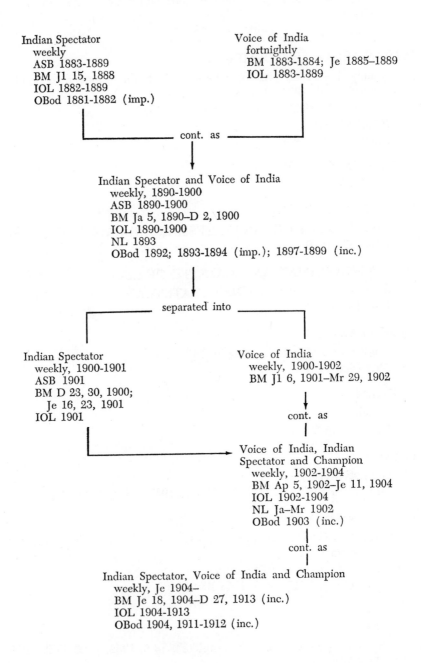

Indian Spectator
 weekly
  ASB 1883-1889
  BM Jl 15, 1888
  IOL 1882-1889
  OBod 1881-1882 (imp.)

Voice of India
 fortnightly
  BM 1883-1884; Je 1885–1889
  IOL 1883-1889

cont. as

Indian Spectator and Voice of India
  weekly, 1890-1900
  ASB 1890-1900
  BM Ja 5, 1890–D 2, 1900
  IOL 1890-1900
  NL 1893
  OBod 1892; 1893-1894 (imp.); 1897-1899 (inc.)

separated into

Indian Spectator
  weekly, 1900-1901
  ASB 1901
  BM D 23, 30, 1900;
   Je 16, 23, 1901
  IOL 1901

Voice of India
  weekly, 1900-1902
  BM Jl 6, 1901–Mr 29, 1902

cont. as

Voice of India, Indian
 Spectator and Champion
  weekly, 1902-1904
  BM Ap 5, 1902–Je 11, 1904
  IOL 1902-1904
  NL Ja–Mr 1902
  OBod 1903 (inc.)

cont. as

Indian Spectator, Voice of India and Champion
  weekly, Je 1904–
  BM Je 18, 1904–D 27, 1913 (inc.)
  IOL 1904-1913
  OBod 1904, 1911-1912 (inc.)

JANMABHOOMI
Gujarati daily, 1934–
DLC p. 1958, 1964
PU 1950–(fairly complete)

KAISER-I-HIND
Gujarati weekly, 1881–
DLC p. 1944-1952; Jl–D 1953; F 1957–

LOKAMĀNYA
Marathi daily, c. 1920–
founder: Krishna Prabhakar Khadilkar (associate of B. G. Tilak on
  KESARI, *Poona*)
DLC p. D 9, 1950–D 1957
HEW film D 1950–D 1957

MORNING STAR
weekly
EC S–N 1831

NATIVE OPINION
Marathi and English weekly
ASB Ja 6, 1867–1889
BM Mr 12, 1865
NL 1905

NAVASHAKTI
Marathi daily, 1932–
DLC p. Ja 1963–
HEW film 1963
ICU 1962–
PU 1948–(fairly complete)

THE ORIENTAL NEWS
weekly
EC S–D 1853, F–D 1854, 1856-1857

THE PARTY LEADER
irregular (weekly, monthly)
CU film Mr 24, 1942; F–Mr, Je–Jl, Ag–O 1943 (inc.); Ja 25–Mr 14,
  1944

THE STAR
weekly, F 10, 1946–
DLC F 10, 1946–My 4, 1947 (2 issues missing)

STAR OF INDIA
IOL S–D 1870; 1871

THE STUDENT
irregular (monthly, fortnightly)
CU film F, Je, N 1942; Ja, Mr, Jl–O 1943; Mr 22–My 22, Jl 22, S 7,
O 22, N 22, 1944; Ja 22–S 21, O 27, N 30–D 15, 1945; Ja 5-21,
Ap 13–Jl 6, 1946

THE SUNDAY NEWS OF INDIA
weekly, Ag 3, 1947–D 31, 1950
pub. by TIMES OF INDIA; replaced by Sunday issue of TIMES
OF INDIA Ja 7, 1951
DLC D 19, 1948; Ja 2, 1949–D 31, 1950 (scattered issues missing)

THE SUNDAY STANDARD
weekly
DLC Ap 16, 1944–D 31, 1961

TIMES OF INDIA
daily, My 18, 1861–; also 3x/wk ed., dropped S 28, 1861
pub. simultaneously in Bombay and Delhi; see Chart II
ASB 1861–to date
BM Ja 1, 1862–Je 29, 1863 (inc.); 1864-1865 (inc.); Jl 2, 1866–D 31,
1867 (inc.); Mr 20, 1911–Ap 30, 1940; Ja 27, 1941–Ap 3, 1943; N
17, 1943–S 9, 1950; F 23, 1951–
CU film S 1, 1951–1955; newsprint thereafter
DLC Ja 1, 1931–1951; film 1952–
EC 1861–Je 1866; Ja 1867–My 1925; Ja 1926–Je 1929; O 1929–1940;
1948–
HEW film D 1949–D 1961; 1963
ICU 1962–
IDC 1893-1964 (667 reels)
IEN N 1925–D 1936
IOL 1861-1889; 1914-1939; 1940-1947; 1950-1951 (inc.); 1952-
IU 1952-
MH p. Ag 1949–Ag 1958 (54 reels)
MicroM film 1861-1895
MILC 1952-
NcD 1956-
NL 1863; 1865-1868; 1870; 1872; 1886-1943; 1953-
NN Je 2, 1919–Ag 31, 1922; Ap 1924–N 9, 1940; D 1, 1940–1950;
film 1951–
OU Ap 15, 1951–
PU 1948–(fairly complete)
WaU 1942-1945 (fairly complete); 1947-
WU p. Ag 1, 1949–F 27, 1962
Note: for additional libraries holding positive film for 1949-1958,
see *Newspapers on Microfilm.*

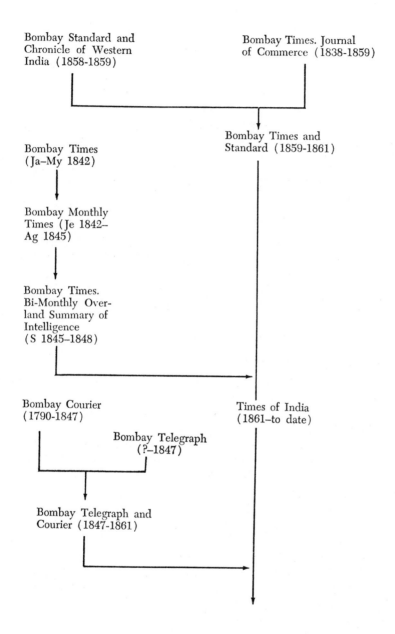

TIMES OF INDIA. OVERLAND SUMMARY
  weekly
  BM D 28, 1864–D 26, 1868
  IOL 1876-1914
  MnU 1870-1890

TIMES OF INDIA. OVERLAND WEEKLY (MAIL)
  BM Ja 2, 1885–Je 24, 1922
  OBod 1917-1934 (inc.)

TIMES OF INDIA. ILLUSTRATED WEEKLY
  continued as ILLUSTRATED WEEKLY OF INDIA, F 3, 1929
  DLC Ja 7, 1920–Ja 27, 1929

VOICE OF INDIA
  see Chart I, INDIAN SPECTATOR

Calcutta

ADVANCE
  daily, 1929–; Sunday issues called SUNDAY ADVANCE, Je 18, 1944–
  founder: J. M. Sen Gupta
  ed. G. C. Chakrabarty
  DLC Ap 1, 1944–D 31, 1948 (large gaps); Ja 25, 1951–D 29, 1953
    (large gaps)
  NL Jl 1931–N 1942; 1944-1945; Ja–S 1946

AMRITA BAZAR PATRIKA
  F 20, 1868–O 1871, pub. in Amrita Bazar, Jessore District, Bengal;
    moved to Calcutta D 21, 1871
  1868–Mr 21, 1878, Bengali and English; 1878–, English only
  weekly 1868-1891; F 19, 1891–, daily
  c. 1877, circulation 1500; "The Government regard it as an able and
    honest, but extremely anti-English paper" (Digby, CR:65 [1877])
  Amrita Bazar Patrika office, 1869–
  DLC N 20, 1941–D 31, 1961; n. & p. 1962–
  HEW film Ja 1962–D 1963
  IaU 1945-1951 (fairly complete)
  ICU 1962–
  IU My 1912–Jl 1939; Ja–Ap 1940; 1952–
  MILC 1891-1894; My 1912–N 1921; Ja 1922–Jl 1946; Ja–My 1947;
    F 1949–My 1951; Jl 1951–S 1955; O 1956–D 1959; Ap–D 1960
  MnU n. F 24, 1950–D 1958
  NL 1891–(fairly complete)
  NN My 1920–D 1921 (weekly ed.); n. 1951-
  PU 1948–(fairly complete)

ANANDA BAZAR PATRIKA
Bengali daily, 1878- or 1922-
DLC p. Ap 8, 1944-
HEW film Ja 1944–D 1960; 1963
ICU 1962-
PU 1948-

THE ANGLO-INDIAN; A WEEKLY NEWSPAPER AND REVIEW
1880-
absorbed THE ANGLO-INDIAN GUARDIAN Ag 28, 1880
NL Ja–Je, Ag–D 1880

THE ANGLO-INDIAN
1886-
NL 1886

THE ANGLO-INDIAN GUARDIAN
weekly, Ag 3, 1878–Ag 1880; continued as THE ANGLO-INDIAN;
A WEEKLY NEWSPAPER AND REVIEW Ag 28, 1880
ed. Thomas S. Smith
NL Ag 1878–Jl 1880

THE ANGLO-INDIAN RECORDER: A MEDIUM FOR ANGLO-
INDIAN REPRESENTATION
Ag 15, 1912-
pub. from Methodist Press
NL Ag–D 1912

ASIATIC MIRROR AND COMMERCIAL ADVERTISER
weekly, 1793?-
ed. in 1799: Charles K. Bruce; in 1814 Rev. Samuel James Bryce, a
Presbyterian minister, purchased the paper and it was then ed. by
James Ralph; ceased pub. before 1823
BM My 22, 1793; Mr 7, 1798
DLC scattered nos. Je 5, 1805–Je 19, 1819

BĀNGLĀRA KATHĀ
Bengali weekly
DLC Je 11, 1945–My 12, 1947 (inc.)

BASUMATI
Bengali weekly
DLC n. 1955-1956

BENGAL CATHOLIC HERALD
1847?-
BM Jl 3, 1858–O 22, 1859; My 19, 1860–N 16, 1861; D 28, 1861; Ja
18–My 3, 1862; N 12, 19, 1864

BENGAL CHRISTIAN HERALD
BM F 2, 1872; N 6, 13, 1874

BENGAL CHRONICLE
3x/wk, 1823?-
ed. James Sutherland; incorporated with INDIAN GAZETTE OR
CALCUTTA PUBLIC ADVERTISER in 1829; see Chart III, FOR-
WARD
DLC O 23, 1828 (vol. 5, no. 50), O 30, N 1, 6, 8, 20, 22, 29, 1828
NL 1827-1829
OBod Jl 14–D 1826

BENGAL COURIER
after O 1, 1834 incorporated with BENGAL HURKARU AND
INDIA GAZETTE; see Chart III, FORWARD

BENGAL HERALD OR WEEKLY MESSENGER (or, INTELLI-
GENCER)
(Bengali title: BUNGA DOOT)
My 1829–1844; printed in English, Bengali, Persian and Nagri
characters
founders and/or close associates in pub.: Nilratan Haldar, Robert
Montgomery Martin, Rammohun Roy, Dwarkanath and Prasanna
Kumar Tagore
incorporated THE ORIENTAL OBSERVER AND CALCUTTA
LITERARY GAZETTE (or, according to Digby, CR:65 (1877),
THE ORIENTAL OBSERVER incorporated the CALCUTTA
LITERARY GAZETTE and BENGAL HERALD); after 1844 in-
corporated into "Weekly Supplement Sheet" of BENGAL HUR-
KARU AND INDIA GAZETTE; see Chart III, FORWARD
IOL 1843
IU n. 1829; 1842; 1843
NL My–D 1829; 1841-1843

BENGAL HURKARU (HIRCARRAH)
weekly, Ja 20, 1795 (or 1798?)-; daily, Ap 29, 1819–1866; see Chart
III, FORWARD
established by Dr. Charles MacLean, later deported for disagreeing
with the government
ed. 1799-, William Hunter; other editors: Sutherland, Kaye, D. L.
Richardson, McPherson, Moor, James Hutton, Henry Mead, Alexander Forbes; 1864-1866, S. E. J. Clarke
DLC 1805 (missing F 12, My 14); scattered issues in 1818, 1828,
1834
HEW film Ag 1822–Jy 1855; Ja 1856–Je 1859; Ja 1860–D 1866
IOL 1822-1866

MicroM n. & p. 1822-1865
NL Jl 1824–1826; F–Je 1827; Ag–D 1828; 1829; Ja–Je 1832; Jl–D 1833

THE BENGALEE

    1858 or 1862-1932; weekly to 1897, daily thereafter

    founder and ed. Girish Chandra Ghosh; Surendranath Bannerjee also ed.

    to Ap 16, 1931, called THE BENGALEE; thereafter mofussil editions continued to be called this, while the town edition went through the following changes: Ap 17–Ag 8, 1931: CALCUTTA EVE-NING NEWS (THE BENGALEE); Ag 11, 1931–Ag 3, 1932: THE BENGALEE (CALCUTTA EVENING NEWS); Ag 4-16, 1932: CALCUTTA EVENING NEWS (THE BENGALEE); Ag 17, 1932, succeeded by THE STAR OF INDIA

    BM D 30, 1871; Mr 9, 1872; Jl 18–Ag 29, 1874; Ja 2–N 20, 1875; Ja 8, 15, 1876; Mr 21, 1929–Ag 3, 1932 (inc.)

    DLC Ja 1, 1907–Ag 16, 1932 (fairly complete)

    IEN N–D 1925 (inc.); 1926-1931; Ja–Ag 1932

    IOL 1876-1917

    MILC N 1919–D 1921; 1923

    NL 1891; 1894-1896; 1898; Jl–D 1900; 1901; 1903; 1905-1917; Ja–Mr, Jl–D 1918, 1923-31; Ja–Ag 1932

BRITISH INDIA

    weekly

    BM F 18–Mr 11, 1905

BUNGA DOOT

    see BENGAL HERALD OR WEEKLY MESSENGER

CALCUTTA CHRISTIAN HERALD

    IOL 1844-1845

CALCUTTA CHRONICLE AND GENERAL ADVERTISER

    weekly, Ja 1786-

    ed. William Baillie

    BM Ja 4, 1787–D 30, 1790

    DLC Ja 7–Jy 22, 1790 (in rare book room)

    NL 1792; Ja–N 1793

CALCUTTA COURIER

    1795 or 1799-1830, 2x/wk; new series Ap 1832-, 3x/wk

    proprietors in 1799: Thomas Hollingbery and Robert Khellen (or Kneln); ed. of new series: George Prinsep

    ASB 1832

    BM Ja 12, 15, 1839

    IOL 1832-1842

    NL 1832-1833; 1835; 1838-1842 (inc.)

CALCUTTA EVENING NEWS
see THE BENGALEE

CALCUTTA EXCHANGE GAZETTE AND DAILY ADVERTISER
daily
DLC S 1, 1820 (vol. 2, no. 291), S 4-11, 1820 (bound with CAL-
CUTTA JOURNAL OR POLITICAL, COMMERCIAL AND LIT-
ERARY GAZETTE, S 1-11, 1820); My 2, 1845; N 5, 10, 1849; My
11, 1854

CALCUTTA EXCHANGE PRICE CURRENT
weekly
DLC My 6, 1830
West Bengal Secretariat Record Office, Calcutta: 1820-1858 (10 vols.)

CALCUTTA GAZETTE AND COMMERCIAL ADVERTISER
daily, O 1, 1828-
pub. and ed. Villiers Holcroft
IU n. 1828
NL O 1828–S 1829

CALCUTTA GAZETTE OR ORIENTAL ADVERTISER
Mr 4, 1784–1823?
pub. Francis Gladwin
BM Mr 4, 1784–Ja 4, 1787
IDC 1784-1964 (as part of series with FRIEND OF INDIA and
STATESMAN)
IOL 1784; 1786-1823

CALCUTTA GAZETTE (CALCUTTA GOVERNMENT GAZETTE)
HEW film Ja 1815–Mr 1832
IOL 1815-1832
MicroM 1815-1832
MnU p. 1815–Mr 1832
NN film 1815-1832; 1903-1940 (all but 1939-1940 indexed and almost
complete; listed under Bengal: Government Publications)

CALCUTTA GENERAL ADVERTISER
see HICKEY'S BENGAL GAZETTE

CALCUTTA JOURNAL OR POLITICAL, COMMERCIAL AND LIT-
ERARY GAZETTE
O 2, 1818-1823; 2x/wk to 1821, then daily (Calcutta's first daily)
ed. James Silk Buckingham (until his deportation Mr 1, 1823, to
London, where he founded the ORIENTAL HERALD); Mr. San-
dys ed. until its license was revoked. The paper "relentlessly ex-
posed the administration of India." When the paper closed, Dr.
Muston used the press for THE SCOTSMAN IN THE EAST.
DLC F 19, 1819; S 1-11, 1820

CALCUTTA LITERARY GAZETTE
weekly (Sun.)
ed. David Lester Richardson
see BENGAL HERALD OR WEEKLY MESSENGER

CALCUTTA MORNING POST
1795 or 1798-; weekly, then daily
ed. in 1799: Archibald Thompson, Paul Ferris, Morely Greenway;
ed. c. 1818: Mr. Heatly
DLC few scattered nos. 1806-1808 (N 7, 1806 = vol. 15, no. 756)
HEW film Ja 1812–D 1813
IOL 1812-1813
MicroM n. 1812-1813
NL F–D 1810

CALCUTTA MUNICIPAL GAZETTE
weekly
BM N 15, 1924–D 21, 1929; Ap 5, 1930–F 22, 1947 (1939-40 inc.)
HEW film My 1952–O 1954; N 1955–O 1956; Ap 1958–Ap 1959
IOL 1924-1936

CALCUTTA PUBLIC ADVERTISER
see THE INDIAN GAZETTE, OR CALCUTTA PUBLIC AD-
VERTISER

CALCUTTA SPECTATOR
1913-
NL Ag–D 1913; Ja–Ag 1914

CALCUTTA STAR
daily, 1840-; incorp. into THE MORNING CHRONICLE
IU n. 1843
NL Jl–D 1843; Jl–D 1844; Ja–Je, Ag–D 1845; Ja–Je 1847; 1848–Je
1850

CALCUTTA TELEGRAPH
see THE TELEGRAPH

CALCUTTA TIMES
weekly
DLC Ja 12, 1819 (vol. 6, no. 267), F 6, 9, 16, 1819

CAPITAL, INDIA'S LEADING FINANCIAL PAPER
weekly
IOL 1928-1948
MILC 1931-1941 (vol. 86-106)

THE CITIZEN
daily, 1851-
NL Jl–D 1851; Jl 1852–Je 1856

THE COLUMBIAN PRESS GAZETTE
1824-
Proprietor and ed. Monte de Rozario; incorp. into BENGAL HUR-
KARU between 1828 and 1833; see Chart III, FORWARD

COMRADE
see *Delhi*, COMRADE

DAILY COMMERCIAL AND GENERAL ADVERTISER
daily
DLC Je 7, 1819

DAINIKA BASUMATI
Bengali daily, c. 1880
DLC p. O 14, 1946–S 1947; S 22, 1950–Ag 1952; S 1953–D 1957;
Ja 1960-
HEW film O 1946–S 1947; S 1950–Ag 1952; S 1953–D 1957; 1960
ICU 1962-

DAINIKA VISVAMITRA
Hindi
ICU 1962-

THE DEMOCRAT. A WEEKLY ANGLO-INDIAN PUBLICATION
pub. Dignum Brothers, 1940-1941
contained mostly international news
NN vol. 3, no. 1-10, 12; vol. 4-vol. 5, no. 4 (D 14, 1940–Je 21, 1941)

EASTERN STAR
weekly, 1839-
NL 1848

THE EMPIRE
ceased pub. Ag 11, 1920; continued as NEW EMPIRE
BM Jl 15, 1910–Ag 10, 1920

THE ENGLISHMAN
1821–Ap 1934; daily, then weekly; Sunday ed. known as THE
JOURNAL
founder and ed. J. H. Stocqueler
title variations: 1821–S 1833 JOHN BULL IN THE EAST
O 1, 1833–1860 THE ENGLISHMAN
1860-1861 THE ENGLISHMAN AND MILITARY CHRONICLE
(*but* DLC lists under this title O 10, 1849 [vol. 11, no. 283]–
O 27, 1849)
1861–Ap 1934 THE ENGLISHMAN
Ap 1934 incorp. with THE SUNDAY STATESMAN
BM My 1, 1874–Ja 8, 1896; Ja 1, 1908–Mr 26, 1934

IEN N 1925–Mr 26, 1934
IOL 1834-1930
NL 1833-1879 (inc.); 1880–Mr 1934

ENGLISHMAN'S OVERLAND MAIL
weekly; continued as THE ENGLISHMAN. WEEKLY SUMMARY
BM My 28, 1887–O 21, 1891
IOL 1875-1891

THE ENGLISHMAN. WEEKLY SUMMARY
incorp. with THE SUNDAY STATESMAN
BM O 28, 1891–Je 29, 1922; Ja 7, 1926–Ja 26, 1928 (inc.)
DLC Ja 4, 1900–Ja 26, 1928 (37 vols.; missing O 13, 20, 1916)
IOL 1891-1914
OBod 1917-1923

ENQUIRER
weekly
IU 1934 (vol. 1, nos. 1-6)

FORWARD
O 25, 1923-; daily to My 11, 1936, weekly My 18, 1936-
title variations: O 25, 1923–Ap 25, 1929 FORWARD
My 1, 1929–My 3, 1929 NEW FORWARD (q.v.)
My 4, 1929–S 1933 LIBERTY (q.v.)
S 1933- FORWARD; see Chart III, p. 466
founder: Deshbandhu Chittaranjan Das
incorp. THE INDIAN DAILY NEWS and THE INDIA GAZETTE
Ap 15, 1924; see Chart III
DLC Ap 11, 1924–Ap 25, 1929; N 3, 1933–N 16, 1936; scattered nos.
in 1937; Ja 2, 1939–Je 1, 1940
IEN N 1926–My 3, 1929
IOL 1948
MILC O 1923–Ap 1928 (inc.); O 6, 1933–F 8, 1934; Ap 24, 1934–
F 15, 1935
NL Jl 1925–Ap 1929; O 1933–1935; 1937-1941; Ja–Ag 1942

FRIEND OF INDIA
weekly; pub. at Serampore Ja 1, 1835–Ap 15, 1875; moved to Calcutta Ap 24, 1875
ed. Meredith Townsend
title changes: 1835-1876 FRIEND OF INDIA
1877-1883 FRIEND OF INDIA AND STATESMAN
1884-1885 INDIAN STATESMAN
1885-1894 STATESMAN AND FRIEND OF INDIA
1894-1909 FRIEND OF INDIA AND STATESMAN
1909-   THE STATESMAN (q.v.)

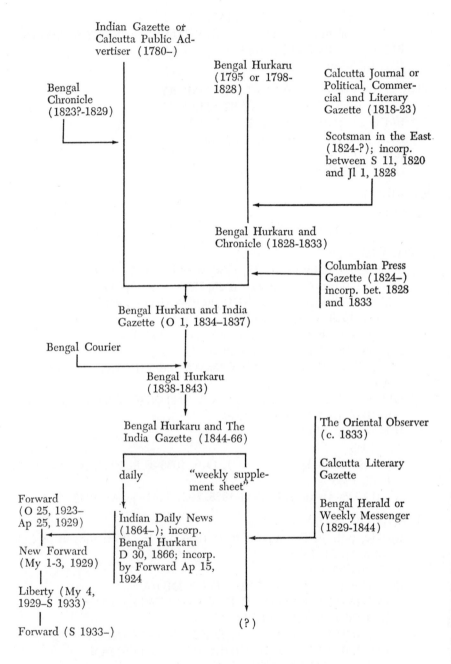

Indian Gazette or
Calcutta Public Ad-
vertiser (1780–)

Bengal Hurkaru
(1795 or 1798-
1828)

Calcutta Journal or
Political, Commer-
cial and Literary
Gazette (1818-23)

Bengal
Chronicle
(1823?-1829)

Scotsman in the East
(1824-?); incorp.
between S 11, 1820
and Jl 1, 1828

Bengal Hurkaru and
Chronicle (1828-1833)

Columbian Press
Gazette (1824–)
incorp. bet. 1828
and 1833

Bengal Hurkaru and India
Gazette (O 1, 1834–1837)

Bengal Courier

Bengal Hurkaru
(1838-1843)

Bengal Hurkaru and The
India Gazette (1844-66)

The Oriental Observer
(c. 1833)

Calcutta Literary
Gazette

daily   "weekly supplement sheet"

Bengal Herald or
Weekly Messenger
(1829-1844)

Forward
(O 25, 1923–
Ap 25, 1929)

Indian Daily News
(1864–); incorp.
Bengal Hurkaru
D 30, 1866; incorp.
by Forward Ap 15,
1924

New Forward
(My 1-3, 1929)

Liberty (My 4,
1929-S 1933)

(?)

Forward (S 1933–)

ASB 1838-1841; 1843; 1846-1855; 1862; 1864; 1866; 1868; 1870; 1872–
Mr 1882

BM Mr 1, 1838–N 3, 1859; Ja 2, 1874–1909

DLC n. Ja 7–D 30, 1841; Ja 5, 1843–D 25, 1845; Ag 6–N 29, 1872; Ja
10–Jl 15, 1873; Jl 23, 1874–Ap 15, 1875; MS index 1844-1845; Ap
24, 1875–D 26, 1881; Ja 2–My 22, 1883

IOL 1835-1909

MicroM n. & p. 1835-1914

OBod 1835-1858; 1871-1888; 1900-1904

GANAVARTA
Bengali
DLC p. Ja 1957–D 1960

GUARDIAN. A CHRISTIAN WEEKLY JOURNAL OF PUBLIC
AFFAIRS
pub. John Burton and James Mackenzie, 1823-
MILC 1928-1953

HABL-UL-MATIN
Persian weekly
MH n. S 12, 1904–Jl 27, 1906 (year 12, nos. 2-44; year 13, nos. 1-46)

HICKY'S (or HICKEY'S) BENGAL GAZETTE, OR THE ORIGINAL
CALCUTTA GENERAL ADVERTISER
weekly, Ja 29, 1780-
BM Ap 1/8, 1780–Mr 16/23, 1782
IOL 1781-1782
MicroM 1780-1782
MnU p. Jl 22, 1780–Mr 30, 1782
NcD 1780 (inc.); 1781-1782
NL Ja 29, 1780–Ja 5, 1782

HINDOO PATRIOT
vernacular weekly, 1853-1892; daily 1892-1923?
proprietor: Babu Madhuudan Roy
ed. 1861, Harish Chandra Mookerjee; 1861-, Kristo Das Pal
"India's First National Newspaper" appeared on the masthead during one period. "Its political faith is loyalty to the British Crown
and justice to the millions." (Digby, CR:65 [1877])
ASB F 1, 1875–1891
BM D 10, 1857; Je 24, 1858; scattered issues 1859-1863; F 16–D 21,
1874; Ja 11, 1875–Ag 5, 1922 (inc.)
IOL 1876-1888

THE HINDU INTELLIGENCER
weekly, 1846-1857
founder and ed. Kasi Prasad Ghose
NL 1849; 1853-1855; Ja–Je 1857

HINDUSTAN STANDARD
daily, O 2, 1937-
ed. Dhirendranath Sen
DLC S 8, 1942; Ap 8, 1944–D 31, 1961; n. & p. 1962-
HEW film 1963
ICU 1962-
NL O–D 1937; 1938-

HIRCARRAH
name changed to BENGAL HURKARU (*q.v.*)

INDIA GAZETTE
probably the same as THE INDIAN GAZETTE, OR CALCUTTA
PUBLIC ADVERTISER (*q.v.*)

INDIAN AGRICULTURIST
IOL 1876-1916

INDIAN CHARIVARI
fortnightly
ASB Ja 1876–Je 1877

THE INDIAN DAILY NEWS
daily, 1864–Ap 15, 1924
founder: George Roe Fenwick; later purchased and ed. by James
Wilson
incorporated BENGAL HURKARU AND INDIA GAZETTE D 30,
1866; incorp. by FORWARD Ap 15, 1924; see Chart III, FOR-
WARD
DLC Je 1, 1914–Ap 10, 1924
IOL 1867-1916
NL 1864-1866 (inc.); 1868-1888 (inc.); 1890-1924 (inc.)

THE INDIAN DAILY NEWS. BI-WEEKLY EDITION
DLC S 14, 1912–My 27, 1914

THE INDIAN DAILY NEWS. OVERLAND SUMMARY
weekly
IOL 1875-1885; 1894-1898

THE INDIAN DAILY NEWS. SATURDAY EVENING EDITION
BM Ja 2–Je 26, 1869; 1870

INDIAN ECONOMIST
IOL 1869-1875

INDIAN EMPIRE
BM Jl 10, 1861–Je 25, 1862 (inc.)

INDIAN FINANCE
TNJ Ja 1958-

THE INDIAN GAZETTE, OR CALCUTTA PUBLIC ADVERTISER
N 1780-; weekly 1782-1822; 2x/wk 1822-1829; 3x/wk; daily N 1830-
pub. 1780: B. Messink, Peter Reed; 1799: William Morris, William
Fairlie, J. D. Williams
ed. Sir Herbert Compton; 1822: Dr. John Grant
incorp. BENGAL CHRONICLE; incorp. with BENGAL HURKARU
between O 30, 1829 and N 19, 1834; see Chart III, FORWARD
BM F 20, Jl 23, 1781; F 16–D 28, 1782; Ja 3–D 26, 1785; Ja 26, 1818;
Je 25, 1838
DLC scattered nos. 1792; 1801; 1803; 1806-1808; 1828
HEW film Ja 1782–D 1788; Ag 1822–D 1843
IOL 1783-1788; 1822-1843
MicroM 1782-1788; Ag 1822-1840; 1842-1843; 1871-1872
MnU p. 1782-1788; Ag 1822-1840; 1842-1843
NL Jl 1831–Je 1832; 1833
NN p. Ja 5–N 9, 1782; N 22, 1783–Je 7, 1784; Je 22, 1784–1788; Ag
1822–1840; 1842-1843

INDIAN LANCET
fortnightly
IOL 1873
MILC Jl 1896–D 1, 1898 (vol. 8-12) (inc.)

THE INDIAN MESSENGER
weekly
pub. Brahmo Mission Press; religious, social, moral and educational
news
BM Jl 6, 1884–Ja 4, 1885
NL vol. 29-32, 35-41 (1912-1913) (inc.)

INDIAN MIRROR
Bengali? daily, 1861
founder Debendranath Tagore
ed. Monomohan Ghosh, Satyendranath Tagore; later Keshub Chun-
der Sen
BM Ag 1, 1861; Ja 5, 1862–S 1, 1863; Ag 1, 1874
IOL 1878-1889
NL Ja–Je 1888; Ja–Je 1891; Jl–D 1892; Jl–D 1893

INDIAN SUNDAY MIRROR
IOL 1878-1881

INDIAN NATION
weekly, 1883-
founder and ed. N. N. GHOSH
IOL 1908-1913
NL 1891; 1894-1896; 1898; 1901; 1908-1910

INDIAN OBSERVER
weekly
after Ap 1871, a continuation of THE OBSERVER; incorp. with
FRIEND OF INDIA
IOL My 1871–My 1872
MicroM 1871-1872

INDIAN POST
BM D 26, 1871

INDIAN STATESMAN
see FRIEND OF INDIA

THE INDIAN TIMES
incorp. with THE CALCUTTA STAR to form the MORNING
CHRONICLE

JAI-HIND
daily, 1947-
founder: Akhil Chandra Dutt
NL 1948-1949

JOHN BULL IN THE EAST
daily, Jl 1, 1821–My 1833
prop. Rev. Samuel James Bryce
ed. James Mackenzie and Robert Macnaughten; then David Lister
and George Pritchard
"to intents and purposes an official government organ"
sold and converted into THE ENGLISHMAN, My 1833
ASB Ja 26, 1828–S 1833
NL 1824-1826; Ja–Je 1827; 1828–Je 1830; 1832

THE JOURNAL
Sunday ed. of THE ENGLISHMAN
BM Ja 5, 1908–D 29, 1912; Ja 4–D 27, 1914

JUNGUNTAR
Bengali daily S 1937-
Amrita Bazar Patrika office, 1937-
DLC p. Jl 1952–D 1953

KALEIDOSCOPE
c. 1828
ed. David Drummond and Henry L. V. Derozio
IU Ag 1829–Jl 1830

LIBERTY
daily except Tues. My 4, 1929–S 1933
succeeded by NEW FORWARD; continued as FORWARD; sus-

pended My 2–Jl 2, 1930 and Ag 4–S 20, 1930 "on account of political troubles"
ed. Satyaranjan Bakshi
DLC My 4, 1929–Ag 1933
IEN My 1929–Ag 1933
MILC My 1929–Ag 1933
NL N 1929–S 1933

MATHRUBHUMI ILLUSTRATED WEEKLY (MĀTRIBHUMI ĀPAPPATIPPŬ)
Malayalam weekly, 1923-
DLC p. 1942-1950

MIRROR OF THE PRESS, OR THE POLITICAL AND LITERARY REGISTER
weekly, My 1, 1830-
IU n. 1830
NL My–O 1830

MORNING CHRONICLE
daily, weekly, daily
Ag 1, 1942–S 30, 1948; moved to Dacca, resumed pub. Mr 20, 1949
founders: Abdur Rahman Siddiqi and K. Nooruddin
DLC 1950: Jl 1-25, Ag 11-22, O 9-14, 16–N 2, 4-14
     1951: F 6-26, Ap 9-22, 24-28, My 7–Je 10, 19-30, Jl 15–Ag 4,
        S 16-21, O 21-27
     1952: Mr 30–Ap 5, 8-13, 15-19, 27–My 3, Je 8-14, Ag 31–D 31
     Ja 1, 1953–Jl 2, 1957 (scattered issues missing); n. & p. 1962-
MILC S 1943–D 1944
NL Ag 1942–Mr 1948

MORNING POST
see CALCUTTA MORNING POST

THE MOSLEM CHRONICLE. A WEEKLY REVIEW OF POLITICS, HISTORY, LITERATURE AND SOCIETY
new series, 1926-1929?
pub. Habibus Sobhan; militantly pro-Muslim, mostly editorial
NN new series vol. 1-4 (inc.)

MOSLEM CHRONICLE AND THE MUHAMMADAN OBSERVER
weekly, 1866-
incorp. THE MUHAMMADAN OBSERVER
IOL 1895-1905
NL 1908, 1926

THE MUHAMMADAN OBSERVER
weekly, 1882-

incorp. by MOSLEM CHRONICLE
NL 1894

MUSSALMAN
weekly, 1906–O 1930; 3x/wk, N 1930–S 1932; daily, O 1932–Ja 1938;
ceased pub. Ja 1938
ed. Majibur Rahman 1920-; moderate Muslim paper
MILC O 14-27, 1932; My 12–S 7, 1933
NL 1923; 1926-1932; Ja–S 1933
NN 1927

THE NATION
daily, S 1, 1948-
ed. Sarat Chandra Bose
DLC Ja 1, 1949–D 3, 1950
NL S 1948–1950

NATIONAL BUDGET AND VERNACULAR REPORTER
BM Ap 11, 1874 (inc.)

THE NATIONALIST
daily
DLC Ap 9–D 31, 1945 (scattered issues missing)

NEW EMPIRE
continuation of THE EMPIRE, Ag 10, 1920-
BM Ag 11, 1920–N 30, 1928 (inc.)

NEW FORWARD
My 1–My 3, 1929; see FORWARD
DLC My 1-3, 1929

NEW INDIA. A WEEKLY RECORD AND REVIEW OF MODERN
THOUGHT AND LIFE
weekly, Ag 12, 1901-
ed. Bipin Chandra Pal
BM My 8–Jl 31, 1893(?)
MILC F 18, 1905–My 4, 1907
NL Ag 1901–F 1903; O–D 1921

THE OBSERVER
became INDIAN OBSERVER My 1871
IOL F 4 –Ap 29, 1871

ORIENTAL ADVERTISER
see CALCUTTA GAZETTE

ORIENTAL COMMERCE REGISTER AND EAST INDIA PRICE
CURRENT
BM Ap 2, 1818–Ja 15, 1819

THE ORIENTAL OBSERVER
  weekly in 1833
  see BENGAL HERALD and Chart III, FORWARD

ORIENTAL STAR
  weekly, 1793- or 1794-
  ed. in 1799: Richard Fleming
  BM Mr 30, 1793
  DLC Ja 3, 1807; Ap 17, 1819; Je 5–Jl 24, 1819

THE PHOENIX
  BM Jl 16, Ag 29, S 2, 4, 1801

PRINCE AND PEASANT
  see REIS AND RAYYET

PROGRESS: A WEEKLY REVIEW OF POLITICS, LITERATURE
  AND SOCIETY
  weekly, 1922-
  NL Ja–N 1923

REFORMER
  weekly, 1831-
  ed. Prosonno Coomar Tagore; Rammohun Roy was assoc. with
    this paper
  IU n. 1833
  NL Mr–D 1833

REIS AND RAYYET. A NEWSPAPER AND REVIEW OF POLITICS,
  LITERATURE AND SOCIETY
  weekly, 1882-
  founder and ed. Sambhu Chunder Mookerjee
  BM Ja 27, 1883–Je 6, 1885; Je 12, 19, 1886; Je 23, Jl 21, D 29, 1888
  NL 1882, 1896
  NN S 23, 1899

ROZĀNA HIND
  Urdu daily, 1930-
  DLC p. O 1942–D 1947; Mr 21, 1948–D 1953

SATYAYUGA
  Bengali
  DLC p. 1952-1953

THE SCOTSMAN IN THE EAST
  daily, 1824-
  ed. Dr. Muston, Bengal Presidency Surgeon
  pub. at the press of the former CALCUTTA JOURNAL, later sold
    out to BENGAL HURKARU
  NL Jl–Ag 1824

THE SERVANT
daily, 1920-
founder and ed. Shyam Sunder Chakravarty
NL Jl–D 1923

STANDARD BEARER
weekly, 1920-1924
ed. Arun Chandra Dutt; superseded by NAVA SAMGHA, *Chandernagore*
NN vol. 1-4 (inc.)

THE STAR OF INDIA
daily, 1932-; not pub. My 31–Jl 12, 1949
succeeded CALCUTTA EVENING NEWS (THE BENGALEE)
Ag 17, 1932
BM Ja 19, 1933–Ap 30, 1940; Ja 22, 1942–Ag 10, 1949
CU p. Mr–Ap 1942; Ap 1943–D 1944; Mr–Ap, Jl–S, D 1945; Ja–My,
S–D 1946; Ap 1947–Ag 13, 1949 (22 reels)
DLC Ag 17, 1932–D 31, 1948; p. Ja 1949–Ag 13, 1949
IEN Ag 17, 1932–D 1936
MH same as CU
MILC n. of CU's p. film
NN Ja 1945–Jl 17, 1946 (inc.)
PU same as CU

THE STATESMAN
daily, 1875-; see FRIEND OF INDIA
BM Ja 1–Mr 31, 1914; Ja 2, 1917–D 30, 1928; Ja 1, 1940-
CaOONL p. 1952-
CU p. Ja 2–Mr 16, 1950; Ag 1, 1951–1955
DLC S 16, 1943–Je 29, 1946 (scattered issues missing); Ja 1, 1947–
D 31, 1951; p. Ja 1952-
HEW film 1952–Mr 1965
ICU 1962-
IOL 1877-1889; 1915-1938; 1939-1951 (inc.); 1952-
MH p. 1952-
MILC 1944-1945 (inc.); n. & p. 1952-1955; p. 1956-
MnU n. Ja 26, 1950–D 1951
NcD Ap 1960-
NcU p. 1957-
NN 1941-1942 (inc.); 1944 (inc.)
PP 1945-
PU 1950-
ViU Ja 1962-
WU p. 1952–Je 1962
Statesman office, 1875-; there is a charge for consulting the files.

THE STATESMAN
weekly, 1909-1923?; see FRIEND OF INDIA
BM Ap 1, 1909–D 27, 1923
IOL 1910-1914
OBod 1917-1923

STATESMAN AND FRIEND OF INDIA
see FRIEND OF INDIA

THE STATESMAN. OVERSEAS EDITION
weekly
BM Ja 3, 1924–Mr 23, 1939; Jl 5, 1945-
CLSU O 27, 1951-
DLC F 2, 1928 (vol. 5, new series, no. 214)–My 14, 1942; O 15,
D 17-31, 1942; Ja 7, 1943–D 30, 1950; scattered runs 1951-1953
MILC 1930-1938; N 26, 1944–D 1945; My 5–D 1951; 1958-1959
NN 1924-1954
OBod 1929–Ja 1941
ViU 1959-1960 (inc.)

STATISTICAL REPORTER
IOL 1869-1877

THE SUNDAY STATESMAN
succeeded THE ENGLISHMAN Ap 1, 1934
DLC S 19, 1943–Je 30, 1946 (bound with THE STATESMAN)
IOL 1950 (inc.); 1951-

SWADHINATA
Bengali
DLC p. 1952-1954; 1956
HEW film 1952-1954; 1956

TELEGRAPH
weekly, c. 1795-; N 26, 1803–N 1, 1806 known as THE CALCUTTA
TELEGRAPH
ed. Holt (or Henry) McKenly
DLC scattered nos. 1803, 1806, 1808

THE TIMES
BM D 7, 1813

VISHWAMITRA
Hindi daily, 1917-
HEW film 1963

WEEKLY MESSENGER (INTELLIGENCER)
see BENGAL HERALD OR WEEKLY MESSENGER

THE WORLD
weekly, then daily; 1791-
DLC Jl 7–N 3, 1792
IOL 1791-1793

Chandernagore (Bengal)

NAVA-SAMGHA

N 1924–Mr 1925; superseded THE STANDARD BEARER, which
was suppressed in Calcutta; NAVA SAMGHA was later suppressed by the French government.
ICU vol. 1 (inc.)

Chittagong (E. Pak.)

AZADI
Bengali daily
DLC p. Mr 3-7, 11-29, Ap 1-12, My 19–D 31, 1962; My 1–D 31, 1963
(inc.); 1964-

EASTERN EXAMINER
daily
DLC n. & p. 1962-

Cochin (Kerala)

THE MALABAR HERALD
weekly, F 25, 1905-
DLC Ap 1, 1944–D 23, 1961; n. & p. 1962

THE WESTERN STAR
weekly, 1864-
NN D 23, 1871

Coorg (Mysore)

JANMABHOOMI
Kannada
DLC p. Ja 1962-

Cuttack (Orissa)

DAINAK ASHA
Oriya daily, 1928-
DLC S 18, 1946–Ap 6, 1951

EASTERN TIMES
daily
DLC n. & p. 1962-
HEW film 1963
ICU 1962-

MATHRUBHUMI
Oriya
DLC film 1962-
ICU 1962-

NEW ORISSA
daily, 1933–Ap 6, 1951
DLC Ap 9, 1944–Mr 2, 1946; Ag 4, 1948–Ap 6, 1951 (scattered issues
missing)

SAMAJA
Oriya daily, 1918-
pub. Servants of the People Society
DLC p. Ap 1944–D 1961; Ja 1963-
HEW film Ap 1944–D 1960
ICU 1962-

UTKALA DIPIKA
Oriya weekly, 1866-1933?
Orissa State Archives 1869-1933 (some gaps)

Dacca (E. Pak.)

ASSAM ERA
incorp. with EASTERN BENGAL to form EASTERN BENGAL
AND ASSAM ERA (*q.v.*)

AZAD
Bengali daily
DLC p. 1957 (inc.); O 17, 1961–D 1964 (inc.)

BENGAL TIMES
2x/wk; N 1905, absorbed by EASTERN BENGAL AND ASSAM
ERA
IOL 1876–N 1905
MicroM 1876-1908

DACCA NEWS
weekly, 1856-
BM 1856–Jl 31, 1858
HEW film Ap 1856–N 1858
IOL 1856-1858
MicroM 1856-1858
NL Ja 1857–D 1858

DACCA PRAKĀS
Bengali weekly, c. 1874
DLC p. F–Je 1939

DAILY TELEGRAPH AND DACCAN HERALD
IOL 1876-1889

EAST BENGAL TIMES
MILC Mr 1933–Je 1934 (inc.); Ag 4-18, 1934; F 2, 1935–Ap 24, 1937;
O 9, 1937–Jl 2, 1939 (inc.)

EASTERN BENGAL ASSAM ERA
2x/wk
incorp. BENGAL TIMES N 1905
IOL 1905-1914
NL 1915

ITTEFAQ
Urdu
DLC film Ja 1962–D 1963

THE MAIL
1952-
DLC Mr 27, 1954

MORNING NEWS
see *Calcutta*, MORNING NEWS

PAKISTAN OBSERVER
daily, Mr 11, 1949-
DLC Ap 28, 1950–S 29, 1951 (missing 66 nos.); D 16, 1954–D 31,
1961 (several nos. missing)
NcD Jl 1959
NjP n. 1961

PASBAN
Urdu daily
DLC film 1962-

SANGBAD
Bengali
DLC p. 1955

Delhi (Old and New)

ANSĀRĪ
Urdu daily, 1935-
DLC p. Ja 1, 1943–S 7, 1947; N 21, 1947–Ap 1, 1950 (inc.)

ASIAN RECORDER
ICU 1955-

BHĀRATĪYA SAMĀCHĀRA
Hindi, 2x/wk
DLC Ja 1945–Je 1949; p. Mr 1941–My 1945

COMRADE
Ja 14, 1911–O or N 1914
pub. in Calcutta 1911-1912, Delhi thereafter
ed. Mohammad Ali
HEW film Ja 1913–N 7, 1914
MicroM n. 1913-1914

CROSSROADS
weekly, Ap 29, 1949–S 27, 1953; suspended pub. Jl 22–D 9, 1949;
absorbed PEOPLE'S AGE in 1949; absorbed by NEW AGE S 27,
1953
CU Ap 29–My 20, Je 3, D 31, 1949; 1950–O 5, 1951; O 19–D 28,
1951; Ja 4–S 27, 1952; Ja 4–S 27, 1953

DAILY CHRONICLE
merged with DAILY GAZETTE, *Karachi* in 1870 to form CIVIL
AND MILITARY GAZETTE, *Simla*

DAILY TEJ
Urdu daily (see also TEJ WEEKLY)
carried signed articles by Shraddananda, founder of Shuddhi move-
ment
DLC Ap 27–Je 29, S 28–D 6, 1950; Ja 6–F 8, 1951 (inc.) p. My 2–
Je 1, Jl 2, Ag 1–S 30, O 18, 1953; 1962-
HEW film 1963
PU 1948-

DAILY WATAN
Urdu daily, 1929-
DLC p. S 3, 1946–Je 1952; D 1952–D 1953

DAWN
daily, O 26, 1941–S 3, 1947; plant wrecked by mob S 14, 1947; moved
to Karachi Ag 15, 1947; see *Karachi*, DAWN
CU n. 1944–Ag 1947
DLC n. O 26, 1941–Ag 31, 1943; Ja 1–S 3, 1947
HEW film O 1941–S 3, 1947
MILC S 1, 1943–Mr 5, 1945 (inc.)
NN n. 1944–Ag 28, 1947 (inc.)
NNC p. O 26, 1941–S 3, 1947

DELHI EXPRESS
daily, D 1, 1951–Je 30, 1953
succeeded INDIAN NEWS CHRONICLE; succeeded by INDIAN
EXPRESS, Delhi ed.
DLC 1951-1953

DELHI GAZETTE
English (and Urdu?) weekly
ASB Ja 3–D 1838; 1840-1841; Ja–Je 1853
IOL 1837-1859; 1877-1889

DELHI TIMES
weekly
BM Ja 4, 1956-

EVENING NATIONAL CALL
daily
DLC F 8, 1943 (vol. 2, no. 38); Mr 2, S 24, 1944

GAZETTE OF INDIA
HEW film 1957-1959
NN 1912 to date (inc.); n. 1943-1956; p. 1957-

HINDUSTAN
Hindi daily, 1936-
DLC p. S 1946-
HEW film S 1947–D 1960
ICU 1962-

HINDUSTAN TIMES
daily, 1923-
founder: Malaviyaji
CtY 1950-
CU n. S 14-
DLC S 11, 1943–D 1961; n. & p. 1962-
GAU 1961-1962
HEW Ja 1962–D 1964
ICU 1962-
MILC 1951- (inc.)
MnU n. F 17, 1950-1959
NcD 1950-
PU 1948-

HINDUSTAN TIMES
weekly, 1923-
DLC 1945-
MILC 1951-1953

HINDUSTAN TIMES. OVERSEAS EDITION
weekly
CaQMMIIS 1952-
DLC Ja 1, 1953 (vol. 4, no. 1)–D 28, 1961
IOL 1950 (inc.); 1951-
MILC F 1952–Je 1957

NcU 1953-1959
ViU 1952- (inc.)

ILLUSTRATED HINDU WEEKLY
DLC p. O 1942–N 1947

ILLUSTRATED TEJ WEEKLY
see TEJ WEEKLY

INDEPENDENT INDIA
daily except Mon.; title changed to THE VANGUARD on an unknown date
NN Ag 30, 31, 1943; S 1, 1943–Je 18, 1946; Jl 1–N 28, 1946; D 4,
1946–Mr 1, 1947

INDIAN EXPRESS
daily; succeeded DELHI EXPRESS Jl 1, 1953
Sunday ed. entitled SUNDAY STANDARD
DLC Jl 1953–D 31, 1961; n. & p. 1962-
HEW film Ja–Mr, Jl–D 1963
ICU 1962-

INDIAN NEWS CHRONICLE
daily, Ap 4, 1947–N 29, 1951; succeeded by DELHI EXPRESS D 1,
1951
DLC 1947-1951 (scattered issues missing)

JAN YUG
Hindi
DLC p. Ag 1952–D 1953

JANG KI KHABREN
English, 2x/wk
DLC N 18, 1943 (vol. 4, no. 92)–S 9, 1945 (scattered numbers only)

MARKAZI ITTILA'AT
Urdu fortnightly
ed. A. S. Ayengar
DLC p. 1941–S 1947; F 1948–Je 1949
IAU 1947, 1949

MILAP
Urdu daily
DLC p. Ap 1949–Jl 1952; Mr 1953–D 1961
HEW film 1954-1960

THE MOFUSSILITE
see *Meerut*, MOFUSSILITE

THE NATIONAL CALL
daily, -N 8, 1949
DLC Ap 3, 1944 (vol. 13, no. 92)–N 8, 1949 (few issues missing)

NAVBHARAT TIMES
Hindi daily, 1947-
DLC p. Ap 1947–D 1954; My–D 1955; My 1956–D 1961; Ja 1963-
HEW film Ap 1947–D 1960; 1963
ICU 1962-

PATRIOT
ICU 1962-

PEOPLE'S AGE
Ag 2, 1942–F 20, 1949
title changes: Ag 2, 1942–N 18, 1945 PEOPLE'S WAR
N 25, 1945–F 20, 1949 PEOPLE'S AGE
Ap 29, 1949–S 27, 1953 CROSSROADS (*q.v.*)
CU Ag 2–D 1942 (inc.); 1943; Ja 2, 1944–F 20, 1949

PRATAP
Urdu daily, 1919-
DLC p. Ag 1946–D 1961; Ja 1963-
HEW film Ag 1946–D 1960; 1963
ICU 1962-

SANMĀRGA
Hindi daily
DLC Ag–D 1950 (inc.)

THE STATESMAN
daily, Ja 19, 1931-
DLC S 11, 1942; O 1, 1942–D 31, 1961; n. & p. 1962-
HEW film 1963
ICU 1962-

SUMACHAR HINDOOSTANI
BM Ja 6, 1862–F 28, 1863

SUNDAY STANDARD
Sunday ed. of INDIAN EXPRESS

TEJ WEEKLY
Urdu, 1923-; until 1947, known as ILLUSTRATED TEJ WEEKLY
DLC p. Ap 18, My 9–Jl 21, 1944; O 28, N 4, D 9, 1947–Je 1954; Ja
10–D 31, 1956; 1958; F–D 1959; Ja 1960–D 1961
ICU 1962-

TIMES OF INDIA (Delhi edition)
weekly
DLC n. & p. 1962-
ICU 1962-

THE VANGUARD
daily; absorbed INDEPENDENT INDIA
MILC Ja 1945–Je 1946 (inc.)

VISHWAMITRA
Hindi daily, 1942-
DLC p. Ja 1944-

WATAN
see DAILY WATAN

Dera Ismail Khan (W. Pak.)

MUJĀHID
Urdu weekly, 1932-
DLC p. 1948-1949 (inc.)

Dhanbad (Bihar)

COALFIELD TIMES
weekly
DLC Ap 4, 1948 (vol. 1, no. 50)–Jl 11, 1948; O 9, 1949–D 8, 1961;
n. & p. 1962-

Dibrugarh (Assam)

THE ASSAM TRIBUNE
weekly, 1938 or 1939-
pub. in Gauhati Je 21, 1946-
DLC My 5, 1944–Je 14, 1946

Ernakulam (Kerala)

THE WEEKLY KERALA
S 7, 1957-
DLC S 7, 1957

Gauhati (Assam)

ASAM BANI
Assamese
DLC My 26, Ag 4, S–O 1961; p. Ja 1962-

THE ASSAM TRIBUNE
weekly Je 21–S 27, 1946; daily S 30, 1946-
see also Dibrugarh, THE ASSAM TRIBUNE
DLC Je 28, 1946–D 31, 1961; n. & p. 1962-
HEW film Ja 1962–D 1963
ICU 1962-
NL 1954-

[483]

Hubli (Mysore)

HUBLI GAZETTE
Kannada weekly
DLC p. O 1944–D 1946

JAI HIND
Kannada weekly, 1939-
DLC 1947–D 1953

SAMYUKTA KARNATAKA
Kannada
DLC p. My–D 1953

Hyderabad (A.P.)

ANDHRA JANATHA
Telugu daily
DLC p. 1962-
ICU 1962-

DAILY NEWS
2x/wk, Ag 1947-
ed. B. R. Chari
Daily News office: complete files "available to bona fide researchers only"

HINDI MILAP
Hindi
DLC p. S–D 1953

INDUS TIMES
DLC n. & p. 1962-

JARIDA-I-ALAMIA SARKAR-I-ALI (HYDERABAD STATE GA-
ZETTE)
Persian 1869-; Urdu c. 1885-1948; weekly
Government official publication
Andhra Pradesh State Archives: nearly complete files

REHNUMA-E-DECCAN
Urdu daily
founded by Ahmad Mohiuddin as REHBAR-E-DECCAN; assumed
present name S 1948
DLC film 1961
Office of the editor: files since Jl 2, 1949 "can be shown only to those
researchers who can produce a certificate from an educational
institution"

Imphal (Manipur)

PRAJATANTRA
Manipuri
DLC p. 1962-
ICU 1962-

Indore (M.P.)

CENTRAL INDIA TIMES
English ed., weekly
DLC S 5, 1934 (vol. 6, no. 23)–S 11, 1935; Ja 22–D 23, 1936; Ja 6, 27, F 10, 17, 1937

Jammu (Jammu & Kashmir)

KASHMIR POST
1956?–Jl 28, 1960, weekly; Ag 1960-, daily
pub. from Srinagar in summer months
DLC D 6, 1958 (vol. 3, no. 28)–D 29, 1960; n. & p., 1962-
ICU 1962-

Jeypore (Madras)

PRAJĀBANĪ
Oriya weekly
DLC p. Mr 1944–D 1952

Jubbulpore (M.P.)

SUBH CHINTAK
Hindi, 2x/wk, 1887-
DLC p. O 1942–D 1950

Jullundar (Punjab)

AKĀLĪ-PATRIKA
Punjabi daily, 1920-
DLC Mr 16–Ag 10, 1947 (inc.); p. My–S 1948; Mr 1950-
HEW film Ja 1954–D 1959
ICU 1962-

AKĀLĪ-PATRIKA
Punjabi weekly
DLC p. 1951-

NAYA ZAMANA
Urdu
DLC p. Je 1953–D 1954

Kanpur (U.P.)

SIYĀSAT
Urdu daily
DLC p. S 5–D 5, 1950 (inc.); 1952-1953

Karachi

ANJAM

Urdu daily
DLC p. Je 17–Jl 30, 1950; Ja 21–Ap 30, Jl 6–D 31, 1953; Ja 26–
D 31, 1961

AZAD

Sindhi daily
DLC p. Mr 4–S 18, 1947

BALUCHISTAN-E-JADID

Urdu
DLC p. Ja–Jl 1948 (big gaps)

CIVIL AND MILITARY GAZETTE

Karachi ed., daily, F 1, 1949-; see *Lahore*, CIVIL AND MILITARY
GAZETTE
succeeded THE DAILY GAZETTE
DLC F 3, 1949–Mr 31, 1953 (several issues missing)

THE DAILY GAZETTE

1877–Ja 30, 1949
succeeded by the Karachi ed. of CIVIL AND MILITARY GAZETTE
DLC Ja 29, 1943; Ap 1, 1944–Ja 30, 1949

DAWN

daily (slightly irregular); see also *Delhi*, DAWN
pub. simultaneously in Delhi and Karachi O 26, 1941–S 14, 1947;
continued as THE HERALD Ap 1, 1950; resumed former title
Ap 4, 1950
BM 1951–My 30, 1953
CaOONL p. 1951-
CLU p. 1951-
CLSU p. 1951-1954
CST p. 1951-1953
CU 1944-1955 (few scattered nos. missing)
DLC N 13-16, 1947; N 26, 1947–Mr 9, 1948; Mr 29, 1948–Mr 31, 1950;
Ap 4, 1950–Je 30, 1955; film Ja–O, 1951; Ja–F, 1952; p. Jl 1955-
HEW film N 26, 1947–S 1964
IOL 1951–My 30, 1953
MH 1951-
MILC p. & n. Ja 1952–D 1955; Ja 1956-
MnU n. Ap–D 1950, N–D 1951
NcD Jl 1960-
NjP p. 1951-
NN 1945-1950; p. 1951-

PU 1950-
NNC p. 1944–Ag 1947; p. 1951-1956

DAWN GUJARATI
Gujarati
DLC film Ja 1962-

THE HERALD
daily, Ap 1-3, 1950; see DAWN
DLC Ap 1-3, 1950; bound with DAWN

JANG
Urdu daily
DLC film 1961-1962

THE KARACHI DAILY
DLC Ja 24, 1943 (vol. 7, no. 2000)

MEHRAN
Sindhi daily
DLC film 1962-

MORNING NEWS
daily
DLC n. & p. 1962-

SIND GAZETTE
daily
IOL 1910-1914

THE SIND OBSERVER
daily; incorporates STAR OF INDIA (?)
DLC S 7, 1942 (vol. 21, no. 242); Ja 25, 1943; Ap 2, 1944–Mr 17,
    1950 (fairly complete)

THE TIMES OF KARACHI
incorporating EVENING TIMES
DLC My 23, 1955 (vol. 3, no. 141); D 29, 1955; Ja 1–Ap 30, 1957;
    S 1, 1957–D 28, 1959

Kathmandu (Nepal)

COMMONER
ICU 1962-

GURKHA PATRA
Nepali, 1890's-; monthly, then weekly, then daily
DLC p. Ap 1949–Ja 1952

NEPAL TAIMS
Nepali
DLC p. 1957

Kottayam (Kerala)

DEEPIKA

Malayalam
DLC p. Ap 1944–Ap 1948; Ap 1949–D 1953

MALAYALA MANORAMA
Malayalam
DLC p. Ja–O 1959; Ja 1962-
HEW film Ja 1962–D 1963
ICU 1962-

Kozhikode

MATHRUBHUMI
Malayalam daily 1923-
DLC p. Ap 1944–D 1953; Jl 1954-
HEW film Ap 1944–D 1960

Lahore (W. Pak.)

AFAQ
Urdu daily
DLC F 20-28, Mr 1–Je 4, 1962 (inc.)

AKALI
Punjabi
DLC p. Mr 1947-

ASAAR
Urdu daily
DLC p. Ja 1, 1953; My 20–Je 30, Ag 1–D 31, 1953 (inc.)

CIVIL AND MILITARY GAZETTE
pub. in Simla 1872–F 12, 1949; thereafter pub. simultaneously in
Lahore and Karachi; weekly, then daily
formed by mergers with DAILY CHRONICLE, *Delhi* in 1870(?),
INDIAN PUBLIC OPINION AND PUNJAB TIMES, *Lahore* in
1876 (or 1886 or 1896), and DAILY GAZETTE, *Karachi* in 1949;
suspended pub. My 13–Ag 13, 1949
BM N 3, 1906–Ap 30, 1940; Ja 24, 1941-
DLC Mr 24, 1943; Je 1945–Mr 6, 1953; Jl 2, 1953–D 31, 1961 (scat-
tered issues missing); n. & p. 1962-
IOL 1876-1914; 1947-1949 (inc.)
MnU n. Mr 4–D 1892 (inc.); Ap 1950-1959
NL 1873-1875 (inc.); Jl–D 1923; 1941-1950; Ja–Je 1951; 1952-

EASTERN TIMES
continued (?) as THE MORNING POST My 1, 1948?
daily
BM Ap 4, 1939
DLC O 11, 1942 (vol. 11, no. 107)–Ap 9, 1948

EHSĀN
Urdu, 1934-
DLC p. O 1942–Jl 1947

IMRŌZ
Urdu daily
DLC p. Mr–D 1960, Ja 1962-
HEW film Jl 7, 1950–D 1955; Mr–D 1960

INDIAN PUBLIC OPINION AND PUNJAB TIMES
2x/wk, then daily; absorbed by CIVIL AND MILITARY GAZETTE
in 1876 (or 1886 or 1896)
BM N 28, 1876
IOL 1870-1876

LAHORE CHRONICLE
2x/wk, 1849-1868
ed. Munshi Mohammad Azim
IOL 1851-1868

MAGHRABI PAKISTAN
Urdu
DLC p. Ja 1952–Mr 1953; 1954

THE MUSLIM OUTLOOK
daily except Mon.
NN Jl 11–D 21, 1925 (inc.); Ja 1–N 26, 1926

NAWA-I-WAQT
Urdu weekly, then daily
ed. Shabar Hasan and M. R. Imrani
DLC p. Ap 1949–D 1950; Mr 1952–D 1954; 1962-
HEW film Ap 7–D 29, 1950; Mr 1952–D 1954
IAU 1940; 1941; 1944; 1945

PAKISTAN TIMES
daily
DLC F 20, 1947 (vol. 1, no. 15)–Je 30, 1957; p. Ja 1956-
HEW film Ja 1956–D 1961; Ap–S 1962
MILC n. & p. 1956-
MH p. 1956-
MnU n. 1950-1955

NcD 1957-1959 (inc.)
PU 1950-

PRATĀP
Urdu and Hindi, 1919-
expressed views of Mahāsabha and Arya Samāj
DLC Ag 29, 1946–Ag 10, 1947

THE TRIBUNE
see *Ambala*, THE TRIBUNE

ZAMĪNDAR
Urdu daily, 1903-
ed. Zafar Ali Khan; represented Muslim point of view in Shuddhi and
   Sangathan movements
DLC p. F 1946–O 1948; Ja–N 1952

Larkana (W. Pak.)

CHĀNDKĀ
Urdu (or Sindhi) weekly
DLC Je 1936–Mr 1948 (inc.)

Lucknow (U.P.)

THE ADVOCATE
2x/wk, 1888-
incorporated THE INDIAN UNION, *Allahabad*
NL Mr–D 1923

AN-NADVAH
Urdu monthly, 1904-1916; new series 1940-1942 (?)
founder and first ed. Shibli No'mani; ed. of new series Abul Hasan
   Ali Nadvi
CaQMMIIS 1904-1916 (inc.); 1940-1942 (inc.)

JANAYUGA
Hindi
DLC p. 1957-1960; 1963-

KAUKAB-I-HIND (THE STAR OF INDIA)
1886-1908
missionary sheet, in transliterated Urdu (Roman script)
NN nos. of vol. 19, 20, 22-34, 38, 41

THE MUSLIM REVIEW
pub. by The Madrasat-ul-Waiseen; religious propaganda
NN vol. 40 (Ja–Mr 1933)

NATIONAL HERALD
daily, S 9, 1938-; suspended pub. Ag 15, 1942–N 29, 1945
founder: Jawaharlal Nehru; official Congress journal

CU O 1951-
DLC 1945-1961; n. & p. 1962-
HEW film 1963
ICU 1962-
InU S 1946-
MnU n. Mr 1950–D 1959
NL 1953-
NN Jl 17–D 25, 1946 (scattered issues)
PU 1947-

NAVAJIVAN
Hindi daily, 1947-
DLC p. Ap 25–D 30, 1950 (inc.); Jl 1951–D 1953

NAYĀ SABERĀ
Hindi
DLC p. 1950 (inc.); 1951

PĀÑCHAJANYA
Hindi
DLC p. S 28–D 28, 1950 (inc.)

THE PIONEER
3x/wk, 1865-1869; daily 1869-
pub. in Allahabad 1865–Jl 1933; Lucknow thereafter
founder: George Allen
first ed. Rev. Julian Robinson
ASB Ja 3, 1873–1930
BM Ja 2, 1865–D 29, 1869; 1870-1874; Ag 18–O 21, 1939; Ja 1, 1952–
    Ja 14, 1954
CU S 20, 1951-
DLC Ap 10–Ag 30, 1945; Ja 2–Mr 31, 1946
HEW film 1870-1884
IOL 1870- (inc.)
MicroM n. 1870-1912
MicroP n. Je 1919–1922; Ap 1924–1926; S 1931–Jl 1948
NcD 1870-1872; 1873 (inc.); 1874-1884
NL Ja 1867–My 1943; 1953-
NN Je 1, 1919–S 10, 1922; Ap 1924–Jl 15, 1948
OBod 1917-1931
OII 1932-1937

Madras

ANDHRA HERALD
weekly, 1947-
PU 1948-

ĀNDHRA PATRIKĀ
  Telugu daily, 1908-
  ed. K. Nāgēsvara Rāu
  DLC p. Ap 26, 1944–S 1947; Mr 23, 1948-
  HEW film 1963
  ICU 1962-

ĀNDHRA PRABHA
  Telugu daily, 1938-
  DLC p. Ag 18, 1950–1958
  HEW film Ag 1950–D 1958

THE ATHENAEUM
  1837-1862; 3x/wk to 1847, daily thereafter
  IOL 1844-1861

THE ATHENAEUM AND STATESMAN
  daily, 1862-; cont. from THE ATHENAEUM
  IOL 1862-1864

THE ATHENAEUM AND DAILY NEWS
  cont. from THE ATHENAEUM AND STATESMAN
  ASB Ja 1876–D 1883
  BM Ja 1, 1875–Ag 29, 1885
  IOL 1864-1865

THE ATHENAEUM OVERLAND
  weekly ed. of THE ATHENAEUM AND DAILY NEWS
  IOL 1875-1885

CARNATIC TELEGRAPH AND MADRAS EXCHANGE GAZETTE
  2x/wk, 1853-
  NL My 13–D 13, 1858; 1860

COMMERCIAL CHRONICLE AND INDIAN DAILY NEWS
  daily, O 2, 1851-
  NL O–D 1851

DECCAN TIMES
  weekly
  DLC Ap 16, 1944 (vol. 10, no. 45)–Jl 8, 1956
  MILC 1948-1949, 1 vol.

DINAMANI
  Tamil daily, 1934-
  DLC p. Ag 17, 1950–D 1953; Ja 1955–D 1959
  HEW film Ja 1950–D 1953; Ja–Je 1955; Ja–Je 1956; Jl 1957–D 1958

DINAMANI KADIR
  Tamil weekly, 1934-
  DLC S 10, 1950-

DINASARI
Tamil daily, 1944-
DLC p. Ja 1947–D 1951

EASTERN GUARDIAN
weekly, 1850-
NL 1851

THE EDUCATIONIST. THE ONLY ALL-INDIA EDUCATIONAL
WEEKLY
1906-
NL Ap 1907–D 1908

FEDERATED INDIA
weekly
MILC N 24, 1937–D 28, 1938

FORT ST. GEORGE GAZETTE
NN 1912–Je 1940 (inc.)

GENERAL ADVERTISER AND JOURNAL OF COMMERCE
2x/wk, 1856-1861; Jl 1, 1861-, cont. as THE MADRAS ADVER-
TISER
NL vol. 5 (Ja–Je 1851)

THE HINDU
weekly S 20, 1878–1889; daily except Sun. 1889-
The Hindu office, n. complete file
BM Ja 23–D 31, 1947; Ja 1, 1952–O 13, 1953
CU 1945-1949; S 9, 1951-
DLC Dak ed.: My 17, 1941–D 31, 1943; My 1–D 30, 1944
    Town ed.: O 1–D 31, 1942; Ja 1943–Je 1955; film Jl 1, 1955-
IaU 1945-
ICU 1962-
IOL Jl 1929–D 1951
MILC D 1929–Mr 1930; S 1930–D 1931; S 1932–Ja 1933; My–D 1933;
    My, Jl–N 1934; F–N 1935; S 1944–N 1953; Ja 1954–D 1955
MnU n. Mr–D 1950
NcCQ Ja 1962-
NN D 1929–N 1932 (very inc.); Je 1940–S 1944 (inc.); Ja 1945–Je
    1947 (inc.)
OII 1949- (inc.)
PU 1948-

THE HINDU WEEKLY EDITION
weekly (Sun.)
title changes: -1915 HINDU WEEKLY EDITION

[493]

1937-1941 THE HINDU ILLUSTRATED SUNDAY EDITION
Ag 24, 1941–Mr 1942, THE HINDU
Mr 29, 1942- HINDU WEEKLY EDITION
BM Ja 29–D 28, 1947 (inc.)
DLC F 14, 1907 (vol. 12, no. 7)–D 30, 1915
  Town ed.: 1942-1946, bound with THE HINDU
  Dak ed.: 1941-1944, bound with THE HINDU
IOL 1916-1928; 1939-1950 (inc.); 1952-
NN Ja 1945–Ap 1947
OII 1950-

HINDU WEEKLY REVIEW
DLC N 30, 1953 (vol. 1, no. 17)–D 28, 1959
NcU 1953 (inc.), 1954-
ViU 1959–1960 (inc.), 1961-

HINDUSTAN
Tamil weekly
DLC Mr 2, 1947–Ap 16, 1950

THE HIRCARRAH
BM Ja 7–O 14, 1794

THE INDIAN EXPRESS
daily; Jl 5, 1953, Sunday issue is THE SUNDAY STANDARD (of
  Bombay and Delhi)
DLC Ag 18, 1950 (vol. 18, no. 258)–Ap 22, 1959
MILC Jl 28–O 19, 1933 (inc.); F 17–My 10, 1934; Ag 1934–Ja 1935;
  My–N 1935

INDIAN REPUBLIC
daily, Ja 20, 1949–My 13, 1953
DLC Ja 21, 1949–My 13, 1953

INDIAN STATESMAN
BM D 10, 17, 1859; Ag 10, S 7, 21, 1861

KOUMI HULCHUL
see MUSLIM PATRIOT

THE MADRAS ADVERTISER
Jl 1, 1861-; cont. from GENERAL ADVERTISER AND JOURNAL
  OF COMMERCE
NL Jl–N 1861

MADRAS CHRISTIAN HERALD
weekly 1842-
NL 1842; 1847-1848; 1859

MADRAS COURIER
  weekly, 1785- (or 1790-)
  founder: Richard Johnson, a gov't printer
  ed. in 1791: Hugh Boyd
  ASB My 14–D 1816; 1819-1821; 1823-1824; 1827
  BM My 12, 1790–Ap 19, 1792; Ja 19, 1819
  IOL 1795; 1798-1818

MADRAS EXAMINER
  2x/wk, 1852-1863
  NL 1852-1854; 1863

MADRAS EXCHANGE GAZETTE
  incorp. with CARNATIC TELEGRAPH AND MADRAS EX-
    CHANGE GAZETTE

THE MADRAS GAZETTE
  Ja 1, 1795-
  founder: R. Williams
  BM Ja 1–F 28, 1795; Ap 27, My 18, Je 8, 22–Jl 6, 1799; Mr 18–D 30,
    1809
  DLC Jl 14, 1810, supplement

MADRAS MAIL
  daily, 1867-; absorbed MADRAS TIMES (?)
  Je 7, 1942-, Sun. issue pub. as THE WEEKLY MAIL; see MADRAS
    WEEKLY MAIL
  founder: Charles Lawson
  BM Mr 3–Ap 6, 1883; Mr 31–Ap 2, 1887; F 10, 1888-
  CtY 1950-
  DLC S 7, 1942; N 9, 1944; Ap 9, 1945–Ap 30, 1946
  IOL 1871-1889; 1915-1938; 1939-1951 (inc.); 1952-
  NL 1894-1900 (inc.); 1903; 1906-1908 (inc.); 1912-1913; 1918; 1922-
    1943

MADRAS NATIVE HERALD
  BM Ja 4–D 20, 1845; Ja–N 1861

MADRAS OBSERVER
  BM S 26–O 31, 1861; Ja 2–Ag 28, 1862

MADRAS STANDARD
  1841–Jl 1914; 3x/wk, then daily
  Jl 1914, purchased by Annie Besant and B. P. Wadia, and ed. by
    Annie Besant; became NEW INDIA Ag 1, 1914
  IOL 1887-1889

MADRAS TIMES
  daily
  ed. James Hutton
  BM F 22, 1883
  IOL 1858; O 1860–1914
  MicroM 1858-1914

MADRAS TIMES. OVERLAND EDITION
  weekly
  IOL 1876-1914
  OBod 1900-1904

MADRAS WEEKLY MAIL
  according to DLC, "serial is that of THE SPECTATOR, est. 1836";
    from Je 7, 1942, was Sun. issue of MADRAS MAIL
  BM Ap 16, 1891–S 30, 1926; Jl 7, 1927–Ag 23, 1934
  DLC Ap 8, 1945–Ap 28, 1946
  IOL 1886-1914; 1950-
  OBod 1917-1934 (inc.)

THE MAIL
  see MADRAS MAIL

MALE ASYLUM HERALD
  2x/wk
  IOL 1833-1836; 1841-1842

MUSALMĀN
  Urdu daily
  DLC p. Jl 1944–D 1953; 1957-1961
  ICU 1962-

MUSLIM HERALD
  weekly, Ap 1924–O 1925
  pub. M. A. A. Ghatala
  NN vol. 1-2 (inc.)

MUSLIM PATRIOT
  (formerly KOUMI HULCHUL); new series, 1907; weekly
  NL Ap–O 1907

THE NATIVE STATES AND UNITED INDIA
  weekly, O 6, 1904-
  formed by amalgamation of THE NATIVE STATES and UNITED
    INDIA
  DLC O 6–D 29, 1904 (bound with UNITED INDIA)

NEW INDIA
daily, Ag 1, 1914-; cont. of MADRAS STANDARD
ed. Annie Besant
BM O 1, 1914–N 30, 1925; Ja 1, Ag 31, 1926; Ap 11–S 29, 1928 (evening ed.); Ap 10, 1928–Ja 31, 1929 (morning ed.)

NEW AGE
(a later paper also bears this title)
CU n. N 1938; My 1939

THE SPECTATOR
3x/wk, 1836- (or 1844) 1858
founder: James Ochterlony
IOL 1844-1858

SUNDAY TIMES
weekly
DLC Ap 2, 1944 (vol. 16, no. 26)–S 14, 1952

SWADESAMITRAN
weekly, then daily; 1879 or 1880-
ed. G. Subramanya Aiyer, who later founded THE HINDU
DLC S 4, 1946-; p. S 1947-
HEW film S 1946–D 1960; 1963
ICU 1962-

SWADESAMITRAN. ILLUSTRATED WEEKLY
Tamil, 1929-
DLC S 1946-

UNITED INDIA
weekly, 1902-1904; O 6, 1904- combined with THE NATIVE STATES
to form THE NATIVE STATES AND UNITED INDIA
DLC Ja 7–S 29, 1904 (bound with THE NATIVE STATES AND
UNITED INDIA)

UNITED SERVICE GAZETTE
2x/wk in 1847
manager: Captain Langley
BM F 26, 1839

WEEKLY MAIL
see MADRAS WEEKLY MAIL

Mangalore (Mysore)

KANTEERAVA
Kannada, 2x/wk, 1919-
DLC p. Ap 1944–D 1953; Ja 1957–D 1961

Masulipatam (A.P.)

JANMABHUMI
weekly
pub. S. Ganesan
ed. 1920-1930, M. Krisharao; then B. P. Sitaramayya
contained political comment of a Gandhian nature
absorbed CURRENT THOUGHT
NN scattered holdings

Meerut (U.P.)

THE MOFUSSILITE
change of place of pub.: Meerut, 1847-1852
                                 Agra, 1853-1859
                                 Meerut, 1860-1868
                                 Delhi, 1869
                                 Ambala, 1870-1874

IOL 1847-1874

Monghyr (Bihar)

MONGHYR SAMACHAR
Hindi weekly
DLC p. Ap 1944–D 1947; Ja–S 1949 (inc.)

Mussoorie (U.P.)

THE HILLS
BM D 12, 1861

Mysore (Mysore)

MYSORE GAZETTE
IOL Jl–D 1915

Nagpur (Maharashtra)

DAILY LOKMAT
Hindi (or Marathi), 1930-
DLC p. My 5, 1950–D 1953

HITAVADA (HITABAD)
weekly, 1910-; daily 1943-
originally in Marathi; English 1911-
CU Ag 1951-
DLC Ap 1, 1944–D 31, 1961; n. & p. 1962-
HEW film Jl–D 1963
ICU 1962-
NL 1953-

MAHARASHTRA
DLC p. 1945

[498]

New Delhi

See *Delhi*

Nilgiri (Madras)

NILGIRI NEWS
3x/wk; after 1903 cont. as SOUTH OF INDIA OBSERVER, *Ootaca-mund*
IOL 1879-1900; 1902

Patna (Bihar)

ĀRYĀVARTA
Hindi daily, 1939-
founder: Hon. Sri Kameshwara Prasad Singh, Maharajadhiraj of Darbhanga
DLC p. My–D 1949; Ja 13-25, F 1, Mr 28–My 31, S 1-30, N 1–D 31,
1950; Ja 1–F 2, Jl 23, 29, 30, Ag 1, 6–D 12, 1951; Ag, O–D 14,
1952; Ja 1953–D 1961
HEW film My 1949–D 1960; Ja–Ag 1963

BIHAR AND ORISSA GAZETTE
NN 1912; 1922-1923 (inc.)

BIHAR TIMES
weekly
absorbed by THE SEARCHLIGHT in 1894

BIHAREE
weekly
absorbed by THE SEARCHLIGHT in 1897

INDIAN NATION. AN INDEPENDENT NATIONALIST DAILY
daily, 1931-; suspended pub. 1932, resumed 1934
founder: Hon. Sri Kameshwar Prasad Singh, Maharajadhiraj of Darbhanga
ed. Sachin Sen
DLC S 5, 1942; Ap 1, 1944–D 31, 1961; n. & p. 1962-
HEW film Ja 1962–D 1963
ICU 1962-
NL Ja 1954-

NAVARASHTRA
Hindi
DLC p. 1953

NEPAL SANDESH
Nepali (Nagari script)
ICU 1962-

THE PATNA TIMES
weekly
incorp. BEHAR OPINION
DLC Ja 29, 1939 (vol. 16, no. 3)

THE SEARCHLIGHT
c. 1894; 2x/wk, 1918-; 3x/wk, 1930-; daily, 1941-
incorporated BIHAR TIMES, 1894 and BIHAREE, 1897
DLC Ap 10, 1944–D 31, 1953; n. & p. 1962-
HEW film 1962-1963
ICU 1962-
NL 1955-

THE SUNDAY INDIAN NATION
weekly (Sun.)
DLC Ap 2, 1944 (vol. 2, no. 14)–D 29, 1946; bound with INDIAN
NATION

Peshawar (W. Pak.)

FRONTIER ADVOCATE
DLC p. Ja–Ap 1948

ITTALA'AT-E-SARHAD
Urdu, 2x/wk
DLC N 1947–S 1950 (inc.)

KHYBER MAIL
weekly, 1932–F 17, 1950; daily, F 26, 1950-
DLC Ap 7, 1944–D 31, 1961

SHAHBAZ
Urdu
DLC p. Ja–N 1952, 1953

Poona (Maharashtra)

ALLEN'S INDIAN NEWS
BM Jl 19, 1854

DAILY TELEGRAPH AND DECCAN HERALD
2x/wk; incorp. DECCAN HERALD, 1886
EC 1886–Ja 1916
IOL 1879-1889

DEENBANDHU
Marathi weekly, 1876-
DLC p. Mr 1947–D 1953; F 1957-

DECCAN HERALD
2x/wk or 3x/wk; incorp. with DAILY TELEGRAPH, 1886 to form
DAILY TELEGRAPH AND DECCAN HERALD
EC My 1861–Mr 1863
IOL 1876-1878

KESARI
Marathi weekly, Ja 1881-
first ed. Gopal Ganesh Agarkar; then Bal Gangadhar Tilak; 1920-,
Narasingh Chintaman Kelkar
DLC p. Jl 1943–S 1949; Ja 1954-
EC 1900-1902; 1905-1931
HEW film Jl 1943–S 1949; 1954-1960
Kesari office, complete files

MAHRATTA
weekly, Ja 1881–1920
first ed. Bal Gangadhar Tilak; 1896-1918, Narasingh Chintaman
Kelkar
Paper's motto: *Malo mori quam demorari* (I would prefer death to
dishonor)
EC Ja 5, 1913–D 1919
Kesari office, complete files

POONA OBSERVER AND CIVIL AND MILITARY JOURNAL
daily
IOL 1876-1906

POONA OBSERVER AND DECCAN WEEKLY REPORTER
EC My 1852–1856; 1858; 1861–Jl 1862; 1871–Je 1915

SERVANT OF INDIA
MILC Ap 1936–Jl 27, 1939 (inc.)

Prayag

SAPTAHIKA
Hindi
DLC p. S 1946–Ag 1948

Rawalpindi (W. Pak.)

TAMEER
Urdu
DLC p. Ja–Ag 1952; 1953

Secunderabad (A.P.)

DECCAN CHRONICLE
daily, 1938-
ed. K. R. Rattabiraman

DLC n. & p. 1962-
HEW film Ja 1962–D 1963
ICU 1962-
Deccan Chronicle office, complete files; apply to Circulation Manager one week ahead of time

Serampore (Bengal)

FRIEND OF INDIA
see *Calcutta*, FRIEND OF INDIA

FRIEND OF INDIA. OVERLAND EDITION
weekly
BM Ag 16, 1866

INDIAN REFORMER
BM Ja 10, 1861–N 28, 1862; S 18, 1863

SAMACHAR DARPAN
Bengali, My 23, 1818–1852? ("written in Serampore Bengalee . . .
frequently containing English sentences dressed up in Bengalee
words"); Bengali and English, Jl 11, 1829–1837; one Persian ed.
printed, My 6, 1826
weekly, 1818-1831; 2x/wk, Ja 11, 1832–1834; weekly, N 8, 1834–1841
eds. 1818-1840, J. C. Marshman
1842-1843, Bhagabati Charan Chattopadhyay
My 3, 1851–Ap 24, 1852, Meredith Townsend
NL 1831-1837

Simla (Punjab)

CIVIL AND MILITARY GAZETTE
see *Lahore*, CIVIL AND MILITARY GAZETTE

THE PIONEER DAILY BULLETIN
daily, 1895-
NL My–O 1909

SIMLA TIMES ADVERTISER
entitled SIMLA TIMES, 1890–Jl 16, 1894
weekly, 1890-
NL 1894-1897; 1907-1908

THE TRIBUNE
see *Ambala*, THE TRIBUNE

Sukkur (W. Pak.)

ALHAQ
weekly
NL 1907-1910 (vol. 8-12) (inc.)

PART III: NEWSPAPERS

Sylhet (E. Pak.)

THE ASSAM HERALD
weekly
DLC Ap 1, 1944 (vol. 6, no. 8)–Ap 5, 1947 (scattered issues missing)

THE SYLHET CHRONICLE
weekly
DLC My 9, 1944 (vol. 24, no. 6)–F 12, 1946 (big gaps)

THE WEEKLY CHRONICLE
weekly, 1900-
devoted to social, political and educational topics
NL 1904; Ja–My 1908

Travancore (Kerala)

DEEPIKA
Malayalam daily, 1887-
DLC Ja 1945–Ap 1948; Ap 1949-

Trichur (Kerala)

KERALA CHRONICLE
daily
DLC n. & p. 1962-
HEW film Ja 1962–D 1963
ICU 1962-

APPENDIX TO THE AUTHOR INDEX

[References are to items, not pages]

Dube, S. P., G102
Emmott, D. H., F337
Gupta, B. L., G103
Hajela, G. L., D693
Jones, M. E. Monckton, D698
Kakitsubo, M., D699
Kamath, S., D312
Kiell, Norman, G104
Manoharan, T., J117
Mathews, V. T., J118
Mohan, Radha, G105
Patel, M. H., J120
Ram, Mali, J121

Ramana, Duvvuri V., J122
Ramkrishna, Reddy, G., J123
Rao, B. S., J124
Raychaudhuri, T. C., E160
Roy, Manomohan, J126
Sen, S. N., A480; B210, 1323; D728,
    814; E107; F241; G13
Singh, S. Ganda, B1345
Sinha, Harischandra, J129
Smith, I. T., D951
Srivastava, Igbal Narain, G106
Strachey, Richard, D953
Varma, Gyan C., J131

AUTHOR INDEX

[References are to items, not pages]

Abbas, K. A., C243, 453
Abbasi, Mohammad Madni, B741
Abbasi, Yusaf, C244
Abbot, Freeland K., F950, 951
Abdul Ali, A. F. M., Al, 2, 143, 226, 227, 268, 269, 416; B931-33, 1194; D484, 657; F280, 694, 892
Abdul-Hadi, Hafez, G100
Abdul Latif, Syed, F116, 490
Abdul Wadud, Kazi, E165
Abdullah, Syed Muhammad, F525
Abhayambal, Udayam, G39
Abir, M., B1562
Abraham, Baby, H45
Acharya, N. K., G62
Acharya, P., F117
Achuta Rao, D. S., A317-19
Adam, Leonhard, B572
Adams, George, D250
Adams, Walter, D742
Adarkar, B. P., D743
Adenwalla, Minoo D., B460; C59, 376; I1
Adyanthaya, N. K., D819
Adye, John, B742, 1563
Afaq, S. S., F551
al-Afghānī, Djamāl al-Dīn, C454
Afzal, Qaiser, F552
Aga Khan, B376; F952
Agarwal, Ram Charan, J102
Agarwal, S. K., H99
Agarwal, Shri Narayan, D757
Agarwal, Sushila, L68
Agarwala, A. N., E243
Agarwala, R. K., J64
Agaskar, M. S., G21
Agharkar, S. P., F1118
Ahluwalia, M. L., A417-19; B65
Ahluwalia, Madan Mohan, C60; I32
Ahluwalia, S. S., J1
Ahmad, A. F. Salahuddin, B27; L1
Ahmad, Aziz, C455-58; F553, 554, 953-56
Ahmad, Badrud-din, B576
Ahmad, Enayat, B1275
Ahmad, M. B., B28
Ahmad, N., J2
Ahmad, Nafis, B1033, 1034
Ahmad, Qeyamuddin, B1035, 1385-87; C459, 460; D851; L79
Ahmad, Rafiuddin, C461
Ahmad, Safi, B1276; G15
Ahmad, Zulieda P., J28
Ahmad Khan, Muin-ud-din, El; F957-64
Ahmad Khan, Shafaat, C462

Ahmed, Manzooruddin, I99
Ahmed, Q., D98
Ahmed, Sufia, K24
Ahmed, Ziauddin, F965
Ahuja, R. L., L22
Aitken, Benjamin, D367; F1046
Aiyanger, S. Krishnaswami, D99
Aiyar, P. S., A681
Aiyer, P. S. Sivaswamy, B743
Aiyyar, K. R. Venkata Raman, B1217
Akhmedzianov, A., C463
Akhtar, S. M., J80
Alaev, L. B., A495; D100, 485; F118
Alexander, Horace G., C246, 377, 378; D368
Alexander, James, D101
Alexandrowicz-Alexander, Charles Henry, D658
Ali, Ameer, B1388; C464-467; D102, 251, 820
Ali, Hamid, B577
Ali, Hashim Amir, F829
Ali, Mohammed, C468; F437
Ali, Muhammed Mohar, F1, L86
Ali, Rahmat, C469
Ali, S. Amjad, F966
Ali, S. Wajid, F281, 440
Ali, Saiyad Murtaja, F967
Allan, James J., A520
Allchin, F. R., F119
Allen, Grant, B1
Almaula, Nalin I., J106
Alsdorf, Ludwig, F120
Alur, V. B., F121
Ambirajan, S., D7, 852; J3
Anand, A. S., G85
Anand, Mulk Raj, C248; F555
Andal, F556
Anderson, A420
Anderson, D. Y., D758
Anderson, Lily Strickland, F679
Andrews, A. Piatt, D853
Andrews, C. F., A682, 683; C379-81, 470, 471; D966; E2, 128; F282, 830
Andronov, I., B1564
"Anglo-Indian," B377
Anjanaiah, Nalabala, J29
Ansari, A. S. Bazmee, A3, 4, 228, 229, 270-72, 496, 521-23; B461, 934, 1277, 1278, 1389, 1390; E167; F122, 439, 440, 558-61, 968-70
Ansari, Mohammed Abdus Salem, I100
Ansari, Zafar Ahmad, F971
Anstey, Vera, D8
Antonova, K. A., A70; D9, 104; F2, 123

[505]

AUTHOR INDEX

Dmitriev, G. L., B1572
Dobbin, Christine, B617
Dobie, Marryat R., F32
Dobson, J. O., F469
Doctor, Manilal M., A701
Dodwell, H., B240, 990; D499, 876; E35
Dodwell, Marcia, F470
Dolbeer, Martin Luther, Jr., L89
Dole, N. Y., H196
Doriaswami, S. V., D769, 877-82
Douglas, R. B., F985
Dover, Cedric, F159
Dravid, N. A., D29
Drummond, J. G., H126
d'Souza, A. W. P., A251
Dua, Shiva, K5
Dubey, Satya Narayan, C109, 110; I35
Duff, M. E. Grant, B286, 287, 365; E298, 299
Dufferin and Ava, Marquess of, D388
Dufferin, Harriot, F1135
Duncan, Jonathan, B1234
Dunn, T. O. D., F582-84
Dunnicliff, H. B., D568
Durand, A. G. A., A551
Durand, H. M., B1423
Dutt, Bhupendra Lal, C14, 111
Dutt, Jatindra Mohan, C498, 499
Dutt, K. N., B1106
Dutt, L. P., D618
Dutt, Romesh C., D139, 389; F33
Dutt, Sudhindra K., B991
Dutta, Bhupendra Nath, E144
Dyer, A. Saunders, B1377

Eagleton, C., A386
Eapen, Karippacheril Chakko, L6
Ebright, Donald Fossett, L90
Eddison, John C., J67
Edwardes, Michael, F34, 1136
Edwardes, S. M., A164; B1424
Edwards, Thomas, E183, 184; F587-89, 713, 1063
Egerton, W. E., C112
Elliot, F. A. H., A656
Elliot, R. H., F35, 36
Elliott, Charles, D390, 391
Elliott, V. C., L28
Elliott, W. Y., C275
Elmhurst, Leonard K., F840
Emerson, Gertrude, C391
Eno, Enola, L75
"Eropmar," D302
Erskine, William, F38
Eustis, F. A., B1108
Evans, Walter B., I108
Ewart, J. Spencer, B794
Ewbank, R. B., D437
Ewer, W. N., C393

Eyles, D., H28
Ezekiel, Hannam, D883

Fagan, Henry Stuart, D392
Fagan, P. J., E41
Fagan, Patrick, E185
Fallon, Pierre, S.J., F1065
Fanshawe, Arthur, B390
Faruqi, Khwaja Ahmad, F587
Faulkner, P. Leo, C501
Fawcett, Henry, D884-86
Fawcett, Millicent Garrett, E42
Fawcett, R. H., B795; D773
Fernandez, T., A280
Feroze, S. M. A., F716, 717
Filliozat, Jean, F162, 1137
Fink, H. R., B619; E45
Finley, Mark, B1534
Firminger, Walter Kelly, B620, 993, 1110, 1111, 1202; D774, 775; F39, 1066
Firozuddin-Sayyid, L29
Fischel, Walter J., D680; E186
Fischer, J. F., D141
Fisher, Humphrey, F986
Fisher, Thomas, F338
Fitchett, W. H., B1427
Fitzgerald, R. C., B496
Floris, George A., C393
Foley, Rudolph X., H67
Fontera, Richard M., B1574; H68
Foot, Isaac, E46
Forrest, George W., B112, 391-94; F163, 1139
Forrest, R. E., D33
Forster, E. M., E301
Fortescue, John W., B1353
Foster, William, B994; F668-73
Fournian, Charles, B1428
Fowler, F. J., H170
Fowler, William, D776
Franda, Marcus F., C15
Franklin, C. S., L91
Franklin, William, A17
Franks, H. George, D303
Franz-Willing, Georg, B1429
Franzer, Major General, A415
Fraser, Andrew H. Lovat, B395, 396, 898; C114; F339, 340, 476
Freemantle, W. H., F910
Fremantle, S. H., D620
French, J. C., A90
Frere, H. Bartle E., E255
Friedman, H. J., H69
Fritz, Henry E., K29
Frykenberg, Robert Eric, B1236, 1237; E187; H143
Fukazawa, Hiroshi, A165, 166; D142; E47, 48

[512]

Wadia, C. N., A142
Wadia, D. N., F260
Wadia, P. A., E226
Wagle, N. B., F261
Wali, *Maulvi* Abdul, B1190
Walker, A., A411
Walker, G. H. W., D985
Walker, Mary, F1112
Wallace, Robert, B882
Walter, Howard Arnold, C566; F1043
Walters, H. Crawford, E290
Walters, Henry, E164
Wang Liang-ch'un, C451
Ward, A., B451
Ward, H. C. E., A316
Ward, Major, B1270, 1271
Warne, Frank W., F1113
Warren, W. Preston, E227
Wasti, S. Razi, B452; C567, 568; F433; I122
Waters, G., F1180
Watson, A., B1617
Watson, Francis, C452
Watson, Robert Spence, C240
Watson, Vincent C., H89
Waugh, A., D96
Webb, M. de P., D756
Wedderburn, David, B1561
Wedderburn, William, B374, 453-56; D366
Weeks, Edwin Lord, E124
Weiner, Myron, I77
Weitbrecht, H. H., F1114
Weitzman, Sophia, H136
Welch, Colin, B1524
Wells, J., B227
West, Raymond, B706
Westbrook, W. F., C242
Westmacott, E. Vesey, E223
Weston, A. T., F434
Wheatley, John, B228
Wheeler, Richard S., I123
Wheeler, Stephen, B457
White, Edith M., F262
White, G. S., B707
Whynant, Neville, F263
Wickins, Peter, B1525
Wight, Robert, B1271
Wilcox, Wayne Ayres, I124
Wilkins, Charles, F522
Wilkinson, Theodore S., L16
Willcocks, James, B885
Williams, Donovan, F1181; H60
Williams, G. R. C., A494
Williams, L. F. Rushbrook, B563; C374, 375

Willson, Amos L., Jr., L17
Willson, W. S. J., B564
Wilson, Prof., B1027
Wilson, C. E., F1116
Wilson, C. R., B1028-31
Wilson, H. H., F949
Wilson, L. B., H140
Windmiller, Marshall Louis, I78
Winterton, Earl T., B565, 566
Wise, James, E228
Wiser, Charlotte Viall, C375
Wodak, E., D964
Wodehouse, C., F524
Wohlers, Lester P., H226
Woldman, Joel M., C518
Wolpert, Stanley A., I56
Wood, J. S., D965
Wood, W. H. Arden, E229
Wood, W. Martin, D986
Woodhouse, T., E126
Wordsworth, W. C., F783
Wright, H. R. C., D97, 247, 575-77
Wylie, David T., B1032
Wyndham, Horace, B886

Xavier, P. F. Francis, F1117

Yamadatta, C569
Yamunacharya, M., F658
Yapp, M. E., A605; E230
Yate, A. C., B887
Yate, Charles E., B459
Younghusband, Francis E., B567, 568, 1373
Younghusband, G. J., A606
Yu Sheng-wu, B1618
Yusuf, Nur Jehan Mohammed, H95
Yusuf Ali, A., B569, 888, 1619; F435, 1044

Zachariah, Kunniparampil C., E132; K23
Zacharias, C. W. B., D352
Zacharias, H. C. E., C58
Zafar Khan, Moimuz, H90
Zaida, R. H., J27
Zaidi, Z. H., A607; B1108, 1193
Zakaria, Rafiq Ahmed, I125
Zaman Khan, Shah, J62
Zbavital, Dushan, F885-90
Zellner, Aubrey A., L48
Zetland, Marquess of, B570, 571; C570
Zoberi, Z. H., H61
Zollinger, Melly, D535
Zunuddin, Mir, B1272
Zvelebil, Kamil, F550, 659, 784
Zwemer, S. M., F1045

DISSERTATION INDEX, BY UNIVERSITY

[References are to items, not pages]

SUBJECT INDEX

[References are to items, not pages]

'Abd al-'Azīz al-Dihlawī, Shāh (1746-1824), F1003
'Abd al-Hayy, Abu'l Hasanāt Muhammad (1848-1886), F999
'Abd al-Kadir Dihlawī (1753/54-1813), F1000
Abdālī, see Durrāni
Abkari Mehal, D249
Achin, A81
Adam, Gov.-Gen. John (fl. 1823), B109
Adam, Rev. William (fl. 1822), F1105
Addiscombe, F452; uniforms, B876
adi granth, A425
adult education, F427
Afghan wars, see Anglo-Afghan wars
al-Afghānī, Jamāl al-Din (1838-1897), C458, 539
Afghanistan, A525, 540, 541, 543, 550, 562, 566, 567, 572, 573; H222; evacuation of, A528, 552; trade, D717
Afghans, A443, 517, 556, 569; C474; G80, 83, 84; H190; and Sikhs, A493; society, A554
Afsōs (1736-1809), F570
Aga Khan, III, see Sultan Muhammad Shah
Agarkar, Gopal Ganesh (1856-1895), C162
Age of Consent Act (1891), E258
agency houses, D672, 739; J92
Agra, A287; B1284, 1285, 1303, 1309; H149; customs, D259; durbar, A601; economy, D14; famine, D425; in 1857, B1415; industry, D446; land revenue, D192
Agra College, F482, 486
agricultural banks, D321
agriculture, D284-352; J49-58; and co-ops, D434; crop statistics, D349; labor, D637, 648; J51; Royal Commission on (1926), D345
ahl-i-hadith, F1001
Ahmad, Mirza Ghulām of Qādiān (1839-1908), F984, 991. See also Ahmadiyya
Ahmad, Muhsin al-din (Dudu Miyān) (1819-1860), F959, 964, 1007
Ahmad Shahīd, Sayyid (1786-1831), A443; F950, 963, 964, 975, 997, 998, 1002, 1012, 1033, 1035, 1036
Ahmadiyya, F982, 985, 986, 990, 1037, 1040, 1041, 1043. See also Ahmad, Mirza Ghulām
Ahmed Khan, Syed (1817-1898), C137, 458, 516; F544, 976, 1017, 1023, 1027;

educational movement, L81; on 1857, B1435; C145; political thought, F1034; I117; religious thought, F1014; social thought, F1039. See also Aligarh movement
Ahmedabad, municipal government, B892; wages, D836
Ahmedullah, Maulvi, F1030
Ahsanullah Khan, Hakim, B1432
air force, B868
Aiyar, Dr. Swaminatha, F73
Ajmal Khan, Hakim, see Khan, Hakim Ajmal
Ajmer, A505, 508
Akali Sikh movement, C319, 357
Akhar Allāhābādī, Sayyid Husayn (1846-1921), F608
Akhbar-i-Dehli, F743
Akhbar-ul-Haqaiq, F753
Akhbar-i-Malwa, F754
Alexander III of Russia (1845-1894, r. 1881-1894), A483
'Alī, Mohammad (1879-1930) and 'Alī, Shaukat (1870-1942) ("Ali brothers"), C10, 400, 543
'Alī, Maulana Muhammad (1874-1951), F1040
'Alī, Nawab Muhammad, B1263
Aligarh, B1328; H156; college, see Mohammedan Anglo-Oriental College; diary, B1302; movement, C509, 516, 519; L83; prices, D848
Alipore Jail Press, F735
Alison, Archibald (1792-1867), B66
'Alivardī Khān (1676?-1756, r. 1740-1756), B984, 1001, 1006, 1016; D676, 747
All-India Congress Socialist Party, C270, 361; I73
All-India Hindu Mahasabha, C305; F902
All-India Muslim League, C288, 323, 512, 513, 544, 567; I103; foreign policy, C507; foundation, C528
All-India Peasant Union, C36, 321
All-India Trade Union Congress, D650
all-parties resolution, C276
Allahabad, B1304; High Court, B623; population, E155
aluminum, D556, 559
Amān, Mīr, F609
amani system, D106
Amātya, Rāmachandrapant, A205
Ambāla, A521, 596-98; durbar, A586
Ambapani, B1457

[533]

orphans, E11
Osmania University, F489
Ostend Company, A62, 67
Oudh, A226-67; B1263-1330; G15-20;
H150, 153, 162; administration, A262;
B1263, 1291, 1318; annexation of,
A235; B1287, 1290; begums, B1324;
ceded provinces, B1296; D201-204;
courts, B678; economy, D66; educa-
tion, F389, 390; and 1857, D189;
H182; land after 1857, B1289; land
settlement, D124; J37; loans, A237,
238; police, B712; revenue system,
A261; salt tax, D579, 580; tahsildar,
B1314; D204; talukdar, D194, 218;
treaty (1837), B1320
Oudh Irregular Force, B840
Outram, B1372
Oxford, and Tagore, F859, 876

P. and O. Company, D763; E123
Paine, Thomas (1737-1809), C174, 175
Pakistan, B461, 510; C484, 526, 536,
549, 550, 552, 553, 563; F978; I99;
agriculture, D307; boundaries, B553,
1033, 1034; constituent assembly,
I106; constitution, B500; C487; I100,
104, 120, 123; economy, D78, 88;
foreign policy, C507; geography, I101,
109; J2; governor-general, B547; Indo-
Pakistan trade, D697; origin, C457;
I108, 113; population, B554; press in,
F716; railways, D797; relations with
India, H223; tea, D603; theory of,
C455, 477, 478
Pal, Bipin Chandra (1858-1932), C19,
74, 110, 130, 178, 186, 219; bibliog-
raphy, C216
Palamau, B1419, 1498
Palestine, C418
Palk, Gov. Robert, B1267
Palmer, William, A384
Pānchālamkurichi rebellion, B1251
panchayat, trials at Poona, A157. See
also subheading, local government,
under states
Pande, Sitaram (1795-1861), B770
Panikkar, Kavalam Madhava (1896-
1966), B1481; F153, 1049
Panipat, battle of (1761), A153, 202,
206, 207, 211, 532, 595
pan-Islam, C493, 504
Panjab, see Punjab
Panjabi Akhbar, F761
paper industry, D454, 455, 480; J67
Paris, peace of, B1611
Parks, Fanny, B1191
Parsis, E93, 94, 200, 216, 226
partition (1947), B482, 506, 508, 551,
553-55; C500, 527, 561; H175; dem-

ography, E142; economic effects, D96;
migration, B511, 543, 548. See also
transfer of power
Patel, Sardar Vallabhbhai Jhaverbhai
(1875-1950), C250, 340
Patel, Vithalbhai Jhaverbhai (1873-1933),
C51
Pathans, A587; in Central India, G25
Patkum, B1131
Patna, B962, 1054, 1067; D551, 657;
defense, B1145; and 1857, B1452;
land, D98; massacre (1763), B946,
977, 978, 1010; village survey, D136
Patna College, F512, 523
patriotic fund, A535
Patwardhan, Gangadhar Shastri, A300
patwari, D201
Paull, James, B1157
Pearse, Col. Thomas Deane (1742-1789),
B860
peasant proprietorship, J33
peasant uprising, C29, 36, 201. See also
kisan sabha
Peel Commission Report, B782
penal code, B669, 685
perjury, B656
permanent settlement, see subheading,
permanent settlement, under states
Perron, General, A97
Perry, Sir Thomas Erskine (1806-1882),
B350
Persia, B846; H222
Persian, language, F525, 536, 542; news-
papers, F694, 699, 703, 723, 750, 752,
755, 766, 775
Persian Gulf, H203
Peshawar, A435, 550, 559; disturbance
(1860), A534; trade, D726
petitions, to Parliament, B185
Petrie, William, B207
petroleum, D544
Phalke, D. G., F4
Phayre, correspondence, B134
Phillips, William, B1584
Pigot, George, Baron (1719-1777),
B1252, 1259
pilgrims, tax on, F908, 920
Pillai, Ananda Ranga (1709-1761),
A110; B1232; D99
Pindaris, A240; B1144, 1145; G25, 31,
35
Piney hills, B1270
Pitman, Major Robert, A385
Pitt, William (1759-1806), B239
Pitt's India Act (1784), B116, 132
plague, F1139, 1180
planning, D77, 285; J14; in Bengal, D74;
Bombay plan, D36, 50
Plassey, battle of (1757), B995, 999,
1008, 1017

[557]